DIMENSIONS
OF THE
HOSPITALITY INDUSTRY

An Introduction

DIMENSIONS
OF THE
HOSPITALITY INDUSTRY
An Introduction

Paul R. Dittmer
New Hampshire College

Gerald G. Griffin
New York City Technical College
of the City University of New York

VNR VAN NOSTRAND REINHOLD
New York

Library of Congress Catalog Card Number 92-17463
ISBN 0-442-00770-1

I(T)P Van Nostrand Reinhold is an International Thomson Publishing company.
       ITP logo is a trademark under license.

Printed in the United States of America

Van Nostrand Reinhold   International Thomson Publishing GmbH
115 Fifth Avenue   Königswinterer Str. 418
New York, NY 10003   53227 Bonn
                                   Germany

International Thomson Publishing   International Thomson Publishing Asia
Berkshire House,168-173   221 Henderson Bldg. #05-1
High Holborn, London WC1V 7AA   Singapore 0315
England

Thomas Nelson Australia   International Thomson Publishing Japan
102 Dodds Street   Kyowa Building, 3F
South Melbourne 3205   2-2-1 Hirakawacho
Victoria, Australia   Chiyoda-ku, Tokyo 102
                                   Japan

Nelson Canada
1120 Birchmount Road
Scarborough, Ontario
M1K 5G4, Canada

16 15 14 13 12 11 10 9 8 7 6 5 4 3

Library of Congress Cataloging-in-Publication Data

Dittmer, Paul,
   Dimensions of the hospitality industry : a college introduction /
   Paul R. Dittmer, Gerald G. Griffin.
      p.   cm.
   Includes bibliographical references (p.   ) and index.
   ISBN 0-442-00770-1
   1. Hospitality industry—Management. I. Griffin, Gerald G.,
1936- . II. Title.
TX911.3.M27D583   1992
647.94'068—dc20   92-17463
                                           CIP

CONTENTS

Preface

This text is intended for courses that introduce students to the broad world of hospitality and tourism and to the curricula that will prepare them for managerial careers in these fields. It consists of nineteen chapters, divided into six parts. Each of the six provides coverage of a primary area commonly treated in introductory courses, as indicated below:

Part	Area covered	No. of chapters
I	Introduction/overview	1
II	Historical foundations	3
III	Food and beverage	3
IV	Lodging	3
V	Travel and tourism	3
VI	Business fundamentals: the hospitality perspective	6

The book has a greater number of chapters than most instructors are inclined to use in a one-term course. In the authors' view, the number of chapters is a virtue—one this text shares with many introductory texts in business. Our goal has been to provide instructors with a choice of chapters that cover the subjects included in their individual course outlines. We believe this is the best approach to meeting the needs that vary from one to another.

In developing the text, we have attempted to make flexibility a key feature. For example, elimination of any one of the six major Parts will not make it difficult to use others. Thus, instructors in programs that do not include food service courses can choose to ignore Part III, Food Service Perspectives. In programs without lodging courses, instructors may prefer to skip Part IV, Lodging Perspectives. And in programs without travel and tourism components, instructors can disregard Part V, Travel and Tourism Perspectives. In those programs in which students take a number of courses in general business, it may be possible to skip Part VI, Hospitality Business Perspectives.

Although instructors in many programs will choose to include the Parts of the text that introduce the principal areas covered in their curricula, some may prefer to take a contrary approach: to assign the Parts that are not linked to the specifics of their programs. Instructors in programs that do not offer courses in food service, for example, may choose to assign the relevant chapters in this text to provide their students with some introduction to this important area.

Instructors will also find considerable flexibility within the Parts of the text. If desired, it is perfectly feasible to use just one or two of the chapters in a Part. In Part II, Foundations, for example, some will choose not to assign Chapter 2, the Development of the Hospitality Industry: A sense of the history of hospitality can be developed from Chapters 3 and 4 alone. Similarly, some instructors may prefer not to assign the "planning" chapters—Chapter 7 in Part III and Chapter 10 in Part IV—or one or more of the chapters in Part VI.

In addition, because the number of end-of-chapter questions is more than most instructors will be inclined to assign, they will be able to make selective use of these for written response or for in-class discussion. Answers for all end-of-chapter questions can be found in the *Instructor's Guide*, which also includes a number of other materials designed to assist those adopting the work. The *Instructor's Guide* is available on request from the publisher: Van Nostrand Reinhold, 115 Fifth Avenue, New York, NY 10003.

Overview

The following is an overview of the text:

Part I gives a profile of the hospitality industry and is intended to provide a sense of its scope. At the same time, it introduces the three principal areas addressed in college majors—food service, lodging, and travel and tourism—and two key concepts: *moments of truth* and *cycles of service*. Finally, it addresses some issues of particular concern to students: career opportunities, education, and experience required to pursue those opportunities; and both the advantages and disadvantages of working in these fields.

Part II traces the history and development of travel and hospitality in the Western world. Chapter 2, the first of the three chapters in this Part, sketches the growth of travel and hospitality from earliest times through the Greek and Roman empires, the Middle Ages, and the period up to the Industrial Revolution in England. The other two chapters are concerned with travel and hospitality in the United States. Chapter 3 deals with the period from colonial times through the nineteenth century. Chapter 4 deals with the twentieth century. The history and development of three important segments of the industry—hotels, resort hotels, and restaurants—are treated individually in these two chapters.

Part III offers a broad introduction to food and beverage. Chapter 5, the first of three chapters, identifies the size and scope of the industry, describes many characteristic types of food and beverage operations, and explains a system for classifying establishments in the food service industry. Chapter 6 deals with food and beverage operations from a systems perspective. Chapter 7 defines the terms *product line* and *service product* as they relate to food and beverage operations and provides insight into planning food and beverage facilities.

Part IV provides a broad introduction to lodging. Chapter 8, the first of three chapters, identifies the size and scope of the industry, describes many characteristic types of lodging establishment operations, and discusses various ways of classifying and rating lodging establishments. Chapter 9 deals with lodging operations from a systems perspective. Chapter 10 defines the terms *product line* and *service product* as they relate to lodging operations and provides insight into planning lodging facilities.

Part V introduces travel and tourism. Chapter 11 discusses various travel motivators, describes the role of governments in travel and tourism, and identifies the size and scope of the industry, as well as its several components. Chapter 12 focuses on the people and businesses that sell travel, defines the term *package*, and describes various types of travel packages. Chapter 13 deals with modes of travel—the various transportation services upon which the travel industry depends.

Part VI provides an introduction to those basic business subjects normally covered in Introduction to Business courses, but from a hospitality perspective. The fundamentals of organization, management, marketing, human resources management, and managerial accounting are introduced and illustrated, using examples taken from the world of food service and lodging. The final chapter addresses a number of significant issues that are likely to be of increasing concern to hospitality managers in the years ahead.

Acknowledgments

In developing this text, we were fortunate to have the cooperation and assistance of the people whose names and affiliations are here recorded. Some of these individuals may feel their contributions were minor. We strongly disagree: Even brief comments and the most casual of conversations can suggest ideas and change views, and thus have profound impact on a work in progress. With that in mind, we sincerely and publicly acknowledge and thank the following for their assistance:

Patricia S. Bartholomew, Frank C. Constantino, Allen M. Freedman, Stephen K. Holzinger, and Fedele J. Panzarino of the Hotel and Restaurant Management Department, New York City Technical College of the City University of New York; William Fulham, Instructor, and Julie Rain, Administrative Assistant, Department of Hospitality Management, as well as Richard Pantano, Library Director, and Edward Daniels, Research Librarian, all of New Hampshire College; Francis M. Domoy, Richard F. Marecki, Warren Sackler, and and Carol B. Whitlock of the School of Food, Hotel, and Travel Management, Rochester Institute of Technology; Robert A. Heath and Edward F. McIntyre of the Birmingham (United Kingdom) College of Food, Tourism, and Creative Studies; Kevin Bedard, General Manager of Canopy's Training Restaurant, Rochester, New York, operated by the Economic Opportunity Center SUNY Brockport; Andrew R. Schwarz of the Hospitality Division of Sullivan County Community College; David C. Dorf of Dave Dorf Associates; Marianne Gajewski, Lisa Gates, and Kathleen Wood of the Educational Foundation of the National Restaurant Association; Allan Sherwin of ATI Career Institute; Kathryn K. Griffin of The Big Twinkie; James Bardi, Director Hospitality Management Program, of Pennsylvania State University, Berks Campus; Edward Sherwin, Chairman, Hotel-Motel/Restaurant-Club Management, of Essex Community College; K. S. Chon, Associate Professor, of the University of Nevada/Las Vegas; Gary K. Vallen, Professor, of Northern Arizona University; Gus Katsigris, Director, Food and Hospitality Services Institute, of El Centro College.

Through the many months required to produce this work, the extraordinary professional staff of Van Nostrand Reinhold has been most patient, helpful, and supportive. In particular, Judith R. Joseph, Pamela Scott Chirls, Julie Markoff, Anthony Calcara, and Amy Shipper all deserve a public salute for their special efforts on our behalf. So does Elyse Rieder, who did an exceptional job of researching and collecting the photographs used in the book. All readily bring to mind a fine old word: mettle.

Finally, we gratefully salute our wives, Barbara and Charlene, who soldiered on in so many ways for so many months. Their understanding as the work progressed calls to mind another fine old word: forbearance. Without their cooperation and support, the manuscript would never have been completed.

If this text is successful—that is, if it is a useful addition to the growing number of professional texts available for students planning managerial careers in hospitality and tourism—much of the credit will be due to the people whose help we are delighted to have had this opportunity to acknowledge. If not, the responsibility is wholly that of the authors.

Paul R. Dittmer
Gerald G. Griffin

April, 1992

Introductions

Dimensions of the Hospitality Industry:
An Overview

1

LEARNING OBJECTIVES

After reading and studying this chapter, you should be able to:

1. Distinguish between the manufacturing and service sectors in an economy.
2. Define hospitality and describe the scope of the hospitality industry.
3. Identify the two principal segments of the hospitality industry and list the major types of businesses in each.
4. Describe the relationship between the hospitality and the travel and tourism industries.
5. Discuss the historic role of entertainment in the hospitality industry.
6. Distinguish between travel agents and tour operators.
7. List and explain the three elements that make the hospitality industry unique.
8. Discuss the special characteristics that distinguish hospitality and other service businesses from those that manufacture products.
9. Define the terms moment of truth and cycle of service; then discuss the significance of each for the hospitality industry.
10. Discuss career opportunities in the hospitality industry and the qualifications commonly sought by hospitality employers.
11. Describe the advantages and disadvantages associated with careers in the hospitality industry.

INTRODUCTION

You are about to begin studying one of the most interesting and fastest growing industries in the modern world economy—the hospitality industry.

The hospitality industry is one part of a larger group of industries that collectively make up the service sector of the economy. The economy is divided into two sectors: The first consists of companies that manufacture tangible, physical items known as products; the second is comprised of individuals and organizations that perform services for people and businesses. The service sector includes enterprises covering a broad range of occupations—law, interior decorating, dentistry, accounting, nursing, automobile repair, food preparation, and haircutting, to name a few.

In years past, the manufacturing sector was the dominant force in the economy, accounting for the largest part of the economic growth that so changed the nation in its formative years and through the first half of the twentieth century. In recent years, the service sector of the nation's economy has been growing at a much faster rate than the manufacturing sector. And the businesses that make up the hospitality industry have been growing at an even faster rate than other service industries. Thus, opportunities are being created in extraordinary numbers in every part of the hospitality industry.

Since the 1950s, the hospitality industry has been of growing importance to the economic life of the nation and has been leading the way in providing new opportunities for individuals from every age group and every ethnic, racial, and socioeconomic background. Professional economists predict that the hospitality industry will continue to grow in the years ahead. This suggests that there will be ever greater numbers of career possibilities for men and women who choose to become hospitality professionals and who prepare themselves for these new opportunities.

As we begin our investigation into the hospitality industry, we will devote this first chapter to some basic elements: identifying the industry, creating an overview of it, contrasting it to other industries, and pointing out its distinctive characteristics. Finally, we will point out some of the opportunities the hospitality industry offers the men and women who prepare to take advantage of it.

A DEFINITION OF HOSPITALITY

The word *hospitality* has ancient roots, dating from the earliest days of Roman civilization. It is derived from the Latin word *hospitare*, meaning "to receive as a guest." Several related words come from the same Latin root, including *hospital*, *hospice*, and *hostel*. In each of these, the principal meaning focuses on a host who receives, welcomes, and caters to the needs of people who are temporarily away from their homes. "To receive as a guest" is a phrase that implies a host prepared to meet a guest's basic requirements while that guest is away from home. The requirements of a guest in these circumstances have traditionally been food, beverages, and lodgings or shelter. Many would add to this some form of incidental entertainment, even though a number of hosts clearly have limited or ignored this as an element of hospitality.

The Basics of an Industry

The traditional view, of course, takes us to the heart of the hospitality industry. If hospitality is the act of providing food, beverages, and lodging to travelers, then the hospitality industry is the collection of businesses that do this. Some may offer entertainment, incidental or otherwise. But we choose to treat this as somewhat apart from the principal subject of this text, which is food, beverage, and lodging — the basics of hospitality.

This description brings to mind two important distinctions between the hospitality industry and other service enterprises:

1. The hospitality industry provides food, beverages, lodging, or some combination of the three that other businesses would provide only on the most incidental basis.

2. It provides services primarily to *travelers* in a broad sense of the term; whereas other service businesses ordinarily deal with customers who are local residents, not travelers.

This definition also distinguishes the hospitality industry from businesses in the manufacturing sector of our economy. Manufacturers do not normally sell services. Instead, they make products that are sold to consumers through regional systems of local wholesalers and retailers, with some notable exceptions.

There are those who will be quick to point out a potential problem with our view of the industry. Clearly, sometimes a service provided for travelers is also provided to local residents. Restaurants and hotels that provide food, beverages, lodging, or some combination of these to residents of their local neighborhoods are excellent examples.

Those concerned with the question of the residential or nonresidential nature of customers in a hotel dining room will soon recognize the futility of attempting to make useful distinctions. Regardless of where the customers live, the staff must offer the same menus and provide the same level of service to all. Although the hospitality industry evolved as a means of providing food, shelter, and entertainment for travelers, these services appealed to local residents, as well; and increasing numbers have come to take advantage of them over time. Today, some hospitality enterprises may service local residents only, and never attend to the needs of any travelers. For practical and definitional purposes, then, those providing food, beverages, and shelter are considered part of the hospitality industry whether or not their customers are actually travelers.

The hospitality industry has become closely linked to travel and tourism, and to certain related recreational activities selected for their ability to "entertain"— casino gambling, skiing, and golf, among many. Because most hospitality educators believe that these should be covered to an extent in any hospitality management curriculum, we have adopted that view in the preparation of this text. Accordingly, we will treat travel, tourism, and various recreational activities as necessary or desirable adjuncts to the study of hospitality management; and we will deal with them separately in a section following those devoted to the traditional elements of the hospitality industry.

SCOPE OF THE HOSPITALITY INDUSTRY

From the above material, it quickly becomes apparent that there may be any number of businesses in the hospitality industry, which is not evident from the definition. The definition is really quite broad; therefore, at this point we will discuss some of the varied enterprises that make up each of the two principal segments of the industry—food and beverage, on the one hand, and lodging on the other.

Food and Beverage Segment

Everyone is aware of the seemingly limitless array of organizations that provide food and beverage service to the public. Today, these include every conceivable type of establishment between a brightly colored fast-food[1] restaurant and one offering elegant, ultraexpensive continental or French cuisine.

No matter what type of food travelers and nontravelers alike desire, there must be food service available to them at the appropriate hour for breakfast, lunch, dinner, supper, snacks, and so on.

The public looks for food service everywhere: hotels, motels, factories, dormitories, highways, cruise ships, city streets, trains, offices, airlines, national parks, airports, bus terminals, shopping malls—any place outside the home where people can be found living, working, or playing. There are commercial restaurants of every description around us every day: fast service restaurants selling hamburgers, or chicken, or pizza, or pasta, or hero sandwiches; ethnic restaurants selling Chinese, Mexican, Italian, Latin American, German, Indonesian, Indian, and many other types of meals; specialty restaurants serving seafood, or steaks, or pasta, or

---

[1]Although the term *fast food* is very common, many believe *fast service* or *quick service* are more suitable terms. We will use all three interchangeably in this text: Those learning about the hospitality industry should be familiar with all three.

chicken, or vegetarian items; restaurants organized around particular themes, such as railroad cars, English pubs, railroad stations, medieval pageants, opera, or the circus; and a range of others—expensive, inexpensive, noisy, quiet, elegant, dingy, brightly lighted, or dark; serving great food, terrible food, and every kind in between.

And food service establishments abound outside the usual restaurant settings: in Disney World and other theme parks; in schools and colleges; in hospitals and homes for senior citizens; in prisons and halfway houses; in shelters for the homeless. There are carts in the streets and vending machines everywhere; even supermarkets and other food stores now offer food service.

Those familiar with the history of our industry will recognize that taverns traditionally have been establishments that sold both food and beverages and provided some form of entertainment, however limited. Some taverns even made overnight accommodations available for travelers. In fact, in the seventeenth century, laws were passed in New England requiring that each community provide a tavern for the "entertainment of travelers."

The tavern, pub, inn, ale house, or public house served as social center—a place to which travelers and local residents could go to find "entertainment." And it served society in this manner throughout the eighteenth and nineteenth centuries, long before the invention of such pervasive modern devices as phonographs, movies, radios, televisions, videos, tape decks, and compact disk players. People gathered in the taverns, where local residents could mingle with travelers—to share news of wars, plagues, famines, or natural disasters and to discuss local politics or gossip about their neighbors. Sometimes it was only to find a quiet, warm place by the fire; normally it created an occasion for a mug of beer, a tankard of ale, or even a glass of wine.

In the twentieth century, the role of the establishments selling beer, ale, wine, and other beverages has changed to some extent. As we shall see, the role of taverns has become enlarged in the modern world. Their role as entertainment centers has diminished, but they are meeting new needs in society—needs that did not exist before the introduction of some of the modern world's technological innovations. Most are no longer called taverns: The terms *bar* and *cocktail lounge* have been devised for those that serve some of these new needs.

Hotels and restaurants have long been in the business of selling drinks—as accompaniments to food, because their customers began to expect it, or because they discovered it was profitable. The terms *food* and *beverage* became ever more closely linked, and both hotels and restaurants began to use terminology that illustrated the linkage: *food and beverage manager,* and *food and beverage department* became common and remain so. Alcoholic beverages have become closely linked to hotels, restaurants, and other establishments that sell food. Therefore, because our industry treats food and beverages together as one segment of the industry, we will do the same in this text.

The Lodging Segment

The lodging segment of the hospitality industry obviously includes the more familiar kinds of establishments that have long offered shelter to travelers—the hotels and motels that we see on city streets, along highways, near beaches, and close to airports, ski slopes, theme parks, lakes, and national parks. Those who are less familiar with the industry may not realize that some lodging facilities, called *inns, motor hotels, lodges,* or *motor inns,* are simply hotels or motels using different names. And that there are lodging establishments using some very different terms and selling some very different lodging concepts from those of the traditional hotels and motels: *bed and breakfast, resort hotel, resort condominium, conference center, extended stay, time-sharing,* and *all-suite*—all terms that must be addressed in a discussion of the lodging segment. Then there are lodging establishments that are known for the special facilities they offer: ski lodges in Colorado, and casino hotels in Las Vegas and Atlantic City are good examples.

In many ways, campgrounds and transient trailer parks are lodging establishments and, in their own special ways, so are school and college dormitories, summer camps, and health spas. All attend to the lodging needs of those away from home.

In other parts of the world, the signs for lodging establishments may display some unfamiliar words—such as *parador:* an old Spanish monastery or castle converted to use as a hotel; *pension* or *pensione:* a French or Italian home at which guests are provided with room and board; *chateau:* a French castle or elegant country home used as a hotel; *ryokan:* a Japanese inn at which traditional customs are observed; and *hostel:* a lodging facility at which inexpensive accommodations are provided for students and others, typically on a not-for-profit basis.

Lodging signs also bring us some of the world's best-known names in hospitality: Hilton, Sheraton, Holiday Inn, Marriott, Ramada, Days Inns, Quality Inns, and Hyatt, to name just a few. All these—and many others, as we shall see—help make up the dynamic and growing lodging segment of the industry.

TRAVEL AND TOURISM

Two key terms that arise in any discussion of the hospitality industry are *travel* and *tourism.* They are typically used together as an umbrella term to refer to those businesses providing primary services to travelers. These include the traditional hospitality businesses and a number of others closely linked to them. The term *travel and tourism* includes food and beverage operations, lodging operations, and related enterprises in the fields of entertainment, recreation, and transportation, as well as travel agencies and tour operators.

A

A luxury hotel in Honolulu, Hawaii, the Sheraton Moana Surfrider. (Photo 1989 David Franzen; courtesy ITT Sheraton Corp.)

B

A resort hotel in Beverly Hills, California, the Regent Beverly Wilshire Hotel. (Photo by Martin Elkort; Los Angeles Convention and Vistors Bureau.)

C

An all-suite hotel in Fort Lauderdale, Florida, the Guest Quarters Suite Hotel. (Courtesy Guest Quarters Suite Hotel, Fort Lauderdale, Florida.)

D

A bed and breakfast inn in Moretown, Vermont, Schultzes' Village Inn. (Courtesy Vermont Travel Division.)

Examples of the various segments of the lodging industry in the United States, reflecting the diversity of guests' choices as well as work environments.

Entertainment and Recreation

Entertainment, as an element in the hospitality industry, has its roots in the traditional duties of a host entertaining his guests, whether they be neighborhood residents or travelers from afar. The host has always felt an obligation to minister to any of his guests' needs, not only for food and beverages and for lodging, but also for entertainment.

Beginning centuries ago, innkeepers, tavern-keepers, and their descendants have attended (in varying degrees) to guests' needs for entertainment. Some simply talked to their guests; others told stories, truthful or otherwise; some provided games (darts, draughts, backgammon, or chess, for example); others engaged jugglers and traveling minstrels.

In our time, the entertaining of guests has included the modern equivalents of these ancient traditions, but it has not been limited to these. Today, the concept of entertaining guests is far broader. Guests are being offered all manner of inducements in the form of entertainments and recreational activities to attract them to particular properties. Golf, tennis, casino gambling, backpacking, concerts, swimming, boating, and handball are among the many examples of steps in this direction.

In some cases, local governments and businesses have worked together very closely to turn an entire community into a desirable destination for travelers. For example, casino gambling and celebrity entertainment are two of the principal reasons that people go to Las Vegas, Nevada. The more traditional elements of the hospitality business are almost incidental players here.

The Las Vegas Strip, where casino gambling and celebrity entertainment are the main attractions for visitors, and the traditional elements of the hospitality business—food, beverages, and lodging—are almost incidental. (Courtesy Las Vegas News Bureau.)

Disney World has taken a logical next step, developing a resort environment that includes a vast array of food and beverage, lodging, and entertainment facilities within its walls. The entertainment facilities include shows, rides, and exhibits so spectacular that a guest has no opportunity to seek or think about any other entertainment during his time at Disney World. This is one example of a complete recreational center that, in itself, becomes the object of travel. To guests, the food, beverage, and lodging is relatively incidental; they travel to Disney World for the spectacle of it all.

Transportation

It should be obvious that all travelers, regardless of destination, require some way of getting from one place to another. That is a major purpose of the transportation business—making it possible for people to go from one place to another. There are many ways to do this, from the primitive and simple to the modern and complex. One can ride on the back of an animal, or in a supersonic jet, or use any number of other possibilities. The more common ones are automobiles, recreational vehicles (RVs), buses, ships, trains, and airplanes.

Those preparing for professional careers in any part of the traditional hospitality industry should be aware of the long-standing importance of transportation to the survival of hotels, motels, restaurants, and closely related enterprises. Links between the transportation and hospitality businesses are as old as history, and developments in either have normally led to changes in the other.

Nations and states with the best transportation networks tended to develop the healthiest economic systems and the most advanced hospitality industries.

Travel Agencies and Tour Operators

Travel agencies and tour operators are modern additions to the travel and tourism world. Neither existed before the middle of the nineteenth century, but both have become central to the survival of many businesses in the hospitality industry.

A *travel agent* is one who sells travel services in a travel agency. Transportation and lodging are the most common; meals may be included in the price of some lodging. Although a travel agent may make individual reservations for airline tickets and hotel rooms for some clients, much of the business volume in many travel agencies consists of selling travel services assembled by others into "packages." In the travel business, a *package* is a bundle of related travel services offered to a buyer at a single price.

There are many types of packages available through travel agencies. Some include only a limited number of services—an airline ticket and a rental car, for example, or a hotel room and tickets for a ski lift. Other packages are more inclusive and may provide the buyer with a round-trip airline ticket, rental car, hotel room, all meals, access to such features as golf courses and tennis courts, and tickets to various events.

Most travel agencies selling packages do not put the packages together. This is done by *tour operators*, wholesalers who make the necessary contacts with hotels, airlines, and other providers of travel services, and devise packages that they believe will appeal to retail buyers. Like all wholesalers in all businesses, they are volume purchasers who are able to negotiate lower prices because of their high-volume purchases. They are typically able to offer any collection of travel services at a price lower than the individual consumer or his travel agent would be able to arrange.

Many resorts owe their survival to travel agents and tour operators. So do operators of other hospitality enterprises that depend for their livelihood on the sales volume provided by guests at these resorts. Resorts on some of the Caribbean islands, for example, find that up to 80 percent of their guests have been booked by travel agents. And the vast majority of other international travel arrangements are made by travel agents.

HOSPITALITY AS A UNIQUE INDUSTRY

One major premise of this chapter is that hospitality enterprises are unique, in contrast both to other service enterprises and to manufacturers of durable goods. It will be useful to point out three elements in the hospitality industry that tend to make it unique:

1. Hospitality operations provide their customers with service products, rather than durable goods.
2. Unlike durable goods, service products cannot be manufactured and stored for future sale.
3. Hospitality operations provide their service products—food, beverages, and lodging—primarily to travelers.

ACHIEVING QUALITY STANDARDS AND UNIFORMITY. Manufacturers of durable goods have the advantage of being able to establish and achieve quality standards for products such that all units of a given product will be uniform. Service businesses have the ability to establish quality standards for the service products they offer, but very limited ability to achieve uniformity. To illustrate, let us compare the manufacturing of toys on an assembly line to the "manufacturing" of service products in a hotel.

The toy manufacturer designs a toy, determines the parts required to manufacture it, creates a process to assemble them, sets up an assembly line, trains workers to do particular jobs in the assembling process, then begins to manufacture units of product. Any problems that develop can be corrected before any of the toys are sold. If the company has a labor problem—a strike, for example—the manufacturer can resolve the problem and resume production, and consumers purchasing the toys will not be able to tell from examining the product that the company had a problem. If there is a shortage of raw materials, the company can close, or slow down production until supplies are again available. The consumers who purchase the toys will never be able to determine that the problem existed by examining a unit of the product. And if the manufacturer finds that units of the product fail to meet established quality standards, they can be prevented from reaching the market, or the entire product line can be withdrawn from sale until the problems are corrected. Again, the customer will not be able to examine units of product and determine that the manufacturer had production problems.

It is much more difficult for a hotel to insure uniformity in the quality of the service products it offers customers. For example, if part of the labor force decides to strike, the hotel must continue to serve customers as best it can, even if this means reducing or eliminating some services. If the kitchen staff is unable to produce food of the desired quality because the chef has accepted a job elsewhere and taken most of the kitchen staff with him, the hotel must continue to open its dining room—even knowing that food preparation may be substandard until new workers with suitable culinary skills can be hired. If the laundry does not deliver an adequate supply of clean linen, the hotel must improvise in some fashion so that rooms can be prepared for expected guests. And because customers are in the hotel while management is dealing with any or all of these difficulties, it is probably impossible to prevent the guests from knowing about problems at the hotel. Whenever management is having difficulty providing the level of service quality it intends to offer each guest, it must make every effort to improve its service while continuing normal business, even though some customers will not be receiving the level of service intended.

PRODUCING AND "STORING FOR FUTURE USE". Another important difference comes from the fact that manufacturers of durable goods can produce and store their products for future use, whereas providers of service products cannot. The company manufacturing toys can schedule production of the toys to meet its own needs without regard for immediate demand and can store the excess until such time as there is demand for the product. For example, the Christmas season is a time of increased demand for toys. Manufacturers produce toys year-round and store them until demand increases during the Christmas shopping season. Production can be scheduled to meet the needs of management—to maintain a year-round staff of limited size, and to avoid overtime pay during times of peak demand, for example.

Hotel operators, on the other hand, cannot control the rate of service production and cannot store units of service products for future use. A hotel is selling a service, and the quantity "manufactured" must meet current demand. A hotel with all rooms occupied requires more staff than when only half the number of rooms are occupied. If demand is very weak, a hotel may be forced to close some or all of the facility. Seasonal resort hotels have always had this problem, and many summer hotels close for the winter when the demand for rooms is too weak to justify remaining open.

A hotel cannot manufacture service products for inventory, producing and storing them for sale later, when there is demand. Servers in a dining room cannot "serve" unless there are guests seated in the dining room. There is no way for management to direct servers to serve in the absence of guests, then somehow store that service for future use. Therefore, there is no "inventory" of service products available for a food service manager to draw upon if the dining room becomes busy. To accommodate these customers, the manager must have additional workers on hand, being paid, and thus ready and willing to provide the required services on demand. That is the only sense in which hospitality managers can be thought to have any inventory of service available.

If the number of customers seeking service at any one time exceeds the capacity of the servers on duty to provide that service, some customers will simply have to wait or be forced to go elsewhere. A hotel must provide service when needed, which means that the rate of production is controlled by the market rather than by the producer. If there is excess demand for a given service during certain periods, that excess demand must remain unfulfilled. If all hotels in a given city are booked to capacity, additional rooms cannot be created to meet sudden demand, and potential customers must either find alternative accommodations or postpone travel until rooms are available.

PROVIDING SERVICES TO THE TRAVELERS. The final element that makes the hospitality industry unique is its special relationship with the traveler, defined as one who is away from home. The hospitality industry has a unique responsibility to provide service products to travelers at the times these services are needed. That may be day or night, workdays or holidays—often when other businesses (producers of both durable goods and other service products) are closed.

Taken together, these elements distinguish the hospitality enterprise from other businesses. Because it is unique, successful management of the hospitality enterprise requires a special approach: one particularly well suited to use in those businesses that provide services directly to the individuals who use the services—hotels, motels, and restaurants among them. An understanding of the special characteristics of hospitality management will require closer examination.

SPECIAL CHARACTERISTICS OF HOSPITALITY MANAGEMENT

Those engaged in selling or providing service products typically deal directly with final customers, meeting them face-to-face on an ongoing basis. Manufacturers of durable goods typically never meet the final purchasers of their product. The toy manufacturer does not know the children who receive their toys and seldom truly knows the extent to which the children are pleased or disappointed with them. Some customers may write the toy manufacturer to express pleasure or disappointment and some may return toys to the manufacturer for repair or replacement, but that is usually the extent of customer contact with the manufacturer.

A hotel, on the other hand, is in the business of providing its service products directly to customers. Its employees come into daily contact with guests and often receive immediate feedback about the hotel's quality of service. Many customers express their impressions of the service quality by complimenting or complaining to the staff. For many customers, the level of service quality is determined by an individual event or contact with a particular member of the staff: a clean room, slow service in the dining room, a friendly and helpful desk clerk, or some similar item.

Unlike the manufacturer, the hotel cannot test the service product ahead of time or take back poor service products as one would take back inferior durable goods and replace them. If customers perceive service to be satisfactory, they will be pleased. If it is perceived to be otherwise, the customer impression of his treatment by the establishment will be poor. Each customer's impression of a hospitality service has expectations of a particular level of service quality. To the extent that the service meets or exceeds expectations, the customer is satisfied. If not, the customer is unhappy. An opportunity to satisfy a guest, and possibly to transform a first-time purchaser into a loyal customer may be lost because of poor service. Service products must be right the first time.

Often, service that is perceived as unsatisfactory is actually the result of differences in individuals' cultures and backgrounds. When this is the case, it is called *cultural collision*. For example, some Americans equate good service with fast service. Yet in many parts of the world, the time taken to perform a given task can be twice that taken in the United States. In some cultures, this is because people are in no hurry and tend to move slowly. In others, it is considered rude to appear to be rushing customers through their meals. Americans visiting these differing cultures sometimes return home complaining about poor service, when in fact the service was not poor by the standards of the country and the hotel visited. It was simply a case of cultural collision.

From this discussion, it should be apparent that uniformity is more common, easier to attain, and more desirable in businesses producing a durable good, rather than a service product. Those manufacturing durable goods can afford reasonable levels of production error, because products that do not meet established standards can be prevented from reaching customers. Hospitality managers and others providing service products have very limited ability to control the actions of employees. Some do not know when the service quality provided by their employees is below the levels intended by management. Others—the more enlightened among hospitality managers—realize that service should not be uniform, but should be tailored to the specific needs and perceptions of the individual customer.

MOMENTS OF TRUTH

Jan Carlzon, president of Scandinavian Airlines, wrote a book[2] published in 1987, in which he employs the term *a moment of truth* to describe any contact between a customer and a business that gives the customer an impression of the business and from which the customer makes judgments about the business.

A customer makes a judgment about a business each time he or she has contact with any element in that business. For example, in a hotel a guest may first make contact with the hotel business when her taxicab stops in front of the entrance. The initial impression made by the outward physical appearance of the building may be the first moment of truth. If the guest expects the taxi door to be opened by a doorman, his presence or absence may be the next moment of truth. The next may be found in the doorman's attitude, or demeanor, or the manner in which he performs his job. Other moments of truth will come from the guest's contacts with the room clerk and bellman, a ride in the self-service elevator, and first reaction to her assigned room.

Many other moments of truth will occur during the course of this guest's stay in the hotel. Finally, her overall impression will reflect every contact made during the period and will include a number of judgments about the business: how efficiently it is run, whether or not it is customer-oriented, how competent the employees are, how well the establishment meets the needs of its customers, and the level of its service quality. In a fully occupied hotel of 500 rooms, there are thousands of moments of truth occurring every day.

The sum total of the guests' moments of truth become the perception and impression of the hotel and its service quality. If the majority of guests judge the moments of truth to be positive, the hotel will have a positive reputation. If not, the hotel's reputation will be negative, and decreasing levels of business will be the likely result.

Hotels sell service. In a very real way, service is their only product. Like the product of the manufacturer, it cannot be sold in volume over long periods of time if it is perceived in the market as being of poor quality or offering insufficient value for the room rates asked—at least as long as customers have an alternative. But unlike the manufacturer, the management of successful hospitality operations must proceed differently from the management of manufacturing operations: The hospitality establishment must do it right the first time.

---

[2]Jan Carlzon, *Moments of Truth* (Cambridge: Ballinger Publishing Co., 1987).

CYCLES OF SERVICE

Karl Albrecht, in his 1988 book, *At America's Service,* carries this concept further. He states that a customer views an organization in terms of the chain of events from the beginning of his experience with an organization to the end of the experience. He calls these *cycles of service.* Albrecht states that a cycle of service "is a natural, unconscious pattern that exists in the customer's mind, and it may have nothing in common with your 'technical' approach to setting up the business."[3]

He indicates that service businesses are often set up and run in a fashion designed to achieve some specific goals established by owners or managers and that working to achieve these goals may impede one's ability provide positive moments of truth and satisfy customers' needs. For example, a hotel may be run to achieve maximum profit. In the eyes of management, this may mean that they should establish policies that would minimize staff and maximize their efficiency. This may translate into instructions that the housekeeping staff should be intent on getting rooms ready for occupancy each day without regard for special requests of arriving guests. It may mean establishing policies in the kitchen and bar that do not allow servers to take orders for items other than those listed on the menu. Or it may lead to minimizing supervisory staff to a point where customer problems cannot be appropriately handled.

The guests, on the other hand, are not aware of these policies and are concerned with their own comfort and enjoyment of the hotel facility. They experience moments of truth from the beginning of their stay to their departure, and these represent a cycle of service that leaves an impression of satisfaction or dissatisfaction with the hotel.

It is important to note that the above policies many work very well in an operation producing durable goods. There, a good manager may be considered one who is best able to establish and carry out specific policies and routines that minimize costs and maximize output. The important goal is the production of appropriate numbers of units at the minimal cost, each of which meets the quality standards established for the item. Disaffected workers and difficult working conditions may not be of real consequence to management, as long as the products sold to customers meet the quality standards established by management, and production volume can be maintained at suitable levels.

The results of such policies in a service enterprise, however, would necessarily be quite different. A hotel's policies must be customer oriented, not product oriented. If both managers and staff members work cooperatively to insure that all aspects of operation will lead to positive moments of truth for guests, the resulting cycles of service are more likely to produce satisfaction. Policies and procedures

[3]Karl Albrecht, *At America's Service* (Homewood, IL: Dow Jones-Irwin, 1988), p. 33.

must be sufficiently flexible so that staff can individualize treatment of guests. Further discussion of this and related topics will be deferred to Chapter 15.

From previous discussion, one can begin to see the importance of managing hospitality operations in a manner that maintains service quality at suitable levels. This is one of the great challenges in the hospitality management professions, all of which demand dedication and long hours of work. For those prepared to meet the challenges of hospitality management, the rewards can be bountiful. It will be useful, now, to look at some of the many opportunities available to those who plan careers in the hospitality industry.

CAREER OPPORTUNITIES IN THE HOSPITALITY INDUSTRY

Until several years ago, management personnel in the hospitality industry were not expected to be college educated. Those interested in hospitality management typically began their careers by taking lower-level jobs to learn about the industry and eventually worked their way up through the organization. This commonly took many years. In hotels, men typically started as elevator operators, information clerks, or bellmen; whereas women began as reservations clerks or typists. The same was true in restaurants: People started as waiters, waitresses, order clerks, or bookkeepers.

Educational Requirements

Although it is still possible to begin a career in hospitality the same way, such opportunities are diminishing each year. Today, those starting careers in hospitality management are more and more likely to have some formal education obtained in one of the postsecondary programs developed in the last twenty-five years to prepare men and women for such careers. Whether they have earned certificates, diplomas, or degrees at the associate, baccalaureate, or graduate level, growing numbers of hospitality managers and management trainees have studied formally to prepare for their chosen careers.

Experience Requirements

Although many begin their careers in management training positions, it is important to note that starting positions are not filled solely on the basis of educational background. Experience in the field is still an important consideration to many employers, and a number of students have found that good work experience gained while attending classes has been instrumental in their finding good jobs after graduation. Depending on conditions in labor markets and accepted norms in various regions, education alone may not be enough to earn one a management training position. In many instances, those in the industry insist that graduates gain real work experience in conjunction with education; and most hospitality management students today should seek part-time employment during the academic year or full-time employment in the summer. Potential employers are typically more inclined to offer good starting jobs to students with valid work experience behind them. Classrooms and laboratories where hospitality operations are simulated are very different from the real world of hospitality, and it is possible that some individuals who enjoy the challenge in hospitality classrooms may not like actual working conditions in the industry.

Entry-Level Management Positions

The multifaceted nature of the hospitality industry suggests that the opportunities available are in a number of different areas. In hotels, individuals might be given such job titles as: management trainee, assistant front-office manager, night auditor, banquet sales representative, assistant restaurant manager, assistant food and beverage controller, assistant housekeeper, and assistant steward. In some motels and smaller hotels the available job titles could include: assistant manager, banquet manager, and assistant food and beverage manager.

In restaurants and similar food service operations, analogous positions might carry such titles as: management trainee, assistant manager, dining room manager, unit manager, steward, bar manager, banquet manager, or food-and-beverage cost controller, depending on an individual's level of experience.

The size of an operation often determines the particular job title, and the authority and responsibility associated with a job title will vary greatly with the size of a property. For example, an assistant manager in a 50-room motel might be the only person on duty in the front office and therefore would be responsible for taking reservations, operating the switchboard, checking guests in and out, and solving guests' problems. An assistant manager in a 500-room hotel would have very different, higher-level responsibilities, such as supervising a sizable staff of specialists each of whom was responsible for one of the many tasks required in lodging operations.

The specific job that a particular individual is offered may be heavily dependent on overall qualifications. After all, employers are likely to consider many aspects of an applicant, trying to match her to the requirements of a particular job. In order to do this successfully, they must attempt to assess all of an applicant's attributes, not simply her technical knowledge.

Qualifications and Employer Assessment

Some of the factors commonly included in such an assessment are grades, outside interests, participation in organizations, past employment record, ability to communicate effectively, attitudes, and interpersonal skills. Good grades demonstrate dedication to achievement and willingness to work hard, as well as ability. A broad range of interests in sports, music, drama, and other areas normally indicates that the applicant is well rounded. Participation in organizations such as fraternities, student government, and professional groups give the employer some idea of a person's social skills and leadership abilities. Past employment is examined to see if the applicant has a stable work record, which can be an indication of reliability in the future. Employers also assess the attitudes of applicants, looking for those who are willing to devote the necessary time and effort to a task, even if it means temporarily sacrificing other activities. They look for applicants who are willing, cooperative workers, able to do the work required of them. Finally, employers search for those with good interpersonal skills. Because hospitality is a "people business," it is critically important that employees are able to communicate effectively with guests.

ADVANTAGES AND DISADVANTAGES OF WORKING IN THE HOSPITALITY INDUSTRY

All jobs have positive and negative elements, and those in the hospitality industry are not exceptions. But people view the characteristics of jobs quite differently. Although one aspect of a given job may be considered to be positive by one individual, another may view that same aspect in a negative light. For example, evening work suits some people well, but others dislike it intensely. Similarly, clerical work suits many, while others find it tedious. Rather than attempt judgments about what may be positive and negative, we will merely outline the conditions generally found in the industry.

Wages and Salaries

Generally, wages and salaries are determined by such factors as the adequacy of the labor supply, the level of skills required for particular jobs, the extent to which unions influence wages, and various regional considerations. The hospitality industry is labor intensive, and many of the jobs require relatively low levels of skill and education. Generally, entry-level jobs requiring neither specific education nor previous experience tend to command the lowest wages. Those having jobs requiring specific training or previous experience—in pastry production, for example—are paid somewhat higher wages. Starting salaries for recent college graduates with majors in hospitality management tend to be "average" when compared with similar jobs in other industries. Salaries for jobs in middle and upper management are often considered quite good, and many regard them as excellent. In general, larger organizations often pay more than smaller organizations for similar work and, within a given region, wages and salaries in affluent urban areas tend to be higher than those offered in rural and poorer urban areas.

Work Environment

The work environment in hospitality operations can be quite good compared with other industries. First-class and luxury hotels are often considered fine places to work, with their opulent surroundings and clean environment. The idea of spending one's working hours in contact with wealthy and famous guests is appealing to many. In better properties, employees are typically provided with excellent meals, and some management employees may be permitted to eat in the dining rooms of the hotels. Further, some hospitality organizations provide exceptional work sites: Caribbean beaches, resort areas with pools, tennis courts, golf courses, and a host of other superior facilities.

On the other hand, conditions can be viewed as less than satisfactory in some older, poorly maintained hotels, and in a sizable number of individually owned restaurants. The front offices of some hotels are without air conditioning, which can be unpleasant in sultry summer months. In others, aging equipment that continually breaks down can present working conditions that would be considered unsatisfactory. Kitchens can present other problems: Those with poorly maintained equipment and those with improper ventilation can be uncomfortably hot and very difficult to work in.

Hours and Days of Work

Because the industry caters to travelers, who may seek hospitality services at any hour of the day or night, a vast number of hospitality operations are open when other businesses are closed. Except for some resort properties, hotels are open and staffed twenty-four hours a day, seven days a week, including holidays. New employees, including managers, are often required to work evenings and weekends. Employees typically have one or two days off each week, depending on the establishment. The days off are not likely to be Saturdays or Sundays for the new employee; weekend days off are usually reserved for employees with seniority.

On the other hand, some consider working on weekends to be an advantage. It gives them time off during the week when shopping malls and recreation facilities are often least crowded. By the same token, those who work evening shifts look forward to having daylight hours for activities that would be difficult or impossible at night: boating, golf, and tennis, for example. In some cases employees work according to a system known as *alternating watches*, where an individual may work a normal day shift for one or two weeks, then an evening shift for a similar period. This provides variety and satisfies the lifestyles of many. Those who are in the resort industry often work very hard during times when their friends are playing but are able to take vacations when others cannot—during cold winter months, when those in some other industries cannot possibly get away from their desks. This also gives them opportunities to vacation when resort areas are least crowded and rates are lowest.

New managers in the hospitality industry are often asked to work longer hours than they would in other industries. A work week of 50 to 60 hours is not uncommon. Neither are workdays of 10 to 12 hours. However, because much of a hospitality manager's workday involves talking to interesting guests, most who do this have no complaints about the length of the day.

It should be noted that the spouses and family members of some hospitality managers object to the specific hours, or the long workdays, or the somewhat unusual days off that can be common in this industry. However, the family members of anyone aspiring to a successful career in management in any field must recognize that long hours are likely to be among the requirements. Hospitality is not unique in that respect.

Travel Opportunities

One of the attractions of a career in the hospitality industry is the potential it offers for travel. A number of chain organizations in the hotel/motel segment of the industry customarily transfer management employees from one property to another every few years. Some restaurant chains do so, as well. Both lodging and food service chains are more likely to transfer management employees during periods of expansion, when their expertise is needed in new units. Some transfer management-level employees at the time of promotion; others transfer managers periodically to reduce the risk of long-term managers becoming "stale."

Another advantage of a career in hospitality is that job opportunities are not restricted to particular cities or regions, as in some other industries. Hospitality businesses can be found in literally every region, city, and town; and individuals can find positions available wherever they choose to live, regardless of climate or geography. Hospitality is very much an international profession.

There are those who make their careers in hospitality specifically because of the travel opportunities the industry provides. There are even some who plan to take advantages of the travel opportunities by taking winter jobs in warm resort areas—Florida, for example—then resigning to accept summer jobs in the cooler resorts of New England and the North Central or Rocky Mountain states. For those who enjoy travel, a career in hospitality can satisfy a need that might be difficult to meet in some other field.

Nevertheless, some individuals truly dislike travel and may take all possible steps to avoid it. Many in the hospitality industry have families and find it very difficult to move, particularly if there are school-age children or elderly parents involved. Many are settled members of their communities and have close ties they are unwilling to break. A substantial number own homes, which they may be unwilling or unable to sell. Others merely prefer to stay in communities where they have lived for many years. Those who prefer not to move from one region to another must be more particular about the types of positions they seek or the organizations from which they seek employment. It is possible, after all, to work for an independent city or resort hotel or motel or for an individual food service establishment for many years without having to face the prospect of moving to a new geographical area.

Opportunities for Advancement

In a number of businesses, youth has traditionally been a barrier to rapid advancement: Promotions in these businesses have been slow, and managers on the higher levels have normally been close to retirement age. In some businesses, it may be necessary to wait, sometimes for years, until openings occur within the company and advancement becomes possible. Generally, this has not been the case in the hospitality industry.

In hospitality, there is a long tradition of *mobility*. Employees at all levels have almost always found it possible to change jobs readily, and many have done so with great regularity. The transient nature of the industry has generally meant that opportunities for higher-paying jobs have continually been available to qualified individuals. Thus, if an individual working in a given hotel or restaurant decides she has little possibility of promotion, she can readily find another position—often a better one!—in another hotel or restaurant.

The hospitality industry has ample opportunities for people of all ages. It is not uncommon for restaurant managers, resident managers, marketing directors, food and beverage managers, executive housekeepers, and others in equally responsible positions to be in their mid- to late twenties. At the same time, many of those in the hospitality industry are people who are in their second or third careers—people who discovered the appeal of a career in hospitality after a number of years in some other, possibly less interesting field. Except for the extremes, neither youth nor age is a disadvantage in this industry.

A PEOPLE-ORIENTED PROFESSION

Because the hospitality industry serves the needs of the traveling public, the majority of people working in this industry—and virtually all of its managers—are in constant contact with guests and customers. Ours is a people-oriented profession. Individuals preparing for careers in hospitality must understand that their responsibilities are likely to include daily interaction with customers to meet their needs and to solve their problems. Social skills and the ability to communicate effectively with others are important assets for anyone planning such a career.

If a reasonable number of your interests and preferences match those detailed in this chapter, you may find the hospitality industry a suitable choice for your career. If so, you are likely to find many exciting and rewarding career opportunities available to you. Reliability, dedication, willingness to work hard, and an interest in meeting customers' needs and solving their problems are the primary requisites for success in this field.

SUMMARY

In this chapter, the distinction between the manufacturing and service sectors of an economy is drawn, and the scope of the hospitality industry within the service sector is defined and described. The relationships among travel and tourism, travel agents, tour operators, transportation, entertainment, and the hospitality industry are explored. The elements that make the hospitality industry unique are identified, as are the characteristics that distinguish hospitality and other service enterprises from manufacturing. The terms *moment of truth* and *cycles of service* are defined and discussed, and their significance for the hospitality industry is described. Career opportunities available in the hospitality industry and both the advantages and disadvantages of hospitality industry employment are explored. Finally, good social skills are identified as a valuable asset for those planning careers in hospitality management.

QUESTIONS

1. Distinguish between the manufacturing and service sectors in an economy.
2. Define the terms *hospitality* and *hospitality industry*.
3. Identify the two principal segments of the hospitality industry and list the major types of businesses in each.
4. What is the scope of the travel and tourism industry? What is the relationship of the hospitality industry to the travel and tourism industry?
5. Historically, what kinds of entertainment have hospitality enterprises provided for travelers?
6. Discuss the relationship and the importance of transportation to the hospitality industry.
7. Define the terms *travel agent* and *tour operator*.
8. List and discuss the three elements that make the hospitality industry unique.
9. What special characteristics of the hospitality and other service industries distinguish them from manufacturing?

10. Define the terms *moment of truth* and *cycle of service* and discuss the significance of each for the hospitality industry.

11. Does the study of hospitality management appear to be more important or less important today than in the past? Why do you suppose that this is the case?

12. What advantages would you expect holders of hospitality degrees, diplomas, or certificates to have in applying for their first management training positions? Why?

13. List several jobs that a new graduate of a hospitality management program could reasonably expect to be offered as a first job in a large hotel? In a small hotel? In a restaurant?

14. List and explain the significance of six qualifications hospitality employers commonly look for in applicants for management trainee positions.

15. For you, personally, what are the positive, appealing aspects of a career in the hospitality industry? What are the negative, unappealing aspects?

16. Why are social skills important for people working in the hospitality industry?

Foundations

The Early Development of the Hospitality Industry

2

LEARNING OBJECTIVES

After reading and studying this chapter, you should be able to:

1. *Explain how the history of travel and the history of the hospitality industry are interrelated.*
2. *List the reasons people have always had for travel.*
3. *Identify the types of hospitality enterprises common in the Egyptian, Greek, and Roman empires and describe their principal characteristics.*
4. *Describe the hospitality services generally available to travelers in the period between the Fall of Rome and the Renaissance.*
5. *Discuss conditions faced by travelers seeking food, drink, and lodging at Western European inns during the Renaissance.*
6. *List and explain the principal political, economic, and social developments in the early modern period that led to improvements in travel and in the hospitality services available to travelers.*
7. *Identify the principal changes in the hospitality industry that resulted from the invention of the steam engine and the development of rail travel.*
8. *Describe the principal contributions of Cesar Ritz and Auguste Escoffier to the hospitality industry.*

INTRODUCTION

The authors believe that everyone planning a career in the hospitality industry should have a healthy curiosity about the present state of the industry and about its history—those facts and trends that shed light on the industry as we see it in the late twentieth century. Every hospitality manager, as an educated person, should understand the industry. That is, she should know more about it than the relatively limited information necessary for doing her job each day. In our view, all managers should have sufficient knowledge to discuss any aspect of our industry, current or historic, with co-workers, superiors, and subordinates.

To that end, as well as to the development of an appreciation of the industry's classic and historic roots, we have written these three chapters. They do not constitute a complete and comprehensive history of the hospitality industry worldwide and in its many manifestations: Such a history would require volumes. However, the material presented here will provide a suitable foundation for understanding the development of our industry, and may impel some—those who find themselves intrigued by the historical information presented here—to study the history of our industry, further at the undergraduate or the graduate level.

This and the following chapters will stress the development of the industry, pointing out the close relationships that have linked food service and lodging to travel and transportation. The first of these three chapters will be devoted to a study of the hospitality industry from its earliest recorded history in the Middle East to its later manifestations in Western Europe, concluding with its development in England through the late nineteenth century. This first chapter sets the stage for the next two, which address the development of the hospitality industry in the United States from Colonial times to the present.

AN OVERVIEW

Those beginning to study the history of the hospitality industry soon recognize that the development of the industry is inexorably tied to the development of transportation and the economic growth of cities, regions, and even nations.

Transportation and economic progress are clearly interdependent: they tend to develop together. Historically, those nations that achieved high economic status in a given era had transportation networks that were more advanced than those of other nations at the time. Examples of economic prosperity and superior transportation abound: The Roman Empire of twenty centuries ago, and the British Empire of the nineteenth century are excellent examples. By contrast, and in our own time, nations that are part of the so-called "Third World" offer typical examples of inadequate transportation networks and relative economic distress. To the student of hospitality history, it soon becomes quite clear that growth and development in our industry has tended to occur most commonly in those nations that

1. were the most economically successful at the time, and
2. had the most highly developed transportation networks.

Throughout recorded history, the hospitality industry has existed to serve the traveler. Inns, taverns, and restaurants—and later, hotels and motels—existed to provide services for the traveler, who required food, drink, and shelter while away from home. Historically, there have been a number of common reasons for people to travel, including

1. making a living,
2. gaining education,
3. observing religious requirements,
4. immigrating/emigrating,
5. restoring or maintaining health,
6. seeking recreation, and
7. visiting family or friends.

Some of these have been of greater importance than others at given times in history, but all have caused people to be away from home and in need of the basic necessities of food, drink, and shelter. Thus, travel has produced a need for hospitality enterprises.

From the earliest days of human history, much travel has been dependent on the existence of roads of one sort or another. Whether people traveled on foot, or on the backs of animals, or in vehicles pulled by animals, or in the mechanized vehicles of the last 100 years, roads were a key element in the development of travel and transportation systems. As we shall see, each segment of the hospitality industry changed and grew as roads improved.

Improvements in roads were accompanied by improvements in modes of transportation. As transportation improved, travel became less arduous and more people traveled. The development of railroads in the nineteenth century, for example, made it possible for travelers to reach their destinations faster and in greater comfort.

Later, such developments even made it possible and practical to create additional travel destinations. Henry Flagler, for one, became very successful as a hospitality executive in Florida in the late nineteenth century by acquiring small railroads and extending them to provide transportation to hotels he developed in resort areas. The increased numbers of travelers to these resort areas created the need for additional hotels and restaurants. In more recent years, the government of Mexico built an airport in an underdeveloped area on the Gulf Coast that led to the development of the resort area known as Cancun.

These are just two examples that demonstrate the interdependence of transportation and the growth of hospitality businesses throughout history. As we explore that history in the balance of the chapter, from earliest known records through the late nineteenth century, many additional examples will be evident.

As one follows the history of the industry, it is also interesting to note changes in the nature of innkeeping, as well as changes in both the role and the status of the innkeeper in society. Until the nineteenth century, the inns and taverns in much of the world were filthy, indifferently managed, and typically shunned by those who could avoid them. Innkeepers were considered to belong on the very lowest rungs of society's ladder and were frequently thought to be disreputable, dishonest individuals. Significantly, however, the innkeepers of America have been considered respected members of society from the earliest times, and their establishments have often become social centers in their communities.

Before sketching the history of our industry, it is useful to look at the following list of some terms used over the centuries to refer to various hospitality establishments. Many of these terms are still used in some parts of the world, although the meanings may have changed a bit over time.

ale house	posting inn
caravanserai	public house (pub)
coaching inn	punch house
coffee house	restaurant
grog shop	tavern
hotel	tippling house
inn	victualing house
motel	wine shop
ordinary	

Interestingly, the terms most frequently encountered today—hotel, motel, and restaurant—are of comparatively recent original. *Hotel* and *restaurant* are of French origin, having come into English usage during the last half of the eighteenth century: *hotel* about 1760, and *restaurant* about 1770. *Motel* is a modern American term that appears to combine the words *motor*, either for automobile or motor highway, and *hotel*, originally to indicate a lodging operation situated along a highway, typically accessible by motor transit.

Historically, *tavern* and *inn*—and their equivalents in other languages— have been the more common terms. Both have always been used to refer to establishments that provided food and drink to travelers. At various times, both *tavern* and *inn* have also been used to mean an establishment offering sleeping accommodations as well as food and drink. Sometimes taverns offered lodging but inns did not; at other times, the reverse was true. At times, one of these provided food and drink to local residents, whereas the other was prevented from doing so by law. Meanings changed from time to time and from one location to another, such that a *tavern* in one locale might have been known as an *inn* if it had been differently situated, and two tavern-keepers in different parts of the world might actually have been in rather different businesses from one another.

However, one should not become confused by the terminology. The important point to remember is that the particular term used to identify any premodern hospitality operation is far less important than the fact that every one of these was in business to meet the continuing, basic needs of people away from home.

BEGINNINGS
The Sumerians

The recorded history of the hospitality industry begins with the Sumerians, a group of people who inhabited an area known as Mesopotamia, near the Persian Gulf, by about 4000 B.C. Much of this area, covering part of the modern state of Iraq, was particularly fertile, making some of the Sumerians prosperous, as well as skilled, farmers and cattle breeders. The Sumerians were a clever people: They made and used flint and bronze tools and decorated pottery; and they were adept at building, creating substantial temples dedicated to their gods. Sumerian skill at farming enabled them to raise and harvest sufficient grain to support artisans and craftsmen who could devote their time and talent to endeavors other than farming—toolmaking, building, and pottery making, among them. The Sumerian farmers were eventually able to produce such abundant harvests that they had surplus grain available to trade. Sumerians are often credited with inventing money and writing, both critical elements in the evolution of business.

By about 3000 B.C., some Sumerian farmers were selling grain to peoples in other parts of this region, thus being the first, also, to develop *trade* in the modern sense of that term. From available evidence, the Sumerians invented money and a written language as means for recording and settling their commercial transactions.

In addition to growing, consuming, and trading grain, the Sumerians became skilled at converting it to alcoholic beverages—beers, primarily; and these became the most widely and commonly consumed beverages at all levels of Sumerian society. The Sumerian beverages were probably safer to drink than their water.

Politically, the Sumerians organized themselves into city states, much as the Greeks did some centuries later. Because these city states covered a comparatively large geographic area, trade required overnight travel from one area to another. Sumerian traders thus sought the services required by travelers in every century: food, drink, and shelter. It is entirely likely that the hospitality industry began nearly 5,000 years ago, with the Sumerians of 3000 B.C.

Early Hospitality Businesses

Local Sumerian taverns were probably among the first hospitality businesses. These were drinking establishments, catering to people who lived in the immediate neighborhood. These taverns served various beers and provided a gathering

An ancient bas relief depicting the trading of flax. From as early as 3000 B.C., Middle Eastern traders engaged in commerce—requiring food, drink, and shelter as they traveled from one area to another—facilitated the origins of the hospitality industry. (Courtesy New York Public Library Picture Collection.)

place for local residents to discuss the issues of the day. Some of these taverns attracted disreputable characters—known criminals and others of unsavory reputation, who met at the taverns to plot crimes. Tavern-keepers, spouses, and barmaids who catered to these people soon developed unsavory reputations of their own among the citizens of their communities.

A number of these taverns had other rooms, akin to bedrooms, which reportedly had many interesting uses: Illicit sex was one, and sleep after excessive drinking was another. Occasionally these rooms were used to accommodate travelers overnight, but this was fairly uncommon.

Early Regulation of Taverns

History abounds with examples of such establishments. Although they were commonly tolerated, sometimes local or national governments attempted to regulate them. The first recorded effort was made by Hammurabi, a king of Babylon who ascended to the throne in 1792 B.C. He devised a set of laws, carved in stone, known as the Code of Hammurabi. One provision required that any customer planning crimes in a tavern be reported to the authorities by the landlady of the tavern. The penalty for failure to do so was death. Hammurabi's code also forbade diluting drinks with water or giving "false measure." Interestingly, the death penalty was to be imposed for these crimes, also, with the miscreant killed by drowning.

At this time in history, taverns had such terrible reputations that revered religious figures—certain high priestesses, who were considered to be in communion with the gods—were forbidden to visit them. Any who did were to be sentenced to death—by burning.

The reputations of early inns were no better than those of the taverns. In fact, in one ancient language the word for *inn* was the same as the word for *brothel*. But this was not the only type of inn; there was at least one other kind—on the trade routes to distant lands.

Early Traders Need Hospitality Services

By 2000 B.C., a considerable amount of trade had developed among the peoples of the Middle East. Many were earning their living from trade and were following established routes to trade for exotic goods. They required hospitality services as they pursued their long journeys, and enterprising individuals set up businesses to meet the needs of these travelers. These enterprises, known as *caravanserai*, provided food and shelter. They could be described as early examples of inns. Their reputations were similar to those of taverns of the period: They were often dirty, bug-infested places, which travelers preferred to avoid whenever possible. The following is a description of one of these:

> After some experience of Kuchan [the city], and especially of its *caravanserai* [inn], I felt the strongest desire to get away from it. Of all the wretched localities of this wretched East, it is one of the worst I have been in. To people at a distance, the petty miseries one undergoes in such a place may seem more laughable than otherwise; there they do not tend to excite the hilarity in the sufferer. For four days and nights at a stretch I did not enjoy ten minutes unbroken rest. All day long one's hands were in perpetual motion, trying to defend one's face and neck against the pertinacious attacks of filthy bluebottles, or brushing ants or various other insects off one's hands and paper. With all this extra movement, each word I wrote occupied me nearly a minute. Dinner involved a perpetual battle with creeping things and was a misery that seldom tempted one's appetite. As for the time spent on the top of the house, lying on a mat, and which it would be a mockery to call bedtime, it would be difficult to say whether it or the daylight hours were the more fraught with torment. Every ten minutes, it was necessary to follow the example of the people lying around, and to rise and shake the mat furiously, in order to get rid, for a brief space, of the crowds of gigantic black fleas, which I could hear dancing around, and still more distinctly feel. After sunset the human inhabitants of the *caravanserai* mounted to the roof and sat there in scanty garments, smoking their kaliouns [pipes] and talking or singing until long after midnight.[1]

---

[1]W. C. Firebaugh, *The Inns of Greece and Rome: and a History of Hospitality from the Dawn of Time to the Middle Ages* (Chicago: F. M. Morris Company, 1923), p. 25.

Over the millennia, each of the dominant civilizations of the Mesopotamian region—Sumerian, Assyrian, Babylonian, Hittite, and others—was overcome by superior force. Although each civilization vanished, the basic elements of the hospitality industry established during this period continued to function. But to regard the dirty, dangerous, unhealthy taverns and inns of the period as hospitality enterprises at all requires a considerable redefining of terms, as well as stretching the imagination.

EMPIRES: 3200 B.C. TO A.D. 476

While several civilizations were thriving in the region around the Persian Gulf, as just discussed, there were civilizations with very different roots developing around the Mediterranean Sea. They occurred at several different times from 3200 B.C. to A.D. 476—a period known to historians as the Empire Era. During this time, three significant empires flourished: the Egyptian, the Greek, and the Roman.

We do not mean to suggest that these parts of the world were the only areas where civilization was developing. Nor are we implying that these were the only areas where trade, travel, and the conditions for the evolution of a hospitality industry could be found. History clearly indicates otherwise. There is evidence,

The Via Appia (Appian Way), one of the many systems of roads that were built during the era of the Roman Empire. A variety of hospitality services—inns, taverns, and escorted travel—arose as transportation networks were built throughout the Roman Empire, as well as in the empires of Egypt, Greece, and China.

for example, that a road system was built in China around the year 2300 B.C. and that there were small road systems in northern Europe as early as 4000 B.C. There are also clear indications of developing civilizations in India by 2400 B.C. Limited commercial trading existed between northern Europe and the Mediterranean. And some evidence suggests trade between northern Europe and China, although this was limited by the hardships involved: It took as long as three years to transport silk from China to Europe. These are just some examples showing that a number of civilizations were developing around the world during this period.

Because of the advanced levels of their civilizations, the wealth of information available about them, and the direct influence they had on the development of the modern hospitality industry, we will restrict our discussion of this era to the empires of Egypt, Greece, and Rome. In its turn, each of these empires built and improved transportation systems and developed hospitality services for increasing numbers of travelers. These developments reached their zenith during the Roman period, with the creation of a transportation network that surrounded the Mediterranean and extended to such distant points as England, France, and Germany.

The important contributions of these three empires to the development of the hospitality industry are examined in the following sections.

Egypt

The Egyptian Empire developed slowly over several thousand years. By about 3200 B.C. various groups had been united under one government. The Egyptians are considered the first people to have created a political entity we could recognize as a nation, as opposed to a group of city states. They developed a government to rule a large number of people in an organized manner, with a hierarchy of civil servants dividing responsibilities for various aspects of governing. Their government was headed by a *pharaoh*, their term for a king.

The famed pyramids were built as tombs for the pharaohs. These were constructed as early as 2700 B.C. and became tourist attractions that people traveled great distances to view. They may well have been the first "man-made" tourist attractions!

Travel was not uncommon in ancient Egypt. In addition to traveling to see the pyramids, people traveled to see other sights, to trade goods, to transact government business, and to attend religious festivals.

There is evidence to suggest that the ancient Egyptians may have been the first to organize massive festivals, religious and otherwise, and to see that food service and lodging was provided for the crowds attending. Thus, the ancient Egyptians may have been responsible for beginning the activity we now call *tourism*.

The Great Sphinx and the Pyramid of Chefren at Giza (c. 2500 B.C.). Since their construction visitors have traveled to marvel at the awesome majesty of these monuments to the pharoahs. (Courtesy Egyptian Tourist Authority.)

Greece

Ancient Greek civilization began to develop about 1100 B.C. It evolved in the form of independent city states that tended to be fiercely competitive. In the early years, major battles involving the peoples of Sparta and Athens took place. No unified Greek nation developed until the middle of the third century B.C., when Philip of Macedon united the city states. His son, Alexander the Great, built an empire that surrounded the Mediterranean and extended as far east as India.

The Greeks were dedicated travelers. By 356 B.C. their land and sea travels had made them dominant in the Mediterranean region. They had established colonies that stretched their empire as far west as Spain and even to the north coast of the Black Sea. Travel to these distant colonies was risky, at best: The traveler was likely to be shipwrecked or to fall victim to piracy at sea, or robbery on land. Nevertheless, many Greeks traveled to great religious centers, particularly Delphi and Olympia, to take part in games and competitions and to consult their oracles.

Inns and taverns became reasonably common throughout the Greek world. As in the Middle East, they had the reputation of being particularly dreadful places and their proprietors were considered among the lowest forms of human life. They, too, commonly adulterated drinks with water and engaged in various criminal activities. Some were particularly adept at extortion and espionage. They were almost universally despised by citizens with wealth, status, and power. These members of Greek society would not enter inns and taverns under any circumstances.

If a member of a government agency visited one, he risked his colleagues' having nothing further to do with him.

The following, written by a poet of the time, provides a picture of a Greek inn of the period:

> Hostelry, o'errun with vermin, the poet, bitten till deplete of blood, salutes thee. Not to thank thee for having sheltered him one night on the borders of a dark highway; the route is miry as that which leads to Hades—but thy cots are broken down, the lamps smoky; thine oil is rancid, the lamps mouldy, and since last autumn there are white worms in thine emptied nut-shells.[2]

In contrast to the inns and taverns, restaurants in ancient Greece were often respected and served fine food. It would appear that there were some inns with good food and habitable accommodations, although it seems that these were relatively few.

Wealthy Greeks indulged in private banquets, at which slaves served the finest food available. Their manner of dining differed from ours: They typically reclined on couches at banquets. Servants would pass trays of such great delicacies as sea urchins, sturgeon, and garlic, which was eaten by itself. Women and children did not eat with the men. They ate in another part of the household— often in the kitchen.

The two most important contributions the Greeks made to the development of the hospitality industry appear to have been

1. their language, which became universally accepted as the language of international trade; and
2. their currencies, which were widely circulated, accepted, and trusted as the medium of exchange for monetary transactions.

The general acceptance of the Greek language and currencies throughout the empire made travel and trade comparatively easy and thus played an important role in increasing the volume of both. And as travel and trade increased, so did the demand for the hospitality services of food and lodging.

Rome

The Roman Empire dates from the time peasant farmers from central Europe settled at approximately the site of present-day Rome. By about 500 B.C. the Romans had established a government that provided for the election of some officials by citizens. The Romans were ambitious and pursued international power by both military and nonmilitary means. They aggressively increased their terri-

---

[2]Ibid., p. 68.

tory and as they did so, their influence grew. In 146 B.C., after many years of conflict, the Romans were finally victorious over the Greeks, and Greece became a Roman protectorate. Roman efforts at territorial expansion continued, and by the time Rome had conquered most of western Europe and the Middle East, inns and taverns were well established throughout the empire.

Travel within the empire was relatively safe and easy, compared with earlier times. Several factors accounted for improved travel conditions:

1. The traveler needed only one currency—Roman coins—to travel anywhere in the empire.
2. The excellent system of roads the Romans built throughout Europe made travel faster and easier.
3. The traveler needed to know only Latin or Greek, the languages of business and government, to communicate fairly easily in any part of the empire.

These factors contributed to the development of an economic prosperity in Rome that surpassed any previously known. All manner of goods flowed to Rome from every part of the world at that time—some because of conquest, most because of trade—and many citizens of Rome became wealthy.

With a stable government and peace in all parts of the empire, Romans could devote their attentions to making money. A middle class began to develop, and this growing middle class traveled—sometimes on business, and sometimes for pleasure. When it was for pleasure, the trip might be to witness spectacular events, to see the wondrous sights outside Rome, or to take vacations.

Spectacles—events pitting groups of war prisoners against each other in fights to the death, for example—drew people to Rome from many parts of the empire. These events, and others with similar aims, were copied by cities in outlying areas and served to increase tourism.

Sightseeing was quite popular, as well. One of the favorite tours was an excursion through Greece, to see the temples, religious sanctuaries, and magnificent works of art. Egypt was considered an excellent destination for the curious traveler who could afford a trip to visit the pyramids.

Vacations for rest were also popular, and a number of resorts were built to accommodate the newly affluent Roman. One example can be found in a resort complex on the northern shore of the bay of Naples. It became a playground for wealthy Romans, who would travel over 100 miles to vacation there. The trip to Naples took over a day, so travelers spent the night at roadside inns or at *diversoria*, resting places some of the wealthy owned along the roads.

Although there were a few good inns reserved for military and government personnel and a very few fine resorts available only to the wealthiest of citizens, the general quality of the average taverns and inns available to members of the public at large was poor. And although inns were numerous along the great Roman roads, the upper classes did not patronize them if they could find any conceivable alternative.

An interesting description of the manner in which the wealthy traveled is provided by Firebaugh:

> Wealthy travelers, who knew beforehand what the penury common to inns had in store for them, took their precautions far in advance whenever the chance of the road obliged them to apply there for lodgings: in the manner of Epicurean Philoxenes . . . , who only traveled when preceded by a train of slaves loaded with wines and everything proper and necessary for even the most educated and delicate of tastes. . . .
>
> When wealthy and powerful transients arrived at such establishments, it was with an entire train of slaves and sumpter mules, minions, lapdogs, carriages, and all the panoply of ostentation. They also carried with them a complete culinary apparatus, and on some occasions, when the highest caste was involved, portable garden plots with growing melons and early vegetables were transported. . . .
>
> In early times, the inns of this class were no better than hovels, badly roofed, and insecurely fastened. In Petronius, the revelers return to their miserable sanctuary at night and cannot get in because the old beldame, their landlady, had been swilling so long with her customers that you could have set her afire without her knowing it.[3]

When Mount Vesuvius erupted in A.D. 79, it buried the city of Pompeii, preserving the city as it existed in its last moments. Recent excavations have revealed a number of interesting buildings, one of which is an inn with a room decorated with four paintings. One of these shows a male customer fondling a young woman who is attempting to resist his advances; a second shows two men gambling; the third depicts three women drinking; and the fourth shows a group of men, apparently drunk, being ejected by the landlord.

The innkeepers of ancient Rome had terrible reputations, so bad that

1. the wife or mistress of an innkeeper or tavern-keeper was exempted from the laws against adultery;
2. innkeepers were not allowed in military service because the military was considered an honorable profession;
3. they were not normally permitted to bring legal actions in Roman courts;
4. nor were they permitted to act as guardians for minor children.

There were exceptions. The Romans built special establishments along the great roads, which served as posting houses. Excellent accommodations were available, and travelers could rest themselves and their horses. These establishments were often relatively luxurious, but they were not for the ordinary traveler. One had to be a high government official with a special pass—a *diplomata*

---

[3]Ibid., pp. 123–24.

tractatorium—to use them. These passes were extremely difficult to obtain and were prized by those with sufficient influence to get them.

Although the typical Roman inn was of very poor quality, Roman food, by contrast, was often excellent. It was not consumed in their inns, however. The Romans, particularly the wealthy, had lavish meals at home and at banquet facilities adjacent to the public baths.

The Romans were particularly fond of delicacies from other countries. The Roman armies brought back such items as wine from various European countries, truffles from Greece, peaches and walnuts from Persia, and cantaloupe from Africa. These were all served at private banquets, along with fish and shellfish from the Mediterranean and meat and poultry raised locally.

Wealthy Romans employed Greek cooks and spent great amounts of money entertaining their friends, often in luxurious dining rooms attached to one of the many public baths. One such man, Marcus Apidius, is said to have tasted all of the rare foods he could find, and unable to locate new eating pleasures, committed suicide. Another historian states that Marcus Apidius felt he had insufficient funds—he had just under a ton of gold bullion left—to maintain his standard of living, so he had no choice but to commit suicide!

The Roman public restaurants of the day served more ordinary food to the population. In the ruins at Pompeii there are a number of small restaurants that remind one of present day fast-food establishments. They share a single basic design and appear to have been set up to prepare and sell essentially the same, very limited menu. They may have been operated by one person, or by one small group, much like a modern small company. It is thus conceivable that these Romans should be credited with the establishment of the first restaurant chain!

By the late fifth century A.D., the Roman Empire was in serious decline. In A.D. 476 the last of the Roman emperors was deposed by the Byzantines, who ruled much of the area to the east and south of present-day Italy—lands that had once been part of the Greek, then the Roman empires. After the collapse of the Roman Empire, the Byzantine Empire became dominant in the eastern Mediterranean for the next thousand years.

DECLINE AND REVIVAL: A.D. 476 TO A.D. 1300

During the later years of the Roman Empire, Christianity gained followers and eventually became the predominant religion in western Europe. The Holy Land became a focal point for travelers, particularly the Cave of the Entombment, the site of the Crucifixion, the Mount of Olives, the cities of Jerusalem and Bethlehem, the Dead Sea, and the River Jordan. However, as the empire began to crumble, pilgrimages to the Holy Land became less and less safe.

After the fall of the Roman Empire, sumptuous foods disappeared from the diets of western Europeans and were replaced by very simple fare. About 90 percent of the population returned to farming and other forms of agriculture.

Cities began to crumble and some virtually disappeared. Commerce nearly ceased, and the middle class no longer existed.

The Dark Ages

This period, known as the Dark Ages, was marked by invasions into the more civilized areas of Europe that had once been the Roman Empire. The invaders were so-called barbaric tribes of north central Europe. Travel and tourism—whether for business or pleasure—virtually ceased. Limited travel took place, primarily for religious reasons: Some brave souls made pilgrimages to Rome and to the Holy Land. As a commercial enterprise, innkeeping nearly disappeared, except for local taverns and a few inns scattered throughout Europe. This was the age of *feudalism*, a system whereby land was given by a ruler in return for loyalty and service.

Throughout this period, the Roman Catholic Church was thriving, gaining both spiritual and political control over the life of Europe. The Church, through its monasteries, filled the vacuum created by the demise of the commercial hospitality industry. In effect, the Church took over the job of feeding and housing travelers—religious and lay people alike. The monasteries of the Church were self-sufficient enterprises. Members of the religious orders were skilled farmers. Vegetables and herbs were usually grown within the monastic walls, and members of the orders raised animals for meat and grew grapes for wine. Perhaps the most famous of these monastery/shelters for travelers was the hospice of the Great Saint Bernard, located in the Alps 8,110 feet above sea level. Construction was completed in the year 962. Travelers were not charged for lodging, but those who were able to pay were expected to leave a generous donation. In the cold, snowy winter, the hospice would send out the Saint Bernard dogs to find and rescue lost travelers. Undoubtedly there was a flask of wine accompanying the dog to provide libation for weary, lost travelers.

There were a number of famines in France and England during this period. It is said that France suffered ten famines in the tenth century, then twenty-six more in the eleventh and twelfth centuries. England experienced a famine about every fourteen years during this time. Where there was famine, there was also cannibalism. In some of the more isolated regions of central Europe, killer bands roamed the countryside, waylaying travelers, cooking their flesh, and selling it to the highest bidder. Purchasers may have been told that the meat was pork or mutton.

RENAISSANCE: A.D. 1350 TO A.D. 1600

Renewed Travel and Trade

By about A.D. 1350 some degree of safety had returned to the roads, and travel and trade increased. Travel and trade created the conditions that would lead to the rise of the middle class in the economic life of Europe. In this period, the monasteries continued to be the principal providers of hospitality services to travelers in all economic strata.

Hospitality in the Monasteries

In many of the monasteries, there were separate buildings that were run by the brothers as dormitory-like shelters for travelers. Both the poor and the middle classes might be accommodated in the same establishment. Some might be traveling for business—to trade or to attend one of the many commercial fairs held during the period, often on lands owned by the Church. Others might be on religious missions or pilgrimages, similar to the famous pilgrimage described by Chaucer in the Canterbury Tales. Wealthy travelers also sought accommodation in the monasteries but were likely to be housed in more luxurious surroundings, sometimes with the abbot in charge of the monastery.

Increasingly, people were traveling, and providing hospitality services for them became burdensome to the religious houses. The Church was having difficulty accommodating so many travelers in a limited space: The monasteries were simply "overbooked." The Church continued willingly to provide hospitality for the poor; Christian charity was an important element in the Church's mission, after all. It continued also to provide for the nobles, who were wealthy; they could and did make large financial contributions, so that serving them made good political sense, as well. But the middle classes, who could neither make large contributions nor claim poverty, experienced more and more difficulty finding accommodations in the monasteries.

Commercial Accommodations for Travelers

Gradually, some taverns, inns, and wine shops began to make accommodations available to middle-class travelers; and the Church began to take the position that since the middle classes could afford to pay for the hospitality services available outside the monastery walls, it was entirely just that these travelers be directed to such establishments. Clearly, the Church played a role in the development of the hospitality industry during this period.

Thus, the number of inns began to grow. Most were quite small by today's standards: An inn of twenty-five to thirty rooms was considered large. But the standards of comfort and cleanliness varied greatly from country to country and region to region.

Tavern Signs

During this period—until the nineteenth century, in fact—most people could neither read nor write. Taverns and inns developed signs with distinctive pictures so that people could identify and direct other people to them. The signs varied but were usually of animals or birds. A weary traveler would be directed to the sign of the bull, or the black swan, or the lion or duck. These signs survive today and are found on many taverns and inns, particularly in the United Kingdom.

The Discomforts of Travel

Traveling was uncomfortable at best. Many roads of the period were more like trails, and travelers intending to go any distance would go by horseback. Women normally did not travel because of the rigors of the road and the dangers associated with travel. Therefore, inns did not have provisions for women. The bedroom of an inn furnished with one or more large beds, each of which would sleep five or six people, was not unusual. In such places, the traveler would go to bed with his clothes on and share the bed with several strangers. The realities of travel were such that women avoided it until the late nineteenth century.

Food Service During the Renaissance

During this period there were no *restaurants*, as we know them. No dining rooms offered meals to the public at large. In England, there were taverns, public houses (pubs), ale houses, and inns. None of these were primarily dining establishments; to the extent that they served food, it was normally only for travelers who had no other place to eat. As in other times and places, they were ordinarily avoided by the wealthy upper classes, who dined and entertained in their homes.

When banquets were served in the home, it was customary for many platters of different foods to be put on the table at once. People seated at the table would help themselves with fingers or knives. Forks were not common until the seventeenth century. Diners would place the foods selected on *trenchers* in front of them. These trenchers were originally pieces of stale bread. The bread acted to absorb the liquids from the food. When a course was finished, all platters of food would be removed from the table, and others would be brought in—an additional course. At the conclusion of the meal, the trenchers would be removed and served to the dogs or to the poor.

Table Manners

Concern over correct social behavior increased during this period, and rules to be observed at the dinner table developed.

Writers of the period instructed their readers not to blow their noses with their fingers and not to go scratching at that part of the male anatomy that they called "codware." People were instructed, as well, not to poke the food on their plates with their fingers. Such behavior was reported to be unpleasant and annoying to one's neighbors at the table.

Some people were inclined to return bones to the serving platters after chewing the meat from the bones. This was considered incorrect: The proper place for these bones was the floor! There were also rules against "breaking wind" at the table—a polite burp was acceptable, and a tribute to the fine fare provided by the host, but the release of digestive gases was not.

Innkeeping

The monasteries that had been housing travelers since the fall of Rome continued to do so. When it could be obtained, this free housing was preferred to local inns. Innkeepers resented this unfair competition, and as students of the Reformation know, at this time a number of Church practices were considered offensive. In England in 1539, Parliament passed an act that suppressed the 608 religious houses. Under King Henry VIII, the monasteries were closed and the lands given to many of the king's supporters, which helped insure the unification of England under one strong government. One unintended consequence of this upheaval was that travelers could no longer find accommodations in monasteries. This greatly stimulated the innkeeping business and dramatically increased the number of inns in England.

Tourism in the Sixteenth Century

The sixteenth century also saw the beginnings of an activity known as the "Grand Tour." Wealthy English would send their sons to tour Europe to "finish their educations" on a tour that might last as long as three years. Because most of the activity of the Renaissance was centered there, the Italian peninsula was a principal destination. Young men might spend an entire year learning about the arts and humanities.

France was another important stop on the tour, and young men spent many months there, as well. Paris was an important cultural center at the time. However, the French Riviera was carefully avoided because it was a notorious gathering spot for pirates!

As previously indicated, women did not commonly engage in travel. In general, they were responsible for managing the home and rearing children. Because they did not hold positions in the business world of the day, they had no occasion to travel for business. And travel was very dangerous. Forests and other rural areas were infested with highwaymen who preyed on travelers. In addition, inns were not equipped to provide privacy to anyone seeking overnight accommodations.

EARLY MODERN: A.D. 1600 TO A.D. 1800

This was a particularly important period in the development of the hospitality industry. One critical element was the development of roads, which facilitated the use of the stagecoach between cities. Roads built by the Romans before A.D. 500 had not been maintained after Rome fell, and thus they had decayed. Moreover, after the fall of Rome, there had been no comparable central governments in Europe to build or maintain road systems. At first, roads were likely to be little better than trails. With continued use, a trail would come to resemble some of the primitive dirt roads found in rural communities. However, because no government was responsible for maintaining roads, maintenance was left to the discretion of the owners of the land through which a road passed. Therefore, although it was possible to go from one population center to another by stagecoach, it was extremely difficult, and sometimes dangerous, because of the condition of the roads.

Introduction of the Stagecoach

With the introduction of the stagecoach, regular stagecoach routes were established, and so-called *coaching inns* soon followed. At the coaching inns, tired horses were exchanged for fresh horses; and stagecoach passengers were fed and given opportunities to rest, frequently overnight. Travel was difficult, since the roads were often mud-soaked and full of potholes. One can imagine how uncomfortable it was to ride in a stagecoach all day. In a pamphlet published about 1672, John Cresset writes:

> What advantage is it to Man's health to be called out of their Beds into these Coaches an hour before day in the morning, to be hurried in them from place to place, til one hour, two, or three within night; insomuch that, after sitting all day in the summertime stifled with heat, and choked with dust; or the Wintertime, starving and freezing with cold, or choked with filthy fogs, they are often brought into their Inns by Torchlight, when it is too late to sit up and get Supper; and next morning they are forced in the coach so early, they can get no Breakfast?[4]

He goes on to tell of the rigors of traveling, describing the unpleasantness of getting out of a coach stuck in the mud to lighten the load, the long delays occurring when a wooden wheel breaks, and the general incivility of the passengers with whom he is forced to share the coach.

Other developments of the period included an increase in the quality of inns, the application of English common law to the hospitality industry, and in France, the reintroduction of restaurants for public dining.

---

[4]Albert E. Richardson, *Old Inns of England* (New York: Benjamin Blom, Inc., 1972), p. 6.

Innkeeping Comes Under English Common Law

English common law forms the basis of U.S. law and many of the principles developed in seventeenth-century England remain in force in the United States today. Prior to the application of common law to inns, which occurred in the 1600s, innkeepers ran their inns as they chose. Many would refuse to accommodate travelers, even though rooms were available. Sometimes they did this because they did not like the appearance of the traveler; or they simply did not like being disturbed after they had retired for the night. Some unscrupulous innkeepers were in league with highwaymen or with guests who would harm or steal from other, unsuspecting guests.

Early common law required innkeepers to receive all travelers, providing that the innkeeper had space available and the travelers were in fit condition to be received. This typically meant that they were not to be drunk, diseased, or known to be dishonest or rowdy. Time of arrival was not a consideration—no matter that the traveler appeared at the inn at 3:00 A.M. Later common law established two principles now thought basic in the hospitality industry: An innkeeper was taken to be an insurer of guests' property and was required to make reasonable provision for guests' safety. These principles are still reflected in our laws today.

Improvements in the Quality of Inns

By the 1700s the inns in England were much safer and more comfortable, although the standards varied from one inn to another. Richardson writes:

> The tired traveler, arriving at one of the large solid inns of the latter eighteenth century, would have generally been justified in expecting the highest degree of "comfort and elegance." If the coach was timed to stop for half an hour to change horses and enable the passengers to dine, the waiters would be standing at the door in readiness to assist him with his hat, shawl, and coat. The landlord and landlady would be waiting in the hall, where there would be a good display of cold meats, game pies, cheeses, and pastries on view in a special glazed cupboard. The coffee-room or dining parlour would reveal an immense central table, round or rectangular, laid in readiness for the meal, with good plated cutlery and spotless table-linen. Some inns could boast a special dining-room for coach passengers, while the upstairs bedrooms, each with its curtained four-poster and good plain furniture, often of mahogany, including mirror, a washing-table, and a wig-stand, were generally known by individual names such as the Moon, Star, Crescent, or Paragon.[5]

In contrast to the above, the Dean of Exeter, a clergyman, writes to a friend in 1767 that he "cannot commend the inns at Plymouth, they are like those in other seaports, neither very neat nor quiet."[6] A gentleman by the name of Arthur Young

---

[5]Ibid, p. 20.
[6]Ibid., p. 20.

kept a list of inns he visited when touring the south of England, and wrote that six of the thirty-seven were "very bad and very dear [expensive]."[7] Of one named the Bush at Wanstead, he wrote that it was "dirty and dear, but civil."[8]

Post Houses

The mails were an important element in the development of the hospitality industry during this period. Until the late 1700s, the mail in England was carried on horseback by messengers known as *post-boys*, who were able to ride at about six miles per hour. Any letter usually took several days to go even 100 miles. With the development of stagecoaches, mail carrying was gradually transferred to stage-coach lines. These had established routes and contracts that provided that mail be delivered within specific amounts of time. Because of these provisions, stagecoaches began to travel faster. Teams of horses were run at full speed for approximately ten miles, at which point the stage stopped at a post-house to change horses. A new team would be hitched to the stage, and the process would be repeated.

Post-houses were much like the coaching inns described earlier. Thus, they were equipped to feed drivers and passengers or accommodate them overnight. Locating the inns along coach routes ensured that the inns would serve a steady supply of customers arriving by stagecoach. Even in the eighteenth century, location was an important element in the success of a hospitality enterprise!

Food Service in Coffee Houses and Taverns

Until the late eighteenth century, no public restaurants existed as we know them today. In England, there were establishments known as coffee houses where one could get light snacks, and there were taverns that served a daily "ordinary"—a main meal at a fixed price. Most people consumed their meals at home. The wealthy had their own cooks; and when they entertained, they usually did so in their own homes. Inns were primarily for travelers and did not normally serve meals to local residents.

Restaurants

The food service element of the hospitality industry changed dramatically and forever in France in 1765. In that year, a man named Boulanger was a soup vendor in Paris, operating a small business selling soups and broths. These were known as *restaurants*, a French word meaning restoratives. Soups and broths have long been noted for their ability to fortify the weary or to restore energy, and Boulanger was one of many such sellers of soup and broth in Paris at the time.

[7]Ibid., p. 21.
[8]Ibid., p. 21.

For reasons that are unclear, Boulanger decided to add an item to his product line—a dish made of sheep's feet with a sauce. Perhaps some had requested it; perhaps he was merely trying to make his small business different from others. In any event, the *traiteurs*—members of a caterers' guild who prepared roasts and meats for consumption in private homes—objected on the grounds that he was preparing and selling a ragout, and that only *traiteurs* were permitted to sell ragouts and similar foods under existing French law. They brought an action against him in court.

After careful study of the *traiteurs'* position, the court decided that Boulanger's selling of the dish did not constitute a violation. The case created much publicity and interest, and led to a decree authorizing both traiteurs and restaurateurs to serve guests within their establishments. After a while, this resulted in the development of public dining rooms in which guests could be seated and served the food and drink of their choice.

Boulanger is usually credited with creating the first *restaurant*, which has come to mean an establishment with a dining room open to the public where varied foods could be purchased and consumed. Technically, however, he merely reinvented a form of food service enterprise that had existed many centuries earlier, but had disappeared during the Dark Ages: After all, the forerunners of Boulanger's "restaurant" had existed centuries earlier in ancient Greece and Rome.

In the late eighteenth century the restaurant business took another leap forward. During the French Revolution, the common people of France revolted against the monarchy, taking control of the government and of the properties of wealthy aristocrats, many of whom were executed. Cooks and chefs who had been employed by the aristocrats were suddenly without jobs. Unemployed cooks and chefs had to find ways to earn their living, and many opened food service establishments. After the French Revolution, restaurants began to proliferate in Paris and in other parts of France.

Another type of food service establishment to develop in France at this time was the cafe. *Café* is the French word for *coffee*, and it is probable that these cafes were the French equivalents of the English coffee houses. At first they may have served only snacks, just as the English did. It is likely that the proprietors of these establishments soon began to use their highly developed culinary skills to prepare more elaborate items—certainly to the delight of their customers.

These developments in France in the late eighteenth century mark the beginnings of the modern restaurant industry, which embarked on a period of growth and development in the early nineteenth century that continues to this day.

THE INDUSTRIAL ERA: FROM 1800

The Industrial Revolution, which dates from the mid-1700s, started in England with the development of mechanized means for doing work that formerly had been done by hand. It was an age of invention. Steam engines, other machines, and the developing concept of the factory were key features that changed forever the way work would be accomplished. It was no longer necessary to depend on water and water wheels for power. With steam engines, power could be made available in locations that had no access to water transportation. This led to the development of mill towns—later, cities—in many locations across England and Scotland formerly thought suitable only for agriculture. The greatest period of growth for these new communities and work-sites followed the invention of the railroad in 1825. This began the development of a transportation network designed to move raw materials and finished goods from place to place.

Rail Travel and the Hospitality Industry

The significance of the railroad in the development of the hospitality industry cannot be overemphasized. It became apparent nearly immediately that railroads could transport people, not simply goods, and thus reduce traveling time from one point to another: Passengers could reach their destinations quickly and in relative comfort. The trip from London to Bath, England, a distance of 110 miles requiring 11 hours to travel by stagecoach, took only 2.5 hours by rail.

As the rail network grew, stagecoach operators began to lose much of their business. Government contracts to carry the mail were not renewed. New contracts were negotiated with the railroads, and it was not long before the principal postal routes were in the hands of the railroads. People soon abandoned stagecoach travel, as well. This led to the demise of most stagecoach lines in a very few years. As the coach lines disappeared, the coaching inns lost their traditional sources of business and were forced to find new markets, or close.

The development of railroad networks—first in England, then in other nations—had a greater effect on the hospitality industry than had any other single development since the fall of the Roman Empire. Passenger traffic on the railroads led to the establishment of railroad stations, which became obvious locations for new hospitality businesses in England and in other nations that developed rail networks. Inns, taverns, restaurants, and later, hotels opened in or near railroad stations. In England, examples include the Charing Cross Hotel and the St. Pancras Hotel in London and the Queens Hotel in Birmingham. In Scotland, there were St. Enoch's Hotel in Glasgow and the Station Hotel in Perth. Later, in the United States, there are such examples as the Biltmore Hotel and the Commodore Hotel, built in New York City near Grand Central Station.

Equally important, the Industrial Revolution brought business opportunities that led to new levels of prosperity. In addition, as trade between nations expanded—first through Europe, and then worldwide—increasing numbers of people were required to travel for business, and this led to a need for many more hospitality enterprises.

Public Dining

In the last quarter of the nineteenth century, some important changes began to appear in the hospitality industry. Until then, eating meals away from home was done of necessity rather than by choice. Business travelers and those working in factories, shops, and offices ate meals away from home because they could not return home for meals during the working day. Whenever possible, people preferred to dine in the privacy of their homes.

Because public dining was not popular, many hotels were constructed without dining facilities. It was the normal custom for hotel guests to have meals in their quarters—room service, in today's terms. In the hotel dining rooms that did exist, the patrons were all men: It was not customary for women to dine in public.

By 1880, dining out had begun to gain acceptability and some small measure of popularity. One of first steps taken in that direction occurred in 1875, in the Albemarle Hotel, London, when a dining facility was opened for the "accommodation of both ladies and gentlemen." By this time, the term *restaurant* had come into common English use but referred to the dining room of a hotel.

In London, more luxurious hotels began to appear, some of which were known both for the excellence of their guest accommodations and for the superiority of their food. One of the best known of these properties was the Savoy, opened by an entrepreneur named Richard d'Oyly Carte in 1889. In the Savoy, d'Oyly Carte employed two men who would become famous throughout the world: Cesar Ritz and Auguste Escoffier.

Cesar Ritz

Cesar Ritz was born in 1850 in Switzerland, the thirteenth child in a large family. His early days in the hospitality industry did not suggest that his was to be a brilliant future: He was dismissed from his first two jobs, one as an apprentice wine waiter and the other as an assistant waiter. After this inauspicious beginning, Ritz drifted to Paris where he obtained and lost other jobs before taking a waiter's job in the most fashionable establishment in Paris at that time, the Voisin. He quickly learned that the wealthy in Paris wanted, demanded, and appreciated excellent service. Soon, the wealthiest and most famous of the Voisin's clientele were asking for him by name. His reputation grew, and he became a maitre d'hotel, then restaurant manager at the Grand Hotel at Nice. Because of his superior abilities to please the wealthy, he was always able to work in the finest properties, some of which were being used by Thomas Cook's organization to accommodate those on luxury tours of Europe.

Before long, he progressed to hotel manager, and in 1870, at the age of 27, was offered a job managing the Grand National Hotel in Lucerne, Switzerland. The hotel was not a profitable venture when he assumed the manager's job, but Ritz was able to turn it into one with his deft management skills. He inspired the staff and the chef with his own enthusiasm and principles of good service, and he organized luxurious and fabulous entertainment for his guests. Soon the hotel became one of the most popular in Europe, and Cesar Ritz became one of the most respected hoteliers in Europe.

Auguste Escoffier

Auguste Escoffier was four years older than Cesar Ritz. His career began in Paris, and he was soon employed at some of the finest properties of the time in France. Escoffier and Ritz had worked together at the Grand Hotel, Monte Carlo, before Ritz became manager of the Savoy. Recognizing the need for a superior chef to enliven a dull menu in this new luxury hotel, Ritz sent for Escoffier.

Escoffier is noted for his many contributions to the improvement of cuisine and service. He is the only chef ever to be given membership in the French Legion of Honor, a distinction bestowed on him by the President of France in 1920. His principal contributions include

1. simplifying classical cuisine;
2. simplifying menus;
3. reorganizing the kitchen staff into the *classical brigade*[9];
4. revolutionizing banquet service by serving only one or two dishes at a time, rather than the older, established practice of serving a whole table full of dishes at once;
5. naming dishes after famous people (Melba toast, Peaches Melba, and Melba Sauce were named for the opera star Jennie Melba);
6. writing the *Le Guide Culinaire* (a culinary text and collection of recipes used by several generations of chefs).

Following the success of the Savoy, a number of other luxury properties were opened in London, including the Waldorf, the Strand Palace, and Claridges, to name but a few. All of these survive to this day.

With the dawn of the twentieth century, various social, political, and economic forces affected the development of the hospitality industry. Of particular importance were World War I, the Great Depression of the 1930s, and World War II, all of which had more negative than positive impact on the industry. In the early years of the twentieth century, the central focus of hospitality industry development shifted to the United States, as we shall see in the following chapter.

---

[9]This divided the kitchen staff into specialized departments on the basis of types of foods prepared, in contrast to the earlier method, discarded by Escoffier, that had each chef prepare an entire meal—from appetizer onwards.

SUMMARY

In this chapter, the historical development of the hospitality industry is explored, from the earliest civilizations in the Middle East, through Egypt, Greece, Rome, and western Europe, with special attention to developments in England from the fifteenth to the late nineteenth centuries. Economic links between hospitality and several other industries are described, and improvements in methods of transportation and the economic development of population centers are illustrated. Various types of early hospitality enterprises are described, along with the principal characteristics of the establishments and their owners. The growth of the industry through the fall of Rome, the role of the Church in providing hospitality services during the Dark Ages, and the importance of several social and economic phenomena in the rebirth of the hospitality industry during the Renaissance are traced. Finally, various elements that fostered dynamic change in the industry during the early modern period are illustrated, including the development of road networks, stagecoaches, and postal networks, the reinvention of the restaurant in eighteenth-century France, and the extension of English common law to the business of innkeeping. The growth of the hospitality business in the Industrial Era is described, and the invention of the steam engine, the development of railroad networks, and acceptance of "dining out" by the public at large are cited as principal determinants of the industry's development.

QUESTIONS

1. Explain why the history of the hospitality industry is tied closely to the development of transportation.
2. List at least five reasons why people have always traveled.
3. What contribution(s) did the Sumerians make to the development of travel?
4. What kinds of establishments do the authors suggest were probably the first hospitality businesses?
5. Why did the first hospitality establishments have poor reputations?
6. What were the characteristics of a typical inn of the approximate year 2000 B.C.?
7. What is the most important contribution of ancient Egypt to the development of the hospitality industry?
8. What were the two most important contributions of ancient Greece to the development of travel?

9. Were Greek inns generally clean and well-run? How good were their restaurants?

10. Of what significance was the Roman road system to the development of travel?

11. Travel during the period of the Roman Empire became relatively safe and easy, compared with how it had been. Why?

12. Some Roman inns were clean and offered excellent accommodations to those they served. Explain.

13. Why did the business of innkeeping virtually disappear during the Dark Ages? Where did travelers stay?

14. What was the "Grand Tour?"

15. What impact did an A.D. 1539 act of the English parliament have on the innkeeping business of that era?

16. During which period in European history did the stagecoach become a common method of transportation? What effect did this have on innkeeping development?

17. When and where did public restaurants first become common? What caused them to increase in numbers?

18. How did the invention of the railroad and the development of railroad networks affect the development of the hospitality industry?

19. Why did the Industrial Revolution increase the number of inns in Europe?

20. Identify Auguste Escoffier. List three important contributions he made to the development of the hospitality industry.

21. Identify Cesar Ritz. What was his role in the history of the hospitality industry?

The Hospitality Industry in the United States I:
Beginnings Through the Nineteenth Century

3

LEARNING OBJECTIVES

After reading and studying this chapter, you should be able to:

1. *Identify and describe the earliest types of hospitality establishments in America.*
2. *Identify a number of significant historic hospitality establishments described in the chapter and enumerate the principal features of each.*
3. *Discuss the impact of railroads on the development of both city hotels and resort hotels in the nineteenth century.*
4. *List and discuss the characteristics of nineteenth-century American city hotels that made them unique in their time.*
5. *Describe the dimensions of the fire problem in city hotels in the nineteenth century.*
6. *List and discuss the economic and social conditions that fostered the growth of the food service industry in the nineteenth century.*
7. *Name six types of food service establishments common in major American cities in the nineteenth century.*
8. *Identify the following individuals and describe the principal contributions of each to the development of the hospitality industry: Samuel Coles, Samuel Fraunces, Isaiah Rogers, Harvey Parker, Potter Palmer, Henry Flagler, and Fred Harvey.*

INTRODUCTION

The development of the hospitality industry in the United States has been unique, having no precise parallel in any other country. There appear to be a number of contributing reasons for this, including the vast size of the country, the multinational character of the people, the formation of the transportation system, and the unique political and economic systems operating in America. A number of factors, listed below, have set the American hospitality experience apart from that in the rest of the world.

1. Since the time of the earliest settlements in the late sixteenth century, a larger proportion of the American people have traveled greater distances than have the people of other nations; consequently Americans have patronized hotels and restaurants in greater numbers.
2. The American political and economic systems have made it possible for the financially successful to build grand hotels as monuments to their success, even if the properties they built were unprofitable. These systems have also enabled ambitious, hard-working people of limited means and little education to become successful in hospitality businesses.
3. Although other nations have long relied on railroads as their major means of intercity travel and transportation, at the end of World War II America began to rely heavily on automobiles and airplanes as its principal means. Today, the automobile accounts for over 80 percent of all intercity travel in the United States. Airplanes account for approximately 17 percent, and railroads less than 2 percent. The major difference between American modes of transportation and those used in other nations has caused hospitality operations to develop very differently in this country.
4. In the United States, innkeeping has always been considered an honorable and respected profession. This is in stark contrast to the tradition of innkeeping in other nations, as discussed in Chapter 2.
5. American hotels have always been "public places"—establishments used by local residents as social centers and places for entertaining. In other nations, inns and hotels were used only by travelers—at least until the late nineteenth century. In these countries, the local populace frequented taverns, but not hotels.
6. The multicultural nature of the American population has led to a greater diversity in the kinds of restaurants established here, in contrast to those established in other countries.
7. Several unique hospitality concepts originated in the United States and were later imitated in other nations. These include
   a. large grand hotels,
   b. restaurant chains,
   c. franchises, and
   d. motels.

In this chapter and the one that follows, we will explain these unique American developments and provide examples to illustrate.

HOSPITALITY IN AMERICA: FROM COLONIAL TIMES THROUGH THE EIGHTEENTH CENTURY
Ordinaries, Taverns, and Inns in Early America

The earliest known example of an American hospitality enterprise existed in Jamestown, Virginia, in 1610. Because the Jamestown settlement did not survive, there is no reliable information about it. Therefore, the beginning of the American hospitality industry is usually said to be 1634, when Samuel Coles opened an establishment in Boston that was named *Coles Ordinary*. It was a tavern—the first tavern of record in the American colonies, and probably the first inn, as well. It was quite successful, lasting well over 125 years: When John Hancock became governor of Massachusetts in the eighteenth century, Coles Ordinary was still in business and was renamed Hancock's Tavern.

The terminology used in the colonial period to identify these establishments may be confusing. Throughout the colonial period, the terms *ordinary, tavern,* and *inn* were all used to refer to the same basic institution—an enterprise established to provide food, drink, overnight accommodation, or some combination of these to travelers, local inhabitants, or both. Over time, *tavern* became the more common term from New England to New York; *inn* became favored in the Pennsylvania region; and *ordinary* was more common in the South.

The word *ordinary* is an old term, used originally in Great Britain to describe a midday meal served at a fixed price in a tavern to the local inhabitants. The term also came to mean the *tavern* itself. The ordinary offered no menu and no choice: The tavern-keeper served whatever he had decided to prepare for that day. Ordinaries in New England were under strict Puritan guardianship, and were not allowed at one point to charge more than 6 pence for a meal and 1 penny for a quart of ale or beer.

Opening and closing hours were enforced by the Puritans; and men who drank too much were punished. The punishment could be severe: Miscreants could be put in *bilbos*—long iron bars with shackles that slide back and forth—set in the stocks, and whipped. Records show that one, Robert Wright, was fined 20 shillings and put in the stocks for an hour for being "twice distempered in drink." Robert Coles—no relation to Samuel Coles—was fined 10 shillings and ordered to wear a sign on his back that read *DRUNKARD* in large letters. Unfortunately, this penalty did not cure him. A year later he was at it again, and that time the badge of disgrace was made permanent: He was ordered to wear a large *D* around his neck. Lists of names of drunkards such as Coles were given to taverns in other towns and the proprietors were warned not to serve liquor to these people under penalty of losing their licenses.

The number of ordinaries in the New England colonies grew. They were considered important establishments, and sometimes the courts directed that ordinaries or public houses be opened in communities where they did not exist. In 1656 the General Court of Massachusetts made towns responsible for sustaining an ordinary. For example, Concord, Massachusetts, was fined by the court for not having an ordinary, and was directed to open one. In 1644, the colonial records of Connecticut ordered "one sufficient inhabitant in each town to keep an ordinary, since strangers were straitened for want of entertainment." It was recognized early in the colonial period that the traveler needed a place to eat, drink, and find accommodation. Inducements were offered to a person willing to keep an ordinary. These included exemption from church rates and school taxes, grants of land, or pasturage for the owner's cattle.

Early ordinaries existed not only to accommodate the traveler, but also to serve as gathering places for the local townsfolk. They were important centers for the exchange of news and served as places where public questions could be debated or public opinion sampled. In addition, they were places for local residents to seek refreshments—ale, beer, and cider among them. In wintertime, taverns were particularly popular places. For example, during church services, people became very cold in the unheated churches and meeting houses while they sat listening to long sermons. After the services, the men flocked to a welcoming nearby tavern to warm up.

Innkeeping in the Colonies

Unlike the innkeepers in England, American innkeepers have always been respected members of the community, and inns located in cities and towns were generally clean and well run. When one traveled into the countryside, however, the quality of the taverns and inns was less reliable, ranging from "very uncomfortable" to "quite nice." In these less populated areas, anyone who could both build a log hut and supply liquor could put up a *Tavern* sign. Those who did would then go to the woods nearby, shoot some kind of game, and put it into a pot to cook. The result was used to feed the "guests," and was known as *potluck*.

The practice of sharing a bed with strangers had disappeared in Europe by the 1700s, but it persisted in America, particularly in the rural inns or taverns. In *Palaces of the People*, Arthur White writes:

> On entering one of these taverns and asking for a single bed, you are told that your chance of getting one depends entirely on the number of travellers who may want accommodation for the night, and if you obtain possession of a bed by promising to receive a companion when required, it is impossible to say what sort of companion may come. . . .[1]

[1]Arthur White, *Palaces of the People* (New York: Taplinger Publishing Co., 1970), p. 114.

Palaces of the People also includes an interesting description of one rural inn of this period:

> It [the description of the inn] will answer for nineteen out of twenty of all we have stopped at during our journey. The outer door opens into a large dirty room full of smoke, used as a sitting room for men folks and also as a bar room, for in one corner, generally in the angle, you will see a cupboard with two or three shelves, on which are arranged in bottles the different coloured liquors. I suppose the colour is about the only difference you would have found in them; the brandy, gin and whisky generally came from one distillery, in Ohio, with the addition of burnt sugar and juniper berries to suit the taste of their customers.
>
> From this room you would enter the family sitting room, also used as a dining room for travellers and out of that usually a kitchen and small family bedroom. The upper storey, although sometimes divided into two rooms was often left as one, with beds arranged along the sides. . . . As for the table they set — well, I suppose they did the best they could, for certainly there were few dainties to be purchased that winter for love or money. . . . In many, a pot hung over the wood fire, a frying pan and a baking pot being about all they had. . . . Meals usually consisted of bread, butter, potatoes, and fried pork; now and then you might get a few eggs but not as far west as Michigan City. . . .[2]

The Oldest Continually Operating Tavern in America

New York City, one of America's oldest cities, has had its share of firsts. One of special interest to the student of hospitality history is Fraunces Tavern, a tavern in the lower part of the island of Manhattan known as *Wall Street*, now New York's financial center. Actually located at the corner of Broad and Pearl Streets, it has the honor of being the oldest continually operating tavern in the nation and has some interesting history associated with it.

The building was built in 1719 as a private residence, which it remained until about 1757, when the owner moved uptown to a better neighborhood, a practice that persisted in New York City for generations. In 1762 it was sold to a West Indian named Samuel Fraunces, who converted it to a tavern that he named the Queen's Head. After operating it for a short time, he leased it out for several years but returned to operate it in 1775 because he was unable to sell it. He continued to run it throughout the Revolutionary War, but it was not actually known as Fraunces Tavern until 1783, after the war.

One of his customers was George Washington, whom Fraunces served when the General met with his staff at the tavern to plan various war campaigns. When the British occupied New York City, Fraunces continued to operate the tavern. Although his customers were then British generals, Fraunces remained loyal to the Revolutionary cause, serving as a spy for the American Army. Fraunces frequently

[2]Ibid., pp. 111–112.

sent word about British plans to General Washington. In fact, Fraunces has sometimes been characterized as the first American intelligence agent!

The First Hotel Building in the United States

In 1794 the first structure designed specifically as a hotel was constructed in New York City near Wall Street. Aptly named the City Hotel, it occupied a large site on the island of Manhattan—on the west side of lower Broadway near Trinity Church. The hotel had 73 guest rooms, simply furnished but spacious and comfortable. It offered room service to its guests and was the largest hotel in New York until 1813. For $2, it offered a room and meals—breakfast at 8, dinner at 3, tea at 6, and supper at 9.

Its two proprietors were men named Jennings and Willard. Willard served as host, room clerk, bookkeeper, and cashier, while Jennings supervised food preparation and the operation of the dining room. Both were said to be very good at remembering names and faces and were generally considered excellent proprietors. For a period of several years, the City Hotel was the social center of New York, the setting for many important banquets, dances, and political events. Although it survived until 1849, it had long since lost its early splendor.

There has always been an important difference between American hotels and those of Europe. From their earliest days, American hotels—the City Hotel, and its successors—were considered to be gathering places for the local community, whereas European hotels were not considered to be such until the twentieth century.

THE HOSPITALITY INDUSTRY IN THE NINETEENTH CENTURY
City Hotels in the 1800s

From 1800 to approximately 1880, a large number of city residents lived in hotels or in rooming houses and boarding houses that closely resembled small hotels. Those who could not afford private homes had no other choice. There were no apartments as we know them today: The first apartments in America were constructed in New York City in 1880. Consequently, over 50 percent of the rooms in the typical city hotel were occupied by permanent residents. There were hotels available for people of various income levels, and virtually everyone in need of rooms could find something affordable. Some hotels appealed to those employed in the immediate area; others catered to those in particular professions or income strata. All were usually very busy. Unfortunately, we know most about those that earned grand reputations as the finest available in their times and comparatively little about the others.

"PALACES OF THE PUBLIC". Those famous American hotels of the past about which much information survives have been dubbed "Palaces of the Public," a title that refers not only to the public nature of American hotels, but also to their elegance. In many small cities, the local hotel was the finest, most splendid structure in the city. In larger cities, there were commonly several competing to be the best— having installed the latest in modern conveniences and often becoming self-sufficient cities within cities. Many featured such amenities as barber shops, libraries, billiard rooms, hair salons, ticket offices, florists, and cigar stands. Some eventually provided dining service for over twenty hours a day.

It is particularly interesting that the palatial hotels of this nature—the so-called "grand hotels"—were found only in America, until the later years of the nineteenth century. Grand hotels were clearly an American invention.

THE TREMONT HOTEL, BOSTON. The first of the truly grand hotels in America was the Tremont Hotel, a purpose-built property that opened in Boston at the corner of Tremont and Beacon Streets in October 1829. By every standard of the times, it was a luxurious enterprise. The Tremont was three stories high and boasted 170 guest rooms and a dozen public rooms. It was the first hotel to have

1. bellboys;
2. clerks whose responsibilities were limited to the front desk;
3. a carpeted lobby and a large, carpeted (200-seat) dining room, both with gas-lighted chandeliers;
4. bathing rooms (eight)—probably steam baths—located in the building,
5. private rooms—both singles and doubles—all equipped with doors having locks and keys for guests;
6. French cuisine;
7. a washbowl and pitcher in each room with a free bar of soap;
8. the first inside toilets, called *water closets*, located in the basement of the building; and
9. a mechanical device known as an *annunciator* in each room, which made it possible for a guest to signal the hotel front office merely by pushing a button.

The ceilings of the Tremont were exceptionally high, and any floors not carpeted were done in black and white marble. The furniture was native, carved walnut. Although the list of "firsts" above may not connote a very luxurious operation by today's standards, one must remember that we are describing a property that was constructed thirty years before the Civil War—long before the advent of electricity, modern plumbing, and telephones. The Tremont was an extraordinary, luxurious hotel for its time. The designer of this remarkable property was a young man of 27 named Isaiah Rogers.

THE ASTOR HOUSE, NEW YORK. John Jacob Astor, a well-known American business tycoon, watched the success of the Tremont with great interest and decided that if a luxury hotel could succeed in Boston, one could do so in New York. Moreover, Astor decided to build a hotel in New York that would exceed the luxury of the Tremont. He proceeded to plan the Astor House, which was completed in 1836.

To design his hotel, Astor employed Isaiah Rogers, who was rapidly becoming known as the premier hotel architect in America. Rogers designed a hotel that was "more grand" than his Tremont. In addition to all the features that had first appeared in the Tremont, the Astor House contained not eight, but seventeen bathing rooms, larger public rooms, and two new devices known as *showers*, which were located in the basement. The guest rooms were furnished with black walnut, and the floors were covered with Brussels carpets. In addition, all rooms were provided with gaslight, and the Astor House was the first hotel to be fully illuminated with gas.

The Astor House was a hotel of 309 rooms on five floors. One of the more interesting problems in operating the hotel involved the gaslights. Guests were not used to the gaslight, which was a new invention at the time. They were accustomed to candles, which were normally extinguished when people went to bed. Because guests were accustomed to extinguishing their candles by blowing them out, some guests took the same approach with the gas lighting fixtures, often with disastrous results. Those who did extinguish the gaslights failed to realize that raw gas was escaping from the unlighted fixtures, and substantial numbers died—some from asphyxiation, others from explosions that occurred when they lighted matches to reignite the gaslights.

Although it was a modern, elegant property when first built, the Astor House had considerable difficulty keeping up with the improvements that appeared in the new hotels being constructed in New York each year. In 1875, after fewer than forty years, it had to be closed for renovation and modernization. It soon reopened and continued to operate, but as a less luxurious property. It was finally closed in 1913.

OTHER GRAND HOTELS OF THE ERA. The Tremont in Boston and the Astor in New York established models for more ostentatious American hotels. In Boston, grand hotels constructed included the Adams House in the latter 1840s, the Revere House in 1847, and the original Parker House in 1855. New Yorkers were awed by such properties as the Howard Hotel in 1839, the New York Hotel in 1844, the Metropolitan in 1852, and the St. Nicholas in 1853. The St. Nicholas was the first hotel costing more than a million dollars to build—nearly $2 million, actually— and became the largest in the city after an 1856 addition increased its size to 500 rooms.

Similar growth and development was occurring in other cities, as well. In New Orleans, both the St. Louis Hotel and the St. Charles Hotel opened in the late

The Revere House, Boston (top), built in 1847, and the St. Nicholas Hotel, New York (bottom), built in 1853, were among the several grand hotels that were constructed in the large urban centers of mid-nineteenth–century America. This first wave of "palaces of the public" offered their guests the latest in modern conveniences. (Top: lithograph by S. W. Chandler & Co.; bottom: lithograph by F. Oppenheimer, courtesy Museum of the City of New York; both images courtesy New York Public Library Picture Collection.)

1830s, soon after New York's Astor House. Philadelphians witnessed the opening of the American House in 1844 and the Washington House in 1845. In Buffalo there was the American Hotel, which opened in 1836, the same year as the Astor House. Further west, the citizens of St. Louis were justly proud of their Planters' Hotel, which opened in 1841.

In Boston, after its 1855 opening, the original Parker House became very popular, and was considered far more modern than the Tremont Hotel. This perception was one of the factors that led to the decline and eventual closing of the famed Tremont. Charles Dickens, the famous British novelist and lecturer, spent several days in the Parker House when he was on a lecture tour of the United States in 1867. Local newspapers reported that he caused a sensation when people lined up at the hotel to obtain his autograph.

None of the grand hotels of the period, including those discussed above, was more than five stories high. There were two reasons for this. First, the hotels were built of wood, and wood construction is not suitable for tall buildings. Of equal importance was that the elevator had not yet been invented, so guests had to climb stairs to get to their rooms. This made the rooms located on the upper floors less popular and less expensive than those on the lower floors. The absence of elevators helps to explain the popularity of bellboys in the luxury hotels: Guests no longer had to carry their own baggage up flights of stairs to their rooms. Years later, after the first elevator installations in hotels, about 1859, the industry would witness an eventual reversal in the rates for rooms: Those on higher floors became more popular, and more expensive, than the less popular rooms on lower floors.

It should be noted that fire was a constant danger in these wood buildings. The situation was serious enough when rooms and corridors were lighted with candles, which could accidentally start fires if knocked over or if placed too close to flammable materials. The problems were considerably worse when the newly invented gaslight became the principal means of illumination. With candles, fire had been an obvious threat, and both guests and employees were vigilant; the introduction of gas brought the added threat of explosions, which might precede and precipitate devastating fires. During this period, before water was available above the first-floor level of buildings, hotels were regularly destroyed by raging fires in which many lives were also lost. Seeing a hotel destroyed by fire, then watching it being rebuilt to open the following year was a normal experience for the citizens of large American cities.

It is important to understand that this period between the opening of the Tremont (1829) and the start of the Civil War (1860) was one in which more new hotels were opened than at any time in our history until the 1920s. This could not and would not have occurred unless there had been a dramatic increase in the number of people traveling. This increase was directly related to the development of a network of railroads that became the primary means of transportation for people seeking to go from one to another of the growing cities in the United States. As in England, locations near railroad stations were quickly seen to be ideal for hotels, and the race was on in every city and town with a railroad station to build hotels close by. Tired travelers, emerging from the stations after long journeys on trains, typically sought the nearest hotel to find food, shelter, and rest.

CHICAGO'S HOTELS. Perhaps the most important railroad center of the age was then developing in Chicago. As the city and the railroad industry grew, so did

*This etching of the enlarged train shed at Grand Central Depot, New York City, reflects the growth of rail travel in the United States throughout the nineteenth century, which contributed to the development of both the hotel and resort industries as it advanced across the country. (*Frank Leslie's Illustrated Newspaper, *26 November 1870; courtesy New York Public Library Picture Collection.)*

the hotel industry. In 1837, the entire population of Chicago was only 4,170. By 1860, the city had grown to over 200,000 and had a sufficient number of first-class hotels to be able to host the second Republican national convention. This was the convention that nominated Abraham Lincoln. The list of grand hotels in Chicago at that time included a new Tremont, opened in 1850 to replace a prior Tremont that had burned, and which, in turn, had been the replacement for yet another Tremont that had also burned! The new Tremont cost $750,000 to construct and was at first considered too palatial for Chicago. Nevertheless, it quickly became a grand success and was enlarged twice. By 1868, it had reached nearly 300 rooms.

A year after the opening of the new Tremont, the Briggs House opened. The management claimed that it was the largest hotel west of the Alleghenies. The Briggs House was a favorite of Abraham Lincoln, who had made it his campaign headquarters during his first candidacy for President.

THE PALMER HOUSE, CHICAGO. Another of Chicago's first luxury hotels was the original Palmer House, a 227-room property that opened in 1870. Unfortunately, a great fire swept through Chicago in 1871, destroying most of its hotels, including the Palmer House.

After the great Chicago fire, the city began to rebuild, and many new hotels appeared. Twenty-three new first-class hotels opened within two years, including the Palmer House, the Grand Pacific, the Tremont, and the Sherman, which collectively became known as the "Big Four." By then, Chicago had a population of over 300,000 people.

The story of Chicago's Palmer House is interesting. Potter Palmer was an extremely successful businessman who made a fortune selling cotton, textiles, and other goods. He was also a man who believed in Chicago and its future. He purchased more than 100 parcels of land and buildings along State Street, tore down the old buildings, and widened the road. He built a number of new buildings, including one that he leased to Marshall Field, the famous department store proprietor. Another of these was the original 225-room Palmer House, which many Chicago residents called "Palmer's Marble Palace."

Just three months before the Palmer House opened, Palmer had married the daughter of a wealthy Chicago landowner. The early success of the hotel encouraged Palmer to plan and construct an even larger hotel as near the original as possible. This new property was to contain 650 rooms on eight floors and was under construction when the great Chicago fire started. Both hotels were destroyed, but Palmer was able to rescue the plans for the newer property; and he used them as the basis for planning yet another Palmer House. When this new hotel was finished, it was a huge success—the most popular hotel in the history of Chicago—and Bertha Palmer, Potter's wife, was toasted as "queen" of the city. The Palmers occupied a suite in the hotel and entertained presidents, princes, and wealthy friends and acquaintances there for many years. Potter Palmer died in 1902, but the hotel prospered until 1924, when it was torn down and replaced by a new Palmer House with 2,250 rooms at a cost of over $20 million. The Palmer House was purchased by Conrad Hilton in 1946 and continues to be operated by the Hilton organization. It remains an elegant property, with its large cathedral ceiling in the lobby, and the famous Empire Room, which has featured many famous entertainers over the years, including Guy Lombardo, Ted Lewis, Maurice Chevalier, Sophie Tucker, and Jimmy Durante.

SAN FRANCISCO'S HOTELS. The success of the hotel industry in Chicago was paralleled in San Francisco. In 1848, San Francisco was a small western town, still part of the Mexican Territory. The "hospitality industry" consisted of one small tavern, just one-and-one-half stories high. Gold was discovered in that part of California and the California gold rush started in 1849. Millions of people flocked to California to make their fortunes; and in the next twenty-five years, the population of San Francisco grew to 160,000. As the population grew, so did the hospitality industry: new hotels, restaurants, taverns (saloons, actually), and other enterprises, which could best be described in a book of this nature as "entertainment centers," were opening almost daily.

One of the earliest hotels of San Francisco was another Parker House, built in 1849 by Robert Parker who, coincidentally, had come from Boston. San Francisco's Parker House was noted for its high prices, gambling hall, and large ballroom. It set the standard for prices: When other similar properties were built, they, too, charged very high prices. With "gold fever" in the air, people were not very concerned about high prices. It was reported that a cigar stand at the Union Hotel rented for $4,000 a month and that the operator of the cigar stand, even at that high rent, was still able to make a handsome profit.

By 1859, a number of other grand—even opulent—hotels had been built. The list of these included the Occidental (400 rooms) and the Cosmopolitan, both of which opened in 1859. Perhaps the most expensive hotel to be constructed in San Francisco during this period was the Grand Hotel, built in 1869 at a cost of more than $1 million for a property of just 200 rooms!

Transcontinental railroad service began in 1869 with the joining of the Central Pacific and Union Pacific railroads. As one might expect, a number of fine hotels were constructed along this route to the West. By the end of the century, there were several very fine hotels in cities west of the Mississippi. In fact, a reporter for one of Chicago's newspapers, the *Century*, wrote that two of the three finest hotels in the country were then located in the west. One was the Palace Hotel in San Francisco; the other was the Brown Palace in Denver. Perhaps not surprisingly, as the third in this trio of best hotels in America, the reporter chose one in his native Chicago—the Auditorium.

THE PALACE HOTEL, SAN FRANCISCO. The Palace Hotel in San Francisco was completed in 1875 at a cost of almost $5 million. It contained 755 rooms and boasted of having the same elegant features offered by the best of the New York and Boston hotels—and a few that even New York and Boston lacked. It was said that the Palace was so large that some guests had difficulty finding their rooms. One writer offered advice for those who experienced this problem: The best plan was to "pretend you are full, let yourself loose, and cuss. Someone will come and guide you to your room."

The rooms in the Palace Hotel were twenty feet square—very large rooms, even by today's standards. The dining room was 155 feet by 55 feet, the largest in the world at the time. The hotel had a large number of private dining rooms, reading rooms, and parlors, and even had card rooms. The Palace was furnished with upholstered furniture made with native hardwood. Operations were not profitable for the first ten years because of the huge cost of constructing the hotel. However, over the years it became extremely successful. The Palace was the pride of San Francisco and was said to be earthquake proof, earthquakes having been a matter of some concern as early as the late nineteenth century. Although it did survive the historic earthquake that rocked San Francisco on April 18, 1906, it burned to the ground in the ensuing fire that leveled the city.

THE BROWN PALACE, DENVER. The Brown Palace in Denver had only 440 rooms, compared with 755 in the San Francisco Palace, but was as elegant as any hotel in the world when it opened in 1892. The immense lobby was eight stories high, with a stained-glass interior roof, onyx walls, and tile floors with elaborate

Greek designs. The public rooms in the Brown Palace were dispersed throughout the building rather than all on one floor—the more usual practice in hotels built both before and after the Brown Palace. These public rooms were grandly decorated in Louis XVI style. The hotel featured five honeymoon suites, known as *bridal chambers* and described by hotel management as "too beautiful and delicate for use." The daily rates for these suites were outrageously high—as much as $100, the equivalent of more than one year's salary for many American workers at that time! The other bedrooms in the hotel, half of which had private baths and many of which had fireplaces, were decorated in fifty shades of yellow—from cream to gold.

THE WALDORF-ASTORIA, NEW YORK. As a fitting climax to the nineteenth-century growth of the hotel industry in the American city, two hotels were built in New York City on Fifth Avenue between 33rd and 34th Streets on the sites of mansions owned by feuding members of the Astor family. The first, opened in 1893, was the Waldorf, built on the site of William Waldorf Astor's mansion at the corner of 33rd Street; the second, opened in 1897, was the Astoria, built on the site of the mansion owned by Colonel John Jacob Astor at the corner of 34th Street. Colonel Astor was the grandson of the John Jacob Astor who had been responsible for the original Astor House over 60 years earlier. The two properties were joined by a passage, from the day the Astoria opened. In addition, their names were soon joined by a hyphen, and the Waldorf-Astoria quickly became one of America's finest and best-known hotels.

The Waldorf-Astoria occupied the 34th Street site for over thirty years, but closed in 1928 when the level of real estate taxes had rendered its operation unprofitable. The site was sold to a new corporation that planned to build the world's largest office building. That office building—the Empire State Building— occupies the site to this day.

Resort Hotels in the 1800s

In the nineteenth century, while the great developing network of American railroads was providing the means for the economic development of the many and growing regions, cities, and towns of America, it was also putting in place a mechanism that would make possible a new period of growth and development for a group of hospitality operations that came to be known as resort hotels.

RAILROADS AND RESORT HOTELS. The resort hotel industry in the United States could not have developed without railroads. The reason for this is apparent when one considers the distance of many nineteenth-century resort hotels from population centers, as well as their relative inaccessibility by any other means of transportation available in the nineteenth century. In this period, it was not uncommon for families of means to spend entire summers or winters at resort hotels. A mother and her children—sometimes with servants—would remain at the resort hotel from week to week. But the father would spend only weekends with his family, traveling by train from a city to the resort at the end of the work week and returning to the city on Sunday evening or Monday morning to earn the money to pay for it all.

EARLY RESORT HOTELS. By the beginning of the nineteenth century, the resort hotel industry had begun its earliest period of development in the East. By 1789, for example, weary city dwellers in New York were being advised in advertisements to seek relaxation at Deagle's Hotel far from the noise and crowds of the city—in a then-rural part of Manhattan Island near what is now 155th Street and Amsterdam Avenue. Deagle's, the earliest known resort hotel on Manhattan, offered harassed New Yorkers opportunities for quiet fishing, and other ways to relax, and ushered in a period of growth for this new form of American hotel enterprise.

The 1800s saw the opening of many of America's important resort hotels and resort areas. In Cape May, New Jersey, the Congress Hotel was in operation in 1812, and was known for its sweeping verandas, which made it possible for resort guests to enjoy the cooling ocean breezes in summer. The Catskill Mountain region, located in an area between 70 and 130 miles northwest of New York City, traces its beginnings to the opening of the Catskill Mountain House in 1823. And by the 1820s, White Sulphur Springs in what later became West Virginia had begun to develop its reputation as a spa.

THE HOMESTEAD, HOT SPRINGS. An early and very famous resort hotel was The Homestead, in Hot Springs, Virginia. The property was acquired in 1832 by Dr. Thomas Goode, who then planned and developed it and continually made improvements to the property. By 1850, the Homestead was said to have approximately 15,000 visitors annually. It continues to be one of America's premier resorts.

THE GRAND HOTEL, POINT CLEAR. Another early resort hotel was constructed in Point Clear, Alabama in 1847 by a Mr. Chamberlain. Named the Grand Hotel, it was 100 feet long, with forty guest rooms on two floors. Adjacent to the hotel were separate structures that housed the dining room and a bar. This original Grand Hotel building served as headquarters for Confederate blockade runners during the Civil War and was a hospital for wounded soldiers of the Confederate Army. It was the only resort hotel to be hit by cannon fire during the war. The original buildings are long since gone; but they have been replaced by more modern structures, and the resort continues to prosper.

Founded in 1832 and still in operation, The Homestead in Hot Springs, Virginia (shown above as it appeared in 1891), was one of the first resort-spas in the United States. Fostered by the spread of the railroad, resorts were opened on the New Jersey Shore, in the Catskill Mountains, and in other areas previously considered remote. (Courtesy The Homestead.)

THE GREENBRIER, WHITE SULPHUR SPRINGS. In White Sulphur Springs, located in Virginia until West Virginia became a state in 1863, the mineral waters were said to have wonderful curative powers. This attracted people to the area, including presidents of the United States, as well as wealthy individuals with various illnesses. The growing popularity of the waters resulted in the eventual building of the original Greenbrier Hotel, called the Grand Central Hotel in 1857. Several of the buildings had been constructed many years earlier, including The Greenbrier Museum, built as a private home in 1816. Many wealthy and famous people who had heard of the mineral waters and their alleged healing powers rented rooms there. The Grand Central Hotel was seldom called by its given name. Guests usually referred to it as " The White," or "The Old White," either in reference to its white-colored exterior or to its location: White Sulphur Springs.

Guests of the Old White included such notables as President Martin Van Buren, Senator Henry Clay, the future King Edward VII, and General Robert E. Lee. It was renamed The Greenbrier in 1861 but was closed during much of the Civil War. Over the years, The Greenbrier has gone through several periods of financial difficulty, and has been owned by a number of individuals and corporations. The original property has been entirely reconstructed. A new 250-room building was added in 1913 and was expanded to 580 rooms in 1930. The Greenbrier was one of the first resorts to be classified as a five-star property—a rating it has continued to earn every year since.

THE BALSAMS, DIXVILLE NOTCH. In New England, another interesting resort property was developed in northern New Hampshire near the Canadian border. Named the Balsams, it was built in 1866 and was under continuing development up to the beginning of World War I. For over 100 years, The Balsams has been considered one of the finest resorts in New England. Although the majority of the grand summer resorts of New England have long since closed because of their inability to operate profitably as summer-only ventures, The Balsams was able to convert to year-round operation successfully and is still considered a premier resort.

WENTWORTH-BY-THE-SEA, PORTSMOUTH. Also in New Hampshire, the Wentworth-by-the-Sea, in New Castle, near Portsmouth, is typical of many of the fine resorts that were developed after the Civil War. Construction of the original building was started in 1873. Until the property closed as a resort hotel in the mid 1980s, the Wentworth-by-the-Sea was considered an elegant property. This is one of the many resort properties in New England and elsewhere that have found it difficult to survive in an ever-changing travel market.

THE GRAND HOTEL, MACKINAC ISLAND. Further west, in Michigan, there is a beautiful resort, the Grand Hotel located on Mackinac Island, in Lake Huron. No automobiles are permitted on the island, which makes this a unique resort. Transportation is by horse and carriage or bicycle, only. The hotel, billed as the largest summer hotel in the world, was first opened for business in 1887. It was a retreat for wealthy and famous people from Chicago and other nearby areas. Mackinac Island is only three miles long by two miles wide, and the hotel is situated to provide guests with spectacular views of the lake. The Grand Hotel is still in operation and is still quite popular.

HENRY FLAGLER, RESORT DEVELOPER. For most of the resort hotels of the nineteenth century, the railroad was the principal means of access. The close relationship between railroads and resort hotels can perhaps best be illustrated by examining the business career of Henry Flagler.

Flagler, who was a partner in John D. Rockefeller's Standard Oil Company, became wealthy and retired at the age of 53. He went to Florida to relax in 1883; but like so many successful entrepreneurs before and since, he could not leave business behind. He was enchanted by the Florida climate and by its unspoiled beauty and decided to investigate the possibilities for profitable real estate development. In 1885, he began construction of the Ponce de Leon Hotel in St. Augustine, on the Atlantic coast of Florida. He planned that the hotel would cater to the wealthy but soon realized that it would be very difficult to attract the clientele he wanted because of the poor transportation in the area. He started to buy the small railroads in the region and eventually controlled most railroad service in the state.

With his control of an excellent transportation network, Flagler was able to build a number of fine resort hotels throughout Florida—including such well-known properties as the Palm Beach Hotel, the Royal Poinciana, and the original Breakers in Palm Beach.

RAILROAD NETWORKS. By the end of the nineteenth century, entrepreneurs in the United States had developed a network of rail lines for both passengers and freight that was second to none in the world. Today, it may be difficult to comprehend the importance and complexity of the rail system, most of which has vanished. For example, the Mount Washington Hotel in New Hampshire's White Mountains was easily accessible by rail from all major cities in the Northeast. Guests typically checked in for all or part of the summer, arriving by train with trunks full of their summer wardrobes. Today, although the hotel is still in operation, the passenger trains no longer come, and guests arrive by automobile and bus. The passenger rail networks serving our resort areas—the Catskill Mountains, the New Jersey shore, and many others—are gone now, and the names of the railroad companies, once household words, are nearly forgotten. The Hudson River Railroad; the Ulster and Delaware River Railroad; the New York, Ontario, and Western Railroad; the Delaware and Hudson Canal Company Railroad; the Delaware, Lackawanna, and Western; these, and hundreds of others, with thousands of miles of track, are now just names for historians. But they were once lifelines, for the guests and employees who made America's resort hotels the great successes they were in the nineteenth century.

Restaurants in the 1800s

Restaurants in the United States are generally considered to have their origins in the ordinaries, inns, and taverns of Colonial America. These older terms persisted through the seventeenth and eighteenth centuries. By the beginning of the nineteenth century, *ordinary* had all but disappeared as a synonym for *inn* or *tavern*. However, by this time we begin to see instances of a comparatively new term of French origin, *restaurant*, that was to become dominant. By the beginning of the nineteenth century, inns, taverns, and restaurants had become common in the major American cities and were thoroughly integrated into the fabric of American society.

FACTORS AFFECTING RESTAURANT DEVELOPMENT. The development of the restaurant business in urban America is closely linked to the Industrial Revolution. By the early nineteenth century, two factors were beginning to have significant impact on the development of restaurants:

1. Manufacturing industries were expanding, creating a growing need for labor in cities and towns.
2. Agricultural methods and technology were improving, resulting in increased farm production on the one hand, and less need for farm labor on the other.

Those who left rural America to seek jobs in urban areas faced the problem of locating living quarters, which became increasingly difficult as the urban population grew. The first apartment buildings did not appear until about 1880. Until that time, people lived either in private homes, which were expensive, or in less expensive alternatives: rooms they rented in early hotels, in boarding houses, or in lodging houses. Boarding houses included meals in their rates. Some gave guests excellent meals, whereas others served food of very poor quality. Hotels and lodging (or rooming) houses did not provide meals, and residents typically had no access to cooking facilities. This led them to seek food in the various kinds of restaurants that developed in this period.

THE VARIETY IN CITY RESTAURANTS. The vast majority of these establishments tended to be very simple and plain, serving basic inexpensive meals to those who needed them: factory and office workers, most of whom lived too far from their jobs to go home for their midday meals. Other regular customers were those who did not have facilities for meal preparation at home. After all, cooking stoves were first patented in America about 1815 and did not become common in home kitchens until about 1850.

In the last half of the nineteenth century, a wide variety of food service enterprises were to be found in America's growing cities: street vendors; lunch carts and lunch wagons; lunch rooms in office buildings; taverns, both common and elegant, offering "free lunch"; hotel dining rooms; ethnic restaurants in ethnic areas; sandwich shops; cheap restaurants, known as "five-cent houses," and others known as "fifteen-cent houses," which served a portion of hot meat with potatoes, pickles, bread and butter for that price; these and many others were common.

OYSTER HOUSES. One of the most popular and inexpensive American foods of the period was the oyster, found in the Atlantic Ocean in large beds near the East Coast. They appealed to people of all backgrounds and were as popular in their time as hamburgers have become in ours. They were very cheap, and the types of establishments that specialized in serving them were known by many names: oyster house, oyster cellar, oyster saloon, and oyster wagon were all common terms. People consumed them in vast numbers, to the extent that many of the oyster beds were depleted. As this occurred, the price of oysters rose, and they began to lose their popularity, except in a few superior establishments.

One of these was Ye Olde Original Oyster House in Boston, now known as Ye Olde Union Oyster House, which opened in 1826. It is one of the oldest continuously operating restaurants in America, with an extensive menu that includes a large number of seafood entrees in addition to the oysters for which it is named. The semiprivate stalls, or booths, and the oyster bar itself are reported to be original furnishings.

CHANGING SERVICE TECHNIQUES. One particularly important development in the nineteenth century was a change in the techniques of service. Until about 1830, hotels and boarding houses were serving table d'hôte meals, just as inns and taverns had done for generations: Each meal was served at an appointed hour, at which time guests were seated at long tables preset with all foods constituting the meal. Guests helped themselves from platters, bowls, tureens, and other serving dishes. Competition among diners for the choicest foods could be fierce, and entire meals were frequently consumed in ten minutes or less.

In hotels, a later and more civilized approach was to divide the meals into courses, which were served by waiters. Meals were still served at appointed hours and guests were still seated at long tables, but the earlier every-man-for-himself approach was eliminated. Waiters moving with military precision would serve each course to one guest at a time. The foods would typically be placed on sideboards to which waiters would go to select the items requested by each guest.

Ye Olde Union Oyster House, Boston, was established in 1826. Offering their patrons inexpensive fare, oyster houses were among the most popular restaurants on the East Coast in the 1800s. (Courtesy Union Oyster House, Boston.)

In one hotel in New York, the regimented procedure described below was being observed in the dining room by 1835:

1. Guests were called to dinner by the ringing of a gong.
2. Uniformed waiters quickly marched guests to seats at long, rectangular tables, in a fashion reminiscent of military drill.
3. The headwaiter rang an official bell to signal his waiters, who moved quickly to the kitchen, returned with covered tureens of the soup of the day, and strategically positioned themselves at attention at their stations.
4. The headwaiter rang his bell again, and waiters deposited soup tureens on tables in unison, then proceeded to serve the soup as quickly as possible to all guests at the table.
5. The headwaiter rang his bell yet again to signal the waiters, who proceeded in unison to cover the tureens and remove them to the kitchen.
6. The following courses were served from sideboards by the waiters, who used techniques which were far less flamboyant than those employed for the soup course.

Later, with the introduction of the European Plan and printed menus, diners were given additional opportunities to select their foods. With this development, both fixed hours for meals and long tables for guests began to disappear. Eventually, dining rooms were open for meals for periods of several hours, and guests would dine at hours they chose.

CITIES KNOWN FOR NUMEROUS FINE RESTAURANTS. By the last years of the nineteenth century, all of America's great cities were able to boast about the quality of the meals available in some of their restaurants. The cities with truly outstanding reputations for fine dining were San Francisco, New Orleans, and New York.

SAN FRANCISCO. One individual wrote the following about the quality of the restaurants in San Francisco:

> The restaurants out there, ever since I can remember, have been about the best in this or any other section of the land. The French cuisine predominates, yet there are ever so many Italian restaurants. And for Chinese food—well I'm told that the best Chinese restaurants in all of China are right in San Francisco!

After the Gold Rush, the population of San Francisco grew dramatically, setting the conditions for equally dramatic growth in the restaurant industry. Within a very few years, San Francisco was noted for its variety of fine restaurants, including Lazzuro's (Italian), Manning's (Oyster house), The Mint (Southern), Zinkand's (German), and Jacques' (French).

NEW ORLEANS. In New Orleans, one of the fine old establishments is Antoine's, which opened in 1840. Known for its superior seafood specialties, Antoine's is owned and operated by the family of the original owner, Antoine Alciatore, an immigrant from Marseilles, France. Other popular establishments included Moreau's, Begue's, Les Quatre Saisons, and Le Pelerin.

NEW YORK. Perhaps the most important American city for fine dining throughout the nineteenth century was New York, which took pride in its many restaurants. The list was long and varied, and included such famous names as Taylor's, Sherry's, Rector's, and von Mehlbach's—an establishment opened in 1842 that changed its name to Luchow's in 1882. It operated under von Mehlbach's name until purchased by a young, industrious waiter named August Luchow, who had immigrated from Hanover, Germany, a few years earlier.

DELMONICO'S. Perhaps the most famous, and certainly the most interesting of New York's restaurants was Delmonico's, originally located on William Street, in lower Manhattan, near Wall Street. Delmonico's opened as a simple coffee and pastry shop in 1827 and grew to be a vast restaurant and private catering establishment. Reportedly the best and most expensive restaurant in the country, it was operated for several generations by members of the Delmonico family. As the commercial center of the growing city continued to move, the owners of Delmonico's kept pace by changing the location of the restaurant. In 1897, Delmonico's made its last move, to 5th Avenue and 44th Street, where it prospered for many years. Eventually, surviving members of the family grew tired of the restaurant business, and Delmonico's closed forever in 1923.

Delmonico's was the first restaurant to print its menu in both French and English. It boasted an unusually long menu: 327 items, each of which was available every day, assuming that the necessary supplies could be purchased. Delmonico's also played a role in the emancipation of women: It provided both room and food for luncheon meetings of an organization of prominent women in an acceptable social setting, thus enabling the members for the first time to appear unescorted in a public restaurant.

THE EARLIEST AMERICAN RESTAURANT CHAINS. A particularly interesting chain of restaurants was started along the southwestern route of the Atchison, Topeka, and Santa Fe Railroad in 1876 by an immigrant from England named Fred Harvey. He had extensive experience in food service and as a railroad mail clerk. He had observed the poor food and terrible service provided for railroad passengers traveling to the west, and he devised a system to improve it.

Under contract with the railroad, he established restaurants at stations for passenger dining. Railroad personnel were trained to distribute menus to passengers, record their selections, and inform the restaurant staff of these selections before the train reached the station. This was accomplished by means of a complex system of whistle signals. Meals were cooked to order and were nearly ready for passengers when trains reached the stations. They were served quickly and efficiently by waitresses who became known as Harvey Girls. The delays resulting from passenger dining were kept to an absolute minimum. Harvey's standards were high, and the meals were considered excellent. They were also inexpensive— because Harvey was not charged by the Atchison, Topeka, and Santa Fe for shipping his food supplies by rail.

The first restaurant in the Harvey chain was opened in Topeka, Kansas in 1876. By 1883, he owned a total of seventeen restaurants and hotels. Among Harvey's contributions to the growth of chain restaurants were centrally developed menus, identical uniforms for all waitresses in the organization, a central commissary, and strict quality control.

Another interesting chain grew from a single restaurant in New York City operated by William and Samuel Childs—Childs' Restaurant. By 1898, the Childs brothers were successfully operating nine restaurants in the city. That year, they introduced a new concept in restaurant dining: the cafeteria. Customers were able to select foods from long counters, place their selections on trays, and pay for the foods at the end of the counter. This was a great success, and was widely imitated by food service operators across the nation, including Horn & Hardart, Bickford's, and a number of others.

RESTAURANTS IN HOTELS. Perhaps the most important restaurants in the United States during the 1800s were not the independent, individually owned establishments, but those restaurants located in the principal hotels of major American cities. Because these hotels could afford to hire the finest chefs from Europe and because they were the social centers of their cities, where the elite entertained, the food service available in these establishments eclipsed that available in most private restaurants. For example, the Parker House in Boston had an unsurpassed reputation for fine food. The owner, Harvey Parker, paid the chef $5,000 per year when a good chef could be hired for less than $500.

In his book *The Palace Inns*, Brian McGinty has reproduced a typical banquet menu for the Parker House[3]. (See page 80.) This menu is typical of those offered by fine hotels during this period.

The Waldorf-Astoria was another hotel known internationally for its excellent cuisine. In fact, at one period in its history, the original Waldorf-Astoria was better known for its exceptional food than for its fine accommodations. Food service has been supervised by some of the best people in the field. The Waldorf-Astoria was the setting for Oscar Tschirky, known worldwide simply as Oscar of the Waldorf, to cater brilliantly for many years to the wealthy and famous personalities who frequented the hotel.

---

[3]Brian McGinty, *The Palace Inns* (Harrisburg: Stackpole Books, 1978), pp. 29–30.

Another hotel noted as much for its *haute cuisine* as for its grandeur was the Palace Hotel in San Francisco. The Palace maintained a staff of 150 waiters, and management claimed that the Palace chefs could prepare the national dishes of any country in the world, without exception, in the manner of chefs of that country. And on many occasions they proved that they could.

Oysters on Shell

SOUP
Green Turtle Soup
Tomato Soup

FISH
Boiled Bass, Egg Sauce
Baked Cod, Claret Sauce

BOILED
Leg Mutton
Capons and Pork
Ham, Champagne Sauce
Turkey, Oyster Sauce

COLD ORNAMENTED DISHES
Mayonnaise of Chicken
Boned Turkey, Decorated
Aspic of Oysters
Lobster Salad
Partridges, with Truffles and Jelly

ENTREES
Sweet Bread, Green Peas
Frican eau Veal
Compote of Pigeons
Fillet of Beef
Oyster Pattie
Macaroni Au Permesan

ROAST
Mongrel Goose
Turkey
Leg Mutton
Chickens

GAME
Black Ducks
Snipe
Black-Breast Plover
Partridges
Grass Birds
Yellow Leg Plover
Woodcock
Widgeon
Peep Quail

PASTRY
Birds Nest Pudding
Cup Custard
Lemon Pie
Apple Pie
Calf's Foot Jelly
Charlotte Russe
Squash Pie
Sago Pudding
Madeira Jelly
Mince Pie

FRUIT
Apples, Pears, Oranges, Walnuts, Peaches, Grapes,
Almonds, Raisins

ICE CREAM
Vanilla, Pine Apple, Roman Punch

Coffee and Olives

SUMMARY

In this chapter, the earliest types of hospitality establishments in America are identified and described. The impact of railroads and railroad travel in the nineteenth century on the hospitality industry in general, and on city hotels and resort hotels in particular, is examined in detail. Significant hotels of the nineteenth century are identified and the characteristics that made them unique described. The ever-present problem of hotel fires is also discussed. Various economic and social conditions that fostered the growth of the food service industry are listed and described, and a variety of types of food service establishments common in the period are named. In addition, the following individuals are identified and their principal contributions to the hospitality industry enumerated: Samuel Coles; Samuel Fraunces; Isaiah Rogers; Harvey Parker; Potter Palmer; Henry Flagler; and Fred Harvey.

QUESTIONS

1. Explain the meaning of the term *ordinary*. What was its role in the life of a seventeenth-century community?
2. What was the difference between a tavern and an inn in seventeenth-century America?
3. What difference was there between the status of the early American innkeeper and that of his counterpart in Europe?
4. Describe the conditions that might face the traveler spending the night in a rural American inn in the seventeenth century? What were the accommodations likely to be? Comment on the probable levels of comfort and cleanliness.
5. Discuss the role of Samuel Fraunces and his tavern during the Revolutionary War.
6. Hotels in the United States have always been considered "Palaces of the Public." Explain.
7. What was the first purpose-built hotel structure in the United States? Where was it located and when was it built?
8. Name the property that is considered to be America's first luxury hotel. Where was it located? When was it built? List five features that made it an outstanding hotel for its time.
9. Name the New York hotel designed and built to rival the luxury of the Tremont. Who designed it? How was it illuminated?
10. Why were no hotels built in the early nineteenth century above five floors in height?
11. The period between 1830 and 1860 was one in which more new hotels were opened in America than at any other time until the 1920s. Why?
12. What characteristics of the hotels built before the Civil War made fire in them an ever-present danger?
13. What was the impact of railroad development on Chicago in the twenty-five year period between 1835 and 1860?
14. What characteristics of the Palace Hotel, San Francisco, and the Brown Palace, Denver, led to their being known as "grand" hotels?
15. Why were railroads important to the development of the resort hotel industry?

16. How does the career of Henry Flagler illustrate the close relationship that developed between railroads and the resort hotels in the nineteenth century?

17. Describe early nineteenth-century changes in agriculture and manufacturing that set the stage for significant growth in the restaurant industry.

18. Discuss the role of boarding houses and lodging houses in the development of the food service industry from 1800 to the start of the Civil War.

19. List six kinds of food service establishments that could be found in major American cities in the period after the Civil War.

20. Which three American cities were reputed to have the best restaurants in the late nineteenth century? List the names of three restaurants in each city during this period.

21. What restaurant had the reputation for being the finest individual restaurant in the United States in the late nineteenth century? Why?

22. Of what importance to the development of the restaurant industry was the chain of restaurants started by Fred Harvey?

23. Describe the service technique used in one New York hotel around 1835.

24. Why were the grand hotels in nineteenth-century America able to develop reputations for providing food and service of a quality exceeding that available elsewhere in major American cities at the time?

25. What distinguished the food service operation of San Francisco's Palace Hotel from that of other American hotels of the late nineteenth century?

The Hospitality Industry in the United States II:
The Twentieth Century

4

LEARNING OBJECTIVES

After reading and studying this chapter, you should be able to:

1. *List the important inventions of the late nineteenth century and describe the impact of each on the hospitality industry.*
2. *Identify each of the following and describe their principal contributions to the development of the hospitality industry: Ellsworth M. Statler; Conrad Hilton; Howard Johnson; J. Willard Marriott, Kemmons Wilson; Ray Kroc.*
3. *Describe in general terms the important developments in the three principal segments of the industry—hotels, resort hotels, and restaurants—in the period between 1900 and 1945.*
4. *List and discuss the economic and social factors that led to increased travel by Americans in the period after 1945.*
5. *Describe the principal changes that took place in hotels, resort hotels, and restaurants in the post–World War II period.*

INTRODUCTION

Following a golden age of invention in the late nineteenth century, there had been some dramatic changes in American life. Electricity, for example, was beginning to replace gas to illuminate homes and offices. Henry Ford and others were further developing the recently invented automobile, which promised new and improved methods of motor transport. Streets and roads were being paved and otherwise improved in cities, towns, and rural areas so that people could take full advantage of the new automobiles. The telephone was becoming common, making voice communication possible over long distances, just as the railroads had made rapid transit between cities and regions a reality. These and other important developments were moving America toward becoming the world's foremost economic power. This dramatic increase in economic development gave rise to more travel for Americans than they had ever known before, setting the stage for the major developments in America's hospitality industry.

The first two decades of the twentieth century were a time of rapid growth in American business. This growth produced an increase in travel, particularly business travel. Long-distance trips were still primarily by train, but use of the automobile was becoming increasingly common. New paved roads were constructed and more and more of the older roads were paved. In many parts of the country, it was becoming possible to drive an automobile from one city to another without using the dirt roads of earlier decades.

The first recorded journey across the United States by automobile was undertaken in 1903 by a physician from Vermont named Jackson. It took Dr. Jackson 69 days—from May 23rd to August 1st—to drive from New York City to San Francisco. Many of those days were spent in hotels, waiting for the automobile to be fixed and for parts to be shipped. America's roads were not yet well suited to long-distance driving.

CITY HOTELS FROM 1900 THROUGH WORLD WAR II

The first half of the twentieth century was perhaps the most important in the history of the hotel industry in the United States. It was both an unprecedented period of growth and later, a period of economic depression that led to many hotel company failures. One hotel organization that began and grew dramatically in the early years of the century, survived the economic downturn, and managed to prosper in the years that followed was that founded by E. M. Statler.

The Early Career of E. M. Statler

Ellsworth Milton Statler, the man most responsible for the development of the modern commercial hotel, was not raised in the hospitality industry. Born in 1863, he started work at the age of nine in a glass factory in Wheeling, West Virginia. He worked twelve hours a day to earn $.50; the rate of pay was $.25 for six hours of work. By the time he quit the job, at the age of twelve, he was being paid $.45 per six-hour shift—$.90 per day.

One of Statler's older brothers worked at a local hotel, the McLure House in Wheeling. He was a bellhop, a term derived from the desk clerk's practice of pressing a small bell to call the "boy" who carried baggage to guests' rooms. Ellsworth applied for a job as a bellboy but was rejected at first because of his age. He persisted and was finally given a job in 1875. He was paid at the rate of $6 a month plus tips.

Statler was a hard worker, and by 1878 he had been promoted to head bellboy. Soon thereafter, he became night clerk and learned more about the operation of a hotel. After two years in that job, the owners decided to close the hotel for renovations, and Statler was faced with the loss of his job and income. He found work in a steel mill until the McLure reopened six months later. The owners wanted him to return, but he would do so only if he were given a lease on the hotel's billiard parlor, which opened off the lobby. The owners agreed, and by his early twenties Statler had become the lessee of the McLure's billiard parlor. Under Statler's management, it became a very successful enterprise, and he soon took over the railroad-ticket concession, as well. Statler continued to find new and profitable business ventures, eventually operating a bowling alley and a restaurant — the Pie House. These ventures provided him with a $10,000 a year income — very much higher than average for the period. In addition, he had sufficient leisure time to pursue his lifelong favorite sporting activity — fishing.

THE ELLICOTT SQUARE RESTAURANT. Statler did some of his fishing in Canada, and as he was returning from one of these excursions in 1894, his route passed through Buffalo, N.Y. He recognized business opportunities in Buffalo and decided to plan a traditional 500-seat tablecloth restaurant in the basement of a new Buffalo office building. When it opened in 1895, he named it the Ellicott Square Restaurant. Buffalo had a reputation for being a poor location for restaurants because the population tended not to patronize them. However, because of his early success with the Pie House in Wheeling, Statler believed that he was an excellent restaurateur and could change the habits of Buffalonians.

His experience soon proved otherwise: The restaurant nearly failed. He discovered that the people of Buffalo were simply not interested in patronizing his restaurant. Because he did not want to go into bankruptcy, he met with his creditors to gain time during which he would try other ideas. They agreed, and he made changes until he found one that made the restaurant financially successful: He installed turnstiles and charged customers $.25 in advance for all they could eat! By 1901, the restaurant was entirely successful, and Statler was out of debt. In addition, he had saved $60,000 from the profit that he would use to launch his hotel career.

STATLER'S FIRST HOTEL. His opportunity came quickly. A World's Fair — the Pan American Exposition — was planned for Buffalo in 1901, and Statler devised a scheme to open an incredible two-story, rectangular wood structure that would contain 2,084 rooms and accommodate 5,000 guests. It was to be a temporary structure, covered with a thin layer of plaster to make it appear substantial, although simple to tear down after the fair closed. Statler invested all of his profits from the Ellicott Square Restaurant to construct it, and it opened in time for the fair. Unfortunately, the fair was a financial disaster, largely because it was the site of the assassination of the then President of the United States, William F. McKinley. The hotel was never able to attract more than 1,500 paying guests on any one night, but Statler was somehow able to make a profit from the venture. One of the reasons was probably his policy of requiring all guests to pay for their accommodations in advance. *Skippers* — guests who leave hotels without paying their bills — were common problems to hoteliers at the time, and Statler determined that he would eliminate them.

STATLER'S SECOND HOTEL. His next venture was the Inside Inn, a hotel he operated at the Louisiana Purchase Exposition, a World's Fair that opened in St. Louis in 1904. The fair was not a financial success: It closed sooner than planned; but by the time it closed, Statler had been able to earn $361,000 in profits from operating the hotel. During this period, he received terrible burns from a coffee urn that blew up as he was inspecting it, and he nearly died. He did recover, however, after a long period of recuperation in a wheelchair.

THE BUFFALO STATLER. Using the profit earned from operating the hotel at the St. Louis Fair, Statler began to plan a new hotel for Buffalo, New York. His new 300-room hotel opened on January 18, 1908. It was named the Buffalo Statler and is considered to be a milestone in the history of the hotel industry: It was one of the first modern commercial hotels to cater to the ever-growing number of traveling businessmen, offering them the following:

1. private bath in every room;
2. circulating ice water in every bathroom;
3. telephone in every room;
4. full-sized, lighted closet in every room;
5. light switch on the wall just inside the door of each room;[1]
6. free newspaper delivered to every guest's room each morning;[2]
7. mail chute that ran from the top floor to the lobby, so that guests could post letters without leaving their floors.

The advertising motto of the hotel was "A room with a bath for a dollar and a half," an incredible value for travelers at the time.

THE STATLER CHAIN. The Buffalo Statler was very successful, and E. M. Statler began to open additional hotels bearing his name, thus creating a group of properties assigned the modern term *chain*. Eventually he owned or operated

---

[1]Other hotels had a pull chain hanging from the light fixtures that guests had difficulty locating in the dark.

[2]Each guest-room door had a slot cut out at the bottom so the paper could be slipped through.

properties in Cleveland, Detroit, New York, Boston, and most other major American cities. When he died in 1928, Statler controlled a larger number of hotels than anyone in history.

Statler had no formal education after the age of 9. He was a self-educated man who learned from employees, guests, friends, and business associates all his life. He developed a philosophy of hospitality that is perhaps best summarized by the following quotation from the Statler Service Code: "Life is service. The one who progresses is the one who gives his fellow human being a little more, a little better service."

The Plaza Hotel in New York

During the years when Statler was developing his Buffalo property and expanding his holdings, many individuals, partnerships, and corporations were designing and building new hotels in cities all across America. In New York City, nearly a mile from the nearest railroad, a new hotel opened in 1907. Named the Plaza, it was actually the second hotel of that name to occupy the site. The first, erected only seventeen years earlier, was torn down so that the new 800-room Plaza could be built.

The world-famous Plaza is a particularly notable establishment, an excellent example of the great American "Palaces of the Public." Interestingly, it is one of

One of the most famous hotels in the world, the Plaza Hotel in New York City. Along with E. M. Statler's several luxurious hotel properties, the Plaza was among the most important hotels built in the United States before World War I. (Courtesy the Plaza Hotel.)

the few successful hotels anywhere to operate without a sign. In addition, the Plaza has been continuously operated as a luxury hotel since 1907 — an unusually long period. Managers have been known to boast that those who would not recognize the Plaza without a sign clearly do not belong there. In the early years, up to 90 percent of the rooms and suites in the Plaza were occupied by permanent residents. This provided financial stability and helped to assure the hotel of a prosperous future.

Other Well-Known Hotels

Other important hotels constructed in the period before World War I included the Copley Plaza (1912) in Boston; the McAlpin (1912) and the Biltmore (1916) in New York City; the Willard (1901) in Washington D. C.; and Statler properties in Cleveland (1912), Detroit (1915), and St. Louis (1918).

"The Golden Age of Hotels"

The decade of the 1920s — popularly known as the Roaring Twenties — was a particularly important period of hotel development. It has been characterized as the "golden age of hotels" because of the large number of hotels constructed, their size, and the very high occupancy rates they were able to maintain.

The opening curtain had gone up on the era nearly a year earlier than the 1920s in New York City with the opening of the Pennsylvania, a 2,200-room hotel located just across the street from a major railroad terminal — New York's famed Pennsylvania Station. The Pennsylvania opened for business in January 1919 and was the world's largest hotel at the time. Although the building was owned by the Pennsylvania Railroad, it was operated by E. M. Statler. It was his first venture in New York City.

The Pennsylvania was a vast enterprise. When it opened, the chef's staff was reported to consist of ". . . 9 bakers, 10 pastry bakers, 4 ice-cream chefs, 9 butchers, 12 cold meat cooks, 9 roast cooks, 12 sauce cooks, 9 fry cooks, 6 vegetable girls, 4 soup cooks, 4 banquet chefs, 8 pot washers, 4 cleaners," and others too numerous to list. Many years later it became a Hilton hotel — the Statler Hilton — when Statler's chain was purchased by Conrad Hilton in 1954.

Many important hotels were built during the 1920s, including the Ritz Carlton (1927) and the Statler (1927) in Boston; the Roosevelt (1924) and the New Yorker (1927), both in New York City; the Biltmore (1927) in Santa Barbara; the Mayflower (1925) in Washington D. C.; and both the Palmer House (1924) and the Stevens (1928) in Chicago. The Stevens, a 3,000-room property, was later purchased by Hilton and renamed the Conrad Hilton. It long served as the headquarters of the Hilton organization and was the world's largest hotel for many years.

Occupancies during the 1920s were the highest the hotel industry had ever known. Annual guest-occupancy rates for many American hotels averaged above 80 percent during this period. New hotels were almost instant successes, and it seemed as though hotels could not be built quickly enough to satisfy the increasing demand for rooms. This high demand was one consequence of a booming economy that had led to great increases in travel for business purposes. And given the improvements in railroads, automobiles, and roads, long-distance travel was far easier than it had ever been in history.

Many of these business travelers were salesmen assigned to sales territories that covered large geographic areas. Great numbers of them traveled from city to city by railroad. Because of the nature of their work, they were away from home for long periods. In order to keep their baggage to a minimum, many left their dirty laundry at hotels when they checked out, requesting that it be washed and held for their return. Hotels opened charge accounts to keep records of the amounts owed for this service, and many labeled the accounts *Hold Laundry*. Some salesmen were reputed to have their clothing spread out in hotels all across their sales territories. An arrangement such as this was mutually beneficial: Salesmen could limit the amount of clothing they had to carry and were assured that clean clothes would be waiting for them when they checked into hotels; at the same time, hotel managers knew they could count on repeat business from these salesmen who were certain to return for their laundry.

Hilton, America's Best-Known Name in Hotels

No discussion of this era would be complete without mention of Conrad Hilton, the most recognized name in the history of the hospitality industry. Unlike E. M. Statler, Conrad Hilton had embarked on a successful career prior to going into the hotel business. He was a banker in New Mexico and purchased his first hotel—the Mobley, in Cisco, Texas—in 1919 with an investment of $5,000. The owner of the Mobley decided to try drilling for oil, rather than stay in the hotel business. Hilton happened to be in Cisco on bank business at the time and discovered the hotel was for sale.

Hilton was very successful at operating the Mobley. He used some of the techniques employed by innkeepers over many centuries: He increased occupancy by renting each room to two, three, or even four persons every night. They were prospectors and oil field workers who did not know one another; but they were all desperate for sleeping accommodations, which were in short supply in the area. Hilton, who lived in the hotel, was even known to rent his own bed and sleep in a lobby chair on occasion. He was obviously able to achieve maximum revenue from the hotel under these circumstances.

Hilton acquired seven hotels in the area in a very short time, expanding as fast as his credit rating would permit. He knew the banking business well, and he had maintained contacts who would lend him the funds to make the necessary down payments on hotel properties. His business philosophy was to borrow as much as possible on each of his hotels in order to expand as rapidly as possible. This worked well as long as hotel occupancy rates were high. However, when occupancy rates dropped during the depression of the 1930s, Hilton was unable to meet the payments required by this heavy debt and lost several of his properties in bankruptcy proceedings.

The Great Depression

The Great Depression began in October 1929 and continued for the next decade. During this period, banks failed and firms, large and small, went out of business. Because the government did not insure against bank failures back then, many people lost their life savings. Unemployment rose to alarming rates and people were sometimes out of work for years. Nature compounded the economic problems in some parts of the country: Prolonged drought was followed by dust storms, and land that had once been fertile could no longer be used for agriculture or to support livestock. Some limited recovery began in 1933 and slow progress continued. However, historians tend to agree that the Great Depression continued until the production demands of World War II reduced unemployment and brought the nation a measure of prosperity.

During the depression, the hotel industry experienced the same problem as other industries—sharply reduced sales volume. The hotel business closely follows business cycles and is therefore profitable when the economy is healthy and unprofitable during economic downturns. The explanation is fairly simple: Profitability in the hotel business is closely linked to travel. During periods of prosperity, more people travel, for business and pleasure. During a recession or depression, individuals and businesses reduce the amounts they had formerly spent on travel and related expenses, including food, beverages, and lodging. As a consequence, hotel occupancy rates plunge. Occupancies for those hotels that were able to survive the Depression were often below 50 percent, a level that is typically below the break-even point for most hotel operations.

One of the few hotels to open during the Great Depression was the world-famous Waldorf-Astoria, which opened in New York in 1932. The new location was 301 Park Avenue, between 49th and 50th Streets. Actually, it was the second hotel to use that name, the first one being located further downtown (see Chapter 3).

World War II: The End of the Depression

World War II brought an end to the Great Depression. It also brought renewed prosperity to the hotel industry. Many of the hotels in major cities had higher rates of occupancy than ever before or since. Virtually all economic activity was being directed toward the war effort and many products, including building materials, were unavailable for civilian use. Thus, no commercial hotel construction was taking place. At the same time, there was a dramatic increase in travel by civilians and by government personnel, including the military. Gasoline was rationed, so people relied increasingly on public transportation for long-distance travel.

Many hotels had failed during the depression, and a number of these hotel buildings had been converted to other uses. Consequently, there was an inadequate supply of hotel rooms available to meet the wartime demand. The existing hotels were busier than anyone had ever thought possible. Day after day, hotel desk clerks would spend eight hours facing unending lines of weary travelers wanting rooms. Travelers to many of the major cities—New York City and Washington, most notably—found it nearly impossible to get rooms. Many hotels failed to honor reservations; others would not even take reservations. It was a desperate time for travelers. National hotel occupancy percentages reached a record annual average well above 90 percent.

RESORT HOTELS FROM 1900 THROUGH WORLD WAR II

By the early years of the twentieth century, several important factors were beginning to affect the quality of life for the American work force—changes that would become significant for the operators of resort properties as the years wore on.

Leisure Time in America

In this period, some Americans began to have measurable amounts of leisure time. Most had very little, but it was more than their parents had ever known. At the same time, some had enough disposable income to be able to make plans for their newly found leisure hours. For most, there was little time and little money, but they went about enjoying the little there was.

There were day trips to everywhere by train or by boat, and later, by car as well. The seashore, a park, a zoo, an historic site—Americans were visiting them all. These visits introduced them to new possibilities, including hotels, rooming houses, and boarding houses catering not to business travelers, but to those with a day, a weekend, or a week of leisure time. Increasingly, those who could afford it began to stay a while.

Vacations

By 1915, growing numbers of white-collar and government workers were being given paid vacation time of one or two weeks a year, and many, with their families, began to take vacations—a nearly revolutionary concept in the industrialized world. As unionized industrial workers began to obtain increased benefits through collective bargaining, many began to pressure their union leaders for vacations with pay. Although it was not easy for the unions to win paid vacations at the bargaining table, they were making gradual progress in this area by 1929.

As time went by, those who could afford it began to travel somewhat farther away. In the New York area, for example, there were a number of possibilities: For those of limited means, a day at the beaches of Coney Island; for others with greater incomes, the extensive rail network offered opportunities for weekends or weeks at destinations in the nearby Catskill Mountains of southern New York and the Pocono Mountains of eastern Pennsylvania. By the mid 1920s, over 200 resort properties in the Catskills alone catered to holiday seekers, principally from New York City.

There were other possibilities, as well. The beaches along the New Jersey coast were always very popular with New Yorkers and Philadelphians. President Grant had said of Long Branch, one of the New Jersey resorts: "In all my travels I have never seen a place better suited for a summer residence. . . ." In the early twentieth century, packed trains from New York City arrived at the New Jersey resort towns on summer weekends at the rate of twelve or more each hour.

The Grand Resorts

The resort hotels developed during this period were many and varied. Many of those enjoyed by white-collar and blue-collar workers have not survived. However, it is likely that they attempted to imitate elements of some of the grand resorts, described in the following sections, most of which continue to operate.

THE BUCK HILL INN. The Buck Hill Inn was originally a summer retreat for Quakers. Its founder was Samuel Griscom, a Quaker from Philadelphia who had inherited several thousand acres of land in eastern Pennsylvania. He became convinced that this beautiful and peaceful area would be an ideal one for a Quaker retreat, and he proceeded to gather together a like-minded group of members of his faith to join him in building an inn and private cottages on the site.

Construction began in 1901. By June 1902, construction had reached the point at which guests could be accommodated while the builders finished construction. Buck Hill Falls was not an easy place to reach, however. Guests from Philadelphia found it necessary to travel first to Trenton, New Jersey, where they boarded trains on the Delaware Valley Railroad and rode to the end of the line. There they changed trains and railroads. After long periods of waiting they boarded trains on the Delaware, Lackawanna, and Western Railroad, which carried them to Cresco, Pennsylvania, the nearest station. From there, they were transported by horse and buggy many miles to the inn. The trip required an entire day, and it was often dark by the time guests arrived.

Over the years, the Buck Hill Inn prospered and was enlarged several times. It relied primarily on Quakers from the Philadelphia area for business, and strict rules were in force for several decades. Alcoholic beverages were not permitted in the public areas. Neither was card-playing. Automobiles were prohibited until 1916. It was a quiet, peaceful, slow-paced resort.

By the 1930s, the inn had gained a nationwide reputation, and the strict rules were no longer observed. In later years, a conference center was added and the inn operated year-round, reportedly as the largest resort in Pennsylvania. However, after a period of severe economic difficulties, it was forced to close in 1991.

THE POCONO MANOR INN AND GOLF CLUB. At about the same time the Buck Hill Inn was under construction, another resort was being built on a nearby site in the Pocono Mountains. Interestingly, this property, the Pocono Manor Inn, was also started by a group of Quakers. They conceived of it as a place where they could relax and enjoy their quiet way of life uninterrupted by the world at large. Although it was started as a summer resort, the Pocono Manor Inn became a year-round operation in 1908, making it one of the first year-round resorts in the East.

The inn was so popular that eventually it was expanded to 280 rooms. Beginning with the Depression, however, it went through a period of decreased occupancy and inadequate revenues. Consequently, the buildings and grounds were neglected for some years and reached a serious state of disrepair. Fortunately, an entrepreneur from Atlantic City, Samuel W. Ireland, saw great potential in the property and purchased it in 1967. He planned and directed a complete renovation of the resort, adding new rooms and such features as a meeting center, ski lodge, indoor swimming pool and tennis courts, to the existing golf course, outdoor pool, and other recreational facilities. Renamed the Pocono Manor Inn and Golf Club, it presently has 275 guest rooms and is considered one of the leading resort properties in the region.

THE BROADMOOR HOTEL. One of the premier resort properties in the United States is located in Colorado, near Pikes Peak. Near the bottom of this 14,000-foot mountain, in Colorado Springs, stands this classic example of the elegant resort hotels of the West. Named the Broadmoor Hotel, it was founded by Spencer Penrose, an entrepreneur who had attempted to purchase the Antlers, a hotel in downtown Colorado Springs. He had not been able to do so and had decided instead to purchase another property outside of town. This had once been an established hotel operation but had burned down, been rebuilt, failed, and been converted to a girls' school. Existing facilities were inadequate for the resort, so construction began in 1917 and the new resort hotel opened in 1918. It was one of

Colorado's first nationally known resorts. The architects were the firm of Warren and Wetmore of New York City, designers of New York's Grand Central Station, Biltmore Hotel, and Ritz-Carlton Hotel, among other important buildings.

The Broadmoor quickly became a success. All through the 1920s, the Penroses entertained many wealthy and famous people, and their Broadmoor became a fashionable place for New York society. It is said that one of the reasons for this success was Penrose's preparation for Prohibition: The Broadmoor allegedly had on hand one of the largest liquor supplies in the United States when Prohibition began in 1920.

This period of success for the Broadmoor ended with the onset of the Depression. Occupancy rates and guest counts dropped sharply, and Penrose was forced to reduce operating costs. He cut the size of the staff drastically and it is reported that bellmen and waiters earned only their tips.

After World War II, improving economic conditions brought prosperity back to the hotel. New facilities and new rooms were added during the 1960s and 1970s, and today the Broadmoor is a five-star resort with 560 rooms.

THE ARIZONA BILTMORE. Another of America's grand, five-star resorts—the Arizona Biltmore—is located just 800 miles south of Colorado Springs, in Phoenix, Arizona. It was built in the style of America's best-known architect, Frank Lloyd Wright, who participated in its design. At the time the hotel was built, Phoenix was a very small community in a large valley—Paradise Valley, which was essentially desert. The Biltmore was situated on a large tract of barren land in the northeastern part of the city, near the foothills of the mountains that surround the valley.

The Biltmore was designed and constructed by Albert Chase McArthur, an architect and disciple of Wright. It opened in 1929 and was sold later that year to William Wrigley, Jr., the chewing gum manufacturer. Wrigley built a mansion for his personal use on a knoll overlooking the hotel. His home was visible for miles around; the resort hotel was not.

Interestingly, the Arizona Biltmore was originally open only during the winter months. Phoenix is normally extremely hot during the summer months, and it is only the development of suitable air conditioning systems that has made it possible for resort hotels in the region to stay open year-round.

After World War II, the population of Phoenix began to increase dramatically. As the city grew, the Biltmore was eventually surrounded by newly constructed homes and businesses. In 1973, the Wrigley family sold the hotel to Talley Industries.

In the summer of 1973, while it was closed for the installation of a sprinkler system, a major fire damaged the property. Repairs were made promptly and it reopened for the start of the guest season later that year.

The Arizona Biltmore, Phoenix, Arizona, as it appeared in 1936. Fostered in the early twentieth century by an increase in leisure time and the availability of paid vacations, the "grand resorts" of the United States provided their patrons with respite from the pressures of an industrialized society. Originally intended as a seasonal resort—open only during the winter months, serving primarily individual guests—the Arizona Biltmore now operates year-round, hosting groups and conventions as well. (Courtesy Arizona Biltmore/Westin Resorts.)

The Arizona Biltmore is typical of seasonal resorts that have found it increasingly difficult—in some cases, impossible—to survive solely on individual guest business. The "seasons" are too short to generate the necessary sales volume. In order to extend the season, the Biltmore began booking conventions and other group business. The Biltmore, in particular, however, enjoys a reputation for restricting its group business to periods of the year when comparatively few individual reservations are booked.

THE BOCA RATON HOTEL AND CLUB. A fourth five-star hotel built during this period is the fabulous Boca Raton Hotel and Club, which was originally opened in 1926. It was envisioned as a palatial establishment by Addison Mizner, a successful architect who had become famous in Florida for designing many of the homes and other properties there. He wanted to turn the 17,500-acre site into "a happy combination of Venice and Heaven, Florence and Toledo, with a little Greco-Roman glory and grandeur thrown in." His grand plan included a castle with drawbridge in the middle of a man-made lagoon—for himself! He was not able to construct all he originally had in mind, but all that he did build used the best and most expensive materials available. One of his creations was a luxurious 100-room hotel that cost $1.5 million dollars to build—a fortune in those days for such a small establishment. He named it the Cloister Inn. He would use this name again later for a property he designed in Sea Island, Georgia.

The Cloister Inn was not financially successful. It was open for only three months before it was forced to close. It was then sold to Charles Dawes, a former Vice President of the United States. It was sold again in 1928, to Clarence H. Geist of Philadelphia. Geist closed it and spent millions of dollars converting it to a private club by adding rooms, swimming pools, and other features to the original building. He brought the total number of rooms to 400 and reopened the facility in 1930 under a new name: the Boca Raton Hotel and Club. During World War II, it was taken over by the United States Army and used as a training facility.

In 1956, the Boca Raton Hotel and Club was purchased by Arthur Vining Davis, who set up a corporation to own and operate it. His corporation, Arvida, built a twenty-seven story tower, which added new guest rooms and a convention center. The property has been under continuous development since then and now is one of the larger resorts in the area, with 1,000 rooms, 29 meeting rooms, 4 outdoor swimming pools, 7 dining rooms, an 18-hole golf course, 22 tennis courts, and a half-mile of private beach.

THE CLOISTER RESORT. A particularly well-known resort hotel located in the South is the Cloister Resort, a five-star resort hotel located at Sea Island, Georgia, one of the "Golden Isles of Georgia." It was a creation of Howard E. Coffin, an automotive engineer who was both yachtsman and hunter. During a trip to the area in 1911, Howard visited the islands and became intrigued with their beauty. He decided to invest in real estate in the islands. He built a large home and a game reserve on one of them and spent much of his leisure time there. When he learned that the state was planning to build a causeway that would link the mainland with Saint Simmons Island, directly west of Sea Island, he saw potential profit and immediately began to purchase as much land as possible. Eventually he acquired title to 6,000 acres on Sea Island, one of the smaller islands, and began to plan a resort for the site.

The original hotel opened in 1928. Although it contained only forty-six rooms, it was an elegant property that attracted wealthy people seeking a peaceful seaside area. There was an excellent beach—almost five miles long—and sufficient land for the development of additional recreational facilities. Today, activities available at the Cloister include golf, tennis, skeet shooting, and horseback riding. It even has its own orchestra that plays nightly. The hotel has been enlarged and now has 264 guest rooms.

RESTAURANTS FROM 1900 THROUGH WORLD WAR II

The early years of the century saw the development of some new food service establishments, such as diners, drive-ins, hamburger restaurants, roadhouses, and ice-cream stands. These years also gave rise to trends that were to become increasingly important. The growing popularity of the automobile, for example, led to the development of different kinds of restaurants along the highways of America. Roadside diners and drive-ins were typical.

Diners

Diners became common after 1897, when the cities of Boston, New York, and Philadelphia began to replace their old horse-drawn trolleys, called *horse cars*, with the new electric variety. Many of the horse cars were sold to dealers who refitted them with stoves and dishes, then resold them as lunch wagons. Later, after World War I, larger well-lighted, furnished, and fully equipped versions were manufactured especially for use as diners—restaurants that were seen by many as imitating for the middle class something of the glamour that had once graced the Pullman dining cars on the railroads. By 1930, dozens of manufacturers were building diners, which became typical features of the highways, cities, towns, and villages of America. They were everywhere.

Drive-ins

Drive-in restaurants were an important development of the automobile age. J. G. Kirby, of Dallas, Texas is credited with the idea for the drive-in restaurant. In 1921, he opened the first of a chain of these, calling it Pig Stand. These were small restaurants within large parking lots that featured food served to customers in their parked automobiles. The idea was widely copied. Orders were taken by young men and women, conveyed to the kitchen, and served when ready. The food was served on special trays that hooked onto the frame of the open automobile window, and customers could eat without leaving their cars. In some drive-ins, servers were equipped with roller skates to speed service. Drive-ins were very popular from the 1920s until nearly 1960.

White Castle: The First Fast Food Hamburger Chain

The origins of the hamburger restaurant chain can be traced to Wichita, Kansas and the opening of the first White Castle in 1921. This featured a portion of ground beef cooked on a grill and served between halves of a sliced roll with fresh onion. No one knows who originally invented the hamburger, or where, or in what year. But it is certain that Walter Anderson and E. W. (Billy) Ingram, the founders of the White Castle system, were responsible for the first fast food hamburger restaurant chain.

White Castle had many imitators, the best known of which was the White Tower. White Castle considered the White Tower imitation flagrant and sought the assistance of the courts to stop it. White Castle sued White Tower in the Minnesota courts, and White Tower sued White Castle in the Michigan courts. At the request of White Castle, the case was transferred to federal court. Hearings, decisions, and appeals consumed several years. Finally, in 1937, the U.S. Court of Appeals affirmed a lower court decision in favor of White Castle, ordering White Tower to stop operating its business in such a manner as to confuse the public—making it

The first fast food hamburger restaurant chain in the world, White Castle. Founded in 1921 by Walter Anderson and E. W. (Billy) Ingram, White Castle survived early legal battles with an imitator and still operates successfully today. (Courtesy White Castle.)

difficult to distinguish between the identity of restaurants in the White Castle system and those of the White Tower.

Prohibition

By the end of World War I, a long-standing political disagreement between two groups of American voters was about to be resolved—at least temporarily. The groups were the "drys" and the "wets"—those in favor of prohibiting the sale of all alcoholic beverages, and those opposed. By 1919, a sufficient number of states had ratified an amendment to the Constitution that made the manufacture, transportation, and sale of alcoholic beverages illegal. This amendment, the 18th, ushered in Prohibition, a period later known as the "Noble Experiment." Prohibition went into effect in 1920 and lasted until 1933. Its impact on the restaurant industry was profound.

Prohibition led to the demise of a number of established restaurants. Unable to sell wine, spirits, and beer, some could not attract sufficient customers by serving food alone; others were not able to earn sufficient profit without selling drinks. Customers looking for drinks by the glass or alcoholic beverages by the bottle soon found them available in a new, illegal, and highly profitable type of establishment known as the *speak-easy*. The number of these grew very quickly. Soon millions drank in the speak-easies; millions more drank at cocktail parties in private homes. By 1929, the police commissioner of New York estimated that there were approximately 32,000 speak-easies in the City, about twice the number of licensed and unlicensed saloons before Prohibition. Some speak-easies survived both Prohibition and repeal and have become particularly well known. These included two of New York's finest—the famed '21 Club and El Morocco.

Prohibition led to the development of an establishment known as the roadhouse—a roadside restaurant that sold alcoholic beverages, alone or as accompaniments to meals, and that provided live or recorded music for dancing. These were formidable competitors for restaurateurs who chose not to break the law. After repeal, many of the roadhouses were able to continue in operation as legitimate restaurants.

Marriott and the Beginning of Restaurant Franchising

Another chain to develop in the 1920s had some units that were drive-ins and others in which the customers walked up to outdoor stands to order a specific product: root beer. Roy Allen and Frank Wright established the organization in California, and the root beer was called A & W, for Allen and Wright. They were very successful and soon developed the idea of selling franchises—contracts that permit others to use the name of the parent company and to sell its products or services under conditions defined in a contract.

In 1926, two young men became partners in the purchase of the A & W franchise for Washington, D.C. One was a young college graduate named J. Willard Marriott; his partner was Hugh Colton. They opened their first store in the summer of 1927. By fall, with the arrival of cooler weather, sales began to drop, and Marriott quickly decided to enlarge the product line. He removed the A & W logo and adopted the name Hot Shoppe, principally because of the spiced Mexican foods he was selling. From this simple beginning has come the Marriott Corporation, one of the world's leaders in the hospitality industry.

Howard Johnson

The first entrepreneur to promote franchises aggressively was Howard Johnson, founder of the company that bore his name. The first franchised Howard Johnson restaurant opened in Massachusetts in 1935. Under the contract, it was owned and operated by the builder, Reginald Sprague, who was to purchase ice cream and other products from Johnson's firm. By 1940, there were over 130 Howard Johnson restaurants along the eastern seaboard.

Although World War II brought a record volume of business to the hotel industry, Howard Johnson's restaurants fell on hard times. Gas rationing restricted the distance that people could drive, which kept potential customers from many of the properties located along highways. Many were closed for the duration of the war because of lack of business. After the war, they were reopened, heralding a period of great prosperity for the chain. The Howard Johnson name and reputation were already well established, and the organization was able to compete favorably for new locations on the developing interstate highway network and elsewhere.

Because of their standard physical features—including the orange roofs—their excellent ice cream, and reputation for products of consistent quality, the Howard Johnson restaurants became a model organization for others.

Other Restaurants of the Period

Other interesting establishments to develop during this period included those that were acceptable to unescorted women, typically shoppers: tea rooms, women's exchanges, and the restaurants found in department stores.

Finally, some of America's best-known restaurants opened in this period. In New York, these included Pavillon, the Stork Club, and the Rainbow Room; in

New Orleans, Galatoire's, Arnaud's, and Brennan's; and in San Francisco, Taidsch Grill, Schroeder's, and Marchand's.

THE HOSPITALITY INDUSTRY AFTER WORLD WAR II

The end of World War II marks a turning point in the hospitality industry. After 1945, the industry embarked on a period of dramatic and previously unequaled change. Travel, transportation, dining, and accommodations—literally every aspect of the hospitality enterprise—were affected.

Up to World War II, the average American did not travel very often or very far. The only people to travel long distances frequently were businessmen and theatrical people, who could not earn their livings without traveling, and the wealthy, who had the time and money to travel for pleasure. The work week for the average American was five and one-half or six days and those who were able to take vacations were not necessarily given vacations with pay. The cost of long-distance travel for vacations was quite beyond the financial ability of most Americans. For the majority, "travel" might mean an occasional trip to the sea-shore or a not-too-distant lake, or a short journey to visit relatives in a nearby community.

Mass Travel

After World War II, great numbers of Americans began to travel. Three of the many reasons for this that were of special significance for the hospitality industry were:

1. Economic life was changing for many Americans. More industries were becoming more unionized and the contracts that resulted from collective bargaining provided for shorter work weeks, higher wages, and more fringe benefits. Vacations with pay became nearly universal for both unionized workers and for nonunionized "white-collar" workers who had held their jobs for the stipulated prerequisite periods: One year was a typical minimum. In general, Americans in all walks of life began to have more leisure time than ever before in history. This set the stage for increased travel.
2. Modes of transportation were changing. The railroads were in decline, and the automobile became the primary means of private transportation for local and long-distance travel. The airplane was increasingly regarded as the major means of public transportation for long-distance travel. With

increased volume and improved technology, travel also became more affordable. This led to the development of new travel destinations.

3. Major improvements were made in America's highways. With the decline of the railroads and increased reliance on motor vehicles—both trucks and cars—the development of a national network of superior, limited-access highways became an important public concern. There had been major highways for a number of years in all regions of the country. There had never been, however, any coast-to-coast, border-to-border network of limited-access, interstate highways. Planning for this national system began during the administration of President Eisenhower, and construction proceeded in the following years.

The changes described above—increased leisure time, improvements in the comfort of travel, reductions in the time it required, and greater economic prosperity—had a significant negative impact on hotels. The average number of nights a traveler would stay in a given city or resort hotel declined; and as the years passed, that number continued to decrease, with dramatic effect on the industry. There were many positive effects, as well: Greater amounts of leisure time, ease of travel, and increased disposable income created a growing number of actual and potential customers for hospitality services.

HOTELS AFTER WORLD WAR II
Motels Develop

To the increasing numbers of Americans traveling by automobile and airplane, many of the grand old hotels located near major railroads stations were no longer appealing to or convenient for travelers. Those traveling by automobile sought accommodations in new, more convenient locations.

The new American traveler—both working class and middle class—was not accustomed to the formality of the traditional hotel. Nor was he willing to pay the prices and tip the great numbers of uniformed hotel employees found in the traditional establishments. Moreover, the traditional city hotel did not provide on-premises parking. This new traveler wanted a clean, comfortable room at an affordable price and wanted ready access to his automobile. The business traveler, who had formerly used the train, was also becoming a confirmed automobile traveler. He could carry more in the trunk of his car than he ever could in a train. He found it easier and cheaper to travel by car.

The demand for convenient accommodations for automobile travelers led, inevitably, to the development of the motel. There had been establishments providing roadside accommodations for motorists since the earliest uses of the automobile for long-distance travel in the 1920s. There were two types of these accommodations: groups of small individual cabins, known as *tourist courts*, which offered parking space near the cabins; and private homes, known as *guest houses*, in which spare bedrooms were rented to transient guests. Neither of these forerunners of the motel constituted a significant element in the lodging industry.

Early Motels

Early motels were usually built, owned, and operated by individuals or couples, not by chains. They were typically purpose-built, single structures, all on one floor. Parking was free and convenient: The car was normally parked just outside the door of the rented unit.

The motel was a very informal place, such that the motorist without a coat and tie did not feel out of place. He stopped at an office to check in, pay for his accommodations, and pick up the key; then he drove to the room, parked his car, and carried his own luggage. There was no one to tip. There were seldom any food service facilities, so the traveler had to walk or drive to a restaurant to eat. These motels were simple, and they were comparatively inexpensive, but there were not many of them.

The best and most sought-after location for a motel at the beginning of the motel age was on a main highway close to a city or town. It was generally agreed that a motel should be located on the right-hand side of a road, because travelers driving to a city would be more inclined to turn right into a motel parking area than to turn left across oncoming traffic. As the interstate highway network was developed, the exits from these highways became the preferred locations for motels.

Kemmons Wilson and the Holiday Inns

In the early 1950s, a building contractor named Wilson from Memphis, Tennessee, while driving with his wife and children on a family vacation, took special notice of the difficulty they had finding acceptable, reasonably priced places to spend the night. He conceived of an improved motel, which would offer many of the services of the traditional hotel but would be situated more conveniently for the increasing numbers of people who traveled by automobile. When he returned home, Wilson began to plan the construction of a motel that was to become the first Holiday Inn. It opened in 1952.

Kemmons Wilson's Holiday Inn was so successful that he constructed another nearby. Thus began the development of an organization that would eventually control more guest rooms than any other in the world. Wilson's special talent was in identifying sites for the location of successful motels. The growth of his chain kept pace with the development of the interstate highway system: Wherever an exit was planned, Wilson would be one of the first to determine if that exit were an appropriate location for one of his Holiday Inns.

An early Holiday Inn hotel (c. 1955). Following World War II, the typical American traveler—either working or middle class, and usually traveling by automobile—required affordable accommodations convenient to major highways. One of the first establishments to satisfy this need, Holiday Inn kept pace with the development of the interstate highway systems, and at one time controlled more guest rooms than any other hospitality organization in the United States. (Courtesy Holiday Inn.)

Older Hotels Begin to Change

While Wilson and others were building motels in the 1950s and 1960s, the established center-city hotels, many of them near the disused railroad terminals, were aging and becoming ever more costly to maintain. Some were indifferently maintained, and most were threatened with loss of business to the new booming motel industry.

A number of the older, decaying properties were finally forced to close; they simply could not compete. In other properties, management added staff to the sales departments and began to look for new ways to survive. Some hotels sought to lure long-term residents by advertising appealing weekly and monthly rates.

Some attempted to compete directly with the new motels by merely changing their signs. Many—typically those that lacked meeting and banquet space but had access to parking—began to call themselves *motor hotels* and *motor inns*, to suggest that the automobile traveler would be as satisfied in these accommodations as he was in a motel.

Many of the hotels that had served the individual commercial traveler attempted, often successfully, to develop tour business—groups of vacationers traveling together, typically by bus or airplane. At about this time, tour wholesalers started to reserve large numbers of rooms at these older hotels, because they were able to negotiate comparatively low rates.

Hotels with adequate meeting and banquet space made efforts to attract special varieties of group business—conventions and business meetings. These ranged from sales meetings to trade shows, from fraternal to political meetings, and from alumni reunions to educational seminars. Center-city hotels became increasingly popular sites for all of these.

Finally, an older center-city hotel attempting to survive would adopt any combination of techniques to fill the vacant rooms. It was not unusual to find a hotel sales staff aggressively competing for both convention and group business; while the banquet manager sold wedding parties, the front office manager sold rooms on weekly and monthly rates. Many of these hotels were very large, and it required skill and imagination to produce adequate sales volume flowing from the vast number of banquet, meeting, and sleeping rooms they contained.

Hotel Construction Begins Anew

Unfortunately for the older center-city hotels, their competition was not limited to the new motels being constructed around the perimeters of cities. A new and lively threat was developing much closer than the outskirts of the city: Builders and developers had started a new era of hotel construction. For most cities, this new era saw the first hotel construction since the earliest days of the Great Depression thirty years before. In many American cities, new hotels were being built and opened at a record pace. In New York, for example, new properties constructed between 1960 and 1965 included the New York Hilton, the Americana (now the Sheraton Centre Hotel and Towers), the Summit, the Regency, the City Squire, and several others. This was in a city which had not seen any hotel construction since the Waldorf-Astoria had opened in 1932.

A number of the new center-city hotels constructed during this period were purpose-built, designed specifically to cater to large groups of people. They were truly convention hotels in every sense, with meeting rooms for hundreds of people and banquet rooms for thousands. For many of these, convention and other group business accounted for at least 80 percent of the sales.

The Jet Age

Another important development that had profound effect on the hospitality industry was the introduction of commercial jet aircraft in 1958. Because of their increased speed, flights between cities took less time, and this improved people's perceptions of travel: Because it consumed less time, it was less arduous than ever before. More people began to travel by air, and as new—and later, larger—models of aircraft were introduced, the relative cost of long-distance travel began to decrease. Round-trip fares between cities became less than one-way fares had been when piston aircraft were used, and the time to travel between cities was cut by nearly half.

International Operations

The introduction of commercial jet aircraft also made international travel for masses of people a practical possibility for the first time in history. Americans began to go abroad in great numbers, and visitors from other countries began to come to America. This led to more business for the lodging properties in many cities—particularly, at first, for those on the East and West Coasts with international airports. Later, when international arrivals and departures become common at other airports, hotels in those cities were also able to benefit.

One of the outcomes of increased international air travel was the development of international hotel operations: American hotel chains that had formerly restricted themselves to domestic operations began to expand abroad. Until that time, only two major American hotel companies were operating abroad. Intercontinental Hotels, a subsidiary of Pan American Airlines had been international since 1947, when the United States government had suggested that the company construct hotels in Central and South America as an aid to the economic development of those regions. And Hilton Hotels had become international in 1949 with the opening of the Caribe Hilton in San Juan, Puerto Rico.

Most hotel companies were focused on the burgeoning American market during this period and were slow to go into the international area. Eventually others did so, and today most American chain operations are international in scope.

Within the last 40 years, the world has become smaller, so to speak. Worldwide television coverage of major events, greater numbers of international travelers, and major investments of foreign capital in the U.S. have caused economic interdependence. British, Asian, and Japanese firms, increasingly, are partners in the U.S. hospitality industry. There can be little doubt that this trend will continue in the foreseeable future.

RESORT HOTELS AFTER WORLD WAR II

We have observed how the decline of the railroads and the increased use of automobiles began to affect traditional hotels in the cities and towns of America after World War II. These developments also had a significant and lasting impact on America's resort hotel industry.

Changes in Ground Transportation Affect Resort Hotels

In New England, for example, the summer resort hotels historically had catered to guests who had arrived by rail and stayed for weeks and months. With changes in transportation, it become more difficult—eventually impossible—to reach these properties by rail; and more guests began to arrive by car, particularly as the quality of the roads improved. People in cars obviously have greater mobility, so that guests tended to stay for shorter periods. Guests used their new-found mobility to visit other areas, see new sights, and try different hotels and, later, motels. Because areas that had been difficult to reach by train were often much easier to reach by car, some properties gained business while others lost it.

Some of the New England ski areas, formerly accessible principally by train, were much easier to reach by car, particularly as the train service deteriorated. Guests with private cars also found that the car simplified the daily transit problem of getting from hotel to ski slope. As time went on, developers began to plan and construct hotels closer to the slopes and accessible only by car, which helped to sound the final death knell for rail travel in the ski areas. Later, the automobile gave impetus to the development of new ski areas that would clearly not have been built if rail travel had remained the primary means of access.

Airlines and Resort Hotels

While resort hotel operators across America were attempting to adjust to the impact of growing automobile use, the airplane was also becoming increasingly popular with vacationers and other, traditional guests of the resort hotel.

Public acceptance of air transportation did not happen suddenly. Just after the end of World War II, a comparatively small number of people began to fly. The number began to grow gradually, as the comfort and conveniences in aircraft improved. Nevertheless, general acceptance required some years.

Changes in the Resort Hotel Industry

As people began to accept air transportation as a common means of travel, several changes took place in the resort hotel industry. And just as the acceptance of air travel occurred gradually, so did these changes.

1. Nearby resort hotels accessible with reasonable ease by rail or by automobile—including many fashionable properties in the East—gradually lost their traditional business. Many of their former guests found new destinations easily reached by air. These included the Caribbean islands, the beaches of Waikiki, and the historic cities and sights of Europe.

2. Resort hotels in remote locations—including many in the West—that had always been difficult to reach were made readily accessible by the airlines. It became convenient for residents of the East Coast, for example, to fly to Colorado to ski for a short time. Previously, such trips took more time and were less comfortable. Those who made such trips tended to stay longer to justify to themselves the time and trouble the journey represented.

3. Some resort areas that had remained small, because of the time and cost incurred by travelers in reaching them, began to grow as air travel made them more accessible and the cost of flights decreased. Some destinations— the Hawaiian Islands and Las Vegas, Nevada, for example—grew quickly. After the introduction of commercial jet aircraft in 1958, the number of visitors to Hawaii increased, reportedly by 500 percent between 1959 and 1967.

4. Later, as remote areas became accessible, imaginative developers began to plan and construct resort hotels—and even new resorts—in areas where none had previously existed. Vail, Colorado is an excellent example.

5. Operators of chain hotels, recognizing the outstanding potential for growth in resort areas, gradually developed various types of properties in domestic and international locations. Privately developed resort hotels began to include the names Sheraton, Hilton, and Marriott. This was because many independent resorts were sold to the chains or were managed by them. Two properties in Phoenix, Arizona are excellent examples: the Camelback Inn, which was sold to Marriott Corporation, and the Biltmore Hotel, which was managed by Western International. Both of these are luxurious, five-star operations.

6. In order to remain competitive, to retain their capable staffs, and to generate sufficient dollar volume to meet growing overhead costs, seasonal resort hotels—both the older traditional properties and their newer competitors—increasingly began to remain open year-round.

Year-Round Operation

Resort properties were forced into year-round operation because they were no longer able to survive as single-season businesses. The costs of operation and the investment necessary for construction made the short-season operation impractical if the hotel was to make a profit. The Arizona Biltmore, discussed earlier, is one excellent example. Resort hotels that were not able to adapt to the changing times—particularly those in New England—soon failed.

Other Developments in the Resort Hotel Industry

The following decades constituted an ongoing period of change for the resort industry. Additional changes occurred that have continued to alter the nature of the resort hotel and the markets it seeks.

An era of "instant" resort development began. Developers acquired large areas of land and created complete resorts, with the typical amenities, all within a short period. Complete resort operations—the Dorado Beach Hotel built by Rock Resorts, for example, and such theme parks as Sea World and Disney World—became both popular and successful. Many of the earlier, more traditional resort hotels, started as small operations, expanded as their fame and success increased. The new resorts, however, were large operations when they opened—grandly and imaginatively designed and constructed for instant and continuing success.

Resort Hotels and the Convention Market

In order to generate volume in their "off" seasons, resort hotels began to move into markets that had formerly been the provinces of the large center-city hotels: conventions and other business meetings. To survive, many resort properties competed with commercial hotels for as much convention and meeting business as they could attract. Eventually, many resort operators found that they grossed more on this kind of business than they did from their traditional customers—families and individual guests.

RESTAURANTS AFTER WORLD WAR II

After World War II, the restaurant industry entered a period of development that was linked in many ways to changes taking place both in the American culture and in other segments of the hospitality industry.

Women in the Work Force

One of the most important of these had its origins during World War II. When men were drafted into the armed forces, labor shortages occurred in business and industry. The solution was to hire women to fill the jobs, so that, by war's end, millions of women were employed full time. Many had never before been employed, discovered that they enjoyed working for wages and salaries, and did not want to be full-time homemakers or housewives.

Economic Expansion

After the war, men discharged from the armed forces returned home to resume their lives. Considerable economic disruption was expected but comparatively little took place: The economy expanded to meet the demand for consumer goods resulting from the end of the war. Gasoline, for example, had been rationed during the war, and automobiles had not been produced for the consumer market in 1943, 1944, and 1945. Demand in this area was very strong in the years immediately following the war, and the number of jobs for workers in automobile plants expanded considerably.

The Restaurant Industry Grows

Gradually, the interaction of an expanding economy, higher levels of disposable income, increased leisure time, and greater numbers of automobiles on the road led to significant growth in the restaurant segment of the hospitality industry, in particular.

As automobile travel increased, the traveling public needed more restaurants to stop at. Local restaurants often were not convenient to travelers and it was difficult for them to determine food quality and prices. This set the stage for nationally recognized images and price structures that the traveling public could rely on.

RENEWED GROWTH FOR HOWARD JOHNSON'S CHAIN. Howard Johnson's was one of the first restaurant companies to benefit. Many of these restaurants, closed during the war, reopened soon thereafter. At the same time, Americans resumed the practice of driving for pleasure, which they had been forced to curtail during the war. Many were stopping at restaurants on these trips away from home. A substantial number were uncomfortable with the idea of eating in strange establishments and elected to stop at the familiar and trusted Howard Johnson's, with its orange roof. His business boomed.

New Chains Develop

A number of other food service chains that were developed in the late 1940s and early 1950s employed some of the same techniques as Howard Johnson. Creating brand names—which came to represent in consumers' minds a particular product, price, level of quality, and perception of service—was one technique. Another was to build into each restaurant physical characteristics that made it instantly recognizable as one of the units in a particular chain. To be successful with these techniques, millions of dollars were spent on advertising—especially in the new national medium that had become commercially available in 1947: television. Some of the organizations to do this were Kentucky Fried Chicken, Dairy Queen, Denny's, Dunkin' Donuts, Burger King, Jack-in-the-Box, and Googie's, among others. With the establishment of this general operating pattern, the era of so-called "fast food" had begun.

MCDONALD'S. Of all the fast food companies to develop in the United States, the most clearly and consistently successful has been McDonald's. Interestingly, Ray Kroc, who is responsible for its ultimate success, was not its founder. The original idea and the early development of the chain was the work of two brothers born in Manchester, New Hampshire, after whom the company is named—Richard and Maurice McDonald.

The McDonald brothers had been in the restaurant business for some years by 1948, which was to become a particularly important year for our industry. By then they had become tired of the personnel problems common in the restaurant business and were looking for a new method of operation to free them of the burden. After considerable discussion and planning, they attempted an operating method that reduced their former dependence on highly skilled staff members. Their method was similar to the assembly line used in the manufacturing industries. They devised an operation offering a limited menu of products prepared by unskilled workers who had been carefully trained to perform simple tasks in a repetitive manner. Each product was thus the result of a number of simple tasks performed by several workers. It became possible to hire people with limited educational background and no food service experience and to train them quickly. Because of the assembly-line format, it was easy to respond to demand by producing large numbers of products quickly, and to do so at low labor cost. Because the jobs were unskilled, wages and labor costs were very low compared with competitors'.

One of the first McDonald's, Des Plaines, Illinois (c. 1955). Employing the assembly-line method to produce a limited menu, the McDonald brothers devised their formula for success. Later, under Ray Kroc's management and marketing strategies, McDonald's grew to become one of the most successful foodservice businesses in the world. (Courtesy McDonald's Corp.)

The McDonald brothers were successful, and they were beginning to sell franchises when their success came to the attention of Ray Kroc.

RAY KROC AND MCDONALD'S. Ray Kroc was one of the most influential restaurant operators in the history of our industry. He was 52 years old in 1956 when he noticed on a trip to San Bernardino, California that people were lining up to purchase hamburgers from a stand owned and operated by the McDonald brothers. He learned that they were selling franchises, and he bought a franchise that allowed him to open McDonald's restaurants anywhere in the State of Indiana. Over the next few years, Kroc opened a number of units but had numerous disagreements with the McDonald brothers over various policies and procedures. Eventually, Kroc offered to buy the business from the McDonalds, and they accepted his offer and retired from the business.

Under Kroc's management, McDonald's became extraordinarily successful, internationally as well as within the United States. His strengths were his ability to organize and standardize and his marketing ability. He made franchising common in the restaurant business. Today, the company he founded accounts for a greater dollar volume of sales than any other restaurant company in the world.

THE GROWTH OF ADDITIONAL SPECIALIZED CHAINS. By the third quarter of the twentieth century, the seeds had been sown for still more national food service chains, many of which grew by selling franchises. The chains typically offered limited menus of specialized, standardized items for consumption, either on the premises or for takeout, as the customer preferred. These organizations included Arthur Treacher's, Kentucky Fried Chicken, and Pizza Hut, among others. Some chains developed around particular themes—Victoria Station, the Magic Pan, Trader Vic's, and the Red Barn, for example—whereas others were defined by the specialty foods they offered—Taco Bell, Red Lobster, Steak and Ale, Spaghetti Factory, and more. Another group catered to families—Friendly's and Denny's were two. Some of these chains have not survived—Arthur Treacher's and Victoria Station, for example—whereas others have continued to succeed.

Changing Tastes in Dining Out

The variety of restaurants in the preceding discussion suggests that Americans have shown a broad taste in their restaurant selections in the years since World War II and that the industry has responded with many types of restaurants. Prior to 1940, dining out was reserved for special occasions for most Americans. As our standard of living has risen, dining out has become more common. For many people, dining out is now considered an everyday experience, part of a normal lifestyle. The term *dining out*, however, conveys varying images to people. And a dining-out experience that some might consider pleasant, can induce horrified groans in others. The beauty of a dining-out experience, like beauty itself, is in the eye of the beholder.

In any event, the trend toward dining out has caused the restaurant industry to grow in size and scope and to become one of the fastest growing industries in the United States. In the following chapter we will discuss along what lines the restaurant industry has developed as a result of the growth in demand for food service.

SUMMARY

In this chapter, late nineteenth-century inventions that helped change the hospitality industry are identified, and the impact of each is described. Significant developments are discussed that occurred in three segments of the industry—hotels, resort hotels, and restaurants—from the turn of the century through 1945. Economic and social factors that led to increased travel by Americans in the period after 1945 are identified and discussed, as are the principal changes that took place in hotels, resort hotels, and restaurants in this same period. The contributions of several important figures—including Ellsworth M. Statler, Conrad Hilton, Howard Johnson, J. Willard Marriott, Kemmons Wilson, and Ray Kroc—are also examined.

QUESTIONS

1. List three important inventions of the late nineteenth century and briefly describe the impact of each on the hospitality industry of the early twentieth century.
2. What were E. M. Statler's principal contributions to the development of the hotel industry?
3. Name the property that is generally considered the first modern commercial hotel and describe five features that distinguished it from competitors. What was the advertising motto of the hotel?
4. List three reasons that the 1920s were considered the "golden age of hotels."
5. Describe one means used by hoteliers in the 1920s to help ensure return visits by traveling salesmen.
6. What effect did the Great Depression have on the hotel industry? What happened to levels of occupancy during this period?
7. Are hotels affected by recession, depression, prosperity, and other changes in the economy? Why?
8. What caused the high levels of hotel room occupancy during World War II?

9. In the early twentieth century, some American workers were beginning to have measurable amounts of leisure time. What kinds of activities does the text indicate were available to the American worker on his day off?

10. Name two resort hotels that were started as resorts for Quakers? Where were they located?

11. Name four five-star resort properties built and opened between 1900 and 1930.

12. List and describe four types of restaurants that developed in the early twentieth century.

13. What was *Prohibition?* What was its impact on each of the following: taverns, fine restaurants, roadhouses?

14. Who founded the Hot Shoppe restaurants? What circumstances led this individual to start the first of these establishments?

15. What were Howard Johnson's principal contributions to the restaurant industry?

16. Identify the three factors which led to an increase in the number of Americans traveling after World War II?

17. What economic and social conditions led to the increase in the number of motels built after 1950?

18. Who was the founder of Holiday Inns? What circumstances led him to build the first of these?

19. Faced with declining business volume after 1950, older, center-city hotels devised ways to attract new business. List three.

20. Over a period of time, the public came to accept air travel. What was the effect of this on the commercial hotel industry? On the resort hotel industry?

21. What effect did the decline of the railroads after World War II have on resort hotels in New England?

22. After World War II, the interaction of several forces led to significant growth in the restaurant industry. List four.

23. Name five restaurant organizations that were among the first to use television advertising to establish their images and reputations.

24. Who founded McDonald's? Who first sold McDonald's franchises?

25. What were Ray Kroc's two principal contributions to the development and eventual success of McDonald's?

Food Service Perspectives

Dimensions of Food and Beverage

5

LEARNING OBJECTIVES

After reading and studying this chapter, you should be able to:

1. *Cite the percentage of gross national product (GNP) attributable to food and beverage service.*
2. *Identify the importance of the food and beverage industry as an employer of women, minorities, and teenagers.*
3. *List and discuss the three principal reasons cited in the text for increased demand for food service.*
4. *Define food service and a food service enterprise.*
5. *List and discuss the five most important elements of a food service operation.*
6. *Describe each of the characteristic types of food service establishments in the chapter.*
7. *Define beverage service and a beverage service operation.*
8. *List nine reasons for patronizing beverage service establishments.*
9. *List and discuss the three terms used to describe the focus of beverage service establishments.*
10. *Identify the major categories in the National Restaurant Association's classification system for reporting industry sales.*

INTRODUCTION

The eating and drinking establishments of their homelands were recreated in America by immigrants from Europe in the seventeenth century. They have always enjoyed a high degree of popularity in America. As we discussed in previous chapters, seventeenth- and eighteenth-century taverns sold alcoholic beverages of various types—beer, ale, wine, and rum among them—and most served food, as well. Many served a midday meal, known in some parts of the country as an "ordinary." Many were popular social centers in their communities.

In the nineteenth century, the number and variety of food and beverage operations grew at an amazing pace. This was when the foundations of the modern food and beverage industry were developed. Restaurants and taverns of all sorts served meals relatively inexpensively. People who lived in lodging houses, where there were no cooking facilities, ate many of their meals in inexpensive restaurants. At the same time, there were also a number of hotels and restaurants providing the finest of food and wines in luxurious surroundings to the growing number of wealthy Americans. The nineteenth century was an important time of growth for the industry.

By the beginning of the twentieth century, Americans had access to a number of different types of restaurants—diners, cafeterias, roadhouses, and hamburger stands, to name a few. And the concept of *dining out*—making an important occasion out of the dining experience, with the finest of food and beverages served in a pleasant environment—began to play a growing role in American life.

The Size of the Industry

The food service industry ranks as one of the largest in the United States. A recent publication of the National Restaurant Association (NRA), the industry's principal trade association, states that "eating and drinking places are first among all retailers in the number of establishments and the number of employees." Today, there are over 710,000 eating and drinking establishments, employing over 9 million people. Information published by the NRA reveals that the food service industry employs more women, more teenagers, and more members of minority groups than any other in America. Approximately 60 percent of food service workers are female, and a large percentage are under 30 years of age. Almost two-thirds are high school graduates. The number of managerial and administrative positions in the industry is approaching 500,000.

One out of every four retail outlets in the nation is an eating or drinking establishment. Nearly three out of four had annual sales under $500,000 in one recent year. Approximately three out of four are single-unit operations. One out of every three is a sole proprietorship, an establishment owned by one individual.

On a typical day, food service establishments provide approximately 30 percent of American adults with lunch, and nearly 25 percent with dinner. Of those patronizing these establishments, over 50 percent are men. On this typical day, over 55 percent of adult men eat out, compared with under 50 percent of adult women. Well over 70 percent of the adult population eats at a restaurant once a month. Younger adults eat out more frequently than older adults: On a typical day, over 65 percent of younger adults eat out, compared to under 35 percent of those over 65. Nearly 50 percent of all consumers visit a restaurant on their birthdays, and the most popular day for eating out is Friday.

The growth of food and beverage sales has been continuous. In 1970, NRA figures placed food service sales at $42.8 billion. By 1975, sales volume had grown to 70.3 billion. By 1980, it had grown to approximately 120 billion, and the 1980 figure had nearly doubled by 1990. Although these figures are not adjusted for inflation, they point out the extraordinary growth in that ten-year period. Today, food and beverage sales account for over $250 billion. This is nearly 5 percent of the gross national product (GNP) of the United States—generally defined as the value of all goods and services sold. By any measure, this is indeed a major industry.

Although a great number of establishments in our industry offer both food and beverages to their customers, it is not a universal practice. The majority of food service operators do not sell alcoholic beverages. Because of this, and because

Foodservice industry sales in the United States doubled from 1980 to 1990. According to an NRA survey, foodservice establishments serve 25 to 30 percent of adults either lunch or dinner every day. (Courtesy Stouffer Hotels.)

there are significant differences between food operations and beverage operations, we will discuss the food service and beverage service segments of the industry separately in this chapter.

FOOD SERVICE

As suggested by the statistics of the NRA, the demand for food service has grown at a very rapid pace in recent years. In today's world, even children are patronizing food service establishments at very early ages—having their "happy meals" at McDonald's—then continuing to patronize McDonald's and restaurants in general in their adult years. Today, many adults eat out several times each week—more than ever before in our history. Studies have shown that the average American eats more than one out of three meals away from home. The National Restaurant Association reports that 43 percent of the money Americans spend on food is spent in food service establishments.

In addition, the frequency of eating out is increasing. Americans are consuming more meals away from home each year, and nationwide food service sales continue to increase dramatically. Experts have predicted that Americans will soon be eating half of all meals away from home.

Several reasons are commonly cited for America's increased demand for food service. These include

1. increased discretionary income,
2. smaller families, and
3. changing lifestyles.

Increased Discretionary Income

The first of these is very significant: The average American has more discretionary income than ever before. Individuals have more money to spend as they choose, and growing numbers are spending a substantial amount of it in food service establishments. For most Americans today, having a meal or a snack in one or another of the restaurants or other food service operations that we see everywhere is an unremarkable, everyday occurrence.

Smaller Families

Another reason that Americans patronize food service operations more frequently is a decrease in the size of the family. One explanation for this is that more women are in the work force and are choosing to postpone having children. In fact, many are choosing to have fewer children altogether. In two-earner households, with both adults tired at the end of the day, going out to eat or having a meal delivered has become an acceptable alternative to preparing the evening meal at home. And it is probably easier to go out with a small family than with a large one.

Changing Lifestyles

The daily routines of families are considerably different from what they were thirty or more years ago: Americans are less inclined to prepare evening meals at home, as we just discussed. The term *two-earner household* implies that one individual no longer stays at home all day to take primary responsibility for food shopping, meal preparation, and cleaning up after a meal.

Another change in lifestyle that affects the food service industry is that neither young people attending school nor working adults are carrying their lunches from home to the extent that they did in years past. Students and workers have food service readily available at very low cost at school, at work, or at any number of fast food establishments nearby.

Similarly, each individual in today's family has a greater degree of independence than in the past. Each makes more personal decisions about his or her life than before. And more family members have automobiles and can, for example, easily decide to go to a food service establishment for a meal with friends, rather than have the meal at home. In some households, it would be difficult to identify an evening meal period at all: Family members may come home at different times and either prepare their own meals or elect to go to a restaurant to eat. This would have been unusual a generation ago.

At the same time, the increase in the number of wage earners in America has led to a decrease in the number of family members trained in the art and science of food preparation. In many households, there is no longer anyone able to prepare an excellent meal. Thus, for holiday meals and other occasions for celebration, many are depending on restaurants.

FOOD SERVICE DEFINED

Food service may be defined as providing fully prepared foods for immediate consumption on or off premises. Food service establishments are those engaged in providing food service. These establishments include not only the obvious examples of restaurants and college dining halls, but also the salad bars and sandwich counters in food markets and such "distant relations" as food vending machines.

Food service enterprises range from full-service restaurants to self-service buffets, from fine restaurants to takeout operations, and from company cafeterias to hamburger stands. And food service operations may be either commercial—those operated with the aim of earning a profit—or noncommercial—those operated primarily for the convenience or welfare of those served, rather than primarily for profit. In the sections that follow, we will examine in more detail the various kinds of food service establishments and the kinds of service they offer.

VARIATIONS AMONG FOOD SERVICE ESTABLISHMENTS

Anyone who has observed the variety of food service establishments will agree that there are significant differences from one to another. These differences are the result of decisions made by owners and managers about the five most important elements of a food service operation:

1. Menu items
2. Food quality
3. Menu prices
4. Service
5. Ambiance

Menu Items

Perhaps the most important difference among food service enterprises can be found in the menu items offered. Some establishments present the customer with a menu consisting of several pages, listing many kinds of dishes. This is common in establishments open for long hours daily and serving a varied group of customers. By contrast, other food service operations offer a very limited menu: one that may include only a very few luncheon or dinner items—two appetizers, three entrees, and two desserts, for example.

Some establishments specialize in particular menu items—such as ethnic or regional dishes. Ethnic dishes are those associated with a particular culture; regional dishes are those characteristic of a particular geographic area—New England or the South, for example. Regional establishments sometimes cater to the tastes of those living in the region in which they are located: A menu for a restaurant in the South might feature catfish, black-eyed peas, and hush puppies. These items would not normally be found in the North, except in establishments specializing in regional southern dishes. Similarly, a substantial number of restaurants on the coast of New England sell Maine lobster, New England clam chowder, and New England boiled dinner—items one would not commonly find on menus in the South.

Some establishments restrict their menus to specialty foods. Specialty foods are those belonging to a particular food family, such as vegetarian, seafood, or pasta. Others do not specialize but instead offer menus that appeal to a broader range of customers. School and college food service operations typically take this approach. They try to serve foods that appeal to many different groups of students.

Food Quality

Food quality is defined as the degree of excellence in food products. Food quality may vary greatly from one food service establishment to another. In the final analysis, variations in quality result from decisions made by management to establish a given level of quality. In general, the level of quality is determined by the interplay of three elements:

1. the quality of the food ingredients used,
2. the professional skill of those preparing the food, and
3. the time and effort expended on food preparation.

The quality of the food products prepared is determined largely by the quality of the ingredients used. For example, no one can prepare an appealing tossed green salad using wilted lettuce and unripened tomatoes, or an excellent fisherman's platter using fish caught several days before and refrigerated improperly. In addition, a food service operator must know that many fresh foods are graded for quality and that items of a given quality may be entirely unsuited for use in certain dishes. Oranges used for freshly squeezed juice may be entirely unsuited to displaying on a buffet or using in fruit baskets delivered to guests' rooms in a hotel.

Another important element in determining food quality is the professional skill of those preparing the food. Some food preparers are trained in one of the excellent colleges and institutes offering culinary degrees and diplomas or in one of the splendid apprenticeship programs in Europe. Others have learned on the job, from mentors willing to train them. Some claiming to be professionals have never really learned very much about food preparation but only pretend to know. Still others lack the intelligence, the ability, or the will to excel at food preparation.

Each food service operator must determine the amount of time and effort that should be devoted to preparing food for customers. As a general rule, food that is prepared on premises from fresh ingredients should be better than food purchased in a frozen, canned, or other pre-prepared state. The latter is known as *convenience food*, a term used to refer to food products that have been processed prior to purchase, thus reducing in-house preparation time.

The reasons for not preparing all food products from fresh ingredients vary. In some establishments, the kitchen staff lacks the professional skill to prepare products equal to the convenience items. In others, hiring skilled personnel would make the cost of labor too high and cause menu prices to be more than customers would pay. For many, convenience items are of acceptable quality. Sometimes the convenience foods are of better quality than those available fresh. And for many chain operations, in which management wants products of uniform quality used throughout its chain, convenience foods provide the most reasonable means of achieving uniformity.

Menu Prices

Menu prices can vary greatly from one food service operation to another. On one hand, some charge low prices and attempt to be successful by making a small profit on each of a large number of sales. Others charge low prices for very different reasons: They are providing a service for a specific group of people—club members or hospital patients, for example—and no attempt is being made to earn a profit. On the other hand, some charge high prices knowing that they will attract fewer customers. Each sale, however, normally results in a comparatively high profit, enabling the operator to prosper with fewer customers than the lower priced establishment. Other reasons for variations in menu prices relate to differences in operating costs, numbers of customers required for profitability, and the image the operator intends to project for the establishment.

Service

Food operators may provide a number of different service arrangements for their customers. Establishments are often differentiated from one another on the basis of these service arrangements, which include table service, counter service, room service, self-service, and takeout or delivery service.

Table service: For table service, servers normally take customers' orders selected from menus or their equivalent, then deliver the foods to the customers seated at their tables. There are many variations on this basic procedure, as well as several specific forms of service, including those known as American, Russian, French, and English. These will be described in greater detail in Chapter 7.

Counter service: For counter service, customers are served food across a level surface called a counter. They may be either seated at the counter or standing, and they may consume the food at the counter or at some other location within the establishment.

Room service: For room service, customers are situated away from a normal dining area, typically in a hotel room or a hospital room. Food is transported to the individual's room and "served."

Self-service: For self-service, customers select foods from an array of displayed items; then they carry the items, with or without a tray, to some location in the establishment to consume them. Cafeterias, buffets, and salad bars are three common examples of self-service arrangements.

Takeout or delivery service: Takeout or delivery service differs markedly from the others: The menu items are expected to be consumed off premises and are packaged accordingly. With takeout, the customer collects the food on premises and carries it out before consuming it. With delivery service, the customer places an order by telephone or fax, then waits for the food to be delivered. Some establishments offer takeout service only; others offer only delivery; and others offer both.

There are no general rules about the types of service offered by food service establishments. Some offer only one type—table service, for example. Others provide more than one type—possibly table service and counter service. Still others may employ all of these in their efforts to please the greatest number of customers.

Ambiance

In the food service industry, *ambiance* is a term used to refer to the aesthetic or emotional impact of an establishment on its customers. It has any number of elements—furnishings, lighting, sound, decorations, themes, table settings, employees' appearances and attitudes, and so on—all aspects of the establishment's environment. In a professionally designed restaurant, the ambiance is never left to chance: It is carefully crafted to achieve a particular impact.

The elements of ambiance vary greatly from one establishment to another. Some—often family restaurants—are typically bright, cheerful, and informal. Others are far more formal, featuring subdued lighting, crisp white linen, fine china and glassware, highly polished silver, and a professionally trained staff. Still other establishments—those that cater to college students, for example—are more likely to be lively, noisily informal, and feature current, popular music. Those attempting to create romantic settings may be dimly lighted and provide soft

A restaurant's ambiance is one of the most important elements of the dining experience. Beneath its stained-glass dome, the Garden Court of San Francisco's Sheraton Palace Hotel has elegantly served dignitaries from all over the world. (Courtesy San Francisco Convention & Visitors Bureau.)

background music. One of the reasons that the units in a chain operation are the same is that this helps insure that all will have similar ambiance.

CHARACTERISTIC TYPES OF FOOD SERVICE ESTABLISHMENTS

Because of the large number of variables in food service establishments, most attempts at classifying them are not very successful. The classifications are either too simple to be of any value—"with or without parking," for example—or too complex to be useful, with categories based on the many possible variations in menu, food quality, prices, service, atmosphere, and so on.

However, because people discuss food service establishments, describing them and comparing one to another, some terms have become commonly accepted. Those that follow are characteristically regarded as describing types of food service establishments. One must remember, nevertheless, that they do not constitute any real system of food service classification because they are not mutually exclusive: To describe a single food service operation, it is commonly necessary to use more than one of these terms.

FAST FOOD. Fast-food establishments are those that serve foods for which there is little or no waiting. Many of those in the industry are beginning to identify them as *fast service* or *quick service* restaurants,[1] in recognition of the fact that the service is fast, not the food.

In fast-food restaurants, customers wait on line for access to a counter at which they order food from a very limited menu. Often the food is prepared and packaged ahead of time and the customer's choices need only be picked up by a server and delivered to the customer—on a tray or in a bag, depending on whether the customer intends to consume the food on or off premises. Fast service operations are relatively low priced. Examples include McDonald's, Burger King, Dunkin' Donuts, Kentucky Fried Chicken, Wendy's, Roy Rogers, and Nathan's.

So that the concept works, a high degree of standardization is required: Management typically sets rigid standards for procedures, portion sizes, and packaging. *Procedures* are methods for doing work; *portion sizes* are the quantities of specific menu items that are to be served each time a given item is ordered; *packaging* is the particular container or wrapping in which a single portion of a given menu item is to be served.

Other prerequisites to successful operation of a fast-food restaurant typically include an almost inflexible menu, specialized equipment for preparing the foods on the menu quickly, and a staff properly trained to use the equipment efficiently and serve a large number of customers in a short time. A fast service restaurant is a

[1]As indicated in Chapter 1, all three terms are used interchangeably in this text.

very well organized enterprise — designed to operate with staff that can be trained quickly and easily.

TABLE SERVICE. A table service establishment is one in which customers are seated and served at tables. Individuals may be escorted to their tables by an employee known by a title, such as *host* or *hostess*, or may select their own tables. They may be given printed menus from which to select foods or these may be selected from an equivalent device, such as a sign or a chalkboard.

At the customer's table, an employee may suggest particular menu items and will normally make note of the item or items selected. The selections are conveyed to the kitchen, where the food is prepared. Selections are served to customers when prepared, with the delivery suitably timed if several items have been ordered by one individual. The individual doing the serving (*waiter* or *waitress* or *server*) is typically the one who has taken the customer's order.

In most table service restaurants, the customer is presented with a bill at the conclusion of service. The bill is commonly called a *guest check*, and the customer is expected to pay, charge, sign, or otherwise attend to the bill at that moment. In some establishments, the bill is settled directly with the server; in others, it is settled with a cashier who is typically stationed near the exit. Exceptions occur in operations that include meals with room prices.

ETHNIC. An ethnic food service operation is one that specializes in foods associated with a particular culture. Among the most common of these are Chinese, Mexican, Greek, Japanese, German, Italian, Spanish, and Indian.

Ethnic restaurants vary considerably in menu, food quality, menu prices, service, and ambiance, even within a specific ethnic grouping. Chinese restaurants, for example, may serve foods from one or more of four regional cuisines — Peking, Szechuan, Canton, and Shanghai — each of which differs from the others. Some Chinese restaurants offer table service; others offer counter service or takeout. Some ethnic restaurants use high quality ingredients and prepare the finest of foods; others use food of lower quality in order to keep menu prices low.

SPECIALTY. A specialty food service enterprise is one that features foods of a particular type, such as seafood, pancakes, chicken, vegetables, steaks, doughnuts, omelettes, or sandwiches. The possibilities for specialties are many and varied, as are the establishments that feature them. Some limit their menus almost exclusively to the specialty, while others use the specialty item as the focal point of the menu but add other items to broaden the establishment's appeal and attract additional customers.

Specialty restaurants can vary considerably in menu items, food quality, menu prices, service, and ambiance, and this can be true even within one specialty. For example, some seafood operations may specialize in shellfish; others feature a more varied assortment of fish and shellfish on one menu. Some have extensive menus, limited only by the availability of particular items in the markets; others may restrict their menus to a very few items that are always available.

Some operators will insist on purchasing fresh seafood daily for their establishments, and others will use frozen products. In some parts of the country one or another item may be readily available and very popular with diners, while that item may be rare or virtually unsalable in another geographic area. Equivalent differences can be easily observed in relation to menu prices, service, and ambiance from one specialty establishment to another.

FINE DINING. Establishments in this category are those that emphasize high quality foods, expertly prepared and professionally served. Few convenience foods are used, and most foods are prepared from fresh ingredients. Such restaurants are typically among the most formal and are often among the most expensive.

Service is a particularly important element in the fine dining experience, but the type of service may vary from one restaurant to another. Some may offer elegant French service, and others, Russian, or American.

The term *fine dining* gives no indication of the nature of the foods served. The menus may be ethnic, such as Swiss or northern Italian; they may feature specialties, such as seafood; or they may rely on the skill of a chef to prepare dishes unique to the restaurant. Other possible variations among fine dining establishments

The importance of service in a foodservice establishment varies with its aim, ambiance, and menu. At a restaurant or banquet catering establishment featuring fine dining, as shown below, knowledgable, professional service is of the utmost consequence, regardless of the menu's content. The different styles of service— American, Russian, French, and English—are covered in Chapter 7. (Courtesy The Manor.)

include number of items on the menu: Many offer extensive menus with a few special creations that change frequently, whereas some others—often among the finest restaurants in an area—offer only one or two entrees that change daily. In some, which typically require reservations, customers may be given no choice at all: They are served the several courses that constitute the dining experience planned by the chef.

LIMITED MENU. An establishment that offers a limited menu is one in which management has made a conscious decision to restrict the number of items on the menu. This may be a small but varying number; or it may be a specific, unchanging number—as in a steakhouse that offers only three entrees, all of which are sirloin steaks of varying weights. Sometimes there may be only one basic menu item, such as pizza or hamburger, for which a large number of variations are available—often in the form of toppings. Other kinds of restaurants with limited menus may feature chicken, hot dogs, lobster, omelettes, or roast beef, among other possibilities.

The quality of limited menu establishments can vary considerably. The steakhouse may offer the finest aged beef in the state, or the steaks may be of a quality such that miniature hacksaws are required to cut them. Menu prices in limited menu establishments may vary as well—from the minimum common in hot dog stands to some extraordinarily high prices in some of the finest steakhouses. And it should be apparent that ambiance can vary as dramatically, as can menu price, from one to another—from the hot dog stand to the steakhouse.

CHAIN RESTAURANTS. Chain restaurants are those that are linked in some way. For some, ownership provides the link: Two or more establishments that may or may not resemble each other in any way have common ownership. For others, the links are provided by common name, appearance, and products, or some combination of these. For those in the well-known national chains—Wendy's, Pizza Hut, and Kentucky Fried Chicken, for example—all three apply. In some instances, all units in a given chain are under common ownership; more frequently, groups of units in one geographical area may be commonly owned by some entity other than the national organization. For example, Burger King owns some, but not all, of the restaurants bearing that name; groups of Burger King restaurants are owned by other companies, and some are owned by individuals.

Chain restaurants vary considerably in their other characteristics, as well as in their identification as chains. Their menu items range from pizza to steaks and from hamburgers to seafood. Some, such as McDonald's, are relatively inexpensive; others—Red Lobster, or Houlihan's, for example—are less so. Food quality and service vary as well. Some offer table service; others, only counter service. Some feature takeout; others do not. Nevertheless, the ambiance in chain restaurants affiliated by product is typically the same from one unit to another.

THEME RESTAURANTS. A theme restaurant is one designed around a particular theme, such that the theme is used or reflected in every element of the establishment's ambiance. For example, if the circus were selected as the theme, the interior of the restaurant might be decorated to resemble some idealized version of the interior of a circus tent, complete with trapeze; the servers might be costumed as circus performers; the menu might be printed to look like a circus program; and the menu items named for circus acts—a hamburger special described possibly as the "Lion, King of the Burger Jungle." Other possibilities for themes are railroad cars or stations, antique automobiles, colonial America, the old West, Medieval dining, World War II, kitchenware—the number is endless, limited only by human imagination.

With theme restaurants, the obvious differences from one to another are in the ambiance: Any developer of a theme restaurant or chain would clearly make every effort to avoid resemblance to any other food service establishment. Menu items and service would typically be closely linked to the theme and the atmosphere. Food quality and menu prices would vary considerably from one theme establishment or chain to another.

"TOPS". *Tops* is a shorthand term used by some to refer to food and beverage operations located on the top floors of hotels or other tall buildings, usually located in some part of a major city where there is an interesting or spectacular view. One of the finest examples can be found at the top of one of the twin towers of the World Trade Center in New York: Windows on the World, a luxurious restaurant on the 107th floor that offers a stunning view of the city and its harbor.

Some "tops" restaurants have been specially constructed so that either the floor or the entire room turns, revolving to give customers panoramic and ever-changing views of the city as they dine.

"Tops" vary as greatly as other food service operations. Some offer foods and service of excellent quality, while others may not purchase the finest ingredients and hire the most talented professionals to prepare and serve their food. Similarly one may present the appearance of a very formal atmosphere and select menu items accordingly, while another strives for a high degree of informality in atmosphere and menu to attract larger numbers of younger customers.

Menu prices vary among "top" restaurants, but as a group their prices tend to be higher than those in similar restaurants that are not located at the top of a building. Menu prices in "tops" reflect the higher costs of construction and operation, as well as the premium one would expect to be charged for the privilege of dining at an establishment that may represent not only the pinnacle of a building, but also the very essence of business or social success.

FAMILY RESTAURANT. A family restaurant is one that caters to family groups—parents with children and other contemporary family groupings. In order to appeal to families, operators must make a number of important decisions with respect to menu, food quality, menu prices, service, and ambiance.

Family restaurants, usually include a sufficiently broad range of items on the menu that there is something for those of every age—parent, child, and grandparent. Some have special menus for children under a given age. These menus may be separate from the regular menu or may be in one section of it.

Family restaurant menu items are typically low to moderate in price, in tacit recognition that the American family faces difficult collective financial burdens and is either unwilling or unable to spend large amounts of the family's limited disposable income on restaurant meals. Menu prices reflect food quality and owners usually attempt to match food quality to their customers' perceptions of quality. Atmosphere in family restaurants tends to be informal: At their best, they are cheerfully decorated, bright, and well lighted; and they radiate a sense of welcome to their customers.

CAFETERIA. A cafeteria is a food service establishment that permits the customer to see the foods available and to make selections from among those displayed—in many cases making possible the selection of the actual portion the customer will consume.

Cafeterias impose a greater degree of self-service on their customers than most other establishments. Food portions are individually plated and priced; and the customer is typically expected to take a tray through an area where foods are displayed, make selections, place them on the tray, and take the tray to a station where the prices are totaled. In some establishments, the customer pays for the food at that point; in others, the customer is given a bill that must be paid at the exit. In either case, the tray is then carried to another part of the establishment, where the food is either consumed or packed for takeout.

BUFFET. A buffet is a type of service characterized by a long table or counter on which a selection of varied foods are attractively displayed, on platters, in bowls, and in other suitable vessels. Typically, each diner carries a plate, determines selections, places desired quantities of selected foods on the plate, then takes the plate to a table to consume the food. A set price is usually charged for each person, regardless of particular foods or quantities selected, and diners are commonly permitted unlimited access to the buffet. This is to encourage diners to take smaller portions and revisit the buffet as desired.

CATERING. Catering is preparing and serving food to groups of people gathered for a specific purpose, such as attending a meeting or celebrating a wedding. Some caterers prepare and serve food only in their own halls; others prepare food in their own kitchens, but serve only in premises provided by their clients. Some will both prepare and serve in premises provided by the client. Some will agree to any of these arrangements. Those in the catering business are normally very flexible and are willing to meet any reasonable requests for particular foods. Most are prepared to offer the client preplanned menus at various price levels for various types of functions—and to adjust any of these to meet the client's particular needs or desires.

Catering has several advantages over normal restaurant operations. Functions are always booked in advance, so management knows the number of people to expect and can easily determine the proper quantity of food to serve. Staffing and food purchasing, therefore, can be planned precisely, making it possible to estimate costs accurately in advance and thus plan a predetermined profit on each function.

A large number of restaurants are simultaneously in the catering business. Some restaurants have separate rooms used primarily for catering, and others are able to close off part of the public dining area to accommodate groups. The food for these groups is typically prepared in the restaurant's single kitchen: There is no special kitchen set aside for catering.

Many city hotels are in the catering business in a major way. These hotels often have both special kitchens and dining facilities for catering. In the hotel business, catering is done by what is commonly known as the *banquet department*. This represents one part of hotel food and beverage operation that is typically quite profitable. Some hotels staff their banquet operations with part-time or full-time employees who work only in this area.

INSTITUTIONAL FOOD SERVICE. *Institution* is a term used to refer to a wide variety of service organizations, public and private, that attend to one or another of many possible public needs. Schools, colleges, hospitals, nursing homes, and prisons are some common examples of institutions. An institutional food service operation is one whose principal purpose is the preparation of food for those associated with a particular institution. Students in grade schools, patients in hospitals, and inmates in prisons are all examples of those served by institutional food service operations.

Institutional food service operations are established primarily to meet the needs of the institutions in which they operate by providing food to those working in or using the services of the institution, willingly or otherwise. In some instances, they are confined to the institutions and must be fed—as in hospitals, nursing homes, and prisons. In others, because of institutional decisions or public policy, food service is made available for those who want it—as in schools, colleges, and similar settings.

Institutional food service operations may be run on either a profit or not-for-profit basis and may be managed either by the institution or by some outside food service contractor.

Institutional food service operations are similar to several other types of food service operations—business and industry food service and airline catering are two examples. None of these are operated primarily for public dining; they are intended to provide food service for those constituting a particular group—children in a school, passengers on an airplane, or employees of a corporation.

BUSINESS AND INDUSTRY FOOD SERVICE. Business and industry food service operations are those that provide food during working hours for employees of particular firms in their offices or factories. As in the case of institutional food service, they may be operated on either a profit or not-for-profit basis and may be managed by the firm whose employees they serve or by some outside food service contractor.

In large firms, it is not uncommon to find several food service operations at one site preparing foods at several levels of quality, for various types of service and price levels and for different groups of employees. For example, within a specific building one might find a cafeteria serving adequate foods at moderate prices for workers earning modest salaries, a table service restaurant with more elaborate meals at higher prices for midlevel managers, and a fine dining facility for the executive staff.

AIRLINE CATERING. Airline catering is the business of providing food prepared and packaged for service by an airline crew during a flight. The food is prepared by an airline catering organization at a central facility, called a commissary, where it is suitably packaged in serving containers. It is transported to planes in storage units that will keep food warm or cold, as required, until it is served. The storage units are stowed in specially designed units on the plane and served by flight attendants at appropriate times.

An airline catering operation may be owned by the airline it serves, by another airline, or by one of a number of hospitality firms, large and small, that have gone into this specialized business. Marriott, Sky Chefs, Dobbs, and Trust House Forte are some of the leading names in this field.

CLUB FOOD SERVICE. Club food service operations are those that provide food service in membership establishments known as clubs. Many types of clubs—golf, tennis, athletic, luncheon, college alumni, fraternal, social, to name a few—are organized to appeal to people with some common interest.

Food service operations in clubs range from very simple and inexpensive to those that provide some of the finest food and service available—from hot dog stands near a swimming pool to spectacular dining rooms with fine linen, china, and glassware, and elegant professional service. Private clubs restrict service to members and their guests; some clubs, however, are open to the general public.

STAND. A stand is a stationary, open-air food service establishment without a dining room facility. Customers walk to a counter to order and obtain foods, then consume the foods at the counter or elsewhere, as they prefer. Examples include hot dog stands at beaches, and roadside stands selling ice cream, hamburgers, or cider, among other possibilities.

COFFEE SHOPS. Traditionally, a coffee shop was an establishment with a limited menu, to which customers typically would go to order coffee and some other item—a donut, a sandwich, or a slice of pie are common offerings. They did not provide full meals. Coffee shops tended to be small, usually offering seating on stools at a counter. Some provided a limited number of tables or booths. Today, many have more extensive menus resembling those of diners, as described below.

DINER. A diner is normally a moderately priced, full service restaurant, typically open very long hours—sometimes twenty-four hours a day—serving breakfast, lunch and dinner from a single, multipage menu. In most diners, the customer can order any meal at any hour—breakfast at 11 P.M., for example.

The modern diner is a direct descendant of the establishments discussed in Chapter 4. The exterior design has evolved from trolleys and railroad dining cars of an earlier period, but only older diners display any of the characteristics of the diners of earlier times. There is little physical similarity between today's diner and one built 60 years ago.

NEIGHBORHOOD RESTAURANT. A neighborhood restaurant is one that caters to the needs, tastes, and preferences of those who live or work nearby. In general, they reflect the character of the neighborhoods in which they are found. Some are inexpensive, and others less so. Some are actually quite expensive, depending on the neighborhood.

More than any other type of establishment, the neighborhood restaurant depends for survival on repeat business from people in the area. Thus, owners of neighborhood restaurants must pay particularly close attention to their customers' likes and dislikes. Failure to do so will have a greater negative impact, more quickly, than would be the case in other types of establishments.

DRIVE-THROUGH. A drive-through is an operation at which a customer can drive a vehicle to a window to obtain and pay for food without ever leaving the vehicle. Having received the food, the customer drives away to consume the food elsewhere. In effect, these can be considered the descendents of the drive-in restaurants of the 1950s and 1960s.

The process limits the kinds of foods that can be sold. They tend to be preportioned items, prepared in advance and easily packaged for takeout—in other words, the typical products of the fast service restaurants. In fact, a number of the chain restaurants specializing in fast service products have been very successful in providing drive-through service for their customers.

TAKEOUT. A takeout is an operation that prepares foods for consumption off premises. Foods for takeout may either be fully prepared in advance, then merely packaged when ordered by a customer—or not prepared until ordered. Takeout merely means that food leaves the premises where it is sold. It may be picked up and transported by the purchaser, or delivered, depending on the nature of the operation. Some do both. Most pizza establishments deliver; those offering hamburgers or chicken typically do not.

Some takeout establishments have no facilities for on-premises consumption; they operate exclusively as takeouts. Some are parts of other food service operation that provide seating for customers.

These are some of the terms used in general conversation to identify or describe various kinds of food service establishments. However, one can readily see that no single term will fully describe a given establishment. For example, the term *fast service* conveys that a customer should be able to obtain food quickly in such an establishment, but it does not provide information about the kind of food served or the extent of its menu. To describe the establishment more completely and usefully, we would have to say, for example, that it is a fast service restaurant with a limited menu, specializing in chicken. Similarly, to describe a particular restaurant as one dedicated to fine dining is to imply that it features foods of high quality, that it is probably expensive, and that it offers table service. But the term *fine dining* tells us nothing about the kind of food served, the type of service, or the ambiance. And because the quality of ethnic, specialty, and all other restaurants can vary so greatly, simply stating that a particular establishment is "Italian" tells us next to nothing about it. We would need to know a great deal more to describe it fully.

BEVERAGE SERVICE

Society has not always viewed the consumption of alcoholic beverages favorably. On the whole, however, American society has generally tolerated "drinking" and has even encouraged it under some circumstances, provided it was not done to excess: Many today believe it has therapeutic value when consumed in moderation. Everyone recognizes its dangerous and debilitating effects when consumed to excess.

During the 1920s, the sale of alcoholic beverages was illegal under provisions of the Volstead Act. Nonetheless, this did not stop Americans from drinking. Drinking establishments called *speak-easies* were very popular. Making alcoholic beverages at home—the so-called *bathtub gin*, for example—was a hobby for many Americans; and illegally transporting and selling alcoholic beverages—*bootlegging*, in the vernacular of the period—made rich men of many underworld characters.

After the repeal of the Volstead Act in 1933, the authority to regulate the sale and consumption of alcoholic beverages was returned to state and local governments. Laws passed in the years since 1933 have resulted in great variations from one state to another, and even from one community to another within a state. The extent of these variations is so great that it is quite beyond the scope of any introductory text. A few examples will illustrate.

All states and almost all local communities allow properly licensed establishments to serve alcoholic beverages in one form or another—by the glass or by the bottle, or both of these. In a few communities, the sale of alcoholic beverages in any form remains illegal. In some of these, however, a customer can bring his own alcoholic beverages, and the establishment will provide the glassware, ice, mixer, or whatever combination of these the customer requires. In some states, customers cannot be served alcoholic beverages unless they are seated. In others, customers are not permitted to order drinks at a bar then carry their own drinks from the bar than one drink in front of a customer at any given time. In others, a customer can carry a drink to his table, but only one. If the customer wants a drink for a companion, he cannot have it; the companion must get his own.

All states now prohibit the purchase of alcoholic beverages by anyone under the age of 21 years. This was the result of a decision by the federal government to withhold federal highway funds from any state that did not raise the drinking age to 21.

BEVERAGE SERVICE DEFINED

There are several possible ways to define beverage service. In this text, we will define *beverage service* as providing alcoholic and other related beverages for consumption on premises. The term *beverage* includes all alcoholic beverages and any nonalcoholic beverages typically prepared by bartenders. The beverage service establishment is one that provides beverage service for its customers. In many cases, the beverage service establishment provides its customers with food as well: Food sales may even constitute the major source of sales revenue.

REASONS FOR PATRONIZING BEVERAGE SERVICE ESTABLISHMENTS

There are a number of reasons commonly cited for patronizing beverage service establishments. These include

1. Dining
2. Seeking entertainment
3. Socializing
4. Discussing business
5. Meeting new people
6. Getting away from home
7. Killing time
8. Relaxing
9. Drinking

These are some of the many possible reasons for going to beverage service establishments. For most of the people who patronize these establishments, drinking would appear to be a secondary consideration. In fact, data reveal that sales of alcoholic beverages have actually decreased in recent years; whereas sales of nonalcoholic drinks have increased a great deal. This may indicate that patrons of beverage service establishments are switching from alcoholic to nonalcoholic beverages, because they never had been drawn to these establishments, in the first place, primarily to consume alcoholic drinks.

There are doubtless reasonable numbers who patronize these establishments primarily to purchase and consume alcoholic beverages. They appear to be a minority, however. To the extent that they abuse alcohol, the social pressures to modify their behavior continue to grow, particularly for those who drive.

THE FOCUS OF BEVERAGE SERVICE ESTABLISHMENTS

Because customers patronize beverage service establishments for different reasons, those who operate such businesses attempt to appeal to their potential customers by featuring or emphasizing those elements that they hope will attract customers. These elements can be grouped into three catagories, each of which we will characterize as a focal point for operations.

Beverage service establishments can be distinguished from one another on the basis of this focus. Each beverage service operator will have established one of the following as primary:

1. Food
2. Entertainment
3. Beverages

Food

Many establishments that provide beverage service place primary emphasis on their food. These tend to be food service establishments that provide beverages as accompaniments to food. Many of the characteristic types of food service establishments described earlier in the chapter—ethnic, theme, family, fine dining, tops, neighborhood, and others— have this focus. They make beverages available before, during, and after meals: Customers may order cocktails before dinner, wines with the meal, and any of various after-dinner drinks—such as liqueurs or dessert wines. To many customers of these establishments, beverages are integral parts of the dining experience. Many would probably not return if the establishment no longer offered beverages with the food.

These businesses may be regarded as both food service and beverage service establishments. They serve beverages to satisfy the expectations of their customers and because drink sales are profitable. But their emphasis, their principal business

A beverage service establishment, such as the hotel lounge shown above, may have a variety of focuses on food, entertainment, or beverages in order to attract potential customers. (Courtesy Stouffer Harborplace Hotel, Baltimore, Maryland.)

focus, tends to be the food, which normally provides greater revenue than the beverages.

Some of these establishments may also offer entertainment—live piano music during dinner, for example—but only as a secondary element. The principal focus is food.

Entertainment

In other establishments, primary emphasis is placed on entertainment. Entertainment is a very broad term, encompassing any number of possibilities. It can range from sports events on television to professional musicians—bands, pianists, or singers—from coin-operated games to horse races at a track, or from professional team sports to theatrical companies. Such establishments as night clubs, gambling casinos, theaters, piano bars, racetracks, and sports arenas provide beverage service to those who have come for the entertainment features of these establishments. For many customers the beverages are an indispensable element in the entertainment.

In some of these establishments, there is no charge for the entertainment. The cost to management may be so low that there is no need to recover any of that cost from customers. This would be the case if the entertainment consisted of sports events on television. However, professional entertainers can be very costly, and the owner of an establishment featuring professional groups might attempt to recover the cost of the entertainment by selling tickets or by imposing either a cover charge or a minimum. A *cover charge* is an amount per person added to the total bill incurred for food and drink. A *minimum* is the least amount each customer is permitted to spend; those spending less are charged the minimum.

Many of these establishments also offer food—excellent food, in some cases. For example, some dinner theaters feature professional performances of musical productions. They offer food and beverages as well, but their principal focus is clearly the entertainment.

Beverages

In a vast number of beverage service establishments, the primary emphasis is clearly and conspicuously on the beverages themselves. Some may give away simple salty foods to stimulate beverage sales. Others may provide entertainment in the form of background music from a radio. The focus of these establishments is very clear and simple: They sell beverages and have little or no interest in any other possibilities. Many neighborhood bars are of this type. Closely related to these are the typical bars at airports or railroad stations that cater to those waiting to board planes or trains.

Some beverage service establishments, although focusing primarily on beverages, make some attempt to broaden their appeal. They may, for example, provide a wider range of foods than salty snacks—sandwiches, hamburgers, or a few hot foods in a steam table located near the bar; but the food even in these is typically of secondary importance. Some attempt to provide a limited kind of entertainment for their customers—coin-operated games, for example. In all of these, however, the principal focus is on neither the food nor the entertainment: It is on the beverages.

There are several terms used to identify those establishments in which beverages are the primary focus—including *tavern, inn, saloon, cocktail lounge,* and *bar.* Historically, the distinctions among these were well known and generally accepted. That is no longer the case. It is perfectly possible, today, to see an establishment identified by its owner as a *tavern,* then to find another nearby, virtually a duplicate of the first, called a *cocktail lounge* by its owner. Such terms are not readily distinguished from one another any longer.

Strange as it may seem, no one ever speaks of a beverage service industry. In our industry, beverage service is treated as part of food service; and the data related to establishments selling beverages and to beverage sales are commonly reported with food service data. Thus, when an individual mentions the food service industry, it is unlikely that he means food service alone: He is probably referring to the combined industries known by the single term *food service industry.*

NATIONAL RESTAURANT ASSOCIATION CLASSIFICATION

A number of years ago, the National Restaurant Association (NRA) developed a classification system for the food service industry, primarily to report information about the industry's total sales. Table 5.1 illustrates the NRA's classification

TABLE 5.1 Food Service Industry Food and Drink Sales Projected Through 1992

	1989 Estimated F&D sales ($000)	1991 Projected F&D sales ($000)	1992 Projected F&D sales ($000)	1991–1992 Percent change	1991–1992 Percent real growth change	1989–1992 Compound annual growth rate
Group I – Commercial Food Service[1]						
Eating places						
Restaurants, lunchrooms	$ 72,726,986	$ 79,191,833	$ 83,230,616	5.1%	1.3%	4.6%
Limited-menu restaurants, refreshment places	65,774,810	73,569,740	78,278,203	6.4	2.6	6.0
Commercial cafeterias	4,174,076	4,566,907	4,813,520	5.4	1.6	4.9
Social caterers	2,085,494	2,378,689	2,552,333	7.3	3.5	7.0
Ice cream, frozen-custard stands	1,954,828	2,063,810	2,142,235	3.8	0.0	3.1
Total eating places	$146,716,194	$161,770,979	$171,016,907	5.7%	1.9%	5.2%
Bars & taverns	8,952,440	8,554,056	8,733,691	2.1	-2.7	-0.8
Total eating & drinking places	$155,668,634[2]	$170,325,035	$179,750,598	5.5%	1.7%	4.9%
Food contractors						
Manufacturing & industrial plants	$ 3,668,914	$ 3,845,156	$ 4,133,543	7.5%	3.7%	4.0%
Commercial & office buildings	1,214,147	1,314,153	1,403,515	6.8	3.0	4.9
Hospitals & nursing homes	1,566,756	1,822,344	1,964,487	7.8	4.0	7.8
Colleges & universities	2,569,246	3,174,252	3,417,277	7.6	3.4	10.0
Primary & secondary schools	1,136,942	1,287,055	1,369,426	6.4	2.6	6.4
In-transit food service (airlines)	1,317,056	1,598,421	1,787,035	11.8	5.8	10.7
Recreation & sports centers	1,724,842	1,948,908	2,073,638	6.4	2.6	6.3
Total food contractors	$ 13,197,903	$ 14,990,289	$ 16,148,921	7.7%	3.6%	7.0%
Lodging places						
Hotel restaurants	$ 12,215,486	$ 12,922,223	$ 13,672,397	5.8%	2.0%	3.8%
Motor-hotel restaurants	553,558	551,310	560,682	1.7	-2.1	0.4
Motel restaurants	836,480	811,573	809,138	-0.3	-4.1	-1.1
Total lodging places	$ 13,605,524	$ 14,285,106	$ 15,042,217	5.3%	1.5%	3.4%
Retail host restaurants[3]	$ 9,244,637	$ 10,642,710	$ 11,442,349	7.5%	3.7%	7.4%
Recreation & sports[4]	2,786,597	2,968,367	3,130,912	5.5	1.7	4.0
Mobile caterers	808,862	835,366	872,957	4.5	0.7	2.6
Vending & nonstore retailers[5]	5,239,124	5,427,539	5,764,046	6.2	2.4	3.2
TOTAL GROUP I	**$200,551,281**	**$219,474,412**	**$232,152,000**	**5.8%**	**1.9%**	**5.0%**

Group II—Institutional Food Service—Business, educational, governmental or institutional organizations that operate their own food service

Employee foodservice[6]	$ 1,987,334	$ 1,870,618	-1.2%	$ 1,919,462	2.6%	-1.2%
Public & parochial elementary, secondary schools	3,477,870	3,747,123	0.2	3,897,008	4.0	3.9
Colleges & universities	3,758,748	4,212,719	-0.5	4,368,590	3.7	5.1
Transportation	1,089,452	1,283,035	7.2	1,430,293	11.5	9.5
Hospitals[7]	8,396,380	9,433,761	1.8	9,962,052	5.6	5.9
Nursing homes, homes for aged, blind, orphans, and the mentally & physically disabled[8]	3,667,376	3,967,470	2.0	4,086,494	3.0	3.7
Clubs, sporting & recreational camps	2,068,991	2,250,128	1.5	2,364,427	5.1	4.5
Community centers	608,040	718,379	7.0	775,849	8.0	8.5
TOTAL GROUP II	$ 25,054,191	$ 27,483,233	1.4%	$ 28,804,175	4.8%	4.8%
TOTAL GROUPS I & II	$225,605,472	$246,957,645	1.8%	$260,956,175	5.7%	5.0%

Group III—Military Food Service[9]

Officers' & NCO clubs ("Open Mess")	$ 697,031	$ 684,938	-3.2%	$ 689,048	0.6%	0.4%
Food service—military exchanges	$ 358,907	$ 361,606	-6.1	$ 353,289	-2.3	-0.5
TOTAL GROUP III	$ 1,055,938	$ 1,046,544	-4.2%	$ 1,042,337	-0.4%	-0.4%
GRAND TOTAL	$226,661,410	$248,004,189	1.8%	$261,998,512	5.6%	4.9%

Footnotes:

1. Data are given only for establishments with payroll.
2. Food and drink sales for nonpayroll establishments totaled $4,787,186,000 in 1989.
3. Includes drug and proprietary store restaurants, general-merchandise-store restaurants, variety-store restaurants, food-store restaurants, grocery-store restaurants (including portion of deli merchandise line), gasoline-service-station restaurants and miscellaneous retailers.
4. Includes movies, bowling lanes, and recreation and sports centers.
5. Includes sales of hot food, sandwiches, pastries, coffee and other hot beverages.
6. Includes industrial and commercial organizations, seagoing and inland-waterway vessels.
7. Includes voluntary and proprietary hospitals; long-term general, TB, mental hospitals; and sales or commercial equivalent to employees in state and local short-term hospitals and federal hospitals.
8. Sales (commercial equivalent) calculated for nursing homes and homes for the aged only. All others in this grouping make no charge for food served either in cash or in kind.
9. Continental United States only.

Reprinted by permission of the National Restaurant Association.

system and provides some interesting data about total food and drink sales for the years shown.

Note that all food and beverage enterprises are divided into three groups:

Group I is the largest, representing the majority of both food and beverage establishments and sales. It encompasses those establishments whose primary business is food service, beverage service, or some combination of both. All are profit oriented. This does not mean that every one of them actually earns a profit but that they are being operated with the intention of profitability.

Group II is for food service establishments operated by organizations whose primary focus is in some other field. Food service is not their primary business: They choose to operate their own food services for the convenience of employees, students, patients, or customers, rather than have firms from Group I run them. Some are operated for profit; others are not.

Group III is military food service, a relatively small part of the industry.

Within Group I, the largest category is called *Eating places*. This includes establishments operated primarily as food service businesses, not those that are part of other businesses. There is no attempt to differentiate among them on the basis of size, type of food served, or food quality. Eating places are divided into several types, including full menu restaurants, limited menu restaurants, cafeterias, caterers, and ice-cream stands. Bars and taverns are separately listed in this category.

The second category in Group I is *Food contractors*. These are commercial firms that provide food service in other establishments (commercial and noncommercial), such as banks and other financial service operations, office buildings, factories, hospitals, colleges, primary and secondary schools, transportation services, and recreation and sports centers.

The third category in Group I is food service operations in *Lodging places*.

The final category in Group I is a collection of commercial food service operations that do not belong in other categories, including restaurants in drugstores, food stores, and recreation centers, as well as mobile caterers and vending machines.

Group II encompasses food service operations that are a part of some larger enterprise and are operated by that larger enterprise, but not for commercial purposes. This group includes school, college, and university food service, and food service provided by hospitals and nursing homes.

Group III includes only those military food service enterprises where people pay for food—officers' clubs, NCO clubs, and the like. Because those in military service do not purchase their meals, the vast number of meals prepared daily for those in the military are not reflected.

Note that some operations listed in Group I appear at first glance to be duplicated in Group II. For example, Colleges and Universities are listed in both Group I and Group II. The Colleges and Universities listing in Group I includes food services operated by an outside profit-oriented food contractor, such as Saga, Canteen, or some other. Listing is Group II, however, is for colleges and universities that operate their own food service establishments.

The principal reason for developing the NRA system was to provide a means for reporting quantitative data about industry size and dollar sales. Establishments are divided into specific categories, and information about each establishment is classified accordingly.

Because this system is not and cannot be concerned with the very real and significant qualitative differences among establishments evident in our industry, we must use other terms to take these into account—*family restaurant, offering table service, moderate prices,* and *ethnic Italian food,* for example; or *cocktail lounge focusing on entertainment, featuring live piano music.* We must use the kinds of terms discussed earlier in the chapter to make meaningful distinctions among the various types of food service and beverage service operations. Both approaches are useful. The first enables professionals and the public at large to distinguish one operation from another, and the second facilitates the collection and reporting of statistical information about a vast and important industry.

SUMMARY

In this chapter, the size of the food and beverage industry is illustrated. Three explanations for the increase in public demand for food service are offered and discussed. A definition is provided for the term *food service,* and five important elements of food service operations that differentiate one from another are discussed in detail. An extensive list of characteristic types of food service establishments is provided, and each is described in detail. *Beverage service* is defined, and the principal reasons for patronizing beverage service establishments are listed. A rationale is presented for distinguishing one beverage service establishment from another on the basis of focus. Finally, the classification system used by the National Restaurant Association to collect and report statistical information is presented and explained.

QUESTIONS

1. What percentage of gross national product has been attributable to food and beverage sales in recent years?

2. What is the rank of the food service industry as an employer of women? Of teenagers? Of members of minority groups?
3. Approximately what percentage of America's retail outlets are eating or drinking establishments?
4. What are the three reasons commonly cited for America's increased demand for food service in recent years?
5. Define *food service*. What is a *food service enterprise?*
6. What are the five most important elements of a food service enterprise? Illustrate by example how changes in each can affect the character of a food service enterprise.
7. Define each of the following characteristic types of food service establishments and cite one example of each: fast service; table service; ethnic; specialty; fine dining; limited menu; chain restaurant; theme restaurant; "top"; family restaurant; cafeteria; buffet; catering; institutional food service; business and industry food service; airline catering; club food service; stand; coffee shop; diner; neighborhood restaurant; drive through; take out.
8. Cite a particular food service establishment in your area, an adequate description of which requires the use of four of the terms in question #7.
9. Define *beverage service*. What is a *beverage service enterprise?*
10. List nine common reasons for patronizing beverage service establishments.
11. Identify three beverage service establishments in your area that attract customers by featuring or emphasizing food.
12. For the establishments cited in your response to question #11, indicate how each differs from the other two with respect to menu items, food quality, menu prices, service, and ambiance — the five most important elements of a food service operation.
13. Identify three beverage service establishments that attract customers by featuring or emphasizing entertainment.
14. Identify three beverage service establishments that attract customers without featuring either food or entertainment. Do these provide any kind of food? What kind?

15. Distinguish between a commercial and a noncommercial food service operation.
16. Which of the three major groups in the National Restaurant Association's food service classification system accounts for the greatest dollar sales annually? Which, the least? What is the principal difference between the establishments in Group I and those in Group II?

Food and Beverage Operations:
A Systems Approach

6

LEARNING OBJECTIVES

After reading and studying this chapter, you should be able to:

1. *Define the terms* system *and* subsystem.
2. *List and describe the seven operational* subsystems *required for preparing and serving portions of food or beverages.*
3. *List and explain the four critical issues that a purchasing* subsystem *must address.*
4. *Distinguish between perishables and nonperishables.*
5. *List the three primary goals of a receiving subsystem and explain the importance of each.*
6. *Identify the four goals of a storing subsystem.*
7. *Describe the primary aims of the subsystem for issuing.*
8. *Name the four objectives that a subsystem for producing food or beverage products is designed to accomplish.*
9. *Identify the purposes of each of the following: sales histories, production sheets, standard recipes.*
10. *Compare the goals of subsystems for selling in profit-oriented operations with those in operations which are not profit-oriented.*
11. *List and describe three techniques used to achieve the goals of a subsystem for selling portions of food and beverage products.*
12. *Describe the purpose of the subsystem for serving portions of food and beverage products.*
13. *List four food and beverage subsystems indirectly related to preparing and serving portions of food and beverage products to customers.*

14. Illustrate the interrelatedness of the subsystems for preparing and serving food and beverage products.

INTRODUCTION

The previous chapter was devoted to examining the size and scope of the food and beverage industry and to imparting some sense of its great importance in American life. With that objective accomplished, we will now turn to a subject that is typically of the greatest interest to those choosing to prepare for careers in the food service industry: food and beverage operations.

Given the array of types of food and beverage establishments discussed in the previous chapter, it should be apparent that the operating details differ greatly from one to another. The operating details of a hot dog stand at the beach or a county fair will differ greatly from those of a sophisticated city restaurant dedicated to fine dining. Similarly, those of a student cafeteria at a college will differ from the operations of a neighborhood restaurant serving ethnic fare to a family clientele. The differences from one to another would be apparent upon consideration of the five most important elements of each, identified in the previous chapter: menu items, food quality, menu prices, service, and ambiance. Similarly, operations differences would be apparent from one type of beverage enterprise to another: The neighborhood bar focused on beverages would differ from the fine restaurant focused on food.

In the authors' view, it would not be productive in an introductory text to attempt detailed descriptions of the many operational *differences* evident in the food and beverage industry. Discussions of such differences are best deferred to advanced courses dealing with the specifics of food and beverage operations. We will turn our attention, instead, to similarities.

Interestingly, any food or beverage enterprise, although defined as part of the service sector of the economy, is also engaged in preparing units of "product"— portions of food and drink—for customers. This is a somewhat simplistic view of the food and beverage enterprise, but customers tend to think of our industry as one that provides them with portions of food and drink. Portions of food and drink are simply the most obvious elements of the service product, which should be defined to include every conceivable element of the customer's experience with the food and beverage enterprise—lighting, visual appearance, service quality, service techniques, atmosphere, and attitude of all members of the staff, to name the more obvious.

The purpose of this chapter, then, will be to identify some important points of similarity in operating details from one establishment to another that may be obscured by the vast array of differences. We will define and describe a number of elements and processes that all food service and all beverage service enterprises have in common. To accomplish this aim, we will treat the food or beverage enterprise—any food or beverage enterprise—as a system.

SYSTEM DEFINED

A *system* can be defined as a whole unit consisting of a set of interrelated parts coordinated to accomplish a set of goals.

Each part has a specific function in the whole unit and each of the parts of a system can be called a *subsystem*. The human body provides an example. The body consists of a set of subsystems with such names as *alimentary, circulatory, respiratory*, and many others, designed to accomplish a particular set of goals, the most important of which is to sustain life. To that end, the alimentary system provides nourishment to the cells via the circulatory system, which moves blood through the body, interacting with the respiratory system in the lungs, where carbon dioxide is exchanged for life-sustaining oxygen. If any one of these systems malfunctions, the others are affected and the results are felt throughout the organism. In any system, changes in a subsystem affect both the whole system and the other subsystems.

Systems can best be understood in terms of an input–output model such as that in Table 6.1.

TABLE 6.1 *Input–Output Model*

INPUT $\longrightarrow$ SYSTEM $\longrightarrow$ OUTPUT

In order for a system to function, resources are required. The system treats these resources as inputs, which it transforms in order to produce outputs. The nature and complexity of the inputs and outputs vary from one system to another. For the human body—a very complex system—these resources include air, food, and water—some of the inputs to the system. The human body takes these and other inputs, transforms them in complex ways, and generates a host of outputs. The overriding one is life itself. Others include the many manifestations of life—the ability to compose musical works, to construct buildings, and to do untold numbers of other things that human beings do—including planning and operating food service enterprises!

FOOD AND BEVERAGE SYSTEMS

Food and beverage systems require inputs—the traditional inputs or resources required by any economic enterprise: land, labor, and capital. In our industry, these are more familiarly referred to as *physical, human*, and *operational resources*. *Physical resources* are the building in which the enterprise operates, the equipment used in its operation, and the food and beverage materials used to generate outputs. *Human resources* are all the personnel of the establishment—managers, cooks, servers, cleaners, and so on. *Operational resources* are the funds employed and the knowledge required to use the funds appropriately.

Food or beverage systems use subsystems to transform the inputs and generate output. The subsystems may be identified as the following:

purchasing	producing
receiving	selling
storing	serving
issuing	

These subsystems are essential for all food or beverage operations—from hamburger stand to catering hall, and from neighborhood bar to hotel cocktail lounge—and are necessary for preparing and serving portions of food or beverages. Each of these will be described in detail, and we will explore their interrelationships.

The possible outputs of food and beverage systems are many. Ideally, some of the outputs will reflect the accomplishment of goals established by the owner. Typical goals may include earning a profit, providing the best service or the finest food and wines in the region, providing a venue for the best performers in show business, or meeting the needs of particular groups—patients in a hospital, or members of a club, for example.

Table 6.2 expands upon Table 6.1. It integrates the specific inputs and outputs of the common food and beverage enterprise with the subsystems required for operation.

The student reading about food and beverage systems may find it useful to refer to particular food and beverage operations. Case Studies 6.1, 6.2 and 6.3 describe three food and beverage operations that, at first glance, differ markedly from one another. These illustrations are included so that the student can learn that these three seemingly different operations—and any others the student may know from firsthand work experience—have much in common with one another.

TABLE 6.2 *Inputs and Outputs of Common Food and Beverage Enterprise Subsystems*

Inputs ⟶	System ⟶	Outputs
funds	purchasing subsystem	profit
equipment	receiving subsystem	food products
food supplies	storing subsystem	beverage products
beverage supplies	issuing subsystem	reputation
human resources	production subsystem	
building	selling subsystem	
	serving subsystem	

The first of these is an independently owned specialty restaurant with a limited menu. The second is an employee food service facility operated for a bank by an independent-business food service company. The third is an English-style pub specializing in imported beers and ales, and offering very limited food service.

CASE STUDY 6.1   *The Steak Shack is a family-owned and operated restaurant located in a middle-class suburb, twenty-three miles from a city of 250,000. It is open six days for dinner only, and closed all day Sunday. The goals of the Steak Shack include meeting the dining needs of those local residents seeking steaks and a limited number of related items, moderately priced, with efficient, friendly service.*

The restaurant is the sole tenant in a purpose-built, stand-alone building surrounded by parking for up to 50 cars. The interior consists of a dining room; a cocktail lounge and bar; production area consisting of food preparation, dishwashing, and storage areas; offices; dressing rooms and lavatories for staff; and men's and women's restrooms for customers. The dining room seats 100 at tables for two, four, or six people, and the tables can be combined when necessary for larger groups. The cocktail lounge, adjacent to the dining room and seating 30 at tables for two or four, is used principally by customers having predinner drinks. In this cocktail lounge, there is a bar seating 12. During busy periods, two bartenders at this bar prepare all drinks for the bar, the cocktail lounge, and dining room.

The production area includes facilities for receiving, storing, and issuing foods and beverages. In addition, this area has facilities used to prepare food for cooking; ranges and other equipment for cooking, and counters for dispensing finished food products to servers. The production area includes facilities and equipment for dishwashing, pot washing, and waste disposal.

Office space is limited. Manager and bookkeeper share one office, where the computer is located. The other office is used by the chef, who manages back-of-the-house operations and does all purchasing, except for beverages: These are purchased by the manager.

The menu consists of three appetizers, two soups, a salad bar, and eight entrees—four steak, one chicken, one roast beef, and two fish. Customers are given a choice of French fried or baked potatoes, and either of the two vegetables of the day. Desserts are limited to two pies, cheesecake, and two flavors of ice cream. Coffee, tea, and milk are available. The customary selection of beers, wines, and spirits and mixers is available at the bar.

CASE STUDY 6.2	*The staff dining room is a facility located in the corporate headquarters of the Mountain Bank and Trust Company in a large city in the West. It is not open to the public: The*

bank provides the facility and subsidizes the costs of operation. One of the bank's goals is to provide staff members with good food at very reasonable prices during working hours, so that they don't have to leave the bank. Another is to provide efficient service so that staff members can eat within the allotted time. The service is operated by Marecki Foods, a regional company specializing in business and industry food service. Marecki has a contract to provide the service for a set fee per month.

The facility is located on the second floor of the bank's new headquarters building, constructed just four years ago. The dining, kitchen, and storage facilities are all attractive and modern; and the bank insists that they be properly cleaned and maintained by the food service contractor.

The facility is open from 7 A.M. to 3 P.M., and limits service to breakfast and luncheon. Menu selections are limited. Breakfast items include juices, cold cereals, muffins, pastries, eggs, bacon, sausage, and the usual breakfast beverages. Daily luncheon items include a choice of three sandwiches, extensive salad bar, two hot entrees, several desserts, and choice of beverages.

Employees pay as they enter. At breakfast, they pay $1.25 for cold selections with beverage and $2.50 for full breakfast. At luncheon, they pay $4.00, regardless of their selections. At the end of each month, the food service contractor bills the bank for the difference between revenues and expenses, plus the monthly fee.

Employees take trays, flatware, and napkins at the entrance to the facility. Foods are attractively displayed on several buffet islands. Employees make their selections and carry these to tables in the dining room, which seats 120 persons at tables for two and four. Employees bus their own trays, but there are two food service employees in the dining room to clean tables.

CASE STUDY 6.3	*Frog's Pub is an American recreation of an English pub, located in a prosperous and growing city of 250,000 people in the Middle West. It is in the downtown area on a*

street known locally as "Restaurant Row"; and it attracts large numbers of customers at lunch, after work, and throughout the evening hours. The owner's goals include providing an eating and drinking place for those seeking something out of the ordinary. Another is to provide a casual atmosphere in which customers will relax and feel at home.

Frog's occupies rented premises in a four-story brick building. Customers enter a large room that gives the appearance of an authentic English pub, and with a long bar along one side of the room. The bar has stools to seat thirty customers. Seventy-five additional customers can be seated at tables.

At the bar, two bartenders prepare drinks for customers at the bar as well as for those seated at tables. Table service is provided by three servers, aided by one individual who clears and cleans tables. Food is prepared in a small kitchen at the rear of the establishment by a chef who has one assistant. There is a small dishwashing machine operated by a third individual. All food and beverages are stored in the basement. Dressing rooms for the staff and a small office for the manager are also located in the basement.

Frog's is different from any other establishment in the region: It offers thirty-six imported beers and ales, many of them English. While spirits and some wines are available, the vast majority of customers order the specialty beers and ales, in spite of relatively high prices per glass or bottle. Food accounts for a comparatively small percentage of dollar sales, and the food menu is restricted. It includes eight items that serve as accompaniments to drinks or as appetizers. The remainder of the menu includes several sandwiches and three hot items that are changed daily. Limited desserts and both coffee and tea are available. All menu items have names that sound British.

Purchasing

The first of the food and beverage subsystems is *purchasing,* a necessary first step in any production process. All food or beverage enterprises must establish subsystems for purchasing.

The goal of a subsystem for purchasing foods or beverages for production is to ensure the availability of suitable materials for the preparation of units of food or beverage products and for other related uses. These materials must be available when needed; should be in sufficient, but not excessive quantities and of appropriate quality; and should have been purchased at suitable prices.

There are four critical issues that any purchasing subsystem must address:

quantity
quality
price
space

QUANTITY. Food and beverage operators cannot successfully ask customers to wait for deliveries. When a customer reading the menu in Frog's Pub requests a glass of Bass ale or an order of shepherd's pie, the owner is expected to have the items on hand. The purchasing subsystem must be designed to ensure that foods, beverages, and other necessary materials are available when needed so that menu items can be produced on demand. One means for accomplishing this is to establish daily routines for evaluating existing supplies of raw materials, assessing needs for the upcoming period, and placing orders as required. A satisfactory purchasing subsystem must have established procedures for maintaining suitable quantities of supplies.

For the Steak Shack, it is obviously important to maintain adequate supplies of steak. This can be accomplished by placing regular orders with a supplier. Assuming that the supplier delivers only on Tuesdays, it is necessary to order a sufficient quantity to last for one week. The individual responsible for ordering must know the quantity used in a normal week and know when larger or smaller amounts than normal may be needed. A good purchasing subsystem is designed to help determine proper quantities for purchase.

QUALITY. Product quality is another critical issue. The food and beverages must be of a quality acceptable to customers and should be consistent. There are degrees of quality, and products need not always be of the highest quality obtainable; but they should be of the quality that meets customers' needs and preferences. Some would add that the quality should always match the image the establishment attempts to convey. If, for example, the Mountain Bank is attempting to convey to its employees the image of a caring employer, foods available to them in the dining facility—even the simplest foods—should be of consistently good quality. The purchasing subsystem should be designed to ensure the purchase of products of consistent quality each time the food and beverages are ordered.

The quality of any item purchased should also be appropriate for its intended use. For example, when the steward in the Mountain Bank buys oranges for fresh orange juice, she buys Valencias or Temples, which are juice oranges, rather than California navels, which are eating oranges. The latter are more expensive and yield less juice. If someone were mistakenly to purchase the Californias, the bank's operating costs would be higher than necessary; and the quality of the orange juice would be lower than desired.

Any subsystem designed for food purchasing must take into account the two different categories into which all food purchases are divided: perishables and nonperishables.

Perishables are those foods that will keep for only short periods before they begin to lose their quality—to spoil and become unusable. They are typically fresh foods, such as meat, fish, fruit, and vegetables. Fresh vegetables will retain sufficient freshness for several days; fresh fish, by comparison, does not, and must be used much sooner. Perishables must be ordered frequently, sometimes each day. The quantity ordered is, of course, limited to anticipated demand.

Nonperishables are those foods that will keep for extended periods before spoiling. They typically come in cans, jars, bags, bottles, and boxes. Some are dried or frozen. Nonperishables are ordered infrequently and can be ordered in larger quantities because these items have longer shelf life than perishables.

The terms *perishable* and *nonperishable* are not normally used in beverage purchasing. This does not mean, however, that shelf life for beverage products is unlimited. Some beverages—draft beers, for example—have a very limited shelf life and must be kept refrigerated. For bottled beer, shelf life is considerably longer—but not unlimited. By contrast, spirits can be kept indefinitely.

Questions of quality should not be left to chance. Beef tenderloin, the commercial cut of beef used to prepare filet mignon in the Steak Shack, is available at several levels of quality, known as *grades*; and someone must determine which grade is appropriate for intended use in a given establishment. In addition, if customers ordering filet mignon are to receive steaks of the same quality on each visit to the establishment, then provision must be made for ordering the same grade each time beef tenderloins are purchased.

One means for ensuring consistency in the quality of items is to prepare a carefully considered written description of each item to be purchased. This could include such information as grade, size, count, color, type and size of container, degree of freshness, and other characteristics, which vary with the product to be purchased. These descriptions are known as *standard purchase specifications,* and are commonly used to one extent or another in most well-managed food or beverage operations. In the Steak Shack, all beef is purchased to match carefully written standard purchase specifications.

A good purchasing subsystem is designed to ensure that all items purchased are of suitable quality for intended use and are consistent from one purchase to the next.

PRICE. Price is always a critical issue in food and beverage purchasing. The higher the purchase price for raw materials of a given level of quality, the higher will be the cost of the food and beverage products an establishment offers its customers. The purchasing subsystem should facilitate the purchase of the needed quantity of an item at the most favorable price for the quality selected. For example, while the Mountain Bank is willing to subsidize the cost of its employees' meals, it is certainly unwilling to spend money wastefully.

There are several methods used by purchasers to determine the best price for the desired quality. Most commonly, purchasers obtain several quotations for desired products, then select the dealer offering the best price. A good purchasing subsystem makes provision for comparing the prices offered by various dealers for a given item, and selecting the best price. Before purchasing meats for the Steak Shack, the buyer obtains price quotations from three dealers, each of whom has a copy of the standard purchase specifications.

STORAGE SPACE. The final critical issue that the purchasing subsystem must take into account is storage space. Storage space is always limited, and decisions must be made as to amounts to be allocated to particular uses. Marecki Foods must determine the maximum quantity of each food item used in the Mountain Bank facility that can be stored in the limited space available. When storage space is severely limited, it clearly becomes necessary to place orders for some items more frequently than would be necessary otherwise. Thus, storage space can affect the timing of purchases. Quantities of any item purchased should never be greater than the storage space available for that item.

As we shall see, if the purchasing subsystem malfunctions—if an establishment lacks proper quantities of food or beverage ingredients to produce for customer demand, or if the food or beverages ingredients are of improper quality, for example—other subsystems will not be able to function properly, and the entire system may be unable to achieve its goals.

Receiving

The second important subsystem for food or beverage operation is that designed for receiving. The subsystem for receiving has three primary aims or goals. It must be designed to verify

1. that the quantity delivered is the same as the quantity ordered;
2. that the quality of the items delivered conform to the quality specified in the order placed; and
3. that the price on the invoice is the same as the price quoted by the dealer when the order was placed.

Food and beverage orders must be received by someone with sufficient knowledge to check carefully and accurately for quantity, quality, and price. Each delivery must be counted or weighed and the quality and price of each item must be verified. Finally, after the verification process is completed, the food is sent to the appropriate storage facility—dry storage, refrigeration, or freezer.

For example, assume the Steak Shack has placed an order for fifteen beef tenderloins, U. S. prime grade, weighing approximately eight pounds each, at a price of $8.50 per pound. When the delivery is received, it is necessary to verify that the beef is prime quality, that the invoice indicates a price of $8.50 per pound, and that the total weight for all fifteen pieces equals the weight shown on the invoice. Experienced receivers would also be certain to check other attributes listed in the purchase specifications, such as packaging, freshness, and thickness of fat cover, for example. If the delivered beef conforms to the order, it would be moved to refrigerated storage.

Should the delivery fail to conform to the order placed, there are likely to be problems in other subsystems, possibly having a negative impact on the success of the overall operation. For example, if the Steak Shack receives only twelve pieces of beef tenderloin, some customers may not be able to have filet mignon. Or if the beef is of a lower grade, the steaks will be less acceptable to customers and the reputation of the restaurant may be negatively affected. If the invoice price is higher than quoted, the profit of the restaurant will be somewhat lower than anticipated.

The receiving subsystem must be able to determine that items ordered are received at the quoted prices, and it must provide for ways to make the necessary adjustments when incorrect items have been sent to the restaurant.

Storing

The subsystem for storing has four primary goals:

1. to ensure the security of purchased materials;
2. to preserve the quality of those materials;
3. to provide ready access to available materials; and
4. to facilitate determination of quantities on hand.

All purchases are stored in one of three places: Food or beverage items that can be stored at room temperature should be placed in dry storage areas; those items that require chilling should be placed in refrigerators; and frozen foods should be stored in freezers. All storage areas should be locked to prevent *pilferage*— an industry term for theft—and it is essential that the storing subsystem make provision for safeguarding all food and beverage supplies. Pilferage is a major cause of unwarranted costs and must be prevented.

The storage subsystem must also ensure that the quality of supplies is maintained. Therefore, to preserve quality, rooms used for dry storage should be maintained at reasonable levels of temperature and humidity; if either or both become excessive, the shelf life of all foods and some beverages will be negatively affected. Refrigerators must operate at the proper temperatures—33 to 40 degrees Fahrenheit for chilled foods, and slightly higher temperatures for draft beers—45 degrees Fahrenheit. Frozen foods belong in freezers that maintain temperatures of 10 degrees below zero, Fahrenheit.

Another consideration in preserving the quality of food items is potential for odors and flavors from some food products to affect other foods stored nearby, particularly if foods are improperly wrapped or covered. In the Mountain Bank,

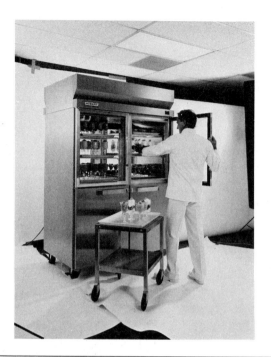

Along with price and quality, storage space and equipment are the factors taken into account when formulating a purchasing subsystem. Perishables are usually stored either in a refrigerator or freezer (left); nonperishables are most frequently stored in cans, jars, bottles, and boxes, and organized on shelves for inventory control (right). (Left: courtesy Hobart Corporation; right: courtesy InterMetro Industries.)

employees of Marecki Foods store eggs and other dairy products in a different refrigerator from that used for fish because these products would take on the odors of the fish very quickly.

One final consideration in preserving the quality of food in storage is taking all necessary steps to see that foods in dry storage are secure from contamination by rodents and other vermin. The owner of the Steak Shack must be careful to see that any items in bags and boxes are carefully protected from invasion by these perennial pests.

Providing ready access to stored food and beverage supplies is another key aim of the subsystem for storing. When a food or beverage item is needed from storage, it is clearly important that the storage facility be organized so that items can be obtained quickly and easily.

In most establishments, items are stored by category. In a food storage facility, canned fruits are stored together, as are spices. In beverage storage, spirits are stored together: The scotch whiskeys, for example, would be kept separate from the ryes and the bourbons. Each item has a predetermined location, and supplies are placed in these locations after they have been properly received. When an item is needed, an employee familiar with the storage facility goes to the location of the needed item and gets the desired quantity. Thus, the owner of the Frog's Pub can quickly and easily obtain a bottle of dry gin to replace one that has just been emptied at the bar.

When all stored items are kept in predetermined locations, it is easier to assess the quantity on hand of any food or beverage item and to make a judgment about whether to place an order for an additional quantity on any given day. Thus, the subsystem for purchasing is closely linked to that for storing: It is necessary to obtain accurate data from the storage subsystem concerning quantity on hand if the purchasing subsystem is to function properly.

ISSUING. The subsystem for issuing is designed to insure that materials for production are released to authorized personnel in the correct quantities at suitable times. This goal can be accomplished in any of several ways. For example, the owner of the Steak Shack may limit access to food storage to the chef, who would be the only individual with keys. Another possibility would be to have one employee whose work station would be the food storage area and who would give supplies only to those requesting them on special forms bearing the chef's signature.

If accurate records of issues are maintained by employees of Marecki Foods, on paper forms or by some other means, the issuing subsystem may also provide data to other subsystems. With data from both the receiving subsystem about goods received and from the issuing system about goods issued, methods can readily be devised for maintaining perpetual inventories of goods, the value of that inventory at any given time, cost of the foods or beverages issued, and considerable additional information.

PRODUCING. The subsystem for producing has four primary goals. It must be designed to produce food products and beverage products.

1. in suitable quantities,
2. of appropriate quality,
3. in a timely manner, and
4. with minimal waste.

The production of a menu of food or beverage products is a complex business. Some items are very simple to prepare — merely placing bottles of beer in a refrigerator to chill or arranging portion-packs of breakfast cereals on a breakfast buffet. Others are equally simple, but most require additional preparation — sometimes quite extensive preparation. The extent of this varies from item to item and from one establishment to another.

Every establishment does some of this preparation daily before opening for business. For example, the owner/operator of a simple hamburger stand must do some basic work before he can produce hamburgers: He moves several boxes of frozen hamburger patties from a freezer to a convenient location next to the grill, then places a corresponding number of packaged sliced rolls nearby. Both hamburger patties and rolls must be handy when the stand opens and customers begin to order hamburgers. He may even open several packages of rolls and place a few open rolls on plates just before opening. If this basic work is not done, service will be very slow, and both sales levels and revenues are likely to be lower than desired.

In the Steak Shack, prime ribs of beef and baked potatoes must be cooked ahead of time because of the length of the cooking process. The steaks must be portioned in advance because these items should be ready for broiling when customers' orders reach the kitchen. Similarly, the chef in the Mountain Bank prepares the tuna salad for sandwiches before the lunch hour begins. And at Frog's Pub, the bartender cuts pieces of lemon peel and sections of lime as garnishes for drinks, then fills several bar containers with ice from the kitchen, and places opened bottles of various spirits and mixers in predetermined, easy-to-reach wells located under the bar. Employees producing food or beverage products do such work in advance so that guests may be served quickly and efficiently.

Many food and beverage employees commonly describe this as preparing their *mis en place*, a French culinary term that means having everything in place. Thus, with the *mis en place* ready, the bartender in Frog's Pub and the chef in the Mountain Bank are ready to serve customers the foods and drinks of their choice without any unnecessary delay.

A significant problem with many food items is determining the quantities to prepare in advance. The proper quantity of any item is that amount that will enable the establishment to serve the item to each customer who orders it without delay, and without leftovers at the close of business. Ideally, the last portion of any item prepared for any given day will be served just as the establishment is about to close for the day.

At best, this is very difficult. Most would say it is next to impossible. Chefs normally do not know the precise number of customers who will order a given menu item. And without a precise number, they are likely to prepare too much or too little. If too little is prepared, some potential customers will be disappointed, and sales revenues may be less than would otherwise have been possible. If too much is prepared, leftover , unsold quantities may be unusable for their originally intended purposes. For example, the chef in the Steak Shack must prepare roast prime ribs of beef in advance. If too much is cooked, it is difficult to use the remaining amount the next day; and if too little is cooked, some customers will be disappointed when told that none is left. Unless the chef can find some suitable alternative use for the leftover beef, it may go unused, then spoil, and be discarded.

Because of their need to set production targets in advance, many food service operators have incorporated into their production subsystems some useful techniques adapted from the manufacturing sector. These are:

1. Sales histories
2. Production sheets

Sales Histories.   As the name implies, *sales histories* are records of the number of customers served during past periods and the number of portions sold of each menu item. Some establishments maintain records of portion sales by day of the week, whereas others find alternative approaches preferable. The data may be obtained from a computerized cash register or by manual means.

A sales history should include additional important information, such as inclement weather and out-of-the-ordinary events—holidays, strikes, special sales in nearby stores, road construction—any data that will shed light on the sales records for a given meal, day, or other period.

It has often been said that the best indicator of future human behavior is past human behavior. Thus, the sales history for a given establishment will provide the food service operator with some rational basis for predicting the total number of customers likely to patronize the establishment on a given day and for making some reasonable assumptions about which menu items they are likely to order. The collection of such assumptions for a given day becomes the basis for judgments about the quantities of particular menu items to prepare for the day.

Chefs preparing the raw ingredients and basic preparations for the day's service. The challenge is to prepare only as much as is needed for the day or meal period, based on sales histories and production sheets. (Courtesy Cryovac.)

Production Sheets.   A *production sheet* is a list of menu items that will be prepared for a specific day or meal period, along with the amount of each item for production personnel to prepare. Some production sheets will also indicate particular recipes to be used in preparation.

The initial entries on a production sheet are normally made by a food service manager after the sales history has been reviewed and evaluated. When completed, the form is given to the kitchen staff as a work plan for the day. It provides cooks with essential information for them to do their work.

Consistent quality is critical to food service success. The quality of food and drinks is established by management. Among the factors considered in establishing quality levels are the tastes and desires of the clientele and the menu prices that will be charged. The Steak Shack and other fine dining establishments typically use the very finest ingredients for their food and beverage products and try to prepare foods from only the freshest ingredients. Chefs in such establishments prepare basic stocks, for example, from high quality ingredients—then use these stocks to produce excellent soups and sauces. At the bar, "top-shelf" liquor is used in drink preparation; and, usually, larger portions of liquor are poured when drinks are ordered. Moderately priced establishments, however, are more likely to use some convenience foods, such as frozen vegetables and frozen breaded shrimp, and to select U. S. Choice steaks, rather than the U. S. Prime served to customers in the Steak Shack. Drinks may be prepared using less costly liquors and the quantity used in drinks may be smaller.

In both food production and beverage production, product quality and cost are established by means of the recipes selected for cooks and bartenders to use in preparing food and drinks. The recipes are normally selected with great care, after comparing a number of similar recipes. The recipe selected for the preparation of any food or beverage is that which management believes will produce a desirable product at a satisfactory cost. It must be of suitable quality and acceptable to customers. The recipe finally selected for producing a given menu item is known as a standard recipe.

Standard Recipes.   The *standard recipe*—a recipe that has been established as the correct recipe to use each time a given item is prepared—is a very important element in the production subsystem. Standard recipes insure that menu items will be prepared the same way each time, using the same ingredients, proportions, and methods. This provides consistent quality and does so at a cost that can be planned in advance.

It is clear that many menu items—food or beverage —can be prepared several different ways. Each variation would result in a product of different quality, taste, and cost. Yet each of these products could be listed on a menu by the same name. For example, a seafood newburg can be prepared using many expensive ingredients—lobster, shrimp, and scallops—or it can be done cheaply using inexpensive fish with very little of the more expensive ingredients. In the first instance, the cost and quality will obviously be higher than will the latter. It is very important for managers to determine which shall be the standard recipe for each item produced. In establishments that use standard recipes, customers can reasonably expect the same quality food and drinks, which taste the same every time they come to the establishment.

SELLING. One of the principal aims of a subsystem for selling food and beverage products is maximizing customer satisfaction. In such not-for-profit establishments as the Mountain Bank, this is likely to be the sole purpose of the subsystem. In the Steak Shack, Frog's Pub, and other profit-oriented enterprises, the subsystem designed for maximizing customer satisfaction has a second goal: to maximize revenue.

The difference between the goals of the selling subsystems in these two types of establishments has to do with the difference between the noncommercial goals of one type of system and the commercial goals of the other.

Therefore, two possible goals of subsystems for selling are to maximize

1. customer satisfaction and
2. revenues.

To achieve the goal or goals of their subsystems for selling, food and beverage operators use several techniques. They are

1. sales-oriented menus,
2. visual sales devices, and
3. personal selling.

Sales-Oriented Menus.   A menu is a list of the items offered for sale in a food or beverage enterprise. Food menus normally list these items by category and in the same sequence in which they are customarily ordered. A dinner menu for the Steak Shack would list appetizers first, followed by soups, salads, entrees, vegetables, desserts, and the usual nonalcoholic beverage accompaniments for meals: coffee, tea, and milk. By contrast, beverage menus normally list contents by category alone. Typical categories include aperitifs, cocktails, spirits, wines, beers and ales, cordials, and dessert wines.

A good menu, however, is much more than a simple list of food or beverage items for sale. It is a sales tool that will influence customers' orders and the dollar amounts they spend. Good menus are carefully designed to be attractive and are written in language intended to promote sales. Some menus give special emphasis to the items that yield the greatest profit per sale.

Developing successful menus is a complex process. Many food and beverage operators use professional consultants, whose many years of experience are of invaluable assistance in preparing this important sales aid. Some of the important elements of menu-making are

1. selecting food/beverage items to include,
2. determining the best location for each category/item,
3. writing item descriptions that are sales-oriented, and
4. making numerous art and design decisions.

Developing an effective menu is one of the critical steps in food and beverage planning and will be discussed in greater detail in the following chapter.

Visual Sales Devices.   In addition to the menu, there are other visual means for increasing food and beverage sales. Small signs, colorful pictures, tent cards, and other printed items for tables or counters can make customers aware of menu items that they might not otherwise have considered. So can posters on walls or windows. Visual displays of desserts on a cart, lobsters in tanks, or racks of wine bottles provide similar suggestions to customers.

Another useful approach is to use service techniques that draw the attention of customers to items being artistically prepared or served. In some very fine restaurants, the preparation at tableside of such foods as Caesar salad, veal piccata, or cherries jubilee, by thoroughly professional servers, may provide visual suggestions to other diners. Similarly, sales can be influenced by skilled servers trained to carry attractive plates of food so that they are easily viewed by customers.

Personal Selling.   Personal selling requires that servers be trained to do more than simply take orders for food and beverage products. The servers in a food or beverage enterprise are the sales force of the establishment and have the potential to influence the number of sales and the particular items sold. In the Steak Shack, servers who are properly trained can often sell appetizers, soups, wines, or desserts to customers who might otherwise order entrees alone. In addition, servers can influence customer choices by suggesting those items that provide higher profit.

Servers adept at personal selling are usually those who provide greater customer satisfaction. And satisfied customers, who have enjoyed the food and beverages suggested by their servers, typically leave larger tips—partially because they are satisfied and partially because their checks are higher. After all, tips are commonly calculated as percentages of customers' total checks.

SERVING. The subsystem for serving food and beverage products is designed to deliver portions of food or drink to customers in a manner consistent with the goals of the establishment.

In addition to the food and beverage items featured, their enticing descriptions, and their location on the menu, a menu's design and the success of its interpretation of the establishment's theme is important in making the menu an effective sales tool.

Because the goals of the Steak Shack, the Mountain Bank, and Frog's Pub are quite different from one another, they have established differing subsystems for serving customers.

Service in the Steak Shack is typical of that found in many American restaurants. At the Steak Shack, once customers are seated, servers appear promptly to suggest drinks and distribute menus. Dinner orders are taken when drinks are served, with appetizers, soups, and dinner wines being suggested by the servers. Customers are invited to visit the salad bar. After the entrees, servers present dessert menus and suggest after-dinner drinks. Dishes are cleared by the server, who takes them to the kitchen. Checks are placed on tables as soon as the last items are served, and customers are asked to pay the cashier as they leave.

By contrast, employees of the Mountain Bank pay as they enter, then serve themselves by selecting from the array of food displayed. Employees are expected to clear their own dishes, by placing their trays on a conveyor belt located near the exit. One person is employed to clean the tables. Marecki Foods has chosen this method of serving to meet the bank's objective of quick, efficient service within the planned meal periods.

In Frog's Pub, the primary emphasis is on beverages, rather than food. Customers choosing tables can either obtain their own drinks quickly from a bartender and carry the drinks to tables or wait to order from a server. Customers at tables order foods from servers; those seated at the bar order food and drinks from a bartender. At lunch, extra servers are on duty to provide very fast food service. The servers are responsible for clearing all tables.

In all three establishments, washing dishes, glasses, and flatware is an important adjunct to the serving subsystem. Dirty dishes, glasses, and utensils are returned to the kitchen, separated into appropriate racks, then sent through a dishwashing machine. When clean, they are placed where needed to serve additional customers: clean dishes in the food preparation areas, glasses at the bar, and flatware in the dining room.

As we will see in the following chapter, there are a number of specific styles of service that professionals should have clearly in mind when planning food service operations. Each has specific characteristics, and each is more suited to achieve some goals than others.

OTHER FOOD AND BEVERAGE SUBSYSTEMS

The subsystems described above are the obvious ones, familiar to those who have worked in any food or beverage operation. These are the subsystems required for preparing and serving portions of food or beverages to customers. However, these are not the only subsystems needed to operate a food or beverage enterprise. There are many other subsystems in food and beverage operations that are required for proper system function—subsystems for accounting, marketing, training, controlling, and maintaining the equipment and the premises, among others. Because these are only indirectly related to our present, narrow focus—preparing and serving portions of food and beverage products—these other subsystems will be discussed in later chapters.

THE INTERRELATEDNESS OF FOOD AND BEVERAGE SUBSYSTEMS

At the beginning of this chapter a *system* was defined as a whole unit and *subsystems* as intrinsic parts of the unit, each of which is necessary for the whole unit to function properly. It should be apparent that all of the essential subsystems of a food or beverage operation—producing, serving, marketing, accounting, and controlling, among others—must function effectively and in concert for the operation to achieve its goals. The accounting subsystem, for example, must function properly to record revenues and expenses accurately, or poor management decisions may be made about the operation of the subsystem for preparing and serving portions of food and beverage product.

Within the subsystem for preparing and serving portions of product, the purchasing and receiving subsystems must work together in a coordinated way to provide the necessary foods and beverages for proper operation. If either of these two subsystems fails to operate properly, unfortunate consequences may result. For example, the production subsystem could be unable to prepare the proper quantity of food or beverage products or to prepare products of the proper quality. This, in turn, could result in customer dissatisfaction, or loss of revenue, or both of these. Similarly, failure of the storage subsystem to prevent spoilage and theft could produce analogous difficulties in the production subsystem: inability to produce the required products in the face of an inadequate supply of the necessary ingredients for particular food and beverage items. If the production subsystem does not turn out the necessary menu items at the appropriate quality and cost, the selling subsystem will not be able to perform its role in helping to meet system goals. Finally, if the subsystem for serving is not functioning as it should, sales may not reach required or intended levels, and profits will suffer. And if sales volume is lower than intended, items purchased in quantities suitable for higher levels of sales volume may also spoil, leading to unwarranted costs.

Because their behavior is interrelated, all subsystems in a given operation must be functioning properly and in a coordinated way for the food or beverage operation to achieve its goals. When subsystems do not perform as designed or intended, other subsystems are affected, and the overall system is unlikely to achieve its goals in the manner and to the extent possible.

Finally, it is quite possible that while all of the subsystems in a given food or beverage operation may be functioning as planned, the operation may fail to achieve its goals because of changes in the external environment. For example, an economic downturn that brings a high level of unemployment to an area is likely to reduce the number of customers patronizing certain kinds of food and beverage establishments. Facing a decline in the customer base, an operator should reexamine both goals and the subsystems designed to achieve those goals and make appropriate changes, as required, for survival. Food and beverage systems should be in constant interaction with their environments.

Now, having examined the operational subsystems required for producing portions of food and beverage products, we turn to some of the planning that must necessarily precede the establishment of food and beverage operations. Planning for food and beverage operations will be the subject of the next chapter.

SUMMARY

In this chapter, food and beverage operations are examined from a systems perspective. *System* and *subsystem* are defined, and subsystems for preparing and serving portions of food and drink are named: purchasing, receiving, storing, issuing, producing, selling, and serving. Examples of three different types of food and beverage operations are provided—Steak Shack, Mountain Bank, and Frog's Pub—and each of the food and beverage subsystems previously named is illustrated in terms of these three examples. Finally, the interrelatedness of these subsystems is emphasized and offered as a basis for comprehending the complexity of food and beverage operations.

QUESTIONS

1. Define each of the following terms:
   a. system
   b. subsystem
   c. perishable
   d. nonperishable
   e. sales history
   f. production sheet
   g. standard recipe
2. Identify the four critical issues that a purchasing subsystem must address and describe the significance of each.
3. List the three primary goals of the subsystem for receiving and explain their importance.
4. Identify the four goals of a subsystem for storing foods and beverages.

5. Describe the primary aims of a subsystem for issuing foods or beverages.

6. Name the four objectives that should be accomplished by a subsystem for preparing portions of food and beverage products.

7. Compare the goals of subsystems for selling portions of food or beverage products in profit-orientated operations with those in operations that are not profit oriented.

8. List and describe three common techniques used to achieve the goals of a subsystem for selling portions of food and beverage products.

9. Describe the purpose of a subsystem for serving portions of food and beverage products.

10. List four food and beverage subsystems that are only indirectly related to the subsystem for preparing and serving portions of food and beverage products.

11. Describe the interrelatedness of the seven subsystems for preparing and serving portions of food and beverage products.

12. Write brief descriptions of the seven subsystems for preparing and serving portions of food and beverage products in any establishment with which you are familiar.

13. Visit a nearby food or beverage operation with which you are unfamiliar. Keep a systems perspective in mind as you do so. State the goals of the system from your point of view. Is the system achieving these goals? Why, or why not? Do you see each of the seven subsystems in evidence in this establishment? Describe each briefly.

Planning Food and Beverage Facilities

7

LEARNING OBJECTIVES

After reading and studying this chapter, you should be able to:

1. *List and discuss the necessary prerequisites to planning a food and beverage facility.*
2. *Define the term product line and identify the elements in the service product line offered by food and beverage operations.*
3. *Identify and describe eight styles of service for food and three for bars.*
4. *List and discuss six principal considerations in the layout and design of a food area.*
5. *List and discuss the three major considerations in the layout and design of a dining area.*
6. *List and discuss the three major considerations in the layout and design of a beverage area.*
7. *Identify the seven principal considerations in menu development and describe the significance of each.*

INTRODUCTION

In the previous chapter the underlying similarities among food and beverage establishments were shown by using examples from three specific operations: The Steak Shack, Mountain Bank, and Frog's Pub. In addition, these served to illustrate the subsystems common to all operations preparing and serving portions of foods and beverages, to demonstrate the interrelationships of these subsystems, and to familiarize students with the basic subsystems they will work with if they pursue careers in food and beverage operations.

The previous discussions of food and beverage subsystems serve as the foundation for this chapter, which will provide students with an understanding of some of the important concepts that lie at the heart of planning food and beverage facilities. Specifically, students will gain insights into four key factors in food and beverage planning:

1. Product line
2. Styles of service
3. Facilities layout and design
4. Menu preparation

PREREQUISITES TO PLANNING FOOD AND BEVERAGE FACILITIES

The first step in planning a food or beverage facility is to establish a concept—an imaginative and unifying idea of the operation that will serve to focus the resources required for its creation. This concept originates with the owner or with some other individual or firm commissioned to create it.

One element in the concept is the type of establishment the operation is to be. Some of the many possibilities were discussed in Chapter 5, including fast service operations, fine dining establishments, family restaurants, cafeterias, ethnic restaurants, specialty restaurants, bars, taverns, and cocktail lounges, among others.

Each of these can attract specific customers. Ethnic restaurants, for example, attract those who seek the particular foods characteristic of a given ethnic group—Chinese, Italian, Greek, or Indian, among many other possibilities. Fine dining establishments typically attract those who have the financial means and the desire for the higher-quality foods and more elegant service offered by these establishments. Specialty restaurants attract customers looking for the specialties offered—steak, seafood, pasta, pancakes, or some other. Some food service operations—in schools, colleges, nursing homes, and hospitals, for example—typically serve those who have little or no choice of places to eat and often make extraordinary efforts to please their customers (some of whom think of themselves as captive diners). Similarly, neighborhood taverns and bars tend to attract customers who live nearby, and airport bars typically attract transient customers who are waiting for planes to arrive or depart. Each establishment attracts customers who patronize it because of the food, or the beverages, or the sevice, or the atmosphere, or the location, or some combination of these, and because they are willing to pay the prices charged by the operator.

In order for a food and beverage operation to be successful, there must be an adequate number of potential customers within reasonable distance who will be willing to patronize it. In addition, the establishment must attract a sufficient number of actual customers to enable it to meet its goals. Location, then, is a key element in determining whether or not a given type of establishment will succeed.

Some locations would not provide sufficient numbers of potential customers to support particular types of establishments. For example, fine dining establishments are normally unsuccessful in working-class communities, principally because those living in the community cannot afford to pay the prices such establishments must charge to be profitable. In addition, residents of the community sometimes dislike the food such restaurants offer and the service they provide. Similarly, some ethnic restaurants fail to succeed in certain locations because the type of food they offer does not appeal to a large enough segment of the population. By the same token, bars and taverns are typically unsuccessful in communities where the consumption of alcoholic beverages is discouraged by social or religious custom.

To assess the potential for the successful operation of a particular type of food or beverage establishment in a specific location, it is advisable to obtain such relevant information as: the number of potential customers for the type of food, beverages, and service planned; the extent to which there are competitive establishments; the cost of constructing the necessary facility; the availability of a suitable labor pool; the dollar amounts potential customers would be likely to spend; and the potential for profitable operation at the projected level of revenue and expense. All the relevant considerations would be included in a *feasibility study*—the name given to an investigation of a given project's likelihood for success. Further discussion of feasibility studies and their importance in planning hospitality facilities can be found in Chapter 10.

For purposes of the present chapter, we will assume that the individuals planning a potential food or beverage operation have attended to the necessary preliminaries, having determined that the type of establishment planned can be successful in the location selected. At this point, a potential operator must become familiar with a number of laws and regulations affecting food and beverage operations.

Any applicable laws and regulations—federal, state, or local—must be taken into account. Health codes, fire codes, building codes, zoning regulations, and licensing requirements are among the most common. Each of these provides specific direction about what an owner can and cannot do in creating and operating a food or beverage enterprise. These vary considerably from one state to another and even from city to city within a given state. For example, health codes in some states require that operators provide the staff with lavatories other than those intended for customers. A facility built without staff lavatories would probably require costly reconstruction before it would be permitted to open. And this is just one example of the many possibilities.

Before proceeding to plan facilities, individuals lacking full knowledge of the laws and regulations that apply in given locales must have professional advice from lawyers, architects, food and beverage consultants, and others with the necessary expertise. Failure to factor this information into the planning process can lead to costly errors.

Having attended to all the necessary prerequisites discussed above, the next step in the planning process is to direct attention to the products that will be offered to customers of the establishment.

PRODUCT LINE

Product line is a term used in marketing and retailing to refer to a group of products having similar characteristics. Some common examples of product lines are shoes, luggage, or jewelry. We will borrow that term from retailing and use it to mean the group of service products that a hospitality enterprise offers, based on the concept developed for the establishment. The hospitality service product line offered by food and beverage operations has three elements:

1. Food, beverages, or both of these
2. Services
3. Ambiance

Every food service operation has a group of service products that includes all the food products the operator intends to offer, at present and into the future. Some, such as Kentucky Fried Chicken or Red Lobster, specialize in one type of food—chicken, fish, or some other—and offer additional items that serve as accompaniments to those featured. Any number of specialized food products can be found as key elements in food operations today. Sandwiches, pasta, pizza, hamburgers, crepes, ice cream, or hot dogs are all good examples.

Some operators choose to offer an entirely different service product line, consisting of beverages—all the beverage products an operator intends to offer to customers, now and into the future. Bars and taverns specialize in beverage products.

In some establishments, both food products and beverage products are available to customers. In a restaurant devoted to fine dining, for example, the operator typically offers both beverage products and food products. Similarly, some taverns also offer meals to their customers. But the service product line offered in food and/or beverage establishments has more to it than specific food and beverage products.

Another important element in any food or beverage service product line is *service*—the range of services associated with the specific food and beverage products. This second element includes all the services the operator intends to offer to customers, now and into the future. The more obvious services are the styles of service adopted for dining rooms—American, French, or some other, as well as variations on the basic styles, such as weekly buffets, possible use of dessert carts, or occasional use of table-side cooking. Other services include food preparation in the kitchen, friendliness on the part of the staff, dishwashing, valet parking, attended coat rooms, background music, special attention to birthday celebrants, complimentary photographs of customers—even entertainment: musicians, clowns, or magicians, for example.

The third element in the hospitality service product line in food and beverage operations is perhaps best identified as the *ambiance* of the establishment. This element includes those essential details—some tangible, some intangible—that give a specific food and beverage operation its distinctive character. These essential details include theme, lighting, uniforms, furnishings, cleanliness, fixtures, decorations, table settings, and any other related features that customers see or sense and that contribute to the total atmosphere of the establishment.

These elements—food, beverages, services, and ambiance—are the components of the hospitality service product line offered by any food and beverage operation. Some choose to add such other product lines as retail foods, gifts, or souvenirs. In this text, we will limit our discussion to the primary service product line cited above and treat all others as being outside the normal scope of food or beverage operations.

The type of food or beverage establishment planned helps define the product line that will be offered. If the type is ethnic, then the product line will emphasize those food items common to the particular ethnic type. If it is a specialty steak house, the product line will obviously emphasize steak. The product line in a food or beverage establishment includes a complete list of all items that the establishment is prepared to offer over time, whether or not they appear on a menu on any given day. Thus, the product line should include every food item that management intends to include on menus at one time or another.

Whatever constitutes the product line to be offered by a particular operation, it is desirable that all elements be identified and defined in advance because much of the planning will be based on the components of the product line. For example, the specific food products will be the basis for the menu that will be offered to customers, and detailed information about these items will facilitate proper kitchen planning.

This list will be much larger than the menu offered to customers on any given day. Menus change, and the list of items that constitute the menu for a particular day should be drawn from the predetermined list.

It is important to recognize that the lists of items that constitute the product line never reach a state in which they can be considered final or complete. Change is constant and continuous in hospitality operations: Dishes are being added to and removed from the list of food products; new drinks and brands are being added to the list of beverage products, while others are being eliminated; any number of changes may be made that will affect the service and the ambiance. It is critical, however, to develop preliminary lists of the particular items that will constitute the product line at opening because of their central role in planning.

In establishing the list of food products for a particular operation and the subsequent menu that will be offered at opening, an operator should have knowledge of:

1. customers' food and service preferences;
2. prices acceptable to customers;
3. skills required to prepare selected items;
4. availability of labor with the necessary skills at suitable wage rates.

For example, the final selection of particular pieces of equipment for a kitchen should not be done until the preliminary list of food products has been developed. The question of whether or not a given piece of equipment should be purchased can best be answered by referring to that list. If it is needed to prepare items appearing on the list, it should be purchased; if there are no menu selections requiring its use, it should not be purchased unless a specific future need can be predicted.

An establishment that serves only pizza obviously needs kitchen equipment that is very different from that required in a luncheonette serving only soups and sandwiches. And an ethnic restaurant serving Chinese food prepared in woks needs very different kitchen equipment from that of a neighborhood restaurant offering an Italian menu. Similarly, a restaurant specializing in deep-fried and broiled menu items needs different equipment from that of one offering convenience foods heated in microwave ovens. Kitchen equipment, once purchased and installed, limits the possibilities for adding new items to the list of food products. Great care must be exercised in determining the selections that will be offered—on both the original menu and future variations. Therefore, establishing the list of food products is clearly the first key element in planning a food and beverage facility.

Over the long term, many food and beverage operations elect to change the original product line, adding and deleting a few items or even making far more radical changes. They may not be able to do so easily. It may be necessary to teach the staff new skills so that they can prepare new menu items; and it may be necessary to purchase new equipment or even to redesign some parts of the facility.

STYLES OF SERVICE

A second key element in the planning of food or beverage facilities is determining the style of service to offer. As indicated in Chapter 5, there are a number of possible styles of service; and the operator must establish the one that will best achieve the goals of the food or beverage facility. He or she must choose one or

more of the styles of service described in the following list or develop some hybrid
based on these:

1. American service
2. Russian service
3. French service
4. English service
5. Cafeteria service
6. Buffet service
7. Takeout/delivery service
8. Room service

Cafeteria service (top) *and buffet service* (bottom) *are among the several styles
of service used by food service establishments. Both types shown rely on food
displays and self-service, minimizing service staff and giving the customers freedom
to help themselves. (Top: courtesy Business Food Services, Inc.; bottom: courtesy
Stouffer Concourse Hotel at Los Angeles International Airport.)*

There are three styles of bar service, each of which is associated with one of the three types of bars. These are:

1. Front bars
2. Service bars
3. Special-purpose bars

All of these will be discussed in the following sections.

Food Service

In most well-organized food service operations and in all fine dining establishments, there are standard procedures for serving food—serving techniques that management believes will provide maximum customer satisfaction. Most use one of the following, with adaptations, as required.

AMERICAN SERVICE. American service is characterized by food portioned and plated in the kitchen and carried to diners by servers. Virtually everyone has experienced some form of American service. In too many cases it has come to mean simply transporting plated food from the kitchen to the dining room and placing the plates in front of diners in any manner that suits the server. Sometimes the food is served from the right, sometimes from the left, and occasionally from across the table. In some establishments, plates of food are even passed from one diner to another until they reach the individuals who have ordered them.

In the view of the authors, none of these methods of delivering food should really be called American service. These are simply ways of transporting food expeditiously—similar to placing cartons of goods on a warehouse conveyor belt, and just about as inviting. True American service involves a great deal more than that.

In proper American service, plates of food are placed before diners from the left. To do this correctly, servers use their left hands. Beverages are served from the right with the right hand. Plates and glassware are removed from the right. When a course is removed, the flatware for that course is also removed, even if it has not been used. At the conclusion of the main meal, prior to coffee and dessert, all plates, glassware, and salt and pepper shakers are removed and the table is crumbed. Appropriate silver is served with dessert.

American service has the advantage of being relatively simple, and comparatively little training is required for servers to achieve proficiency.

RUSSIAN SERVICE. Russian service is characterized by food arranged on serving platters in the kitchen for maximum eye appeal, then carried to a serving stand near the table. The server uses the right hand to place empty warm plates in front of each diner from the diner's right. The platter of food is shown to those at the table for their visual delight, then transferred from serving platter to diners' plates. To do this, the server balances the platter on the left hand, then uses fork and spoon with the right hand to serve the food—which is done from the diner's left. Beverages are served from the right. All dishes, glassware, and flatware are removed from the right.

Russian service, sometimes mistakenly called French service, is used in many of the finer restaurants of Europe. It is elegant: Food arrives at the table beautifully arranged on silver serving platters and is presented to diners prior to being transferred to their plates. It also has the advantage of facilitating the delivery of food at the correct serving temperature—a common problem with American service. The serving platters are very warm, and the plates set in front of diners are also warm. Both contribute to maintaining the proper temperature for the food ordered. Russian service is particularly well suited for serving soups, which come to the table in hot tureens and are served into warm bowls.

A variation on Russian service is often used at large banquets. Servers wearing white gloves will carry large silver serving trays, each of which will be used for a single menu item—filet mignon, for example. A server will proceed around a table placing single portions of meat before diners on plates previously set in place. That server will be followed by others who have food to accompany the meat—potatoes and vegetables, most commonly. In this fashion, large numbers of people can be served very quickly with both elegance and grace—if the servers are suitably trained.

FRENCH SERVICE. The most expensive and most elegant service used in restaurants is French service. It is sometimes called *gueridon service*, named after the specially equipped cart or trolley on which food is transported from kitchen to dining room: a gueridon, equipped with gas burner for table-side cooking.

French service requires a staff of four:

chef de rang, who is in charge of the service staff. A chef de rang takes diners' orders, supervises the service, finishes the preparation of some foods on the gueridon at table-side, and attends to any carving, slicing, or boning of meat, fish, or poultry.

demi chef de rang, who assists the chef de rang, takes drink orders, and serves food under the chef de rang's direction.

commis de rang, a waiter in training who will serve some items, clear the tables, and perform other duties as directed.

commis de suite, who takes orders to the kitchen and brings food from the kitchen on the gueridon. He will assist in clearing tables and perform other duties as needed.

In French service, the gueridon is wheeled to a position close to the diners' table and is used by the *chef de rang* to complete the cooking of food. He expertly carves or slices the meat, fish, or poultry, then places the food on plates. It is served from the diners' right. Beverages are also served from the right, and all plates and glassware are removed from the right. One can appreciate the great expense, skill, and time required to perform this kind of service. For that reason, it is used only in the most expensive restaurants.

Additionally, French service requires more square feet of floor space per seat than other types of dining room service. Aisles must be wider than normal to accommodate the gueridon, and tables must be placed farther apart than normal to provide room for the *chef de rang* to finish the preparation of the food.

French service takes a considerable amount of time compared with other forms of service. For that reason, establishments that use it must charge high prices to compensate for the relatively fewer number of customers they can serve in the course of a meal period.

ENGLISH SERVICE. English service is seldom, if ever, used in restaurants. It would only be used in those few private homes that employ a staff of servants. English service is often thought of as "mine host" service, because the main entree—a roast of beef or lamb, or a turkey, for example—is placed in front of the host who carves and plates it at the head of the table. A server then takes each plate and sets it in front of the diner from the diner's right. Beverages are also served from the right. Vegetables, potatoes, and other foods are either put on plates from a side stand prior to service or passed from one diner to the next in bowls—family style. All dishes and glassware are removed from the right. As with American service, the table is cleared of flatware, glassware, and salt and pepper, and the table is crumbed prior to dessert.

CAFETERIA SERVICE. Cafeteria service is characterized by prepared foods displayed so that customers can view the array of offerings prior to making selections. Hot foods are in warmers and cold foods are packed in ice or stored in reach-through refrigerators. Many foods are preplated for the convenience of diners selecting those items. Diners typically have trays and proceed to the area where the kinds of foods they want are displayed. If a customer wants a sandwich, he goes to the area where the prepared and wrapped sandwiches are displayed and takes the one he chooses. If he wants a hot entree, he goes to that part of the display where they are kept; and a server plates the item selected by the customer. Each item is usually priced separately. After the customer finishes making selections, he proceeds to a cashier who adds and totals the prices of all items selected. The customer pays the cashier and takes the tray to a table.

Variations of this procedure are common. In some cafeterias, customers receive a bill at the cashier's station but do not pay until they exit the restaurant. In others, employees may carry customers' trays to tables.

There are several types of cafeteria service. They are:

1. Straight line
2. By-pass line
3. Shopping center

Straight Line.   As the name suggests, in straight line service, one customer follows another along a long line of displayed foods. Each customer reaches the cashier in turn, at the end of the display. This form of service is perhaps the easiest to set up but has the disadvantage of providing the slowest service. The speed of the line matches that of the slowest customer.

By-Pass Line.   To speed up service, many cafeterias have established by-pass lines. These enable customers to skip a section of the cafeteria line and proceed to the section where the foods they wish to buy are displayed. For example, many cafeterias have separate sections for salads and hot items. Customers who want only salads go to that section of the display, select their salads, and get back in line at a point beyond the hot food section. Those seeking hot foods go to the hot food section, make their selections, then proceed to the cashier.

There are several variations on the by-pass line. One variation resembles the teeth in a saw, with foods displayed on counters that are at angles to one another. Another variation has recessed sections in the line, so that individuals who do not want any foods in the recessed section pass it by, proceeding to another part of the line.

Shopping Center.   The shopping center approach is to arrange foods by type at *islands*—free-standing stations. It eliminates the appearance of a single line. Customers take trays to the specific stations containing the foods they wish to buy, make their selections, then proceed to a cashier to pay. This approach is becoming increasingly popular, particularly in establishments where many customers arrive at one time.

Cafeteria service has several advantages over table service. Customers can obtain their food selections quickly and consume their meals in a very short time. Large numbers of people can be served very quickly in a cafeteria setting. Customers can select whatever they wish—anything from a full meal to a cup of coffee. There is no pressure to take a great amount of food, although the better cafeterias have very attractive displays, and frequently customers will take more food than they intended because it looks so appealing. Since customers serve themselves, they typically do not have to tip servers.

Cafeterias make it possible for people with limited incomes to eat out more frequently. They are particularly popular in the southern part of the United States, where a large number of retired people are on limited budgets, and in schools where large numbers of students must be served at one time.

BUFFET SERVICE. Buffet service differs from cafeteria service in several ways. Trays are not used: Customers take plates and proceed to select and place on their plates foods displayed on the buffet. Items on the buffet are not individually priced: There is one fixed price for the meal regardless of the items selected or the quantities of food taken by customers.

Restaurants often use buffet service, either for such functions as wedding receptions or for specific meals—breakfast, or Sunday brunch, for example. Buffet service is sometimes used in restaurants as the primary means of serving food. This type of service has the advantage of minimizing the service staff required and offering faster service. Because diners do not have to study menus, wait for a server to take the order, and wait for food to be prepared and delivered, it can be much faster than table service. Patrons merely go to the buffet when they are ready, make their selections, and return to their tables to eat the food selected. One disadvantage is that management has less control over the amount of food consumed. Typically, customers help themselves and can normally go back to the buffet as many times as they like.

Many hotels and restaurants schedule buffets frequently to use up excess food. After all, buffets typically do not have set menus, except for a few specific items, and this allows the chef considerable latitude to prepare many different items—and even to use up leftovers.

TAKEOUT AND DELIVERY SERVICES. Takeout and delivery services are becoming increasingly popular. These forms of service are characterized by food being consumed off premises. In many establishments, customers are given a choice of coming to the establishment to pick up food or of having it delivered to their homes or offices. Many restaurants offer takeout and delivery services in addition to their regular table service. Although there may be some extra cost associated with packaging foods for consumption off premises, takeout and delivery services effectively increase the sales capacity of the establishment without necessitating an increase in its physical size.

Perhaps the most popular types of takeout and delivery establishments are those associated with common ethnic foods—Chinese food and pizza. Many of the food service establishments featuring these foods do not even have seating for customers. Because of this, they find it possible to operate in relatively small quarters and thus keep their operating costs to a minimum.

ROOM SERVICE. Although room service is most commonly associated with hotels, hospitals also provide room service for their patients. This type of service differs from others in one major way: Food is moved to and served in the room of the guest or patient.

Room service is not classified as takeout or delivery service. The food does not leave the premises, and it is served in a guest's or patient's room rather than in a traditional dining facility. This type of service is particularly labor intensive, typically requiring a greater number of servers per meal than other forms of service. In hotels offering room service on a twenty-four–hour schedule, both kitchen and service staff must be on hand to prepare room service orders when the dining room is normally closed. Hotels charge higher prices for items on the room service menu than for equivalent items served in traditional dining rooms. Although they charge higher menu prices, however, hotels often lose money on room service, offering it merely as an accommodation to guests. The higher labor costs associated with room service operation commonly make it unprofitable.

Beverage Service

The term *beverage* requires definition. Beverages are those alcoholic and nonalcoholic drinks typically prepared by bartenders, rather than the items listed as beverages on food menus—coffee, tea, and milk, among them.

Food being delivered to a hotel room. Typically requiring an increased kitchen and service staff due to advance preparation, room service makes menu items more expensive than in traditional dining facilities. (Courtesy Wyndham Hotels and Resorts.)

As indicated previously, three types of bars are used in beverage operations; and an understanding of beverage operations requires that one know about these three and comprehend their differences. The three types of bars are:

1. Front bar
2. Service bar
3. Special-purpose bar

FRONT BAR. A front bar is a fixed counter for beverage service, open for business on a regularly scheduled basis, and directly accessible to customers. Front bars are permanently fixed in particular locations within establishments. Many of these establishments are open long hours daily, but the days and hours of operation are determined by owners within the parameters of state and local laws.

Front bars are the most common of the three types of bars. At the typical front bar, customers walk to the bar, where they are greeted by a bartender who takes their orders and prepares and serves their drinks. Beyond the point at which the drink is served, there are many possible variations. Customers may or may not consume their drinks at the bar. In some establishments, customers can remain at the bar, sitting on stools or standing as they drink. In others, customers may carry their drinks elsewhere. Sometimes the bartender acts as a cashier, collecting for each drink as it is served. Sometimes the bartender records a given customer's drinks on a paper form called a *guest check*, which the customer settles before leaving. Occasionally, there is a cashier at the bar who does not act as a bartender but who serves as cashier for the establishment.

SERVICE BAR. A service bar is a counter at which a bartender prepares drinks but does not serve them directly to customers. Drink orders are given to the bartender by servers who take the orders from customers and serve the drinks when ready.

Service bars are frequently located in kitchens and similar areas that are neither visible nor accessible to customers. In other instances, a service bar may be visible but not accessible: Some service areas are too small for customer access to be feasible; others are behind glass walls; some are in establishments in which the level and extent of service is such that any appearance of self-service would be unseemly.

Some service bars are permanently located in fixed positions. Others are mobile—bars on wheels that can be moved from one location to another as needs dictate. Still others are temporary—folding tables set up quickly, possibly draped or otherwise covered, then dismantled when no longer needed. What differentiates service bars from others is not the degree of permanence but the fact that customers are not permitted access to a service bar. Customer access is not a characteristic of a service bar.

SPECIAL-PURPOSE BAR. A special-purpose bar is one that, although directly accessible to customers, is open only for a defined period to accommodate a special need. Special-purpose bars are most commonly used in banquet or catering businesses to accommodate guests at special functions—parties, dances, or the receptions preceding special events. At special-purpose bars, customers have direct access to a bartender: They order and receive drinks just as at a front bar. But although a front bar is open on a regularly scheduled basis, the special-purpose bar is open only to accommodate the beverage service requirements of those present at the event. When the event is over, the special-purpose bar is closed. Thus, special-purpose bars are open for varying periods—some long, others short, depending on the length of the event.

Special-purpose bars can be permanent, mobile, or temporary. Some are permanent, built into the physical structure of a banquet room. Others are mobile—bars on wheels that can be moved from one location to another. Still others are merely tables, or counters, folding or otherwise, that are fitted out to be used as bars when required.

In planning for beverage service, it is necessary to give thought to the purpose a bar or bars will serve in the establishment. In some establishments, managers consciously decide to restrict beverage service to a service bar located in the kitchen. Some may do this because they do not like the physical appearance of a front bar in the establishment. Others may do it to reduce the noise level in an establishment: Bars are typically noisy. Still others may do it to discourage patronage by those who would be interested only in sitting at a front bar. In contrast, some restaurant operators elect to have both front bars and service bars. This arrangement makes it possible to provide beverage service in the dining room without placing unwarranted demands on the front bar and also to use the front bar as a holding area for customers who are waiting to be seated. Many of these establishments provide tables in the front bar area to facilitate its use as both cocktail lounge and waiting area for diners. Other establishments having side rooms that can be used to accommodate groups for functions often use special-purpose bars to serve the guests attending these functions. Some, in fact, have a front bar, a service bar, and special-purpose bars, the number of which is limited only by the number of functions that can be accommodated at one time.

Another consideration in planning for beverage service is the type of service that will be used for wines served to guests in a dining room. Essentially, *wines* are the fermented juices of fruits—grapes, principally—although there are some exceptions. There are three types of wines: sparkling, still, and fortified.

Still wines are those that do not continue to ferment after the wine is bottled. Cabernet sauvignon and chablis are two of the better-known still wines. *Sparkling wines* are those in which the fermentation process continues after bottling. This produces the carbon dioxide that gives sparkling wines their characteristic "fizziness." Champagne is the best known of the sparkling wines. *Fortified wines* are still wines to which brandy has been added, thus increasing the alcoholic content. Sherry is among the best-known fortified wines.

Proper planning for beverage service requires knowledge of the techniques for serving wines. These are described as follows:

Still Wines.   Still wines may be sold by the glass or by the bottle. The finer the wine, the more likely it is to be sold by the bottle. When wine is sold by the bottle, the following is a commonly used serving procedure:

After taking the order, the server brings the wine to the table and presents it for approval to the guest who placed the order. The server holds the bottle in a manner that facilitates inspection of the label. When approved, the bottle is opened, which normally entails removing the cork with a corkscrew. The cork is inspected by the server to be sure that it remains moist and that its odor indicates a good wine—one that has not gone bad. The cork is then presented to the guest for inspection. Next, a small amount of the wine is poured in the guest's glass to be examined for clarity, color, and aroma. If these are satisfactory, the guest sips the wine. If the taste is satisfactory, the guest approves the wine and the server pours for those at the table who will be drinking it. If the bottle is not empty, the server leaves it on or near the table for refilling glasses later in the meal.

Sparkling Wines.   Sparkling wines are not normally sold by the glass because opened bottles lose their effervescent character. When they are sold by the bottle, service technique is essentially the same as that for still wines. The major exception is in the removal of the cork, which never entails the use of a corkscrew: The corks in bottles of sparkling wine are removed by hand, very carefully, to prevent the cork from being projected some distance by the pressure in the bottle. As the cork is removed, it produces the "pop" that is characteristic of sparkling wines.

Fortified Wines.   Fortified wines are not normally sold by the bottle. They are sold by the glass and poured at the bar by a bartender.

Clearly, it is important in planning any food or beverage establishment to determine in advance the type of food service and beverage service that will be offered so that equipment and space needs can be factored into the planning.

FACILITY LAYOUT AND DESIGN

Once the product line has been established, it becomes feasible to design an appropriate facility, to select the specific kinds of equipment required and the number of pieces of each, and to plan suitable equipment layout for each area of the facility.

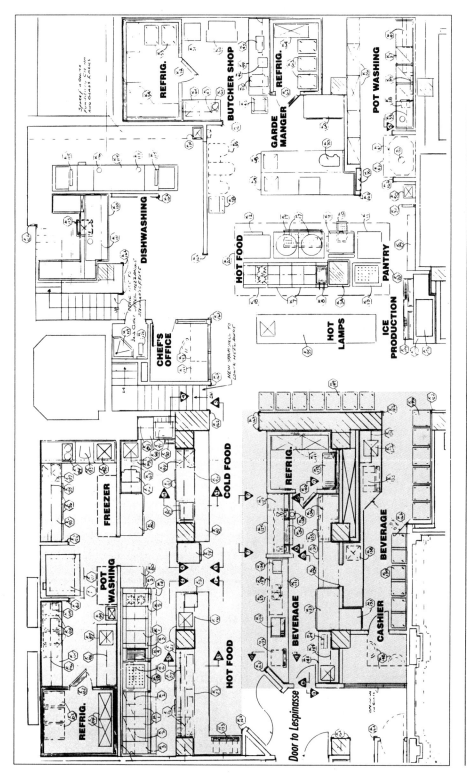

The floor plan of the 5,000-square-foot kitchen designed for the St. Regis Hotel in New York City. Actually two kitchens in one, the facility will serve the hotel's signature restaurant, its smaller food court, cocktail lounge, room service, all functions and banquets, as well as staff meals. In consideration of the kitchen's volume of production, the design of the space, equipment, lighting, ventilation, and materials and traffic flow are all geared to accommodate and maximize efficiency in its day-to-day operations. (Blueprint courtesy Anthony J. Gaeta, Inc., International Food Service Consultants, Bay Shore, New York.)

For the present discussion, we will assume that food and beverage operations have three parts. The first is a food area, where the food products are prepared. This includes the kitchen and such related facilities as food storerooms, refrigerators, and freezers. The second is a dining area where customers may consume food, or food and beverages. The third is a beverage area, where the beverage products are prepared. This includes at least one bar and at least one storage facility for liquor, beer, and wine. If an establishment has a front bar, we will consider it part of the beverage area, rather than part of the dining facility.

It is clear that there can be many variations on these basics. Most food service establishments, for example, do not sell alcoholic beverages and thus have no need to plan bars. In contrast, some beverage service establishments do not sell meals and have no need for kitchens. And some food service establishments, which operate on a takeout or delivery basis, have no need for bars or dining facilities. Therefore, in the discussion that follows, the reader should understand that comparatively few establishments need to plan for all three of the areas described.

Layout and Design of a Food Area

The food area is that part of the facility where food products are prepared. It includes subareas for the functions listed below. Note the extent to which they correspond to subsystems discussed in the previous chapter.

Purchasing.   This is normally an office with a desk for working, a file cabinet for keeping records, a computer work station, and space for meeting quietly with the sales representatives of vendors.

Receiving.   This is an area that contains equipment used to verify that the goods received conform to the orders placed. Quantity, quality, and price must all be checked. To do this properly, it is necessary to plan an area that is easily accessible to delivery drivers and large enough to hold an entire normal delivery.

Storing and Issuing.   This area normally provides three types of facilities for storing foods: dry, refrigerated, and frozen. A dry storage facility, typically called a *storeroom*, is maintained at normal room temperature. It is used to keep a reasonable supply of bags, bottles, boxes, and jars of food that need not be refrigerated or frozen. This storeroom must be large enough so that shelves can be constructed and foods can be stored in an orderly manner on those shelves. Refrigerated facilities—reach-in or walk-in refrigerators— are used to store meats, fish, vegetables, dairy products, and any other foods that will spoil if not kept cold. Freezers—reach-in or walk-in types—are required to store those items that are purchased in a frozen state.

Producing. In a food service operation, this is the kitchen. Most kitchens require two production areas: one for advance preparation and another for the final preparation of foods immediately before they are ready to be served. The advance preparation area is for basic preparation of foods that will later be transferred to another area for final preparation. The final preparation, or finishing area is for making foods ready for service.

Serving. This is the location where finished products are transferred from preparation staff to servers. This is true even in self-service operations—cafeterias and buffets among them—where the customers are also the servers.

The layout and design of an efficient food area, one that contributes to smooth day-to-day operation, is critical. Efficient layout and design takes the following into account:

1. Space
2. Equipment
3. Lighting
4. Ventilation
5. Flow of materials
6. Traffic flow

SPACE. If a food area is to run efficiently, adequate space should be provided for the activities associated with purchasing, receiving, storing and issuing, producing, and serving food. The amount of space allocated for each area will vary from one establishment to another, depending on such considerations as products, type of service, type and amount of equipment, and number of personnel required to prepare and serve food. For example, a fine dining establishment with an extended menu is likely to require more preparation area than a limited menu restaurant with five entrees that require only microwaving. While it may be possible to plan sufficient space for every kitchen need in a new facility, older facilities being converted to food service use may lack the ideal amount of space for a specific use. In such circumstances, compromise may be necessary.

EQUIPMENT. Two considerations determine the equipment to purchase: products and preparation methods.

Product line is a key determinant in equipment selection. If the line is to include Chinese food, the equipment needs will be very different from those in operations featuring chicken or Italian food. Similarly, specialty restaurants serving pizza require different equipment from those serving hamburgers. In contrast, family restaurants with varied menus require more varieties of equipment than do specialty restaurants.

The equipment in food areas varies considerably from one establishment to another. In some, one might see stock pots, kettles, mixers, steamers, and the other heavy equipment characteristic of kitchens preparing large quantities of food from raw, primary ingredients. This heavy equipment may include broilers, ranges, conventional ovens, microwave ovens, deep-fat fryers, and a number of other possibilities. In other food areas, the equipment may be limited to a few counters used to arrange food on small platters just before they are microwaved. Needs vary from one operation to another and choice of equipment should be based on the food products prepared.

Many food items can be prepared a number of different ways, and it is important to establish a preparation method for each food item before purchasing equipment. Chicken, for example, can be fried, sauteed, deep fried, baked, roasted, boiled, or broiled. If an operation establishes deep frying as the proper preparation method for a particular chicken entree, then a deep fryer—or more than one—should be on the list of equipment to purchase. Similarly, if soups are to be prepared from stocks made in the establishment, then suitable equipment to produce the stocks—stock pots, or steam kettles, depending largely on volume—should be on the list. If the product list includes a large number of frozen convenience foods, it would be necessary to purchase a larger freezer than would be required if the restaurant were to use mostly raw, fresh ingredients. The number of examples illustrating this point would be endless.

It is important to recognize that once equipment decisions have been made and the equipment has been purchased and installed, it may be extremely difficult to change the product list in any significant way. For example, some specialty restaurants have found it impossible to enlarge or change their menus because they have neither the appropriate equipment nor the space in the kitchen to add that equipment.

LIGHTING. For employees to work efficiently, they must have sufficient light. In some operations, light is required so that employees can attend to the detailed work required for the elegant presentation of foods. In others, light may be required so that employees can read portion scales and be certain that they are providing the correct number of ounces or grams in a portion.

The amount of light provided by a lighting source is measured in lumens. Light is quickly dispersed, however, and the amount of light at a particular workstation will be considerably less than what is given off nearer to the lighting source itself. More light will be available at the workstations if wall and ceiling surfaces are light colors: Light colors reflect light; dark colors absorb it. The amount of light on a surface, such as a work table, is measured in lumens per square foot, or foot-candles. One lumen per square foot is equal to one *foot-candle*, a term whose origin precedes the invention of electric lights. A foot-candle of light is the amount of light that can be measured at a distance of one foot from an ordinary candle. Lighting experts suggest that employees need at least 60 foot-candles of light for ordinary work and about 110 foot-candles of light for detailed work.

VENTILATION. Adequate ventilation is another basic requirement for people at work. The air they breathe should be clean—free from smoke and other pollutants. And it should be at a temperature at which they can work in reasonable comfort.

Because kitchens produce smoke and odors, the air must be changed continually. If not, air quality will deteriorate as levels of smoke and odors rise. In addition, temperatures in the kitchen will rise quickly from stoves, ovens, and other heat-producing equipment in use, and the air will become unhealthy. The proper rate of air exchange in a kitchen is determined by the type of cooking, the type and amount of equipment used, and the height of the ceiling. In heavily used kitchens the rate of air exchange may be as high as fifty times per hour.

It is important to note that the air pressure in the dining room and other rooms should be higher than that in the kitchen. When such is the case, air will flow from the dining room to the kitchen, not the other way around. If air pressure were higher in the kitchen, the dining room would receive the smoke and odors from the kitchen.

Fresh air may come from any of three different sources: other rooms in the facility, outside, or a ventilation system in the establishment.

MATERIALS FLOW. Work areas and equipment should be arranged so that foods can proceed smoothly and logically from the receiving area to the storing and issuing area. From there, foods should move smoothly to the producing area for advance preparation and final preparation, and from there to the serving area.

To facilitate this smooth and even flow, the receiving area and all equipment required for receiving is typically located near a rear entrance to a food service facility. The storing and issuing area and the attendant equipment and facilities—storeroom, refrigerators, and freezers—should be located close to the receiving area. The producing area and its equipment should be located close enough to the storing and issuing area that advance preparation and final preparation can be accomplished expeditiously. The serving area should be close to the finishing area so that foods can be served as quickly as possible once they are ready.

The arrangement of equipment in each area is determined, in part, by the extent of the work to be done in the area and the number of staff members available to do it. A large establishment may set up a specific station for broiling, another for frying, and yet another for sauteeing, and provide each of these with appropriate equipment. Smaller establishments, not having the volume of work to justify a specific station and staff, may combine these three in a single station. And that station would clearly have less equipment of any one type than each of the three stations in the larger establishment.

Dishwashing equipment has traditionally been placed near the entrance from the dining room, so that servers returning to the kitchen with soiled china, glassware, and flatware can place these things in a convenient spot before proceeding to pick up food. But because the noise associated with the handling of dishes can often be heard in the dining room, some establishments have installed conveyor systems. With these systems, dishwashing areas can be located some distance from the kitchen entrance with soiled items moved to the dishwashing area by the conveyor belt.

TRAFFIC FLOW. People working in food areas must be able to move around without interfering with the work of others. They are all working in aisles, real or potential. In general, there are two kinds of aisles: traffic aisles and working aisles. They should not coincide: Employees moving about the food area in traffic aisles should not interfere with those storing, issuing, or preparing food, for example, in working aisles. Traffic aisles should be wide enough to permit the passage of personnel and equipment. Working aisles should be wide enough to give employees sufficient space to move with reasonable freedom as they work. In a serving area, for example, space is required to accommodate both personnel returning soiled china and linens from a dining room and those picking up foods to be served in the dining room; and there must be adequate space for the anticipated number of personnel to go about their work without crowding.

In planning a food area, then, adequate space and suitable equipment must be provided for purchasing, receiving, storing, issuing, producing, and serving food. Similarly, adequate lighting and ventilation must be provided in all parts of the food area. Finally, the food area should be arranged to facilitate efficient movement of personnel and materials.

Layout and Design of a Dining Area

A number of considerations are of particular significance in the layout and design of a dining area. These include:

1. Space requirements
2. Traffic flow
3. Lighting

SPACE REQUIREMENTS. The amount of space devoted to seating in the dining room will be determined by the type of service, the variety and mix of table sizes, and decisions of management about space between tables.

As previously discussed, some types of service require more space than others. French service, for example, requires considerable space between tables so that the gueridons characteristic of French service can be moved table-side. American service, on the other hand, requires comparatively little space between tables—just enough for servers to walk quickly carrying plates or trays.

Table sizes and their mix in the dining area will also influence the amount of space required to accommodate a given number of diners. Tables for two, or four, or six, or eight customers require varying amounts of floor space. Round tables require different amounts of space than square or rectangular tables. Knowledge of the number of tables of each shape and size will help determine the total number that can be accommodated in a dining area of a given size. Round tables, for example, require slightly more space than squares. It takes only one-half the space to seat eight persons at one table as it does to seat the same eight persons at four separate tables accommodating two persons each. Tables intended to seat two persons can be purchased in various standard sizes ranging from 24″ × 24″ to 30″ × 36.″ An establishment catering to families will have a greater number of tables accommodating larger parties than one that caters to couples. Establishments offering luxurious evening dining will require larger tables than those offering only breakfast or lunch.

The distance between tables is determined by management. The distance selected will influence the number of customers who can be accommodated in a given area. Many managers see no difficulty in having customers seated very close to one another. Others prefer to seat customers at greater distances from one another and to preserve the privacy of their conversations. In the former, a greater number of customers will be seated; in the latter, fewer can be seated.

TRAFFIC FLOW. Traffic in a dining area must move smoothly. Traffic patterns should be planned to avoid cross traffic between customers and service personnel and among the service personnel. Service personnel must be able to move freely and conveniently within the facility. In some places, this means, for example, that servers must be able to move into and out of a serving area to pick up food orders and to deposit soiled china and flatware for washing. In other kinds of establishments, it may mean that employees must be able to move about the dining area to clean tables and get rid of disposable paper and plastic food packaging.

The measures taken to facilitate free movement vary from one type of operation to another. In table service restaurants, for example, the servers' exit from the dining area to the kitchen is typically located some distance away from the street entrance used by customers. In establishments that do not provide table service, the area where customers order or select foods is typically near the street entrance. In part, this is to facilitate freedom of movement for customers carrying foods.

Lavatories are installed in locations such that traffic to and from the lavatories will not interfere directly with servers or other customers. If servers are required to pick up plates of food in a kitchen, it is important to have two doors between the kitchen and dining areas—one for traffic going into the kitchen, and the other for traffic coming out. If only one is provided, accidents can result from service staff coming and going into the kitchen at the same time. And the farther apart these two doors are placed, the better the traffic flow.

LIGHTING. There are two primary considerations in dining area lighting: the amount of lighting and the type. The decision to have a well-lighted dining area as opposed to one dimly lighted is based on the atmosphere management is attempting to create. Some establishments—those specializing in evening dining, for example—are dimly lighted to create an intimate atmosphere. In some, the lighting is so dim that older customers may have difficulty reading the menu. In contrast, other establishments may be brightly lighted. Some of these are family establishments; others are operations that feature an interesting or unique theme.

There are two basic types of lighting—direct and indirect. The bulb providing direct lighting can be seen, and the light shines directly into the room. In indirect lighting, light shines toward the ceiling and walls and is reflected back into the room. Direct lighting produces shadows, but less light is required to achieve a given degree of brightness. Indirect lighting is softer and produces no shadows; but more indirect lighting is required to reach a particular level of illumination than would be required with direct lighting.

In planning a food area, adequate space and suitable equipment must be provided for those purchasing, receiving, storing, issuing, producing, and serving activities associated with the service product line. By contrast, space requirements, traffic flow, and lighting considerations should be of prime concern to the planner when designing the layout of a dining area. Knowledge of the type of service, the variety and mix of table sizes, and decisions of management about space between tables are critical to determining space requirements. The ambiance, or atmosphere—a critical factor in overall success—is determined largely by the layout and design of the dining area.

Layout and Design of a Beverage Area

The beverage area is that part of the facility where the beverage products are prepared. It includes subareas for the functions described below.

Purchasing. The beverage purchasing area is where decisions are made about the quantities and kinds of beverages to be purchased. Orders for beverages are often placed from the purchasing area by telephone or by direct contact with sales persons, if that is consistent with state law and the policies established by management for beverage purchasing.

Receiving. The beverage receiving area is where beverage purchases are delivered and it is verified that the beverages delivered conform to the orders placed. In many small establishments, the beverage receiving area is the bar; in larger establishments offering both food products and beverage products, one receiving area is likely to exist for both.

Storing and Issuing.   The size of the area for storing and issuing beverages varies greatly from one establishment to another. The variations stem from differing needs based on the size of the establishment, the number of customers served in a given period, and the complexity of the beverage product list. In a small neighborhood bar, the storing and issuing facility may be only a small closet located near the bar; in a large hotel or restaurant doing high-volume business and offering a complex array of beverage products, at least two separate areas will be used for storing and issuing beverages. One of these will be a locked storeroom, maintained at normal room temperature, which will be used for storing liquors and may be used for storing mixers and any alcoholic beverages that are not refrigerated. Another will be a locked, refrigerated room for the storage of beers, ales, and those wines that require chilling.

Those restaurants that offer their guests choices from wine lists must keep reasonable supplies of bottled wine on hand. Some of the finer restaurants maintain wine inventories worth thousands of dollars. These are typically kept under secure conditions in climate-controlled storerooms known as *wine cellars*.

Wine cellars should be maintained in an organized manner, so that particular wines can be located quickly when ordered by customers. To accomplish this, wines are normally classified by type, and each individual wine is given a number. The still wines and sparkling wines are stored on their sides in special racks or bins designed for storing wines. The number assigned to each wine is both printed in the wine list and posted on the bin or rack where the corresponding wine is stored. This makes it easier to find any wine ordered by a customer.

Producing.   Beverage products are typically produced at bars, and establishments offering beverage products make provision for some or all of the three types of bars described previously: front bars, service bars, and special purpose bars.

Bars can be built in various shapes and in any desired size. The layout and design of a bar will be determined by the use that management plans for the bar. If the bar is to be used only as a service bar, it probably will be compact—no larger than required to prepare and serve a projected number of drinks in a given time period, with some space allocated for storage. In contrast, if it is to be a front bar used in a cocktail lounge that also serves as a holding area for customers waiting to be seated in a dining area, it probably will be considerably larger—providing work space for several bartenders and counter space to accommodate a substantial number of customers seated at the bar. The sizes of special purpose bars vary with the number of customers to be served.

There are three specific parts of a front bar that should be incorporated into its design: bar, back bar, and under bar.

The term *bar* is used normally to refer to that physical device in a barroom or taproom that fills several purposes: It is a counter where bartenders can serve drinks to customers; a convenient surface used by customers who consume drinks; a surface on which bartenders may prepare drinks; and a serving station where servers may pick up drinks for consumption elsewhere.

A *back bar* is a storage and display facility located behind a bartender. The top surface is used to hold shelves on which are displayed bottles of some or all of the wines and liquors available at the bar. Glassware may be displayed here as well. The compartments underneath are used for storage of bar supplies, which may include beers, wines, liquors, mixers, paper supplies, or any other item used at the bar. If the facility is refrigerated, it may be used to store bottled beers and such food supplies used in beverage production as milk, cream, lemons, limes, and various fruit juices.

An *under bar* is a work area under the bar surface, containing equipment and supplies used by bartenders. The work area will have "stations"—one for each bartender, and the number of stations will govern the number of bartenders who can conveniently work at the bar at any one time. A station consists of one steel sink for ice, surrounded by wells to hold bottles of frequently used liquors and mixers. In addition to these stations, the under bar has sinks or a machine for washing glassware and a sink for disposing of liquids and washing bar equipment. There may also be work space for preparing drinks and for storing supplies and equipment and additional refrigeration facilities.

Serving.   This is the area where finished beverage products are transferred to servers, to customers, or to both of these. These transfers take place at one of the three types of bars just discussed and described earlier in this chapter: front bars, service bars, and special purpose bars.

In designing a beverage area, the planner must include adequate and suitable equipment for those purchasing, receiving, storing, issuing, producing, and serving activities associated with the beverage product list. Just as in the food area, adequate lighting and ventilation must be provided in all parts of the beverage area. Finally, the beverage area should be arranged to facilitate efficient movement of personnel and materials.

MENU DEVELOPMENT

In the previous chapter, a menu was identified as

1. a list of food or beverage items offered for sale;
2. the primary sales tool for any food or beverage operation.

Printed menus typically begin with those items served first—starters and soups—and end with those served last—desserts and beverages. Customers tend to read menus from top to bottom and from left to right. Thus, a one-page menu would list appetizers at the top and desserts and beverages near the bottom. Two-page menus would tend to list appetizers at the top of the first page, followed by soups, salads, entrees, and any other items in sequence, carrying over to the second page.

Menu development is an important aspect of planning in food and beverage operations. It will therefore be useful to present and discuss seven principal considerations in menu development. These are:

1. Product suitability
2. Product variety
3. Ingredient availability
4. Staff time and capability
5. Equipment capacity
6. Product salability
7. Item profitability

These must each be discussed.

PRODUCT SUITABILITY. This consideration refers to the need to see that each item on a menu is a suitable one for the clientele, the time of day, and the season of the year. One assumes, of course, that a feasibility study and other preliminary work has established an acceptable concept for an intended market, and that the question of product suitability has thus been addressed. Beyond that, it is necessary to refine the list of items offered, according to time of day and season. Breakfast items, after all, are normally quite different from dinner items. Less obviously, such items as hearty beef stew and warm apple pie are likely to be more popular on winter rather than summer menus.

PRODUCT VARIETY. To obtain the broadest appeal, menus should include a sufficient variety of items to attract the greatest possible number of customers. The extent of the variety required to do this will vary from establishment to establishment. Even a specialty restaurant will usually have some variety within its specialty. It will also have some items on its menu outside of the specialty, so that those who do not care for the specialty items will have alternatives. Even units in the nationwide hamburger chains, which formerly sold only hamburgers, now have such other items as chicken, pizza, fish, and salad.

INGREDIENT AVAILABILITY. All restaurants must limit their menu items to those that are available in the marketplace. It is true that most menu items are available year round; but during parts of the year some fresh vegetables and fruits either are not available, are available in limited quantities or at very high prices, or are of inferior quality. For example, in New England fresh corn is unavailable in January and blueberries are available only at very high market prices because they must be imported from other countries. During some periods, the only tomatoes available at reasonable prices come from "hot houses" and their quality is inferior to those available during the normal growing season.

STAFF TIME AND CAPABILITY. Because of the high cost of skilled labor, many restaurants employ cooks whose training and skill are limited. In such instances, management would be wise to avoid offering menu items requiring special skills to prepare. Management must be careful to choose items that the kitchen personnel can prepare within the limits of their skill. Similarly, if staff members have the requisite skills but cannot prepare a given item within the space of time available, it is best left off the menu.

EQUIPMENT CAPACITY. Although establishment of the food product list makes possible the selection of equipment for an establishment, conversely, the equipment selected serves to limit the items that can be included on a menu. In fact, available equipment often determines which of the specific items from the complete list will actually be offered at any one time. For example, a kitchen with one deep-fat fryer would be unable to produce French fries, deep-fried chicken, and deep-fried fish during the course of one meal. The reason for this is that the fat will transfer odors and flavors from one item to another, thus affecting the taste of all products cooked in it. Similarly, a kitchen having limited broiler space or oven space must be careful not to offer too many menu items at once that require the use of these pieces of equipment.

PRODUCT SALABILITY. The location of items on a menu will greatly influence their sales appeal. Studies show that consumers who have not come to restaurants with particular menu items in mind tend to select the items that first catch their eye. Because of this, food service operators often emphasize menu items in such a way as to capture the customer's attention quickly and to sell the featured item. One way is to print these items in larger or bolder type. Another is to enclose the item in a box on the menu and position it in a place that customers will see first. On a one-page menu, this is typically in the upper center, where customers' eyes usually focus first.

Other studies have shown that customers tend more to purchase items appearing at the top of a list than those near the bottom. Thus, managers commonly list their most profitable items first or nearly first on the list of entrees and those that are least profitable near the bottom.

Another useful sales technique employed by the operators of many chain restaurants is to display pictures of items on the menu. These may be either photographs or artists' renderings. Colorful and appealing, they tend to increase sales of the items pictured.

Most managers agree that as much time should be devoted to writing menu descriptions as might be spent writing an expensive advertisement to place in a newspaper or a magazine. Each item description should be thought of as an advertisement; if the description makes the item sound appetizing, it will increase sales. After all, it is more probable that a customer will order a "U.S. Prime filet mignon: eight ounces of America's finest beef, broiled to perfection the way you want it done, then topped with a giant mushroom cap and served sizzling on one of our hot steak platters" over a simple menu listing of "broiled steak." Menu descriptions should always be honest and accurate and include information about method of cooking, major ingredients, and presentation. Menus are designed to tempt the appetite, and a customer should be able to visualize an item just by reading the menu description.

ITEM PROFITABILITY. In food service, one measure of profitability is the difference between the selling price of an item and its *food cost*—the cost of the ingredients in that item. The resulting figure can be called *item gross profit*. The item gross profits from all item sales in a given period go toward meeting other costs of operation for that period, including labor costs, rent, and insurance. If the sum of the item gross profits for a period are greater than these other costs, the operation has earned a profit for that period. If the costs are greater, a loss results.

In general, it is advisable to price menu offerings at levels that will ensure suitable item gross profits. By doing so, managers ensure the profitability of each individual item. Then, provided the establishment sells a sufficient number of portions of each item, management may achieve its financial goal for the period. In commercial operations, the financial goal is usually profit; in not-for-profit operations, it is more likely to be simply meeting all expenses for the period. If it is not possible to price a menu item accordingly and still sell an acceptable quantity of it, the item should probably be removed from the menu.

Further discussion of establishing selling prices for menu items and other hospitality products will be deferred to Chapter 16 (Hospitality Marketing).

There is no more important selling device in any food service operation than its menu. A good menu requires considerable time and effort to produce but is well worth it. Menu development is an interesting combination of art and science and clearly one of the keys to successful food service operation.

The four key factors in food and beverage operations discussed in this chapter—product line, styles of service, facilities layout and design, and menu preparation—are important concepts that lie at the heart of planning for food and beverage operations.

However, the concepts presented in this and the two preceding chapters are only the specific technical elements that differentiate food and beverage operations from other types of hospitality operations—lodging operations, for example. There are many other aspects to planning and operating an enterprise, whether profit making or not-for-profit. These include developing an organization plan, a marketing plan, and a budget; managing the operation; assessing its financial position; and planning its future course. These will be topics for discussion in Part VI: Hospitality Business Perspectives.

SUMMARY

In this chapter, concept development, feasibility study, and understanding of applicable laws and regulations are introduced as prerequisites to planning for food and beverage operations. Product line, styles of service, facilities layout and design, and menu preparation are presented as four key factors in food and beverage planning. Food, beverages, service, and ambiance are identified as the primary elements in the service product line offered by food and beverage establishments. American, Russian, French, English, cafeteria, buffet, takeout/delivery, and room service—the eight primary styles of service found in food operations—are identified and described, as are the styles of service associated with three types of bars: front, service, and special purpose. Layout and design considerations for food areas, dining areas, and beverage areas are discussed. Finally, the seven principal considerations in menu development—product suitability, product variety, ingredient availability, staff time and capability, equipment capacity, product salability, and item profitability—are identified and discussed.

QUESTIONS

1. What are the necessary prerequisites to the planning of food and beverage operations?
2. Define the term *product line* as it is used in food and beverage operations.
3. What are the elements in the hospitality service product line offered by food and beverage operations?
4. Describe each of the following styles of service:
   a. American
   b. Russian

      c. French

      d. English

      e. cafeteria

      f. buffet

      g. takeout/delivery

      h. room service

5. Why does French service normally require more space per customer than other forms of dining room service?

6. Distinguish between the three types of cafeteria service.

7. List the steps in service of still wine.

8. Identify the purpose and use of the following types of bars and describe the style of service associated with each.

      a. front bar

      b. service bar

      c. special-purpose bar

9. List the six considerations that the authors state must be taken into account when laying out and designing a food facility. Describe the importance and significance of each.

10. What is a lumen? A foot-candle? How many foot-candles do experts suggest for normal kitchen work? For detailed work?

11. Why is it necessary that air pressure in a dining room and in other rooms adjoining the kitchen be greater than that in the kitchen itself?

12. Distinguish between traffic aisles and working aisles.

13. Explain the importance of space, traffic flow, and lighting in the layout and design of a dining area.

14. In what ways do the arrangement and size of tables in a dining room influence the amount of space required for a given number of customers?

15. Distinguish between direct lighting and indirect lighting. Why might food and beverage operators choose to use each one?

16. List and describe the three principal parts of a front bar.

17. Explain the importance of each of the seven principal considerations in menu development listed below.

      a. product suitability

      b. product variety

    c. ingredient availability

    d. staff time and capability

    e. equipment capacity

    f. product salability

    g. item profitability

18. Identify the three elements that should be included in the description of each menu item.

19. Write a menu description for roast prime ribs of beef, including in your description the elements identified in question 18 above.

20. How is *item gross profit* calculated?

Lodging
Perspectives

IV

Dimensions of Lodging

8

LEARNING OBJECTIVES

After reading and studying this chapter, you should be able to:

1. *Define the term* lodging property *and identify several types of properties covered by the definition.*
2. *Discuss the size and scope of the commercial lodging industry in terms of numbers and types of properties of various sizes.*
3. *Identify the approximate number of persons employed in commercial lodging and the annual sales volume generated.*
4. *List and discuss five key elements in a lodging operation that differentiate one lodging establishment from another.*
5. *Describe the characteristics commonly associated with each of the following terms:* inn, hotel, motel, lodge, *tourist home/guest house,* bed and breakfast, hostel, condominium, *and* hospital.
6. *Identify the principal characteristics of each of the following specialized types of lodging establishments:* motor inn, transient hotel, residential hotel, resort hotel, traditional resort, all-inclusive resort, *resort condominium,* resort motel, guest ranch, commercial hotel, convention hotel, all-suite hotel, extended-stay hotel, conference center, casino hotel, health spa, boarding house, lodging house, dormitory, *and* nursing home.
7. *Identify ten lodging operations that are directly or indirectly associated with transportation.*
8. *List three means traditionally used to classify commercial lodging establishments.*

9. *Identify and describe the six categories that make up the American Hotel and Motel Association's most recent system for classifying commercial lodging properties.*
10. *Name and describe the four rate plans that include food and the one rate plan that does not.*
11. *Identify the two national organizations that rate commercial lodging establishments and list five factors used by each in making their ratings judgments.*

INTRODUCTION

Previous chapters have described the historical development of the lodging industry, but a recap here might be useful. Clearly of ancient origins, the lodging industry dates back to the beginnings of trade nearly 5,000 years ago. Its development has paralleled the development of trade, travel, and transportation throughout civilization.

But the modern age of travel and trade can really be traced to the beginnings of the Industrial Revolution in the mid-eighteenth century. The development of railroads and the increasing prosperity brought by industrial growth contributed greatly to making travel more common. The coaching inns of an earlier era were replaced by larger properties—hotels—which were typically located near railroad stations.

Innkeeping in the United States developed in a manner similar to the way in which it developed in western Europe. Unlike his European counterpart, however, the American innkeeper was always a respected member of the community. Although many rural American inns of the seventeenth and eighteenth centuries were uncomfortable, those located in cities and towns were generally better. Laws and societal values in many communities regulated eating and drinking in taverns.

In America, as in Europe, the Industrial Revolution was responsible for a period of unprecedented growth in the number of people traveling and in the distances they traveled. By the early 1800s, grand "palaces of the public" were being constructed in the developing cities. Unlike in Europe, these hotels were community centers for local parties, dinners, receptions, and political events. They were often the most elegant and impressive structures in these cities. By the third quarter of the century, cities across the country were linked to one another by a network of railroads, and many of these cities were boasting of the quality of their luxury hotels.

In the twentieth century, mass production of automobiles and a developing system of paved roads began to make travel easy for Americans. Eventually, the national government sponsored the development of a coast-to-coast network of roads, which facilitated the transportation of goods around the country. With the resulting economic growth, the United States grew strong in the world economy, and Americans became prosperous. Many American businessmen found it necessary to travel in the course of their work, and some Americans had sufficient disposable income to travel for pleasure. This increase in travel for business and for pleasure led to an expansion of the lodging industry that continued until the Great Depression of 1929, the most severe shock in history to the nation's economic system. During the depression, the number of people traveling declined dramatically, leading to numerous bankruptcies and general economic hardship for the lodging industry.

In the early 1940s, business and military travel associated with World War II brought renewed demand for lodging services, and the industry experienced a period of great prosperity. After the war, new directions for the industry were charted by Kemmons Wilson with his Holiday Inn concept. During the 1960s, new large hotels were constructed by growing organizations with names such as Hilton, Sheraton, and Marriott. And although the automobile had become America's favorite vehicle for travel, the airplane had replaced the railroad as the primary means of public transportation for long-distance travel. By the time commercial jet aircraft were introduced in 1958, airports were becoming favorable locations for lodging establishments.

The lodging industry continues to evolve, seeking new customers by offering new and different kinds of lodging establishments each year. Increasing amounts of travel continue to create opportunities for imaginative lodging developers.

LODGING PROPERTIES DEFINED

Lodging properties may be defined as establishments that charge fees for providing furnished sleeping accommodations to persons who are temporarily away from home, or who consider these accommodations their temporary or permanent homes. Many of these establishments also provide food, beverages, cleaning services, and a range of other services normally associated with travel and commonly sought by travelers.

The above definition includes transient and residential hotels, motels, and inns, as well as resorts, college dormitories, hostels, boarding houses, condominium rentals and other related establishments. It even includes the accommodations aspect of hospital operations.

Many lodging properties provide accommodations to both travelers and nontravelers. The Plaza Hotel in New York City is an excellent example: At one time shortly after it opened, up to 80 percent of those staying in the Plaza considered it their permanent home. There are many properties that cater almost exclusively to permanent guests, providing them with many of the same services that other properties offer to travelers and temporary guests.

THE COMMERCIAL LODGING INDUSTRY

The commercial lodging industry is one segment of the lodging industry. It is the group of profit-oriented lodging properties—hotels, motels, inns, and similar establishments—that provide transient accommodations and operate as businesses.

The American Hotel and Motel Association reports that the commercial lodging industry in the United States consists of approximately 45,000 properties, ranging in size from small inns with fewer than 10 rooms to giant hotels with over 3,000 rooms. About 70 percent of the properties have fewer than 75 rooms. These small establishments account for approximately 20 percent of the 3,000,000 rooms available in commercial lodging establishments in the United States. At the other extreme, only about 3 percent of the properties have more than 300 rooms, but these establishments account for 23 percent of the total number of rooms available. The remaining 27 percent of the properties range in size from 75 to 300 rooms and account for 57 percent of the rooms available. It is apparent that typical commercial lodging establishments are quite small and tend to be owned by individuals or by partnerships or small corporations. Many small properties are managed by their owners.

In total, the commercial lodging industry in the United States generates more than $63 billion in sales each year, representing about 1 percent of the gross national product. The industry employs appoximately 1.6 million people, full time and part time.

The American Hotel and Motel Association reports that 25 percent of today's lodging customers are traveling for business purposes, 24 percent are attending conferences, and 31 percent are vacationing. Another 20 percent are traveling for any of a number of personal reasons.

VARIATIONS IN LODGING ESTABLISHMENTS

Any keen observer of the variety of lodging establishments is certain to note significant differences from one to another. These differences are a result of decisions made by owners and managers about five key elements in a lodging operation:

1. Services
2. Accommodations
3. Decor
4. Rates
5. Target clientele

These elements are generally used to define and differentiate among lodging establishments. Each will be discussed in the sections that follow.

Services

The range of services offered to guests varies considerably from one lodging establishment to another. At one end of the scale are guest houses that offer little more than a bed in a room and bathroom facilities down the hall. At the other end, are luxury properties that offer a complete range of services. These include 24-hour room service, valet and laundry service, secretarial service, hair stylists, health clubs, pay-per-view sporting events and films, in-room bars stocked with a selection of beverages, in-room safe boxes, concierge service, and extensive maid service that incorporates placing fresh towels twice a day, turn-down service at night, and wake up coffee or tea in bed in the morning. In between these two extremes are most lodging operations that provide full or limited food and beverage service, color television, telephone, and private bath. Many motels limit their services to a private room with bath, telephone, and television. Ice and snacks may be available in a vending machine located in the hallway.

Accommodations

The types and sizes of accommodations also differ from one lodging property to another. The types of rooms vary from the bunk room with bath down the hall, provided by some inexpensive ski lodges, to the elegant suite with bedroom, private bath, living room, dining area, and small kitchen, offered by many luxury hotels. The most common type of accommodation is a bedroom with private bath. The room will contain one or two beds, each of which is designed for one or two people. Other furnishings will depend on the nature of the property and the size of the room.

Room sizes vary considerably from one establishment to another. In properties built before World War II, some of the rooms are tiny—designed for single individuals, and providing just enough space for a small bed, a dresser, and one chair. In many of the properties built in more recent years, the minimum number of square feet allocated was 200 for a unit consisting of room and bath. That was considered very small; lower priced motels, for example, would usually allocate nearly 250 square feet. Fine hotels, moreover, would typically allow 450. In contrast, some other, newer properties here and in Europe have rooms that are even smaller—150 square feet and less. These properties are designed to operate profitably at rates that are even lower than those of the lower priced motels.

Many properties provide accommodations other than the typical unit of bedroom and bath. The sizes of these will also vary—both with the type of property and the nature of the accommodation. It is quite possible, for example, for a unit with two bedrooms, two baths, and a living room in an inexpensive hotel to contain fewer square feet than a unit with one bedroom, one bath, and living room in a luxury property.

One of the five key elements in a lodging operation—along with accommodations, decor, rates, and target clientele—the services offered by lodging establishments vary considerably. For example, concierge service (opposite top left), usually accompanied by various room, valet, and maid services; pool facilities (opposite top right), often with adjoining food service; and a health club or spa (opposite bottom left), which sometimes may also offer exercise classes and massage services. At seasonal resorts or resort hotels, the recreational services are most important: (from opposite bottom right to above right) skiing, golf, and horseback riding are only a few of several services offered by lodging establishments to attract a particular target clientele. (Clockwise from opposite top left: courtesy Stouffer Concourse Hotel, Denver, Colorado; courtesy Stouffer Cottonwoods Resort, Scottsdale, Arizona; courtesy Utah Travel Council, Salt Lake City, Utah; courtesy Hospitality Franchise Systems. From left above: courtesy Stouffer Esmeralda Resort, Indian Wells, California; courtesy Stouffer Presidente Los Cabos.)

Decor

The decor of a lodging establishment—the style and layout of its interior furnishings—determines its atmosphere. The higher the quality of the furnishings, the higher the degree of luxury the establishment will be perceived to offer. At one end of the spectrum are lodging establishments with simple, plain decor, and inexpensive furnishings. At the other, there are the elegant—those that employ highly skilled interior decorators to plan the decor and to select each item with great care, from fine period furniture to the simplest ash tray.

Lodging establishments belonging to a given chain are often noted for a particular style and type of decor. They may feature the same color scheme and style of furnishings in all their properties, so that customers in these properties may not be able to distinguish between the rooms in the chain's Boston unit and those in its Los Angeles unit.

Rates

The fees charged by lodging operations for the sleeping accommodations they provide are commonly known as *rates*. In hotels and motels, one speaks of *room rates*, for example, as the fees charged guests who rent rooms. Rates for rooms vary from one locale to another and from one property to another, as do the charges for the various additional services a lodging facility may offer.

Generally, room rates are much higher in major cities than in suburban locations because of the higher costs of construction and operation. Some cities are well known for their high room rates. New York, for example, has traditionally been the most expensive city in the United States for hotel rooms; and London, Paris, and Tokyo are very expensive cities for lodging accommodations in their respective countries.

Target Clientele

Throughout history, people opening lodging establishments have always attempted to attract particular types of customers. Four thousand years ago, lodging operators had caravans of traders in mind and set up their establishments on trade routes. In seventeenth-century England, lodging operators had stagecoach passengers in mind when opening their coaching houses. More recently, American companies opening hotels in major cities near railroad terminals were targeting railroad travelers. Today, we see lodging operators building properties along highways and at airports for much the same reason.

Targeting particular groups of potential customers has become a sophisticated endeavor. Properties are being designed and built to accommodate travelers at a number of different price levels, from low to high. Others are designed and built to accommodate the needs of a particular clientele—ski lodges, for example.

Taken together, the five elements we have just discussed—services, accommodations, decor, fees, and target clientele—determine the nature of the lodging property.

Major metropolitan centers tend to have numerous lodging properties of widely varying types. These range from limited service to full service; from small, plain rooms to large, luxurious rooms; from the simplest to the most ornate decor; from very cheap to extraordinarily expensive; and from those targeting bus travelers to those catering to corporate executives and show business personalities. Smaller communities also have variety, of course, but tend to have less of it.

CHARACTERISTIC TYPES OF LODGING ESTABLISHMENTS

As in the case of food establishments, the number of possible variables in lodging establishments makes attempts at classifying them very difficult. Most classification systems are either too simple—urban, suburban, and rural, for example—or too complex, to be useful: It can take dozens of categories to account for the variations from one operation to another in services, accommodations, decor, rates, and target clientele.

Nevertheless, owners and operators of lodging establishments do select terms to identify their establishments to the public. A lodging property that is about to open in a community may be described in local newspapers by such terms as *motel*, *lodge*, or *inn*. Because the public tends to associate different characteristics with the various terms used and to select or avoid lodging establishments on the basis of their interpretation of the terms, it is useful to list and discuss the most common. One must remember that this list does not constitute any real system of lodging classification because the terms do not represent mutually exclusive categories. Very many lodging operations can be described by two or more of these terms.

Most people have heard the names used to identify lodging establishments—hotel, motel, inn, motor inn, resort hotel or motel, condominium, lodging house, residential hotel, tourist home, guest house, bed and breakfast, guest ranch, hostel, hospital, and dormitory, among them. Each of these conveys an impression of the kind of establishment identified. No one believes that a hotel is the same as a dormitory, for example. These are clearly very different from one another, and someone opening a hotel would be making a terrible mistake to identify it as a dormitory; it would not appeal to those seeking traditional hotel accommodations. The following is an examination of the characteristics commonly associated with these terms.

Inn

The term *inn* was brought to the United States from England in the early seventeenth century. Originally, the term meant an establishment that provided rooms, food, and entertainment to both travelers and residents of the local community. Over the years, the term came to be used to describe any one of three different types of hospitality enterprises:

1. A small, typically rural, lodging establishment that may or may not serve food
2. A larger property—or one that may have once been known as a hotel—that wishes to convey an image of smallness and caring for their customers
3. A restaurant or bar that has no sleeping accommodations available.

Hotel

The term *hotel* was used traditionally to identify a lodging facility of two stories or more that provided sleeping accommodations and other services for its guests. In the United States, there has been a tendency to build hotels in or near the business centers of cities, towns, and villages and to regard them as centers of social and political activity.

Hotels have commonly offered housekeeping services and luggage-carrying assistance, as well as food, beverages, telephone, and other services. The extent of these services varies from property to property. Some hotels provide the full range: restaurants; bars; cocktail lounges; room service; hair stylists; exercise salons; computer, photocopy, and fax facilities; laundry; dry cleaners; gift shops; check cashing and other financial services; newsstands; travel agencies; drugstores, and others. Other hotels provide nothing beyond sleeping accommodations and housekeeping services.

Motel

The term *motel* traditionally described a special variety of lodging establishment that catered to travelers with automobiles and provided self-service parking on premises.

The original motels were single-story properties providing basic sleeping accommodations to overnight travelers. They were inexpensive, offering free parking and housekeeping service, but little else. Staff was kept to a minimum to keep costs down. There were none of the services normally associated with hotels—room service, bellmen, restaurants, and the like. Motels were located on the outskirts of cities and towns and catered to those who did not want the expense and formality of a hotel. Later, many had adequate land to expand and to add swimming pools, which helped to differentiate motels from hotels, and to attract new customers.

Over the years, many motels evolved into properties that so resemble hotels that it is impossible to identify any differences. Many are multistoried, provide full services, and are located in the centers of cities.

Lodge

The term *lodge* was traditionally used to describe a lodging establishment associated with a particular type of activity, such as *ski lodge* or *hunting lodge*. This type of lodge was a smaller establishment, typically in a rural setting, that provided food and housekeeping services to guests who came to be with others engaging in the same activity.

Many lodging proprietors have used this term instead of the term *inn* in order to make clear that the primary emphasis of the establishment is providing transient accommodations for those engaging in some specific activity. As suggested above, the term *inn* can be confusing.

A substantial number of properties are known as *motor lodges*. For all practical purposes this is merely another name for a motel.

Tourist Home/Guest House

Tourist home and *guest house* are terms used to describe private homes in which the owners rent spare bedrooms to transient guests. No meals are served to guests in these establishments. These are not normally business ventures in the usual sense; they are more often sources of extra income for those whose primary income comes from somewhere else.

Bed and Breakfast

Bed and breakfast establishments have long been popular in Europe. In recent years they have been gaining popularity in the United States. They are close relatives of tourist homes and guest houses: Owners of private homes rent rooms to overnight guests. They differ in one important respect: A full breakfast is included in the rate. Some people prefer to stay in bed and breakfast establishments because they are smaller, more intimate, and less expensive than hotels and motels and because the proprietors of many offer a degree of hospitality seldom equaled in commercial properties.

Hostel

Hostels are inexpensive lodging establishments that typically cater to younger transient customers. They provide little or no service. The typical hostel provides a bed for the night and offers no frills. Some provide a community kitchen, in which guests may prepare their own meals. Everyone staying in a hostel is expected to participate in keeping it clean. There is usually a limit to the number of nights an individual is allowed to stay.

Condominium

Condominium is a relatively new term that identifies a furnished housing unit with kitchen area, living room area, sleeping area, and bath.

Condominiums take many forms. They can be free-standing single units; individual units among several built as a single structure; sections or segments of hotel facilities; or units in a residential apartment facility.

Condominiums are distinguished from other types of lodging establishments by their ownership characteristics: Each condominium unit in a complex is independently owned, but the management of the complex provides maintenance for the outside and the common inside areas of the facility for a monthly fee. In addition, the grounds and other facilities are usually owned jointly by all of the condominium owners.

Many owners rent their units to permanent or transient guests. Those located in resort areas are called resort condominiums. Major corporations— Marriot, for example—have built large condominium developments in recent years, sold the individual units, and retained the management of the condominium development.

Hospital

In many respects, a hospital can be regarded as a specialized lodging facility. *Hospitals* provide sleeping accommodations and many of the same services provided by hotels—including housekeeping, room service, telephone, television, and a pharmacy—and often such additional services as hair stylists, gift shops, and lending libraries. A principal difference is in the clients served: Hospital guests are known as *patients*, and all are in the hospital for medical reasons.

These are the general terms used to identify lodging establishments. In addition to these, one should be familiar with the following list of more specialized terms, used to describe some of the many other lodging operations that abound.

Motor Inn

Motor inn is a term that came into use as an alternative to the term *motel* and originally described a motel property whose proprietors wished to convey the concept of free parking and the traditions of an inn—a kind of modern inn. During the 1950s and 1960s when older hotels were no longer in favor because of competition from motels, many hotel properties that had parking facilities on premises or nearby changed their names from hotel to motor inn in order to compete with motels.

Transient Hotel

A *transient hotel* is one that is designed to cater to temporary guests—people who have need of accommodations for a comparatively few nights. The guests may be business people, groups of sightseers, government employees, members of the armed forces, students, or any persons seeking temporary lodging.

Residential Hotel

In contrast to transient hotels, some hotels have traditionally provided accommodations for long-term guests—individuals who consider the hotel their temporary or permanent home. Establishments that offer traditional hotel services—food and beverages, laundry and dry cleaning, telephone, and the like, for those who choose to live permanently in hotels—are known as *residential hotels.* A considerable number of people stay for long periods in these hotels. They enjoy and are willing to pay for daily maid service and other services that a particular hotel may offer.

Some transient hotels emulate residential hotels. They set aside a number of rooms or suites for permanent guests. Many well-known hotels have permanent guests, and some have whole sections of the hotel building set aside for resident guests. Perhaps the most famous of these is New York's Waldorf-Astoria. One section of the hotel, known as the Towers, caters to permanent guests. The Towers has a separate entrance for its guests and provides a full range of the finest hotel services for them.

Resort Hotel

The term *resort hotel* is commonly used to describe lodging establishments that feature enjoyable or beneficial—often healthy—recreational activities for their guests. Swimming, tennis, and golf are among the most common, although many others are possible. Some resorts have only limited recreation facilities on premises and provide their guests access to other recreational facilities nearby.

Resorts have traditionally catered to customers who stayed for several days or several weeks. In past generations, many resorts had guests who would stay for an entire season. While this is no longer common, some resorts still have guests who stay for extended periods.

As discussed in previous chapters, the United States had a tradition of developing resort accommodations in rural areas. Today, many resort properties that were once in rural settings find themselves situated in suburban or urban areas. Older resort hotels in Miami Beach, Phoenix, and San Diego, for example, are actually located in or near city centers: Metropolitan centers have grown up around the resort properties.

Many resort hotels that once catered exclusively to vacationers now cater to those attending meetings and conventions. Thus, it is becoming increasingly difficult to distinguish between resort hotels and transient hotels.

Various types of resort properties exist. These include:

TRADITIONAL RESORT. A *traditional resort* hotel is one with recreational facilities on its premises. The rates include some or all of the meals. Entertainment is usually free, but liquor, gratuities, and many recreational activities are extra. Rates are charged on a daily or weekly basis.

ALL-INCLUSIVE RESORT. An *all-inclusive resort* is one that includes everything in one weekly rate—airfare to the resort, sleeping accommodations, all meals, liquor, gratuities, entertainment, and activities. The best known of these is Club Med.

RESORT CONDOMINIUM. A *resort condominium* is one that is located in a resort area or on a resort property. Some resort hotels have resort condominiums on their properties. The condominium units differ from regular guest rooms: They have kitchen and living room facilities, as well as the traditional sleeping accommodations. Customers may prepare their own meals in the condominium kitchen or dine in the resort's dining room. In addition, they have access to all the recreational facilities of the resort.

Many older resort hotels that were lacking business have transformed themselves into resort condominiums by selling their hotel rooms to investors and using the money to develop the property.

RESORT MOTEL. *Resort motels* are simply motels located in resort areas. Many of them serve food and most of them have limited recreation facilities.

GUEST RANCH. *Guest ranches* are resort properties that emphasize horseback riding and related activities. They are typically small properties of fewer than 100 rooms, which provide housekeeping services, food, and other seasonal recreational facilities—swimming, tennis, and hunting, for example.

Guest ranches are typically very informal and attempt to suggest the rough and ready, informal democratic spirit that we have come to believe was characteristic of the old West.

Commercial Hotel

Commercial hotel is a term used to refer to a specialized property: one that caters to business travelers such as executives and sales personnel in need of transient lodgings. The term dates from the early twentieth century, when a number of newly constructed hotels—Statler's Buffalo property among them—were designed to accommodate single business travelers, providing the types of rooms and services that would appeal to these anticipated guests.

In recent years, as the mix of travelers has changed, the term has come to have less significance. Today, there are probably no hotels that accommodate only "commercial" guests; most cater to a more varied clientele.

Convention Hotel

This is a term used to designate a very specialized type of hotel: one that focuses on conventions as the primary source of business. A *convention* is a gathering of people sharing some business, professional, social, or avocational interest and is characterized by meetings, exhibits, and related activities regarding that interest.

Some convention hotels were specifically designed to accommodate convention business; others set their sights on conventions only after newer properties—motels, for example—began to capture their other business.

The principal difference between convention hotels and other hotels is in specific facilities available for convention groups. These include at least one large ballroom or similar meeting room and a substantial number of other meeting rooms nearby. Convention hotels also have the capacity to prepare and serve food and beverages to large numbers of people in banquet rooms, as well as in several public dining rooms and bars. Convention hotels normally do not limit their business to convention groups; they routinely accommodate individual reservations to maintain the highest possible level of occupancy.

All-Suite Hotel

Suite is a term used in lodging operations to describe an accommodation consisting of a living room—sometimes called a *parlor*—plus a minimum of one bedroom and bathroom. Many have some type of kitchen facility. Some properties offer suites that have several bedrooms and baths.

All-suite hotels do not offer the traditional bedroom and bath accommodations provided by most hotels. They offer only suites. These include facilities for limited cooking. The all-suite hotels typically have no restaurants or bars, and most have no public meeting rooms. Many, however, provide some form of limited food service or beverage service, or both. Free breakfast buffets in the lobby, food vending machines in designated areas, and in-room bars are some of the possibilities. The elimination of restaurants, bars, and public meeting rooms reduces construction and operating costs and enables the owners of all-suite properties to offer guests larger accommodations at competitive rates.

Extended-Stay Hotel

A relatively new term, *extended-stay hotel*, is used to describe a property that caters to those who intend to stay longer than typical transient guests and who seek accommodations other than the traditional bedroom and bath. The typical extended-stay hotel provides a homelike environment and attempts to minimize the resemblance to other commercial lodging facilities.

Accommodations in extended-stay hotels would tend to resemble those in a fine garden apartment complex—a suite consisting of kitchen, living room, bedroom, and bath and recreational facilities for swimming and other forms of exercise. Suites in extended-stay hotels commonly feature exterior entrances, with parking by the door.

Conference Center

Conference center is another relatively new term used to describe a facility designed especially for meetings and conference business. They are typically located in suburban and rural areas and are designed to provide a setting that is relatively free of distractions. Thus conference centers tend to be conducive to concentration and learning and are selected by groups that require such settings for productive work.

Conference centers typically accept only group business. Given high operating costs in some regions of the country, however, some conference centers accept individual reservations during slack periods in order to maximize revenues.

Casino Hotel

Casino hotel is a term used to refer to transient hotels that house gambling casinos. These hotels have allocated major amounts of space to casino gambling, which includes games of chance using cards or dice—blackjack, roulette, and poker, for example—and slot machines. Casino gambling, illegal in most parts of the United States, is a major attraction for many Americans; and the casino hotels are very popular with vacationers and conventioneers. Operators of casino hotels also provide lavish entertainment—nationally known artists and professionally staged shows—as added attractions.

Until recently, casino hotels in the United States have been found only in the state of Nevada and in Atlantic City, New Jersey. However, casino gambling is now being permitted on Mississippi riverboats by the states of Illinois, Iowa, Louisiana, and Mississippi, as well as on growing numbers of Indian reservations. With this increase in the number of legal sites for casino gambling, it is possible that new casino hotels may be constructed in states other than Nevada and New Jersey.

Because casino gambling can be a very profitable enterprise, casino hotels can be very desirable properties to own. In successful casino hotels, the major share of profits comes from gambling operations, rather than from lodging or from food and beverage. Casino hotel operators commonly give free lodging, food, and drinks to guests who routinely wager large amounts of money—these are the so-called *high-rollers*. Obviously this is done to attract their continuing patronage.

Health Spa

Health spa is a general term given to lodging establishments that focus on providing some form of beneficial, health-related services. Each tends to specialize—in weight reduction, cosmetic therapy, or drug or alcohol rehabilitation, among others.

For obvious reasons, health spas typically do not accept guests other than those seeking the health-related services in which they specialize. Some even restrict admission to those referred by physicians.

Boarding House

A *boarding house* is a residential facility that provides lodging and meals for guests who normally consider the facility their home, whether temporarily or permanently. The services they offer are typically restricted to limited housekeeping and meals, which tends to distinguish them from residential hotels. They are inexpensive, compared with residential and other hotels. In the past, boarding houses were much more common than they are today.

A boarding house may be as small as a private home, or it may be a larger facility, resembling a small hotel. Rates are commonly charged on a weekly or monthly basis and include both lodging and meals.

Housekeeping services in a boarding house are typically very limited: Daily maid service is unlikely, and cleaning services may be restricted to once a week. In some, guests clean their own rooms and exchange soiled for clean linens in an office on the main floor. Food service is typically two or three meals a day served at specified hours or during specified time periods.

Lodging House

Essentially, a *lodging house* is a boarding house that does not provide meals. The weekly or monthly rate is for the lodging alone. Lodging houses, also known as rooming houses, were more common in the past.

Some lodging houses offer kitchen privileges—free use of a common kitchen, provided the user leaves the facility clean after each use.

Dormitory

Typically, the term *dormitory* is used to refer to a lodging facility affiliated with some educational or other institution that provides sleeping accommodations for those in residence. It is this institutional affiliation that differentiates a dormitory from a lodging house.

The characteristics of dormitories are extremely varied. Some have daily maid service; others have none. Some have private rooms with private baths;

others have rooms shared by several people and bathrooms shared by all residents of one floor. Some have kitchen facilities; others prohibit cooking. In most, food service is available, often in a separate facility. If food is available, it may be provided only to those who pay extra for it. In some instances, the fee charged includes both room and board—in which case, residents usually eat in a food service facility.

Nursing Home

A *nursing home* is a residential facility that provides lodging and food service for people requiring nursing or related care. Those residing in nursing homes tend to be temporarily or permanently infirm, physically or mentally.

Some cater to the elderly; others assist patients recovering from major surgery. Some specialize in the care of chronically ill children; others, called *hospices*, deal with the terminally ill. The services provided vary from one establishment to another and, for obvious reasons, are closely linked to the needs of the residents.

Other Lodging Operations

There is one entire collection of lodging operations, vaguely related to one another by their direct or indirect association with transportation—water, rail, air, or highway. These include cruise ships; freighters that accept passengers; riverboats; overnight passenger ferries; specialized commercial sailboats, or windjammers; railroad sleeping cars; planes with sleeping accommodations for passengers on long international flights; specially-fitted charter buses used for golf tours and similar purposes; completely furnished and outfitted motor homes, campers, trailers, boats, or barges rented on a daily or weekly basis; and lodging facilities known as *boatels*, located at marina developments. None of these constitutes a major segment of the lodging industry, but each employs some or all of the techniques and procedures of lodging operations. These will be discussed in Chapter 9.

CLASSIFICATION OF LODGING ESTABLISHMENTS

It is important to recognize that many of the transient lodging establishments just enumerated cater to more than one type of business. In major cities, many accommodate residential guests on weekly or monthly rates, because they are not able to maintain a sufficiently high level of occupancy with transient trade alone. In contrast, some transient hotels do not accommodate residential guests, but maintain high levels of occupancy by attracting several types of transients: business travelers, vacationers, and those attending conventions, for example. It is quite common to find a single hotel property that has characteristics of two or more of the many types that one encounters in this dynamic industry. This has been a major difficulty to those attempting to develop useful classification systems for lodging properties.

Many attempts have been made to classify lodging properties. Some have classified them by location: For purposes of statistical analysis, one industry publication divided properties into these five categories:

Center city
Suburban
Highway motels
Resorts
Airport hotels

Others have classified them by size:

Under 75 rooms
From 75 to 149 rooms
From 150 to 299 rooms
Over 300 rooms

Another system divided properties into five types:

Transient hotels
All-year resort hotels
Seasonal resorts
Residential hotels
Condominium hotels

In two of these—the first two—every property can be placed in one or another of the categories. However, each of the categories includes properties that are so different from one another that the classification system does not reveal much about any of them. The third classification scheme presents one very great difficulty: No one can be sure of the proper category for those establishments having both residential and transient guests, for example.

Another classification system of interest is that used by the Bureau of the Census, a branch of the United States Department of Commerce, and by some organizations that report industry statistics. This system separates properties into four categories:

Full-service
Economy
All-suite
Resort

The following language accompanies a table in which lodging properties are divided into these categories:

An *economy property* is defined as one that offers clean, standard-sized, fully furnished modern rooms at usually $10.00 to $20.00 per night below the rate of typical full-service motor hotels. Their customers do not need food facilities, banquet rooms or meeting facilities, indoor recreation areas, or entertainment. An *all-suite hotel* doesn't have rooms, only suites. A *suite* differs from a hotel room by several characteristics. Generally, there is a separate bedroom, and guest amenities often include 'extras,' such as a wet bar or microwave and in some cases a full kitchen. A *resort hotel* is a lodging facility providing an environment conducive to leisure and recreation and an ambiance of isolation/destination while providing a full range of leisure-oriented amenities. . . .[1]

This system is intended to be used for reporting data obtained from surveys — rates, averages, and similar variations — of some characteristic types of lodging properties. Some lodging properties are not included — bed and breakfast establishments, hostels, and others.

A student trying to understand the scope of the lodging industry is better served by a system published recently in the *Business Travel Planner*, the official lodging directory of the American Hotel and Motel Association. This approach separates commercial lodging establishments into the six categories described below, based on a property's room rates, services, and quality. The categories[2] are:

Limited-Service Budget Motels

"These facilities offer simple, basic, clean rooms. They will offer towels, linen, and soap. Private bath and two double beds are the norm. They will not offer bellmen, food service, or recreational facilities. . . ." There are about 22,000 of these properties in the United States, including about 372,000 rooms.

Limited-Service Economy Motels

"These guest rooms will feature color television, telephone, and an upgraded room decor. Probably not offering food service, they will be close to restaurants and have vending machines for food and sundries on the property. . . ." There are about 10,000 of these establishments, with approximately 672,000 rooms.

Full-Service, Mid-Priced Motels and Hotels

"An ambiance of greater interior and exterior design. Will have 24-hour front desk attendant, offer food service of limited hours and usually offer laundry and dry cleaning services. Extra room amenities, such as shampoo, as well as

---

[1]Bureau of the Census, *Statistical Abstract of the United States*, (Washington, DC: U. S. Department of Commerce, 1990), p. 786.
[2]Detailed descriptions of the categories are taken from the *Business Travel Planner*, North Amer. Ed., Sept.–Nov., 1990, p. 17 (Oakbrook, IL: Official Airline Guides, Inc.)

upgraded quality of linens are the norm. Limited recreational facilities are offered. . . ." There are about 4,500 of these, with about 552,000 rooms.

Full-Service, Upscale Hotels

"A generally better quality and more luxurious surroundings are offered in this category. Restaurants will be of a better quality, room service (in some cases 24 hours) is offered. A health club and swimming pool, concierge/guest services manager will also be found here. . . ." There are about 3,500 of these properties, including approximately 573,000 rooms.

Luxury Hotels

"Lavish surroundings with smooth service in marble and polished brass lobbies. Guest rooms that offer the ultimate in in-room amenities. Often ranked among the finest hotels in the world, services include 24-hour room service, haute cuisine restaurants, concierge service, and personalized service from an attentive staff. . . ." There are about 4,000 of these, with about 831,000 rooms.

All-Suite Hotels

"The most important innovation since the motel, all-suite properties are rapidly growing across America. The all-suite hotel offers separate sleeping and living quarters. The suite can accommodate up to six guests. A small kitchen area, with refrigerator, wet bar, and microwave are usually featured. Complimentary breakfast and evening refreshments are usually standard. This concept is perfect for a small group or family and business travelers who may use their guest room for work or entertaining. . . ." There are approximately 800 properties in this category, with nearly 100,000 rooms. Some experts predict that about half of all new lodging construction will be in this category.

Useful as it is for some purposes, this approach also leaves out a number of the characteristic types of lodging properties—guest houses, residential hotels, and most bed and breakfast establishments, for example.

Thus, in the light of the foregoing discussion, a person attempting to learn about the lodging industry will find no single classification system for lodging properties that is both useful and includes all properties. Some are useful, but leave out large numbers of properties; others include all properties, but are not particularly useful.

MEAL SERVICE IN LODGING ESTABLISHMENTS

As indicated above, a number of lodging establishments provide food service to guests. Some offer very limited food service—vending machines, for example— while others provide room service and several public restaurants. Some hotels quote room rates that include food service; some do not include food service with the room rates; and others offer their guests a choice. The following are the accepted terms used to describe the various arrangements:

American Plan (A. P.)   American Plan rates include three meals daily: breakfast, luncheon, and dinner. In some properties, these meals may include a full choice of the menu; in others, choices may be restricted to certain menu items, with other, more expensive items available at an extra charge. In some, it can mean unlimited quantities of unlimited selections — anything the guest chooses from the menu. More commonly, it means a choice of one item in each menu category: one appetizer, one entree, and so on. In years past, many resort hotels offered American Plan rates. In recent years, the popularity of the American Plan has decreased markedly, except in those hotels in which alternative food service is not readily available.

Modified American Plan (M. A. P.)   Modified American Plan rates include breakfast and dinner. Luncheon is available, but for an extra charge. This plan has become popular at resort operations. It was devised to satisfy those guests who objected to being charged for luncheons they did not eat, either because they were sightseeing and found it inconvenient to return to the dining room for lunch, or because they finished breakfast late in the morning and were not hungry at lunch time. Other guests were weight conscious, and did not want to consume three hearty meals in any one day. Resort owners responded by offering rates that did not include lunch.

Breakfast Plan (B. P.)   The Breakfast Plan, sometimes called the Bermuda Plan, includes a full breakfast with the quoted room rate. Although the particular term was not used, this plan has been common and popular in many parts of Europe for years. However, rising operating costs have made it necessary for many European hotels to impose a charge for the full breakfast. In the United States, the Breakfast Plan survives as the standard in bed and breakfast establishments and a few other properties. Many all-suite hotels serve full breakfast; some impose the extra charge, just as in the European hotels.

Continental Breakfast Plan   The Continental Breakfast Plan includes a light breakfast with the room rate. The composition of the light breakfast varies from one establishment to another. In some, it is limited to juice, Danish pastry — also known as sweet rolls in some parts of the country — and a choice of coffee or tea. In others, it can include an array of juices, fruits, pastries, croissants, rolls, bagels, and doughnuts, and a choice of regular and decaffeinated coffee and tea.

A number of hotels and motels offer this plan to attract business travelers and other guests accustomed to having very light breakfasts — possibly just juice and coffee — in the morning. When some operators in an area have done this, others have had to do it also in order to remain competitive: Continental breakfasts are very popular.

European Plan (E. P.)   Rates quoted under the European Plan include no meals. Ironically, the European Plan has become the standard in most American transient hotels; this was not the case through most of the nineteenth century.

Although many hotel guests choose to dine in the restaurants operated by hotels, many do not. Hotel-keepers have found that guests staying for two nights will commonly have one evening meal in the hotel restaurant and the other away from the hotel, depending on their sense of security about the area in which the property is located.

The weather often plays an important part in helping a guest decide whether or not to patronize the hotel's restaurant. If the weather is poor—rain or snow, for example—guests will stay in; if it is good, they are more likely to go out.

Some resort hotels with long traditions of offering American Plan rates alone are now giving their guests a choice of American Plan, Modified American Plan, Breakfast Plan, or European Plan. Guests who select any of the latter three can still order other meals in the hotel restaurant. However, they must order from the menu and pay separately for meals not included in the plan they have selected. Prices for these meals are normally somewhat higher than for the same meals taken as part of a meal plan.

RATINGS OF LODGING ESTABLISHMENTS

Another method of differentiating one lodging property from another is to consult a guide that rates hotels and motels.

Because quality of lodging operations varies from one establishment to another, in some parts of the world, including some European countries, lodging establishments are rated for quality by government agencies. In the United States, no government agency performs any similar service for the traveler. There are, however, two well-known private organizations that judge the quality of lodging operations and publish rating guides based on these judgments. The first of these is the Mobil Corporation which, in collaboration with Prentice Hall trade division, publishes the *Mobil Travel Guide*. The second is the American Automobile Association, which publishes the *Tour Book*. The *Mobil Travel Guide* is sold through many commercial outlets and may be purchased by anyone; the *Tour Book* is distributed only to members of the American Automobile Association.

Neither of these guides lists all lodging establishments. The publisher of each reserves the right to determine which to include. All properties listed are recommended by the rating organization. Unlisted properties are merely unlisted: They may be superior, equal, or inferior to a listed property. In every region of the country one can identify numerous small properties with fine accommodations, food, and service that are not listed in the rating guides.

The following is the rating scale used in the *Mobil Travel Guide*[3]:

*	Good; better than average
**	Very Good
***	Excellent
****	Outstanding—worth a special trip
*****	One of the best in the country

The principal areas evaluated by Mobil include quality of physical structure, furnishings, maintenance, housekeeping, and overall service. Each property listed in the Mobil guide must undergo an annual review, so no rating is ever final.

The five-star rating is awarded by Mobil to a comparatively small number of properties, which represent the finest in the United States. This top rating is extremely difficult to achieve: New York City, for example, has many excellent hotels; but as this text is written, only one has the five-star rating.

The tour books published by the American Automobile Association use a rating scale based on diamonds, rather than stars. Rated establishments can be awarded as many as five diamonds. The five possible ratings signify the following:[4]

- ◆ Provides good but unpretentious accommodations. Establishments are functional, emphasizing clean and comfortable rooms. They must meet the basic needs of comfort, privacy, cleanliness, and safety.
- ◆◆ Maintains the attributes offered at the ◆ level, while showing noticeable enhancements in decor and/or quality of furnishings. They may be recently constructed or older properties, both of which cater more to the needs of a budget-oriented traveler.
- ◆◆◆ Rated establishments offer a degree of sophistication. Additional amenities, services, and facilities may be offered. There is a marked upgrade in services and comfort.
- ◆◆◆◆ Are excellent properties displaying a high level of service and hospitality. Properties offer a wide variety of amenities and upscale facilities, both inside the room, on the grounds, and in the common areas.
- ◆◆◆◆◆ Are renowned. They exhibit an exceptionally high degree of service; striking, luxurious facilities, and many extra amenities. Guest services are executed and presented in a flawless manner. The guest

[3]Mobil Oil Corporation, *Mobil Travel Guide* (Englewood Cliffs, NJ: Prentice Hall, 1991).
[4]© Copyright American Automobile Association. Reproduced by permission.

will be pampered by a very professional, attentive staff. The facilities, service, and operation of the property help set the standards in hospitality and service.

The American Automobile Association publishes the following list of factors taken into account when rating lodging establishments:[5]

Exterior	Security
Management and staff	Bathrooms
Housekeeping	Parking
Room decor	Guest services and facilities
Maintenance	Soundproofing
Room furnishings	

As with the Mobil Guide, the top rating is very difficult to earn, although the American Automobile Association typically awards more top ratings than Mobil. Interestingly, the guides often differ in their judgments about specific properties. As with Mobil, no American Automobile Association rating is ever final: Field representatives annually reinspect all properties listed in the Tour Book.

SUMMARY

In this chapter the term *lodging property* is defined. Data are provided to illustrate the size and scope of the commercial lodging industry, including number of properties, number of employees, and total annual sales. Five key elements of lodging operations that differentiate one lodging establishment from another are listed and discussed. Numerous characteristic types of lodging establishments are described— both commercial and noncommercial, as well as both generic and specialized. Several approaches to classifying commercial lodging properties are identified, including one used by the Bureau of the Census and another in the *Business Travel Planner*, the official lodging directory of the American Hotel and Motel Association. Various rate plans are identified—several that include food with room rates, and one that does not. Finally, the two national organizations that rate the quality of lodging operations for consumers are identified and their rating scales illustrated.

QUESTIONS

1.   Define the term *lodging property* and list ten types of lodging properties that fit the definition.

---

[5]As published in the *Tour Book: New York*, An Annual Travel Guide of the American Automobile Association. (Heathrow, FL: 1991.)

2. Briefly describe the size and scope of the commercial lodging industry. Include data in your response to indicate number of properties, number of persons employed, and approximate gross sales annually.

3. What percentage of guests in commercial lodging establishments are:
   a. Traveling for business purposes?
   b. Attending conferences?
   c. Vacationing?
   d. Traveling for personal reasons?

4. List five key elements in a lodging operation that differentiate one lodging establishment from another.

5. Describe the impressions lodging property owners tend to convey to the public by selecting the following terms to identify properties.
   a. Inn
   b. Hotel
   c. Motel
   d. Lodge
   e. Guest house
   f. Bed and breakfast
   g. Hostel
   h. Condominium
   i. Hospital

6. Identify the principal characteristics of each of the following:

a.	Motor inn	k.	Convention hotel
b.	Transient motel	l.	All-suite hotel
c.	Residential hotel	m.	Extended-stay hotel
d.	Resort hotel	n.	Conference center
e.	Traditional resort	o.	Casino hotel
f.	All-inclusive resort	p.	Health spa
g.	Resort condominium	q.	Boarding house
h.	Resort motel	r.	Lodging house
i.	Guest ranch	s.	Dormitory
j.	Commercial hotel	t.	Nursing home

7. In the chapter, the authors discuss a number of lodging operations that are thought of more commonly as *modes of transportation*. Cruise ships are one example. Name ten others.

8. Identify the categories used to classify commercial lodging properties by:
   a. Number of rooms
   b. Location
   c. Types of properties

9. Identify the inadequacies inherent in each of the three classification systems identified in question 8.

10. List and describe the six categories that comprise the system used in *Business Travel Planner*, the official lodging directory of the American Hotel and Motel Association.

11. Define each of the following:
    a. European Plan
    b. American Plan
    c. Modified American Plan
    d. Breakfast Plan
    e. Continental Breakfast Plan

12. Given a 200-room commercial hotel in the business center of one of America's ten largest cities, which of the five plans identified in question 11 would be appropriate to offer transient guests? Why?

13. Given a 350-room beachfront resort property located in Miami Beach, Florida, which of the five plans identified in question 11 would be appropriate to offer transient guests? Why?

14. Identify the two national organizations that publish widely recognized ratings of commercial lodging establishments. List five factors used by each for determining these ratings.

Lodging Operations:
A Systems Approach

9

LEARNING OBJECTIVES

After reading and studying this chapter, you should be able to:

1. *Define the terms* system *and* subsystem.
2. *Identify the inputs, systems, and outputs of a basic lodging operation.*
3. *Identify six additional services offered by some, but not all, lodging operators.*
4. *List and state the goals of the four subsystems associated with front office operation and describe the functions of each.*
5. *List the advantages of using electronic locks, rather than traditional locks with metal keys.*
6. *Describe three possible variations of the checkout procedure used by hotels, motels, and similar facilities.*
7. *Identify two common problems that have induced lodging operators to overbook reservations.*
8. *Describe a minimum of ten tasks that may be assigned to the housekeeping subsystem.*
9. *List a minimum of ten tasks required to make a room ready for occupancy.*
10. *Describe three ways in which work is assigned to room attendants in hotels, motels, and similar properties.*
11. *Discuss the key differences between security measures used in large center-city hotels and those used in smaller rural and suburban properties.*

12. *Identify the kinds of services normally associated with a front service subsystem.*
13. *List three uses of the telephone subsystem.*
14. *List and describe the three types of food service offered in lodging establishments.*
15. *Explain the importance of a recreation and entertainment subsystem to resort and gambling lodging properties.*
16. *Identify the following subsystems and describe the function of each in lodging operations: a. Banking services; b. Guest laundry; c. Dry cleaning services; d. Office services; e. Health facilities; f. Newsstands; g. Shops*

INTRODUCTION

The previous chapter was devoted to examining the size and scope of the lodging industry. We identified characteristic types of lodging establishments and discussed several classification systems. In addition, we identified several rate plans that include food service and described two rating systems used for lodging properties. With that as background, we now turn to the subject of lodging operations and proceed to examine it from a systems viewpoint.

As discussed in the previous chapter, lodging establishments may offer any number of different services to guests. Some lodging operations offer very few — simple guest houses having only rooms with a bath down the hall, for example. Others present a full range — elegant luxury hotels, for example, offering 24-hour service, laundry and valet services, concierge service, 24-hour maid service, secretarial services, hair stylists, and many other services.

Lodging establishments also vary greatly in size and in target clientele. The simple guest house may have only one or two rooms to rent, whereas the large, complex hotel may have over 3,000. Similarly, some lodging operations cater to business travelers, while others specialize in convention business. Still others offer permanent accommodations to those who consider the hotel their home, while some provide temporary accommodations to people on vacation.

It should be apparent from the broad range of possibilities for service, size, and target clientele that many of the details of operation differ from one to another. For example, compare a resort property to a city hotel. The resort is likely to provide recreational activities — golf, tennis, and swimming, for example — requiring specialized staff and equipment. In contrast, the city hotel might offer specialized services to appeal to high-level business executives — in-room computers and fax machines on each floor, possibly — requiring different kinds of specialized staff and equipment. While there are obvious differences between these two — and between any two different types of lodging properties—there are a number of important similarities. All lodging properties provide accommodations for guests, and all provide some services—although the services may be very limited in some properties. As we will see, however, the points of similarity are of far greater importance than the many apparent differences.

The purpose of this chapter will be to identify some of the important similarities in lodging establishments that are sometimes obscured by the vast array of differences. We will define and describe a number of important elements and processes that lodging operations have in common. To accomplish this, we will treat the lodging enterprise—any lodging enterprise—as a system.

SYSTEM DEFINED

The term *system* has previously been defined as a whole unit consisting of a set of interdependent and interrelated parts, coordinated to accomplish a set of goals.

Each part has a specific function in the whole unit, and each of the parts of a system can be called a subsystem. The automobile provides an example. An automobile is a system designed primarily for the transportation of people and goods. It consists of a number of subsystems—electrical, motor, and drive, among others—each of which plays an important role in achieving the goals of the main system. The electrical subsystem, for example, has a battery to store the energy required to start the engine. In turn, the engine powers a generator that keeps the battery charged. These two are interdependent: Neither can operate as intended unless the other is operating properly; both are necessary for the automobile to achieve its intended goal—the transportation of people and goods.

Systems can best be understood in terms of an input–output model, such as that in Table 9.1.

TABLE 9.1 *Input–Output Model*
INPUT $\longrightarrow$ SYSTEM $\longrightarrow$ OUTPUT

In an automobile, one of the inputs is fuel, which provides energy for the motor to run. The output is a force that goes to the drive subsystem, which enables the automobile to move.

Lodging systems also require inputs—the resources required for the lodging system to work. Lodging operations use three kinds of resources—physical resources, human resources, and operational resources—as inputs. In lodging, the physical resources include buildings, furnishings, and machines. The human resources include people doing jobs with titles such as *desk clerk* and *housekeeper*. The operational resources include paper supplies, linens, and money. These inputs enable lodging systems to produce outputs. Outputs are the results produced—the outcomes of productive enterprise. The outputs of lodging systems reflect the goals established by lodging operators. Clean accommodations are among the most common goals of lodging operations.

These goals can vary from one establishment to another. In some lodging operations, the single significant goal is to provide clean accommodations to transient guests. This could be true in lodging operations catering to the budget-minded traveler. In those catering to people willing and able to spend more than the budget-minded traveler, the goals might include providing a higher level of accommodation and offering additional services—as in a luxury hotel.

A lodging system is composed of subsystems that become systems in themselves. Just as in the example of the automobile, the subsystems are necessary to achieve the overall goals of the system. The number of lodging subsystems and the complexity of each will vary from property to property. Operations accommodating economy-minded travelers will have only a few, simple subsystems. Luxury properties will have many and more complex subsystems.

Table 9.2 is an expanded version of the input–output model. It shows inputs, subsystems, and outputs for a simple lodging system.

LODGING SUBSYSTEMS

Lodging subsystems can be divided into two groups:

1. Those common to all lodging operations
2. Those that are not common to all

Those in the first group are to be found in every lodging operation; without them, one would not be operating a lodging establishment. Those in the second group are used selectively by lodging operators whose goals can best be reached by using one or more of these subsystems.

Group 1 includes three subsystems:

front office subsystem
housekeeping subsystem
security subsystem

TABLE 9.2   *A Simple Lodging System*

INPUTS ⟶	SYSTEM ⟶	OUTPUTS
building	front office	clean room
equipment	subsystem	safe environment
human resources	housekeeping	courteous service
funds	subsystem	satisfied guest
supplies	security	
	subsystem	

Group 2 includes those subsystems needed to offer any of a broad range of other services that are not necessarily available in all lodging establishments. Their availability depends on the goals of the lodging operator. Included in Group 2 are a range of possible services that a lodging operator may provide; the following is a list of some of the more common of these additional services:

1. Front service
2. Telephone service
3. Food and beverage services
4. Recreation/entertainment
5. Parking
6. Other personal services

Lodging operators choosing to provide some or all of these services have two basic options:

1. hire employees to provide the service
2. engage an outside contractor to do so for a fee

For purposes of this text, we will consider that either option results in the addition of a subsystem to the lodging operation — one devoted to providing the service. In addition, guests using the service of the subsystem will consider it part of the lodging operation regardless of whether it is staffed by employees of the lodging establishment or those of an outside contractor.

The student reading about lodging systems may find it useful to refer to particular lodging operations. Therefore, in order to describe the various lodging subsystems and to point out some of the differences from one property to another, we will refer to the three distinctly different types of lodging properties described in Case Studies 9.1, 9.2, and 9.3.

The first of these is a limited service budget motel, catering to economy-minded transient travelers. The second is a full service, upscale resort hotel, which provides accommodations and services primarily for vacationers. The third is a luxury hotel located in a major cosmopolitan city, offering the services associated with this type of property.

CASE STUDY 9.1 *The Value Lodge is a 50-room property located in a small midwestern town adjacent to an exit on Interstate 80. It is owned and operated by a couple named Goodson — Roger and Janet. It is part of a chain — Value Lodges. Roger was an executive for a major company for many years. Eventually he began to dislike the work and felt he was wasting his life, so he decided to open his own business. He had always been fascinated by innkeeping and felt he had a talent for it.*

Because he had no formal training in the business, he decided to work with a chain to receive the necessary training and to reduce risk. The Goodsons sold their home and as many other assets as they could. Because they had limited funds, they could afford only a relatively small property. They answered an advertisement in the Wall Street Journal *placed by the Value Lodge Co. After thorough investigation, they agreed to an arrangement giving them a motel in an excellent location, a Value Lodge sign, a large mortgage, and an obligation to pay various fees to the chain.*

The Value Lodge is a fairly simple 50-room operation. Roger and Janet, as owner–managers, live in quarters connected to the office, where guests check in and out. The 50 units are modern and comfortable— pleasantly decorated, yet simply furnished. Each unit contains two queen-size beds, private bath, color television, two lounge chairs, a dresser with mirror, and a telephone, among other items. The motel has no restaurant, no meeting rooms, no swimming pool, and no recreational facilities. It does have a small dining area with tables, chairs, and vending machines, from which guests may obtain ice, beverages, sandwiches, and snacks. The motel caters almost exclusively to travelers—motorists from Interstate 80 looking for clean, comfortable, overnight accommodations. Most guests check in by late afternoon and are back on the road again early the following morning.

There is a Burger King located across the road and a family restaurant nearby. The Value Lodge Co. has a central system that takes reservations for all units in the chain. Roger and Janet receive about 25 percent of their business from the reservation system.

Roger and Janet take turns in the office during the day. Roger is usually there during morning hours doing the bookkeeping and ordering supplies while Janet supervises the housekeeping. During the afternoon, Roger sees to the maintenance of the grounds and rooms while Janet takes her turn in the office. In the evening, neither stays in the office, but the door to their quarters is open so that they can attend to any needs of the guests, or to any check-ins.

CASE STUDY 9.2   *The Mountain Inn is a 400-room, three-star resort hotel located at a major ski area in Colorado. It is owned by the Mountain Inn Corporation, a company formed by the group of investors that built the property. They have hired the Preferred*

Management Company to run it. The agreement calls for Preferred to receive 3 percent of gross room sales and 10 percent of profits.

The Mountain Inn is a seasonal resort hotel. During the winter months—early November until mid-April—the hotel is a ski resort, catering to vacationers who come for winter sports. During the summer months—from June 1 until September 30—it is a summer resort catering to individuals and groups that come for summer recreational activities and meetings. The hotel closes during the months of October and May.

The 400-room hotel has two dining rooms—one for individual guests and families and the other for groups. It has one large meeting room that can be divided into several smaller ones, as well as coffee shop, pharmacy, hair stylist, several boutiques, indoor pool, exercise room, two racquetball courts, and four outdoor tennis courts.

The hotel is located at the base of a ski slope, within one mile of an excellent golf course. Mountain Inn guests receive special consideration at the golf course. There is an excellent stable nearby for horseback riding. Additional services offered guests include room service from 7 A.M. until midnight, as well as tennis and swimming instruction.

CASE STUDY 9.3 *The Kensington is a 350-room, four-star luxury hotel located in the center of a major eastern city. It is owned and operated by a nationally known chain, but the name of the chain is not used on any signs, linen, literature, or other matter that would be noticed by guests. Management decided that the image of the property would not be improved by being openly linked with this chain.*

All 350 guest rooms are furnished with reproductions of antique furniture. There is always a doorman on duty at the front door to welcome guests, take charge of their cars, and obtain transportation for them. The lobby is all marble and brass. Each elevator is operated by an attendant, even though they can be operated automatically.

The Kensington has a large ballroom with its own kitchen and a separate entrance from the street for guests attending weddings and similar formal functions. The hotel does not have meeting rooms, except for three small rooms that can be used by guests for small meetings.

Other services associated with the hotel include 24-hour room service, concierge, secretarial service, hair stylist, gourmet dining in the Empire Room, cocktails in the Kensington Lounge, pharmacy, indoor pool and exercise room, and extensive housekeeping services that include the service of early morning tea or coffee, fresh towels twice each day, and turn-down service in the evening.

Seventy-five of the Kensington's 350 rooms are presently occupied by permanent guests. The remaining rooms are available for transient business. Guests are served by a staff of 500 people, half of whom have been employed by the hotel for over ten years. The Kensington emphasizes personal service. All staff members—desk clerks, elevator operators, bellmen, and doormen, among others—make a concerted effort to know guests by name. Staff members are expected to be friendly and courteous at all times, and to attend quickly to all reasonable requests made by the guests.

Significantly, all three of these properties are closely related to one another: They provide accommodations to transient guests, and each operates as a hotel or a motel. These have been selected for a simple reason: Hotel and motel properties provide the best and most understandable examples of the subsystems that make up a lodging property. In fact, most of the material in this and the following chapter relates to hotels, motels, motor lodges, and similar properties—the kinds of commercial lodging establishments that are generally of the greatest interest to students preparing for careers in the field.

Group I

As previously stated, the three subsystems in this group—front office, housekeeping, and security—are common to all lodging establishments. However, although this is true, the study of housekeeping or security subsystems in a small boarding house would be much less enlightening than the study of those subsystems in a large hotel, motel, or similar commercial lodging enterprise. Therefore, much of the following discussion relates to those kinds of properties—the kinds illustrated in Case Studies 9.1, 9.2, and 9.3.

FRONT OFFICE. *Front office* is a term commonly used to refer to the location where the front desk is situated within a lodging operation. To guests, the front office represents the lodging property: It is their first point of contact on arrival and last point of contact at departure.

The front office subsystem in a lodging operation is made up of four other subsystems.[1] These are:

1. Check-in
2. Information
3. Checkout
4. Reservations

[1]Sub-subsystems, really. However, using the term would make the language a bit difficult to deal with, so we will simply call these subsystems, too.

The three lodging subsystems common to all lodging operations — front office, housekeeping, and security. Each encompasses a wide variety of responsibilities. The front office (top left) coordinates check-in, guest information, check-out, and reservations. Housekeeping (top right) provides appropriate care for guest rooms, the lodging's linen and uniforms, and the appearance of all common rooms and facilities. Security (bottom) ensures the safety of guests and their property, providing room safes and taking measures against crime, fire, and other dangers. (Clockwise from top left: courtesy Hospitality Franchise Systems; courtesy Boca Raton Resort and Club; courtesy Sentry Group.)

Together, the coordinated activities of these four subsystems comprise front office operation.

Check-in.   *Check-in* refers to a process by which people become guests in a lodging establishment. The goal of the check-in subsystem in hotels, motels, and other lodging operations is to accomplish this process.

Check-in takes place in a *reception area*, another name for that part of a front office known as the *front desk*. Here, guests register, are assigned accommodations, and pick up keys for these accommodations. In the Kensington, the check-in process proceeds in the following manner:

An arriving guest goes first to the front desk, located in the lobby near the main entrance. The *room clerk*, a job title for the person on duty at the front desk,[2] greets and welcomes the arriving guest and asks if she has a reservation. If so, the room clerk asks the guest to *register*, a term which refers to filling out a form known as a *registration card*. A registration card is a printed front office form on which guests record their names, addresses, and other information, including the number of nights a guest expects to stay. If the guest has no reservation, the room clerk will describe available accommodations and rates, thus attempting to "sell" a room to the individual. If successful, the room clerk will ask the individual to register. Once the guest has registered, the room clerk assigns a suitable accommodation.

Although this describes the procedure followed in the Kensington, it is essentially the same in all hotels, motels, and similar commercial lodging operations. In the Value Lodge, arriving guests check in at a small front desk located in an office adjacent to the owners' apartment, rather than in a lobby, but they do so for the same purpose. The equipment used in the process differs considerably from one property to another, as do a number of the procedural details. The important point is that the check-in subsystems in all lodging establishments share at least one common goal: to assign guests to rooms.

In order to be able to assign guests to rooms, room clerks must be able quickly to determine which rooms are occupied, which have been vacated but not cleaned, and which are both vacant and ready. To enable room clerks to do this, lodging establishments use one of two possible means to maintain the necessary information: manual or electronic. The latter refers to computers, of course, and computers are becoming the preferred means in all but the smallest properties. Computers used for guest check-in are typically part of an overall *property management system* — a term for a computer system designed to perform a variety of tasks formerly attended to by manual means.

In some properties — the Value Lodge, for example — the information room clerks need is maintained manually in a device called a room rack; in many other more complex operations — the Kensington, for example — property management

---

[2]There are a number of titles used for this job including *desk clerk, assistant manager, desk attendant,* and *guest services attendant*. For simplicity, we will only use the terms *room clerk* and *desk clerk* in this text.

systems are used. Detailed information about specific equipment and techniques for registering guests is normally covered in a rooms management course.

Today, most hotels, motels, and similar lodging establishments require that arriving guests either pay in advance for their accommodations or present credit identification. Credit identification is verifiable proof that an individual has sufficient credit to cover his or her hotel bill. This typically means that guests are required to present acceptable credit cards. The Mountain Inn, for example, accepts both cash and national credit cards, but virtually all its guests present credit cards at check-in and settle their bills at the time of departure. In contrast, the Value Lodge requires that all guests either pay for their accommodation in cash as they check in or sign credit card vouchers imprinted with their card numbers. Most of its guests pay cash.

After questions of billing have been attended to, guests are given access to their assigned accommodations in one of two possible ways: Either guests are given keys to their assigned rooms or their keys are given to bellmen, who accompany guests to their rooms. In the Value Lodge, there are no bellmen; guests are simply given keys and directed to their rooms. In contrast, room clerks in the Kensington are required to give the keys to bellmen, who always accompany guests to their rooms. At the Mountain Inn, guests are offered their choice of being accompanied by bellmen or finding their own way.

Modern technology has changed the nature of the room keys used in many hotels and motels. Although many operations still use the traditional lock with metal key—the kind inserted into a lock, then turned to unlock a door—growing numbers are now using electronic locks. These are opened by means of plastic cards having information electronically encoded on magnetic strips. To enter a room, the guest inserts the card into an electronic device that reads the code and opens the lock.

Plastic "keys" have several important advantages over traditional metal keys. Hotel and motel operators have constant problems with traditional keys. When lost or stolen, they are sometimes used by burglars to enter rooms illegally and steal guests' money and valuables. In addition, lost keys must be replaced, which is an expensive and time-consuming task in a large property. Some large hotels employ full-time locksmiths, whose jobs are to make duplicates to replace lost keys and to change the locks in guest room doors. The plastic cards eliminate many of the problems associated with traditional keys. No room numbers are visible, so that a lost card is useless to the finder. And changing the codes each time a guest checks out is the same as changing the lock.

Information.   The goal of an information subsystem in hotel and motel operations is to serve the special needs of guests and employees for information about:

1. Guests
2. Goods and services

Guest Information.   The front office serves as a center for guest information. In effect, it maintains a data bank with the names and addresses of current guests, their room numbers, the status of their accounts, and considerable additional information. As guests check in, information about them is added to this data bank; as guests leave, the data bank is changed to keep it current. Thus, the front office of a hotel or motel always has up-to-date information about all current guests and about the status of each room—whether occupied or vacant. This information may be maintained in any number of possible forms: data in a computer, typewritten slips of paper, or handwritten sheets of paper are some of the possibilities. The information is used constantly.

Without this information, any number of routine front office matters would be very difficult. For example, in the Kensington, one of these routine matters is assisting guests who have forgotten their room numbers. When such a guest goes to the front desk, the employee on duty finds the guest's name and room number in its data bank and is thus easily able to give the guest his room number. In the Value Lodge, a small property, the owner has the same need for information, but maintains the records in a very different way: The registration cards are simply kept in a file box in alphabetical order.

In front office work, some of the other tasks that require the use of this guest information include: placing mail and messages for guests in numbered mailboxes that correspond to their room numbers; directing incoming telephone calls to guests' rooms; assisting visitors in finding the guests they have come to see; verifying the room numbers of guests who have signed guest checks in the restaurant or bar; determining the number of occupied rooms that are expected to be vacated by guests checking out on the current day; counting the number of rooms vacant at any given time during the course of a day; determining the *house count*, a term meaning the number of guests registered in the property; advising housekeepers that a room has been vacated so that it can be cleaned; and calculating the percentage of guest rooms occupied.

Information About Goods and Services.   Many transient guests find themselves in strange surroundings when they have registered in a hotel or motel. Most are strangers to the community and need some orientation and assistance. In many hotels and motels, the front office may have maps, guidebooks, and other sources of information to help guests. Room clerks and other employees may be asked to recommend restaurants, give directions to places of interest, or help guests find sources for any number of goods or services that the community offers. The front office in the Mountain Hotel, for example, has maps of the surrounding region that it makes available without charge to guests interested in sightseeing. Similarly, the owners of the Value Lodge provide guests with free copies of a directory listing the locations of all other motels in the chain, from coast to coast.

In hotels, motels, and other lodging establishments that offer services beyond sleeping accommodations, guests normally ask many questions about these services. They may ask about the hours of operation of restaurants, bars, swimming pools, stables, or other facilities; regulations governing the use of the golf course; availability of child care services, hair stylists, or travel agents; details about the kinds of exercise equipment, types of computers and printers, or hair dryers available. An unlimited number of questions can be asked about the facilities and services of the property itself. Consequently, room clerks and other employees are expected to provide all sorts of information to guests quickly and courteously.

Checkout.   *Checkout* refers to a process by which guests terminate their status as guests of a lodging establishment. The goal of a checkout subsystem in hotels, motels, and other lodging operations is to accomplish this process.

There are several variations of the checkout process. In the Value Lodge, overnight guests typically pay their bills in advance at check-in, so most simply leave their keys in the rooms and drive away. Because of the size of the property, the owners normally see or hear guests depart and thus know that the vacated room needs to be cleaned and made ready for its next occupant.

In the Mountain Hotel, the procedure is different. All guests are expected to stop at the front office to settle their accounts and leave their keys. As indicated above, these accounts are created and maintained in the front office. When guests leave, employees update the front office data bank and make the room number available to housekeepers so that the room will be made ready for the next guests.

In the Kensington, in contrast, guests have access to advanced technology that enables them to check out from their rooms, using the television screen to review and settle their bills. While the approaches differ from one establishment to another, the goal is the same in all three: To accomplish the checkout process.

Today, because so many lodging operations require that guests sign credit card vouchers or pay cash at check-in, there are fewer problems with unpaid and uncollectable bills than was the case years ago. Because credit cards can be verified as guests check in, hotels, motels, and similar lodging establishments do not have as many *skippers*, an old hotel term used to refer to guests who leave without paying their bills

Reservations.   *Reservation* refers to an arrangement by which lodging operators hold accommodations for guests who will be arriving at some later time. This may be later in the day on the date the reservation is made or on some date in the future. The reservations subsystem in a hotel or motel is designed to make such arrangements. There are two major goals of reservations subsystems.

One major goal is to serve the needs of people seeking assurance that accommodations will be available to them when needed. Individuals intending to travel to a distant location want to be certain that they will have rooms to stay in when they arrive. Reservation subsystems are intended to meet this need. A potential guest can call or write the reservation office in a hotel, motel, or other lodging establishment to arrange for a room to be held for the necessary number of nights.

The reservations subsystem in a lodging establishment typically consists of an office with some number of employees, known as *reservation clerks* or *reservationists*, who respond to requests for accommodations from potential guests. Requests may be for the coming night, some date in the distant future, or any time in between. These requests usually arrive by telephone, fax, or letter. Each request for a room reservation must be answered promptly with a definite *yes* or *no. Maybe* is never an acceptable response to a potential guest. In order to give definite answers, reservationists must have access to data that include the number of rooms already reserved for a given night; the number of rooms remaining available for those same nights; sold-out dates for which no reservations can be taken; and rates for the rooms available for any given night. Without such information, no reservationist would be able to give a prompt response to someone calling on the telephone to ask about the availability of, say, a room for one person for three nights, beginning next Tuesday. Potential guests need immediate, unequivocal answers to requests of this nature, and reservationists must be able to provide them.

Assuming that an appropriate room is available at an acceptable rate for the nights requested by a caller, the reservationist must record some information quickly. This normally includes name, address, dates for which the room is to be reserved, type of room required, rate, expected time of arrival, and intended method of payment. Some lodging operators may require additional information — telephone number, for example. Many require deposits from guests before they will confirm reservations. Others reserve rooms only for guests who provide national credit card numbers when they make their reservations.

The information taken from guests is recorded either on a paper form or in a computer terminal. If the paper form is used, additional processing is required to add the reservation to others for the same arrival date. If a computer terminal is used, the reservation is automatically added to the reservations data base. The Value Lodge, for example, uses inexpensive paper forms for recording reservations, and files all the reservations for one date in one folder. In contrast, the Kensington has a computerized system, and all reservations are recorded in terminals and thus added to the reservations data base.

Each day, the reservations that have been taken for that particular day are given to the front desk so those on duty will have the names, addresses, and other information about guests who are expected to check in during the course of the day. In the Value Lodge, the owner has a single folder at the desk that contains all reservations for the current day. In the Kensington, the morning desk clerk uses the computer system at the front desk to print the list of reservations for the day. In some hotels, no list would be printed: Desk clerks would use the computer system to look up arriving guests' reservations.

The second major goal of the reservations subsystem is to ensure that the number of rooms occupied each day is as great as possible and that the rates charged for those rooms are the highest possible.

The ideal goal in a hotel or motel is to have every room occupied each night at the highest possible rate. This is obviously the way to earn maximum revenue. Although it is desirable, however, it is nearly impossible to accomplish. In order to come as close to this ideal as possible, an owner or manager must establish a rate structure that will enable reservationists to sell as many rooms as possible. There must be a range of rates that appeal to the target clientele—that group of individuals and businesses that management wants to attract to the property.

Overbooking.   One of the more difficult and interesting problems of lodging operation results from customers who make reservations and either cancel at the last minute or fail to check in. Those who fail to check in are called *no-shows*. Last minute cancellations and no-shows may result in vacant rooms and lost revenue. Potential guests, whose requests for reservations were turned down when it appeared the hotel would be sold out, have then gone to other properties and may be permanently lost.

This problem can be dealt with in several ways. One of these is to *overbook*, which means to take more reservations than the number of anticipated rooms available. Many transient hotels have used this method successfully. They often accept 10 percent to 15 percent more reservations than rooms are available, knowing from historical data that some customers will cancel and others will not arrive to claim their reservations.

A difficulty arises when the hotel miscalculates and the anticipated number of cancellations do not materialize, or more people than anticipated arrive to claim their reservations. When this occurs, some guests must be *walked*—a hotel term meaning to send guests with confirmed reservations to other lodging properties when their reservations cannot be honored.

In recent years, lodging operators have developed new strategies for dealing with the problem. Several methods are used to insure that hotels do not lose revenue because of no-shows. They include:

1. Confirmations that state reservations will only be guaranteed until a given time in the afternoon—5 P.M., for example. Thus, hotels do not need to overbook to any great extent because they can rent rooms to walk-in guests after that time.
2. Requiring a major credit card number when the reservation is made. Many hotels will not accept a reservation without this credit card number.

No-shows are charged for the rooms held for their arrival. The primary difficulty with this process is that customers often state that they did not make the reservation or that they cancelled the reservation, and they refuse to pay. The amount is then billed back to the hotel.

The American Express Company has developed the Assured Reservation plan. Under this arrangement, customers who agree to provide their American Express credit card numbers to the hotel also agree to pay for the room if they do not show. In return, the hotel will guarantee that a room will be available, no matter what time they arrive. Customers can appear at the hotel at any hour of the night and expect to have a room available for them.

Most hotels are not guilty of serious overbooking. Nevertheless, some do make mistakes and find themselves in the position of having to walk guests. When this happens, most hotels and motels attempt to find accommodations for the guest at another hotel, then pay for transportation to the other property. Some even pay for the first night's accommodation.

Resort hotels have long required advance payment for accommodations. The typical resort hotel will require a substantial advance deposit, and some resort hotels require full payment in advance. All have refund policies for customers who must cancel, but they vary greatly. Some will refund only a portion of the advance payment; others will refund the entire amount if the reservation is canceled within two or three weeks prior to scheduled arrival. Some have a sliding scale that provides a percentage refund ranging from 100 percent to 0 percent, depending on when the reservation is canceled. The closer the cancellation is to arrival time, the less of a percentage is refunded. No-shows are seldom a problem with resort hotels that require advance deposits. Thus, many of them do not overbook; and some will overbook only slightly, knowing that a few cancellations will occur.

HOUSEKEEPING. The second major subsystem in lodging operations is housekeeping. The principal goal of the housekeeping subsystem is to provide appropriate care for guest rooms and various other areas in the lodging property. Although this sounds simple enough, it entails numerous tasks, large and small, many of which are very easy for staff members to overlook. However, survey after survey has shown that guests notice and rate overall cleanliness in hotels, motels, and similar properties. These surveys also reveal that positive or negative feelings about housekeeping in a given property play a major role in determining whether or not a guest will return to stay in the property again. In the housekeeping subsystem, even the smallest task can be of very great importance to guests.

Providing appropriate care for guest rooms and other areas in hotels, motels, and similar properties includes changing bed and bath linen, making beds, and cleaning rooms for current guests; doing the same in rooms vacated by guests who have checked out, thus preparing these rooms for new occupants; cleaning hallways and such areas as the lobby, meeting rooms, public bathrooms, and offices used by the management; and insuring the availability of a supply of clean bed and bath linens either by operating an on-site laundry, by using a commercial laundry to wash soiled linen, or by making suitable arrangements with a linen rental company. In addition, the housekeeping departments in some properties have responsibility for looking after the supply of uniforms for uniformed employees in all departments and the *food linen*, the general term for all linens used in a food and beverage department. They also may have responsibility for: redecorating and rehabilitating rooms; looking after articles in the property's "lost and found"; maintaining floors throughout the property—washing and waxing floors, vacuuming and shampooing carpets, for example; washing windows; raising and lowering flags; moving furniture; repairing torn fabrics; attending to the rooms of employees who live in the property; cleaning such outside areas as porches or sidewalks that surround the building. The tasks assigned to housekeeping are limited only by the imaginations of those who make the decisions in hotels, motels, and similar lodging properties.

The operation of the housekeeping subsystem can be complicated. Housekeeping is commonly the largest single department in a lodging operation, and is managed by an individual who is usually given such a title as *head housekeeper, supervising housekeeper,* or *executive housekeeper.* There are many variations. A head housekeeper manages a staff that may include people with such job titles as *maid* or *housekeeper, room attendant, rooms inspector, houseman, laundry manager, linen room manager, assistant housekeeper, floor supervisor,* and many other possibilities. Job titles vary considerably from one property to another.

While many of the particular responsibilities of housekeeping may vary from one property to another, one major responsibility is common to all: giving daily attention to guest rooms occupied the previous night, whether or not the guests in those rooms check out on the current day.

Attending to Guest Rooms.   Each guest room in a property is monitored daily by the housekeeping department to determine whether it is occupied or vacant. In most major hotels and motels, daily comparison is made between housekeeping's determinations and front office records of occupancy so that any differences can be identified and investigated.

When an occupied room becomes vacant because of a guest checkout, the housekeeping office is informed and a maid or room attendant is advised so that the room can be made ready for a new occupant. This entails removing all soiled bed and bath linen from the room; replacing it with fresh, clean linen; making the bed(s), cleaning the bathroom; vacuuming the floor; dusting or polishing furniture; cleaning mirrors; emptying wastebaskets; replenishing supplies of tissue, toilet paper, matches, laundry bags, soap, and such amenities as shampoo, hair conditioner, and shower caps; and checking electric lights, televisions, clock radios, heating/cooling units, hair dryers, shoeshine machines, and other devices to be sure they are working properly. It may also require washing ashtrays; replenishing supplies for in-room coffee- and tea-making devices; restocking supplies for in-room bars; reporting items used from an in-room bar to the front office for billing purposes; checking the number of hangers in closets; and many other possibilities. There can be so much to do in every room in some properties that staff members may be given printed lists of items to be checked.

For rooms that will continue to be occupied by the current guests, the procedures may be essentially the same, although some properties do not change bed linens every day for guests staying several nights. It should be noted, as well, that it is probably not possible to do a thorough job of cleaning when guests' belongings are in the room. This is particularly true when clothes and other items are scattered around the room.

If a room has remained vacant since it was last made ready for a new occupant, it is not normally necessary to do more than check it quickly, just to be sure it is still fresh and clean.

In order to have adequate supplies of linens and other materials available as they work, room attendants normally have mobile carts that can be pushed from room to room. Each of these carts typically has a canvas bag for storing the soiled laundry taken from guests' rooms. All soiled laundry collected in the course of one day is normally taken to a single area for processing, which may entail separating it by type and reloading it in other carts that will be collected by a commercial laundry or linen rental company, or preparing it for processing by the in-house laundry.

In the larger hotels and motels of major cities, the work of room attendants may be inspected by supervisors, who verify that rooms have been properly cleaned and meet the standards established for the property. After a vacated room has been made up and inspected, the supervisor may have responsibility for reporting it ready for occupancy—by informing the front office directly, or reporting it via the housekeeping office. In a number of the smaller properties, room attendants may have little or no immediate supervision and may report directly to the front office.

The number of room attendants and the manner in which their work is assigned varies greatly from one property to another. In some, they are paid by the hour and expected to work at a reasonable pace, completing as many rooms as possible. In others, they are given a work quota for the seven-hour day that is stated in terms of number of rooms or beds that must be done. In still others, they are paid by the room. In most cases, they are assigned a *station*, a term used to describe the particular section of property or the group of rooms assigned to a room attendant. The station may be a complete floor or a specific number of rooms on one floor, for example. Some hotels, motels, and similar properties use a team approach, assigning more than one attendant per room. The amount of time required to clean a room will depend on the number of attendants assigned to it, as well as the size of the room, the number of beds, the extent of cleaning expected each day, and whether or not the room is a checkout. When a room is occupied by the same guests for several days, the amount of time attendants must spend in that room daily is somewhat less than the time they must spend in checkouts.

In those hotels that are considered luxury properties, room attendants normally have more work to do in each room. In some properties they must polish fine antique furniture; in others, they may be required to place arrangements of fresh flowers in rooms daily. In luxury hotels, standards of cleanliness are typically higher than in many other types of properties, so that a greater amount of time is expected to be taken with each room. In many luxury operations, guests may be provided with services not provided in other types of properties. In some, room attendants visit each occupied guest room during the early evening to supply fresh towels, empty wastebaskets, and turn down bedding.

At a property such as the Kensington, these services are routinely performed for each guest. It is necessary, therefore, for the hotel to employ additional room attendants for this purpose. They are supervised by an assistant housekeeper who works an afternoon and evening shift. The Kensington uses housekeeping teams to clean rooms. Two room attendants spend approximately one-half hour working together to clean a typical room—one full hour of working time in each room. This is about 50 percent more time than is spent by room attendants at other hotels in the area.

The Mountain Inn and the Value Lodge assign specific rooms to each room attendant. In the Mountain Inn, each is assigned a permanent station consisting of ten rooms on one floor, which are to be completed in one seven-hour shift. In the Value Lodge, room attendants are expected to do fourteen rooms in the seven-hour shift; and those who complete the work satisfactorily in less time are allowed to do additional rooms for extra pay. Thus, room attendants in the Mountain Inn complete each room in an average of forty-two minutes, whereas those in the Value Lodge take about thirty minutes.

Redecorating and Rehabilitating Rooms. A very important function of the housekeeping subsystem is long-term upkeep. This is the process of maintaining the appearance of guest rooms by attending to the many items that make rooms attractive and appealing to guests—including paint, wallpaper, fixtures, carpeting, furniture, lamp shades, curtains, draperies, and other fabrics. All these must be kept in the proper condition. This may mean touching up the paint on one wall, patching damaged wallpaper on another, or replacing a burned patch of carpet, a damaged lamp, a tattered lamp shade, or a broken mirror—the list is endless. If the quality of guest rooms is allowed to deteriorate, they become less appealing to potential guests and fewer people are willing to stay in them. Over time, lodging operators who ignore this important element of housekeeping find that the establishment has deteriorated below the standards of the original property.

Many hotel and motel operators refurbish guest rooms every few years on a planned rotation system. Each year a certain number of rooms are taken out of service to be completely refurbished. They are stripped, then redecorated and refurnished. One well-known hotel in New York completely refurbishes several floors each year. Over the course of five to seven years, every room in the property is completely redone.

SECURITY. The third of the front office subsystems is that devoted to providing security. Security is one of the most important services provided for guests.

Hotels have both moral and legal obligations to protect guests from harm and safeguard their property. The goal of the security subsystem is to provide the necessary protection to keep guests and their property safe. The extent of this protection varies from establishment to establishment and from location to location. Danger to guests may came from intruders, other guests, or from such hazards as fire or unsafe conditions in the property.

Major metropolitan areas typically have greater crime problems than rural areas, and large hotels in the centers of cities tend to have greater difficulty with burglary and robbery than do small properties in outlying areas. Thus, major hotels in major cities will both need and take greater security measures than their rural counterparts.

Hotels have always attracted thieves. Transient guests, after all, tend to have many of the items thieves seek: cash, credit cards, jewelry, and other valuables. And although all states have laws stating that lodging operators cannot be held responsible for losses of these valuables unless they are deposited in management's safe, many guests fail to do so. Many keep cash, jewelry, and other valuables in their rooms, where it is subject to theft either by professional thieves or sometimes even by unscrupulous employees of the establishment—although this is rare.

In some hotels, motels, and similar establishments, prostitution presents problems. Most major cities have prostitutes who find willing customers among hotel and motel guests. It is not unusual for a guest to meet a prostitute in a bar and invite that prostitute to the hotel room. Sometimes guests give their room keys to prostitutes who promise to come to the hotel room. Sometimes they do. Sometimes, however, they merely give or sell the keys to professional thieves.

Major hotels, motels, and similar properties normally provide safe-deposit boxes for guests. In most establishments, these are located in the front office and are exactly the same as those used by banks. Some, however, provide in-room safes. In contrast, smaller and older properties, including small inns and motels, may provide nothing more than a single safe in the front office where valuables can be placed.

Fire and smoke represent continuing threats in most lodging operations. Sometimes guests accidentally start fires in their rooms. During the day, when people are awake, this is a difficult enough problem; at night, when guests are asleep, it is a terrifying threat to life. Newer establishments have smoke detectors and alarms to signal fire stations and to alert employees. But such systems are not universally required, and fire continues to be a danger. The security department of a large hotel in a major city may include personnel who patrol all floors of the building at night with watchmen's time clocks, looking for any signs of smoke or fire, as well as for any other potential threats to guests.

One very serious threat to the welfare of guests and employees is to be found in any unsafe conditions that exist within the lodging property. Therefore, identifying, reporting, and remedying such conditions is of major importance in any lodging operation. Doing so is not the sole province of security, however; it is or should be one element in the job of every lodging employee. For example, room attendants who note frayed electric cords on hair dryers, lamps, televisions, or other appliances should be trained to report these so that repairs can be made.

Similarly, instances of torn carpets, broken glass, burned-out lights in stairwells, broken chairs or other pieces of furniture, elevators that do not function properly — all such hazards should be reported immediately by the employees who spot them, to prevent unnecessary harm or injury to guests and to other employees.

An important element in providing security for the guests of hotels, motels, and similar properties is that group of individuals known as the security staff. As indicated previously, they may be hotel or motel employees, or may work for an outside company that provides security services on contract.

Larger properties may have some security personnel in uniform, while others work in plain clothes. Many of those employed as security personnel have backgrounds in law enforcement and are trained to spot people who are likely to present problems — potential thieves, confidence artists, prostitutes, and others. Security personnel are often placed in locations from which they can observe everyone who enters and exits the property. Resort properties, such as the Mountain Inn, often follow this procedure. They may employ a director of security, who supervises several security guards who work in plain clothes. Some may observe entrances and exits, while others mingle with guests in bars, nightclubs, and other recreational facilities.

In contrast, the large transient hotels and motels in major cities may install closed-circuit television cameras to monitor entrances, corridors, storage facilities, and other important areas. Properties such as the Kensington commonly have modern closed-circuit television networks that are used to monitor a number of areas in these properties — particularly areas that are deserted at night and those from which food, liquor, and other hotel property may be stolen. In the Kensington and similar properties, employee entrances are typically locked during late evening and night hours, and security guards are posted at these entrances during the day to prevent their use by unauthorized individuals.

Small motels and similar properties cannot normally afford the number and type of security personnel employed in the larger operations just described. In the small property, the owner or manager, who is normally on premises most or all the time, typically serves as the security staff. On a small scale, he or she must attend to all the security routines for which major city hotels employ security staff. Typically, this means keeping watch for suspicious or unusual activities. In the Value Lodge, for example, the owner must note carefully who enters and leaves the rooms and watch for strangers attempting unauthorized entry. The owner of such a property will normally walk throughout his property several times during the evening.

In summary, basic lodging operation is a function of the interactions of three primary subsystems identified above as the components of Group 1—front office, housekeeping, and security.

Group 2

Most commercial hotels, motels, and similar lodging properties provide more than the basics, in keeping with the wishes of their guests. The majority provide additional services, some of which are listed above in Group 2. Because the number of possibilities is so great, we will restrict the following discussion to those listed earlier in the chapter—which are those most often provided by the operators of hotels, motels, and similar properties.

The extent to which these services are provided to guests will vary. Some motels will provide few if any of them and some luxury hotels may provide them all; whereas other hotels, motels, and similar lodging properties will offer a limited number. As discussed, we will consider that the offering of any of these services results in the addition of a subsystem to the lodging operation—one devoted to providing the service. In addition, the subsystem will be considered part of the lodging operation by guests using the service, regardless of whether it is staffed by employees of the lodging establishment or those of an outside contractor.

One of the most common and important of the services and subsystems offered in lodging operations is front service.

FRONT SERVICE. *Front service* is a term used to identify the subsystem that provides an array of niceties for guests. These include attended service at the front door for handling luggage, obtaining taxicabs, and opening doors; escorting guests from the front desk to the assigned accommodations, as discussed in the section on check-in; carrying luggage for guests; opening guest room doors for those having difficulty with their keys; delivering newspapers, mail, packages, or telephone messages to guests' rooms; providing information about restaurants, theaters, shopping, and sightseeing if this is not done at the front desk; making reservations or providing tickets, or attending to both of these, for shows, tours, sporting events, and transportation.

The employees engaged in front service are normally uniformed, and have such job titles as *bellman* or *bellperson, doorman* or *doorperson, baggage porter, concierge, superintendent of service.* People in these positions are typically paid low hourly wages, and receive gratuities or tips from those for whom they perform services.

TELEPHONE. The telephone subsystem has the obvious goal of providing telephone communication service to guests and employees. Additionally, the telephone communication system may be used to provide wake-up services for guests and to send and receive fax messages. In some properties, guest rooms are equipped with the necessary outlets for portable modems for the laptop and notebook computers many guests bring with them.

In past years, large hotels had telephone switchboards staffed by many telephone operators. All incoming and outgoing telephone calls were individually processed by these operators. Individual handwritten charge slips for each local and long-distance call had to be made out and sent to the front office to be recorded on guests' accounts. Frequently, the telephone charges would not reach the front office until after a guest's departure, resulting in uncollectible after-departure charges.

Wake-up calls were individually placed by the morning telephone operators. The process of placing large numbers of individual wake-up calls could be arduous and highly inefficient. If an operator had forty wake-up calls for 7 A.M., it was necessary to make the first of these calls several minutes before 7:00 and to continue ringing until all forty were made. The operator would not be finished with these calls until well after 7 A.M. This frequently resulted in unhappy guests, some of whom would be awakened prior to the time they requested and others who would be awakened later.

Today, the telephone service in many lodging establishments is automated. Guests in many hotels and motels can dial local and long-distance calls directly. Charges are calculated by computerized call accounting systems and automatically charged to guest accounts. Telephone operators in major metropolitan hotels do not make individual wake-up calls to guests: It is now accomplished by computer. And in many properties, guest rooms are equipped with clock radios so that guests no longer need wake-up calls.

In some properties—the Kensington, for example—the telephone subsystem is operated as a separate department, with round-the-clock operator service available. In others—typically smaller establishments such as the Value Lodge— the telephone subsystem is actually part of the front office operation. The desk clerk on duty serves as telephone operator in addition to other duties.

FOOD AND BEVERAGE. The food and beverage subsystem can be critical to the overall success of some lodging operations. For a number of luxury establishments, the quality of the food and beverage products offered in the restaurants and bars are among their major attractions.

For those hotels, motels, and similar lodging operations that offer food and beverage services, the primary goal of the subsystem is to provide food and beverage products and services that meet the quality standards established by the owners and managers.

The food and beverage service offered by lodging establishments can be separated into three distinctly different types:

1. Service in facilities open to the public
2. Service in guests' rooms
3. Service to special groups in banquet rooms

Service in Facilities Open to the Public.   Many commercial hotels, motels, and similar lodging operations operate food and beverage facilities that are normally open to guests of the property and to the public at large. These facilities include formal and informal restaurants—specialty restaurants, coffee shops, snack bars, and cafeterias among them—as well as bars, cocktail lounges, and nightclubs.

The type and quality of food and beverage products and services available to guests in lodging establishments vary, of course, from one establishment to another. Some properties—motels, most commonly—provide only vending machines with packaged foods. Other motels have vending machines that contain frozen meals, which can be cooked with microwave ovens installed in the lobby or near guests' rooms. By contrast, many luxury hotels take pride in providing the finest food and beverage products and services available. These properties have talented staffs of professionals in their food and beverage departments, who are the equals of those in the finest restaurants. In between these two extremes are the majority of hotels, motels, and similar lodging establishments—those that serve guests and customers from the surrounding community foods and beverages that are comparable to those served in most restaurants.

Service in Guests' Rooms.   Most first-class and luxury hotels provide *room service*, a type of service that provides guests with food and beverages that may be ordered from and consumed in their rooms.

The most popular meal for room service is breakfast, even though some hotels provide room service twenty-four hours a day. Room service menus typically include items that are similar to or the same as those offered on menus in the public rooms. However, the prices for items offered on room service menus are normally higher than regular menu prices.

Even with higher prices, however, room service is not always a profitable enterprise. One of the primary reasons is that room service is labor intensive and relatively inefficient. It is necessary to have a separate staff of servers for room service, and these individuals may have few orders and little work much of the time. In addition, delivering room service orders can be a very slow and time-consuming business: Food that comes from the main kitchen often must be transported great distances to guest rooms. For all of these reasons, labor cost associated with a given room service order is higher than that for the same item served in a public restaurant.

Service to Special Groups in Banquet Rooms. Most establishments with extensive food and beverage facilities make concerted efforts to attract banquet business. *Banquet* is a term used to refer to the prearranged service of food and beverages to a group of people in a private room not in use as a public dining room. Banquet business is normally very profitable—often more profitable than restaurant or bar operation—because exact numbers of guests are guaranteed in advance, making it comparatively easy to achieve planned food and labor costs.

The availability of food and beverage products and services in some or all of the above can increase the appeal of a given property to potential lodging customers. Some guests return to particular lodging operations time after time because of the excellent food offered in the dining room or because of the superior wine list available. Some may enjoy the great luxury of having breakfast or some other meal served in the comfort and privacy of a guest room or suite. In some instances, those planning one or another type of banquet function will reserve sleeping rooms in the hotel, bringing revenue that would otherwise not have come to the property. Sometimes groups will select a particular hotel and reserve large numbers of rooms for a convention because the hotel has the capacity to provide banquet service for a very large group—500 or more people. The presence of a food and beverage subsystem can be very important in a lodging operation and can make a difference in the amount of revenue the property can generate both from food and beverage sales and from room sales.

RECREATION AND ENTERTAINMENT. Recreation and entertainment can be major factors in attracting guests to a lodging operation. In some cases, one of these may be the only reason for deciding to go to a particular property. *Recreation and entertainment* is a broad category that can include an array of activities and events that guests find appealing.

One type includes a number of well-known and popular athletic and sporting activities: tennis, skiing, horseback riding, golf, and swimming, for example. However, it may also include such simple possibilities as the ping-pong and billiard tables found in some small family resort properties.

Along with front service, telephone service, food and beverage services, parking, and other personal services, recreation and entertainment are among the second tier of subsystem services offered by lodging establishments. The gambling casino is just one type of activity that operators use to attract guests. (Courtesy Las Vegas News Bureau.)

Another type includes the nightclubs and other showplaces featuring star-quality entertainers that one finds in many mountain and shore resort properties across the country, in the major hotels and motels of Las Vegas and Atlantic City, and on such closely related facilities as cruise ships.

Still another type is the gambling casino, a highly profitable and very popular attraction in many of the hotels of Las Vegas and Atlantic City, as well as on river-boats and in some areas outside the United States. Related to gambling casinos, however distantly, are the bingo games, card games, and coin-operated machines of various sorts that are available in many properties because they appeal to guests.

The operators of lodging properties who believe the addition of one or more of these is likely to increase the appeal of the properties or their profitability, or accomplish both of these at once, will probably attempt to include them.

PARKING. Facilities for parking are of ever-growing importance to guests and lodging operators, as more and more travelers use automobiles—those they own and those they rent. Many properties are so far removed from any public transportation that guests must have automobiles to get around the local area.

Those properties surrounded by adequate land have relatively little difficulty using it for parking—either outdoor parking near the doors to guests' accommodations or on a simple lot, or indoor parking in a purpose-built structure. By contrast, many newer properties have parking facilities within their structures, permitting guests to drive inside buildings and to park their own cars, before proceeding to lobbies to check in.

A number of older hotels in the centers of cities have been forced to arrange alternative parking. Because they had no surrounding land and could not create parking space within their structures, many have had to make arrangements for parking with nearby garages and lots. Some provide pickup and delivery service, so that guests need never go farther than the front door to leave or retrieve their vehicles.

OTHER PERSONAL SERVICES. There are any number of other possibilities for offering personal services to guests of hotels, motels, and similar lodging operations. The following are the most common:

Banking Services.   For the convenience of guests, some lodging operations provide banking services at the front desk. They normally make change, and some cash both personal checks and travelers checks. A growing number convert foreign currencies for dollars, given the increased number of international visitors entering the country.

Guest Laundry.   A large number of hotels, motels, and other commercial lodging operations provide personal laundry service to guests. In many instances, guests can arrange for soiled shirts, blouses, underwear, and other clothing to be collected from their rooms, laundered, and returned to their rooms. Some even provide same-day service. Another approach is to provide self-service facilities for guests to attend to their own laundry—making washers, dryers, irons, and ironing boards available.

Dry Cleaning.   Most properties that provide laundry service also provide dry cleaning services for guests. Guests can arrange to have suits, skirts, trousers, and other garments collected from their rooms, cleaned, pressed, and returned to their rooms. As with laundry, some provide same-day service. Dry cleaning services in hotels are normally referred to as valet services.

Hair Styling.   Many lodging properties provide facilities for men's and women's hair styling. In a few properties, these are still known by the older terms *barber shop* and *beauty salon*, terms that are disappearing from the lodging lexicon. Some facilities offering hair styling may also offer nail care, cosmetics treatments, and related services.

Office Services.   Some hotels, motels, and other lodging properties offer an array of office services, primarily for business travelers. They may provide copy machines, fax machines, computers and printers, modems, typewriters, and tape recorders for dictation. Some have this equipment — as well as such simple items as staplers, staple removers, and paper clips — set up in special rooms for use by guests twenty-four hours a day. A very few will provide personal assistance on request.

Health Facilities.   Because many guests are very health conscious, and because of the increased emphasis on exercise, a number of lodging operations provide a variety of facilities for exercise. Some have health clubs, saunas, and steam rooms on premises. Others have set up a room or an area with exercise equipment. Some have small swimming pools for exercise. Still others assist joggers in finding appropriate routes at various hours of the day.

Newsstands.   In a lodging establishment, the term *newsstand* can refer to a small counter at which a few newspapers and magazines are sold, or to a larger enterprise selling newspapers, magazines, books, candy, cigars, cigarettes, souvenirs, and such personal articles as disposable razors, shaving cream, antiperspirants, toothpaste, and the like.

Language Services.   Hotels, motels, and similar lodging establishments that accommodate tourists and business travelers from other nations often employ individuals who are fluent in two or more languages. Such people can be very helpful to visitors who are not fluent in English.

Other Shops.   Hotels and other major lodging properties in large cities are very likely to rent space to shopkeepers who provide various goods and services to guests, as well as to people from the surrounding area. It is not unusual to find travel agencies, jewelers, luggage shops, and clothing boutiques, among many other possible shops, in the lobby areas of these properties.

The availability of some or all of these commonly increases the appeal of a hotel, motel, or similar lodging establishment to guests. Therefore, the property offering these typically enjoys some competitive advantage over those that do not.

THE INTERRELATEDNESS OF LODGING SUBSYSTEMS

At the beginning of this chapter a system was defined as a whole unit consisting of a set of interdependent and interrelated parts coordinated to accomplish a set of goals. Each of the parts is necessary for the whole unit to function as intended. It should be apparent that the several subsystems that are the very essence of a lodging operation—front office, housekeeping, and security, identified as part of Group 1—as well as those that enhance the quality of the lodging operations—

front service, telephone, food and beverages services, and others, identified as part of Group 2—must function effectively, both individually and as a group, for the operation to achieve its goals.

Within the front office subsystem, reservations must be accurately recorded if the room clerks are to know how many rooms they have available to rent to persons without reservations. Room clerks must properly record information about arriving and departing guests if the housekeeping department is to have accurate data to perform its job. Housekeepers must clean and prepare vacated rooms properly and report the room numbers of made-up rooms to the front desk promptly and accurately so that newly arrived guests can be assigned to suitable accommodations.

In the front services subsystem, bellpersons checking guests into rooms should note and report the numbers of any rooms that are not up to standard—those with burned-out light bulbs, damaged furniture, or dripping faucets, for example. This information helps housekeeping to identify problems and to keep guest rooms in proper condition.

In the food and beverage subsystem, room service employees must accurately verify the names and room numbers of guests ordering from their rooms, so that the items ordered can be delivered to the correct room quickly. Similarly, employees in restaurants must verify the names and room numbers of guests who charge food and beverages, so that the bills of those guests can be properly charged.

Employees attending to guests' laundry and dry cleaning requirements must be particularly careful to obtain and record room numbers correctly, so that garments can be returned to the right rooms and charges for the service can be recorded on the right bills.

Because the subsystems in a lodging operation are interrelated, all must be functioning properly and in a coordinated way for the lodging operation to achieve its goals. When any given subsystem is not performing as designed or intended, other subsystems are affected. For example, if the housekeeping subsystem in the Kensington fails to clean rooms quickly, the front office subsystem will be affected: Room clerks may be forced to tell guests that there will be a delay in assigning them to rooms, thus disappointing some guests and possibly angering some others. In addition, this may affect the behavior of room clerks towards guests.

If one or another of the lodging subsystems fails to operate properly, the overall system will not achieve its goals.

SUMMARY

In this chapter, lodging operations are examined from a systems perspective. Systems and subsystems are defined, and front office, housekeeping, and security are identified as the basic subsystems that are common to all lodging operations.

Front service, telephone, food and beverage, recreation/entertainment, parking, and personal services are identified as six additional subsystems not common to all lodging operations, but used selectively by some operators to aid in achieving their goals. Examples of three different types of lodging operations are provided — the Value Lodge, the Mountain Inn, and the Kensington; and each of the lodging subsystems identified is illustrated in terms of these three examples. Finally, the interrelatedness of these subsystems is emphasized and offered as a basis for examining and understanding complex lodging operations.

QUESTIONS

1. Define the terms *system* and *subsystem*.
2. Name the three subsystems common to all lodging operations.
3. List five common inputs required for a lodging system.
4. List four desirable outputs of a lodging system.
5. List and state the goals of the four subsystems associated with the front office and describe the functions of each.
6. Identify six additional services offered by some, but not all, lodging operators.
7. What are the advantages of electronic locks over traditional locks and metal keys?
8. Describe three variations on checkout procedure used by hotels, motels, and similar facilities.
9. Define the terms *overbooking* and *no-show*. Describe two problems that have caused some lodging operators to overbook.
10. What is the goal of a housekeeping subsystem?
11. Describe ten tasks that may be assigned to the housekeeping subsystem.
12. List ten tasks typically involved in making a room ready for occupancy.
13. Why would a guest room in a luxury hotel take more time to make ready for occupancy than one in an economy motel?
14. Why is it necessary to redecorate or rehabilitate guest rooms every few years? List the kinds of tasks likely to be required for the complete rehabilitation of a guest room in a luxury hotel.
15. Describe several security measures that would typically be taken in a large center-city hotel. Contrast those with security measures typically taken in a small motel in a rural community.

16. List ten guest services normally associated with front service subsystems.
17. Identify three uses of the telephone subsystem.
18. List and describe three different types of food and beverage services that may be offered by food and beverage subsystems.
19. Which of the three types of food and beverage services identified in question 18 is the most profitable? Why?
20. Explain why recreation subsystems are vitally important to the success of many resort and gambling properties.
21. Is it more important for lodging properties in outlying areas to have parking facilities for their guests than for those located in city centers? Why?
22. Define each of the following subsystems and describe their use in lodging operations.
    a. Banking
    b. Guest laundry
    c. Dry cleaning services
    d. Office services
    e. Health facilities
    f. Newsstand
    g. Shops

Planning Lodging Facilities

10

LEARNING OBJECTIVES

After reading and studying this chapter, you should be able to:

1. *Distinguish between durable and service products.*
2. *Identify the three elements in the service product line offered by lodging operations.*
3. *Define the term <u>feasibility study</u> and describe its importance in planning a lodging facility.*
4. *Identify the subjects normally covered in a feasibility study.*
5. *List and describe ten engineering systems common to most lodging properties.*
6. *List and discuss three factors that lead to differences from one lodging property to another in the layout and design of each of the following: a. Front office; b. Guest room; c. Housekeeping area.*
7. *List and distinguish among the types of beds commonly found in the guest rooms of lodging properties.*
8. *List seven types of guest accommodations commonly found in lodging properties and the size range in square feet for each.*
9. *Identify three approaches to obtaining clean linen for a lodging operation and discuss the advantages and disadvantages of each.*

INTRODUCTION

In the previous chapter, the basic similarities of lodging establishments were illustrated by means of three specific operations—the Value Lodge, the Mountain Inn, and the Kensington Hotel. In addition, these examples served to illustrate the three subsystems common to all lodging operations, to demonstrate the inter-relationships among these subsystems, and to familiarize students with the basic subsystems they will encounter if they pursue careers in lodging operations.

The previous discussion of lodging subsystems serves as the foundation for this chapter, which will provide students with an understanding of some of the important concepts that lie at the heart of planning for lodging operations.

Before beginning a discussion of planning lodging operations, it must be pointed out that planning the typical lodging operation is likely to be far more complex than planning the typical food and beverage operation. A person intending to open a modest restaurant is likely to find the work of planning far easier than that faced by someone intending to open a modest lodging establishment. In addition, the amount of money and the length of time required to plan and open a food and beverage operation is far less than that needed to plan and open a lodging operation. These realities clearly help to explain why comparatively few people develop their own commercial lodging operations. Most are planned and developed by corporations.

PLANNING LODGING OPERATIONS

The first step in planning a lodging operation is to establish a *concept*—an imaginative, unifying idea of the operation to serve as the focus for the people, energies, and other resources required to convert it into reality. This concept originates with the person or company that will own the property or with some other person or firm that develops it under commission.

We will begin with one fairly obvious element in this concept: the type of lodging operation to be developed. The person or company responsible for the concept should have in mind some idea of the type or types of lodging operations that might be developed—motel, convention hotel, resort hotel, or some other. A new property is likely to resemble one of the various characteristic types discussed in Chapter 8, or some combination of these.

Those responsible for the concept must clearly understand the nature of the hospitality service products to be offered in the lodging operation they are developing.

Product Line

The term *product* is a very broad one, used to describe two types of products: durable products and service products. Durable products are "goods" with three-dimensional physical characteristics. They can be seen, touched, and produced for inventory and eventual use. By contrast, service products cannot be produced for inventory: They are produced to order. They are services performed for the purchaser. Examples include haircutting, bookkeeping, and room cleaning. The purchasers of these receive, respectively, a haircut, a set of neat and accurate books of account, and a clean and tidy room. The basic products of a lodging operation are service products.

As indicated in Chapter 7, the term *product line* is used in marketing and retailing to refer to a group of products with similar characteristics. We will borrow the term *product line* from retailing once again and use it to mean the service products that a lodging operator intends to offer, based on the concept developed for the establishment. For example, if one intends to operate a budget motel, the service products will be significantly different from those offered by a developer who intends to operate a luxury resort. Each lodging establishment offers its own distinct product line. Sometimes — in the case of individual proper- ties in a motel chain, for example — the product lines offered may be so similar that it is difficult to distinguish between them.

The hospitality service product line offered by lodging operations has three elements:

1. Accommodations
2. Services
3. Ambiance

These are described in the following sections.

ACCOMMODATIONS. Lodging establishments offer accommodations — the most basic element in their service product line. The accommodations element consists of all the accommodations that will be offered to the public. These *accommodations* are the specific rooms, suites, or other facilities to which guests are assigned. All of these, taken together, are defined as the accommodations element in the service product line. Many lodging operations offer specialized accommodations, possibly featuring only one type: suites, for example. Any number of specialized accommodations can be found in the lodging industry today. Two of the characteristic types of properties discussed in a previous chapter offer good examples: budget motels and residential hotels. In contrast, other lodging operations offer a broader range of accommodations, which may consist of both rooms and suites of varying sizes and types.

SERVICE. Another basic element in the hospitality service product line offered in a lodging enterprise is the *service* available to guests. This element is defined as all the services the operator intends to offer. Again, the type of establishment will strongly influence the nature and extent of the services offered. Housekeeping service is the basic service offered by transient hotels, motels, and similar lodging enterprises. Other common services include security, parking, valet and laundry, and front services. Additional services may include background music in elevators and corridors, information about goods and services available in the area, and assistance in making reservations in affiliated properties in distant locations for future nights.

Many operators offer such additional services as entertainment and recreational facilities—normal hospitality-related services that are central to specific types of lodging operations and expected by guests in these operations. Again, the characteristic type of lodging facility established strongly influences the nature and extent of these other services. Thus, entertainment and recreational facilities are central to resort hotel operations. For example, the Mountain Inn described in Chapter 9 offers such recreational services as a swimming pool, an exercise room, and several tennis courts.

AMBIANCE. The third basic element in the hospitality service product line in lodging operations is one often described as *ambiance*. This element includes a vast number of those essentials—some tangible, some intangible—that give a specific lodging operation its special and distinctive character. These essentials include theme, lighting, uniforms, furnishings, cleanliness, wall coverings, fixtures,

Ambiance, accommodations, and service are the three basic elements in the service product line of a lodging operation, used to establish its concept during the planning stage. Shown below is an elegant hotel lobby that immediately communicates the operation's goals and focus. (Courtesy the Four Seasons Hotel.)

fabrics, feelings, decorations, and any other related features that customers see or sense and that help to form their impressions of the establishment. For example, when an arriving guest walks through the front door of a lodging facility, he or she gets an impression of the property from the lighting, furniture, carpet, wall coverings, works of art, and any of the other coordinated elements that make up the lobby area. Similarly, after being assigned to a particular accommodation, the guest gets additional impressions from the elevator, the elevator foyer on her floor, the general appearance of the corridor leading from the elevator foyer to her room, and so on. To a guest, the sum of these and many other impressions constitutes the property's ambiance or atmosphere. Although there is also an ambiance about the guest accommodations, it is important to recognize that these two—the guest accommodation and its ambiance—are so interrelated that they are inseparable.

The discussion above does not take into account that many lodging operations also offer food and beverage products. Some would say that the lodging enterprise that offers food and beverages is offering a second product line. Others would disagree, saying that if food and beverages are offered because of guests' expectations, the food and beverage operations should be thought of as additional services, akin to the recreational facilities discussed above. The Kensington, as described in Chapter 9, offers high-quality foods and beverages. From one point of view, the food and beverages—and the service and ambiance that accompany them—constitute a second product line for the Kensington. From another, the food and beverage operations in the Kensington are services, offered as part of the service element of the service product line, because guests selecting hotels of that type expect high-quality food and beverage products to be available. One can agree or disagree with either point of view.

In summary, the service product line offered by a lodging establishment consists of three basic elements—accommodations, services, and ambiance. Some operators choose to add one or more of an array of other possible product lines by having boutiques, jewelry shops, gift shops, souvenir stands, and other retail shops on premises. Although these are interesting and often desirable additions to a property, they are not essential to the basic lodging enterprise. Therefore, we will limit the following discussion of planning to the facilities required for the basic service product line of a lodging enterprise. Appropriate discussion of planning food and beverage facilities can be found in Chapter 7.

FEASIBILITY STUDIES

Because the development of most commercial lodging properties requires the commitment of major resources—people, funds, energy, and time—it is not undertaken lightly. Before selecting and acquiring land and starting to build a lodging property, a developer will typically employ a consulting firm to conduct a feasibility study. A *feasibility study* is a professional analysis of a proposed project to determine whether or not it is likely to succeed.

The results of a feasibility study are normally presented in the form of a written report, which is discussed in detail with the developer who has ordered it. Feasibility studies typically take months to complete and are likely to cost hundreds of thousands of dollars, depending on the size and cost of the proposed project and the thoroughness of the study.

Although full discussion of feasibility studies is beyond the scope of the present chapter, it is important to have some idea of the work such studies entail and the questions they seek to answer.

While there are no industry-wide standards for the contents of feasibility studies, most typically provide an analysis of each of the the following:

Geographic region	Site
Competition	Project finance
Product demand	Anticipated operating results
Type and size of property	

Each of these will be discussed separately.

Geographic Region

An analysis of the region provides valuable information about the area and its economy. It will include information about the characteristics of the population in general, the work force, the local businesses and industries, and data about highways, traffic patterns, numbers of travelers into the area via ground and air transportation, economic trends, and other relevant data. Such information as age distributions, educational backgrounds, income levels, and spending patterns are of great interest to a developer attempting to determine the extent to which a lodging operation and possible food and beverage facilities in it will be supported locally.

Competition

Analysis of the competition looks at the number and types of lodging facilities in the region, the age and condition of the buildings, and levels of occupancy. It is important to know in advance of any lodging properties that might be in direct competition with the type of facility being planned. Such information plays an important role in determining whether or not the proposed lodging operation has some reasonable chance for success.

Product Demand

Demand analysis assesses the need for a lodging facility of the type proposed and attempts to determine the number of potential guests in the area who might select such a property. It may project the number of rooms likely to be occupied on an average night. Overall, it projects the potential demand for accommodations in the area, taking into account current conditions in the local economy and future projections for its continuing health, as well as any other relevant trends that may be evident.

Type and Size of Property

Assuming the study finds some need for a new lodging operation in the area, it takes into account the economic and demographic data and attempts to identify the type and size of property most likely to succeed. Specifically, the study will use demand data to suggest an ideal number of rooms for such a property to contain. In addition, it will suggest the type of property that guests would be most likely to support.

Site

Site analysis attempts to match a proposed property of a given type and size to a particular piece of land. If the developer has a particular parcel of land in mind, site analysis will assess its suitability for the type and size of property proposed. If no particular site is proposed by the developer, the consultant may identify the characteristics of an ideal site or propose several potentially available sites that would be suitable. Additionally, site analysis includes research into such important considerations as local zoning regulations, building codes, and environmental impact.

Project Finance

The development of any major lodging project normally requires a very large amount of money, particularly when land must be purchased and a building constructed. Thus, before such a project is begun, it must be determined how the project developer will pay for it. One of the important elements of a feasibility study is a determination of the funding level a particular project is likely to require, as well as possible sources for the funds necessary to complete it.

Anticipated Operating Results

One of the main functions of the feasibility study is to see whether or not the project is likely to be financially successful. To determine this, financial forecasts are based on data developed in other parts of the study and on both local and national average figures for labor costs and other expenses. These forecasts are attempts to determine in advance the levels of revenue, expense, profit, and cash flow that the developer would need.

Applicable Laws and Regulations

Although a feasibility study does not normally include a specific discussion of all the laws and regulations—federal, state, and local—that a developer will face in planning a lodging facility, clearly these must be taken into account. Building codes, fire codes, health codes, zoning regulations, environmental regulations, and licensing requirements are among the most common. Each of these provides specific direction about what an owner can and cannot legally do in planning, designing, and operating a lodging enterprise.

Laws and regulations vary considerably from one state to another and even from city to city within a given state. For example, zoning regulations in some areas limit the height of new buildings constructed in the area. Planning a facility that failed to comply with these regulations would make it impossible to obtain a building permit until architects and engineers had redesigned the building to comply with the regulations. And this is just one example of the many possibilities.

Before proceeding to plan facilities, potential owners lacking full knowledge of the laws and regulations that apply in given locales must have advice from lawyers, architects, engineers, professional lodging consultants, and others with the necessary expertise. Failure to factor this information into the planning process can lead to costly errors.

Seven factors—geographic region, competition, product demand, type and size of property, site, project finance, and anticipated operating results—are considered in a feasibility study before the construction of a lodging facility can be financed or begun.

In the present chapter we will assume that the planners of a lodging operation have reviewed a feasibility study, determined that the type of establishment planned can be successful in the location selected, and decided to proceed. At this point, we will turn our attention to the layout and design of the planned facility.

ENGINEERING SYSTEMS

In order to provide the kinds of accommodations and services commonly offered by hotels, motels, and similar establishments, the lodging operator must have an appropriate facility. While recognizing that at times an existing facility is converted for use as a lodging establishment, we will assume for purposes of this discussion that it is a new building that the developer will construct. In either case, the planners—engineers and architects, working with developers and hospitality executives—must make provision for a number of engineering systems that are essential in any building project.

The following are brief descriptions of the basic engineering systems common to most lodging properties. These brief discussions will serve to suggest the degree of complexity inherent in the layout and design of a building constructed for use as a hotel, motel, or similar lodging enterprise.

The engineering systems in a building may include all of the following:

1. Heating
2. Air conditioning
3. Ventilation
4. Electrical
5. Water
6. Transportation
7. Waste
8. Fire safety
9. Energy control
10. Communications

HEATING. In the United States, lodging facilities have heating systems to raise the temperature of water and air in the building, thus providing hot water and warm rooms. Heating systems accomplish this by converting energy resources to heat. Common energy resources include oil, gas, electricity, steam, coal, and solar energy. The selection of one of these over another will depend on availability, relative cost, and particular preferences of the owner/operators of the facility.

AIR CONDITIONING. Technically, air conditioning is any treatment of the air in a building that changes it in any way. Thus, heating, cooling, humidifying, dehumidifying, and filtering are all air conditioning processes. However, the term *air conditioning* is commonly taken to mean improving the comfort level in a facility by reducing the temperature of air, or by controlling the level of humidity in the air, or by doing both of these. There are two types of air conditioning systems used in lodging facilities:

Centralized.   A central system services a number of guest rooms and other facilities, treating the air in one large air conditioning unit and distributing the treated air through ducts.

Decentralized.   A decentralized system relies on individual air conditioning units in each facility to treat the air in that particular facility. In some properties, these are built into the walls of the rooms they service; in others, they may be installed in windows.

VENTILATION. Ventilation systems provide and control the volume of fresh or recirculated air. They ensure an adequate supply of air with sufficient oxygen for human activity. Some ventilation systems also filter the air to remove dust and such undesirable properties as cigarette smoke and cooking odors. Lodging facilities in the centers of major cities commonly filter incoming air to remove the pollutants added to the air by automobile, truck, and bus traffic. Ventilation systems are designed to remove and replace all the air in a given space or room a number of times each hour. That number may vary from a very few times per hour—possibly 6, for example, in a large hotel ballroom—to a great many times per hour: up to 50 in a large hotel kitchen, according to one authority. Ventilation systems are typically linked to heating systems, or air conditioning systems, or both.

ELECTRICAL. Electrical systems are designed to provide for the availability of electricity wherever it may be needed as an energy source in the building. Electrical systems consist of wires of various sizes, as well as the circuit breakers or fuses, switches, and outlets that facilitate their safe use. Electricity is used for three primary purposes in lodging facilities: lighting, heating, and operating specific equipment requiring electric power.

Because of their public nature, many lodging establishments are required to maintain emergency systems to use in the event of a power failure. The nature and extent of the emergency systems vary, depending on state and local regulations. Some are simple battery systems that provide emergency lighting in corridors and other public areas for limited periods; others are complex systems that may include gasoline-powered generators to provide sufficient electricity for lighting and limited elevator service. Many operators install emergency systems that will also provide power for refrigerators, freezers, and computer systems until the regular flow of power resumes.

WATER. The water system consists of those parts of the plumbing system that provide fresh water to various parts of the lodging establishment, including guest rooms, food and beverage facilities, laundry facilities, and public bathrooms, among others.

In many localities, the source of fresh water is a public water supply with water pipes running under the streets. In many remote, rural areas, however, absence of a public water system makes it necessary to use some alternative means to obtain fresh water. Most commonly, this means drilling a well. Another possibility is pumping the water directly from a nearby lake or river. Others, although rare, include collecting it from rainwater and processing salt water from the sea.

Sometimes incoming fresh water is processed before being distributed throughout a building so that its properties may be changed before use. There are various reasons for doing this. One is that the water is too "hard," a term used to describe water containing excessive amounts of calcium and magnesium salts. Another is that the water may contain other minerals or impurities that must be filtered out. Still another is that the water may require the addition of chlorine to make it safe for human use.

Some fresh water—the cold water—is distributed directly to the areas in which it is used. The rest, the hot water, is diverted to the heating system, where its temperature is raised before distribution.

One of the significant engineering challenges in a multistory lodging operation is to design a water system that will provide:

1. adequate water pressure on all floors during periods of peak use. If this is not addressed, guests in rooms on high floors may not be able to obtain adequate water at particular times;
2. an adequate supply of both hot and cold water, so that each water user can maintain the temperature he or she selects for any given purpose. Failure to provide for this may result, for example, is sudden changes in shower water temperatures from comfortable to too hot or too cold, either of which may be unpleasant or dangerous.

TRANSPORTATION. The transportation system in a lodging establishment consists of those facilities used to move guests, employees, equipment, and supplies from one level of the building to another. Its most common components are elevators and escalators.

Wherever feasible, planners of lodging facilities provide for an adequate number of elevators so that those used by guests need not be used for other purposes. These other elevators are often called *service elevators* and are usually located some distance from the guest elevators. They are used for transporting employees, equipment, and supplies from one part of the building to another.

A small, specialized kind of elevator called a *dumbwaiter* is used for moving food, normally for short distances between floors. For example, if the main kitchen in a large hotel is one or two floors below the dining rooms and banquet rooms, a dumbwaiter way be installed to transport food and materials between kitchen and the food service facilities.

Dumbwaiters are not normally used to transport personnel and, consequently, lack the internal operating controls found in elevators. Staff members usually place food and other items in a dumbwaiter, close the door from the outside, and control it by depressing a button on the wall next to the dumbwaiter shaft.

Escalators are normally used to transport large numbers of people for short distances—one or two floors. They are more commonly used with banquet and meeting facilities, so that those attending meetings, dinners, and other events can get into and out of the facility quickly and easily. If it becomes necessary to move large numbers of people into or out of a facility quickly, all escalators can be made to move in the same direction—up or down. With this arrangement, greater numbers of people can be moved more quickly than would be possible using elevators.

WASTE. The waste system in a lodging property is designed to facilitate the removal of solid and liquid wastes produced in the property. Solid waste includes paper, glass, fabric, plastic, metal, wood, and food. Liquid waste is primarily waste water being drained into a sewage disposal system.

Solid waste is normally collected throughout a lodging establishment by employees who transport it to one central area. From there, it can be put out for pickup in plastic bags, trash cans, or dumpsters, depending on type, volume, and local regulations. Alternatively, it can be compacted before being put out, or incinerated on premises. Many large hotels accumulate huge amounts of solid waste daily. In many areas, local regulations now identify certain solid wastes as *recyclables* and require that they be separated and made ready for special handling or collection.

In contrast, the disposal of liquid waste is normally quite simple. In areas with public water supply systems, there are also public sewer systems, and disposal is a simple matter of connecting to that system. In other areas, some other means must be found. The most common alternatives are treatment plants and underground drain fields.

FIRE SAFETY. A fire safety system is designed to detect, contain, or extinguish fires and to alert both guests and employees to the danger. Some are also designed to summon fire and police personnel to the scene. A fire safety system consists of:

1. Sensing devices for detecting heat, smoke, flame, or some combination of these

2. Devices for containing or extinguishing fires, such as doors that close automatically to prevent the spread of fire; sprinklers; and portable extinguishers containing water, carbon dioxide, foam, or other chemicals
3. Warning devices for alerting guests and employees such as fire horns, fire alarms, and flashing lights.

Because of the public nature of lodging establishments, all but the smallest are required by law to have some type of fire safety system. The nature and extent of the systems required clearly vary from one area to another and from one size and type of lodging facility to another.

ENERGY CONTROL. The energy control system in a lodging establishment is designed to manage the use of energy in the building efficiently, minimizing its use and consequent cost. It consists of various devices that turn energy-consuming equipment on and off at optimum times or that prevent excessive use of energy in any system or subsystem. There are four common types of systems:

Time Clock.   This is the simplest and least costly of the systems. It uses time clocks to turn on and off the flow of electricity to such devices as exterior lights, lighted signs, and even swimming pool filtration systems, ensuring that they will operate only when needed and for the proper length of time.

Automatic Sensor.   Some lodging operators control energy costs by installing automatic sensors that detect the presence or absence of people in a room. These are used primarily to turn lights on and off, ensuring that lights are off when there is no one in a room. They may also be used to turn off such appliances as television sets when guests have left a room.

Electric Demand.   These systems are designed to limit the amount of energy of one type that can be used at any one time. This may entail limiting the length of time that a given device can operate continuously or preventing the use of a given device while another is in use. These systems are more commonly used in large buildings where, say, three major air conditioning systems serve different parts of the building. An electric demand control system may be used to prevent two or more from operating together and to limit the length of time that any one of them can run before being automatically turned off to enable a second to operate.

Computerized System.   Computerized systems are the most flexible, efficient, and effective in use today. These are the systems most commonly installed in newly constructed lodging facilities. They can be programed to control energy use and are capable of all the controls exercised by the three systems described above.

Because proper use of an appropriate energy control system can result in considerable savings in energy costs—some manufacturers claim up to 40 percent—planners of lodging properties are normally interested in selecting systems that will produce minimum energy costs for the facilities they design.

COMMUNICATIONS SYSTEM. Communications systems in lodging establishments are designed to enable guests, managers, staff members, and others outside the lodging property to communicate with one another. This system may be as simple as a telephone system used by guests, employees, and managers to reach one another to communicate simple messages. This would be the case in the Value Lodge, for example, where an overnight guest may use the telephone only to call the front desk to request a morning wake-up call so that he or she can get an early start the following morning, or to request information. However, some communications systems in lodging properties today are far more complex.

A typical modern communications system may link telephones, televisions, computers, and various audiovisual devices. The communications may range from telephone calls between front desk and guest room, to interactive televised conferences linking groups in two or more cities via satellite transmission. Or they may involve business travelers using computers with modems in guest rooms or suites to communicate with their offices via telephone lines. They may even provide a means for guests to view and approve their room bills via the television sets in their rooms. The possibilities for developing increasingly complex telecommunications equipment for installation and use in lodging enterprises are growing with each development in this relatively new field. Therefore, those planning new lodging facilities will be challenged to select systems and equipment that will not soon become obsolete as new systems are developed.

FACILITY LAYOUT AND DESIGN

It should be obvious that the layout and design of an entire lodging facility is a difficult and complex project. At this point, we will focus our attention on the layout and design of three important facilities found in lodging operations:

1. An area for activities and records associated with guest reservations, check-in, and check-out: the front office
2. The accommodations themselves: guest rooms
3. An area for attending to housekeeping activities, including the storage of linens, uniforms, and cleaning supplies and equipment: housekeeping.

Because these three areas are so different from one another, the layout and design of each will be addressed separately.

Front Office Layout and Design

To some extent, front office layout and design is determined by the type of establishment the developer intends to operate. In economy motels, for example, front office areas tend to be smaller, simpler, and more compact than in the traditional luxury hotels found in the more affluent areas of major cities.

As described in Chapter 9, front office subsystems deal with reservations, check-in, information, and checkout. The facilities in which these activities take place vary greatly from one property to another. In a 50-room motel, such as the Value Lodge described in the previous chapter, a front office facility is normally quite small. Figure 10.1 is a diagram of the front office of the Value Lodge.

In a larger property, such as the 350-room Kensington hotel, the amount of work and the number of employees make a larger front office facility necessary. Figure 10.2 is a diagram of the front office of the Kensington.

Note that both facilities are designed to deal with the same activities—those associated with reservations, check-in, information, and checkout. As previously noted, these are the activities common to all front office operations, and every lodging establishment should have a front office designed to accommodate the level of activity anticipated in each of those four areas. To that extent, the front

FIGURE 10.1 *Front Office of the Value Lodge*

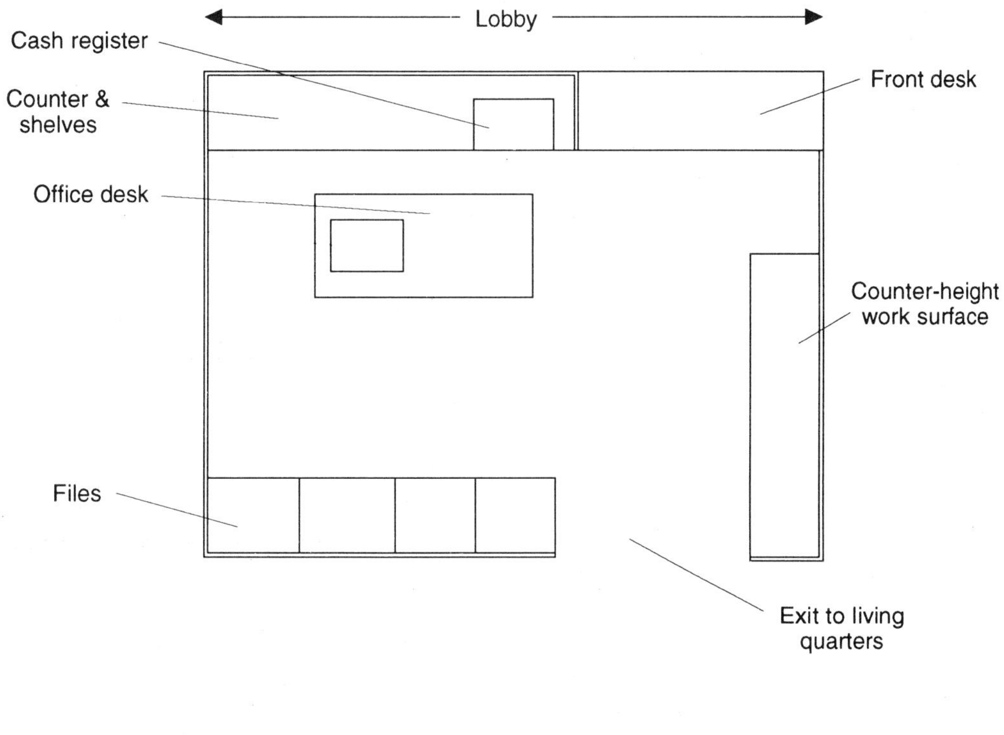

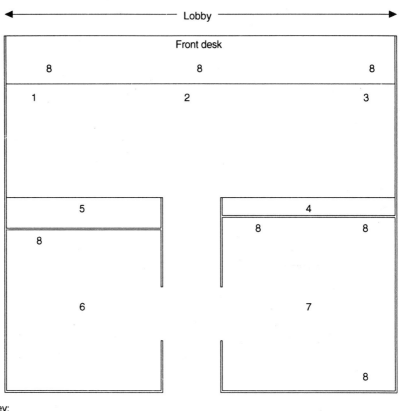

Key:

1 Cashier's area
2 Information area
3 Room clerk's area
4 Wall of mailboxes for
  keys, mail, and messages
5 Counter-height bank of
  safe deposit boxes
6 Office for front office
  manager
7 Reservations office
8 Locations of computer terminals and printers

FIGURE 10.2 *Front Office of the Kensington Hotel*

offices of the Value Lodge and the Kensington hotel are the same. There are obvious differences, however, between the two front offices, and these differences reveal much about the differences between the two properties. The principal differences are:

Size.   In the Value Lodge, the volume of work involving those activities can be handled by one individual in a single small area. The entire front office area, including the front desk, is only 54 square feet: 6 feet by 9 feet. In contrast, the front office area in the Kensington is quite large, encompassing 540 square feet: 18 feet by 30 feet.

Space Allocation. The Value Lodge has one single area in which all front office activities take place, and the volume of each is such that all can be handled by one person. In the Kensington, however, some of the front office activities occur in sufficient volume to require that some employees dedicate their time to specialized work. For example, the volume of financial activities—updating guest accounts, processing guest checkouts, cashing checks, and making change—make it desirable to assign specialists (cashiers) to the work—and to allocate one specific area for their work. The same is true for the specialist employees assigned to deal with reservations, information, and check-ins. In the Kensington, the front office staff is large enough to require supervision by a front office manager, for whom a separate office area has been allocated.

Equipment. In the Value Lodge, the front office requires some simple manual equipment: a room rack that also holds room keys and guests' bills, a cash register, a telephone, and a file cabinet for reservations and for storage of various forms and records. In the Kensington, the front office has an integrated computer system with terminals in each area. For example, the reservations office has a workstation with a terminal in which all reservations are input. A telephone and a fax machine are within reach, as are file cabinets and other storage facilities for reservations and related forms.

Rooms Layout and Design

To a great extent, the layout and design of guest accommodations in a given establishment are determined by the type of establishment the developer intends to operate. In economy motels, for example, guest rooms tend to be smaller, simpler, and more compact than in traditional luxury hotels.

Because beds, the principal furnishings in most guest accommodations, vary considerably in size, it is important to know the dimensions of beds most commonly found in lodging establishments (see Table 10.1).

Most beds are 75″ long. Some guests however, prefer longer beds; and these are readily available to lodging operators who choose to buy them. Some are 78″ long; others may be 80″ or 82″. The latter are often called California lengths.

Table 10.2 indicates typical sizes of guest accommodations in seven types of lodging operations. Note that the number of square feet in each accommodation includes bedroom, parlor or living room (if any), bathroom, and entry area, as well as any closets and other hallways.

TABLE 10.1 *Dimensions of Beds in Lodging Establishments*

Bed	Width
Rollaway/cot	30"
Studio	33"
Single	36"
Twin	39"
Three-quarters	48"
Double	54"
Queen	60"
King	78"

TABLE 10.2 *Typical Size Ranges of Lodging Accommodations*

Type of Lodging Accommodation	Common Sizes of Guest Accommodations (in square feet)
Subbudget motel room	175–200
Budget motel room	225–250
Commercial hotel/motel room	250–325
Luxury hotel/motel room	350–450
Hotel junior suite	400–475
Hotel standard suite	450–550
Suite in an all-suite property	450–700

Figure 10.3 illustrates typical floor plans for guest accommodations in the seven common types of lodging establishments listed in Table 10.2.

The layout and design of guest rooms in the Value Lodge closely resembles that for the budget motel room in Figure 10.3. Each unit has private bath, two queen-size beds, color television, two lounge chairs, and a dresser with mirror, among other items. Units in this property are of uniform size: 236 square feet.

Guest rooms in the Kensington more closely resemble those for the luxury hotel room in Figure 10.3. Some, like that in the diagram, have private bath, one king-size bed, two night stands, a desk/dresser with mirror, and a lounge area consisting of corner table, loveseat, lounge chair, and coffee table. Units in the Kensington hotel are of differing sizes but average approximately 400 square feet. That illustrated is among the largest the property offers.

Note that both guest rooms are designed for the same basic purpose—to provide accommodations for travelers. Every lodging establishment has guest rooms designed to accommodate the needs and desires of the kinds of travelers patronizing the establishment. To that extent, the guest rooms in the Value Lodge and the Kensington hotel have the same general purposes. There are, however, obvious differences between the two guest rooms illustrated; and these differences reveal much about the differences between the two properties. The principal differences are:

Commercial Hotel/Motel Room 312 sq. ft.

Suite in an All-Suite Property 690 sq. ft.

Hotel Standard Suite 546 sq. ft.

Budget Motel Room 243 sq. ft.

Hotel Junior Suite 450 sq. ft.

Sub budget Motel/Room 196 sq. ft.

Luxury Hotel/Motel Room 442 sq. ft.

FIGURE 10.3 *Typical Floor Plans for Guest Accommodations in Lodging Establishments*

285

Size. The typical room in the Value Lodge is approximately 150 square feet smaller than that in the Kensington.

Space Allocation. In the Kensington, some of the additional space has been allocated to some additional furnishings not found in the Value Lodge. In addition, the Kensington hotel room appears to be more open and uncluttered. Some of the extra space is used, quite simply, as space, affecting the ambiance of the lodging product.

Furnishings. In the Value Lodge, the furnishings are better suited to those staying overnight, rather than to those remaining for longer periods. They are not quite as attractive and comfortable as those in the Kensington, which features reproductions of classical antiques. However, the Kensington caters to guests seeking attractive furnishings and who are both willing and able to pay higher rates for more luxurious accommodations.

Housekeeping Layout and Design

As in front office and guest accommodations layouts, the layout and design of a housekeeping area in a lodging establishments is determined, to a great extent, by the type of establishment the developer intends to operate. In economy motels, for example, housekeeping areas tend to be smaller, simpler, and more compact than in traditional luxury hotels found in the more affluent areas of major cities. The housekeeping area in the Value Lodge, for example, is quite small and compact. In the Kensington, by contrast, housekeeping requires considerable space because of the nature of the Kensington as a luxury enterprise and the comparatively large number of employees required to maintain such a property.

The layout of the housekeeping facility in the Value Lodge is illustrated in Figure 10.4. Note that the facility is comparatively simple, having storage space for laundered bed and bath linens and cleaning supplies and providing floor space for the overnight storage of three mobile carts used by the housekeeping staff during working hours.

Figure 10.5 illustrates the layout of the main housekeeping facility in the Kensington.

The housekeeping area in the Kensington includes an office for an executive housekeeper, as well as considerable space for storing bed linens, bath linens, and cleaning supplies. A separate room is set aside for soiled linens. Here, soiled linens are separated and counted before being sent out to a commercial laundry to be washed and folded or ironed.

Note that both housekeeping areas are designed for the same basic purpose—to facilitate housekeeping services for guests. Every lodging establishment has a

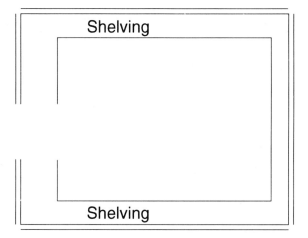

FIGURE 10.4 *Housekeeping Area in the Value Lodge*

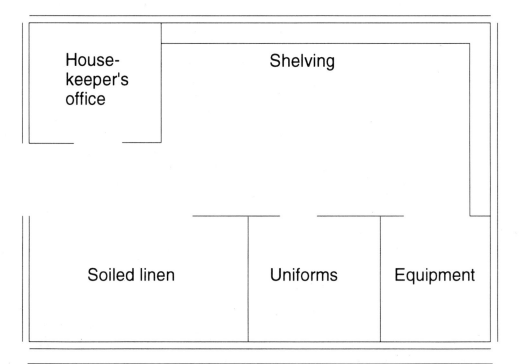

FIGURE 10.5 *Housekeeping Area in the Kensington*

similar area designed to provide the kind and level of housekeeping services preferred by the travelers patronizing the establishment. To that extent, the housekeeping areas in the Value Lodge and the Kensington have the same general purposes. However, there are obvious dissimilarities between the two areas illustrated, which suggest some of the dissimilarities between the two properties. The principal differences are:

Size. Two major factors account for the differences in size between the housekeeping areas in the two properties. The first of these has to do with the number of rooms to be serviced—50 in the Value Lodge versus 350 in the Kensington. Thus, the Kensington must have at least seven times the amount of bed and bath linen. The second reason has to do with the need to store uniforms in the housekeeping area of the Kensington—a need that does not exist in the Value Lodge.

The diagram of the Kensington Hotel does not show the additional housekeeping storage facilities that are located throughout the hotel. Each floor has a housekeeping closet used for storing small amounts of cleaning supplies, guest room supplies, and linens and for housing mobile carts when not in use by the housekeeping staff.

Space Allocation. Besides the space allocated for an office in the housekeeping area of the Kensington, there is also space for storing uniforms for all hotel employees required to wear them. This is not necessary in the Value Lodge, as we have noted. Because the Kensington is an older property, some of the side rooms now used for storage were once used by categories of housekeeping employees no longer found in most hotels: upholsterers and seamstresses, for example. Work formerly done by people in these job classifications is now typically done outside the hotel by independent contractors, making it possible to allocate this space for additional storage.

Equipment. Because it is a luxury property with a large lobby and considerable public space, the Kensington has some heavy, specialized cleaning equipment used to maintain these areas. Because the Value Lodge has no comparable space, it has no such equipment.

In addition, as a luxury enterprise the Kensington makes available to its guests various kinds of equipment not offered to guests in the Value Lodge. Guests in the Kensington can telephone the housekeeping office to obtain such common items as steam irons and ironing boards, and guests visiting from other parts of the world can borrow conversion devices that enable them to use their electrical appliances.

Linen

Caring for linen is one of the major responsibilities of any housekeeping department in any lodging operation. Without adequate supplies of appropriate linen, it is impossible to operate a lodging facility properly.

Linen—bed linen, bath linen, and, in some establishments, food linen—is one of the major problems and largest expenses in a lodging operation. Every bed in every room must be made up and ready for use at all times, whether or not the room is occupied. In addition, the property must have an adequate supply of linen on hand each day to change the linen on each bed, just in case the bed was used the previous night. Finally, there is always some linen in the process of being washed and ironed or folded, whether in the property's own laundry or at that of an outside service. In effect, any lodging operation must have at least three complete sets of linen for each bed and an additional quantity in inventory to replace items that are worn, torn, lost, or stolen. To make up a bed, one would need at least two sheets and one or more pillowcases, depending on the bed and the standards of the property.

In addition to bed linen, housekeeping should have at least three complete sets of bath linen for each guest that the property can accommodate. A set of bath linen would consist of at least one bath towel, one face towel, and one face cloth. Most properties also supply one tub mat for each bathroom. Considerable money is invested in the bed linens and bath linens that lodging establishments need for operation.

Better lodging establishments typically change bed and bath linens for each guest daily. Others—some economy motels and a number of inexpensive resorts—provide guests with changes of bath linens daily and changes of bed linens every two to three days. Still others—boarding houses, typically—are likely to change all linens just once a week. Every responsible lodging establishment would certainly change all linens in any guest accommodation after each checkout.

LAUNDERING LINEN. In general, there are three possible approaches to obtaining clean linen. The lodging operator can:

1. Own linen and install a laundry on premises to wash, iron, and fold it
2. Own linen and send it out to a commercial laundry to be washed, ironed, and folded
3. Rent clean linen

Each of these approaches has advantages and disadvantages.

1. *Owning linen and installing a laundry on premises to wash, iron, and fold it.* Many hotels and motels maintain their own laundry equipment on

premises. Space is set aside for the specialized equipment needed to wash, dry, and iron linens, which may have the name of the property embroidered or woven into the fabric.

Having one's own laundry has several advantages over other approaches. Linen does not leave the premises, so it is easier to control. If linen remains on the premises, it does not get lost as easily as when other methods are used; and personnel do not have to count linen leaving or returning to the building. The lodging operation is not dependent on an outside laundry, which can sometimes be late in returning clean linens, and is thus less likely to encounter the kinds of difficulties caused by linen shortages. Finally, maintaining an in-house laundry is often more cost-effective than the other approaches. In order for a lodging establishment to justify the expense of the investment in equipment and the ongoing cost of operating a laundry, however, the establishment must be large enough to keep the laundry operating several hours each day. Because of its remote location, the management of the Mountain Inn takes this approach.

2.   *Own linen and send it out to a commercial laundry to be washed, ironed, and folded.*   There are many lodging operations that prefer to own their own linen but are not large enough to justify the installation of laundry equipment on premises. In these cases, they must use the services of a commercial laundry. This choice still permits management to choose linen of the desired quality and inscribe it with the property's name, or logo, or both. However, those who send their laundry out to a commercial establishment must separate and either count or weigh all sheets, pillowcases, towels, and other items going to and coming from the laundry. Billing is often a problem when the hotel's count does not agree with the commercial laundry's count. In addition, commercial laundries may lose, tear, or otherwise ruin items sent out to be washed, and this can be a source of difficulty and misunderstanding.

3.   *Rent clean linen.*   Many lodging operators choose to rent clean linen rather than own it and have it laundered either on premises or in a commercial laundry. This is the most convenient of the three approaches: There is no investment in either linen or equipment, and management does not have the problems associated with operating a laundry. Many rental companies do not keep accurate records of the amount of linen returned by lodging operators because it is too time consuming to do so. Thus, lodging operators that rent clean linen may not have to account for it. They simply pay for the number of clean pieces they are sent and return the soiled linen. Laundries may not know how much linen they are losing to any one lodging operation, so they build the replacement cost of the lost linen into the rental prices charged to all lodging operators using their services.

Renting is typically the most costly of the three approaches, which is a distinct disadvantage. Another is that the lodging operator must accept the quality of linen supplied by the rental laundry, except in some special situations in which the rental laundry agrees to purchase higher quality linens for a specific lodging operation.

For many smaller operations, renting clean linen is the most desirable of the three approaches. The Value Lodge uses this approach because the owners of the motel are satisfied with the quality of the linen supplied by the rental company. Also, they lack the time to deal with laundry, choose not to make any investment in linen or laundry equipment, and do not want to add laundry staff to their payroll.

SUMMARY

In this chapter, the planning, layout, and design of lodging facilities are discussed. Lodging products are identified as service products; and the three elements in the service product line offered by lodging establishments are identified as accommodations, service, and ambiance. Feasibility studies are identified as important preliminaries in the planning of lodging facilities, and the topics most commonly addressed in a feasibility study are listed and discussed. Ten engineering systems are identified as basic elements in the design of most lodging properties. The layout and design of three areas central to lodging operations are illustrated and discussed: front office, guest room, and housekeeping area. The layout and design of these three in the Value Lodge and the Kensington hotel are described, compared, and contrasted. Finally, the responsibility of housekeeping for bed, bath, and food linen is addressed, and three approaches to providing clean linens for a lodging facility are described.

QUESTIONS

1. Distinguish between durable goods and service products.
2. Define the term *product line* as used in lodging operations.
3. List and discuss the three elements in the service product line of a lodging enterprise.
4. Identify seven principal subject areas normally analyzed in feasibility studies.
5. List and discuss ten engineering systems found in lodging facilities.
6. Distinguish between centralized and decentralized air conditioning systems.
7. How often should air be changed in the ballroom of a large hotel? In the kitchen serving the ballroom?

8. List four possible sources of water for lodging operations having no access to a public water supply.
9. What are *dumbwaiters*? For what purposes are they used in lodging facilities?
10. What are the principal components of a fire safety system?
11. Identify four common types of energy control systems.
12. What are the activities common to all front office operations that must be taken into account in their layout and design?
13. How would you expect the front office layout and design for a 75-room budget motel to differ from that for a 500-room luxury hotel?
14. Identify by name and size eight types of beds commonly used in lodging properties.
15. Provide the size range in square feet for each of the following: subbudget motel room; budget motel room; commercial hotel/motel room; luxury motel room; hotel junior suite; hotel standard suite; suite in an all-suite property.
16. Compare and contrast the size and furnishings of a budget motel room with those of a luxury hotel.
17. How would the layout and design of the housekeeping area in a 50-room motel be likely to differ from that in a 500-room luxury hotel?
18. Why would there be great differences in the size, space allocation, and equipment found in the housekeeping areas cited in question 17?
19. List and describe the three approaches identified in the text for obtaining clean linen for guest accommodations.
20. Which of the three would you recommend:
    a. to reduce the possibilities for linen loss;
    b. to minimize investment in linen;
    c. to minimize housekeeping payroll costs?

Travel and Tourism Perspectives

V

Dimensions of Travel and Tourism

LEARNING OBJECTIVES

After reading and studying this chapter, you should be able to:

1. *Identify a minimum of ten travel motivators.*
2. *List and discuss eight social and economic changes that have led to more frequent travel.*
3. *Explain the role of local, state, and federal governments in travel and tourism.*
4. *List the four criteria used to determine a person's status as a traveler.*
5. *Discuss several definitions of* traveler *and* tourist.
6. *Identify the three segments of the travel industry.*
7. *Discuss the size and scope of international travel.*
8. *Identify the nations that are the world's leading travel destinations.*
9. *Identify the nations whose citizens spend the most money on international travel.*
10. *Discuss the conditions and documents necessary for international tourist travel to take place.*
11. *Identify the nations that send the most visitors to the United States.*
12. *Describe the importance of domestic travel to the U.S. economy.*
13. *Define and describe the economic, cultural, social, and environmental impacts of tourism.*
14. *Identify several nations, states, areas, and localities that rely on tourism for jobs and income.*

INTRODUCTION

Previous chapters have demonstrated the relationships among economic progress, the development of roads and transportation, the scope of hospitality establishments, and the extent of travel. We have pointed out that those countries having the highest levels of economic progress have had the most highly developed transportation networks and the greatest numbers of travelers. We have shown that hospitality enterprises develop as a direct consequence of the development of transportation and that, as transportation modes change, so too do the locations of hospitality operations. We have discussed the food service and lodging industry in detail and described characteristic types of operations in each industry.

In this chapter we will turn our attention from the specifics of food, beverage, and lodging operations and look directly at the larger industry of which hospitality operations are a part—travel and tourism. We will examine the importance of travel and tourism to various countries and states and will look closely at its impact on their economy, society, culture, and environment. The succeeding chapter will examine the selling of travel and the chapter after that, the transportation systems that make travel possible.

TRAVEL MOTIVATORS

People travel for many reasons. Those listed below are just a few of the possibilities.

- Attending conventions or conferences
- Visiting friends or relatives
- Going on business
- Attending to health-related problems
- Going to a warmer climate
- Resting and relaxing
- Visiting theme parks, exhibitions, or events
- Participating in sports events
- Sightseeing
- Furthering education
- Visiting the birthplace of parents or grandparents
- Attending weddings or funerals
- "Getting away from it all"

Some of these reasons for travel would have been unknown before this century. In the 1600s or 1700s, for example, very few people would have had the time or the money to travel just because they wanted to go to a warmer climate. And no one would have traveled to go skiing or to visit a theme park: No ski slopes or theme parks had yet been developed.

In recent years, a number of important social and economic changes have led to more frequent travel. These include:

EARLY RETIREMENT. The retirement age for a large part of the population is earlier than it used to be. Our social security system grants benefits as early as 62 years of age, and many employee retirement programs are tied to years of service rather than to age. In some retirement programs, particularly government programs, it is possible to work twenty-five or thirty years and receive substantial retirement benefits at age 55. Early retirement leads to greater numbers of travelers as the retirees use their time to see the world.

LONGER LIFE SPAN. The average person can now expect to live well into his or her seventies, and many will live considerably longer. This is in contrast to just a few generations ago, when the average life span was considerably less. This increasing population of people over 60 provides a larger base of travelers—many of whom can well afford to travel for long periods of time.

SHORTER WORK WEEK. Sixty years ago, a six-day work week was standard for most working people. Today, a five-day work week is the standard; and the four-day work week is not uncommon, leaving several days for other activities. The resulting longer weekends, combined with faster and easier transportation, enable many workers to take weekend trips. This may include driving to visit friends and relatives, attending weddings and receptions, and traveling to various places and events that they would not have had time to attend only a few years ago.

MORE LEISURE TIME. Greater amounts of leisure time are now available to most workers. Americans receive more vacation time than ever before. Most receive at least two weeks each year, and many employees work for companies that offer additional vacation time for those with more years of service. Some of the leisure time available to Americans is in the form of holidays, many of which are now scheduled to fall on Mondays and Fridays. These create three- and four-day weekends that allow people to get away. One example is the recent addition of Martin Luther King day. In most states it is celebrated on a Monday in mid-January. This has created a long weekend that has had a major impact on travel destinations. For example, in the Northeast, it has turned a relatively quiet weekend into a record weekend for the ski areas.

GREATER DISPOSABLE INCOME. Many families have more money to spend than ever before. Higher wages and two-earner households account for much of this increase in disposable income. This allows more money to be spent on consumer goods and services, and travel appears to be an important part of what consumers want.

Increased mobility facilitated by improved roads (as shown above, Highway 101 in San Francisco) and other modes of transportation is only one of the important social and economic changes that have led to more frequent travel in the twentieth century. These include early retirement, longer life spans, shorter work weeks, more holidays, greater disposable income, and changes in consumer spending patterns. (Courtesy San Francisco Convention & Visitors Bureau.)

GREATER MOBILITY. Improved roads and better transportation make it easier and more comfortable to travel each year. The interstate highway system is now virtually complete, allowing faster travel between distant points. Most people in the United States are near a major airport or one that provides service to a major airport.

SMALLER FAMILIES. The average family size has decreased. This means that it is easier for the family to travel; and with fewer family members, travel costs less.

CHANGE IN CONSUMER SPENDING PATTERNS. The growth in public and private retirement programs has prompted a "live now" attitude and a feeling that the future will take care of itself. Many people are not as concerned with saving for retirement and are willing to spend their increasing income on travel. Travel has become an important part of the lifestyle of many people.

GOVERNMENT ROLE IN TRAVEL AND TOURISM

In many countries the national government plays an important role in travel and tourism. Some national governments own and operate airlines, as well as the national rail system. Some also own and operate hotels, motels, and other tourist facilities. In addition, most national governments establish tourism goals, gather statistical data, regulate tourist facilities, and advertise internationally to promote tourism.

In the United States, the national government has a much more limited role. The official government agency for tourism is the United States Travel and Tourism Administration (USTTA). It is a part of the U.S. Department of Commerce and is headed by an undersecretary for travel and tourism. The major function of the USTTA is to promote foreign travel to the United States. The USTTA does not directly operate hotels for tourists, nor does it operate a national transportation network.

Statistical data concerning travel in the United States are gathered by the U.S. Bureau of the Census and by various other agencies. However, most people interested in obtaining travel-related data about the United States tend to rely on information from private agencies. The principal private organization providing data in this area is the U.S. Travel Data Center, based in Washington, D.C.

The responsibility for promoting and regulating travel and tourism in each state falls to state governments. All state governments have offices charged with that responsibility, but their names and the departments to which they report vary from one state to another. In some, there is an independent state travel department; in others, the office responsible for travel and tourism is part of a larger department—commerce or transportation, for example.

At the local level, most cities and communities have chambers of commerce that promote tourism in those communities where tourism is important. City governments frequently have convention and visitors bureaus that promote travel to the city. They receive inquiries that they refer to hotels for follow-up action. They provide services to meeting planners that include orientation to the city and introductions to convention hall managers, hotel convention managers, and other suppliers of hospitality services. They frequently act as housing coordinators for groups that come to the city, referring delegates to hotel properties. In many instances, convention and visitors bureaus are funded by means of a tax added to the bills of hotel guests staying in the city. This is not the only approach to funding these bureaus, however. In some cases, their operating costs are met by a combination of private funds contributed by businesses relying on tourism and matching funds provided by state or local governments.

DEFINITIONS OF *TRAVELER* AND *TOURIST*

Most people would agree that a *traveler* is someone who goes from one place to another beyond his normal commuting distance, and a *tourist* is a person who travels for pleasure. However, when one examines those definitions critically, it becomes apparent that categorizing a specific person as a *traveler* or a *tourist* is not as easy as it first appears.

There are four criteria generally used to determine a person's status as a traveler.

1. Distance traveled
2. Residence of the traveler
3. Purpose of the travel
4. Length of stay at destination

Governments, states, and organizations concerned with travel and tourism have definitions of travelers and tourists based on those criteria. The definitions are important: They are used to count and categorize travelers. Unfortunately, government and nongovernment organizations alike do not agree on the importance of each of the four criteria. They have developed different definitions.

The question of who should be considered a traveler is particularly thorny. Should someone who is going to work on a special assignment twenty miles beyond his normal commuting distance or who is going shopping in a city fifteen miles from home be considered a traveler? Should someone who visits a friend in a nearby town and returns home the same day be considered a traveler? Should a person who goes from New Haven, Connecticut, to New York City to see the Yankees play baseball and who then returns home be considered a traveler? If he should stay overnight in New York, does that change his status?

To be counted as a traveler by the U.S. Bureau of the Census, a person must travel to a place at least 100 miles away from home and return. The U.S. Travel Data Center uses a broader definition: A traveler is "any resident of the United States regardless of nationality who travels to a place 100 miles or more away from home within the United States or who stays away from home one or more nights in paid accommodations and who returns home within twelve months, except for commuting to and from work or attending school."[1]

The issue is further complicated when one considers that people often travel for more than one reason. A great number combine pleasure with business when traveling. For example, consider the sales representative who takes his family to Disney World but spends one-half of his time there calling on clients. Is he a tourist

[1] *The 1990-1991 Economic Review of Travel in America* (U.S. Travel Data Center, Washington, D.C.), p. 1.

traveling for pleasure or is he a business traveler? Should a person who goes to a resort hotel for a business convention be considered a business traveler if he spends much of his time playing golf at the resort's country club?

The following are examples of the varying definitions of *tourist*:

In **Virginia,** a tourist is anyone residing outside the state who visits Virginia for vacation or pleasure.

In **Nevada,** a tourist is a resident of any state other than Nevada who visits somewhere in the state while en route, and without regard for trip purpose. This means that anyone who is passing through the state and who stops to visit someone, or who puts money in one of the slot machines located anywhere in the state, is considered a tourist.

Florida restricts the definition of a tourist to any person from out of state who stays overnight and who is in Florida for purposes of recreation and pleasure.

In **Massachusetts**, a tourist is anyone on a pleasure or vacation trip traveling outside his normal commuting distance.

Because travel and tourism are important to the economic health of so many nations of the world, even the United Nations has become involved in establishing definitions. It divides international travelers into *visitors* and *nonvisitors*. Visitors are further divided into two groups: *tourists* and *excursionists*. Tourists are those who spend at least twenty-four hours in a country and who come for almost any purpose—business, holiday, study, health reasons, visiting relatives, and participating in or attending sports. Excursionists are cruise passengers that are housed on board their ships and day visitors who do not stay overnight in a country. Nonvisitors are border workers—those workers who live in one country but work in another—members of the armed forces, immigrants, nomads, refugees, and diplomats. Visitors are counted in the tourism statistics and nonvisitors are not.

Thus, there are no universal definitions of travelers or tourists. It is important that anyone reading and attempting to understand statistical data on travel and tourism recognize that data are often neither comparable nor compatible because of the varying definitions used.

The terms *traveler* and *tourist* are being used interchangeably more and more often. The U.S. Senate Committee on Commerce, Science, and Transportation recently defined *travelers* or *tourists* as "people journeying outside their home community for any purpose except daily commuting to and from work." The two terms are quickly becoming synonyms. For purposes of this chapter, we will accept this. We will use the word *tourist* to mean any traveler who journeys outside his home community for any purpose except daily commuting to and from work, and we will use the words *traveler* and *tourist* interchangeably.

COMPOSITION OF THE TRAVEL INDUSTRY

The travel industry is made up of those firms and people who serve the needs of travelers. Professor Chuck Gee, in his excellent text, *The Travel Industry*,[2] divides the travel industry into three segments:

1. Direct providers of travel services
2. Support services
3. Tourism development

Direct Providers of Travel Services

Direct providers of travel services are those firms and people who are in direct contact with travelers and who provide the services necessary for their travel. They include:

Hotels/motels	Car rental companies
Restaurants	Shops selling travel and tourist products
Camps	Rental companies specializing in campers and
Travel agents	recreational vehicles
Airlines	Entertainment and recreation centers
Trains	National and state parks
Buses	Credit card companies
Cruise lines	

This list does not exhaust the possibilities of direct providers of travel services. However, it shows a good cross section of firms whose primary business activity is to provide a travel service. It is important to emphasize that this category of the travel industry does not include just transportation, hotels, and restaurants. It includes any firm that provides a travel service directly to the traveler: the travel agent who makes the travel arrangements, shops that sell travel mementos, firms and people who act as tour guides for tourists, entertainers who provide music and cultural activities for tourists, businesses that supply rental bicycles, rowboats, or sailboats for tourists, and many others.

Support Services

Support services are the firms and individuals who provide services and supplies to the direct providers and who are dependent on the travel market for a large part or all of their business. They provide the necessary goods and services that allow the direct providers to perform travel services; they include: purveyors of food and

[2]Chuck Y. Gee and others, *The Travel Industry*, 2nd ed. (New York: Van Nostrand Reinhold, 1989), pp. 7–9.

beverages to hotels and restaurants; laundries that supply the linen for lodging properties; firms and individuals who supply the travel mementos to gift shops; employment agencies that specialize in providing hospitality workers; hotel management firms that manage hospitality operations; food service firms that provide the food for airline passengers; and many others.

Tourism Development

Tourism development is a term used to describe individuals and organizations that directly and indirectly affect the direct providers, the support services, and the individual traveler. The category includes those with an interest in travel and tourism but who would not be considered direct providers, support services, or travelers. Examples of individuals and organizations in tourism development include:

1. ***Organizations associated with direct providers:*** These include the American Society of Travel Agents, the American Hotel and Motel Association, the National Restaurant Association, the International Air Transportation Association, and the Cruise Lines International Association. Each of these organizations represents its respective hospitality or travel industry and consists of member firms from those or allied industries. They provide a voice for their industries to Congress and to the public, provide information about their industries to their members, and in some cases, make policy decisions relating to sales of their services or practices of their membership. For example, the International Air Transportation Association establishes international air fares for member airlines.

2. ***Government agencies, including the United States Travel and Tourism Administration, as well as various state and local travel offices:*** These government organizations promote travel and tourism to their countries, states, and localities and are important components of the travel industry.

3. ***Private agencies that promote travel and tourism and gather statistical data:*** One example is the World Tourism Organization — a private organization located in Madrid, Spain. It promotes international tourism, gathers statistical data on world tourism, and is an official consultant to the United Nations. Another important private organization is the World Travel and Tourism Council, located in Brussels, Belgium. It is the newest of the international organizations and has recently published a study of world tourism.

4. ***Schools, colleges, and universities — public, private, and proprietary — that prepare individuals for careers in hospitality and tourism:*** Numerous public and private institutions train cooks, hotel workers, and travel agents. In addition, more than 800 two- and four-year colleges offer

In the United States the responsibility for promoting and regulating travel and tourism falls to each state, usually overseen by the department of commerce, transportation, or tourism. This includes advertising (as shown above) in print, television, and radio, contributing to the development of tourism within the state. (Copyright © Virginia Department of Economic Development — Tourism Group.)

majors in food service, lodging, or tourism. Among the first colleges to develop such programs were Cornell University, Michigan State University, and Pennsylvania State University. One of the first to develop a nationally acclaimed culinary program was the Culinary Institute of America in Hyde Park, New York. The oldest of the four year colleges offering a comprehensive program in travel industry management is the University of Hawaii.

The travel industry is comprised of a broad range of private and government firms and agencies. It is an amalgamation of organizations serving the needs of travelers. Many of the firms within the travel industry have little in common except that their primary business is dependent on travelers.

THE SIZE AND SCOPE OF THE TRAVEL INDUSTRY

Travel is the world's largest industry. In 1990, the World Travel and Tourism Council estimated that world domestic and international tourism spending reached

$2.7 trillion. This represents about 12 percent of the total amount of money spent at the retail level on goods and services. Worldwide, travel and tourism employs more than 112 million people.

The Scope of International Travel

International travel is travel between countries. There has been continued growth in the number of people traveling internationally, as shown in Tables 11.1 and 11.2.

Tables 11.1 and 11.2 show international arrivals only, and do not show the many millions of travelers who restrict travel to their own country.

The alert student will note that the two tables appear to contradict each other. A sizable increase in the number of arrivals occurred across the years shown in Table 11.1, while the percentage increase in international tourism shown in Table 11.2 has declined for each period shown. For example, between 1950 and 1960 the increase in international tourist arrivals was 44,014,000 (69,296,000 − 25,282,000), and the percentage increase per year for that period was 10.6 percent. Yet, between 1980 and 1990 the increase in international tourist arrivals was 166,969,000 (454,875,000 − 287,906,000), but there was only a 4.7 percent annual increase for that period. The explanation is that the base numbers used to calculate the annual percentage increases were larger in the latter period, resulting in a smaller percentage increase. For example, an increase of 500 in the number of visitors to an area from 1,000 to 1,500 would be a 50 percent increase. Yet that same increase of 500 in the number of visitors the next year from 1,500 to 2,000 is only a 33 percent increase.

Of importance to our analysis is that there has been a significant and steady increase in international travel. One of the primary reasons is the decreased cost of transportation relative to income, making it more affordable for everyone. Another is increased vacation time and a greater number of holidays in many countries.

TABLE 11.1 *Growth of world tourism*

Year	International tourist arrivals
1950	25,282,000
1960	69,296,000
1970	159,690,000
1980	287,906,000 (r)
1990	454,875,000 (r)
1991	448,545,000 (p)

(r) revised data
(p) provisional revised estimates
Source: World Tourism Organization.

TABLE 11.2 *Annual increase in world tourism*

Period	Average annual increase in international arrivals
1950–1959	10.6%
1960–1969	8.7%
1970–1979	6.1%
1980–1989	4.7%
1981–1990	4.5%

Source: World Tourism Organization.

World's Leading Tourist Destinations

The world's leading tourist destinations are shown in Table 11.3. A *destination*, as used in this table, is a country that receives visitors. They come by plane, ship, train, or car.

France is the recipient of more international arrivals than any other country. One of the reasons for this is France's central location in western Europe. Residents of western Europe frequently travel through Europe, and France is both an excellent destination and a country that travelers must pass through when traveling by automobile to other countries. France's central location means that many visitors counted in the statistics include people who are passing through France on their way to other destinations.

Second on the list is the United States. Discussion of travel to the United States is found later in this chapter.

The third leading travel destination is Spain. Its sunny, warm climate and its relatively low prices make it a very popular travel destination, particularly for those residents of colder climates. It is thus perhaps the leading vacation country for European travelers. The Spanish government has made a consistent effort to keep the monetary rate of exchange very favorable for visitors in order to attract as many tourists as possible.

Italy, the fourth leading tourist destination, is important historically, particularly because the Vatican is located there; and there is much else to see in Rome, as well as in the rest of the country. Many tours of Europe start or end in Rome.

In nations that are high on the list of tourist destinations, many jobs are created to feed, house, and provide other travel services for tourists. This is important to their economies, a subject that will be discussed in greater detail at the end of this chapter.

TABLE 11.3 *World's leading tourist destinations, 1990*

Rank	Country	Number of arrivals
1	France	53,157,000
2	U.S.A.	39,772,000
3	Spain	34,300,000
4	Italy	26,679,000
5	Hungary	20,510,000
6	Austria	19,011,000
7	United Kingdom	18,021,000
8	Germany	17,045,000
9	Canada	15,258,000
10	Switzerland	13,200,000
11	China	10,484,000

Source: World Tourism Organization.

World's Leading Spenders on International Tourism

Table 11.4 shows the amount of money spent on international trips by residents of the top ten countries in international travel.

The United States leads the list of international spenders. Discussion of U.S. spending abroad is found later in the chapter. Germany is second on the list. The figures shown represent only West Germany, as they were gathered prior to unification. The Germans have always been frequent travelers. A primary reason for this is the economic prosperity of West Germany and the high standard of living in that country. In addition, Germans typically have a great amount of holiday time. On average, they receive ten holidays and six weeks of paid vacations.

Third on the list is Japan. It has become a leading economic power—exporting autos, televisions, cameras, computers, radios, and many other products. It has become a significant member of the world community, and its citizens travel frequently to other parts of the world. The average Japanese worker now receives more vacation time than the average American, and the Japanese government is encouraging its citizens to travel abroad.

It should be noted that the list of leading tourist spenders is made up of the most developed countries and does not include any from the underdeveloped countries. This pattern of travel confirms historical trends.

Current trends suggest that travel will continue to increase. Recent political changes in eastern European nations will allow many who were formerly restricted from traveling by their governments to become part of the world's growing number of travelers. In addition, these former Eastern-bloc countries will become more attractive destinations for growing numbers of international travelers. The world is fast developing a global economy. As nations become more and more dependent upon one another, travel will increase.

TABLE 11.4 *World's leading spender nations on international travel, 1990****

Rank	Country	Amount spent
1	U.S.A.	$38,671,000,000
2	Germany	29,836,000,000
3	Japan	24,928,000,000
4	United Kingdom	17,614,000,000
5	Italy	13,826,000,000
6	France	12,424,000,000
7	Canada	8,390,000,000
8	Netherlands	7,340,000,000
9	Austria	6,212,000,000
10	Sweden	6,066,000,000
11	Switzerland	5,989,000,000

*Excludes international transportation.
Source: World Tourism Organization.

Conditions and Documents Required for International Travel

Before tourist travel between countries can take place, countries must recognize each other through formal, diplomatic channels, the mechanisms for travel between countries must be in place, and the travelers themselves must have the proper documentation.

DIPLOMATIC RECOGNITION. The first requirement for international tourist travel is diplomatic recognition between countries. This recognition can take two forms:

1. *De jure recognition:* The government of one country recognizes that the party in power in another country is that country's legitimate government.
2. *De facto recognition:* The government of a country does not acknowledge the legitimacy of the party governing another country but acknowledges, at least, that that party does govern.

When diplomatic recognition occurs, consular or ambassadorial officials are exchanged, and negotiations take place that establish the procedures and routines for travel. Without recognition, the procedures for travel between two countries cannot be negotiated, and travel between them is normally prohibited.

These procedures for travel are established by consulates or embassies that serve as the official links between two countries. Diplomats work out detailed procedures for travel between the countries and for assistance and protection to travelers. Diplomats also negotiate agreements that facilitate travel, such as landing rights for aircraft.

International travelers must have the appropriate documentation. The basic document needed for visits to most countries is the passport. It is issued to the traveler by his country of residence and provides specific data about the person to whom it is issued, including residence, date of birth, occupation, and citizenship. It also contains a photograph of the passport holder.

In addition to the passport, many countries require a visa. A visa is an endorsement on the passport or other document that shows the passport holder has received the permission of the government of the country he is visiting to enter that country. Visas are usually obtained by applying well in advance of intended dates of travel to a consulate office of the country to be visited.

Passports and visas are stamped by immigration authorities when visitors enter a country. They show the date and port or border of entry. Permission to stay in a country is normally granted for only a limited period of time.

U.S. citizens need only a passport to visit most western European countries — one does not need to obtain a visa or advance permission. Passports are not required for U.S. citizens to visit Canada, Mexico, or most Caribbean nations.

However, valid identification and proof of citizenship are necessary. In some countries a driver's license will suffice; in others, further proof is needed—such as a birth certificate. A visa is required to visit most eastern European, Mideastern, Asian, and African countries. In many South American countries, visas are required for some travelers and not for others. There, visas normally are required for business travelers and those staying for three months or longer.

Additional travel requirements exist in many places. Typical of these are vaccination certificates for diseases that prevail in the countries being visited. As of this writing, cholera vaccinations are required in many African nations, including Angola, Chad, Ghana, and Liberia. Cholera vaccinations are also required in many countries in the Middle East, the Pacific area, and South America. Yellow fever vaccinations are necessary in Bolivia, Brazil, Columbia, Ecuador, and Peru. Malaria vaccinations are required in several countries during certain times of the year when the risk of contracting the disease is great. Smallpox vaccinations are also needed in a number of countries.

Proof of financial ability—a return ticket or a stated amount of cash—and other documentation are also frequently required. For example, to enter Ecuador, a tourist must have a ticket to leave and proof of sufficient funds. A passport is also required, and a visa is necessary for a stay of three months or more. An American traveling to El Salvador must have a passport and visa along with a photograph and a notarized letter from the traveler's employer. In addition, travelers must have police clearance. Presumably, these strict travel requirements result from recent hostilities in the area.

Governments frequently prohibit citizens from visiting countries that are at war, countries where the safety of visitors may be at risk, or countries that have not been recognized. For many years, U.S. citizens were prohibited from visiting China because it did not have diplomatic relations with the United States.

Some countries restrict the amount of money their citizens can take with them out of the country. For example, citizens of Indonesia, Israel, and Malaysia are restricted in this way. Some countries, including India and Burma, prohibit tourists from taking any local currencies out of the country.

Governments sometimes also prohibit citizens of certain countries from entering. As of this writing, Israelis are not permitted to enter most of the Arab countries; and several countries prohibit South African citizens from entering. Most countries do not allow criminals, suspected terrorists, and similar undesirables to enter.

Usually, some goods that visitors can bring with them into countries are restricted. For example, pork products and pornography are forbidden in Saudi Arabia, and many countries limit the quantity of liquor that can be brought in.

Some countries require that departing travelers obtain exit permits: This is true for business travelers leaving Venezuela, for example. When arriving home, travelers must pass through immigration. In the United States, all articles purchased abroad and in the possession of the traveler must be declared, along with the prices paid for them. Officials verify that prohibited goods are not being brought into the country. Prohibited goods include illegal drugs, explosives, firearms, and certain plants, animals, and related items. When necessary, *duty* — an import tax—is paid on goods purchased in other countries. As of this writing, U.S. citizens may bring up to $400 worth of nonprohibited goods into the country ($1,200 if coming from the U.S. Virgin Islands, American Samoa, or Guam; $600 if coming from the Caribbean countries) without paying duty. Amounts over $400, $600, or $1200 are taxed. No tourists are allowed to bring goods intended for resale into the country, without the proper permits.

TRAVEL TO AND FROM THE UNITED STATES

United States citizens have always been leading world travelers. Americans spend more money traveling in other countries than any other nationality ($38.6 billion), as illustrated previously in Table 11.4. Perhaps the most significant reasons for this are:

1. The United States has a large, prosperous middle class, who can afford to travel internationally.
2. Many Americans have roots in other countries. This creates an incentive for people to visit the homeland of their ancestors.
3. Travel is an integral part of the American heritage. We tend to move from one town or city to another frequently, when compared with other nations. Because relatives are located in other areas, we tend to travel distances to see them.
4. It is easier for Americans to travel internationally than for citizens of many other countries. The United States government has established relatively few travel restrictions, making it possible for nearly all Americans to travel outside the country without government interference. The amount of money Americans can take along when traveling outside the country is not restricted, nor is the amount of time they can spend outside the country or their frequency of travel.
5. English is the most widely spoken of the international languages, making it possible for Americans to travel without having to know other foreign languages. In many countries, English is a nearly universal second language, studied in school and spoken by most of the population. Workers in hotels, restaurants, airlines, and other travel services throughout the world speak English.

The United States is also the leading country for tourism receipts ($40.5 billion), as illustrated in Table 11.5.

TABLE 11.5 *World's top international tourism earners, 1990**

Rank	Country	Amount spent
1	United States	$40,579,000,000
2	France	20,185,000,000
3	Italy	19,742,000,000
4	Spain	18,593,000,000
5	United Kingdom	13,935,000,000
6	Austria	13,017,000,000
7	Germany	10,683,000,000
8	Switzerland	6,839,000,000
9	Canada	6,374,000,000
10	Mexico	5,324,000,000
11	Hong Kong	5,032,000,000

*Excluding international transportation.
Source: World Tourism Organization.

TABLE 11.6 *Foreign-visitor arrivals to the United States, 1990 estimates*

Origin	Number (000)
Canada	17,262
Mexico	6,761
Overseas	14,802
Europe	6,548
Asia/Mideast	4,619
South America	1,296
Caribbean	1,143
Oceania	653
Central America	411
Africa	136

Source: U.S. Travel and Tourism Administration, in Somerset R. Waters, *Travel Industry World Yearbook: The Big Picture, 1991* (New York: Child & Waters, 1991), p. 61.

TABLE 11.7 *Overseas-visitor arrivals to the United States, 1990*

Country	Number (000)
Japan	3,148
United Kingdom	2,230
Germany	1,152
France	706
Australia	459
Italy	386

Source: U.S. Travel and Tourism Administration, in Waters, p. 61.

The United States is a vast country with innumerable sights and attractions for foreign visitors. The many features they enjoy include such imposing cities as New York and Chicago with their tall buildings and cultural diversity; the impressive scenery in our national parks; excellent facilities for such sports activities as golf and skiing; and places of special interest such as Disney World, historic Williamsburg, and Sea World.

It is interesting to note which countries send the most visitors to the United States (see Tables 11.6 and 11.7).

The greatest number of foreign visitors to the United States come from Canada and the next greatest number come from Mexico. The proximity of these two countries to the United States accounts for the large number of Canadian and Mexican citizens who visit the United States. It is relatively easy and not very expensive to drive across the border, when compared with the distance and cost associated with overseas travel.

The pattern of travel to the United States from overseas has changed in recent years. Table 11.7 shows where the most overseas visitors to the United States originate.

In recent years, the Japanese have traveled to the United States in very large numbers and now lead the list of overseas visitors. This is indicative of the role of Japan in the world economy and particularly of the importance of the United States as an importer of Japanese goods. We have very strong economic ties to Japan. They have heavily invested in the United States, and we purchase more goods and services from them than any other single country. The Japanese people come to the United States for many reasons, not the least of which is to play golf. It is a sport that they have become enthralled with, one that is very expensive in Japan and therefore available to only a relatively few people there.

The United Kingdom is second in the number of visitors. It has always sent many tourists to the United States. A major reason for this appears to be our common heritage and language. America traditionally has also received large numbers of immigrants from the United Kingdom, although these numbers are not reflected in the tourist statistics.

TRAVEL WITHIN THE UNITED STATES

The scope of travel/tourism in the United States is truly impressive. According to the *Travel Industry World Yearbook*, total spending for tourism services in the United States was estimated at $652 billion for 1990.[3] This represents about 12 percent of the United States gross national product. Stated another way, more than one in every ten dollars spent at the retail level is for tourism-related services.

Table 11.8 reveals some interesting information about travel patterns in the United States.

Several observations can be drawn from this data. Nearly all travelers in the United States use family automobiles or trucks, recreational vehicles (RVs), or airplanes to reach their destinations. Seventy-seven percent of all travel over 100 miles is done by automobile and 19 percent by airplane. Ninety-six percent of all trips taken use these two modes of transportation. Trains and buses are rarely used for long-distance travel. It appears that their primary use is for commuting to and from work.

The major reason that people travel long distances within the United States is to visit friends and relatives—35 percent of all trips. Most of the trips over 100

---

[3]Somerset R. Waters, *Travel Industry World Yearbook: The Big Picture, 1991* (New York: Child & Waters, 1991), p. 16.

TABLE 11.8 *U.S. trip profile, 1989*

Trips to places 100 miles or more from home

Round trip distances	Percent (%) of trips
200–299 miles	23
300–399 miles	16
400–599 miles	18
600–999 miles	13
1,000–1,999 miles	14
2,000 miles or more	11
Outside U.S.	6
Mode of transportation	
Auto/truck/RV	72
Airplane	23
Bus	2
Train	1
Other	1
Trip duration	
No nights	11
One night	15
2 or 3 nights	37
4 to 9 nights	29
10 nights or more	8
Type of lodging	
Friends', relatives' homes	37
Hotel or motel	45
Owned cabin or condo	3
Camper, trailer, or RV	3
Other	5
No overnight stay	11
Primary purpose of trip	
Visit friends or relatives	35
Outdoor recreation	12
Entertainment	23
Business	26
Other	8

Source: U.S. Travel Data Center, *1990 Travel Market Report*, pp. 7, 8.

miles—89 percent of them—involve at least one overnight stay; and a large number of overnight stays are at friends and relatives.

Thus, the statistics confirm the importance of the family automobile to the traveling public. This is in contrast to many other nations, particularly the underdeveloped ones, in which automobiles are not owned by large numbers of people, roads are not as good as in the rest of the world, and train, bus, and bicycle travel are still the primary means of transportation.

THE IMPACT OF TOURISM

Tourism affects every nation and many localities. For some nations and localities, tourism has a major impact on the economy, the culture, the society, and the environment. The effects can be both positive and negative and are greater in some countries and areas than others. Let us examine these effects in more detail.

The Economic Impact of Tourism

Economic impact of tourism is a phrase used to refer to the increased level of economic activity in an area that results from tourism. It is generally measured in additional jobs and income to an area.

Travelers and tourists purchase goods and services. They spend money for transportation, lodging accommodations, food, drink, and entertainment. They also buy gifts and supplies in shops and businesses. The money that is spent for these goods and services comes from outside the area and is brought to the area by tourists as cash, travelers checks, and credit cards. It is not generated from any internal source but is "new" money to the area—money that would not be spent unless travel and tourism occurred.

Tourism affects the economic development of any region to which tourists travel, generally increasing its jobs and income. For example, tourism to Guadaloupe spawned shopping areas and recreational activities. (Photo by Joe Petrouck.)

The direct, or immediate, effect of the additional spending is an increase in the number of jobs and an increase in the income of the area. For example, new hotels, motels, and other lodging establishments must be built to accommodate the travelers. This creates construction jobs to build the new facilities. Once the facilities are built, staff must be hired to operate them. Wages are paid to employees, and these wages are spent in the area to purchase housing, food, clothing, and many other goods and services. The grocery stores and shops affected receive income that they would not have had if the hotels, motels, and other lodging facilities were not built. The lodging facilities must also purchase food and other supplies. If the goods are bought locally, the food purveyors and suppliers of other goods gain income they would not otherwise have received.

Besides these immediate effects, there are also very important "ripple" effects. The additional income that local grocery stores, shops, purveyors, and other businesses receive as a result of tourism allows these enterprises to hire more employees to handle the extra business. These new employees also spend their wages in the local community. So, more jobs are created and more income is generated as a secondary effect of the original new spending. And it does not stop there. There may be third, fourth, and additional rounds of new jobs created as these new employees spend their money locally. Where there was only one restaurant in the area, for example, there may now be several, catering to the tourists, to the enlarged population, or to both.

The total of the increased economic activity is referred to as the *economic impact* on an area. It may be greater than the original amount spent or it may be less, depending on how much of the original new money is spent locally and how much of it is spent outside the area. For example, suppose that a new hotel hires workers who commute from a distance away and that the hotel also purchases its goods and services from firms outside the local area. Under these circumstances, the economic impact on the immediate area would be limited, because very little of the new money would be spent there. This is precisely what has happened in Atlantic City, New Jersey. The legalization of casino gambling led to the construction of many new hotels, but the economic impact in the immediate area has been minimal. There are three principal reasons for this:

1. Gamblers seldom leave the casino hotels and consequently spend very little money in other Atlantic City businesses.
2. Comparatively few casino hotel employees actually live in Atlantic City, so they tend to shop for goods and services outside the city.
3. A major portion of the casino hotels' purchases of goods and services are from vendors located outside the area.

The economic impact of tourism varies considerably from one part of the country to another and from one location to another. Some travel destinations have a very high economic impact resulting from travel and tourism, whereas other destinations do not benefit as much. For example, in Florida tourism is the most important industry in the state. In 1988, $47.9 billion was spent by tourists in that state. This spending directly and indirectly created about 1.5 million jobs and accounted for 24 percent of the state's civilian labor force. The economic impact of tourism is high. This is because most of the wages paid to workers were spent in Florida, and a large proportion of the goods and services purchased by the travel industry came from Florida businesses. By contrast, in Bermuda the economic impact of tourism is relatively low, even though tourism is also the most important industry there, accounting for about 60 percent of the jobs on the island. The impact is lower than in Florida because Bermuda grows relatively little food and manufactures very few products for the travel industry. Although employees do spend their wages in the local community, hotels, shops, and other businesses must buy from the United States and other countries. In both locations—Florida and Bermuda—tourism is the most important economic activity. In Florida, however, the economic benefits from tourism are greater because the direct and indirect economic impacts are greater.

Other important economic benefits are increased government income from taxes and earnings of foreign exchange, or currencies. All states in the United States impose taxes on tourists. Most states have sales taxes on rooms and meals. These are frequently higher than the sales taxes imposed on other goods and services. For example, the state of New Hampshire has a 7 percent tax on rooms and meals; yet it has no sales taxes on any other goods and services sold in the state. New York City imposes special sales taxes on hotel rooms. A traveler staying in a New York hotel may be charged as much as 19 percent in state and city taxes for hotel accommodations.

A very significant economic benefit to many countries is the foreign exchange they are able to earn as a result of tourism. Countries need foreign currencies in order to pay for imported goods and services. For example, when a United States manufacturer of furniture sells beds, tables, and chairs to a hotel in Jamaica the manufacturer wants payment in American dollars, rather than Jamaican dollars, in order that the money can be spent in the United States. As long as tourists or others have purchased goods or services in Jamaica for equivalent value in dollars, the banking system will be able to exchange the Jamaican dollars for American dollars. If there are insufficient sales of tourism or other goods and services in Jamaica, there will be a shortage of dollars to pay for the beds, tables, and chairs. This will eventually lead to higher prices for imported goods and services as the Jamaican dollar becomes less valuable in the world market. On the other hand, if tourism produces sufficient foreign exchange, prices for imported goods and services will not be affected. Many countries, such as Bermuda, for example, trade in U.S. dollars. They accept dollars in payment for tourism, and they purchase goods from the United States with these earned dollars.

Cultural Impact

Tourism can have an important impact on a country's *culture*—the customary beliefs, social forms, and material traits of a racial, religious, or social group. Culture manifests itself in art, dance, religion, food, drink, and other features of the society. Tourism may help preserve native culture, but at the same time it will speed the process of cultural change.

Tourism helps preserve culture when large numbers of people travel to observe it. Music, dances, religious rites and similar activities are performed for tourists and thus become profitable. The repetition of these performances and the profit from them provide an incentive to preserve the past and current culture. It is said that cultural ceremonies on several Caribbean and South Sea islands would have disappeared if tourists were not there to see them.

Travelers frequently go to countries, in part, to sample the native food and drink: Irish stew, German sauerbraten, Italian cannelloni, Japanese sukiyaki and sashimi, for example. These dishes are preserved in their original form for tourists, and thus they remain part of the culture.

Travelers also go to other countries to see the remains of past cultures. The remains of the Roman Colosseum and the ruins of Pompeii, for example, attract large numbers of visitors; and the money spent by tourists helps preserve them.

Over the long term, tourism may bring about changes in the culture of a region or a country. Two important areas that may be affected are food and clothing.

CHANGES IN FOODS CONSUMED. Tourists bring social and cultural values with them when they visit other countries. They may be eager to sample the food of the countries they visit; but they commonly look for a familiar food as well, seeking foods similar to those served at home. Hotels and restaurants willingly accommodate them. The local residents discover these foods and begin to try them, so that eventually some of the foods become part of the culture. For example, imported frozen foods and American whiskey are now popular throughout the Caribbean. This was not the case before Americans began to visit in large numbers.

Fast-food hamburger chains are now spreading throughout the world. McDonald's is now in Russia and throughout Europe, and Burger King has expanded into China. American-style restaurants are now in Japan. Eventually, these foods will become an important part of the diets of the peoples in those countries, and their culture will have been altered. It is said that the many Puerto Rican dishes have all but disappeared from the diets of those living on that island. The Puerto Rican diet now clearly resembles that of the American mainland. San Juan is primarily a city of fast-food restaurants, having typical American mainland cuisine.

Tourism impacts culture in two ways: For example, it may help to preserve art or dance in performance or cuisine in preparation, but may also influence changes in a culture through contact with travelers and the devaluation of once sacred rituals through commerce. Shown above are the Lion Dancers at the Merlion Festival, held on the last day of the Merlion Week. (Courtesy Singapore Tourist Promotion Board; all copyrights preserved.)

CHANGES IN DRESS. Tourism also can change the manner in which local populations dress. Tourists come to countries wearing clothing that is popular at home. These forms of dress are sold in local stores to the tourists, noticed by the local population, and sometimes imitated. As the dress worn by tourists becomes more popular, traditional native dress becomes less used and is gradually replaced. A classic example of this change is taking place in Russia. Levis and other forms of jeans have become very popular and command high prices in that country.

Social Impact

Tourism can also have dramatic—and often negative—effects on social relations in a country. It can affect the way the host society feels about citizens of other countries, and it can also affect behavior of the citizens of the host country. These changes manifest themselves in many ways, including:

1. Resentment
2. Family problems
3. Social problems
4. Increased crime and violence

RESENTMENT. Tourists going to poor, underdeveloped countries sometimes create feelings of resentment and jealousy among the native population. They do this by being demanding, sometimes demeaning, and by showing a tendency to spend excessive amounts of money.

Local workers see tourists check into first-class and luxury hotels. The rates paid by these tourists are usually high by local standards. The room rate charged for one night in some of these properties may be the equivalent of several weeks' wages for a local worker. Some tourists can be very demanding, requiring instant service or a special service that may not be readily available in the area. Other tourists can be demeaning, talking to the hotel staff as if they were inferior.

The considerable amount of money spent by the tourists can create jealousy. Tourists sometimes appear to spend money as if it meant very little. Native workers with lower standards of living become jealous of the more affluent tourists and develop a dislike for them.

If the behavior of tourists is grossly inappropriate, local workers are likely to become resentful and react by being impolite. These feelings are transferred to the local population, as workers go home and discuss events with family and friends. Americans have poor reputations in some countries, because some American tourists have behaved inappropriately and insultingly. Thus, local residents have assumed that all Americans are like the unpleasant ones they have seen at the hotels.

This problem is not restricted to other nations. It can be seen within the United States. For example, tourists from large cities, such as New York, who go to rural areas in New England may appear to local residents to "throw money around." They willingly spend more than the local population feel products and services are worth. The prices of goods and services generally rise in response to this. In reality, prices in the rural areas may be considerably cheaper than in large cities, such that tourists do not feel they are paying too much. Nevertheless, the native population resent them for driving up prices, crowding the highways, polluting the area, and generally "acting superior"; and although local residents typically are willing to take their money, they resent the presence of the outsiders.

FAMILY PROBLEMS. Tourism can affect the family relationships of local residents when one or more members of the family work in the tourist industry. Several years ago a study of Hawaiian families showed that the divorce rate of workers involved in tourism was rapidly rising. The study concluded that women who dressed in native Hawaiian costumes to greet and entertain tourists sometimes faced jealousy from their husbands, who accused the women of carrying on with the tourists. In addition, many of the women began to earn higher wages than their husbands, which led to further problems.

SOCIAL PROBLEMS. Tourism obviously creates the need for labor to work in hotels, restaurants, and other businesses catering to the traveler. Many of these workers come from the local population, but many also come from other locations, and settle in the area among the local population. Communities that may have been populated almost entirely with a single culture find that people of different backgrounds, beliefs, values, and lifestyles are now living in their neighborhoods. The new residents act differently, go to different churches, may speak a different language, and perhaps eat different foods. Past social patterns are upset and cultural collision occurs. If the new residents are accepted by the community, the dissimilar cultures can exist peaceably together. If not, there may be conflict.

INCREASED CRIME AND VIOLENCE. When areas grow in population as a result of tourism, negative changes can take place. A once peaceful, rural community is now an active, bustling one. The increased population brings with it crime and violence that did not exist before. Tourists, who tend to carry larger amounts of money than they would when not traveling, become targets for amateur and professional thieves. Houses and stores are broken into; a larger police force is needed; and natives who did not lock their houses and cars when not in them must now do so.

Environmental Impact

The impact of tourism on the environment can be positive or negative, depending on the specific area and one's personal views. On the one hand, everyone would agree that some tourist areas such as Atlantic City, Miami Beach, or Waikiki do not now have the natural beauty that existed prior to development. On the other hand, many would argue that resort areas such as Bermuda, Nassau, or Maui are nicer, cleaner, and more charming than prior to development for tourism.

Some people feel that more people in an area and changes in an area, such as new roads, hotels, and restaurants, are harmful to the environment. To them *all* tourism is harmful to the environment. The general arguments for each are as follows:

THE POSITIVE ARGUMENT. Development of all kinds has a tendency to destroy the natural as well as the historical and the cultural environments. One cannot develop an area without creating roads, buildings, and telephone lines. In the process, some historical or cultural symbols may be destroyed. Many countries and areas lack the incentive or the economic means to undertake large-scale projects for the conservation of beautiful scenery, rare and interesting natural environments, or historically important sites. The local population may have little use for "unspoilt nature" and will develop these areas in ways that will bring in the most money—whether it be for factories, mining, or some other kind of business.

Tourism changes all that. It encourages the restoration of ancient monuments and archaeological treasures. It provides a reason for the preservation of historical buildings and the creation of museums. The Roman Colosseum would not be preserved if there were no tourists to see it; the same can be said for the Acropolis in Greece—probably the best known "ruins" in the world. Natural scenery and historical sites, as well as traditional towns, become economic assets. Some attractions may be more beautiful than the natural land—golf courses and parks, for example.

Tourism provides not only the incentive but the economic means to preserve the environment. It discourages the development of heavy industry and other unsound uses of the land.

THE NEGATIVE CASE. The benefits of tourism are overshadowed by its side effects. The development of tourism often brings large numbers of people, accustomed to relatively high standards of amenities, to a previously secluded natural or cultural environment. Tourism necessitates the development of roads, airports, food service, lodging facilities, and shops.

In the process, many of the tourist sights are inevitably transformed. At best, their natural attractiveness will be lost as they become regulated tourist areas. At worst, major and often irreversible environmental damage will be caused by a rush to build tourist facilities on the most attractive sites. In many instances the natural environment is lost forever.

Crowds of tourists litter the area and damage the fragile environment. Local water, sewage, and other facilities become overburdened, causing pollution and unclean air. In the long run, tourism, like any other industry, contributes to environmental destruction.

Most people find that neither argument is completely accurate. Perhaps the most compelling argument falls somewhere between these two extremes. If there is to be development—if an area is to have economic progress—tourism is one of the very best alternatives. If properly controlled and regulated, tourism can be the least damaging of any form of economic development and can actually improve the environment of an area. The key to preserving the environment and allowing for economic progress is in controlling the rate of growth, attending to the necessary support (water, sewage, roads), and developing a plan that will preserve the best environmental assets of the area. This usually requires government involvement in tourism planning.

THE IMPORTANCE OF TOURISM (TO NATIONS, STATES, AREAS, AND COMMUNITIES)

Tourism is more important to some nations, states, areas, and communities than to others. In many nonindustrialized nations, for example, tourism is the single most important source of income and economic activity. This is true of Spain and most of the Caribbean islands, where tourism produces about 43 percent of the income for the region. Leading the list of income generators in the Caribbean are the Bahamas, Puerto Rico, Dominican Republic, the U.S. Virgin Islands, and Jamaica. Taken together, these five account for over one-half of the tourist-generated dollars in the region.

The economic importance of tourism is not limited to nonindustrialized nations. Some industrialized countries also rely heavily on tourism to provide foreign exchange. France is now the world's leading travel destination and receives about 10 percent of all international tourists. The United States is a close second. Countries such as the United Kingdom, Italy, and Canada also rely heavily on tourism.

Within the United States, tourism is very important to some states and less so to others. Those states in which tourism is particularly important—where large numbers of tourists visit the state or where tourism generates in excess of 20 percent of the jobs in the state—are frequently labeled *destination states*. Heading the list of destination states is California. It annually receives more tourist dollars than any other state. Other destination states include Florida, New York, Texas, New Jersey, Hawaii, New Hampshire, Vermont, Nevada, Colorado, Arizona, Maine, and South Carolina, among others. In some of the destination states, tourism is the leading industry, accounting for more jobs than any other industry in the state. This is true in Hawaii, Florida, Vermont, Maine, and Nevada.

For many states, tourism is not the leading or even the second leading industry but is still a major factor in the economy, accounting for 10 percent to 20 percent of total employment. This is true in Virginia, West Virginia, Georgia, Tennessee, Louisiana, Michigan, Missouri, Illinois, Wisconsin, Minnesota, North Dakota, Montana, Utah, Idaho, Oregon, Washington, Alaska, Massachusetts, Connecticut, and others.

In some areas and many local communities, tourism is the only significant industry. In these places, most jobs and income can be traced directly or indirectly to tourist dollars. Included in a list of areas where this would be true are such destinations as Cape Cod, Bar Harbor, the White Mountains of New Hampshire, the Catskills, the Poconos, Atlantic City, Myrtle Beach, Orlando (Disney World),

White Sulphur Springs, Sea Island, Great Smokey Mountains National Park, New Orleans, Hot Springs, the Black Hills, Yellowstone, Scottsdale, Sante Fe, Las Vegas, Sun Valley, Yosemite, and Vail.

It would be impossible to list all of the areas in the United States where tourism is the only significant industry. Hundreds of smaller areas, such as Boothbay Harbor, Maine, or Long Beach Island, New Jersey, have only local or regional reputations but rely on tourism for jobs and income.

To many, tourism is the industry of the future. As more people have greater amounts of leisure time, the number of people traveling will increase. As transportation becomes cheaper, faster, and more comfortable, travelers will venture farther and farther from home. As disposable income increases, travel will become even more a part of our lifestyle. As the population lives longer and our medical care enables us to continue to be mobile, larger numbers of older people will travel. These and other changes in society, mentioned at the beginning of this chapter, insure that travel and tourism will continue to be a leading growth industry.

SUMMARY

In this chapter, the dimensions of travel and tourism are explored. The motivators for travel and changes in society that have caused people to travel more frequently are listed. The government role in travel and tourism is examined, and major government and private travel organizations are identified. The terms *traveler* and *tourist* are discussed, and various definitions for each are provided. The composition of the travel industry—direct providers, support services, and tourism development—is explained. The size and scope of international and domestic travel are examined. Conditions and documents necessary for travel are described, as are the economic, cultural, social, and environmental impacts of tourism. Finally, the importance of tourism to nations, states, areas, and communities is discussed.

QUESTIONS

1. List at least ten motivators for travel.
2. Describe eight social and economic changes that have led to more frequent travel.
3. How does the U.S. government's role in travel and tourism compare to that of other countries?

4. What organization gathers most U.S. travel data?
5. List the four criteria used to determine a person's status as a traveler.
6. How does the U.S. Census Bureau define *traveler*?
7. How does the definition of a traveler from the U.S. Census Bureau differ from that of the U.S. Travel Data Center?
8. Distinguish between *visitor* and *nonvisitor*, as defined by the United Nations.
9. List ten examples of direct providers of tourist services.
10. What kinds of firms would be classified as support services to the travel industry?
11. Give one example of each of the four types of organizations or agencies classified as *tourism development*.
12. How much money is spent on world domestic and international travel and tourism?
13. List the countries that are the top three tourist destinations.
14. List the countries that are the top five spenders of tourist dollars.
15. Distinguish between *de jure* and *de facto* diplomatic recognition.
16. What basic document is required for Americans to visit most European countries? Canada? The Caribbean islands?
17. What is a *visa*?
18. List the top five countries for international tourist receipts.
19. Where do the largest number of foreign tourists to the U.S. come from? What accounts for the large number of them?
20. Where do the largest number of overseas visitors to the United States come from?
21. How much money is spent on domestic travel in the United States?
22. Which mode of transportation accounts for the greatest share of domestic travel?
23. What is the primary reason for domestic travel?
24. Explain what is meant by *economic impact of tourism*.
25. How do national governments benefit from tourism?
26. In what primary way does tourism preserve the culture of a nation?
27. In what ways can tourism affect human relations in a society?

28. What are the basic arguments for both the positive and negative environmental impact of tourism? Do you accept either? Why not?

29. List five *destination* states for tourists.

30. List ten areas or localities where tourism is the only significant industry.

Travel Services

12

LEARNING OBJECTIVES

After reading and studying this chapter, you should be able to:

1. Identify five direct providers of travel services.
2. Define and give examples of travel intermediaries.
3. Define the term <u>package</u> as used in the travel business.
4. List the advantages and disadvantages of travel packages over independent travel arrangements.
5. Describe the contents of each of the following types of packages: (a.) All-inclusive; (b.) Fly/cruise; (c.) Fly/cruise/hotel; (d.) Fly/drive; (e.) Motor coach; (f.) Accommodations; (g.) Accommodations and meals; (h.) Family vacation; (i.) Events; (j.) Special-interest; (k.) Affinity group; (l.) Incentive; (m.) Convention and meeting.
6. Explain the advantages and disadvantages of making travel arrangements directly with a supplier of travel services.
7. Describe the typical packages provided by: (a.) Airlines; (b.) Bus tour companies; (c.) Cruise lines; (d.) Hotel companies; (e.) Trains.
8. Outline the importance of travel agents to both travel sales and the traveler wishing to make travel arrangements.
9. Discuss the number and size of travel agencies in the United States.
10. Explain the importance of travel agents to the suppliers of travel services.
11. Outline the prerequisites necessary for a travel agency to sell travel.
12. Define the terms <u>travel wholesaler</u> and <u>tour operator</u>.

13. *Define the term* specialty channeler.
14. *Identify and explain the role of each of the following specialty channelers in selling travel: (a.) Hotel representatives; (b.) State and local tourists offices; (c.) Corporate travel offices; (d.) Incentive travel firms; (e.) Convention and meeting planners.*

INTRODUCTION

In the previous chapter, the dimensions of travel and tourism were explored. The travel industry was shown to consist of direct providers of travel, support services, and tourism development. Data were supplied to show that international and domestic travel has increased steadily over the years, such that the travel industry is now the world's largest industry. (It accounts for more than one in every ten dollars spent at the retail level.)

Mass travel—extensive long distance travel by the middle class as well as by the wealthy—really began shortly after World War II. Prior to that time the middle class generally had neither the time nor the money for long-distance travel, except for job-related purposes, immigration, or some other travel that was absolutely necessary. For many Americans, serving with the armed forces during a war provided the single opportunity for travel that they would have in their entire lives.

Long-distance travel for pleasure was highly unusual for most. After World War II, however, more people had greater amounts of free time to travel. They also had automobiles with which to travel and higher wages to be able to afford travel. Airlines evolved into a major means of public transportation, making it possible for virtually everyone to travel long distances at relatively low prices. The age of large-scale selling of travel to the public began after World War II.

In this chapter, we will provide a broad picture of the travel business: We will describe the two basic options for those intending to travel—then examine the roles of travel agencies, travel wholesalers, travel specialists, and other related organizations in developing travel packages and making arrangements for travelers.

Once a person has made the decision to travel, there are two possible options for making the necessary arrangements: Either get the help of an individual or firm that is in the business of making travel arrangements, or take the do-it-yourself approach.

If the traveler decides to do it herself, she must make direct contact with the supplier or suppliers of the services required and make all necessary arrangements. The traveler must obtain detailed information about fares, schedules, and dates directly from the supplier.

The difficulties associated with making these arrangements have led many travelers to take the other approach: having it done by a travel professional known as an *intermediary*. The term *travel intermediary* refers to a person or firm that makes travel arrangements for individuals or groups. When the arrangements are made by an intermediary, the traveler need only call or visit the intermediary, who can then make all the appropriate arrangements.

One of the more familiar travel intermediaries is the travel agent. A *travel agent* is one who is in the business of making travel arrangements for others. When travelers use the services of a travel agent, travel arrangements can be tailored to their particular needs and desires. Specialized itineraries can be prepared for them. The travel agent inquires into their needs and makes specific reservations for airlines, hotels, transfers, rental cars, or other requirements. If specialized travel arrangements are not required, the travel agent may recommend a common alternative: a package. *Package* is a term used to describe a number of travel services bundled together and sold at one price.

Travel packages are among the most important elements in the travel business. The typical travel agent finds that sales of travel packages represent approximately 25 percent of annual business. Because of the important role they play in the travel business, it is useful to examine the various types of packages and the firms that develop them.

TRAVEL PACKAGES

There are many different kinds of travel packages. Some are group packages, arranged so that a given number of travelers are together for the duration of the package. Others are individual packages that enable the traveler to travel independently of other participants who select the same package. In some instances, the independent package requires that the individual travel at specified times; thus the air transportation may be arranged along with others taking the tour. In other instances, the independent tour does not require a specific departure or return date. Travelers choose those dates for themselves and travel entirely independently of others taking the same package.

Packages can be very different from one another. Some packages are vacation packages to specific locations—a hotel on a Caribbean island, for example. Others are packages with travel to several locations—London, Paris, Rome, and Berlin, for example. Packages may last for only a few days or for a week or longer; and they will vary in price, according to the quality of the package and the length of time involved.

Some packages will provide deluxe accommodations, and others will provide lesser quality accommodations. Some packages are geared to specific activities—golf, for example.

Some packages include all the necessities: travel, accommodations, meals, tips, transfers, sports, and entertainment. Others include only a few: accommodations and a rental car, for example. The firm that assembles the package makes

Located on the southeast Atlantic coast of St. Lucia on 95 acres, five minutes from Hewanorra International Airport. The pastel pink, marble-trimmed central atrium leads to a large swimming pool, open-air cocktail lounge, boutique, theater and modern nightclub. Tiny Maria Island dots the horizon. For ages 2 and over.

Accommodations

Air-conditioned, double occupancy rooms in four-story beach and garden-front lodgings with a private balcony overlooking the ocean. Each has oversized twin beds and a private bathroom with shower. Connecting rooms (request upon arrival) and single rooms (extra charge; request when reserving) are subject to availability.

Restaurants

At the main dining room in the village center, enjoy lavish buffets at breakfast, lunch and dinner. For quiet, intimate dinners served at your table for two or more, visit the open-air Club House for French cuisine, and the new Cadi's Pub for classic American favorites.

Sports and Activities*

- Scuba diving: beginners to experts; near the Pitons (departure 2-3 is a five-minute bus ride from the village); intensive program
- Horseback riding: English and Western; intensive English horseback riding program for all levels of skill
- Windsurfing: experienced boardsailors only; advanced training program
- Tennis: 8 composition courts (all night-lit); clubhouse with showers
- Circus workshops
- Fitness center
- Aerobics/Calisthenics
- Water exercises
- Practice golf
- Archery
- Volleyball/Basketball
- Soccer
- Softball
- Ping-pong
- Bocce ball
- All-day snorkeling picnics and boat rides
- Nightly entertainment and dancing

Beyond the village*

Castries, Soufrière (hot sulfur springs), island helicopter tour, the Grenadine Islands, Martinique, snorkeling excursion, sunset cruise.

Especially for kids

Scuba experience in the pool from age 4-12. Carriage, pony and horseback rides, according to age and ability, with intensive program from age 8*. Go-cart racetrack, complete with traffic lights, road signs and individually-timed races. Kids-only circus instruction and equipment, complete with flying trapeze, trampoline and more, from age 4. Snorkeling, tennis and practice golf for age 6. Basketball, softball and volleyball on smaller courts.

Open-air Petit Club (2-3 years) with air-conditioned nap room, Mini Clubs (4-7 years), and Kids Club (8-11 years), open from 9:00 am – 9:00 pm. Wading pool.

Highlights

- *Dramatic Windward island setting*
- *Plenty for every member of the family*
- *Unique children's program with scuba diving, horseback riding, go carting, circus school and more, plus Kids Free!*

Kids Free — Youngsters 2-5 years are invited to St. Lucia absolutely free of charge! Please refer to page 1 for dates and details.

*Extra charge for horseback riding, scuba certifications, and excursions. Refer to the "General Sports Information" section in the back of the main brochure for more information about our sports programs.

ST. LUCIA
VILLAGE FACTS

Address:
Club Med–St. Lucia
P.O. Box 246
Vieux Fort
St. Lucia
West Indies

Telephone:
(809) 45-46-546

Telex:
341 6324

Fax:
(809) 45-46-017
Incoming calls/telexes/
faxes reach our switchboard;
messages are posted.

Transfers:
Airport: Hewanorra (UVF)
approx. 3 miles from village;
10 minutes by transfer;
approx. $5 one way taxi
fare plus $2 per extra
person
Alternate airport: Vigi (SLU),
approx. 28 miles from
village, 1 hour; approx. $45
one-way taxi fare

Time difference:
EDT all year

Currency:
Eastern Caribbean dollar

National language:
English and Creole

**Languages spoken in
the village:**
English and French

**Form of payment in the
village:**
Traveler's Checks
American Express
Visa
MasterCard
Cash

Laundry:
Washers, dryers, irons and
ironing boards available

Voltage:
220 volts; adapters and
converters are necessary

Car rental:
At village and at airport

**Medical assistance at
the village:**
Infirmary/2 Nurses

**Medical assistance
outside the village:**
Doctor
Hospital 10 minutes from
village

Climate:
Tropical*

	High	Low
November	85	71
December	83	70
January	82	69
February	83	69
March	84	69
April	87	71

*average daily highs and lows

A page from a brochure featuring all-inclusive vacation packages, detailing accommodations, food service, activities, and other points of interest. A myriad of travel packages are available, offering travelers savings through volume sales and the convenience of having most of the important arrangements made. (Copyright © Club Med Sales, Inc. All rights reserved.)

judgments about the combination of services it believes are most appealing and can best be sold to potential customers.

The following are characteristic types of packages sold to travelers:

All-Inclusive Packages.   As the name implies, all-inclusive packages include most or all of the necessary elements of travel. They generally include transportation, accommodations, meals, transfers (that is, ground transportation between an airport and a hotel or similar lodging property), entertainment, sightseeing, sports, taxes, and gratuities. However, they do vary considerably. Some offer all meals; others offer a specified number of meals. Some include admission to special events; others do not. Other specifics in the travel package will also vary.

Fly/Cruise Packages.   Fly/cruise packages include air transportation to and from a point of departure, transfers, and a cruise. Fly/cruise packages are almost always all-inclusive, meaning that the package price includes the cost of air fare, accommodations, all meals, and entertainment. Gratuities and sightseeing are typically extra.

Fly/Cruise/Hotel Packages.   These normally include air transportation, a cruise, and a specified number of nights at a hotel. These packages are typically offered by such cruise line companies as Cunard, which own resort hotels in the general vicinity of the ship's point of departure.

Fly/Drive Packages.   Fly/drive packages typically include air fare and rental car only. They are intended for travelers who prefer to make their own travel plans. Fly/drive packages are usually prepared by airlines in partnership with rental car companies.

Motor Coach Packages.   Motor coach packages are special-purpose bus tours for those interested in shopping, sightseeing, or attending a particular sports event, for example. They are planned by motor coach operators and other tour companies. If a particular tour is to take more than one day, it will normally include accommodations, meals, and entertainment.

Accommodations Packages.   Accommodations packages usually include only lodging. They are really just discounts on room rates. Some are only available for particular seasons or on specified dates. Others are limited to particular numbers of nights. Many international airlines offer very attractive accommodations packages for use in major cities abroad. Accommodations packages sometimes include such additional features as continental breakfasts, transit passes, or theater tickets.

Accommodations and Meals Packages.   Accommodations and meals packages include hotel accommodations and meals. They vary considerably. Some include three meals per day; others include certain specified meals: full English breakfast daily, or dinner the second night, for example. Some include free access to sports facilities, such as golf courses and tennis courts. Others offer discounts on sporting activities. Some also offer sightseeing and other entertainment.

Family Vacation Packages.   Family vacation packages always include accommodations at specific destinations and attractions that appeal particularly to families: Disney World, Sea World, or Busch Gardens, for example. They normally include other appealing features, as well: some type of child care for part of the vacation, for example, so that adults can have time for themselves. These packages are typically designed to provide value to families.

Events Packages.   These are special packages that focus on particular events or performances: football games, festivals, theater, art exhibits, and so on. The possibilities are endless. These packages usually include transportation and admissions to the event or performance—and may include such other features as accommodations, meals, and rental cars.

Special-Interest Packages.   Special-interest packages are designed for groups of people who share a particular interest. It may be in a sport or in a particular hobby. The common interests around which these packages are developed include golf or tennis, photography, wineries, fall foliage, and many others.

Affinity Group Packages.   Affinity groups are groups of people who share a common bond. They may be students in the same college, alumni of one university, members of a social club, a religious organization, or a fraternity or a sorority. They may all be in the same profession: doctors, dentists, or lawyers, for example. Affinity group packages enable the group to share a common experience. It can be a tour, a vacation at a particular resort, a cruise, or any other activity that appeals to the group.

Incentive Packages.   An incentive package is a vacation package sponsored by a corporation and offered to employees as a reward for superior performance—high-volume sales of a product or service, or some other achievement beyond the norm. Some companies offer all-inclusive vacations to Hawaii, for example. Any type of package can be used as an incentive package as long as it provides incentive for employees to improve performance.

Convention and Meeting Packages.   Convention and meeting packages are typically offered by hotels and sponsoring organizations. They frequently include accommodations, meals, sightseeing, and other activities.

Packages have several advantages over individual travel arrangements. They are typically less expensive, because the person or firm preparing the package purchases the travel arrangements in quantity and is able to pass on savings to the traveler. For example, an intermediary putting together a vacation package to London, England, for forty-five people might be able to obtain rooms and meals at a particular hotel for 70 percent of the normal price. The hotel is pleased to sell these rooms at that price, because it is assured of selling a large number of rooms and the cost of providing food for these guests might be less than for regular customers. In addition, the hotel does not have to pay a travel agency commission, because the commission is paid to the travel agent by the intermediary. It is also possible to purchase airline seats at a discount. Some of the savings that result from making these arrangements at discounts are passed on to the purchaser of the package, and sufficient profit is left for the intermediary making the arrangements. The total price of the package is considerably less than it would be for an individual to make the same arrangements on his own.

Another advantage of a package is that the traveler knows precisely what the trip will cost. All essentials of the trip are normally included in the price, and any extra charges are stated in the promotional materials.

Finally, if the travel is complicated, the tourist traveling on a package has to make only a very few decisions. Once the tour package has been selected, there are normally relatively few choices to be made. Many people prefer to travel without having to be constantly making important decisions about where to stay and what sights to see. Good packages assure the traveler that the important events and sights will be seen.

PACKAGE DEVELOPERS
Packages Prepared by Direct Suppliers

Many direct suppliers of travel services develop travel packages. The following is an examination of these direct suppliers and the types of packages they develop.

AIRLINES. Airlines are responsible for creating a large number of packages—the most popular of which are fly/drive packages and accommodation packages. Fly/drive packages are designed for travelers who wish to be on their own. Airlines create these packages to provide incentives for travelers to go to destinations served by the airlines. They frequently offer these packages on days of the week or dates when they are not normally fully booked.

Accommodations packages are also very popular with airlines. These are typically individual travel packages, rather than group packages. Airlines work closely with hotels to provide accommodations at rates that may be below the hotels' normal room rates. Hotels are willing to do this because when they establish links with the airlines, they obtain bookings they might not otherwise get.

Many accommodation packages offered by airlines do not include air fare, and some do not include meals or other normal expenses. For example, American Airlines offers accommodations packages to more than twenty Caribbean islands and has established package rates with several hotels on each of these islands. The basic package rate is very appealing but includes only the hotel room. Transfers to the hotel, taxes, air fare, food, drinks, entertainment, and activities are all extra. Many of the same hotels participating in the American Airlines package plan, however, do allow customers to opt for an all-inclusive rate that includes drinks and some activities.

Other packages offered by airlines are more extensive and may include air fare, as well as other costs. For example, Northwest Airlines offers packages to Bangkok, Hong Kong, and Singapore that include air fare, hotels, land transportation, sightseeing, and entertainment.

Thus, the buyer of an airline package must look very closely at the contents of the package to determine if it indeed contains the elements she is looking for.

BUS COMPANIES. Bus packages are increasingly popular, particularly with senior citizens. These packages are offered by bus companies that own or lease buses and by many other firms that contract with bus companies for required bus service.

Bus tours vary considerably in quality, length, price, and amenities. Some are as short as a few hours, while others may take days. One of the most popular tours is the gambling tour, a bus tour that takes potential gamblers to a casino and returns them to the point of departure. The casino hotels of Atlantic City, New Jersey, play host to many of these tours from the surrounding region—New York, Connecticut, Pennsylvania, Delaware, Washington D.C., and other nearby areas. These tours frequently include bus fare, entertainment, and a number of quarters or gambling chips of sufficient value to make the cost of the tour very reasonable.

Extended bus tours are, by nature, all-inclusive tours, because the people on the tour must be housed and fed. These bus tours, like other all-inclusive tours, vary in quality and in amenities offered. At the economy level, bus tours will stay at budget lodging properties. Meals will offer few if any menu choices and travelers may be charged extra for admissions to events. At the luxury level, those on the tour will be accommodated at luxury hotels, will have a number of choices from the hotel menu, and will not pay for admissions to events.

One of the more interesting professions is that of a bus tour manager or tour guide. He meets the travelers at the point of embarkation and stays with them throughout the tour. Duties of the tour manager include confirming that all reservations for hotels, restaurants, and events are in order, assigning seats and establishing a seat rotation plan on the bus, keeping the tourists informed of sights along the way, keeping order on the tour, making sure baggage gets to hotel rooms and back on the bus, attending to illness and other emergencies, and attending to the 1001 details of a bus tour and needs of the travelers. Tour managers typically are not paid high salaries, but they do receive tips at the end of the tour. In some cases, they also receive commissions from gift shops and other retail establishments when buses stop at these places. Thus, many tour managers are able to make comfortable incomes and live interesting lives.

Domestic bus tour companies generally price their package tours without air fare. International bus tour companies, however, have package prices that also include air fare. For example, Cosmos, a European-based bus tour company, has various packages to Europe. Their 27-day escorted budget tour of Europe can include air fare and offers transfers, tourist class hotels, private baths, twenty-five continental breakfasts, twelve dinners, and visits to various sights. These and other bus tours are sold directly to the public, as well as through travel agents.

CRUISE LINES. Major cruise lines prepare all-inclusive packages that include air fare, transfers to the ship, and the cost of the cruise. Included in the cruise are accommodations, meals, and entertainment. Passengers are required to pay only for drinks, gratuities, and excursions from the ship. Most cruise lines are noted for the quality and quantity of their food. A typical day will include breakfast, lunch, midafternoon tea or snacks, dinner, and midnight buffet.

The cruise lines use a variety of airlines to transport passengers from their home city to the ship. Interestingly, the typical cruise price is usually the same from any city in the United States. This means that cruise passengers coming long distances pay the same as those coming from near the port of embarkation. Usually, cruise lines will deduct the airline portion of the package for those passengers who choose not to take advantage of the "free" air transportation.

Some cruise lines have packages that include one or more nights in a hotel before or after the cruise. These combinations are particularly attractive to those who wish to see the sights while they are in the vicinity of the port. Some offer packages that include a one-week cruise and a second week at a resort hotel owned by the cruise line.

As shown in Table 12.4 on page 344, travel agents account for 95 percent of all cruise sales, virtually all of which are packages. The packages cruise lines create are obviously the most important element in their sales effort.

RAILROADS. As mentioned in earlier chapters, rail travel was once the most important form of pubic transportation. In Europe and other parts of the world, it is still important; but in the United States, rail travel is used primarily for commuter service. Amtrak does issue a Discover America pass; but it is not what one would call a package, because it does not contain features other than the train ride. In Europe, a Eurailpass enables travelers to see Europe relatively inexpensively. In several South American countries, trains are a fairly popular transportation mode for excursions, although the trains are not particularly modern or comfortable. Trains may be part of packages prepared by others, but rail companies typically have not developed packages.

LODGING COMPANIES. Many of the companies operating hotels, motels, and other lodging properties create travel packages that are sold directly to customers, as well as through travel agents. For example, Club Med, one of the largest chains of resort hotels, has all-inclusive packages to their resorts throughout the world. These packages include transportation, transfers, taxes, gratuities, meals, entertainment, and accommodations. Most recreation is also included in the package price, although the resorts charge extra for certain sports, such as golf, horseback riding, and deep sea fishing. In contrast to cruise packages, the price of Club Med packages is not the same from all cities. Those who travel the farthest are charged more than those who come from nearby points. Interestingly, Club Med is now also in the cruise business and offers a cruise package aboard its *Club Med 1*, a motor-sailing vessel, advertised as the largest and most beautiful sailing ship in the world. The vessel has 191 outside staterooms.

Other accommodations packages offered by hotels vary significantly. Many hotels offer packages that include accommodations, all meals, and recreation. Some offer only accommodations and breakfast, plus specified entertainment. There are several all-inclusive resorts that offer packages with accommodations, meals, recreation, sports, gratuities, taxes, and even unlimited drinks at the bar. It is almost impossible to spend money at these resorts.

Packages Developed by Intermediaries

Many travel packages are developed by travel intermediaries. The following is an examination of these travel intermediaries and the types of packages they develop.

TOUR WHOLESALERS AND TOUR OPERATORS. Tour wholesalers and tour operators are important developers of travel packages. As the name implies, a *tour wholesaler* prepares tours and other travel packages and distributes them through retail outlets. The wholesaler organizes the tour, prepares promotional material, and distributes it to travel agencies and other retail firms. Wholesalers may also conduct the tour. *Tour operators* traditionally have been individuals and firms that carry out ground arrangements—for bus tours or guides, for example.

One example of a tour wholesaler that prepares and operates tour packages throughout the world is Collette Travel Service, based in Pawtucket, Rhode Island. This company offers group tours and independent tours to Australia, Europe, Alaska, Africa, Asia, Hawaii, Canada, and the continental United States. The packages range from fly/drive vacations to escorted tours that include land and sea transportation, accommodations, a number of meals, and many of the tour sights. Air fare to the starting destination is additional and is arranged with TWA and other airlines. Collette relies heavily on travel agents to sell their tours.

Of course, when the wholesaler makes travel arrangements, there is a risk that all of the available space will not be sold. If tours are not sufficiently popular, the wholesaler may lose money or may have to cancel the tour.

Any individual or firm can act as a wholesaler. There are virtually no government regulations or requirements for becoming a tour wholesaler. There are more than 2,000 independent tour wholesalers and operators in the United States, although the largest 40 obtain the bulk of the business. One of the major problems of there being so many tour wholesalers and operators is that some go bankrupt, causing serious loss to customers, travel agents, and suppliers of travel services. In recent years, several large tour wholesalers have gone out of business. The travel industry is addressing this problem. The U.S. Tour Operators Association, which represents many of the largest international tour operators, has established a bonding program that assures payment in the event of the failure of a travel wholesaler or tour operator.

In many instances the tour wholesaler and tour operator are two separate firms. The wholesaler makes the travel arrangements for hotel accommodations, meals, and visits to sites along the way. He also prepares the promotional material and distributes it to travel agencies. The tour operator carries out the ground arrangements. He meets the travelers at their departing or arriving point and conducts the tour for the travel wholesaler.

There is increasing overlap in the functions of tour wholesalers and tour operators. Some tour wholesalers arrange all of the details for their tours and also act as tour operators. Some tour operators act as tour wholesalers, preparing tour packages and promotional materials and distributing them to retail outlets. Thus, travel wholesaler and tour operator are beginning to be seen as one; and increasingly all travel wholesalers are being referred to as tour operators.

One exception is firms that make ground arrangements for airlines and cruises. They are referred to as *independent contractors*, not *tour operators*.

Frequently, travel agencies act as travel wholesalers. They do this by preparing package tours themselves and offering these to their own customers and to those of other travel agencies. They make all the necessary arrangements for airline travel, hotels, ground transportation, and places of entertainment. Two of the largest of these firms are American Express and Thomas Cook Travel. Both organizations are tour operators, as well as travel agents.

TRAVEL SALES FIRMS

Travel is sold by two broad categories of sellers: (1) direct suppliers of travel services and (2) travel intermediaries. We will examine the role of each in travel sales.

Direct Providers of Travel Services

In addition to selling through travel intermediaries, the direct providers of travel services—airlines, hotels, and rental car companies, among others—sell their services directly to customers. A large number of sales are made this way, and there are important reasons that this is so. Those travelers who know precisely where and how they wish to travel and who have had previous experience with a particular airline, hotel, or other travel supplier, use this method very effectively. For example, a customer who has previously stayed at a resort hotel can contact the hotel's reservation office, talk with a sales representative, and discuss specific dates, accommodations, rates, and other particulars. She can ask questions about particular accommodations, inquire about programs and events being offered, and make all necessary arrangements directly with the hotel. The traveler has the

Travel is sold in two ways: directly, through suppliers themselves (airlines, cruise lines, hotels, and so forth), and indirectly, through travel agents, travel wholesalers, or other intermediaries. Shown above is a customer representative of a rental car company assisting a client who made his own arrangements to pick up and return his car. (Courtesy The Hertz Corporation.)

opportunity to inquire into any aspect of the hotel's operation and can request special services, if necessary. She can satisfy herself that she has made the best arrangements possible.

Many suppliers of travel services prefer to sell their services directly to the customer. It gives them an opportunity to sell additional or higher-priced services, and suppliers can often achieve a greater profit on these sales. The traveler discussed above may be sold higher-priced accommodations or alternative dates if the hotel is booked for the desired period.

All large airlines, hotel chains, and rental car firms sell their services directly to the public. They have their own central sales offices—locations at which 800-number calls are received and processed.

Most direct suppliers of travel services sell their services to groups, and the larger travel suppliers have sales staff for the express purpose of seeking group business. For example, a large convention hotel will have a convention sales office, staffed with sales personnel who will seek out and attempt to sell to corporations, fraternal organizations, government organizations, and others.

Travel Intermediaries

As we will see, most travel, including packages prepared by direct suppliers, is sold through travel agents and other intermediaries. The primary intermediary is the retail travel agent, who makes travel arrangements for travelers and books them with the suppliers of travel services. It is important to understand that these services are not sold *to* travel agents, but to customers: The travel agent merely acts as an intermediary who makes the travel arrangements.

Other intermediaries include tour wholesalers and specialty channelers, many of whom sell directly to the public, as well as through travel agents.

We will examine the role of travel agents and other intermediaries in the selling of travel.

TRAVEL AGENTS. The most important retail sellers of travel are travel agents. Interestingly, they are a relatively recent addition to the travel industry. The first travel agent was Thomas Cook, a British publisher and lecturer on the evils and sins of alcohol. In 1841 he conceived of the idea of chartering railroad trains to bring his temperance supporters to meetings; and on July 5th of that year he transported 570 passengers round trip on a train from Leicester to Loughborough, England. The distance was twelve miles each way and the reported cost to each passenger was one shilling.

The trip was very successful, and his services were soon sought by others interested in group travel. By 1845 he was organizing relatively complex travel for individuals and groups over several railroad lines. In 1851 he organized tours to the Exhibition in London and in 1855 organized similar tours to the Paris Exhibition. Shortly afterwards he opened an office in London.

Thomas Cook was the first man to organize and conduct an around-the-world tour, a feat he accomplished in 1872. His travel agency business continued to grow, and today Thomas Cook Travel is one of the world's largest travel agencies. The term *Cook's tour* stems from the trips he and his firm have organized.

In the United States, one of the oldest and certainly one of the largest travel agencies to be organized prior to 1900 was the Ask Mr. Foster travel agency. Organized in 1888, it finally reached a size of more than 600 offices. Other large U.S. travel agencies include American Express and the American Automobile Association.

Travel agents are professionals whose expertise is arranging travel for clients. Good travel agents, like good doctors, lawyers, or accountants, are highly trained individuals. They have extensive knowledge of travel destinations, accommodations, transportation, and all aspects of travel. They are able to find the most direct travel route or the least expensive travel route to any destination. They can determine which hotel in a given city is most convenient to a particular site. They can advise travelers about the best time of year to travel to specific destinations. They can find out average temperatures at various destinations and advise customers about the type of clothing to take at a particular time of year. They can tell clients if a visa is needed for a particular country. They can even advise clients on the best routes from the airports to their hotels.

Like other professionals, some travel agents have specialties. Some are particularly knowledgeable about travel in specific parts of the world—Africa, China, or Russia, for example. Others have extensive knowledge of particular types of vacations—cruises or bus tours, perhaps. All travel agents have access to information about the elements of travel, and all should be able to make appropriate travel arrangements for their clients.

Good travel agents have one very important trait in common—the ability to match customers with travel that is suitable for them. For example, assume that a customer goes to a travel agency looking for a vacation on a cruise ship. Each cruise line and cruise ship is different. Some cruise ships are more formal than others—requiring formal dress at meals. Some have music and entertainment that appeals to younger people, and others are more suitable for older adults. Some cruise ships do their cruising primarily at night and dock during the daytime at different ports. A good travel agent will be able to determine which cruise best suits the needs, desires, and budget of each individual. To be able to do so requires an understanding of the customer—the kinds of activities, entertainment, and food he prefers, as well as the most suitable shipboard environment, type of accommodation, size of ship, and price. Only by understanding both the customer and the cruise lines can the travel agent properly match the customer and the cruise. If the travel agent does a poor job of this, the customer will not be satisfied and will blame the travel agent.

Travel agents have immediate access to a wealth of travel information that customers would have to spend long hours looking for if they were to make their own arrangements. For example, a person who intends to fly from Boston to San Francisco would have to spend a great deal of time on the telephone calling each airline that flies out of Boston to ask if they fly to San Francisco. She would have to ask about flight schedules and fares from each of those airlines. If she needed a hotel room in San Francisco, she would have to call someone in California who had access to the yellow pages for San Francisco or in some other fashion determine which hotels were located there. She would then have to call, fax, or write to the hotel inquiring about reservations.

All of this information is readily available to travel agents through computers and publications on hand in their offices. Within moments, a travel agent can determine which airlines fly to San Francisco, the schedules for all flights, and the availability and cost of seats on each flight. He can also advise the customer about which hotels are located in the city, their rates, and their locations and can easily determine the availability of rooms. All travel arrangements including air, hotel, rental car, and insurance can be made by the travel agent in a very short period of time.

And the travel agent can perform all of the above services at no cost to the client. This is because the income to a travel agent comes in the form of sales commissions paid by airlines, hotels, and other suppliers of travel services. This sales commission is normally a stipulated percentage of the price of the particular travel service arranged.

Frequently, travel agents can obtain travel and hotel reservations at lower prices than a customer attempting to make individual travel arrangements can. The agent's familiarity with rates and sales practices of airlines, hotels, rental cars, and other services enables him to search out and sometimes bargain for the cheapest rates.

Thus, under most circumstances, travelers are wise to employ the services of travel agents for travel that requires public transportation, accommodations, rental cars, or other travel services. Good travel agents have the expertise to advise clients on the best travel arrangements and can usually make these arrangements at the same cost or cheaper than arrangements made independently.

Travel agents gain their expertise in a variety of ways. Most of them have been to one or more of the various travel schools—some at colleges and universities and others at private schools that train travel agents. They take courses in travel agency management, geography, computers, ticketing, customer relations, and other travel-related subjects. Nonetheless, experience is a major factor in

An office in a typical travel agency. The most important retail sales channel for travel sales in the United States, travel agents provide the majority of sales for the airline, international hotel, cruise line, and packaged tour segments of the industry. With access to a wealth of information, travel agents can provide their clients with travel arrangements that best suit their needs and expectations. (Courtesy American Society of Travel Agents.)

becoming an expert travel agent. Travel knowledge and expertise is gained on the job and through familiarization trips—referred to as FAM trips. These are trips to resorts, cities, sights, and the like that are sponsored by airlines and by other travel suppliers at the destination. The cost of these trips is usually absorbed by the airlines and the sponsoring organization. The organizations that sponsor FAM trips do so with the obvious objective of creating referrals and bookings from the travel agencies.

The Number of Travel Agencies and Their Size.   Although travel agencies have been in existence since Thomas Cook started in the mid-1800s, not many of them existed until after World War II—the beginning of mass travel. The increase in the number of travel agencies has kept pace with the growth of travel. Table 12.1 shows the growth in the number of travel agencies in the United States.

TABLE 12.1 *Number of U.S. travel agencies**

Year	Number of travel agencies
1984	25,748
1987	30,169
1990	37,807

*Including satellite ticket printer locations.
Source: Airlines Reporting Corporation, in Somerset R. Waters, *Travel Industry World Yearbook: The Big Picture, 1991.* (New York: Child & Waters, 1991) p. 129.

TABLE 12.2 *Size of travel agencies, 1989*

Sales	Percentage (%) of total
Under $300,000	16.3
$300,000–$500,000	13.5
$500,000–$1,000,000	29.1
$1,000,000–$3,000,000	32.6
Over $3,000,000	8.5

Source: Airlines Reporting Corporation, in Waters, p. 132.

TABLE 12.3 *U.S. travel agency sales, 1987*

	$ Billions
Airlines	$37.9
Hotels	7.1
Car rental	5.1
Cruise lines	10.3

Source: Louis Harris 1988 survey for *Travel Weekly,* in Waters, p. 132.

Total dollar sales of all U.S. travel agencies in 1989 was estimated at $79.4 billion, and the majority of agencies booked between $500,000 and $3,000,000 in sales, as shown in Table 12.2.

Airlines provide the largest share of income to travel agencies as shown in Table 12.3.

In 1990 the "typical" agency had total sales—from airline tickets, hotel accommodations, and car rentals, for example—of $2,160,000. The average sales commission received from all sources was 10 percent of sales, which would mean that the amount of money actually received to cover salaries and other expenses, and profit was about $216,000. This "typical" agency employed six full-time travel agents and two part-time agents, 80 percent of whom were women.

From the above data, one can conclude that a travel agency is not a highly profitable business. Most of the income to the agency must be paid to agents in salary, and much of the remainder is used to pay for such overhead costs as advertising, rent, utilities, computer, and telephone, among others.

Supplier Dependence on Travel Agents. Much of the travel industry is highly dependent on travel agencies for survival. Airlines, international hotels, cruise lines, and those firms that prepare tours rely heavily on travel agencies.

TABLE 12.4 *Supplier dependence on U.S. travel agents*	
Supplier	**Estimated percentage (%) of volume booked by travel agents**
Airlines	70 — Domestic
	80 — International
Hotels	25 — Domestic
	85 — International
Cruise lines	95
Rail	37
Bus	Less than 10
Rental cars	50
Packaged tours	90

Source: Waters, p. 131.

Table 12.4 shows the importance of travel agents to the major segments of the travel industry.

The airlines rely on travel agents for 70 percent of domestic business and 80 percent of international business. Cruise lines are almost totally dependent on travel agencies, and some international hotels are very heavily agency dependent.

For the supplier of travel services, several critical reasons exist to promote the use of travel agencies. One of the most important is having sales representatives in all parts of the country. It was shown in Table 12.1 that there are over 35,000 travel agencies in the United States. If the average travel agency has six employees, there are more than 200,000 salespeople working to sell travel. This is a powerful incentive to promote their use, particularly when one considers that agencies are paid only when the agents are successful in selling travel.

This is particularly true for the suppliers of travel services that cannot afford to have sales representatives in all parts of their marketing area. For example, a 200-room resort hotel in the Caribbean obviously could not afford to maintain offices in all the major cities in the eastern United States.

Travel agencies are equally important for the larger suppliers of travel services. Travel agencies enable them, in effect, to expand the number of offices selling their services without increasing their overhead costs. For example, it would be necessary for each major airline to have a sales office in every city in the United States if there were no travel agents to represent them.

Prerequisites for a Travel Agency to Sell Travel.   One cannot open up a travel agency and sell airline, cruise line, or other travel tickets as easily as one can open other types of retail establishments. This is because the travel agency receives its income from the suppliers of travel service, and most of these suppliers will not pay commissions to organizations that they have not approved or that have not been approved by a travel association. Approval to sell travel is only given to a travel agency when it receives an appointment to one or more of the various conferences that represent travel services. The term *conference* does not mean a meeting, as one might think; but it is a regulatory body that sets standards for travel agencies. The following are the most important conference approvals needed by travel agencies:

A.R.C.	The Airline Reporting Corporation
C.L.I.A.	Cruise Lines International Association
I.A.T.A.	The International Air Transport Association

Each conference has specific requirements that travel agencies must meet in order to gain approval and the right to sell the services offered by conference members. Conference requirements are very strict, because travel agents issue tickets and collect funds that must be turned over to the companies whose services they sell. Requirements for conference approval typically include the following:

1. The travel agency must have a manager with at least two years' experience and at least one employee with one year's experience as a travel agent.
2. The agency must have a net worth of about $100,000 or a bond—a type of insurance policy—covering the normal amount of business expected for a period of time.
3. The agency must be clearly identifiable to the public and be open for business a given number of hours (typically at least 35) per week.
4. The agency must pay an application fee and annual fees to the conference, plus additional charges for blank ticket forms and for computer and other costs.

Each conference has its own requirements, but those above are representative of them. Travel agents that receive conference approval can then issue tickets and are entitled to receive commissions on the sale of tickets.

Computer Use in Travel Agencies.   Just a few years ago, travel agents made all travel arrangements by telephone, telex, and mail, exclusively. A travel agent booking an airline seat looked up the schedule in a publication known as the *Official Airline Guide*, then called the airline to find seat availability.

Today, virtually all full-service travel agents make these travel arrangements using one of the computer programs that airlines have developed. American Airlines, with its Sabre system, has a greater number of network users for its program than any other system. United has the Apollo system, and TWA has a system called PARS. These programs enable the travel agent to find out which airlines fly between any two points and the schedule of flights between those two points for any given day. They enable the travel agent to determine seat availability for each flight and the prices for various classes of tickets. If a customer decides to reserve a seat, the travel agent can do so by computer. The computer prints the ticket in the travel agent's office and it is issued to the customer. The entire transaction may take as little as five minutes.

New computer programs now available enable travel agents to obtain information about many hotels. Agents can even obtain layouts of hotel properties and floor plans of hotels, as well as special features they offer and other essential information. Of course, telephone calls and the mail are still important; but fax machines and the computer are quickly replacing older methods of communication at travel agencies.

OTHER INTERMEDIARIES

Specialty Channelers.   Specialty channelers are intermediaries who represent either buyers or sellers of travel services. They make travel arrangements for the parties they represent and do so either directly with the travel supplier or through a travel agent. Because specialty channelers deal directly with travel customers, they exercise great influence over travel suppliers' sales.

Specialty channelers that represent sellers of travel services include:

1. Hotel representatives
2. State and local tourism offices

Hotel Representatives.   A *hotel representative* is an individual or firm that represents a number of hotels and that sells the services of the hotels directly to individuals, businesses, and groups. They are not employees of the hotels; they usually have contractual agreements with the hotels they represent, and they both develop and book individual and group business for these hotels. Hotel representatives may be individuals, travel agencies, or other firms and they are normally located in specific metropolitan areas. Typically, they represent many hotels.

Hotel representatives seeking group business have detailed knowledge of the businesses and groups in their area that require hotel facilities for meetings and conventions. Many hotel representatives are also in close contact with travel agencies in the area and thus provide a link between the hotels they represent and the local travel agencies.

Hotel representatives are able to meet the needs of the businesses and groups they contact because they represent a great number of hotels in many areas. Some hotels will have a number of hotel representatives, one in each of several parts of the country. Hotel representatives make hotel reservations directly. They are compensated by retainers and commissions for the business they bring hotels. Retainers are flat fees paid to professionals for services rendered.

State and Local Tourism Offices.   State and local tourism offices include state tourism offices, chambers of commerce, and convention and visitors bureaus that seek to develop tourism for their areas.

All states have tourist offices that act as intermediaries for hotels and other travel services in their states. They advertise travel opportunities and attempt to connect potential customers with their member properties and organizations. They often have information offices located on highways that direct customers to appropriate travel destinations, properties, and businesses.

Chambers of commerce perform similar functions for local areas. They advertise the local area and refer inquiries to specific properties and businesses. Most chambers of commerce have offices that provide information and assistance to travelers and refer them to local properties.

Most cities with populations over 1,000,000 have convention and visitors bureaus. These bureaus typically focus their attention on attracting groups, businesses, conventions, tours, and the like to their cities. They frequently assist in convention arrangements and often act as housing coordinators for convention groups.

Specialty channelers that represent buyers of travel services include:

1. Corporate travel offices
2. Incentive travel firms
3. Convention and meeting planners

Corporate Travel Offices.   An example of a specialty channeler who represents the buyer of travel services is a corporate travel officer who makes travel arrangements for corporate personnel. Corporate travel officers may make the arrangements directly with suppliers of travel services or they may book through travel agencies. Corporate managers, sales personnel, and employees in various job titles account for a considerable amount of travel, and many corporations have established travel departments to make the necessary arrangements. These travel departments are generally not official travel agencies, because they are not members of the various travel conferences and cannot receive commissions on their travel arrangements. Frequently, however, they make the same arrangements as travel agencies—booking transportation, hotel rooms, and so forth directly with the supplier of travel services. They often work also through travel agencies in the same way as any other customer.

Corporate travel offices are established for a variety of reasons. Sometimes they are established as a convenience to employees, providing a central office where travel arrangements can be made. Frequently they are established so that corporations can control their travel costs. Instructions are given to travel departments on such matters as who is eligible to travel at company expense, whether personnel are permitted to travel first class, how much is allowed for hotel and meals, and other matters. Corporate travel departments greatly influence which airlines and hotels the employees use.

Incentive Travel Firms.   Incentive travel firms are specialized intermediaries that deal directly with corporate clients. They specialize in assembling incentive packages—transportation, accommodations, meals, and entertainment, for example—for corporations that have incentive programs.

Incentive travel companies are of two broad types: those that charge fees for their services and those that receive their fees in the form of commission from the travel suppliers.

Those that charge fees are often referred to as full-service incentive companies. They are employed by corporations to establish an incentive program, prepare the promotional material, supervise the operation of the program, and make the travel arrangements. They make the travel arrangements directly with the suppliers of travel services or through travel agencies.

The second type of incentive travel company does not charge fees but receives commissions directly from the travel suppliers. Travel agencies sometimes have incentive travel departments that specialize in making these travel arrangements. These departments typically do not establish the incentive programs or supervise their operation as a full-service company would. Instead, they limit their activity to providing advice on establishing incentive programs and making the travel arrangements. Incentive travel firms obviously have a great influence over the travel arrangements of the incentive packages they book.

Convention and Meeting Planners.   Convention and meeting planners are employees of or consultants to corporations, government agencies, and other large organizations. Their profession is planning and running conventions and meetings.

Convention and meeting planners organize meetings and conventions ranging from small board meetings to conventions attended by thousands of people. They typically attend to all of the planning details including budget, travel, accommodations, meeting programs, and billing. They supervise the meetings or conventions and ensure their success. Conventions and meetings account for more than $40 billion per year; thus these individuals and firms have influence over large expenditures for travel. They make travel arrangements directly with travel suppliers, or they may work through travel agencies.

SUMMARY

In this chapter the individuals and businesses that sell travel are examined—direct providers of travel service and intermediaries. The term *package* is defined and the advantages and disadvantages of packages are described. Characteristic types of packages are listed and explained in detail, including those provided by direct suppliers and those provided by travel intermediaries. The terms *travel intermediary*, *tour wholesaler, tour operator,* and *specialty channeler* are defined, and their roles in travel are explored.

The importance and significance of travel agencies are examined. The size and scope of the travel agency industry, supplier dependence on travel agents, requirements for a travel agency to sell travel, and the importance of the computer in travel agency operation are discussed in detail. Finally, the role of such specific specialty channelers as hotel representatives, state and local tourist offices, corporate travel offices, incentive travel firms, and convention and meeting planners are described.

QUESTIONS

1. Identify five direct providers of travel services.
2. Define the term *travel intermediary.*
3. Define the term *travel package.*
4. List three advantages of purchasing a travel package over making arrangements directly with the providers of the same travel services.
5. Describe each of the following characteristic types of packages, identifying the features normally included.
    a. All-inclusive
    b. Fly/cruise
    c. Fly/cruise/hotel
    d. Fly/drive
    e. Motor coach
    f. Accommodations
    g. Accommodation and meals
    h. Family vacation
    i. Event
    j. Special-interest
    k. Affinity group
    l. Incentive
    m. Convention and meeting
6. What are the advantages to the traveler of making arrangements directly with the supplier of travel services rather than making arrangements indirectly through an intermediary? What are the advantages to the direct supplier?

7. List and describe the typical packages provided by:
   a. Airlines
   b. Bus companies
   c. Cruise lines
   d. Hotels and motels
8. Who is generally considered to have been the world's first travel agent? For what purpose did he organize his first group tour?
9. When was the first round-the-world tour? Who arranged and conducted it?
10. List six reasons why it is advisable to use a travel agent to make travel arrangements.
11. What is the approximate number of travel agencies in the United States?
12. What are the total annual dollar sales of the "typical" travel agency?
13. What two modes of transportation provide the most income to travel agents?
14. What percentage of sales of international airlines are booked through travel agents? International hotels? Cruise lines?
15. Why are conference appointments necessary for travel agencies? What are the typical requirements for a travel agent to obtain a conference appointment?
16. Explain the importance and role of the computer in travel agency operation.
17. Define the terms *tour wholesaler* and *tour operator* and distinguish between the two.
18. Define the term *specialty channeler*.
19. Define and explain the role in travel of each of the following.
   a. Hotel representatives
   b. State and local tourist offices
   c. Corporate travel offices
   d. Incentive travel firms
   e. Convention and meeting planners

Transportation Services

13

LEARNING OBJECTIVES

After reading and studying this chapter, you should be able to:

1. Trace the history of automotive development from 1801 to 1925.
2. Discuss the importance and significance of the automobile to the American traveler.
3. List the most important rental car firms.
4. Define the term <u>recreation vehicle</u> and discuss its importance in transportation.
5. Distinguish between inter-city motorcoach service and charter service.
6. List three reasons for the decline of inter-city bus service.
7. Discuss the importance of railroads to travel in the United States during the first four decades of the twentieth century.
8. Identify Amtrak and trace its development.
9. Discuss the early history of aviation, and explain the importance of mail contracts to airline development.
10. List and discuss three results of the Airline Deregulation Act.
11. Explain the hub-and-spoke method of routing aircraft.
12. Discuss the history of long-distance travel by ship.
13. Explain the growth and importance of cruising.
14. List the principal appealing features of a vacation cruise.
15. Identify the typical length of today's cruises.
16. List the advantages and disadvantages of travel by freighter.
17. Discuss schooners, charter yachts, river boats, and adventure cruising as alternate forms of pleasure cruising.

INTRODUCTION

The previous two chapters have demonstrated the tremendous growth in travel in the years since the end of World War II. We have pointed out that travel and tourism is now the world's leading industry, amounting to more than $2.7 trillion in sales and accounting for about 12 percent of the world gross product.

Reasons for this include higher disposable incomes, shorter work weeks, longer vacations, greater numbers of holidays, smaller families, earlier retirement, and declining travel costs relative to income, among others.

Another of the important factors in increased travel has been the speed, comfort, and safety of public and private transportation modes: automobiles, airplanes, ships, trains, buses, and recreation vehicles. People are able to get to their destinations more cheaply, faster, more comfortably, and with greater safety than ever before. These transportation modes are the subjects of this chapter. We will examine their historical and current significance, and look at their impact on society. We will begin with a discussion of private transportation—automobiles and recreation vehicles—then turn to various modes of public transportation, including motor coaches, railroads, airplanes, and ships.

AUTOMOBILES AND RECREATION VEHICLES
History of the Automobile

The automobile is an outgrowth of the steam engine. As early as 1801, an Englishman, Richard Trevithick, built a steam-powered passenger-carrying vehicle. It was developed further, and by 1840 there were regularly scheduled "road locomotives," vehicles that could carry as many as sixteen passengers. However, the steam engine was not well suited to automobiles. A lighter and more compact source of power was needed. It took the invention of the internal combustion engine in 1860 to begin the age of automobiles as we know them today. Etienne Lenoir, a Frenchman, invented an engine that ran on illuminating gas. This led to the development of engines that were suitable for automobiles. Two of the first to take advantage of these new developments were Karl Benz and Gottlieb Daimler, who built a factory for internal combustion engines. This in part led to the development of automobile production.

The first production of the automobile in large numbers came in 1891 when a French company, Panhard & Levassor, produced horseless carriages powered by internal combustion engines. By 1900 there were 9,500 automobiles in the world.

Charles and Frank Duryea established the first automotive manufacturing company in the United States in 1895, producing automobiles that looked like a horse carriage without the horse. Just one year later, Henry Ford produced his first vehicle, the two-cylinder "quadricycle." Further development of the automobile came when Henry Leland, founder of the Cadillac Company, conceived the idea of standardized parts that could fit into any automobile of a given make and model. However, it was Henry Ford who invented the techniques for making automobiles on an assembly line. By 1914, using these assembly-line techniques, he developed the capacity to produce a Model T Ford every twenty-four seconds. He sold more than 300,000 of them that year at a price of $850 each. A year later the price dropped to $440, and by 1925 it was $290. This set the stage for the large-scale assembly-line production that has continued to the present day.

The United States was the world leader in automobile production until 1958, annually producing more automobiles than the rest of the world combined. Since that time, the United States has become less competitive, as Japan and other countries have been able to capture a very large share of the automobile market.

Automobile Popularity

In Chapter 11 we noted that the automobile is clearly the most popular form of travel in the United States, accounting for some 85 percent of all long-distance travel. We have almost five times as many motor vehicles registered as any other nation. Table 13.1 demonstrates this.

Worldwide, the average number of people per car is 12. In the United States it is 1.8, a dramatic difference. One of the reasons for this is that many households have more than one car, something that is not as common in other countries. It is important to note that the popularity of the automobile has enabled people to make their homes some distance from their jobs and that the locations of their homes have been in large measure independent of the development of public transportation. This is perhaps one of the major reasons that many parts of the United States have never developed an extensive public transportation system: There was no great demand for it. Another important reason is both sociological and psychological: The automobile is a symbol of individual freedom. It provides

TABLE 13.1 *Motor vehicle registration, 1988*

Country	Number of cars registered	Population per car
United States	141,251,695	1.8
Japan	30,776,243	4.0
West Germany	29,190,332	2.1
Italy	23,500,000	2.4
France	22,370,000	2.5
United Kingdom	20,923,423	2.7
U.S.S.R	15,874,700	18

Source: Somerset R. Waters, *Travel Industry World Yearbook: The Big Picture, 1991* (New York: Child & Waters, 1991), pp. 154–55.

the assurance that one can go wherever one wants at any time; and this is particularly important for those who live in suburban and rural areas where public transportation is neither as common nor as reliable as in other societies.

Rental Cars

One important use of the automobile is for rental cars. There are a number of national and international rental car companies as well as a large number of local companies that rent cars. In addition, many automobile dealerships, gasoline service stations, and other businesses rent automobiles. In total, there are over 5,000 car rental companies in the United States, operating at over 26,000 locations.

The five largest rental car companies account for about 80 percent of all car rentals. Table 13.2 illustrates this.

Most people who rent cars do so because they have flown to a destination and require ground transportation for their local travel. Thus, about 80 percent of all cars are rented at airports and returned to those airports. Business men and women are the primary users of rental cars, but leisure users are taking a larger share, particularly as fly/drive packages become more popular. As shown in the last chapter, travel agents are particularly important to the rental car industry. They reserve about one-half of all rental cars.

Competition in the industry is strong; thus large amounts of money are spent on advertising and various promotional gimmicks.

Recreation Vehicles

Recreation vehicles—vehicles with wheels and temporary living quarters—include motor homes, travel trailers, truck campers, and van campers. They are a significant part of the American scene. About 8 million people in the United States own some form of recreational vehicle, commonly called *RVs*; and about 25 million people regularly use them. They do so on an average of about twenty-three days per year.

TABLE 13.2 *Rental cars: largest companies, 1989*

Company	Worldwide locations	Revenue (billions)	Global market share
Hertz	5,400	$3.1	22.6%
Avis	4,600	2.8	20.4
National	4,630	2.3	16.8
Budget	3,510	2.0	14.6
Dollar	1,312	0.8	5.8

Source: Business Travel News, in Waters, p. 144.

Reflecting the importance of individual freedom and mobility, travel by motor vehicle is the most popular form of travel in the United States, with an average of 1.8 persons per car; compared with a worldwide average of 12. Recreational vehicles enable vacationers to travel to any location accessible by road, and to come and go at their leisure. Following a surge of popularity in the 1970s, RV sales dropped significantly as a result of an increase in fuel prices and an inflationary recession. After a healthy sales recovery in the late 1980s, RV rentals are now on the rise, with travelers flying to their location of choice and renting their vehicle (Courtesy Winnebago Industries, Inc.)

When RVs first became popular in the early and mid-70s, a large number of them were sold. However, gasoline prices increased significantly in the late 70s and early 80s, when there was a recession, and interest rates were very high. This caused the numbers sold to drop dramatically. Table 13.3 illustrates this.

Since the early 1980s, sales of RVs have recovered considerably. Recently, however, sales have again begun to decline, although RV rentals appear to be increasing. Many people fly to destinations and rent RVs for their vacations.

TABLE 13.3 *Recreation vehicle sales*

Year	Sales of RVs
1976	Over 500,000
1980	181,000
1983	335,000
1987	382,000
1988	425,000
1990	391,000

Source: Waters, p. 143.

RVs can range in price from just a few thousand dollars to over $100 thousand. There are many different types. These include fold-down trailers, very large trailers pulled behind automobiles and trucks, campers that fit into the back of pickup trucks, and self-motorized vacation vans of many sizes that are actually homes on wheels.

Motor Coach Service

The terms *motor coach*, *bus*, and *coach* are all used to describe the same transportation mode. The preferred term appears to be *motor coach*.

The inter-city (travel between cities) motor coach industry can be divided into *scheduled* and *charter*. Scheduled buses provide public transportation between towns and cities. They serve about 8,500 communities in the United States not served by any other form of public transportation. In contrast, charter buses are nonpublic and used to carry specific groups of people from one point to another.

SCHEDULED BUS SERVICE. Scheduled motor coach travel has traditionally been used for personal travel rather than for business travel. It is particularly important to those who live in rural areas not served by any other mode of public transportation and for those who seek to travel the most inexpensive way. Until the early 70s, inter-city motor coach transportation was relatively popular. Some 60 million people were transported by inter-city buses in 1970. However, by 1985 that number had dropped to about 35 million. Three reasons for the decline in passengers are:

1. Competition from trains has increased. Trains have been heavily subsidized by the federal government since 1971 and thus have been able to keep fares close to those of buses. Passengers who are able to choose between them have, for the most part, opted for railroad transportation.
2. The construction of the interstate highway system has made travel by private automobile much easier. Although this has made bus service faster, it has also encouraged people to take their own automobiles. Increasing disposable income has made the automobile much more affordable to those who might otherwise rely on bus transportation.
3. Airlines have become the popular choice for long-distance travel, and airline fares have become affordable for many who might otherwise have taken the bus or train.

Prior to 1982 inter-city buses were regulated by the federal government. Schedules and fares were approved, routes were allocated, and competition was limited. In 1982 the industry was deregulated, and this set off an increase in the number of bus companies and a price war. The number of bus companies approved by the Interstate Commerce Commission grew from about 1,500 to about 3,000.

Most bus companies—including the largest, Greyhound and Trailways—lost a considerable amount of money. In 1985 and 1986, large numbers of bus lines were forced to cease operating when insurance rates went from an average of $2,000 per vehicle to $15,000.

In 1987 Greyhound was purchased by a group led by Fred Currey, the former head of Trailways Lines. He then purchased Trailways; and although the name Trailways continues to be used, the United States today is served by only one coast-to-coast bus company.

By 1990 the reduction in passengers, the heavy debt acquired by Greyhound in the takeover of Trailways, and a labor–management dispute led Greyhound to declare bankruptcy in order to prevent creditors from taking over the company. Today, Greyhound is a much smaller company, operating with 25 percent fewer drivers and buses than before.

CHARTER BUS SERVICE. Charter bus service presents a brighter picture. The number of charter buses and tours has been steadily increasing, so that over 50 percent of the motor coach industry traffic can be attributed to charter tours. Charters tend to be profitable, because unlike scheduled inter-city bus service, they can be canceled if insufficient numbers of people make reservations for the tours. Interestingly, most motor coach tours last only one day. A survey done in 1988 showed that there were 976,166 one-day tours compared with 302,593 multiday tours.

RAILROADS
History

In the United States today, the railroad plays only a minor role in inter-city passenger traffic, accounting for about 1 percent of long-distance trips. Nevertheless, the historical role of railroads in the expansion and development of many parts of the United States cannot be ignored. In previous chapters the importance of the railroads was discussed. Railroad stops were natural locations for hotels, and resort hotels were natural destinations for railroads. In some cases—Henry Flagler's hotels, for example—reaching existing hotels was the chief reason a railroad was built.

The number of miles of railroad track in the United States reached a peak in 1916, as shown in Table 13.4. However, the railroads were still the primary means of long-distance public transportation for many years thereafter. All through the 1920s, the 1930s, and most of the 1940s, American railroads provided excellent passenger service. In fact, the railroad cars were generally considered more comfortable than other means of transportation, and the staff was efficient and polite. Trains generally ran on time, and food served in the dining cars of some trains was

TABLE 13.4 *Railroad mileage in the United States*	
Year	Mileage
1830	23
1850	9,021
1870	52,922
1890	163,597
1910	240,439
1916	254,037
1930	249,052
1950	223,779
1970	209,000
1980	200,000

Source: *Encyclopedia Americana* (Danbury, CT: Grolier, 1989), p. 221.

as good as that served in some fine restaurants. During the period of their greatest popularity, railroads accounted for as much as 70 percent of all inter-city traffic.

The best inter-city trains were named, just as cruise ships are named. In fact, the practice of naming trains continues with Amtrak. Some of the famous trains of the past include:

The Panama Limited: Started by the Illinois Central Railroad in 1912, it ran between Chicago and New Orleans.

The Twentieth Century Limited: The deluxe train of the New York Central Railroad, it provided service between New York City and Chicago. It was introduced in 1902 and made its last run in 1967.

The Broadway Limited: It was first run by the Pennsylvania Railroad between New York City and Chicago in 1902 as competition for the Twentieth Century Limited. Amtrak retains a train with this name.

The Super Chief: Started in 1936 by the Atchison, Topeka & Santa Fe Railroad, it traveled between Chicago and Los Angeles.

After World War II, competition from airlines and private automobiles led to a decrease in the number of railroad passengers. Passenger service has never been highly profitable, and decreased ridership caused the railroads to operate at a loss. As a result, passenger service began to deteriorate: Service was perceived as less friendly; cars were not kept in the best condition; and food in dining cars was not up to previous standards. Roadbeds for the railroad track were not well maintained, and train travel was less comfortable than it had been. Railroads were required by

Once an important factor in the expansion of the United States and the development of the hotel industry, rail travel now accounts for only about 1 percent of long-distance trips. Formed by the federal government in 1971, Amtrak is a quasi-public corporation, subsidized 28 to 50 percent by public funds since its inception. In other industrialized countries, railroads are nationalized and more heavily subsidized to keep fares low, and are a significant means of transportation. (Amtrak photo; courtesy Amtrak.)

law to maintain passenger service; but because it was not profitable, they spent less money on the service—with predictable results.

Creation of Amtrak

In an attempt to preserve long-distance train service, the federal government formed Amtrak in 1971. It is a national passenger train service but differs in organization from railroad service in other countries. Amtrak is a quasi-public corporation that is neither nationalized nor completely private. It is independent of the federal government, having its own board of directors and nongovernment employees. At the same time it is financially dependent on the federal government, which regulates it.

Amtrak has never made a profit and has been subsidized each year by Congress. From its inception in 1971 to 1988 Congress has given Amtrak between $500 million and $800 million each year. This has represented 35 percent to 50 percent of its total revenues.

Since 1971, under Amtrak's management, new railroad cars have been added, roadbeds have been improved, service has become much better, and many more people are riding the limited number of trains that Amtrak operates. The greatest number of trains operate in the Northeast corridor, the stretch of track running between Boston and Washington, D.C., serving such cities as Providence, New Haven, New York, Philadelphia, and Baltimore. Amtrak is also slowly adding routes and new equipment. It is purchasing over 100 new bilevel Superliner cars for long distance routes. These cars have sleeping accommodations on the lower level and observation areas on the upper level. In the dining cars, food is prepared on the lower level and served to diners seated on the upper level.

In fiscal 1990, Amtrak had the best performance of any year in its history. It carried a record 22.2 million passengers on inter-city routes and earned revenues of $1.3 billion. The subsidy from Congress was the lowest in history, $475 million. Amtrak was able to generate a record 72 percent of its costs from its operation.

In other parts of the world, railroads continue to be a very important means of public transportation. In some less developed countries, railroads are still the largest carriers of inter-city traffic. In industrialized nations, railroads provide an inexpensive means of traveling between cities and towns and are an excellent alternative to automobile and airplane travel. In virtually all countries in the world except the United States, railroads are nationalized—owned and operated by the national government. They are also very heavily subsidized to keep fares low enough so that anyone can afford to ride them. Japan subsidizes its railroad system with more than $11 billion annually. In Europe, subsidies amount to $5 billion in Germany, $3.5 billion in France, and $3.5 billion in the United Kingdom.

In some countries inter-city train service is quite fast. France has trains that reach 186 mph; Germany has a link between Mannheim and Stuttgart where trains can travel at 155 mph. Japan has its famous "bullet train" that travels at speeds in excess of 140 mph.

AIRLINES

In the United States, air travel has become the primary means of public transportation, accounting for 19 percent of all trips taken over 100 miles. A recent study of the U.S. population showed that 80 percent of all adult women and 75 percent of all adult men have flown in commercial aircraft. Just over half—51 percent of these trips—were for business; the remaining 49 percent were taken for personal reasons. On average, 35 percent of all American adults fly each year. In the history of transportation, however, air travel is a relatively recent phenomenon.

Airline History

LIGHTER-THAN-AIR CRAFT. The first airline, Deutsche Luftschiffahrts AG, was founded on November 16, 1909. It was more commonly known as Delag. Headquartered in Frankfurt, Germany, its purpose was to operate zeppelin airships. These were a particular type of lighter-than-air craft known as *dirigibles* or *blimps*. They were similar in appearance to those seen today in the skies over major sports and entertainment events advertising Goodyear and Met Life.

Lighter-than-air craft have been around for many years. The first successful one was constructed and flown as early as 1852, by Henri Giffard, from Paris to Trappe.

The name *zeppelin* comes from Count Ferdinand von Zeppelin, who designed many successful lighter-than-air craft, constructed of a lightweight frame that was covered by a thin exterior "skin" of aluminum and powered by internal combustion engines. These were an important part of early aviation and transported many passengers throughout Europe and across the Atlantic. The popularity of the zeppelin reached a high point in commercial aviation in 1929 when the *Graf Zeppelin*, a large version of the original Zeppelin, made an historic round-the-world flight—taking 21 days, 7 hours, and 31 minutes. The *Graf Zeppelin* flew until 1940, when it was finally retired. Between 1928 and 1940 it completed 590 flights, including 140 Atlantic crossings, and carried 13,100 passengers.

While the *Graf Zeppelin* was operating, the Zeppelin Company was constructing an even larger ship called the *Hindenburg*. Completed in March 1936, it was the world's largest airship: 808 feet in length and 134 feet in diameter. It had four diesel engines and carried 75 passengers and a crew of 25. However, on May 6, 1937, while the *Hindenburg* was attempting to dock at Lakehurst, New Jersey, fire broke out at the top of the craft near the stern and within seconds the great ship was engulfed in flame. Fortunately, 62 of the 97 people on board escaped. This tragedy effectively ended the development of commercial service in lighter-than-air ships. Interestingly, the tragedy could have been avoided. The ship was designed to be kept aloft by helium, a nonflammable gas. However, because no helium was available at the time, the company elected to substitute hydrogen, a very dangerous, flammable gas.

COMMERCIAL AIRPLANES. The first scheduled air service on a commercial airplane was January 1, 1914, from St. Petersburg to Tampa, Florida. It was accomplished by the newly formed St. Petersburg–Tampa Airboat Line, in a single-engine biplane (a plane with two sets of wings) that was open to the sky. It appeared to be a successful venture, but for unknown reasons the airline continued operations only until the end of March of that year. During the period of its existence it carried a total of 1,024 passengers.

The first international commercial flight was on January 10, 1919, from London to Paris. It was established by the British Royal Air Force primarily to provide transportation for government officials attending the Paris Peace Conference. Flights continued until September 1919. A total of 749 flights were made.

Another attempt at scheduled passenger service in the United States was made by Ryan Airlines in 1925. This was a West Coast airline that flew from Los Angeles to San Diego. That service lasted about a year.

Continual scheduled passenger service did not begin until 1927. It was started by Colonial Air Transport, an airline that had a contract to carry the mail from Boston to New York. It was one of the many airlines that had been carrying mail for the U.S. Postal Service since 1918. In 1926 Congress passed the Kelly Act that authorized long-term mail contracts for airlines. The passage of the Kelly Act led to the founding of many airline companies. All were competing for the contracts to carry U.S. mail; and many, like Colonial Air Transport, carried passengers as well. Many of these new airlines failed; some succeeded; and many of them merged. By 1931 these mergers had resulted in the establishment of such well-known airline carriers as American, Eastern, TWA, and United.

The airlines suffered a major setback in February 1934, when President Roosevelt, feeling that some airlines had been favored when mail contracts were awarded, canceled all air mail contracts. Air mail service was taken over by the U.S. Army Air Corps. This resulted in the failure of many airline companies and reduced competition in air service. In April of that year, mail service was again awarded to airlines, and American, TWA, Eastern, and United received the important contracts. TWA and United were awarded transcontinental mail routes, Eastern was awarded north–south routes, and American was awarded service between Newark and Chicago and between Newark and Boston. Thus, contracts to carry the U.S. mails were an important element in the success of the major air carriers that eventually dominated air passenger service in the United States. Those without mail contracts found it was difficult, if not impossible, to succeed.

One very important airline in American aviation history is Pan American. It began regular mail service between Key West, Florida, and Havana, Cuba, on October 28, 1927. Passenger service on that route began in January 1928. Travelers were charged $50 for a one-way ticket. Over the next few years, Pan American expanded its routes to other Caribbean islands and into South America. By 1934 it was operating 85 aircraft and carrying over 100,000 passengers a year.

In November 1935, Pan American inaugurated transpacific mail service with its new four-motor sea plane, the Martin M-130 *China Clipper*. It departed from Alameda, California, for Manila, in the Philippines, and arrived there almost 60 hours later. Paying passengers were allowed on this flight beginning October 21, 1936. Pan American's new long-distance sea planes were named the *China Clipper*, the *Philippine Clipper*, and the *Hawaii Clipper*. They could carry 41 passengers and had a cruising speed of 157 mph. Pan American subsequently extended this service to Hong Kong.

Airline service over a portion of the Atlantic began on June 16, 1937, when Imperial Airways inaugurated service between Bermuda and New York. Pan American began its passenger service between New York and Southampton, England, on July 8, 1939, with the *Yankee Clipper*, another new long-distance plane. It was a Boeing 314, which carried 17 passengers, each paying a fare of $375.

Begun in 1914 in the United States, commercial air service relied on freight and mail service early on to significantly supplement revenues; following World War II, passenger service increased 50 percent. Developments in aircraft design now accommodate up to 500 passengers for long distance flights, and lower fares have made air travel available to more travelers than ever before. Deregulation, instituted in 1978, eventually contributed to the survival of only a few financially strong carriers, with competition among them intense. (Courtesy United Airlines.)

Most of the planes used on domestic airline routes during the latter 1920s and the 1930s were small, accommodating 8 to 15 passengers. They cruised between 100 and 135 miles per hour. In 1934 Douglas Aircraft introduced its DC-2, a twin engine plane that could travel at a cruising speed of 196 mph. Douglas soon produced a larger version, the DC-3, with a cruising speed of 186 mph. The DC-3 became the workhorse of civil and military passenger service for many years. It is said that the DC-3 was the first plane that could operate profitably without the benefit of a mail contract. There were a total of 10,655 DC-3s built, and several hundred of them are still flying today.

After World War II, airline passenger service began to expand rapidly. In 1946 the world's airlines carried 18 million passengers. By 1949 that figure had grown to 27 million—a 50 percent increase in just three years.

Larger four-engine aircraft were starting to be used extensively. The DC-4 and the Lockheed Constellation were the first of these. Shortly thereafter, the DC-6, DC-6B, the Lockheed Super Consellation, and the Boeing 377 Stratocruiser became the standard aircraft used for long-distance flights. These planes cruised at speeds of about 300 mph and carried 60 to 100 passengers, depending upon the seat configuration. The Boeing 377 Stratocruiser, a two-decked plane, was used primarily for overseas flights: It was designed to provide sleeping accommodations for between 50 and 100 passengers.

The next real advancement in aircraft was the development of the turbojet aircraft. One of the most successful of these was the Boeing 707, which came into service in October 1958. It cruised at 570 mph and carried 179 passengers. The DC-8 was introduced shortly thereafter and began service in September 1959.

Smaller jet aircraft were soon designed for medium- and short-range service. The first of these was the Boeing 727, which has the characteristic high tail section and three rear-mounted engines. It began service in February of 1964 and held 131 passengers. The 727 was a very successful aircraft and prompted Boeing to design later versions of it that accommodate 189 passengers. This airplane has been used by more than 80 airlines.

Perhaps one of the most important developments in air travel was the introduction of wide-bodied aircraft. The first of these was the giant Boeing 747, which went into service with Pan American World Airways on January 22, 1970. The aircraft had 58 seats in first class and 304 in economy class, and a maximum cruising altitude of 45,000 feet. More recent versions of the 747 accommodate as many as 500 passengers.

The 747 is too big and costly to operate on short flights, however; it is designed for long-distance routes. Smaller and less costly wide-bodied aircraft were manufactured about the same time. These include the DC-10, which has a seating capacity of 270 passengers, and the Lockheed L1011, which can carry 330 coach passengers or 272 passengers in a mixed configuration. The DC-10 came into service on August 5, 1971; and the L1011, on April 26, 1972.

Other smaller aircraft have been recently introduced to serve short- to medium-range flights relatively inexpensively. These include the Boeing 737, 757, 767, and the McDonnell Douglas MD-80. These smaller planes are also now used for long-distance flights when there are a limited number of passengers. They feature fuel-efficient engines and many modern advances in airline technology.

Perhaps the most interesting aircraft is the Supersonic Concord, a joint development of Britain and France. It underwent many years of design and testing before it was put into service. It first flew on March 2, 1969, but was not put into service until January 1976. This remarkable plane cruises at an amazing 1,332 mph. It is a slim delta-winged aircraft that accommodates relatively few passengers. It can fly from western Europe to New York, however, in about three hours, enabling it to arrive in New York at a local time earlier than its local time of departure in Europe. It is also very costly to operate; therefore, compared with fares on traditional jet aircraft, the Concord is very expensive.

A major difficulty with the Concord and other supersonic aircraft is the sonic booms they make. These can cause real damage to people and property. As a consequence, restrictions have been placed on their use. For example, in the United States they are not permitted to fly over land at speeds in excess of the speed of sound.

The airline industry in the United States was highly regulated until 1978. The Civil Aeronautics Board (CAB) allocated routes, approved fares, and ruled on mergers. Relatively little competition existed among airlines: Comparatively few were allowed to serve major routes. For example, direct service from New York to Los Angeles might be awarded to only two airlines, which would submit proposed fares to the Civil Aeronautics Board for approval. Knowing the number of potential passengers between New York and Los Angeles, they would submit fares that would guarantee a profit. In return for limited competition, airlines were required to serve cities with few potential passengers, where service was unprofitable.

The Airline Deregulation Act of 1978

The Airline Deregulation Act of 1978 led to major changes in the airline industry. It eliminated the Civil Aeronautics Board and transferred its responsibilities to the Federal Aviation Administration (FAA) and the Department of Transportation (DOT). The Act was designed to increase competition and to provide the airlines with more freedom to choose routes and set rates.

The effects of deregulation can be summarized under three headings:

1. New airlines
2. Lower air fares
3. Mega-carriers

NEW AIRLINES. As a result of deregulation, a number of new airlines were created and competition for passengers increased dramatically. These new airlines included New York Air, Midway Airline, American West, and People Express, to name a few.

Other new airlines were *feeder airlines*—smaller airlines that brought passengers from smaller cities to the major cities, where they could connect with long-distance airlines. Two reasons account for the establishment of many new feeder airlines:

1. Major airlines stopped serving the smaller, unprofitable cities they once were required to serve. One example is Manchester, New Hampshire, for which the only major airline service provided was by Delta. After deregulation, Delta eliminated all flights to Manchester, creating a temporary void in service.
2. It became easier for airlines to gain government approval to establish passenger service. This spawned many new airlines. They filled the void in service that was created when major airlines ceased passenger service to the smaller cities.

Eventually, realizing the importance of this connecting service, the major airlines franchised the smaller feeder airlines or purchased them and created connecting airline service. This had the effect of extending the service of major carriers to cities they would otherwise not serve. Thus, we now have Continental Express, Delta Connection, and American Eagle, to name a few.

LOWER AIR FARES. The increased competition set off a price war that persisted throughout the 1980s. Discount carriers were one factor in the low rate structure. These were airline companies that had lower fares than the major airlines for service between the same two points. People Express is a good example of a discount airline that provided service on new, modern planes, yet charged very low fares. They were able to offer lower fares than competing carriers because they employed fewer people, provided fewer passenger services, and generally kept overhead costs to a minimum. Some discount carriers even refused to pay commissions to travel agents for airline reservations the travel agents had booked. Passengers flying discount airlines generally paid the flight attendants for their flight after the plane was in the air. No food was served, and drinks were sold for cash.

Another factor in lower air fares was the increase in the number of major airlines serving large cities. It is a fact that if one airline lowers a fare, all of the competing ones must also do it. If not, all airlines will lose considerable business to the airline that lowers fares. Air fares are very price sensitive, because much of the public sees little difference between the major carriers. Airline passengers tend to fly with the airline that offers the lowest fare to their destination.

MEGA-CARRIERS. Eventually, many of the new airlines went out of business, and others were merged. The effect has been that the strong airlines—American, Delta, Northwest, and United—have survived, and the weaker airlines—Eastern, Pan American, Continental, TWA, and Braniff, to name a few—have either gone out of business, gone into bankruptcy, or become part of another airline. Airlines that were purchased include Air California (by American Airlines), Western Airlines (by Delta), Ozark (by TWA), and Republic Airlines (by Northwest). Continental, Eastern, Braniff, Frontier, and New York Air were combined with Texas Air to form a very large conglomerate under the ownership of Texas Air. Since then, Eastern, Pan American, and Braniff have gone out of business; and Continental, America West, and TWA, although still flying, have gone through bankruptcy. It appears that the final result of deregulation will be the emergence of a few mega-carriers that will dominate the airline industry. As of this writing, 90 percent of the U.S. air traffic is carried by just eight airlines.

Frequent-Flyer Programs

In an effort to develop a loyal customer base, the airlines have frequent-flyer programs. These are incentive programs that award mileage for travel on their airlines and provide various rewards for accumulation of miles. The awards may include upgrades to first-class seats, free flights, free car rentals, and free hotel rooms. It has been estimated that airlines now owe more than 3 million free round-trip tickets, enough for flyers to travel at least 5.4 billion miles at no cost, as a result of these frequent-flyer programs.

Hub-and-Spoke Routing

In an effort to fill the maximum number of seats on each flight and to simplify scheduling, airlines have developed a system of routing commonly referred to as the hub-and-spoke method. Each airline has several major airports, which serve as hubs providing meeting points for planes coming from outlying cities (spokes). Flight schedules are established so that many planes arrive at the hub at about the same time. Passengers then change planes and proceed to their final destinations. Delta, for example, has a major hub in Dallas. Many flights originating in Boston, New York, Philadelphia, Pittsburgh, Washington, Atlanta, and elsewhere fly directly to Dallas. They are scheduled to arrive in Dallas within approximately one-half hour of each other. On arrival, passengers change planes and proceed to their final destination. Not all flights on any airline are scheduled this way, of course. A number of them still operate as direct flights.

The hub-and-spoke method has advantages over direct routing. The major advantage to the airlines is that flights can be more fully booked. For example, suppose that on a given day, Delta has sold 300 tickets on flights from Boston: 100 for Phoenix, 100 for Los Angeles, and 100 for San Francisco. If it scheduled three direct nonstop flights, one to each of the three cities, each plane would be only about one-half full. However, using the hub-and-spoke method, only one wide-bodied plane need be used. It could be scheduled to go, for example, to Los Angeles. The plane would stop first in Dallas where it would meet other planes coming from New York, Washington, and other cities. Those passengers continuing to Los Angeles would stay on board, whereas those for Phoenix and San Francisco would transfer to other planes that had come from New York and Washington. The Los Angeles plane would be filled from passengers transferring from the New York and Washington flights.

From the viewpoint of the passenger, the advantage of the hub-and-spoke method is that one can fly to virtually any city in the Delta system with only one stop and a change of planes. The disadvantage is that the stop at the hub makes the time to fly from one city to another somewhat longer than a direct flight would be.

For some flights, it is necessary to fly extra distance because it is necessary to go to Dallas. In addition, for those passengers changing planes, there is an increased chance that baggage will be lost. And in the event that one incoming flight is delayed or canceled, passengers due to transfer to that flight will miss their connection and be delayed in Dallas until the next scheduled departure for their intended destination.

Growth in Airline Passenger Traffic

The number of passengers on airlines has grown steadily since World War II. Table 13.5 shows this growth.

The increased number of passengers, however, does not necessarily translate into increased profits for the airlines. Severe competition has kept air fares and profit margins low, so that only those airlines that are financially healthy can operate profitably. It has been reported that U.S. domestic airlines as a group lost $2 billion in 1990. About 91 percent of all passengers were flying at reduced fares that averaged 65 percent off the full fare.

PASSENGER SHIPS

Travel by ship is perhaps the oldest form of public transportation, going back at least to Roman times. For many centuries, travel by ship was on sailing ships. The most famous of these were the clipper ships that carried the American flag around the world during the mid 1800s.

The first successful steamship was Robert Fulton's *Clermont*, launched in 1807 on the Hudson River in New York State. This 133-foot vessel sailed up the Hudson River from New York City to Albany in thirty-two hours, a voyage that normally took four days by sail.

TABLE 13.5 *Worldwide airline passenger traffic*

Year	Passengers carried
1946	18,000,000
1949	27,000,000
. . .	. . .
1975	534,000,000
1980	748,000,000
1985	897,000,000
1990	1,159,000,000

Source: International Civil Aviation Organization, in Waters, p. 146.

The first steamship to travel into the Atlantic was the *Phoenix*, which sailed down the New Jersey coast from New York to Philadelphia in 1809. However, the ship was not built for the high seas and did not venture beyond the sight of land.

The first vessel with steam to cross any ocean was the *Savannah*, which in 1819 went from Savannah, Georgia, to Liverpool, England, in twenty-nine days. It was a full-rigged sailing ship with a steam engine for auxiliary power. The paddles that drove the ship when steam power was used were centered on either side of the ship. The Savannah had luxurious accommodations, with such amenities as rosewood paneling and full-length mirrors. However, it was an economic failure: Passengers were afraid of this new ship because of the fire used to generate steam below decks, and shippers would not send cargo on a vessel they considered unsafe. It made only one crossing and was rebuilt as a sailing ship.

The first regular steamship service on the north Atlantic began in 1838 with two ships: one called the *Great Western*, which sailed from Bristol, England, and the *Sirius*, which sailed from Cork, Ireland. Both ships arrived in New York at about the same time, although the *Sirius* had left Ireland three days earlier than the *Great Western*. Both were powered with steam engines and propelled by paddle wheels.

The next advancement in steamships came with the *Great Eastern*, launched in 1857. Made of iron, it was 693 feet long, weighed 18,000 tons, carried a maximum of 4,000 passengers, and was the largest ship on the seas for 50 years. The *Great Eastern* had five smokestacks—one more than any other ship ever to be built—six masts rigged for sail, a screw propeller, and paddle wheels. Like the *Savannah*, the *Great Eastern* was an economic disaster, never making money. Finally, in 1865 it was assigned the job of laying the first cable across the Atlantic Ocean. It was the only ship large enough to hold the length of cable required.

By 1860 travel abroad by Americans on clipper ships and steamships had reached an annual rate of 26,000 persons. In 1900, the number of American passengers traveling abroad was 120,477 and by 1929 the number had increased to 511,814.

The period beginning with 1900 saw the building of ships weighing much more than the *Great Eastern*. The French, Germans, British, Scandinavians, Italians, and Dutch built huge ocean-going ships with legendary names: *Nieuw Amsterdam*, *Rotterdam*, *Carolina*, *Lusitania*, and *Mauritania*, among others.

The years between 1920 and World War II were those when transatlantic passenger ships reached their highest levels of popularity. Ships of 20,000 tons and more were common, and by 1934 ships of 80,000 tons were being built. The most notable of these were the *Queen Mary*, the *Queen Elizabeth*, and the *Normandy*.

World War II brought a halt to most scheduled passenger shipping. Many of the grand passenger ships were used for troop transports, and some were sunk by enemy submarines. After the war, passenger service resumed. The luxurious *S.S. France* was built in 1961, and the *Queen Elizabeth II* went into service in 1968.

Although the United States has never invested heavily in passenger ships, it did build the *United States* in 1952. At the time, this was the fastest liner afloat, capable of a speed of 35 knots. By this time, however, the days of transatlantic passenger ships were numbered, and the *United States* never carried the numbers of passengers that might have been possible some thirty years earlier. By the late 1960s, the *United States* had to be taken out of service for lack of passengers.

The beginning of the end of transatlantic passenger crossings came in 1957, the first year more people crossed the Atlantic by plane than by ship. Travelers no longer wanted to spend five to seven days traveling to Europe by ship when a plane would take them across the Atlantic in a matter of hours. The last ship to provide scheduled transatlantic service was the *Queen Elizabeth II*, and this was only during the summer months.

Today, most of the grand transoceanic liners are gone. The *Queen Mary* is permanently docked in Long Beach, California, as a tourist attraction. The original *Queen Elizabeth* sank in Hong Kong harbor. The *France* was sold to the Norwegian Caribbean Line, was refurbished, and is now sailing as the cruise ship *Norway*. The *Queen Elizabeth II* is used almost exclusively for long-distance vacation cruising.

Vacation Cruising

Vacation cruising goes back 100 years to 1891 when the P&O line, the world's oldest cruise line, began to offer vacation cruises to distant parts of the world. For generations, taking a cruise meant boarding a ship in Boston, New York, Los Angeles, or some other city—then sailing to ports around the world.

The scheduled lines—those that provided scheduled transoceanic service—had specific year-round routes. However, sales always decreased in winter, which was never a good time to travel by ship. The seas were rough, the winds were fierce, and the temperatures could be frigid. In the mid-1930s, owners of lines that crossed the Atlantic Ocean started scheduling ships for winter vacation cruises to keep them going during the cold months when there was limited demand for transatlantic service. These ships carried passengers from cold-weather ports to warmer climates. New York City was the major port of embarkation. Ships that normally traveled from New York to Europe went on vacation cruises to the Caribbean, South America, and the Mediterranean.

Today, the large seagoing passenger vessels are used almost exclusively for vacation cruising. They are concentrated in the Mediterranean, Caribbean, and on the U.S. west coast. The typical cruise is three, four, seven, or eight days long, although cruises of ten to fifteen days are not uncommon. Extended vacation cruises to distant ports of call are still available on ships such as the *Queen Elizabeth II*, but the greater demand is for short-term cruises that are within the budgets of the average working person.

Worldwide, about $6.5 billion is spent annually on vacation cruises, with 81 percent of it spent in North America. This represents about 3.6 million passengers. The type of person who takes a cruise vacation is changing rapidly. Years ago, vacationing aboard cruise ships was selected by older, more affluent individuals who had the time and the money to spend. In more recent years, the age of cruise ship passengers has become younger, and the length of cruises has become shorter. The average age of the passengers is now under fifty years, the average income is more typical of the middle class, and the average length of the vacation cruise is likely to be three or four days. Most vacation cruises are now informal. Men generally are not required to wear coats and ties to meals. Interestingly, however, only about 5 percent of Americans have ever been on a vacation cruise.

As mentioned in the previous chapter, cruises are sold as packages having air fare, transfers, and the actual cruise all included in one price. The only additional costs passengers on cruise packages must face are those for shore excursions and gratuities.

Cruise ship vacations and getaways are becoming increasingly popular, with a growth rate of about 10 percent each year. Table 13.6 illustrates this.

New cruise ships are being built to accommodate the expanding market. There are nearly 200 cruise ships worldwide, with more being added each year. Most ships carry between 1,100 and 1,600 passengers, but there are some notable exceptions: Some of the newer ships carry more than 2,000 passengers. Examples include the Royal Caribbean's *Sovereign of the Seas*, which carries 2,280 passengers, and its sister ship *Majesty of the Seas*, which carries 2,354. Carnival Cruise Line's *Fantasy* carries 2,025 passengers. There are also a number of smaller ships that carry very limited numbers of passengers. For example, Cunard's *Sea Goddess I* and *Sea Goddess II* each carry 58 couples. Exploration Cruise Line's *Colonial*

TABLE 13.6 *Cruise passenger growth rate*

Year	Passenger growth (%)
1981	1.7
1982	1.2
1983	15.2
1984	9.9
1985	13.4
1986	13.8
1987	11.0
1988	9.5
1989	2.4
1990	9.0 (p)

(p) Preliminary.
Source: Cruise Line International Association, in Waters, p. 145.

Explorer carries only 102 passengers; and Ocean Cruise Line's *Ocean Islander* carries 250.

Although the ages of vacation cruise passengers are younger and the length of the cruises is shorter, the appealing features of cruises have not changed over the years. They continue to be:

1. Food
2. Activities and entertainment
3. Weather
4. Elegance and comfort

Cruise ships normally offer quantities of excellent food. As mentioned in the previous chapter, passengers on vacation cruises are typically offered breakfast, midmorning bullion, luncheon, afternoon tea, dinner, and a midnight buffet supper. Passengers can eat as much as they like, and the high quality of the food is a major attraction.

Cruise ships have an entertainment staff that provides activities all day long. A typical day might start with exercises, or swimming in one of several pools. During the day, ongoing activities include cards, bingo, dance lessons, sports, and movies. If the ship is docked or anchored, there are shore excursions ranging from shopping, to visiting rum factories, to going underwater snorkeling. In the evening there is live entertainment and dancing, as well as more movies.

One of the main attractions for many cruise passengers is the weather. Most voyages take place in the warm climates of the Mediterranean, the Caribbean, or along the Mexican coast. When the weather is cold in much of the United States and northern Europe, the temperatures in the Mediterranean and the Caribbean are very appealing. Vacation cruises in colder climates—Alaska, for example—are restricted to the warmer summer months. Many ships cruise the northern waters in the summer and the warmer waters nearer the equator during the winter.

Modern ships provide a level of elegance and comfort that can be found only in luxury resort hotels and private villas. Facilities on board the larger ships include theaters, night clubs, gambling casinos, swimming pools, saunas, exercise rooms, beauty and barber shops, gift shops, and various sporting activities. Public rooms are tastefully decorated; lounge and deck chairs are plentiful; and staterooms are comfortable. Stabilizers prevent most ships from rolling in high seas, even when the weather is stormy. Thus seasickness, which used to be a problem for some passengers, has been virtually eliminated.

The level of service on many ships is as high as that in luxury hotels. Cabin stewards are available twenty-four hours a day and provide turn-down service in the evening. Food and beverage service is commonly available day and night, and all sorts of recreational activities are available at any given time. Pursers are there to store valuables, cash checks, and convert currencies. Because of the high level of service, a cruise on one of these luxury liners can be an elegant and refreshing experience.

Perhaps the oldest form of long distance transportation, travel by ship is available in several forms. Traditional vacation cruising (shown above) is concentrated mainly in the Mediterranean and Caribbean and off the U.S. West Coast, offering passengers trips of three to 15 days with food, activities and entertainment, and mild weather as the most appealing features. Other types of cruise vessels—including freighters, schooners, charter boats, river steam boats, and barges—are less popular but provide an interesting alternative to cruise ships in both their orientation and destinations. (Courtesy Carnival Cruise Lines.)

Travel by Freighter

Freighters have traditionally provided the least expensive way to travel by ship. Freighter travel receives very little attention; but it is still possible to travel this way, although the advent of the larger container ships has reduced the number of opportunities. Most freighters have a few cabins for limited numbers of passengers. The lines do very little advertising; but arrangements for freighter travel can be made through travel agents or directly with the shipping company. *Ford's Freighter Travel Guide* lists most of the available opportunities for freighter travel. Included in the list of freighter lines that carry passengers are Polish Ocean Line, American President Lines, Ivaran Lines, and Adriatic/Australia/New Zealand Line.

Freighter travel can be relaxing and interesting. There are, however, some possible disadvantages to consider.

1. Schedules are not dependable. Freighters are frequently delayed loading and unloading cargo and consequently do not keep to an exact timetable.
2. Frequent unscheduled stops are common, and ports of call frequently change from those anticipated. Once on board, passengers may find themselves sailing to undesirable places.

3. No planned entertainment or recreation is available; and the food, although very good in most cases, is not up to the standard of cruise ships in variety or quantity.

Nevertheless, some people enjoy the leisurely lifestyle aboard freighters. Many enjoy the adventure, and others enjoy the opportunity to catch up on reading or writing. For some, freighter cruising provides an opportunity to regain physical or emotional health.

Other Forms of Cruise Vessels

For those interested in other forms of water transportation, several interesting choices exist. These include schooners, charter yachts and sailboats, riverboats, adventure cruises, and barges.

SCHOONERS. A number of old-fashioned schooners sail coastal waters on cruises lasting several days. These are typically sail-only ships that have auxiliary power to get in and out of port. Passengers on these cruises are usually expected to assist in pulling up and taking down the sails. They generally sail during the day and anchor in a port for the night.

CHARTER YACHTS. Many people own yachts and sailing vessels but use them only for limited periods of time. Some of the larger ones have permanent captains. Some vessels can sleep four to ten, or more, people; and some of them are available for charter. The resulting income helps the owners defray the high cost of main-taining such boats.

If one is to charter a yacht or sailing vessel without a captain, considerable prior experience is necessary. It is also advisable to have some knowledge of the seas in the area where the charter will occur, as well as an understanding of the weather that one can face. A private charter can be an adventurous holiday, although it is fraught with the dangers that can plague smaller craft on the ocean. But it can also be an absorbing and gratifying vacation. One is not tied to a schedule, as in the case of most other cruises, and the activities associated with private charters—fishing, snorkeling, and sailing—present refreshing alternatives to those on large cruise ships.

STEAMBOATS. On many of the rivers and lakes of the United States, boats operate that have been built to look like nineteenth-century paddle steamers. A number of these have been built quite recently. These craft offer cruises that may last for several hours or several days. For example, the famous *Delta Queen* sails the Tennessee and Cumberland Rivers in the summer, and the *Mississippi Queen* sails the Mississippi River. Each of them takes two- to twelve-day cruises.

On small lakes throughout the United States, facsimiles of steamboats take short inexpensive pleasure cruises. Many of them provide entertainment and food. They offer vacationers an afternoon or evening of relaxing sightseeing.

ADVENTURE CRUISES. Throughout the world a number of so-called adventure cruises take vacationers into jungles and exotic places the large ocean liners cannot go. For example, Epirotiki Line's *World Renaissance* is a 470-passenger ship that sails down the Amazon River and through some rarely visited Caribbean islands. Exploration Cruise Line offers cruises in and around Alaska's glaciers, rivers, and bays on luxury ships that accommodate 200 to 300 passengers. These ships go where larger liners cannot. There are a number of smaller boats accommodating up to 100 passengers that sail the inland waterway on the east coast of the United States. They stop at various Southern towns and cities that are unavailable or infrequent ports to larger vessels. These ports including Palm Beach, Florida, Savannah, Georgia, and Charleston, South Carolina.

BARGES. One of the more unusual forms of cruising is that available on river barges. Primarily operated on the rivers and ancient canals of England and France, these barges provide accommodations for limited numbers of passengers. There are two types: smaller barges accommodating about four persons, and larger barges—up to 100 ft. long—accommodating ten to fourteen passengers. The larger barges have a captain and crew, as well as a chef.

The large barges are very comfortable; they offer private carpeted bedrooms, each with private bath, as well as a dining room and a lounge. The food served on these barges is excellent, prepared by professional chefs. Because they move very slowly—traveling only about five miles per hour—one can actually get off and walk along the canal. It is even possible to leave the barge, go shopping or sightseeing, and take public transportation to catch up to the barge at its next stop.

Arrangements for barge trips are made through travel agents or directly with the barge companies. Package prices for the larger barges compare favorably with ocean cruises. The price typically includes transfers from the major arrival city to the place of embarkation, food and beverages, wines and cocktails, and various activities, including tours and lunches at pubs and restaurants.

SUMMARY

In this chapter the modes of travel are examined. The development of the automobile is discussed and its importance and significance explained. Rental cars are discussed, as is the growing market for recreation vehicles. Reasons are listed for the decline in inter-city motor coach travel and for the growth of charter tours.

The history and significance of the railroad industry are discussed, and reasons are suggested for the decline in railroad service. The formation of Amtrak is explained.

The development of the airline industry is discussed in detail. Its growth and importance to travel are examined and the effects of deregulation are detailed. The significance of the current methods of routing aircraft and establishing ticket prices is explained.

The history and importance of water transportation are examined, as are reasons for the gradual disappearance of scheduled long-distance service. The growth of the vacation cruising industry is also discussed. Travel by freighter is examined, and the advantages and disadvantages of this travel mode are described. Finally, alternative forms of cruising — via schooners, charter yachts and sailboats, riverboats, adventure cruises, and barges — are discussed.

QUESTIONS

1. List the important events that led to the development of mass production of the automobile.
2. Give three reasons why Americans own more automobiles than do citizens of any other nation.
3. List the five largest rental car companies. What percentage of the rental car market can be attributed to this group?
4. Define the term *recreational vehicle* (RV).
5. Why did sales of RVs drop significantly in 1980?
6. List three reasons for the decline in inter-city bus travel.
7. Why is charter bus service profitable while inter-city bus service is not?
8. What percentage of domestic long-distance travel in the United States was by railroad during the 1920s and 1930s?
9. Why did the number of railroad passengers decline after World War II?
10. What is *Amtrak*? What year was it formed? Has it been profitable?
11. What is a *zeppelin*? In which decades of the twentieth century were they used for commercial passenger service?
12. Of what significance was the Kelly Act of 1926 to the development of passenger airlines?
13. When was Pan American's first international passenger flight? Its first Pacific passenger flight? Its first Atlantic passenger flight?
14. In what year was the first turbojet aircraft introduced into commercial service?

15. In what year was the Boeing 747 introduced into commercial service? Which airline was first to use it?

16. In what year was the Concord supersonic jet introduced into commercial service? How fast does it fly? Why is it not allowed to fly over land at supersonic speeds?

17. List and explain three effects of airline deregulation.

18. What is the hub-and-spoke method of routing aircraft? What are the advantages and disadvantages of this method over direct routing of aircraft?

19. In what year did the first successful commercial steamship start to be used? What was the name of the steamship, and who developed it?

20. Name the first steam powered vessel to cross the Atlantic. How many days did the journey take?

21. List the characteristics of the *Great Eastern* that made it a unique ship.

22. During which decade of the twentieth century did transatlantic shipboard travel achieve its highest degree of popularity?

23. What date is considered to mark the beginning of the end of commercial transatlantic passenger ships? Why did this occur?

24. What became of each of the following ocean liners?
    a. *Queen Mary*
    b. *Queen Elizabeth*
    c. *France*

25. In which waters of the world do most cruise ships sail?

26. Why are vacation cruises becoming increasingly popular?

27. List and discuss four main attractions of vacationing on board cruise ships.

28. What are the advantages and disadvantages of travel by freighter?

29. What is a *schooner*?

30. In what ways would a barge trip differ from an ocean cruise?

Hospitality Business Perspectives

VI

Hospitality Business Organization

14

LEARNING OBJECTIVES

After reading and studying this chapter, you should be able to:

1. *Define the term organization.*
2. *Distinguish between the formal organization and the informal organization.*
3. *Explain how the formal organization relates to systems and subsystems.*
4. *Identify each of the following terms: (a.) Authority; (b.) Responsibility; (c.) Delegating; (d.) Accountability; (e.) Departmentalization; (f.) Coordinating; (g.) Span of control; (h.) Unity of command.*
5. *Define an organizational chart and draw organizational charts for the following kinds of business organizations (a.) Line; (b.) Line and staff; (c.) Functional.*
6. *Distinguish between institutional, managerial, and technical levels of an organization.*
7. *Distinguish between and give examples of centralized and decentralized organizations.*
8. *Explain the effect of organizational changes on the formal organization chart.*

INTRODUCTION

The previous chapters have been directed at specific topics unique to restaurants, hotels, and travel and tourism. We now turn our attention to those dimensions of the hospitality industry that have a more general application—organizing, managing, marketing, human resources, and accounting. The material covered in a discussion of these topics is applicable to all businesses, regardless of type. After all, every business—retail, manufacturing, wholesale, or any other—must concern itself with these things.

Over the years, general principles and theory have been developed that cover the areas we will discuss. The application of theory, however, is frequently different for manufacturing operations, retail establishments, and hospitality operations. Our discussion will focus on the application of organization, management, marketing, human resources, and accounting to hospitality businesses.

The discussion of these topics will be introductory in nature. Students generally take separate course work in several of the topics, so no attempt will be made to cover them completely. It is, however, desirable to discuss the basics of each topic in order that the student will gain a better understanding of their importance in the hospitality industry. These discussions will also prepare students for more advanced courses in the subject areas.

This chapter will focus on the basic forms and elements of the organization. Succeeding chapters will cover the remaining topics.

THE MEANING OF ORGANIZATION

The term *organization* is used to refer to a structured body of people established as an entity to work toward the achievement of specific goals or objectives. There are all sorts of organizations. Although some are businesses, others may be fraternities, sororities, clubs, leagues, or federations. Food service and lodging establishments clearly fit the definition, as well. Hotels, motels, and restaurants are organizations made up of people working to achieve particular objectives or goals. Some of the people direct operations, whereas others work at various jobs.

Having objectives or goals is a key element in the establishment of an organization. To be considered an organization, an entity must have a set of objectives, goals, or purposes that cannot be achieved without the collective and structured action of people within the organization. Some organizations consist of people whose aim is to get together for specific social purposes, or to carry out particular charitable objectives. Other organizations consist of people who have goals associated with a business purpose. A bridge club, for example, is an organization whose purpose is to get people together who enjoy playing bridge—a social goal. Similarly, United Way is a charitable organization whose primary goal is to provide financial assistance to worthwhile activities and groups—a charitable purpose.

The parallels with hospitality enterprises are clear. A transient hotel is an organization whose goal is to provide accommodations for people who are temporarily away from home. A restaurant is an organization established to provide food service for people.

So that any group can function and achieve its goals, it must be structured. The word *organized* is commonly used to suggest this. The job of organizing is one of the most important tasks of owners and managers. It involves deciding what work must be done to achieve the goals that have been established, then creating the jobs and job titles necessary to do the work. Most organizations have a president or director whose job is to establish or structure the organization, assign the necessary work to specific individuals, and oversee the operation of the organization.

The importance of suitable structure and organization cannot be over-emphasized. If a business or a fraternal group is properly organized, the work of pursuing its goals can proceed in an orderly manner. If it is not properly organized, there is a risk that its goals may not be achieved. For example, it is necessary in a restaurant that food be ordered, cooked, and served, that money be collected from customers, and that dishes be washed. If the job of collecting money from customers is given to the same person who is washing dishes, he or she would have to leave the dishwashing area to go into the dining room to collect money whenever a customer was ready to pay and leave; or, alternatively, customers would have to go to the dishwashing area to pay for their meals. And if guests were going into the dishwashing area to pay their bills, besides interrupting the dishwasher, the guests would get in the way of servers trying to do their jobs, as well. Confusion would result, and guests and employees would be unhappy. Employing a cashier and stationing him in a position convenient for departing guests, however, or permitting the servers to collect money from guests, would result in a more smoothly functioning organization.

Nevertheless, hiring additional personnel is not always a sign of better organization. In a small thirty-seat restaurant, for example, hiring five people to attend to each of the major functions—purchasing, receiving, storing, issuing, and production—would probably result in inefficient utilization of labor. Labor costs, then, might become too high for the restaurant to be profitable.

Thus, we can redefine an *organization* as an entity made up of people who have been assigned jobs and responsibilities in a way that will allow the work of that entity to proceed as smoothly as possible toward achieving its established goals.

Formal and Informal Organizations

Every enterprise actually has two organizational structures—one formal, the other informal. A *formal organization structure* refers to the division of work among employees, and their relationships to one another based on their jobs. The *informal organization* refers to the personal relationships of people in an organization, regardless of their jobs.

In the formal structure, jobs and job titles are consciously and formally established. Management—one individual or a group constituting a management team—sets up the formal organization, determining the particular tasks that constitute each job and giving each job a job title. Management determines the relationships that will exist among the jobs in the organization and establishes a hierarchy of jobs. This hierarchy indicates which job titles have greater power and responsibility. For example, suppose the general manager of a new hotel is given full authority to organize the entire enterprise. To do so, she divides the work to be done into jobs and assigns job titles for each one. In addition, the general manager establishes the chain of command. The term *chain of command* refers to the formal relationships among jobs in an organization and indicates channels of communication among them. These channels of communication are sometimes called the *reporting structure* of the organization. Figure 14.3 on page 395, for example, shows the formal organization of the Mountain Inn, a resort described in detail in Chapter 9. The room clerk at the Mountain Inn reports to the front office manager, who reports to the rooms division manager. The rooms division manager, in turn, reports to the general manager. The front office manager is the immediate superior of the room clerk. He gives directions and instructions to the room clerk; and, in turn, the room clerk is expected to keep the front office manager informed about events that affect front desk operations.

While the formal organization indicates the formal structure of an organization, the informal organization is the network of personal and social relationships that exists among those in the organization. The informal organization is quite different from the formal organization: It is based on the particular personalities, friendships, interpersonal influences, and abilities of the individuals working in the organization.

Within the informal organization, interpersonal relationships have little or no connection with the positions employees hold in the formal organization. The communications links in the informal organization are typically very different from those in the formal organization. In the formal organization, information moves through structured channels—via direct links between bosses and subordinates. In a hotel, for example, when a cook has a question about the count for a given banquet, he asks the chef. If the chef does not have the answer, she asks the food and beverage manager. If the cook is friendly with a secretary in the banquet office, however, he may simply call the secretary to obtain the necessary information through this informal channel, rather than use the formal network.

The informal organization can also have a significant effect on the way work gets done. For example, when a faucet in a hotel kitchen sink needs repair, a formal procedure for having it repaired usually exists: Cook informs chef, who fills out a

A supervisor oversees her assistant's work while a colleague looks on. Part of the purpose of an enterprise's formal organization is to impose a hierarchy of jobs, relationships, and responsibilities, or chain of command, through the directives of management. (Courtesy Wyndham Hotels and Resorts.)

work order, which is sent to the engineering department, where the chief engineer assigns the job to a plumber. The informal organization may offer an alternative approach: The cook merely tells his friend the plumber about the needed repair work, when the plumber comes into the kitchen for a cup of coffee. The latter approach saves both time and paper and is often the preferred method for dealing with problems.

Positions in the informal organization are typically based on friendship, as well as on real or perceived differences in ability, judgment, understanding, output, influence, or any other characteristic that those in the organization consider valid. An individual's position in the informal organization may be based on holding a specific position in the organization or on having a family relationship with others in the organization. Whatever the reason, the position someone holds in the informal organization may be of greater significance than that assigned in the formal organization.

Assume that one of the eight cooks in a particular restaurant is considered by the manager, the chef, and the other cooks to be especially talented. His work is generally admired by other employees. He is always the first to be asked by the chef to prepare new dishes, then to instruct the other cooks. This talented cook might gain great influence over menu selections, methods of service, hours of work, and other operational matters, because of the position he has in an informal organization. In the formal organization, he is merely a cook—the equal of all other cooks in the establishment. The formal organization does not give him the power and influence he exercises.

FORMAL ORGANIZATION VS. SYSTEMS

In Chapters 6 and 9, the concept of *systems* and *subsystems* was explained, and essential subsystems for food service and lodging properties were discussed. The alert student will be interested in the relationship between formal organizations and subsystems. At first glance, they appear to be similar because both deal with the flow of work and the interdependency of work in an organization. On closer examination, however, a distinction becomes evident. While systems and subsystems are concerned with the parts of the organization required to achieve the goals of the organization, the formal organization is concerned with jobs and job titles within the framework of the systems and subsystems. The essential subsystems in a food service organization are purchasing, receiving, storing and issuing, production, selling, and serving. In a lodging operation the essential subsystems are front office, housekeeping, maintenence, and security. *Formal organization* is the term used to describe how the work and jobs are structured to achieve the goals of the enterprise. The work may or may not be arranged along system or subsystem lines.

In larger organizations, the formal structure, as well as the work and jobs it includes, may closely coincide with the systems and subsystems established for day-to-day operations. For example, in a large lodging operation, a front office subsystem of the kind described in Chapter 9 may also be a department headed by a person having the title Front Office Manager. However, this is often not the case in smaller organizations. In a small property, the front office subsystem and several other subsystems may all appear on the formal organization chart as parts of a single unit or department headed by the general manager. This is the case in the Value Lodge, discussed in Chapter 9 and shown in Figure 14.2 in this chapter.

Similarly, the subsystems for purchasing, receiving, production, sales, and service in a major food service organization might each have a manager responsible for the operation of the one subsystem. But, in a small individual restaurant, the subsystems for purchasing, receiving, and production might be combined under one head—a person with the job title Chef–Steward.

CONCEPTS IN FORMAL ORGANIZATIONS

In order to comprehend the concept of the formal organization, it is necessary to have some understanding of several key terms. These include *authority, responsibility, delegating, accountability, departmentalization, coordinating,* and *span of control.*

Authority

Authority is the power to act—to make decisions and to carry out assigned duties in a job. A room clerk in a hotel has the authority to check guests in. The clerk will quote room rates, engage in limited negotiations regarding rates with people who come to the desk seeking accommodations, and assign specific accommodations once an agreement has been reached. A banquet sales representative in a hotel has the authority to sell functions at the hotel. She has the power to discuss available banquet facilities and services with interested individuals and groups and to negotiate menus, prices, dates, and a range of related items. If agreement can be reached with the clients, she has the authority to commit the hotel to providing the facilities, goods, and services required.

The extent of the authority in each position is established by the person who has structured the organization. The power may be quite extensive, or it may be limited in one way or another. For example, the room clerk just mentioned may have the authority to assign only individual rooms. He may be prohibited from assigning suites — a duty assigned to the front office manager. The same clerk may have the authority to negotiate rates for rooms but may be instructed never to negotiate rates lower than a specified amount. The clerk might be directed to refer to the front office manager those people seeking rates lower than the specified figure. Similarly, the banquet sales representative may have the authority to commit the hotel only to dates within the next six months; those seeking to book functions twelve months in advance might be required to see the banquet manager.

Responsibility

Responsibility is an obligation to perform a task or to do a job in the manner intended by the person who devised the task or job. Responsibility is closely linked to authority: Having authority to perform a given job implies that the individual who has this authority also has an obligation to exercise this authority when necessary. The desk clerk just cited, given the authority to negotiate room rates, has an obligation to do so if necessary to sell a room. By the same reasoning, the banquet sales representative has an obligation to suggest menu items to potential clients.

It is important to understand that one cannot be held responsible for doing work that he or she lacks the authority to do. For example, if the front desk clerk had not been given the authority to negotiate room rates, he would not be held responsible for failing to register customers who rejected rooms because they considered the quoted rates too high. If the banquet sales representative is not given authority to discuss with potential customers menu selections other than those on a printed list, she cannot be held responsible for losing banquet business when menu selections do not appeal to customers.

Before concluding this brief discussion of *responsibility*, it is important to point out a major difference between responsibility and authority. It is possible that someone who has been given authority to perform a task may fail to do it responsibly — in the manner intended by the person who delegated the authority. For example, because a room clerk has the authority to negotiate room rates with potential customers, we cannot assume that he will do it. The clerk may be unwilling to negotiate rates and, as a result, could lose many customers to whom rooms might otherwise have been sold. And because the banquet sales representative has the authority to discuss menu selections with potential customers does not mean that she will necessarily do so. She may be unwilling to take the time to discuss the possible range of menu selections and thereby make potential customers less than satisfied with the final menus. Thus, while it is easy to assign authority to an individual, responsibility cannot be assigned effectively to someone unwilling to accept it. One hopes that those given authority are willing to accept the responsibility that accompanies it. They may or may not, however, be willing to do so; and it is important to understand that responsibility cannot be imposed on anyone by a superior. At best, it can only be accepted by those to whom accompanying authority has been given.

Delegating

The person in charge of an organization—the owner of a restaurant or the general manager of a hotel, for example—generally has the authority to perform all of the tasks in a business. Nonetheless, except for some particularly small operations, he or she has neither the time nor the expertise to do everything that needs to be done. The general manager of a hotel, for example, could not normally check guests in, clean guest rooms, and both prepare and serve meals, as well. Some or all of this work must be assigned to others. The process of assigning tasks and jobs to others is referred to as *delegating*. In a large hotel, a general manager delegates all of the work of the front office to a front office manager, delegates the work of selling hotel conventions and banquets to a director of sales, and delegates other work— housekeeping, food and beverage operations, and maintenance, for example—to other managers.

The work delegated to the front office manager includes that associated with the front office subsystem, as explained in Chapter 9: check-in, information, reservations, checkout. The front office manager cannot do all of the work alone. Thus, the work of checking in guests is delegated to room clerks; the work of taking reservations, to reservations clerks; and the work of checking guests out, to cashiers.

Similarly, the director of sales cannot do all the work delegated to her, so she delegates much of it to people working under her direction. Some of it, including booking banquets, is delegated to the banquet sales representative.

It is important to note that although it is possible to delegate authority, it is not possible to delegate all the responsibility associated with various jobs. The president still has a responsibility for achieving the goals of the organization. The front office manager still has a responsibility for the successful operation of the front office, and the sales manager still has a responsibility for achieving the sales goals of the sales department.

Accountability

Accountability is a term used to describe the process of holding a person answerable for the authority delegated to her. People given specific work assignments are delegated the authority to make decisions regarding that work, and they accept responsibility for the successful completion of the assigned work. If the work is not accomplished successfully, the person may be held accountable and may be reprimanded, demoted, transferred, or fired, as a result.

In the illustration above, if the front office and the sales departments are not achieving some or all of the goals established with them or for them, the department managers—the front office manager and the sales manager—may be held accountable. They may be reprimanded, fired, transferred, or demoted. Similarly, the front office manager and the sales manager each hold the members of their staffs accountable for doing their jobs properly and can take appropriate action when room clerks or sales representatives do not perform their jobs satisfactorily.

The above is analogous to a baseball team. If the owner thinks the team does not win enough games, the manager can be fired, even though he personally did not pitch, bat, or field. Similarly, the manager decides who among the players will pitch, bat, and field. He expects his players to perform in the manner intended; and if they do not, he will hold players accountable for poor performance. He may choose to bench a player when he is batting poorly or to take a pitcher out of the starting rotation when he is not pitching well.

Departmentalization

The process of arranging jobs into groups that work as a unit is called *departmentalization*. Not all hospitality organizations arrange jobs in the same way, but most organizations of the same type tend to have similar arrangements. For example, most larger lodging establishments group jobs related to guest reservations, check-in, checkout, and information into one department known as the front office. Other groups of jobs are collected under such department names as sales and marketing, housekeeping, telephone, food, beverage, accounting, human resources, and engineering. If two or more closely linked departments report to one high-level manager, they are said to constitute a *division*. An example is the rooms division of a hotel. It typically includes the front office department, housekeeping department, telephone department, and front services department. Each of these departments has its own manager, and all four managers report to a rooms division manager. The rooms division manager coordinates the activities of the four.

Coordinating

So that a business may run smoothly and achieve its goals, all elements of the business must work together in synchronization. *Coordinating* is the term that describes what managers do when they organize and integrate work so that members of an enterprise function together to achieve established objectives.

Departments in an enterprise cannot operate independently from one another. Neither can subsystems. Subsystems in a lodging operation, for example, must function effectively, in an integrated way, so that the operation can achieve its goals. In a food service operation the purchasing subsystem, for example, must work closely with the production subsystem, so that the menu can be produced. If members of the purchasing subsystem do not know what is to be on the menu or if they do not know the appropriate foods to order for each menu item, the production subsystem cannot properly produce the menu. Similarly, in a hotel front office, the members of the front desk subsystem must know how many rooms have been reserved by the reservations subsystem in order that they will know how many rooms can be rented to people who do not have reservations.

Besides coordinating activities within their departments, managers must also coordinate the activities of their departments with other areas of the operation so that the entire business achieves its objectives and functions smoothly. For example, the sales department in a hotel must coordinate the activities of the sales department with the reservations department, if the goal of maximum room revenue is to be achieved. It is important that the sales department not book groups at discounted room rates during periods when the reservations department can sell all of the rooms at full rate. It is also important that the sales department make a special effort to book groups into the hotel when the reservations department is unable to obtain large numbers of individual reservations.

Span of Control

Span of control refers to the number of people one person can supervise directly. This is important when an organization structure is being developed, because the span of control effectively determines the number of supervisory personnel in an organization. The greater the span of control, the fewer the number of supervisors.

The extent of the span of control in an enterprise is a matter of debate, with many different opinions. Some management experts feel that five to seven people is an ideal number for one person to supervise. Others feel that a single person can supervise many more than seven and still be an effective supervisor. Most management experts agree that no one number or range of numbers is appropriate in all situations. It depends on the abilities of the people concerned, the kinds of jobs being supervised, and the physical distance between the people being supervised.

Of the eight concepts basic to an understanding of the formal organization—authority, responsibility, delegating, accountability, departmentalization, coordinating, span of control, and unity of command—the concept of span of control reflects a synthesis of the others, and is the subject of some debate in regard to the number of jobs that may be effectively supervised and the appropriate level of supervisory involvement. Above is one example of span of control, showing a hotel kitchen's hierarchy: the executive chef (at left rear) accompanied by his sous and line chefs, the wait staff, the head waiter, and the food and beverage manager. (Courtesy Gardner Merchant.)

When the span of control is limited to a few people, a supervisor or manager is typically able to supervise the activities of these subordinates very closely. The supervisor may actually work alongside those being supervised, doing some of the same work. She can have greater understanding of the work and exercise more influence over the activities of the employees being supervised. When the span of control is extensive, the supervisor will have less opportunity to get involved directly in the activities of subordinates. Thus, they are likely to have more freedom to act independently.

Unity of Command

Unity of command is the term given to the practice of assigning each worker just one supervisor. The reporting structure in an organization should be sufficiently clear so that each worker knows who his supervisor is—whom he reports to. No worker should have more than one immediate supervisor because of the strong possibility for conflicting and contradictory orders.

ORGANIZATION CHARTS

An *organization chart* is simply a diagram of the formal department structure of an enterprise. It shows the jobs or job titles, the reporting structure (the chain of command), and the span of control at each level of the organization.

The work and jobs of any enterprise can be grouped into departments in several ways. Special terms are used to identify each of the types of organizations that result. These include *line*, *line and staff*, and *functional*, among others. Examples of the functional type, however, are not common in individual restaurants, hotels, and motels; they are much more common at the corporate level.

Line Organization

In a *line organization*, a direct flow of authority exists from the top position in the organization through the chain of command to the bottom. Smaller food service and lodging operations typically use a line form of organization. The organization chart shows specific jobs or job titles, the reporting structure, and the span of control. Figure 14.1 shows a line organization chart for the Steak Shack, a restaurant described in Chapter 6.

The lines connecting the job titles are lines of authority. They show the *reporting structure* of the establishment—the manner in which authority is delegated. The chef, head bartender, and dining room manager report directly to the manager. The cooks and dishwashers report to the chef. The bartenders report to the head bartender. The busers report to the servers, and the servers report to the dining room manager.

It is especially important in a line organization to ensure that no employee has more than one immediate supervisor—the practice identified as unity of command. If a person reports to more than one person, a probability exists of opposing or contradictory instructions that will result in conflict and confusion. If the chef in Figure 14.1, for example, were to start giving instructions to servers to serve plates of food from the right, whereas the dining room manager had instructed them to serve from the left, the servers could become confused and frustrated—not knowing which instructions to follow. If the chef wanted an item served in a particular way, the correct procedure would be to inform the dining room manager, who could, in turn, instruct the servers. Similarly, if the manager wanted to change a standard recipe, she should not go directly to the cook preparing that item; the proper procedure would be for the manager to tell the chef, who would in turn instruct the cooks. If the manager did not follow that course, confusion and conflict would be likely to result.

The organization chart does not show which of the subsystems in the organization are the responsibility of particular job titles or positions, except by

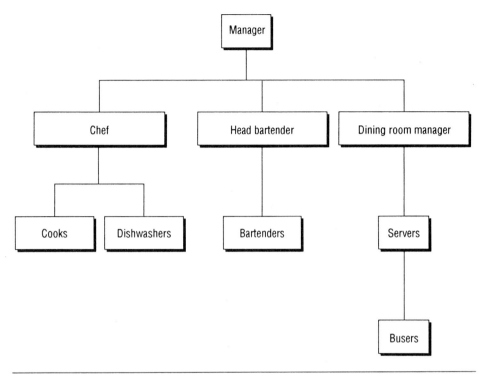

FIGURE 14.1 *Organization chart: Steak Shack*

inference. Authority and responsibility for subsystems are revealed in job descriptions, which are discussed in Chapter 17.

In the case of the Steak Shack, job descriptions have been written and both the authority and the responsibility for the subsystems that purchase, receive, store, and produce food are delegated to the chef. The purchasing of liquor is done by the manager, but the authority and responsibility for the subsystems that store and issue liquor and produce drinks are delegated to the head bartender. The authority and responsibility for the subsystem that sells menu items and serves food are delegated to the dining room manager.

Figure 14.2 shows the organization chart for the Value Lodge, discussed in Chapter 9.

At the Value Lodge, the only employees are the room attendants. The co-owners are the entire management team. Except for cleaning rooms, they perform all the work associated with the several subsystems: front office, housekeeping, security, and telephone. The organizational chart is extremely simple. In small, uncomplicated organizations such as the Value Lodge, a formal organization chart, in written form, is seldom needed.

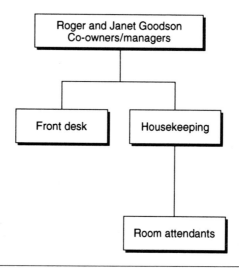

FIGURE 14.2   *Organization chart: Value Lodge*

Line and Staff

As organizations grow, positions are added and the organizational structure becomes more complex. One type of position likely to be added is that known as a staff position. Staff positions provide assistance, expertise, or advice to those who direct the organization. A staff position is without line authority, except for any assistants reporting directly to the individual in the position.

In many of the larger and busier lodging properties, general managers have assistants with such titles as Assistant to the General Manager. These assistants are often assigned special projects, such as supervising the renovation of all kitchens and dining rooms or all guest accommodations, over a period of time. Sometimes these assistants attend to routine tasks that a general manager might otherwise have to perform personally. Thus they free up time for the general manager that can be used to better purpose. In addition, assistants in these staff positions often provide recommendations that can be accepted or rejected by their bosses.

A human resource department is another example of a staff department in hospitality organizations. Human resource departments recruit and screen applicants for jobs, prepare job descriptions, supervise the benefits packages, and perform other services for the line departments.

Typical of staff positions in large chains are legal counsels, advertising specialists, research specialists, and development specialists.

A larger, more complicated line and staff organization is found in the Mountain Inn, discussed in Chapter 9, and is illustrated by the organization chart

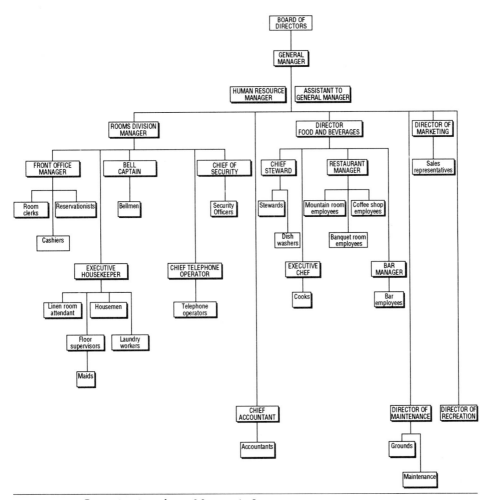

FIGURE 14.3 *Organization chart: Mountain Inn*

in Figure 14.3. It includes two of the staff positions just mentioned—an assistant to the general manager and a human resources manager.

The Mountain Inn has a board of directors and a general manager. Reporting to the general manager are the assistant to the general manager, the human resource manager, rooms manager, chief accountant, food and beverage director, director of maintenance, director of marketing, and director of recreation.

Reporting to the rooms division manager are the front office manager, executive housekeeper, bell captain, chief of security, and chief telephone operator.

Within each of these departments, various managers and workers report to the department head. Reporting to the executive housekeeper are the linen room attendant, the laundry manager, floor supervisors, and housemen. Reporting to the director of food and beverages are the chief steward, the executive chef, the restaurant manager, and the bar manager.

The pharmacy, hair stylists, and boutiques do not appear on the organization chart. This is because they are independent contractors — concessionaires — who lease space for their businesses in the hotel. They do not come under the control of the management.

Each manager has employees reporting to him. For example, the laundry manager has laundry workers reporting to her, and the floor supervisors have room attendants reporting to them.

The span of control is indicated on the chart. The general manager has eight people reporting to him, the rooms manager has five, and the food and beverages director has four. Note that unity of command is evident in the organization chart: Every employee at the Mountain Inn reports to only one manager. Note, too, how closely the organization chart follows the subsystems described in Chapter 9.

The organization chart for the Mountain Inn is not intended to be representative of all resort hotels. Every property has its own unique organization chart with differing titles for department heads; and each reflects the chain of command that management chooses to establish for the particular property.

Another organization chart for a line and staff organization appears in Figure 14.4. This charts the line and staff organization for a restaurant chain.

Functional Organizations

Occasionally one encounters hospitality organizations in which some employees report to more than one supervisor — an apparent violation of unity of command. In these organizations, functional specialists supervise all of the employees doing work in their specialty, regardless of the department or unit to which the workers are assigned. For example, there are some chain organizations in the lodging industry in which some employees in units of the chain have two bosses: (1) the general manager of the individual unit in which they work and (2) a functional specialist in the central office, who supervises all those working within his particular specialty. Chief accountants in the individual hotels may report both to the general managers of those hotels and to the corporate treasurer. Similarly, marketing directors in the hotels may report both to the general managers and to a corporate vice-president for marketing.

The chart in Figure 14.5 illustrates a functional organization in which the director of marketing and the chief accountant report to corporate officers, as well as to the general manager of their hotel.

Assume that the director of marketing in the individual hotel has been instructed to place less emphasis on booking group business and more on individ-

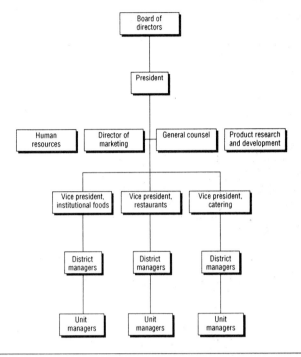

FIGURE 14.4   *Organization chart, restaurant chain*

FIGURE 14.5   *Chain hotel*

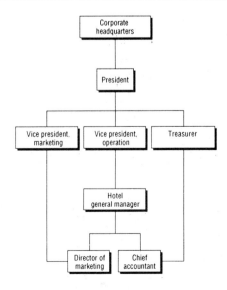

ual room reservations at higher average rates. At the same time, the corporate vice-president for marketing instructs the marketing directors in all hotels of the chain to increase the number of group bookings, even at lower than average rates, in order to maximize occupancy rates.

In another example, consider the case of a hotel night engineer who reports to two bosses: the chief engineer of the hotel, who only works a day shift, and a night manager, who works the same shift. One evening the night engineer arrives for work at midnight to find a note from the chief engineer. It instructs him to change burned out light bulbs in the corridors on all floors in response to a directive from the general manager, who is expecting a large convention group to check in the following day. Before he can begin this project, however, the night manager directs him to repair a malfunctioning walk-in freezer unit in the main kitchen. It contains a large quantity of frozen food that has already begun to thaw. Either of these projects will require most of the engineer's shift to complete.

Clearly, the director of marketing and the night engineer in these properties have conflicting directives from their bosses. Situations such as these can be sources of serious discomfort to the employees who face them. Employees who encounter these situations may eventually resign rather than continue to deal with the conflicting demands of their superiors. Until conflicts such as these are resolved, affected employees are subject to continuing frustration. Similar potential difficulties are inherent in all functional organizations.

Because of this, no hospitality enterprise follows the functional model exclusively—although some parts of some organizations operate this way. When they do, it is normally of necessity rather than by preference. The functional organization model is best suited for enterprises that depend on individuals with highly specialized skills—scientists developing a space program, for example.

LEVELS OF ORGANIZATION

It is common for chain organizations and large individual establishments to have three distinctly different organizational levels: institutional, managerial, and technical.

Institutional Level

The institutional level of an organization directs its attention to factors in the external environment that affect the organization: the national or regional economy; federal, state, and local legislation; consumer trends in food service and lodging; market trends for products purchased by the organizations; and any other issues that have significant impact on the organization. The institutional level is that part of the organization that gathers pertinent outside information, then interprets and communicates it, as necessary, for others in the organization. This is normally attended to by top management and those in staff positions reporting to top management. In Figure 14.4, the president, vice-presidents, and staff reporting to the president would be considered institutional-level management.

Managerial Level

The managerial level of an organization coordinates and controls work, makes normal business decisions, resolves conflicts, and deals with problems in the work environment. The managerial level normally consists of middle and supervisory management. As illustrated in Figure 14.3, the rooms division manager, food and beverage director, front office manager, executive housekeeper, executive chef, purchasing steward, bar manager, chief of security, and restaurant manager of the Mountain Inn constitute its managerial level personnel.

Technical Level

The technical level of an organization includes those who perform the specific activities needed to make the business function. The technical level is normally considered to be those people who do the work associated with their departments. In the Mountain Inn they include the room clerks, reservationists, telephone operators, bellmen, cooks, and maids.

In some organizations employees or managers may operate at more than one level. For example, a chef in a smaller restaurant or hotel may be part of both the managerial and the technical levels, because he not only manages the kitchen but also prepares food. The general manager of a hotel may be considered at both the institutional and managerial levels, depending on the extent to which he is involved in the operation of the hotel and at the same time concerns himself with outside issues.

CENTRALIZED VERSUS DECENTRALIZED ORGANIZATIONS

The terms *centralized* and *decentralized* refer to the extent to which decision making is retained by top management or delegated to those with lower-ranking positions on the organization chart.

In a centralized organization, decisions tend to be made at the top. There is limited delegating of decision-making authority to managers at lower levels.

For example, in a centralized food service chain, purchasing of all foods for the individual units—the restaurants—may be done through a central purchasing office. Requisitions for food supplies are prepared by restaurant managers, and all food orders are placed by the central office. The unit managers do not have the authority to purchase locally, nor do they have the authority to decide which brands they will purchase or what size containers the food will come in. A procedure of this nature enables top management to maintain close control over

In a centralized organization, directives are issued from a top tier of management executives. In a centralized restaurant chain, for instance, a test kitchen located at corporate headquarters (top) may issue inventory guidelines and portion and cooking instructions in order to maintain quality and production control throughout the organization over any items introduced to the menu. In another example, a centralized organization may create a single training facility to eliminate training at the local level, and any inconsistencies in company policy it may create. (Courtesy dāka, Inc., copyright © 1988; courtesy Wyndham Hotels and Resorts.)

the quality and quantity of the foods purchased. It may also make it possible to purchase the foods at more favorable prices than could be obtained by the individual restaurants.

Many centralized restaurant chains do not allow individual restaurant managers to change menu items; menus are prepared at the central office. This enables a central purchasing office to create a standard purchase list of foods for all restaurants in the chain. Many of the organizations that operate this way also do not allow changes in menu prices without the approval of central management. This enables top management to exercise control over profit margins.

Many centralized chains prepare organization charts and job descriptions at the central office for units in the chain. Frequently, all units have the same organization chart, and all operate in the same manner. When this is the case, management personnel can be transferred from one unit to another without the need for additional training.

Many chains have central training facilities for both management and non-management personnel. This takes responsibility for training away from local managers. When training is required at the local level, personnel from the central office are sent to the unit to do the training.

The centralized approach to management allows the top executives to retain much greater control over the individual units in the chain. Managers in these units follow directions and standard operating procedures, making very few decisions for themselves.

Fast-food chains frequently use centralized management techniques. McDonald's is a prime example. Food is purchased centrally and sent to individual units from company warehouses. Standard menus, procedures, and personnel policies are established and written at the central office. Training for managers is done at a central location. McDonald's strives to make each unit in the organization identical to all other units. This ensures that any customer purchasing a particular menu item in any unit will receive the same item he or she would have received in any other unit of the chain.

In decentralized organizations, authority and responsibility are delegated to the lowest practical level. Top management make only those decisions it believes should not be made at lower levels in the organization. In decentralized food service operations, unit managers can select the items to include in their menus, even if these will result in menus that are different from other units in the organization. They can also purchase foods from any purveyors they choose, establish their own formal organizations, and make pricing decisions for their menus.

Advocates of decentralized management believe that it is better that decisions be made at as low a level as possible. They point out that each unit in a chain is subject to local conditions that are unique, and that decisions made in a central office may not consider local conditions. For example, the food preferences of communities differ from one part of the country to another and from community to community. Thus, goes the argument, decisions as to menu items should be left to local managers who are more familiar with local tastes. Many times, they say, food can be purchased more cheaply in a local area than it can be purchased by the central purchasing organization; and sometimes the quality of locally purchased ingredients is better than that of standardized items purchased by a central commissary.

Further, they point out that managers not allowed to make their own decisions do not develop and progress as managers. Good managers, they say, will not continue to work for organizations that stifle their initiative and creative ability. They will soon move on to organizations that allow them to make decisions. Thus, the argument goes, centralized organizations are unable to retain and develop talented managers for promotion to higher levels.

ORGANIZATIONAL CHANGES

Once formal organization charts have been established, they seldom remain the same for long. As organizations increase in size or as management sees additional work that must be done, new positions are created and added to the organization chart.

Similarly, if it becomes necessary to reduce the size of an organization because of lack of business or a reduction in the number of services offered, positions will be eliminated and the chart will decrease in size. When reorganization occurs, positions are frequently combined and one person may be required to perform the duties formerly assigned to two or more in the old organization chart. In the Mountain Inn, for example, a very slow season could make it necessary for the front office manager to eliminate one morning room clerk's position. He might attend to those duties himself in order to save payroll costs. Another option might be to eliminate the cashier's position, combining the duties of room clerk and cashier in one position. In either case, such organizational changes would require revision of a formal organization chart.

SUMMARY

In this chapter the basic principles of organization are discussed. The term *organization* is defined as a body of people established as a structured entity to carry out specific goals or objectives. The distinction between formal and informal organizations is made. The relationship between subsystems and organizations is discussed, and several key terms are defined—including *authority, responsibility, delegating, accountability, departmentalization, coordination, span of control*, and *unity of command*. The concept and purpose of a formal organization chart is discussed and illustrated. Three common types of organization charts—line, line and staff, and functional—are discussed and illustrated. The institutional, managerial, and technical levels of organizations are defined and discussed. Centralized and decentralized approaches to management are explained, compared, and contrasted. Finally, organizational changes and their effects on the formal organization are outlined.

QUESTIONS

1. Define the term *organization*. List four different types of organizations.
2. Contrast the formal and informal organization.
3. How is the departmental structure of the formal organization in a large hotel related to the systems and subsystems required for its operation?
4. Define and illustrate the following terms used in business organizations:
   a. authority
   b. responsibility
   c. delegating
   d. accountability
   e. departmentalization
   f. coordination
   g. span of control
   h. unity of command
5. Why does the authority associated with a given position—room clerk, for example—vary considerably from one hotel to another?
6. Can full responsibility for a given job be delegated? Why?
7. Can a cook be held responsible for the unacceptable taste of a given menu item he prepared if he followed the recipe exactly? Why?
8. Why might the owner of a 2,000-room hotel delegate management of the front office subsystem, while the owner of a 30-unit motel might not?
9. Can all responsibility for the food quality in a restaurant be delegated to the chef? Why?
10. Provide two examples of activities that require the coordination of two departments in a lodging operation.
11. What factors determine the span of control in a hospitality organization?
12. What is the major risk associated with violating the principle of unity of command?
13. Define *organization chart*. Draw organization charts for each of the following types of organizations:

a. line
b. line and staff
c. functional
14. What are the lines connecting the various job titles in an organization chart called? What purpose do they serve?
15. What is a staff position in an organization? Give two examples of staff positions in a large restaurant chain.
16. Provide an example of functional organization in a hospitality enterprise.
17. Distinguish between the institutional, managerial, and technical levels of an organization.
18. Distinguish between and give two examples of centralized and decentralized organizations.
19. What are the major advantages to centralized management in hospitality organizations? To decentralized management?

Managing Hospitality Operations

15

LEARNING OBJECTIVES

After reading and studying this chapter, you should be able to:

1. Define the term <u>management</u>.
2. List and define the three levels of management.
3. Define the term <u>planning</u> as used in management.
4. Categorize plans by time and type.
5. Identify the ten steps in the planning process.
6. Identify the six steps in the organizing process.
7. Define the term <u>directing</u> as used in management.
8. List and discuss three styles of leadership.
9. Identify six motivating factors influencing employees to work toward organizational goals.
10. Define the term <u>management by objectives</u> and list the steps in the process.
11. Distinguish between two opposing sets of assumptions about subordinates, identified as <u>Theory X</u> and <u>Theory Y</u>.
12. Define the term <u>control</u> as used in management.
13. Identify eight control techniques used in hospitality management.
14. List the four steps in the control process.
15. Discuss the relative importance of technical skills, human relations skills, and conceptual skills to managers at each of the three levels of management.
16. List and explain six rules for successful hospitality management.

INTRODUCTION

In Chapter 1, it was pointed out that hospitality operations have special characteristics that differentiate them from many other enterprises: They sell service
products, rather than durable products; and they sell these products primarily to
travelers. Because of the special nature of these service products, managers and
employees in hospitality enterprises are commonly in day-to-day, face-to-face
contact with customers. Hospitality employees are continually interacting with
customers and delivering services. These are the "moments of truth," and the
outcomes are impressions of the enterprise from which customers make judgments.
Some of those judgments have to do with its management.

Because the hospitality industry differs from most others, successful management of hospitality operations is somewhat different from successful management of factories or retail stores, for example. In this chapter we will examine some
basic principles of applied management for hospitality enterprises.

MANAGEMENT DEFINED

Management is defined as a process by means of which available resources are
combined in an effective and structured way to achieve organizational goals.
There are three important elements in this definition:

1. Process
2. Resources
3. Organizational goals

Each of these should be discussed briefly before we proceed.

A *process* is a series of actions or operations that achieve an end. The
management process is ongoing and unending. It is also an abstract process: Those
responsible for managing can be seen deciding, asking, directing, requesting,
ordering, commanding, permitting, mandating, requiring, examining, judging,
agreeing, viewing, inspecting, disagreeing, thanking, and so on. This is how they
do it, and the list of verbs indicating what they do is as endless as the process.

The *resources* available to management are people, money, time, work
procedures and methods, energy, materials, and equipment, among others. People
accomplish work, using energy, materials, and equipment; but people are also
valuable resources for ideas to improve both the service product and the management of the enterprise. Money is used to procure the facilities and materials
necessary to carry out the objectives of the enterprise and to reward people for
their efforts on its behalf. Work procedures and methods help make operations run
smoothly. Energy, materials, and equipment are necessary for the enterprise to
function in the manner intended.

All of the above are combined and used to achieve *organizational goals*. If management is able to combine these resources in ways that will achieve the goals that have been established, we speak of management as being successful. If not, management has been unsuccessful.

LEVELS OF MANAGEMENT

There are three levels of management in the hospitality industry:

1. Top management
2. Middle management
3. Supervisory management

Top Management

Top managers are those at the institutional level of an organization chart, as described in Chapter 14. Typical titles for top managers include *chairman of the board*, *president*, and *vice-president*. In the hospitality industry, one also finds top managers with simple titles such as *owner* (in the restaurant business, for example), and *vice-president* and *managing director* (in the hotel business).

Top-level managers establish goals for an enterprise, organize it, obtain financing, develop plans, make policy, and establish appropriate controls. They also concern themselves with conditions in the external environment that will have some impact on the enterprise. The external environment includes the economy; the local, state, or national political climate; and the social environment. Decisions made by managers at this level affect the entire organization.

Middle Management

Middle managers carry out the policies and directives of top management. Typical job titles for middle managers in the lodging segment of the hospitality industry include *general manager, resident manager, director of marketing*, and *director of food and beverage*. In the food service segment, typical titles include *district manager, area manager*, and *restaurant general manager*.

Middle managers develop plans, make policies, and prepare budgets for the parts of an organization (units or departments) under their jurisdiction. The plans, policies, and budgets for their units must conform to the goals and policies established by top management for the organization as a whole. Middle managers coordinate the work of supervisory managers. Decisions made by middle managers affect the units or departments they supervise.

Supervisory Management

Supervisory management is the level of management that is assigned responsibility for directing nonmanagerial employees. Supervisory managers schedule work, follow budgets, and supervise the work of employees. In the hospitality industry, most department managers are supervisory managers. Typical job titles for managers in this category include *front office manager, restaurant manager, head housekeeper, chef,* and *bar manager.*

It is not uncommon in the hospitality industry to find managers whose duties and responsibilities encompass some of those normally assigned to managers at other levels. A top manager may also have middle-management duties and responsibilities. A middle manager may have some supervisory responsibilities and may even have some of those normally reserved for top managers. A supervisory manager may have both middle-management responsibilities and specific duties normally assigned to technical-level employees in other organizations.

In very small organizations there may be only one manager, who has duties and responsibilities associated with all three levels of management. For example, the Value Lodge described in Chapter 9 has a husband and wife management team. They must attend to such top-level management concerns as the political and social environment of the area, its tax structure, level of inflation, and general

In addition to the top and middle levels, supervisory management is one of the three levels of management in the hospitality industry. The function of management at all levels is to plan, organize, direct, and control to achieve the goals of the company. Shown below is a restaurant manager discussing the weekly work schedule with a member of the wait staff. The number of managers in each level and the extent of their responsibilities varies with the size and type of the organization. (Courtesy Marriott Hotels & Resorts.)

wage structure, and any other area matters that might affect the business climate. At the same time, they are both middle managers and supervisory managers. They make policy and budget decisions, and they also direct and supervise the housekeeping staff.

As the size and complexity of an enterprise increases, it becomes difficult for only one level of management to attend to the responsibilities of all three. As growth occurs, additional managers are employed and differentiation in levels of responsibility becomes more evident. Eventually, with continued growth, it becomes necessary to have the three distinct levels. Managers at each level will then tend to limit their responsibilities to that level.

THE FUNCTIONS OF MANAGEMENT

Management at all levels is often said to have four specific functions:

1. Planning
2. Organizing
3. Directing
4. Controlling

Planning

Planning is the primary task of management. At the level of top management, *planning* is the process of defining goals and objectives for the organization and determining the appropriate means for achieving them. In its broadest sense, planning is an attempt to define the organization's future state: to determine in the present what the organization will look like in the future—one year or five years from now. In the hospitality industry, top management must make plans that will define the service products to be offered in the future, the rate of expansion for the organization, the rate of sales increases necessary to sustain that growth, and the means for financing any of the organization's future plans. These are a few examples of the high-level and long-range planning in which top management engages.

At the middle-management level, planning tends to be more pragmatic and more short term. With knowledge of top management's plans for the coming year, middle managers plan annual budgets for their departments or units, and they make plans for dealing with such related problems as increases and decreases in staffing needs. Their plans are linked to the day-to-day realities of the units or departments they manage.

At the supervisory level, planning tends to be for the very near term. Supervisory managers must make plans for meeting expected levels of demand today, tomorrow, and next week. Their plans deal with such problems as having adequate staff and sufficient food available in the restaurant to prepare and serve the next meal and meals for the balance of the week. Or they may deal, for example, with having enough housekeeping staff and linens on hand in the hotel to prepare for 100 percent occupancy for the next three days. At the supervisory level, chefs plan menus, dining room managers plan schedules for servers and other personnel, and front office managers plan orders for such paper supplies as reservation forms and registration cards.

CLASSIFICATION OF PLANS. Plans are typically classified in two ways: by time and by type.

Time.   Plans can be classified as long term or short term. Long-term plans are those that cover periods greater than one year. Management of such large enterprises as national food service or lodging chains make long-term plans that define expectations for the organization five or more years into the future. Long-term plans may deal with new service products to be introduced, new units to be constructed, new markets to be developed, or any number of other issues related to the long-term health and vitality of the organization. For the top management of chain hotels and restaurants, one of the more important of the long-term plans is that dealing with expansion of the number of units in the chain. This indicates the rate of growth envisioned by management. Although smaller organizations should also engage in long-term planning, they are less likely to do so. In some, top management must assume so many of the duties normally carried out by middle managers and supervisors that they have no time for long-term planning.

Long-term plans tend to be general in nature, rather than specific. The reason for this is the great difficulty of looking more than twelve months into the future. There are too many possibilities for unforeseen changes that can wreck plans carefully made a year or so before. Inflation, recession, war, and such natural disasters as floods, hurricanes, and earthquakes can devastate long-term plans. Because long-term plans typically only provide direction for an enterprise, however, top management makes long-term plans while recognizing that conditions in the external environment are likely to necessitate adjustments to those plans.

Short-term plans are those developed to achieve rather specific goals during the coming year. Managers make short-term plans, usually for under a year, to generate specific amounts of revenues, at specific levels of expenses, in order to achieve specific levels of profit. Short-term plans may also deal with renovating parts of a building, purchasing new kitchen equipment, and other similar immediate capital expenditures. Other possibilities include plans for marketing, training, and staffing—any planning to achieve short-term goals.

Type.   Plans can also be classified by type. Top management makes many different types of plans, including financial plans, personnel plans, building plans, and marketing plans.

Middle-level managers develop budget plans and training plans for their departments, and they plan for the replacement of essential equipment—ranges for the kitchen or beds for the guest rooms, for example.

Supervisors also develop various types of plans. Their plans are for such immediate needs as the scheduling of employees for the coming week and the purchasing of perishable foods for the next three days.

STEPS IN THE PLANNING PROCESS. The planning process follows ten logical steps:

1. Determine objectives.
2. Identify assumptions or premises on which the objectives are based.
3. Identify alternative plans to achieve those objectives.
4. Determine the resources required to carry out each alternative.
5. Assess the impact of each alternative on the enterprise.
6. Select the best plan from among the alternatives.
7. Establish a timetable for carrying out the plan.
8. Determine subsidiary objectives.
9. Develop a budget.
10. Select methods for implementing the plan.

These steps in planning are used by managers at all levels. To illustrate, assume that top management at the Mountain Inn has decided to expand its operation. They have assessed the skiing market and determined that the number of skiers coming to the nearby ski slopes will be increasing in the coming years. They have also looked at current business at the Mountain Inn and found a growing percentage of guests coming to the area to ski. They have decided to expand at the rate of 50 rooms per year for the next five years, for a total of 250 new rooms. These objectives, although very specific, will be subject to change if circumstances change.

The first two steps in the planning process have been accomplished. Objectives have been set and the assumptions on which the goals are based have been identified. The goal is to add an additional 250 rooms over the next five years. The assumption is that the number of skiers coming to the area will increase at an appropriate rate.

Management must then look at alternative plans for achieving the objective of adding an additional 250 rooms. One way might be to build a new wing onto the present structure. Another would be to build a new structure near the present facility. Costs associated with each must be assessed at this stage.

Before proceeding, management must assess the impact of the various alternatives on the enterprise. For example, accommodating an increased number of guests in the new units might create a need for additional parking facilities or increased dining room space. There might also be a need for additional kitchen facilities or even for a larger front office to check in the additional guests.

After considering alternative plans, as well as their cost and impact, management then selects the best plan. Once the plan is selected, a timetable for the project must be established that will indicate when the project will start and how long it will take.

The subsidiary objectives to be accomplished must also be considered. For example, if additional dining room space or additional parking is needed, these objectives must be achieved at suitable times.

At this stage, a budget for the project must be developed. If financing for the project is necessary, it must be arranged before work begins.

The next step is to determine how the work is to be done. For the Mountain Inn project, specialists will be needed: architect, interior designer, and general contractor, among them. Decisions must be made about the layout and design of the rooms, corridors, and other elements of the facility—as well as about furnishings, carpeting, and lighting, among others. In addition, details concerning the heating, air conditioning, and other engineering systems in the structure must be planned.

Essentially, this is the planning process used by managers at all levels. The same planning process is used by middle managers and supervisors. For example, the chef at the Mountain Inn must make plans each Monday to prepare and serve adequate quantities of food for the number of guests expected during the week that begins the *following* Monday. The objective is to have an adequate supply of foods of appropriate quality and variety to meet guests' expectations. The plans are clearly simpler than those required for constructing a new facility, but the process is generally the same. With simple plans, some of the steps may not be necessary.

Organizing

Organizing follows planning as the next logical step in the management process. It is the second function of management. After management has developed plans designed to achieve some objective, those plans must be carried out. That is the purpose of the additional steps in the management process—organizing, directing, and controlling.

Organizing means coordinating the use of resources, human and otherwise, to achieve established objectives. To organize work in a hospitality enterprise, management determines how human and other resources will be combined and activated to achieve established objectives.

Organizing also requires a series of steps:

1. Determine specific work necessary to implement plans and achieve objectives.
2. Group the work into logical patterns or structures.
3. Assign the work to specific people.
4. Allocate the resources required for accomplishing the work.
5. Coordinate the assigned work.
6. Evaluate the results of the organizing process.

Assume that the chef in the earlier example has completed plans to feed the expected number of guests for the following week. The first step in the organizing process is to determine what must be done to carry out the plans. Clearly, food must be ordered and a staff schedule must be set up. The second step is to group the work into logical patterns. To do this, the chef must decide which menu items should be prepared by each of the stations in the kitchen. The third step is to assign the preparation of the various menu items to specific cooks. Next, each cook will be told the number of portions of each item to prepare and will be given recipes to use. Additionally, the chef will make provision for the ingredients to be on hand when needed. Next, he will coordinate the work, synchronizing the efforts of all personnel so as to achieve the established goals. He will make sure that the roasts are placed in ovens in sufficient time to be ready for service, that the vegetables have been cut up and prepared for cooking, that soups and sauces have been prepared. As the work proceeds, he will continually evaluate the results of the organizing process to determine whether or not changes or alterations are required.

In similar fashion, an executive housekeeper must organize the work in that department so that the goals of the department are achieved. Necessary supplies of linen, towels, and other items must be ordered; vacant rooms must be prepared for occupancy; and occupied rooms must be maintained, among many other tasks. The work must be divided and apportioned so that the desired results are achieved. Linen and other supplies must be ordered, and some determination must be made of the number of rooms to be assigned to each housekeeper. Stations must be established for the housekeepers, who must then be scheduled and assigned to stations. Sufficient linen and other supplies must be made available to the house-keepers at each station. The work must be coordinated in such a way that occupied rooms are made up while guests are out and, at the same time, vacant rooms are cleaned and prepared so that they are ready when arriving guests check into the hotel. Finally, the executive housekeeper must evaluate the process, to determine if changes need to be made.

Each of these steps is not necessarily required every day. Once work and satisfactory work patterns are organized, they simply become daily routines. Although they should be reevaluated on a regular basis, they are unlikely to be changed unless new, more effective or efficient ways are found.

Directing

The third management function is directing. *Directing* is the process of achieving organizational goals by leading, motivating, and supervising subordinates. Directing is important at all levels of management, but it is particularly important at the supervisory level. After all, compared with many other businesses, hospitality operations tend to be more labor intensive. This means they require a greater number of employees at the technical level to accomplish their routine daily work. The vast majority of employees report to supervisory managers. In food and beverage operations, the technical-level employees who report to supervisory managers include servers, busers, cooks, dishwashers, and bartenders. In hotels and motels, they include housekeepers, bell staff, room clerks, telephone operators, grounds keepers, sales representatives, and accounting office clerks. Technical-level employees who report to supervisory managers account for as much as 90 percent of all hospitality employees.

Leadership

One important element in the process of directing is leadership. *Leadership* is the ability to persuade others to work toward achieving established goals.

Leadership has always been an important element in all human enterprise. Many agree that leadership accounts for the success of such varied enterprises as businesses, armed forces, governments, religious organizations, and trade unions. Whenever an organization is labeled *successful*, the leader is given the credit. Thus, it is not surprising that behavioral scientists have been studying leadership for a long time. Many have sought to identify the characteristics of leadership.

Unfortunately, all the thought and effort that has gone into the study of leadership characteristics has not produced broad agreement. Behavioral scientists have studied Winston Churchill, Indira Gandhi, Franklin Roosevelt, Joseph Stalin, Margaret Thatcher, Adolf Hitler, Abraham Lincoln, George Washington, Martin Luther King, Jr., Golda Meir, Dwight Eisenhower, Douglas MacArthur, and many others and have found no specific universal characteristics that set them apart from other human beings. They had very different personalities from one another and they often had very different approaches to motivating subordinates. They were as diverse as the people they led.

Behavioral scientists have also looked at the styles used by business leaders who successfully motivate employees to work toward achieving established goals. Although they have not identified any set of universal characteristics exhibited by these leaders, they have documented a number of different leadership styles and found that some seem to work better than others in given situations.

STYLES OF LEADERSHIP. *Leadership* is the ability to influence others to behave in certain ways. To understand leadership, one must focus on the manner in which the leader in an organization gets others to do work. *Leadership style* is the manner in which influence is exercised. There are a number of leadership styles, at least three of which can be identified as basic: autocratic, democratic, and free rein.

An *autocratic leader* is one who uses power overtly, making decisions without consulting others, and issuing orders to subordinates. The autocratic leader is clearly the boss. He or she seldom asks subordinates for comments, suggestions, or opinions. Decisions are made and announced, and orders are given as the boss sees fit.

Leadership is an important element of the directing function of management. Shown above is the democratic style of leadership, where a manager consults with her subordinates and considers their suggestions, comments, and opinions before making decisions that will impact the entire department. (Courtesy Red Lion Hotels and Inns.)

A *democratic leader* is one who normally seeks comments, suggestions, and opinions from subordinates. He or she commonly asks for advice and consults with all affected individuals before making a decision. Whenever possible, the democratic leader prefers that decisions represent the consensus of all parties.

A *free-rein leader* typically prefers that people make their own decisions in matters that affect them. He or she does not make decisions but assists and guides subordinates in deciding for themselves how they wish to solve problems that affect them. The free-rein leader normally permits subordinates to function on a job as they wish, within the limits of organizational policy.

It will be useful to illustrate all three of these within a hospitality framework. Suppose, for example, that a restaurant manager needs to prepare a schedule for servers for the coming week. The way in which she goes about it depends on which of the three leadership styles she uses. If she is an autocratic leader, she simply prepares the schedule without consulting the servers about who will work the various days and shifts. The completed schedule is posted on a bulletin board or distributed to the servers, and each is expected to accept it without question. If she is a democratic leader, she is likely to ask the servers which days each prefers to work. She then prepares a tentative schedule, designed to accommodate as many of their varied needs as possible. The schedule is distributed to servers, but it is subject to change if they do not like it. If she is a free-rein leader, she might call the servers together in a meeting to describe the limits and guidelines for setting work schedules. Each individual server makes his own work schedule, and as long as each one's schedule conforms to the limits and guidelines, it is accepted.

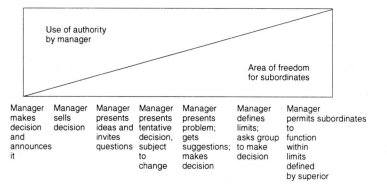

FIGURE 15.1 *Continuum of leadership behavior*

A continuum of leadership behavior ranging from autocratic to free rein was described by Robert Tannenbaum and Warren Schmidt.[1] Figure 15.1 illustrates the Tannenbaum–Schmidt continuum. From this illustration, there are seven ways that the servers' schedule could be prepared. The entire list is as follows:

1. Manager prepares the schedule and presents it, as previously described.
2. Manager prepares the schedule. It is not subject to change, but the manager explains her rationale for the way it was prepared to each of the servers. She sells her decision to them.
3. The manager prepares a schedule, presents it to servers, invites questions, and accepts suggestions for preparing future schedules.
4. The manager prepares a tentative schedule and shows it to the servers, as previously described. Servers can request changes if they find it unsatisfactory.
5. The manager calls a meeting of the servers, discusses the problems of scheduling with them, and solicits ideas and suggestions from all servers. She then prepares a schedule that reflects the ideas and suggestions of the servers.
6. The manager defines limits and guidelines for servers' schedules, then asks the group to prepare the schedule.
7. The manager would let each server prepare his own work schedule, as previously described. As long as each conformed to established limits and guidelines, it would be accepted.

MOTIVATING. Another important element in directing is the ability of the leader to motivate subordinates to put forth their best efforts—to work hard to achieve the established objectives of the organization. Many managers feel that

[1]Robert Tannenbaum and Warren H. Schmidt, "How to Choose a Leadership Pattern," *Harvard Business Review* (May–June 1973), pp. 162–80.

two specific motivators are always sufficient to induce employees to work toward established objectives: money (wages and salary) and job security. Few people will continually strive to achieve organizational goals if they feel underpaid or insecure. Although these two factors are important, however, various studies have shown that other motivators are also very significant. Elton Mayo first illustrated this in a study done in 1927.

Mayo and a group of researchers went to the Hawthorne plant of the Western Electric Company to explore the relationship between changes in physical working conditions and the productivity of employees. One series of tests was conducted to determine the effect on worker output of increases and decreases in the amount of light at work stations. They reduced the amount of light for one group and found that output was not reduced. In some cases, output increased in spite of the decreased amount of light. Mayo was baffled; he could not explain this phenomenon. Eventually he concluded that output had increased, despite adverse conditions, because the workers recognized that someone was taking an interest in their work. The workers felt important and appreciated and were therefore motivated to work harder.

The Hawthorne studies led to further investigations and to a recognition that motivating factors for workers are not limited to money and job security. A number of other positive motivators for workers are now commonly recognized. These include recognition for excellent performance; respect for employees' opinions and judgments; increased responsibility; job advancement; employer interest in the employees' well-being; and opportunities for personal growth.

Management by Objectives.　One widely used technique for motivating employees was introduced in the 1950s by Peter Drucker, an eminent management theorist. Known as *management by objectives* and abbreviated as MBOs, the technique motivates employees by having them participate in establishing their own job-related goals, informing them in advance how they will be evaluated, and then evaluating their performance on the basis of how well they achieve their goals.

Organizations that use MBOs as motivators typically proceed in the following manner:

1. Manager and subordinate meet to discuss the subordinate's past performance and to establish specific agreed-upon objectives for the subordinate to achieve by a specified date.
2. Manager and subordinate jointly develop an action plan that details precisely how each objective will be achieved by a specified date.
3. Subordinate's performance is reviewed on specified dates and compared with results anticipated by the action plan.

Employees who participate in the development of objectives against which their own performance will be measured are likely to accept the objectives as realistic and fair. In addition, they will have a clear understanding of the objectives they are expected to achieve and the time frame in which to achieve them.

SUPERVISING. To *supervise* is to oversee and guide the work of subordinates in an organization. Supervising offers another important means for directing employees. There are any number of ways to supervise: Some pay very close attention to all activities of those they supervise; others take more of a *laissez-faire* attitude, paying very little attention unless some problem becomes evident. The specific approach to supervising taken by a given person is normally an indication of that person's general beliefs about employees in organizations. Some mistrust employees or feel that employees lack the requisite knowledge and skills for performing their jobs. Supervisors with these attitudes and beliefs are inclined to watch closely. In contrast, other supervisors have confidence in those they supervise. They believe that workers have the knowledge and skills required for their jobs and are willing and able to work hard. Supervisors with these attitudes are unlikely to closely monitor those they are responsible for supervising.

Douglas McGregor, another widely respected management theorist, hypothesized two sets of assumptions that managers have about workers that could be used to classify managers as one of two types: *Theory X* and *Theory Y*.

Theory X. A Theory X manager makes the following assumptions about workers:

1. They feel that work is inherently distasteful and should be avoided.
2. They must be coerced, controlled, directed, and threatened with punishment in work situations to get them to perform adequately.
3. They have very little ambition, want to avoid responsibility, and prefer to be told what to do.

Theory Y. A Theory Y manager makes very different assumptions about workers:

1. They do not inherently dislike work, which is a natural activity for human beings.
2. Given appropriate rewards, they willingly work toward established objectives.
3. Under proper conditions, they will accept and even seek responsibility, not avoid it.
4. They work to satisfy other needs besides money and job security. These are personal, social needs.

A supervisor adhering to the Theory X assumptions would be more likely to supervise employees very closely, to correct them constantly, and to pressure them continually to work harder. In contrast, a supervisor whose beliefs matched the Theory Y assumptions would observe employees and would be quick to praise them for work well done. He would also be likely to allow them greater freedom to do work as they saw fit. If the Theory Y supervisor thought it necessary to criticize a worker, it would certainly not be done in front of co-workers.

In the hospitality industry, all kinds of managers exist, providing examples of the various leadership styles, motivational methods, and supervisory techniques just described. How managers direct employees varies considerably from manager to manager and from establishment to establishment. In some instances, autocratic approaches are the rule. In others, more democratic techniques are preferred. Some managers adhere more to Theory X assumptions, while others prefer those of Theory Y.

It is also apparent that changing circumstances can affect the attitudes and behavior of managers toward those they supervise. Under some circumstances managers may be autocratic, and under different circumstances those same managers may be democratic. For example, some managers adopt relatively autocratic leadership styles when directing employees whose jobs require little skill. On the other hand, those same managers may adopt democratic leadership styles when dealing with highly skilled employees.

Given the poor performance and attendance records of some employees, it is easy to understand why a manager may make assumptions about them that closely match those associated with Theory X. Similarly, loyal employees who work hard year after year to achieve established objectives make it equally easy to understand why a manager's assumptions about them will appear very close to those described under Theory Y. Those enjoying the confidence of management are often treated differently from those who do not.

Controlling

The fourth function of management is controlling. *Controlling* is a process by means of which management attempts to regulate and sometimes restrain the actions of people in order to achieve desired goals. It consists of actions and decisions taken by management to assure that desired goals are achieved.

Plans are made to achieve goals and objectives, the enterprise is organized, management directs the efforts of employees, but goals and objectives are seldom achieved unless management controls those efforts and prevents occurrences that could delay or possibly prevent the achievement of those goals.

CONTROL TECHNIQUES. Management uses a number of control techniques. The following is a list of some of the most common in hospitality operations:[2]

1. Establish standards.
2. Establish procedures.

[2]For a detailed discussion of control in the food service industry, see Paul R. Dittmer and Gerald G. Griffin, *Principles of Food, Beverage, and Labor Cost Control* (New York: Van Nostrand Reinhold, 1989).

3. Train employees.
4. Set examples.
5. Observe and correct employees' actions.
6. Require records and reports.
7. Censure and discipline employees as required.
8. Prepare and follow budgets.

Establish Standards.   *Standards* may be defined as rules or measures established for making comparisons or judgments. They are an important element in control, because they provide a basis for determining whether or not actual outcomes conform to planned outcomes. Hospitality managers normally establish three types of standards:

1. Quantity standards
2. Quality standards
3. Cost standards

For example, the chef in a well-organized restaurant develops standard recipes for cooks to follow whenever they prepare a menu item. These recipes are designed to produce a specific number of portions of a particular size, at a given quality and specific cost. The cost of a portion prepared from the standard recipe becomes the standard cost for that menu item. The total recipe cost becomes the standard recipe cost.

Another example of standards can be found in a housekeeping department. The department manager, the executive housekeeper, normally develops standards that identify the number of rooms each housekeeper should be able to prepare for occupancy at the appropriate level of cleanliness in a given time period—normally one work shift. This may be done by observing experienced housekeepers preparing rooms and then making careful judgments either about the number of rooms that should be done in one shift or about the time it should take for a housekeeper to prepare one room. Quantity standards and quality standards are developed from observation. If one knows the wage rate for housekeepers, the standard cost for preparing a room for occupancy can be calculated.

Establish Procedures.   Another control technique commonly used by managers is to establish specific procedures for accomplishing work. *Procedures* are methods employed to perform a job. *Standard procedures* are those that have been established as the correct methods, routines, and techniques for day-to-day operations.

Suppose that a chef must prepare a specific number of portions of a given menu item. The levels of quality and cost are prescribed. Because he cannot do the

One of the techniques employed in the controlling function of management is establishing standards of quantity, quality, and cost. Shown above is a member of the housekeeping department maintaining the appearance of a conference room, an important part of meeting goals of quality and inspiring guest confidence. (Courtesy Ogden Services Corp.)

work himself, he assigns the work to one cook who is given a standard recipe to follow. The standard recipe gives the cook a list of ingredients, the correct quantity of each, and a preparation method to be followed. If the cook follows the standard recipe, the appropriate number of portions of the item, each of desired quality, will have been prepared at the proper cost. On the other hand, if no standard recipe has been developed for the item, the effect will be to leave to the discretion of the cook the ingredients, quantities, quality, and preparation method for the item. Some cooks might prepare the correct quantity but at higher cost or lower quality because the ingredients or preparation methods were different from those the chef had in mind. Other cooks might prepare too many portions, or too few, resulting in excessive or insufficient supplies of the item. Thus, by establishing standard procedures such as standard recipes, managers are better able to control the quantity, quality, and cost of the foods or beverages produced.

Although one would not call it a standard recipe, a specific procedure might also be developed for preparing a guest room for occupancy. It might then become the standard procedure for preparing all guest rooms. Standard procedures are common in the hospitality industry. They are established by managers for such varying purposes as taking reservations, checking in guests, serving dining room customers, and ordering, receiving, and issuing supplies.

Train employees. *Training* is a process by which employees are taught the proper methods and techniques for accomplishing the work they have been hired to do. Training is obviously one of the most effective control techniques managers can use. If employees are not trained to do their jobs in the manner intended by management, they are unlikely to follow standard procedures. For example, one cannot expect a new employee to prepare and plate menu items in the manner prescribed by management without some amount of training. If specific arrangement of foods on plates is important in a particular restaurant, management must provide training so that employees will be able to do the work correctly.

Employee training is an ongoing task for management, equally important in all departments of hospitality operations. Employees can be trained individually or in groups. Some of the methods used for training include:

1. Lecture or demonstration classes
2. Individual on-the-job instruction
3. Seminars
4. Conferences
5. Panels
6. Role playing
7. Simulations

Set Examples.   The examples set by managers in the performance of their jobs are often useful as control devices. This is because employees tend to learn from and emulate the behavior of the managers. If managers speak courteously to customers, employees are more likely to do so. Similarly, if managers are discourteous to customers, employees may be also.

Managers' behavior in performing tasks can influence the way employees perform the same tasks. For example, if a chef has occasion to work alongside cooks plating food and the chef makes the portions larger than the established standards, the cooks will be likely to do the same. Similarly, if a front office manager is assisting room clerks in checking in guests during busy periods and the front office manager assigns guests to unmade rooms, the room clerks will be more likely to do so. Conversely, chefs and front office managers who follow the standards and standard procedures established for doing the work just described will note that cooks and room clerks are more inclined to do their jobs in the manner intended.

Observe and Correct Employee Actions.   If a chef observes a cook using a knife improperly, thus risking a cut finger, or observes another cook preparing too much of some item and throwing away the excess, the chef must speak to the cooks to correct their behavior. If the chef fails to do so, either cook might assume that such work habits are acceptable to the chef. If so, they are likely to continue them. Similarly, if a front office manager observes a room clerk speaking discourteously to guests and does not correct this undesirable behavior, the clerk might assume it is acceptable to speak to guests in that fashion.

One of the important tasks of all managers is to observe the actions of employees as they go about their daily jobs and to correct their performance at appropriate times.

Require Records and Reports. Managers cannot be everywhere at once. In larger organizations, the offices of top managers are frequently located great distances from the sites of individual units. They cannot have very much firsthand knowledge of unit operation from personal observations. Even in individually operated hotels, motels, and restaurants, managers cannot observe all employees at all times. To compensate for their inability to observe the day-to-day performance of all members of the staff, managers commonly require records and reports. This is an important control technique used by managers in most hospitality operations. Records and reports provide managers with information that enables them to make judgments about whether or not their units are achieving goals and objectives. Some of the common reports required by hospitality managers include sales reports, occupancy reports, and expense reports. Analysis of these reports, if done regularly, often enables managers to detect potential problems and to correct small problems before they become large enough to interfere with achieving organizational goals and objectives.

For example, if the occupancy reports for the Kensington Hotel indicate lower rates of room occupancy than expected, management may be able to increase occupancy through intensive sales or marketing efforts. If that is not feasible, it may be possible to reduce expenses so that the desired level of profit can be maintained. In either event, reports provide the information that alerts astute managers to potential problems.

Discipline Employees. Disciplinary action is commonly employed as a control technique. For example, if the financial performance of one unit in a chain of restaurants does not compare favorably with the budget, the unit manager is likely to have this pointed out to him by top management. The possibilities for doing so range from quiet discussion to reprimand. Other possible actions include demotion and termination. On a different level, if a room clerk has been given training so that she will understand and follow certain standards and standard procedures in her work, and she then does not do so, she is likely to be called aside and informed of her shortcomings by her supervisor, the front office manager.

The primary purpose of discipline should be to change behavior. Discipline should be used as a punishment only as a last resort. Literally, *punishment* means to afflict with pain, loss, or suffering. In managerial terms, it means to subject a subordinate to some penalty as a consequence of unacceptable performance.

Discipline should have a positive outcome: After being disciplined, a subordinate should be better able to perform the work expected of her. In contrast, punishment may have a negative outcome: The subordinate may be resentful. Although he may correct some specific aspect of his behavior, his attitude may be such that his overall performance will be poor.

Prepare and Follow Budgets.   Perhaps the most important and most commonly used control technique in business is preparing and following budgets. There are various kinds of budgets prepared by managers, including capital equipment budgets, cash flow budgets, sales budgets, advertising budgets, and many others.

A *budget* is a plan stated in financial terms. It indicates how the various resources of an enterprise are to be used in the period covered by the budget—usually one year. For example, a budget usually includes a dollar figure to pay the total of employees' wages and salaries for the year. That dollar figure is the amount management expects to use in order to have work done for the year. Viewed another way, the budget figure for salaries and wages could be thought of as the maximum amount managers will be permitted to spend to get work done. A manager who gets the necessary work done without spending more than allocated in the budget is normally considered to be managing well, at least in that sense. The manager who exceeds the amount allocated in the budget will probably be called on to explain, particularly if the excessive cost of labor reduced profits anticipated in a profit-oriented enterprise, or led to an unacceptable loss in a not-for-profit operation.

Budgets, as control devices, are developed by owners and higher-level managers so that judgments can be made about the performance of subordinate-level managers. Budgets are important control devices because they provide financial guidelines for all who have authority to spend money. Without budgets, managers have no useful means of assessing whether or not operations are progressing satisfactorily, and whether or not financial objectives are likely to be reached.

THE CONTROL PROCESS. From the previous discussion of control techniques, it is possible to generalize four basic steps that constitute the control process:

1. Establish standards and standard procedures for operation.
2. Train employees to follow established standards and standard procedures.
3. Monitor employee performance and compare actual performance with established standards.
4. Take appropriate action to correct deviations in performance.

One example will serve to illustrate the control process.

The Kensington Hotel's rooms division manager has established a goal of 75 percent occupancy at an average room rate of $250 for the year beginning March

1st. This is believed to be realistic and achievable based on past performance and current trends. It is reflected in the budget for the rooms department. After careful review of existing procedures, he has written and given to the front office manager new standard procedures for taking reservations and selling rooms. Training sessions are conducted in February for reservationists, room clerks, and all other personnel who sell rooms. On March 1st, the new budget year begins. Occupancy and revenue reports are prepared daily. At first, the occupancy and sales revenue figures are on target. A 76 percent occupancy rate is maintained and the average rate per room is $252. By early April, however, reports show that occupancy is remaining high, but the average rate per room has dropped to $228. Investigation reveals that a large number of rooms are being sold at discounted rates. The front office manager traces the problem to one reservation clerk who appears to be selling a large percentage of rooms at rates lower than desired. Discussion with the clerk reveals some misunderstanding of both the objectives and the new procedures. He is given additional training during his normal work day. After the clerk resumes his duties in the reservations office, the average rate soon returns to the $252 level and the level of occupancy continues to be 76 percent.

The example illustrates the four steps in the control process. Standards and procedures were established for room sales; personnel were trained in the new selling procedures; reports were issued so that management could monitor performance and compare results with standards previously established; and appropriate actions were taken when performance deviated from standards.

SKILLS REQUIRED FOR SUCCESSFUL MANAGEMENT IN THE HOSPITALITY INDUSTRY

To be successful in the hospitality industry, managers must be adept at planning, organizing, directing, and controlling the operations for which they are responsible. To be successful managers, they must also have certain additional skills: technical, human relations, and conceptual. All three are necessary.

Technical Skills

Technical skills are those needed to do the specific work associated with such jobs as selling, operating computers, preparing drinks, serving food, checking guests in or out, or maintaining the accounting records of an enterprise.

In smaller establishments, managers need more technical skills than their counterparts in large corporations. This is because managers in these establishments often have responsibilities at or near the technical level. The manager of a small restaurant, for example, may also be the dining room manager who schedules and directs the dining room staff. In that role, it is important to know and be able to demonstrate the specific techniques that constitute good service in that setting. The manager of an operation such as the Value Lodge may also be the room clerk, housekeeper, and bookkeeper. As such, she must have the skills required for those jobs.

Many managers of smaller restaurants and motels must be available to substitute for employees who become ill or fail to appear for work when scheduled. It is not unusual for the manager of a small restaurant to become chef for the day when the chef does not come to work, or for the manager of a small motel to cover the night shift when the regular clerk is ill.

In larger organizations, operational managers are not as often required to perform technical tasks. There is normally sufficient flexibility in the organization to handle emergency situations. For example, even when a cook must leave work early, the executive chef in a large hotel can usually rearrange the work load among kitchen staff so that all necessary work is done. This should not be interpreted, however, as meaning that operational managers in larger establishments do not need technical skills. No chef can effectively supervise kitchen staff unless he also is able to do the job of each staff member. Similarly, a front office manager in a major hotel must be able to take reservations, to check guests in and out, and to respond to guests' requests for information if she is to judge the quality of the work done by various categories of front office employees.

Top managers of large organizations typically require few technical skills because they are not normally engaged in day-to-day operational matters. Most top managers in the hospitality industry have demonstrated extensive knowledge of technical skills at one point in their careers. However, as promotions have moved them further and further from the operational levels in the organization, some of their skills have fallen into disuse.

Human Relations Skills

Human relations skills—the ability to work effectively with others—are particularly important for hospitality managers. There are two reasons for this.

Hospitality managers are constantly interacting with their customers. One of the primary jobs of many hospitality managers is to deal with customer complaints and to solve the problems and issues that arise with customers. For example, dining room managers constantly deal with such problems as boisterous guests, requests for specific food items, customers who overindulge in alcoholic beverages, complaints about the appearance or taste of menu items, and seating arrangements for large parties. Front office managers interact with guests in the same way as dining room managers, but usually deal with them on matters relating to room assignments, room rates, and room amenities, to name just a few.

Along with technical and conceptual skills, human relations skills are necessary to execute the management directives of planning, organizing, directing, and controlling operations. Above, a manager warmly greets an employee arriving to take part in a training program. Hospitality managers must also work diplomatically with customers, dealing with complaints and solving any problems that arise. (Courtesy ITT Sheraton Corp., Boston.)

Secondly, hospitality managers must work closely with staff to fulfill guests' needs. It is imperative that managers and staff work together cooperatively and effectively. If relationships between manager and staff are strained or tense because managers have poor human relations skills, the quality of the service product may deteriorate, and guests are likely to be dissatisfied. In addition, guests are quick to sense tension in the work environment and to realize that employees are not comfortable with their jobs, their managers, or both.

Conceptual Skills

Conceptual skills are skills associated with intelligence. Those with conceptual skills have an ability to think in abstract terms. High levels of conceptual skill are required to formulate new ideas, to see the organization as a whole unit, and to understand the impact external factors will have on the organization.

Although conceptual skills are assets to managers at all levels, they are of particular importance for top managers. Such skills are critical for decision making: Intelligent decisions can be made only when management understands the ultimate effect or impact of these decisions on the organization. For example, a decision to change room rates or menu prices should be made only after manage-

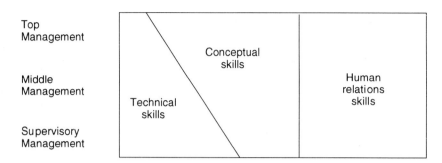

FIGURE 15.2 *Skills needed at various levels of hospitality management*

ment assesses the likely short- and long-term effects of such a decision on revenues and customer counts. Any manager contemplating major decisions of this nature should take into account such factors as economic conditions, competitive advantages, general price levels, and the sensitivity of customers or guests to price changes. Top managers must have the conceptual abilities to make correct decisions on matters that can affect the future of their organization and their subordinates.

Conceptual skills are important to managers at the middle and supervisory levels, also. Managers must comprehend how their decisions and those of their subordinates affect specific operations and subsystems in immediate and remote parts of the organization. For example, a food and beverage manager who decides to purchase food of lower quality to save money must understand the effect that decision will have on such diverse outcomes as menu item quality, customer satisfaction, food and beverage income, and server gratuities. A decision to buy lower-quality ingredients at lower cost may also affect the room sales: Some guests may decide to stay at other hotels if food quality is at a level they find unacceptable.

Figure 15.2 illustrates the need for the three types of skills at the three levels of hospitality management.

RULES FOR SUCCESSFUL HOSPITALITY MANAGEMENT

At the beginning of this chapter, we noted that the hospitality industry is substantially different from many others—that there are essential differences between managing hospitality operations and managing factories or retail stores. Essentially, this is because hospitality operations serve travelers. The hospitality service products sought by travelers must be available when needed—24 hours a day, 7 days a week, 365 days a year.

In Chapter 1 we introduced the term *moments of truth*, which is used to describe any contact between a customer and a business that gives the customer an impression of the business and from which that customer makes judgments about the business. We pointed out that these *moments of truth* occur thousands of times daily in hospitality operations.

In Chapter 1 we also introduced the term *cycle of service*, a chain of events beginning with a customer's first contact with an organization and extending to his last. Each contact is a moment of truth. The guest's overall impression of an enterprise, favorable or unfavorable, is based on the cumulative outcomes of these moments of truth. The overall impressions are those that guests have when they leave the establishment. Undesirable outcomes from some moments of truth can lead to a very poor overall impression, even though the outcomes of most of the guest's moments of truth may have been entirely positive and favorable.

Because hospitality operations are special and different, some of the basic rules for successfully managing hospitality operations are also a bit different, as suggested below:

1. Establish policies that emphasize service quality, service image, and guest satisfaction.

Frequently policies established by managers are designed to achieve worthy objectives, but they lead to moments of truth that have unpleasant outcomes for guests. For example, a policy mandating the closing of a dining room or a swimming pool during periods of low occupancy would undoubtedly save money in staff wages and have short-term financial benefits. Those guests who are inconvenienced because of the policy, however, may feel that the hotel is operated solely for the benefit of the owners.

2. Empower staff members to make reasonable adjustments to policies, rules, and regulations to ensure guest satisfaction.

Policies should not be so rigid that individual needs of guests are ignored. For example, a policy that restricts the preparation of haddock fillets to frying or sauteeing does not take into account the needs of customers who are concerned about fat content. If feasible, servers should be empowered to respond positively to requests for broiled portions. A moment of truth occurs when a guest asks a server for a broiled portion. An unnecessary negative outcome will be detrimental to the goals of the business over the long term.

3. Strive to develop expertise in human relations skills and practice those skills at all times.

This is one of the most important and significant of the skills needed for successful hospitality management. In an industry offering service products and attempting to build a service image, the ability to deal with guests courteously and effectively is clearly a critical key for success.

4. Plan and organize carefully and accurately.

When guests are dissatisfied because of poor planning or poor organization, they are normally not interested in listening to explanations. Unlike durable goods, service products cannot be tested in advance and recalled if they are unsatisfactory. The service product must be right the first time; if it is not, there is no second chance. If the outcome is negative at the moment of truth, the guest may never return.

5. Develop a continuing training program for employees.

The outcomes of customers' moments of truth are less likely to be positive if staff members are untrained or undertrained. Customers do not readily accept poor service and are not interested in learning that service is poor because personnel are untrained. Thus, staff should be trained to an acceptable level of technical proficiency before being permitted to deliver the service product to customers. Training is the responsibility of management.

6. Set up controls that are geared to customer satisfaction and make exceptions when circumstances warrant.

For example, to prevent excess linen cost a housekeeper may establish a control on linen such that sheets are issued at the rate of two per bed. If a guest were to have an accident, however, such as spilling a cup of coffee on his bed, it would be wise to make an exception to the control procedure and to allow additional linen to be issued. It is easy to imagine the rage of a guest in these circumstances if he were told that the wet, coffee-stained sheets could not be changed until the following day because of management's linen control procedures.

SUMMARY

In this chapter the management of hospitality operations is examined. The term *management* is defined and the three levels of management are discussed. The functions of management—planning, organizing, directing, and controlling—are discussed in detail. *Planning* is defined as the process of identifying goals and objectives and determining appropriate means of achieving these goals. Plans are categorized by time and type, and the steps in the planning process are listed and discussed. *Organizing* is defined as determining what work is to be done and assigning that work to individuals in such a way as to achieve organizational goals. The six steps in the organizing process are listed and discussed. *Directing* is defined as the process of achieving organizational goals by guiding, motivating, and supervising subordinates. Several important elements in the directing process are discussed, including styles of leadership, motivational techniques, and supervisory methods. *Controlling* is defined as the process by which management attempts to regulate and restrain the actions of people. Control techniques are outlined and explained. The four steps in the control process are listed and discussed. The skills for successful management in the hospitality industry are outlined as technical skills, human relation skills, and conceptual skills. Finally, six basic rules for successful hospitality management are presented and discussed.

QUESTIONS

1. Define the term *management*.
2. What are the three levels of management? List two job titles normally associated with each level.
3. Define the term *planning* as used in management.
4. Identify the essential differences between long-term and short-term plans.
5. According to the text, plans can be classified by type. List four.
6. List the ten steps in the planning process.
7. Define the term *organizing* as used in management.
8. List the six steps in the organizing process.
9. Define the term *directing* as used in management.
10. Define the term *leadership*.
11. Do behavioral scientists agree on specific leadership traits? Why?
12. List and discuss the three basic styles of leadership. Include at least one example of each.
13. List eight motivators that can lead employees to work to achieve organizational goals.
14. What is MBO? Describe the typical process for developing MBOs for a given employee.
15. What assumptions are at the heart of the Theory X view of workers?
16. What assumptions are at the heart of the Theory Y view of workers?
17. Define the term *control* as used in management.
18. List eight control techniques commonly used by hospitality managers.
19. List and discuss the four steps in the control process.
20. Identify three types of standards commonly used in the hospitality industry and give an example of each.
21. List and discuss the three types of skills that are required at all levels of hospitality management.

22. At what managerial level are technical skills most important? Why?
23. Give two reasons why human relations skills are vital at all levels of hospitality management.
24. At what level of management are conceptual skills most important? Why?
25. List and explain the six rules for successful hospitality management.

Hospitality Marketing

16

LEARNING OBJECTIVES

After reading and studying this chapter, you should be able to:

1. Define the terms marketing and hospitality marketing.
2. List the four key elements of marketing.
3. Distinguish between franchise organizations and referral organizations and discuss the advantages and disadvantages of each.
4. Identify the benefits derived from belonging to a centralized reservation system.
5. Provide examples of "right" locations for various hospitality operations.
6. List the primary considerations in establishing a rate structure for a lodging establishment.
7. List the primary considerations in establishing menu prices.
8. List and discuss five types of promotional activities.
9. List and discuss six media used to advertise hospitality operations.
10. Define each of the following terms: a. market; b. target market; c. market segment.
11. Distinguish between demographic, geographic, and psychographic market segments.
12. Define and discuss the terms marketing mix and market strategy.
13. Define the term marketing plan and list its elements.

INTRODUCTION

The previous chapter stressed the importance of management in achieving the goals of a hospitality enterprise. Good management is, of course, essential to successful operation. The very best management, however, cannot make an enterprise profitable if an insufficient number of customers patronize it. For example, hotels typically must achieve between 55 percent and 65 percent occupancy to be profitable. Restaurants must average a given number of customers per week if they are to be profitable.

This chapter discusses the activities associated with gaining that number of customers required for an operation to achieve its financial goals. These are generally referred to as *marketing strategies*.

DEFINITION OF MARKETING

The American Marketing Association defines marketing very broadly. It states that *marketing* is "the process of planning and executing the conception, pricing, promotion, and distribution of ideas, goods, and services to create exchanges that will satisfy individual and organizational objectives."[1] The above definition can be interpreted to incorporate the following:

1. Determining consumers' needs
2. Creating ideas, goods, and services to meet those needs
3. Establishing profitable prices
4. Taking various sales-oriented actions
5. Making arrangements to get ideas, goods, and services to consumers

In the traditional view of marketing, the ideas, goods, or services purchased by the consumer are used or consumed somewhere other than in the creator's place of business. A manufactured toy, for example, may be used at home, in school, or in any of a thousand other locations. None of those locations, however, is likely to be the factory where the toy was manufactured. In contrast, nearly all of the service products made available to customers by hospitality operators are actually used or consumed in the location where they are produced. In addition, service products are produced to order.

Except for caterers and the operators of takeout or delivery food service establishments, operators of hospitality enterprises do not typically export their service products to the homes or businesses of their customers. Hospitality service products cannot normally be distributed in the same way as toys, automobiles, or cans of condensed soup, for example. They are usually available only where they are produced, and customers or guests normally travel to the hospitality operation to obtain the service product.

[1]"AMA Board Approves New Marketing Definition," *Marketing News*, 1 March 1985, p. 1.

Because of these important differences, marketing for hospitality products is somewhat different than for products intended for use in home or business settings. For example, a transient hotel in a major city and a resort hotel on a Caribbean island must market their service products to people who will have to make a considerable effort to travel to the locations where these service products are available. Similarly, many restaurants successfully market their service products to customers who are willing to travel great distances to patronize these establishments.

Because the traditional meaning of the term *distribution* is unsuitable for use in connection with most hospitality service products, the definition of *marketing* developed by the American Marketing Association must be altered slightly if it is to apply. Our definition will be as follows: For hospitality operation, *marketing* is the process of planning service products, finding the right place to locate, and pricing and promoting products to attract customers and to create exchanges that will satisfy their needs and the goals of the enterprise.

ELEMENTS OF MARKETING

The above definition has four key elements:

1. Product
2. Place
3. Price
4. Promotion

Product

One basic decision to be made in marketing is the nature of the service product(s) to be offered. To some extent, that is defined by the characteristic type of hospitality establishment one intends to operate. Some of the many possible types were discussed in Chapters 5 and 8, including fast-food restaurants, family restaurants, specialty restaurants, fine dining restaurants, upscale hotels, economy motels, resorts, lodges, and all-suite hotels.

Each of these characteristic types of hospitality operations is associated with some general type of service product line. Based on that knowledge, customers seeking a particular type of service product are likely to look for the type of establishment they expect will offer it.

Fast-food restaurants, for example, typically attract customers who want to eat quickly and who are looking for a meal at a reasonable price. The service product line offered to these customers features quick service and relatively low prices. Fine dining establishments, however, are more likely to attract those who are looking for excellent food, exemplary service, and memorable ambiance (and for whom prices are a secondary consideration). The service product line offered customers in these establishments will emphasize these three elements.

Similarly, economy motels typically attract travelers looking for clean, moderately priced accommodations. They are designed for travelers who do not require and do not want to pay for the accommodations, services, and ambiance in high-priced, luxury hotels. In contrast, upscale hotels normally attract business people and other travelers who are willing to pay for the luxury and services these properties offer.

All-suite hotels, on the one hand, attract those who plan to spend considerable time in their accommodations and look for the additional space, conveniences, and furnishings associated with these establishments. Resort hotels, on the other, attract those who plan to use the recreational facilities featured by these establishments. Each characteristic type of hospitality property attracts customers who prefer the prices, facilities, and services commonly associated with that kind of property. Consequently, the service product line offered reflects the desires of the customers attracted to each of those establishments.

Once the characteristic type of establishment has been established, it is not normally changed. Owners of fast-food restaurants do not commonly convert them to fine dining establishments. Nor are luxury hotels very often suddenly converted to economy motor lodges. When this kind of change occurs, it is the exception rather than the rule.

Although hospitality operations do not commonly change their characteristic type, they do frequently *alter* their service product lines. For example, a fast-food restaurant specializing in hamburgers may change its service product line by adding such new foods to the menu as a salad bar, individual pizzas, or breast of chicken sandwiches. Motels can change their service product lines by adding such new features as tennis courts or exercise rooms — or even by making laptop computers and modems available to business travelers.

THE NATURE OF THE HOSPITALITY SERVICE PRODUCT. Hospitality marketing decisions should be based on an understanding of the nature of the service products offered by hospitality operators. As has been pointed out previously, the hospitality service product is produced to order — "manufactured," so to speak, as required by guests. For some, this is a difficult concept to grasp, and an illustration may help. A haircut, for example, does not exist until a stylist responds to a customer's request and gives that customer a haircut. It is done to order, and even if two customers both request identical haircuts, the service product each receives will differ in the details. Haircuts cannot be prepared and stockpiled in advance, any more than hospitality service products can. The stylist can be at her haircutting station, prepared to cut hair. She can have with her all the necessary professional tools, and she can have high levels of professional skill developed from instruction, training, and practice over a number of years. But she cannot produce a haircut until a customer arrives and requests one.

A restaurant meal is similar. The restaurant owner can take great pains to have a beautiful dining room, carefully decorated, lighted, and appointed with fine furnishings, linens, china, glassware, and all other requirements for fine dining. He can employ highly skilled personnel for each job in the establishment, then give them additional training to be sure they are prepared to do their jobs exactly as intended. He can develop an excellent menu and develop standard recipes to be used in preparing each dish. At that point, all is ready. But no hospitality service product called a *restaurant meal* can be produced until a customer arrives, is seated at a table, and orders specific items from the menu. Those foods, along with all attendant services and the ambiance of the establishment, constitute the hospitality service product—the restaurant meal—"manufactured" for that one, individual, customer. Similar illustrations could be drawn for the hospitality service products offered by lodging operators.

In one sense, hospitality service products are among the most highly perishable of all products. Hospitality operators can have ready all the necessary components for the production of their hospitality services. Unless those components are successfully combined into service products to meet the immediate needs of guests, however, no hospitality service product is produced. In a hotel, for example, no service product is produced until a room is sold to a particular guest; it cannot be manufactured today in the absence of guests, then sold twice tomorrow.

A hospitality service product has three components—central, services, and ambiance. Figure 16.1 is an illustration of the hospitality service product concept.

For hospitality service products, the possibilities for central components are foods, beverages, and lodging. The central component of a specific hospitality service product consists of the selection or selections made by the customer from

FIGURE 16.1   *The hospitality service product*

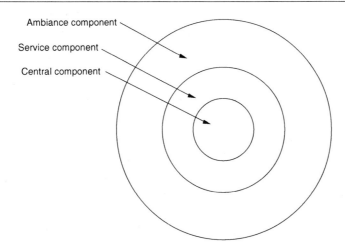

Ambiance component

Service component

Central component

among those offered—foods from a menu or accommodations in a hotel. The service and ambiance components of a given hospitality service product may also depend on specific selections made by customers or guests. For example, a restaurant customer may be given a choice between the main dining room and a satellite room. In that sense, the ambiance component of the hospitality service product received by that particular diner will reflect her choice of rooms.

CHAIN AFFILIATION. An important element in the service product line of a hospitality operation may be its affiliation with a national or regional hospitality chain.

Many privately owned lodging operations are affiliated with regional or national organizations. Examples of national lodging organizations that accept independently owned operations as affiliates include Holiday Inn, Ramada Inn, Best Western Motels, Hilton, and Sheraton. Such restaurant chains as McDonald's, Burger King, Subway, and Pizza Hut have a large number of independently owned restaurants affiliated with them as franchisees.

In the hospitality industry, there are two basic types of affiliations: franchise affiliation and referral affiliation. It is important to distinguish between the two.

Franchise Affiliation. A *franchise* is a contract between two parties—a franchisor and franchisee—that allows the franchisee the right to use the franchisor's

The three components of a hospitality service product—central, service, and ambiance—are sometimes expressed in the organization's affiliation with a chain, whether for lodging or food service. There are two types of chain affiliations: franchise and referral. Shown below is the Sheraton Stamford Hotel, Stamford, Connecticut, part of a national organization that also accepts independently owned operations as affiliates. (Courtesy ITT Sheraton Corp., Boston.)

name, sell its products, and participate in its programs and services under set, specific conditions.

The franchisor typically owns many of its establishments. It will seek independent operators to become affiliates for two main reasons: (1) so that the franchisor can expand its network of establishments at a more rapid rate than would otherwise be possible and (2) so that the franchisor can increase its revenues through the fees it collects from its franchisees.

There are many reasons for independent operators to want to become franchisees. The most important of these are

1. the ability to use a regionally, nationally, or internationally known name with an established image;
2. the ability to profit from regional, national, or international advertising that no single property could afford;
3. access to a national or international reservation network (for lodging establishments);
4. access to training from the franchise organization; and
5. access to professional management assistance and advice from the franchise organization.

Affiliated operations are often able to enjoy more dollar sales than independents. Management training and assistance enables inexperienced operators to avoid costly mistakes. Being part of a franchise even allows developers to obtain credit more easily. After all, lending institutions are usually more willing to finance hospitality establishments with nationally known names than those without such back-up.

There are also disadvantages associated with franchise operations. They include:

1. Inability to manage independently. The franchisee must operate the establishment in accordance with the policies of the franchisor. In most instances, this means that the franchisee must receive franchisor approval for changes in menus, decor, prices, and other operational matters.
2. Conforming to the franchisor's standards of construction and appearance of the establishment. Many franchise organizations have standards for appearance and very strict construction requirements that assure a particular standard of quality.
3. High costs associated with belonging to the franchise organization. All require an initial franchise fee and ongoing fees that typically include
   a. a percentage of revenue,
   b. a fee for advertising,
   c. a fee for access to the reservation network (for lodging establishments), and
   d. a sign-rental fee.

The fees can total between 6 percent and 8 percent of gross sales for the establishment. This means that a motel with annual sales of $5,000,000 per year will pay between $300,000 and $400,000 annually to the franchise organization. Similarly, a restaurant with sales of $2,000,000 will pay between $120,000 and $160,000 to the franchisor.

Some lodging franchisors mandate a minimum number of rooms for franchisees. Unless a property has the required minimum, it is ineligible to join. The franchisors of full-service, mid-price, and luxury hotel and motel chains typically require a minimum of 100 to 150 rooms. Economy motel chains generally have lower limits. Thus, we often see economy motels with fewer than 100 rooms.

Most franchisors have inspectors who visit franchised properties on a regular basis to be certain that the standards of the franchise are being met. If a franchisee is not managing the property according to requirements of the franchisor, it may lose its franchise.

With high fees and strict management requirements, many wonder why any owner of a hospitality operation would want to become part of a franchise. Franchisees often reply that the higher level of dollar sales that comes from the affiliation more than offsets the disadvantages.

Referral Affiliation.   A second kind of affiliation is known as a *referral organization*. For reasons that will become apparent, these are found only in the lodging segment of the industry.

A referral organization consists of some number of independent lodging operations that join together to gain the advantages associated with national advertising and a national reservation network. Like franchise organizations, they establish standards and they charge an initial fee, in addition to various other fees. The similarities, however, end at that point. The referral organization is managed by its members and does not own any lodging establishments. Each property in the referral organization is independently owned and operated, and member properties may have little in common. They will all meet the specified minimum quality standards, but they will differ in their appearance, size, and services.

Initial fees and other ongoing fees are typically lower in referral operations than in franchise operations and controls are much less stringent. Many first-rate lodging operations that could not qualify for a franchise because they do not meet the size or appearance requirements find that referral organizations are excellent alternatives. They have the advantages of national advertising, a reservation network, and a nationally known name but do not have some of the disadvantages associated with franchises. Owners can manage their lodging operations as they see fit. The largest of all of the lodging referral organizations is Best Western, which has more properties than any other lodging organization—including the largest franchisors.

Becoming a franchisee or a referral affiliate is an important marketing decision. Affiliation with either removes some or all responsibility for making marketing decisions from the control of unit managers, and it places that responsibility with the franchisor or referral organization. The image of the establishment and its product lines may be determined by the national organization; and all regional, national, and international advertising and promotion are prepared and placed by the parent organization.

CENTRAL RESERVATION SYSTEMS. One of the most important marketing benefits and a significant service for any lodging franchise or referral organization is its central reservation system. The American Hotel and Motel Association reports that approximately 22 percent of North American lodging reservations are made through central reservation systems. Although this may not seem like a large percentage, one must remember that many independent hotels and motels are not linked to any central reservation system. Those that *are* linked often receive as much as 50 percent of their business through their reservation network.

The concept of automated central reservations goes back to the mid-1960s when Holiday Inn established such a system. Every individual Holiday Inn property would send updated information on room availability to the central reservations computer each day. Travelers could contact any Holiday Inn and make reservations at any other Holiday Inn through a telex machine located in the front office; or they could call the central office and make reservations at any Holiday Inn.

Today, the Holiday Inn centralized computerized reservation system is linked directly with each property in the system. For some properties, this centralized system also keeps track of all check-ins and checkouts. In those properties, managers are no longer required to attend to the updating of the reservation system; it is done automatically.

Some lodging chains and a number of individual hotels and motels are now linked to both airline and travel agency reservation systems. The same computers used by travel agents to make airline reservations can also be used to make reservations for accommodations at a growing number of hotels and motels. Some of the software programs feature sophisticated graphics. This enables the user with the proper graphics monitor to show a potential guest a picture of the hotel and the location of a given room, in addition to much other information about the property.

Place

The second element in hospitality marketing is place. In the hospitality field, *place* as a noun is often a synonym for *location*. The location of a hospitality operation can be an essential element in its marketing effort.

Physical location is critical to the success of many hospitality operations. Ellsworth M. Statler, one of America's most successful hoteliers, once stated that there were three key elements in successful hotel operation:

1. location,
2. location, and
3. location.

Statler knew that having the right location was a critically important factor in the successful operation of a hotel; and that was his way of emphasizing the point.

The characteristics of a "right" location vary from one type of property to another. For example, ski lodges located at the base of ski slopes normally attract many more customers than equivalent properties some distance away from the slopes. Motels located at the exits of interstate highways can be very successful, while similar properties located only a short distance away may fail. In-town hotels located near the business districts or in the more attractive parts of major cities generally have much more business than those located in deteriorating parts of these cities. Resort hotels located on the beachfront will normally attract more guests than those located a block or two away from the beach.

Proper locations can also be important factors in the success of restaurants. A family restaurant must generally be located within a reasonable driving distance of the population it intends to serve. Any fast-food restaurant must be in the immediate vicinity of its customers to attract a lot of customers. For a restaurant and bar at an airport, it is the fact of its location at the airport that is likely to spell success—particularly if it is the only food and beverage operation available to travelers at the airport.

Many successful hospitality operations have been developed to meet perceived needs for hospitality services in particular locations. Cities and towns going through periods of growth frequently attract an increased number of travelers who require such hospitality services as food and overnight lodging. Cities in which existing hospitality properties are old and deteriorating also offer potential opportunities for the successful development of new properties. The same can be true in areas with many hospitality establishments but which have a need for a different characteristic type of property: budget motels in areas that have only expensive full-service hotels, for example, or inexpensive full-service restaurants in residential areas without such establishments. These and many others are examples of potentially good locations for the development of successful hospitality operations by willing entrepreneurs.

Sometimes developers are able to attract customers to areas that have no obvious need for new hospitality services. Examples include the many resort hotels that have been developed in remote areas: the Camelback Inn in Phoenix, Arizona; the Buck Hill Inn, in Buck Hill Falls, Pennsylvania; and the Cloister, at

The location of a lodging or food service establishment—both in general and in relation to its competitors' locations—is a major element of its success. Establishments at remote locations must offer persuasive attractions—climate, scenery, recreational activities—that will inspire guests to travel long distances. (Courtesy Sonesta Beach Hotel Key Biscayne.)

Sea Island, Georgia, for example. These and others like them were successful because of climate and because they offered such features as scenic beauty, beneficial mineral waters, or extraordinary recreational facilities.

For marketing managers at existing properties, physical location is an element of marketing that cannot be altered. One of the major challenges of marketing is to develop a product line that is suitable for the existing location.

In general, hospitality operations with better locations are more appealing than similar operations in poorer locations. In addition, those with the better locations are normally able to charge higher room rates and menu prices than those not so favorably located.

Price

The third element in hospitality marketing is *price*—the prices or rates charged for hospitality services. In general, customers are more easily attracted to hospitality operations charging lower prices than to similar establishments charging higher prices. Price is only one consideration, however, in the consumer's decision to purchase a hospitality service product from one operation rather than from another. The three other elements of marketing—product, location, and promotion—also play an important role in the decision-making process.

Establishing the price structure for any hospitality operation is a difficult process. Unfortunately, there is no simple formula that will enable one to do so. Many judgments must be made, most of which are subjective. Because the service products of lodging operations differ in so many important ways from those of food or beverage operations, methods for establishing price structures for the two differ as well. Because of this, they are discussed separately in the sections that follow.

ROOM RATES. For lodging operations, the following are among the primary considerations at the heart of establishing a room rate structure. Room rates must be designed to

1. attract potential guests during both slow and busy periods;
2. compare favorably with those of competing lodging establishments in the area; and
3. make operations profitable.

During periods when demand for hotel rooms is slack and the competition among lodging operations for the limited number of guests is greatest, room rates are reduced in order to attract as many guests as possible. For example, commercial hotels in major cities have regularly found that weekends and holidays are their periods of lowest occupancy. Many commercial hotels in the Northeast find that January, right after the Christmas holiday period, is the slowest month of the year. Winter weather is at its coldest, and business routinely falls off. Room rates in hotels affected in this way tend to be lower during these slow periods. In contrast, some resort hotels in Florida are very busy on weekends and during holiday periods. They experience their periods of highest occupancy during winter months, when residents of the Northeast are more likely to seek the warm sunshine of Florida.

For purposes of rate setting, resort properties divide their seasons into three periods:

1. **High season:** the peak of the season, when the demand for rooms is greatest. In Florida, high season includes February and March; on Cape Cod, high season is July and August.
2. **Shoulder season:** the period just before and just after peak season. Late fall and early spring in Florida and late spring and early fall on the Cape are shoulder seasons.

3. **Off season:** the period when demand for accommodations is weakest. This is during the summer in Florida and during winter months on Cape Cod.

Resort properties charge their highest rates during high season, more moderate rates during the shoulder season, and their lowest rates during off season.

Package rates are also used during slow periods to attract business. Package rates include accommodations, meals, and various other services. For example, many hotels have weekend packages that include room, meals, and theater tickets for one price. This package price is typically lower than the total that would be charged for those services if purchased separately.

A selection of hotel rate advertisements announcing package "specials" for the weekend, some including meals and other services with accommodations. Hotels must vary rates to remain competitive and to continue to attract business during slow periods and the off and shoulder seasons.

Room rates must also be competitive. If the rates quoted for a given lodging property are considerably higher than those quoted for similar properties in the area, many potential guests are likely to make their reservations at competing properties. If this goes on for a protracted period, it can lead to lower levels of occupancy than those needed for the property to operate profitably. Over time, it may eventually lead to the sale or closing of the property, or to bankruptcy.

Room rates in a commercial property must be high enough so that the total of revenues is greater than the total of expenses for the property. This is to say that the operation must be profitable. Revenues—the total of the specific rates charged to guests—must be sufficient to cover all the costs associated with operating the lodging establishment. If revenues are too low because the rates are too low, the property will operate at a loss. In addition, if rates are too low, it is possible for the property to be very busy at all times, yet not be operating profitably.

One method for determining the average room rate necessary to achieve profit is provided by a formula known as the *Hubbart formula*. The Hubbart formula is a mathematical computation used by accountants and financial consultants to determine the average room rate necessary to cover assumed costs and achieve a given level of profit at an assumed level of occupancy.[2]

MENU PRICES. Menu pricing is one of the most difficult challenges facing food and beverage operators. As with room rates, if food and beverage prices are too high, customers may go elsewhere. If they are too low, the establishment may not be profitable. Establishing menu prices takes into account the following factors:

1. the ingredient costs of each menu item;
2. the cost of labor, including benefits and payroll taxes;
3. overhead costs associated with having a place to do business;
4. the level of skill required to prepare each menu item;
5. the amount of employee time required to prepare menu items;
6. menu prices at competitive establishments; and
7. the effect of menu prices charged on the number of customers attracted.

It should be obvious that food and beverage operations cannot operate profitably if the menu prices charged are less than the cost of the ingredients. And operating costs are not limited to the cost of ingredients: There are labor costs and such overhead costs as real estate taxes, telephone, insurance, heat, gas or electricity for cooking, electricity for lighting, and cleaning supplies, to name just a few. All of these costs must be taken into account before setting menu prices, because

---

[2]For further discussion of the Hubbart formula, see Vallen, Jerome J., and Gary K. Vallen (1991) *Check-In Check-Out*, 4th ed. Dubuque, IA: William C. Brown, Publishers, pp. 199–202.

there must be adequate revenue from the sale of menu items to cover all the costs of operation.

The levels of skill and the amounts of employee time required to prepare menu items must be reflected in the menu prices established. For example, fine dining establishments employ talented and highly paid food preparation personnel, partly because they have the high level of skills required to prepare the menu items, some of which require great amounts of hand labor. In contrast, most fast-food restaurants can operate successfully with relatively unskilled labor earning far lower wages. The menu prices at both these types of establishments reflect the levels of difficulty and amounts of employee time required to prepare menu items. These differences help to account for the higher menu prices charged in fine dining establishments, compared with those of the fast-food restaurants.

For the majority of food and beverage operations, establishing menu prices should be done also with consideration of menu prices in competing operations. Those who ignore the menu prices of their competitors risk having potential customers go elsewhere. This is a particular risk for most fast-food restaurants and for other operations offering homogeneous service products.

A *homogeneous service product* is one that is so similar to those offered by other nearby competitors that customers do not favor one over another. Thus, they purchase on the basis of price. Given equal menu prices for homogeneous service products, customers will patronize the most conveniently located source. Commercial food service operators in competitive environments should normally avoid offering homogeneous service products.

Food service operators who seek to attract a large number of customers usually establish low menu prices. For example, one of the major reasons for the success of fast-food hamburger chains has been this ability to attract many customers by pricing their products low. They are able to make a satisfactory level of profit by instituting strict controls over costs. For many food service operations, low pricing is a key element in marketing.

Each food and beverage operation necessarily has its own cost structure, so it is not possible to provide any universal formula that can be used to set prices for the particular list of items on a given menu. In general, most commercial food and beverage operators attempt to set prices such that the total cost of food and labor combined is no greater than 65 to 70 percent of the sales revenue obtained from particular menus in given time periods.

Promotion

The fourth element in hospitality marketing is promotion. For many, this is the most important of the four.

For hospitality operations, *promotion* is the process of informing, persuading, and influencing customers to purchase a hospitality service product. There are five types of promotional activities:

1. Personal selling
2. Advertising
3. Sales promotion
4. Merchandising
5. Public relations

PERSONAL SELLING. Personal selling requires personal contact between buyer and seller. It typically takes place in a face-to-face encounter but can also take place over the telephone. Personal selling enables the seller or salesperson to communicate directly with the buyer—to ask and answer questions and to use all her personal powers of persuasion to sell the service product.

Because of this characteristic one-to-one relationship, personal selling is the most effective *sales tool*—or means of selling—that any organization can use. It is also an expensive means of reaching potential customers: In terms of the cost per person reached, personal selling is also the most expensive sales tool any organization can use. A salesperson reaches comparatively few customers in the course of any day or week. Such other forms of promotion as television and newspaper ads reach many more people at lower cost per person. Nevertheless, the sheer power of personal selling mandates that it be used to sell some hospitality service products. For example, sales representatives for hotels and catering organizations sell directly to people interested in receptions, banquets, weddings, and similar events. Hotel sales representatives personally visit prospective clients interested in booking conventions and sales meetings. In similar fashion, reservation clerks personally sell rooms over the telephone to prospective guests; desk clerks personally sell accommodations to walk-in customers; and restaurant servers sell specific menu items to customers.

ADVERTISING. *Advertising* is paid, nonpersonal communication directed to potential buyers. A vast number of hospitality organizations advertise their service products. Advertising is costly, however; and most hospitality organizations have limited amounts of money to purchase advertising. The professional expertise of an advertising agency may be required to prepare effective advertisements. In addition, advertising professionals are often the ones best able to place advertising in media that will provide the best results for the available budget. All of this costs money.

One of the important goals in advertising is to reach specific potential customers and to avoid reaching those who cannot or will not purchase the service. The familiar term *market* refers to a group of people who are willing and able to purchase a product For example, the owners of a cruise line would be interested in reaching the *cruise market*, defined as that group of people willing and able to purchase a cruise.

In most cases, the group of people identified as the market for a given type of product is too large to be reached effectively by general advertising. Those who purchase advertising have found it more effective to identify smaller groups of potential customers within the large market.

A specific group of potential customers within a larger market is defined as a *market segment. Market segmentation*—the process of selecting groups of potential customers with common characteristics—is an important concept in marketing and worthy of discussion.

Market Segmentation.   Any hospitality operation that offers service products designed for a particular group of potential customers with common characteristics can be said to have engaged in market segmentation. Markets can be segmented many ways. The three most important for the hospitality industry are

1. demographic segmentation,
2. geographic segmentation, and
3. psychographic segmentation.

These will be discussed individually.

Demographic Market Segmentation.   Demographic market segmentation is the most common way to segment a market. To divide a market into demographic segments means to divide potential consumers into groups with common characteristics such as age, sex, income level, occupation, level of education, marital status, family size, or mode of transportation used for long-distance travel, among many other possibilities. These are important to hospitality operations because the service products provided are typically directed toward those with specific characteristics that can be identified in demographic terms. For example, Club Med operates a worldwide chain of resort properties that appeal to various demographic groups: Some appeal to single individuals; others appeal to married couples; and still others appeal to families. Each of these three types of properties appeals to a different demographic segment of the vacation market.

Income level is another demographic market segment targeted by some hospitality operators. Five-star hotels and restaurants are examples of hospitality operations that appeal to small segments of the market—people with the highest income levels. In contrast, budget motels appeal to different market segments—people of more moderate means.

Another way of segmenting the travel market is by mode of transportation used for long-distance travel. This is of particular interest to some lodging operators. Airport motels and hotels typically depend on airline travelers for the largest share of their business. Motels situated on or near interstate highways depend, instead, on those who travel by automobile.

Geographic Market Segmentation.   Geographic market segmentation divides potential customers into geographic areas. This can be important for those hospitality operations with a large number of customers living in particular geographic areas. For example, a large percentage of the guests patronizing the ski resorts in Vermont reside in and around New York City. Knowing this, many ski resort operators direct their advertising toward this geographic market segment. On a broader scale, government tourism agencies from many nations direct advertising toward specific geographic segments of the American travel/tourism market: Chicago area residents, Southern California residents, and so on. Knowledge of the geographic region from which guests may come is important information to have when making advertising decisions.

Psychographic Market Segmentation.   The personality traits of individuals as indicated by their attitudes, interests, opinions, and lifestyles can be very useful to advertisers. Market segments reflecting these personality traits are known as *psychographic market segments.* Such specific information about potential customers as their recreation, eating, and entertainment preferences can be of considerable interest to those planning to advertise hospitality service products. It is also important when considering which services to offer customers. For example, restaurants that attempt to attract health-conscious customers must be sure to develop menus that appeal to such people. Hotels that target customers who regard daily exercise as an important activity will surely have specific facilities for these guests. And resorts attempting to appeal to tennis or golf enthusiasts must obviously have the necessary facilities on premises, or nearby.

Thus, most advertising is directed at specific segments of a broad market. A specific market segment to which advertising is directed is defined as a *target market.* Identifying and selecting target markets is important because of the high cost of advertising. Directing advertising to specific target markets helps to insure that limited advertising dollars are used effectively.

Advertising Media.   Once a hospitality operation identifies its markets and selects its target markets, advertising can be arranged. The media used to advertise hospitality service products include:

1. Television
2. Radio
3. Newspapers
4. Magazines
5. Outdoor ads
6. Direct mail

Both advantages and disadvantages are associated with the use of each of these for hospitality advertising.

Television. Television is a particularly effective medium for advertising, but it is also very expensive. The effectiveness of television advertisements is based on the combined visual and aural messages that reach the potential customer. No other advertising medium reaches potential customers' eyes and ears simultaneously. Purchasing advertising time on either national television networks or on local television stations is expensive, and only those with substantial advertising budgets are able to afford it. In some parts of the country, however, there are local cable television systems that sell time to advertisers. This form of television advertising is comparatively inexpensive, and growing numbers of hospitality operators are using it to advertise their service products.

Narrow targeting of specific market segments can be achieved by buying advertising time on carefully selected programs or at carefully selected times of the day. For example, some advertisers target their messages to young children by advertising on programs that appeal to children and during the hours when children are most likely to be watching television.

Radio. Radio advertising can be very effective, particularly in local markets. A single spot message can be relatively inexpensive, although advertising specialists generally believe that frequent radio advertising messages are required to have a cumulative effect. As with all other media, rates for radio advertising are determined to a large extent by the number of people reached by the selected radio station or program.

Radio is most appropriately used by those attempting to reach local or regional markets. Radio stations tend to be local in character and each station has a targeted group of listeners. Obviously, the targeted market of the radio station must be compatible with the targeted market of the advertiser for the advertising to be effective.

Newspapers. Perhaps the most popular medium for advertisers is the newspaper. Newspapers have the advantage of assuring that the targeted audience will have the message available to read at any time of the day, unlike television and radio that require the targeted group to be watching or listening when the advertisement is run. Most newspapers target customers geographically rather than demographically: Newspaper readership cuts across age, income, sex, and other demographic lines.

The circulation of most newspapers is localized, although some also have statewide, regional, or national circulation. Advertising costs in newspapers vary considerably, depending largely on circulation—the average number of copies the newspaper sells.

Magazines.   Magazine advertising is very effective for hospitality operations that target demographic or psychographic market segments. Magazines can be used to target both regional and national market segments. Many magazines appeal to specific market segments—unlike newspapers, which reach a more general readership. For example, there are magazines published specifically for golfers, computer enthusiasts, gun collectors, children, sailboat owners, and coin collectors, to name just a few. Hospitality operators seeking to appeal to particular groups can advertise in appropriate magazines, with some assurance that targeted groups will be reached.

Outdoor Ads.   The primary means of outdoor advertising is the billboard — found along roads and highways all across the nation. Billboards, signs, and other forms of outdoor advertising are very effective for many hospitality operations, particularly motels and restaurants. Outdoor advertisements must be very brief: Passengers in automobiles must be able to read them in the very few seconds required to pass one. For hospitality operators, the advertisements are generally limited to a quick message and the location of the service product provider. For some motels, particularly those that are not close to highways, outdoor advertisements are critical factors in their survival.

Many people oppose outdoor advertising on principle, and a number of states have prohibited all outdoor advertising on environmental grounds.

Direct Mail.   Direct mail reaches potential customers via the postal system: Promotional materials are sent directly to them in the mail. Those hospitality operations interested in using direct mail can purchase fairly accurate mailing lists of potential customers sorted into any number of market segments—demographic, geographic, or psychographic. Lists are available that include only people of specified income levels, of specified professions, or residing in specified communities or parts of communities. The number of market segments that can be reached using purchased lists is virtually unlimited.

SALES PROMOTION. A *sales promotion* is an inducement offered by a seller to persuade a buyer to make an immediate purchase. Sales promotions are intended to persuade consumers to take action immediately rather than to wait. In hospitality operations, sales promotions are intended to attract customers to the establishment immediately, or at least to make their reservations immediately.

Hospitality operations frequently offer sales promotions to increase business. Some restaurants offer entrees at reduced prices on specific nights: a 50 percent discount on all fried shrimp dinners on Monday nights, for example. Similarly, hotels or motels sometimes offer packages at discounted rates to attract business during slow periods.

MERCHANDISING. *Merchandising* is a term used to describe those actions taken by hospitality operators to increase sales to in-house customers. Merchandising differs from sales promotion in that sales promotions are aimed at attracting new customers to the establishment; merchandising activities are designed to increase sales to existing customers—diners seated at tables in a restaurant or guests who have already checked into a motel.

Merchandising tools used by hospitality operators include posters, carefully written menus, table tent cards, and displays of breads, desserts, fruits, and wines. Some hotels post attractive signs in elevators to merchandise their food and beverage service products. Some restaurants use dessert carts; others may use tent cards to merchandise specific desserts.

PUBLIC RELATIONS. *Public relations* is a term used to refer to those activities and efforts designed to do one of the following: (1) improve or enhance the image or reputation of an organization; (2) promote the organization's name; or (3) improve its relations with employees, customers, suppliers, stockholders, or any other people or firms thought to be important to the organization.

Public relations activities and efforts can take many forms. Supporting local charities or sponsoring worthwhile activities is one. Writing news releases or holding news conferences to announce worthwhile activities and events is another.

Some resort hotels used to send photographs of guests to the guests' hometown newspapers. This provided valuable publicity for the hotels that did it. Sometimes it had unfortunate consequences for those whose names and photographs appeared in local newspapers, and the practice has largely disappeared.

Each of the four elements of marketing listed and just discussed—product, place, price, and promotion—is used to one extent or another in the marketing efforts of hospitality organizations. In any hospitality organization's marketing effort, the relative proportions of these elements or ingredients make up the organization's *marketing mix*. Target markets and the marketing mix are central to a hospitality organization's marketing strategy.

MARKETING STRATEGY

Marketing strategy is a term that refers to the overall approach used to reach marketing goals. Two main considerations exist in a marketing strategy: targeted market segments and marketing mix. Managers must determine which segments of markets to target. They must also determine the relevance of each of the four marketing elements to the target markets. In general, a marketing strategy should attract potential customers by employing the four marketing elements in appropriate measures. Some give greater importance to product—the specific service products they offer—in developing the marketing strategy. Others rely more heavily on location. Some prefer to emphasize price. Some others place greater stress on promotion. The extent of the emphasis given each of the four elements in an organization's effort to reach target markets describes the organization's marketing strategy.

Product as the Primary Strategy.   Many hospitality operations emphasize their specific service products, using these as the primary marketing tool. Gourmet restaurants, for example, generally rely on cuisine, service, and ambiance to attract customers. Some develop outstanding reputations, and new customers are attracted by the glowing comments made by satisfied customers. Once customers are seated, merchandising is tastefully employed to increase sales. For these kinds of restaurants, price, location, and promotional techniques may play only minor roles in the marketing effort.

Some five-star resort hotels use similar marketing strategies. They emphasize their service products—accommodations, services, and ambiance. Fine hotels do very limited promotion; some use direct mail to former guests as their highest promotional priority.

Place as the Primary Strategy.   In contrast to those that emphasize product, some hospitality operations rely more heavily on place—their locations. The target market of restaurants on interstate highways, for example, are the passengers in cars on the highway—travelers who will need food or refreshment. Some restaurants located on interstate highways do virtually no promotion, have comparatively poor food, and charge relatively high prices; yet they are very profitable because of their locations.

Many independently operated motels also rely on location as their primary marketing tool. Just as with interstate restaurants, their target market consists of travelers on the adjoining highway. Those motels with good locations can be very profitable, while those with inferior locations may find it necessary to develop an entirely different marketing strategy.

Price as the Primary Strategy.   Price is a key element in the marketing strategies of typical fast-food restaurants. Those that are associated with national chains generally have an advantage, because the marketing strategies of these national organizations provide two other important elements for success: considerable promotion and the selection of superior locations. Budget motels use both price and location as key elements in their marketing strategies. Those that are associated with national chains have additional advantages: the central reservations systems to which they are linked and the national advertising done by these chains.

Promotion as the Primary Strategy.   Some restaurants and lodging operations rely heavily on promotion to obtain business. This is true for many restaurants with relatively poor locations. Some use both sales promotions and advertising to attract customers. Hotels and motels with deteriorating facilities, inferior locations, or both are forced to rely on promotions to attract customers. Properties that fall into this category include resort hotels located in declining areas and older center-city hotels that lack modern accommodations and facilities.

THE MARKETING PLAN

A *marketing plan* is a document that incorporates all intended marketing efforts into a plan of action for an organization. It identifies marketing objectives, target markets, and a marketing strategy. It also forecasts the anticipated cost of the marketing plan and the timing for the execution of various parts of the marketing program. Marketing plans are typically prepared for the coming year, although it is possible to prepare longer range marketing plans covering several years.

The specific contents of marketing plans, like the specific contents of feasibility studies, differ from organization to organization. Most would agree, however, that marketing plans should deal with the following:

1. Internal analysis of the organization
2. Analysis of the competition
3. Market assessment
4. Positioning
5. Marketing objectives
6. Target markets
7. Marketing mix
8. Marketing costs
9. Timing

INTERNAL ANALYSIS OF THE ORGANIZATION. Internal analysis examines such important factors as past and present sales, expenses, and profits for the establishment. It also looks at current standards of service, the state of repair of the property and all facilities, and the service products offered to guests or customers. In general, it assesses strengths and weaknesses, as well as opportunities and threats in the near term. It is an objective appraisal of the current state of the enterprise and its operation. An internal analysis evaluates current trends and projects them into the future, providing management with a forecast of the organization's future performance.

Internal analysis is the natural starting point for a marketing plan, because it provides a complete appraisal of the current operation. If owners and managers are satisfied with the current state of profitability, operation, and the property itself, planning will be considerably different than it would be if one or more of these were found unsatisfactory. For example, if sales or customer counts are too low, a new marketing plan will establish appropriate goals and describe a means of achieving them.

ANALYSIS OF THE COMPETITION. Analysis of the competition provides information about significant competitors in the market—their relative strengths and weaknesses and their anticipated plans for the coming period. For example, analyzing the competitors of a given lodging operation may reveal that some have better locations, others have more spacious and attractive accommodations, and still others have more desirable recreational facilities. Analyzing the competitors of a given restaurant may indicate that some have better locations, others have more convenient parking, and still others have less expensive menus.

Sometimes owners or managers are aware of future actions planned by their competitors that will have unfavorable consequences for their own operations. When it is possible to identify competitors' plans, it may be possible to counter them or to lessen their consequences.

It is important to know and understand the nature and extent of one's competitors' advantages and disadvantages. The marketing plan can then tailor actions to overcome their advantages and to benefit from their disadvantages.

MARKET ASSESSMENT. Market assessment provides useful information about various economic, social, and political trends in the markets from which one's customers are likely to come. Such considerations as unemployment, recession, changing food preferences, changing tax laws, and political instability in the market are likely to have predictable effects on businesses.

As discussed earlier in this chapter, markets may be segmented geographically, demographically, or psychographically. Although hospitality organizations are commonly concerned with all three, geographic market segments are particularly important to many.

For restaurants, geographic markets are normally local: Customers are most likely to be drawn from a nearby and comparatively small geographic area. In a city, that might be the surrounding twenty square blocks; in a rural setting, it could be the surrounding twenty square miles. For hotels and similar lodging operations, geographic market areas are normally considerably larger. For a large, well-known hotel in a major Eastern city, the geographic market area could include the Northeastern and Middle Atlantic states. It might even include the entire United States. For a resort property in the Caribbean, it could be even larger.

POSITION. Market position refers to the image an establishment wants to convey to the public. The operator of any food service or lodging establishment normally wants to project an image to the public—an overall impression that will set the establishment apart from similar establishments in the minds of customers. It may be based on price, degree of luxury, convenience, fast service, or some combination of these and other attributes. For example, a family restaurant may establish an image as a moderately priced, informal restaurant with a warm and friendly atmosphere and a menu that offers great variety and a number of items specially prepared for children. This defines the restaurant's market position and differentiates it from other restaurants. It gives it an identity.

The Kensington Hotel would be likely to position itself as a luxury property with elegant accommodations, excellent food, and a high level of personal service. Positioning the hotel in this fashion would distinguish it from many other hotels and create an image intended to attract the target clientele. In contrast, the Value Lodge would be more likely to position itself as an inexpensive motel with comfortable accommodations catering to overnight travelers who do not want to pay for frills.

Many hospitality marketing experts would agree that the market position of a hospitality operation is the basis for the marketing plan. All decisions and actions are based on the desired market position of the organization. If an organization decides to change its current market position, the effort is referred to as *repositioning.*

MARKETING OBJECTIVES. Marketing objectives are the goals that the marketing plan intends to achieve. For a lodging operation, one marketing objective might be to increase occupancy by 5 percent in the coming year, to attract a larger percentage of business from a particular geographic area, or to attract a different demographic or psychographic guest population.

For a restaurant, one marketing objective might be to increase the number of dinner customers by 100 per week for the coming year. Or it could be to increase income by attracting a different demographic population—customers from higher income brackets who will be likely to order more expensive menu items.

Whatever the objectives for marketing, they must be enumerated as precisely as possible. Like any plan, the objectives must be known to all employees so that everyone will be working to achieve the same goals. Obviously, the marketing objectives must be compatible with other plans and objectives of the organization.

TARGET MARKETS. The target markets for the marketing plan must also be identified precisely. As previously discussed, target markets are the specific groups of potential customers or guests that the marketing plan will attempt to reach. The characteristics of the target markets influence the nature of the marketing mix as well as the promotional elements that are emphasized. For example, if a resort hotel identifies residents of the Chicago area as its geographic target market, promotional plans might include spending a considerable portion of the advertising budget in appropriate Sunday newspapers read by those in the Chicago area. Or it might call for personal visits to travel agents in the Chicago area. On the other hand, if the resort identifies golfers as its psychographic target market, a large part of the advertising budget would probably be allocated for specific golf magazines.

Tennis resort and camp advertisements aimed to appeal to their target market, or the specific group of potential customers at which the organization's marketing plan is aimed. Note the varying emphasis on tennis in each of the ads.

MARKETING MIX. The marketing plan must indicate the relative importance the organization will give to product, place, price, and promotion in its marketing effort. As previously indicated, each hospitality operation establishes its own unique marketing mix—one that management feels will best enable the organization to achieve its marketing goals. Some organizations rely heavily on their service product lines. Some rely on their locations, and others attempt to attract customers with low prices. A large number of hospitality operations rely on extensive promotional efforts to achieve their goals. Most hospitality operations incorporate a blend of the four elements in their marketing plans but stress one or two, using these as the foundations of their marketing strategy.

MARKETING COSTS. Marketing objectives and a marketing strategy cannot be established independent of cost considerations. There would be no point to establishing a marketing plan that relied heavily on promotional activities unless one had the resources to carry them out. As management works to develop a suitable marketing strategy, options at various levels of cost must be assessed. It is probable that the marketing strategy developed for a particular organization will be heavily dependent on the resources available. A neighborhood restaurant may be able to afford promotional activities such as wine displays and more attractively designed menus, for example, but may not be able to attempt advertising on television or offering free bottles of good wine to all customers, because of the costs they will incur. Similarly, a resort hotel seeking to upgrade its service product line by building a world-class golf course might find the cost to be far beyond the resources available. The costs associated with implementing a marketing plan become part of the plan.

TIMING. Finally, the timing of the elements of the marketing plan must be determined. To achieve the established objectives, the marketing effort must be coordinated. Each piece must be undertaken at a predetermined time, and the overall relationship of each one's timing becomes very important. For example, promotions designed to stress improved service should not begin until staff members have been given suitable training. Similarly, promotions emphasizing low rates for resort hotel rooms should be timed to increase room sales in the off season, when levels of occupancy are lowest.

Finally, the marketing plan for every hospitality organization should be the result of the dedicated efforts of hospitality managers to devise appropriate means to achieve organizational goals.

SUMMARY

In this chapter the terms *marketing* and *hospitality marketing* are defined. The four key elements of marketing are listed and discussed. The three components of the hospitality service product are identified. Advantages and disadvantages of franchise affiliations and referral affiliations are listed and described. Various considerations in establishing room rates and menu prices are identified. Five types of promotional activities are enumerated and discussed as are six media used to advertise hospitality service products. The terms *market, target market, market segment, marketing mix,* and *marketing strategy* are defined and discussed. Geographic, demographic, and psychographic market segments are identified. Finally, marketing plans and their importance to hospitality organizations are described.

QUESTIONS

1. Define *hospitality marketing.* Why is it different from the standard definition of *marketing* for manufactured products?
2. List and describe the four elements of marketing.
3. Define the term *franchise.*
4. List five reasons that an independently owned hospitality operation might want to become part of a franchise organization.

5. List and discuss three disadvantages associated with becoming a franchisee.

6. Distinguish between franchise and referral organizations.

7. Identify the primary benefit to a lodging property in belonging to a central reservations system.

8. Describe locations that could be described as "good" for each of the following:
   a. Ski lodge
   b. Luxury hotel in a city
   c. Motel near a limited-access highway
   d. Fast-food restaurant
   e. Resort hotel

9. List the three primary considerations in establishing a room rate structure for a lodging operation.

10. Define the following resort hotel terms:
    a. High season
    b. Shoulder season
    c. Off season

11. List the seven factors taken into consideration in establishing menu prices.

12. List and describe five types of promotional activities.

13. Of the five identified in question 12, which is the most effective? Why?

14. Define each of the following terms:
    a. *market*
    b. *target market*
    c. *market segment*

15. Distinguish between demographic, geographic, and psychographic market segmentation.

16. List six advertising media used for promoting hospitality operations and identify two advantages and two disadvantages of each.

17. Which advertising media would be appropriate for each of the following hospitality operations? Why?
    a. A highway motel
    b. A neighborhood family restaurant
    c. A resort hotel catering to tennis enthusiasts

d. A center-city luxury hotel

e. A national chain of fast-food restaurants

18. Define each of the following terms:

a. *marketing mix*

b. *marketing strategy*

19. Identify the purpose of a marketing plan.

20. List and describe the elements of a marketing plan.

Human Resources Management in Hospitality

17

LEARNING OBJECTIVES

After reading and studying this chapter, you should be able to:

1. *Define the term human resources management.*
2. *List and discuss the elements of human resources planning.*
3. *Identify the information required for job analysis.*
4. *List and describe the three parts of a job description.*
5. *Define the term job specification.*
6. *Define the term recruiting and identify ten possible sources for recruiting hospitality employees.*
7. *List and describe the seven basic steps that constitute a standard procedure for selecting the best candidate for employment.*
8. *Identify the three principal elements that should be included in a basic orientation for new employees.*
9. *Describe five approaches for training groups of employees.*
10. *List and discuss three primary objectives of performance appraisal.*
11. *Define the term compensation.*
12. *Distinguish between deferred compensation and the two forms of current compensation.*
13. *Define the term labor union.*
14. *Discuss the resolution of grievances in hospitality operations with union contracts.*
15. *List three important steps taken by management to enhance employee safety in the workplace.*

16. *Define the term* <u>Employee Assistance Program</u> *and list seven issues EAPs often address.*
17. *Identify five ways to improve employee morale in the workplace.*

INTRODUCTION

Hospitality is a labor intensive industry—meaning that many people are needed to do the work required in those enterprises that make up the hospitality industry. In fact, more than 10 million workers are employed in hospitality, making the industry one of the largest in the United States. The industry depends on a work force that includes more female and minority workers than are employed in any other industry. Of all the resources available to hospitality managers, none are of greater value than human resources.

The hospitality industry is also known to have a high rate of employee turnover. Employee turnover rate is calculated by dividing the number of workers hired to replace those who have left in a given period of time by the number of workers employed in that same period. It is not unusual for a hospitality operation to have a 100 percent rate of employee turnover during the course of a year. While many establishments have very loyal employees who have worked at the same place for years, many others are continually seeking new employees, as current employees leave for any number of reasons.

Planning human resources needs, recruiting suitable applicants, selecting new employees, orienting them to the organization, providing them with the proper training, conducting performance appraisals, developing suitable compensation and benefits packages, and attending to various health and safety considerations are important elements in the management of human resources in hospitality organizations. In organizations in which employees are covered by contracts negotiated by labor unions, labor relations constitutes another element in human resources management.

HUMAN RESOURCES MANAGEMENT DEFINED

The activities cited above are the major responsibilities of a human resources manager. In one sense, all managers are human resources managers, because working with people and supervising their activities is a human resources activity and is a major part of any supervisor's job. However, in large organizations, supervisory managers often do not have sufficient time to attend to all the details of recruiting, selecting, and training employees for their departments, particularly in organizations with high rates of employee turnover. In addition, most supervisory managers have somewhat limited knowledge of such other human resources topics as collective bargaining, compensation and benefits packages, and modern training techniques. Most, therefore, need the expert assistance of human resources professionals.

Human resources managers normally occupy staff positions in hospitality organizations. People in staff positions are specialists who provide assistance in their specialties to those in line positions. As specialists, human resources managers relieve line managers of some very time-consuming work and enable them to concentrate on their primary jobs.

Dr. Mary L. Tanke, in her text, *Human Resources Management*, defines *human resources management* as "the implementation of the strategies, plans, and programs required to attract, motivate, develop, reward, and retain the best people to meet the organizational goals and operational objectives of the hospitality enterprise."[1]

Given Tanke's definition, one can generalize the following as principal topics to be covered in a discussion of human resources management in the hospitality industry:

1. Human resources planning
2. Recruiting applicants
3. Selecting applicants for employment
4. Orientation of new employees
5. Training and developing employees
6. Appraising employee performance
7. Compensation programs
8. Labor unions
9. Employee safety
10. Employee assistance programs
11. Employee morale

These are among the most important subjects to address in an introduction to human resources management in the hospitality industry.

HUMAN RESOURCES PLANNING

The first task of human resources management is planning. This cannot be undertaken until management has organized the business—defined the service product line and established the jobs that must be accomplished to achieve organizational goals. Once management has attended to these preliminary steps, the process of human resources planning can begin.

Human resources planning is more complex than simply forecasting the number of workers needed for the various job titles in a hospitality operation.

---

[1]Mary L. Tanke, *Human Resources Management* (Albany: Delmar Publishers, 1990), p. 5.

Instead, it requires that one identify the nature of each job as well as the skills, the level of education, and any other specific qualifications needed to perform it. For example, planning for personnel at the front desk of a hotel is more than simply determining that there will be one room clerk on duty for every eight-hour shift, every day of the week. One must also know and understand the nature of the room clerk's job in the particular hotel, the specific duties assigned to that job, the skills required to carry out those duties, and any other qualifications or attributes that a room clerk should possess. The term given to the process of gathering this information is *job analysis*.

Job Analysis

Job analysis is the first step in forecasting human resources needs. The information necessary to complete job analysis may be gathered in any of several ways. In the hospitality industry, the two most common methods are

1. interviewing workers and supervisors to obtain the information and
2. observing workers on site as they perform the jobs.

Complete analysis requires effective use of both methods. One approach is to conduct in-depth interviews with workers and supervisors during the course of a normal workday. These interviews are typically conducted on premises in a reasonably quiet area, somewhat removed from the actual work site. In some instances they are videotaped to facilitate review. Each interview is carefully structured to elicit the specific information required for the job analysis. Later, interviewers observe both workers and supervisors, taking extensive notes to supplement those taken during the interviews. The interviews and observations are designed to provide information about the following:

1. Job objectives
2. Specific tasks required to achieve objectives
3. Performance standards
4. Knowledge and skills necessary
5. Education and experience required

The data gathered is used to develop job descriptions and job specifications.

Job Description

Once job analysis is completed, job descriptions can be written. As the term implies, *job descriptions* are detailed written statements that describe jobs. In some instances, job descriptions list very specific duties and directions for performing jobs. Job descriptions for particular jobs should answer three important questions:

1. What is to be done?
2. When is it done?
3. Where is it done?

A job description typically has three parts:

1. A heading that states the job title and the department in which the job is located. In some organizations, the heading may include such information as the number of positions with that particular job title, the specific hours, days, or shifts worked by those with the job title, and the supervisor to whom those with that job title report.
2. A summary of the duties of the job, typically written in paragraph form. The summary enables the reader to gain quickly a basic understanding of the nature and purpose of the job. By reading the summaries of all the jobs in a particular department, one could obtain a great deal of information about the department in a very short period. This might be of great benefit to a new manager, for example.
3. A list of the specific duties assigned to the job. These will be as detailed as possible, to the point that well-written job descriptions can be used as step-by-step instructions for doing the work required of those holding the jobs. As we will see, having job descriptions can be of great value to those charged with appraising employee performance.

A job description is particularly important for prospective employees. By having detailed descriptions of the duties required, job applicants and newly hired workers know specifically what is to be done by someone holding a particular job.

Job descriptions are also very important for employers. They enable employers to hold employees accountable for doing the work assigned to a job. Employees who have read job descriptions but fail to perform the assigned work cannot successfully use the age-old excuse, "Nobody ever told me I had to do this."

Job analysis and the resulting job descriptions have the added benefit of forcing managers to assign specific work to each job holder. If all the normal duties of a department are identified with specific job descriptions, the department will be better organized and will operate more smoothly.

Table 17.1 is an example of the kind of job description that one might find in a food service enterprise. Note the degree of detail provided, which can also be of great assistance to those responsible for developing employee training programs.

TABLE 17.1 *Job description: Steak Shack*

JOB TITLE:	Server
SUPERVISOR:	Dining Room Manager
WORKING HOURS:	Schedule varies. Hours and days will vary each week.

JOB SUMMARY

Servers greet seated guests, take orders and serve food and drinks, present checks with last service, and clear/reset tables.

DUTIES

1. Server reports to supervisor one hour before meal period to assist in preparing dining room for opening.
2. Servers are assigned stations in dining room by dining room manager. Schedules are posted each Friday for the following week, which begins Sunday.
3. Servers pour water, take food and drink orders, place orders in kitchen and bar, pick up and serve food and drink, present checks to guests, and clear/reset tables.
4. Service procedures: food is served from guest's left; beverages from right. All china, glassware, and silver are removed from guest's right.
5. Fifteen minutes before the scheduled opening of the dining room, servers are briefed on daily specials, service techniques, and other matters of importance.
6. Tips are pooled. Ten percent of the tip pool goes to bartenders and the remainder is divided equally among servers. Tips are distributed the following day.
7. Servers provide own uniforms as follows: Black pants or skirt; white dress shirt with long sleeves and buttoned cuffs; black bow tie; polished black shoes with flat heels. No high heels. Servers will be given an allowance of $5 per week to care for their uniforms.
8. Standards for personal appearance: Showered or bathed prior to work; underarm deodorant required; clean fingernails; hair clean and neat; no excessive jewelry.

Males:
  a. Clean shaven preferred. Moustache permitted if neat and trimmed.
  b. No facial or ear jewelry.
  c. Hair cannot extend beyond shirt collar.

Females:
  a. No excessive jewelry, makeup, or perfume.
  b. Long hair must be in hair net.
  c. No long false nails.

Job Specification

A job specification outlines the qualifications needed to perform a job. It outlines the specific skills needed, and it describes the kinds and levels of education and experience required. In addition, job specifications typically include minimum qualifications that applicants must have to be considered, as well as appropriate standards that can be used for judging the qualifications of applicants.

Once the job analysis phase has been completed and both job descriptions and job specifications have been written, human resources personnel can begin to plan another critical activity in human resources management: recruiting.

RECRUITING APPLICANTS

Recruiting is a process by which suitable applicants are found for available jobs. It may begin when there are actual vacancies to be filled because employees have left. Alternatively, it may begin in anticipation of vacancies that are likely to occur in the near future. Many hospitality operations have high rates of employee turnover; and recruiting, selecting, and hiring new employees can take considerable time. Because of this, a number of the larger hospitality organizations are continually recruiting, knowing that new personnel will soon be needed.

Human resources personnel have found that applicants for particular jobs can come from any of the following:

1. Recommendations made by current employees
2. Unsolicited resumes received in the mail
3. Walk-ins
4. Classified advertisements in newspapers
5. Public and private employment agencies
6. Recommendations made by trusted vendors who deal with the organization
7. Unions
8. Colleges and universities
9. Industry trade journals
10. Competitors

Economic conditions often determine the extent of the recruiting effort that must be undertaken to fill a given position. During periods of recession, hospitality organizations typically find that very little recruiting effort is required to obtain qualified applicants for most jobs. During such periods, human resources personnel may be inundated with applicants for any open job. When unemployment rates are very low, however, human resources personnel may find it difficult to find applicants. If that is the case, it may be necessary to make a greater effort to find applicants—using many of the sources just listed.

The decision to use or not to use any one of these sources will also depend on the nature of the jobs to be filled. Many hospitality operations with labor contracts are required to seek new employees for jobs covered by the union contract through the union hiring hall. Applicants for jobs other than those covered by a union contract may be obtained through classified advertisements in the help-wanted sections of newspapers. In contrast, entry-level management trainees can often be recruited at colleges and universities. Candidates for supervisory positions and for such skilled titles as *chef* often come from employment

Before recruiting prospective applicants, a human resources manager analyzes the position to be filled and writes up a job description and specifications. Using the many sources available, including classified ads, recommendations made by employees or suppliers, and employment agencies, along with the screening processes of interviews, application reviews, and reference checks, a human resources manager will attempt to appropriately fill a vacant position. (Photo copyright © 1988 Miles Thomas; courtesy Wyndham Resorts and Hotels.)

agencies, or they may be obtained from vendors who supply products to a given hospitality operation.

SELECTING APPLICANTS FOR EMPLOYMENT

The purpose of the recruiting effort is to develop a sizable pool of applicants from which the best person for the job can be selected. In their efforts to obtain sufficient information about applicants to ensure the selection of the best one, human resources personnel use a number of common "tools." These include application forms, resumes, selection tests, interviews, and background checks. The following steps constitute a standard selection process used by many organizations:

1. Preliminary interview
2. Application form
3. Selection test
4. Interview
5. Reference check and background investigation
6. Selection
7. Physical examination

Some or all of these steps are normally at the core of the selection process used by human resources managers in hospitality firms. However, these seven cannot be taken as an industrywide standard: Each hospitality organization normally develops its own preferred routine for selecting the best candidate.

Even among those firms that accept these seven steps as their standard approach to selecting individuals for employment, few would use every one for every job. The higher the level of skill or responsibility associated with a particular job, the more thorough would be the selection process.

Preliminary Interview

Applicants for jobs are typically given preliminary interviews. The purpose of a preliminary interview is to eliminate all applicants who do not meet the minimum qualifications established for the job. Some will lack previous experience; others will not have the specified knowledge or will lack the necessary skills. During this preliminary meeting, the interviewer has an excellent opportunity to describe the job and discuss it with the applicant. This provides the applicant with an opportunity to ask questions about both the job and the organization, and it gives the interviewer some basis for determining whether or not the applicant is minimally qualified.

Provisions of various federal and state laws prohibit discrimination in hiring on the basis of age, race, sex, religion, and national origin, among others. Therefore, employment applications and employment interviews must avoid asking questions that would be illegal under these laws. For example, one cannot ask where applicants were born.

The Application Form

The application form requests job-related information that will help the employer determine if the applicant is qualified.

Virtually all application forms ask applicants to provide name, address, educational background, and past work experience. Some applications request such additional information as awards received, outside interests, and hobbies. Application forms must conform to laws mandating equal employment opportunities for all. Thus, they cannot include questions about the applicant's sex, weight, height, nationality, or religion. Similarly, employers cannot ask applicants to submit photographs with their applications. Other questions that do not relate to the job requirements are also illegal. These include questions about marital status, size of family, and arrest record.

There is one exception to the above guidelines. If it can be shown that specific qualifications are necessary to perform a job, questions relating to those qualifications can be asked—even if they might otherwise be construed as discriminatory in nature. These are called *bona fide occupational qualifications (BFOQ)*. For example, if one is attempting to hire an attendant for a women's locker room at a resort hotel, a question on the application relating to sex can be asked.

Testing

Some organizations require that applicants for jobs complete written tests. Such tests are designed to aid in assessing applicants' qualifications for positions in the organization. There are several types of written tests commonly used for these purposes, including:

1. Skills tests
2. Personality tests
3. Aptitude tests
4. Psychological tests

Written tests, like applications and interviews, must be job related. If the test questions are not job related, the test may be subject to legal challenge and should probably not be given.

Written tests should also meet standards of reliability, objectivity, and validity. A test is *reliable* if a person taking it on several occasions earns similar scores each time. It is *objective* if everyone evaluating the results of a test taken by a given subject arrive at the same score for the subject. It is *valid* if it measures what it is designed to measure. A test that is designed to measure culinary skills should provide results that demonstrably measure those skills. In addition, the test should be *standardized:* Everyone applying for a particular job should receive the same test. Finally, the results should be meaningful, such that the most qualified receive higher scores than those who are unqualified.

Interviews

Those applicants who have demonstrated in initial interviews that they meet the minimum qualifications, and who have filled out applications and passed written tests with acceptable scores, are typically brought back for more extensive interviews. These interviews provide the employer with opportunities to evaluate the applicant, making appropriate judgments about such concerns as a person's enthusiasm, personality, or ability to fit into the organization. These interviews may be conducted by human resources personnel or by the head of the department in which the job is located.

There are two types of questions asked in these interviews: direct and open-ended.

A *direct question* is one that is designed to elicit specific information. Direct questions tend to restrict responses. Examples of direct questions are "What were the duties of your last job?" and "What are your salary requirements?" An *open-ended question* does not seek specific information. Instead, it gives the applicant an opportunity to express an opinion or to provide information. Open-ended questions typically provide insights into an applicant's personality, character traits, and abilities. An open-ended question gives the interviewer an opportunity to make value judgments about an applicant's qualifications and ability to fit into the organization. Examples of open-ended questions are: "What did you like best about your last job?" and "Which of your qualifications do you think our organization will find most valuable? And why?"

Most interviews are a blend of direct and open-ended questions. It is normally considered good practice for the interviewer to elicit some basic, specific information from all applicants with direct questions, then to ask some open-ended questions to give applicants an opportunity to make points in their own favor that might otherwise never have come up.

Reference Check and Background Investigation

By the time all qualified applicants have been interviewed, the interviewer normally has some idea which of the candidates are the most likely finalists for the job. At this stage, it is important to verify the accuracy of all information provided by the applicants, to check references, and in some instances to investigate applicants' backgrounds. Hospitality organizations are liable for the job-related actions of employees, so it is important to make every effort to avoid hiring those whose past histories include theft, assault, battery, and similar antisocial behavior. Interviews can be deceiving. It is possible for a candidate to present himself positively to a prospective employer but to act very differently on the job. Thus, it is important to verify information on the application or resume and to make sure that past job performance and character references check out.

The information obtained through reference checks and background investigations is not always reliable, although the extent of reliability can be improved if one is willing to incur the expense of hiring a private investigator. Sometimes background investigations reveal gaps in an applicant's employment record that cannot be accounted for satisfactorily, and many employers are unwilling to provide information about former employees other than the dates between which they were employed. References are supplied by applicants, and it should be obvious that applicants are unlikely ever to provide the names of people who have anything unfavorable to say. However, one must never accept without verification the information supplied by job applicants. Some reasonable effort must be made to verify all significant information provided by applicants. And if one piece of information proves to be incorrect, every effort must be made to check on other data provided by that applicant.

Selection

Once finalists' references have been checked and their backgrounds investigated to the extent deemed necessary, it is possible to select the finalist to whom the job will be offered. The selection may be made by the human resources department or by the head of the department in which the new employee will work. If the selection is to be made by the department head and prior interviews have been conducted by the human resources department, the department head may want to bring back the finalists for a third interview.

In some cases, the human resources department will complete the entire process and simply send the selected applicant to the department head. This is a common approach for jobs with little responsibility or requiring little interaction with other employees. For most positions in hospitality organizations, department heads usually prefer to make their own final selections.

Physical Examination

The final step in the selection of employees is to require that the individual to whom the job is offered undergoes a physical examination. Job offers are usually contingent on the candidates' passing physical examinations showing that they are free of contagious diseases and physical disabilities that would prevent them from performing their jobs. A job offer may be withdrawn if medical problems revealed by a physical examination are sufficiently serious to prevent adequate performance.

Physical examinations have other purposes, as well. For example, suppose that a physical examination reveals that an employee has a minor physical problem that will not interfere with his work. If that worker later attempts to claim that the problem is job-related, the results of the pre-employment physical will enable the employer to refute the employee's claim.

ORIENTATION OF NEW EMPLOYEES

All new employees should be given a suitable orientation to the organization prior to their first day of work. New employees normally have some concern and uncertainty about beginning a job, and it is important to get them started with as little uneasiness as possible. In addition, some basic information should be given to every new employee. In most well-managed hospitality organizations, basic orientation includes:

1. Organization policies, procedures, and rules. Among the concerns to be addressed are those related to wages, work hours, overtime, sick leave, time cards, insurance, and keys, among others. In the hospitality industry, answers must be provided for such common questions as: "Where should I park my car?" "What meals do employees get?" "How do I get a clean uniform?" "Where do I change into uniform?" "Can employees use any of the hotel's facilities?" "How does the health insurance plan work?" "What is the grievance procedure?"

2. Mission and objectives of the organization. It is important that every employee in the organization work toward the same goals—and that the goals be understood by every employee from his or her very first day on the job.
3. A tour of the work area to point out offices and facilities with which all employees should be familiar. The tour should include opportunities for the introduction of such personnel as the paymaster, the human resources manager, and any others with whom workers should be acquainted.

In many of the larger hospitality organizations, new-employee orientation may be conducted in a group environment such as a classroom. In most of the smaller organizations that tend to characterize the hospitality industry, it is usually necessary for orientations to be done on an individual basis.

Some organizations rely on a mentor system to provide each new employee with a more complete orientation. A new employee will be paired with an experienced employee who will "show him the ropes." For example, a cook who has been with a given hotel for ten years may be made the mentor for a new cook. The experienced cook could give the new cook an orientation tour of the property and kitchen, pointing out such details as the locker room, store room, specific pieces of equipment, requisitions, recipes, uniforms, and refrigerators. The experienced cook might also explain the chef's policies for reporting to work, cleaning equipment, laundering uniforms, and other matters. In the same hotel, a new housekeeper might be paired with an experienced housekeeper, who would show the new employee such details as the location of the locker room, linen room, and employee cafeteria and who would explain various policies and procedures enforced by the executive housekeeper.

TRAINING AND DEVELOPING EMPLOYEES

Training is generally required of all new employees—even those who come to an organization with considerable experience. Every hospitality operation has its own way of doing things—its own methods for performing tasks and accomplishing work. It is important, therefore, that people who already know how to perform a job be shown the specific methods and procedures used by the organization for which they have just started to work. For those who are inexperienced, more formal training is likely to be needed.

Training can be done on an individual basis, or it may be done in groups. Individual training is undoubtedly the most effective, but it is very expensive: The trainer must devote time to training only one person at a time.

Training can be done on the job or off the job. On-the-job training is commonly used with experienced workers, who need only be shown the methods used by the hospitality operation. For example, the new cook cited previously may

Employee training and development are accomplished in a number of ways: through a close mentor relationship (shown above), through lectures and demonstrations, through role playing, through seminars, by reviewing case studies, and through panel discussion. Each approach serves a different purpose at every level of an employee's experience. (Courtesy Four Seasons.)

be put to work immediately under the guidance of an experienced cook, who will show the new cook how to fill out requisitions for supplies, how orders are placed for menu items, and how the establishment garnishes plates of food going into the dining room.

For inexperienced employees, on-the-job training can be used effectively when their work can be easily monitored and corrected before it has negative impact on guests, or when a new employee can work side by side with an experienced worker. For example, the new housekeeper mentioned before can be trained effectively if assisted by an experienced housekeeper. The experienced housekeeper can show the new housekeeper the normal routine for preparing a room for occupancy. She can show the new housekeeper the most efficient way to make beds, clean the bathroom, and attend to all the other tasks that go into making up a room. The experienced housekeeper can monitor the work performed by the new housekeeper, correct mistakes, and suggest those improvements that will ensure that the work is done in the most efficient manner.

In some of the major hospitality organizations, group training sessions are often possible because of the number of new employees who require training. There are many approaches that can be used for group training. These include:

1. Lecture and demonstration   4. Case studies
2. Role playing   5. Panels
3. Seminars

Lecture and Demonstration

The lecture and demonstration approach to training requires that a trainer explain a subject to trainees, demonstrate the skills involved, and respond to questions about the subject during or after the lecture. For example, a trainer may explain the proper procedures for taking orders and serving food, then demonstrate those procedures to trainees. Similarly, a trainer may explain the proper way to sell accommodations and check in guests, then demonstrate the necessary techniques and procedures to room clerk trainees. The lecture and demonstration method is limited in effectiveness, however, unless students are given opportunities immediately to practice what they have learned.

Role Playing

Role playing can be a very effective method of training, particularly when coupled with the lecture and demonstration approach. Role playing enables each student to play a part in a scene created by the trainer. For example, servers can be divided into small groups, with each member of the group taking a turn at practicing serving techniques previously demonstrated. Similarly, room clerks in a group may take turns playing the part of guests while their colleagues in the group practice selling and assigning accommodations.

Seminars

Seminars are group discussions of particular subjects, led by trainers. They are the most useful for management training, in which the input of the trainees is an important part of the learning process. Typically, significant questions are raised by the seminar leader, and each member of the group is asked for his opinion. For example, a large commercial hotel in a major city may hold a seminar on guest relations for middle managers and supervisors. Participants may be asked to discuss the best way to handle guest complaints about noise coming from adjoining guest rooms or about the service in the dining room. Managers would be expected to participate actively in the seminar by expressing their points of view. Their opinions then would be discussed by the others, enabling all present to benefit from the thoughts of their colleagues. This type of training session can be extremely valuable when conducted as part of an ongoing training program.

Case Studies

Case studies are similar to seminars, except the participants are asked to read a prepared case involving a real or imagined situation. The case should provide sufficient information so that the participants can provide opinions on what has occurred and solutions to the problems in the case.

Panels

Panels consist of groups of experts called in by trainers to express their opinions on specific questions for the benefit of an audience of trainees. The panel members are generally asked to comment on timely subjects. They may agree with one another or have differing opinions, thus giving trainees the benefit of hearing several views. Like seminars, panels offer an excellent means of eliciting the opinions of participants. However, the opinions are those of the panel members, not those of the trainees. In some instances—especially with management training groups—trainees are encouraged to question members of the panel and to challenge their views.

Each of the above approaches to training may be used for any of several levels of training, although their purposes vary slightly from one to another. Lecture and demonstration and role playing are best used to teach specific skills. Seminars, case studies, and panels are best used as a part of the ongoing development of employees to improve job performance and to qualify participants for more responsibility within the hospitality organization.

APPRAISING EMPLOYEE PERFORMANCE

Performance appraisal is the process of comparing an employee's level of job performance against the performance standards that have been established for a job. Performance appraisals are among the more important elements of human resources management.

The three primary objectives of performance appraisal are to provide

1. information to employees about their performance relative to established standards (All employees want to know how well they are doing their jobs, and regular performance appraisals give necessary feedback when they may not be receiving it regularly from their supervisors);
2. opportunities for employer and employee to plan for changes in the employee's behavior or to make provision for improvements in the employee's job-related skills; and
3. rational bases for salary review and promotion.

In addition, performance reviews provide employees with opportunities to make suggestions that will improve the operation. These can include changes in service procedures, supervisory concerns, and suggestions that will improve employee morale, among others.

Performance reviews are typically done by department managers. However, because department heads are sometimes not equipped to conduct performance reviews without specific training, human resources personnel may need to run training classes to teach them the proper way to conduct these reviews. In addition, the human resources office often has to prepare the necessary forms used in performance reviews.

Each hospitality organization that conducts performance appraisals has its own forms and methods of reviewing employee performance. Whatever approach is used, the criteria should be appropriate to the work being judged and should be closely linked to the job description. For example, one very common criterion for judging performance is "ability to communicate." This is generally very important for supervisory personnel, but far less so for dishwashers. For a dishwasher, a list of more appropriate criteria would include getting to work on time, cooperating with other members of the staff, and demonstrating an ability to wash dishes with a minimum of breakage. For servers, clean and neat appearance and strong ability to maintain good guest relations are important criteria, but they would not be important for judging a dishwasher.

COMPENSATION PROGRAMS

The term *compensation* refers to all forms of pay and other rewards going to employees as a result of their employment. In the hospitality industry, employees receive two forms of current compensation, direct and indirect, as well as deferred compensation.

Current Compensation

DIRECT COMPENSATION. Direct compensation includes salaries, wages, tips, bonuses, and commissions. Traditionally, the term *salary* is used to refer to a fixed dollar amount of compensation paid on a weekly, monthly, or annual basis without regard to the actual number of hours worked. Wages, by contrast, always take the actual number of hours worked into account: Wages for an employee are calculated by multiplying the employee's hourly rate by the number of hours worked.

Tips—sometimes referred to as *gratuities*—although not paid from an employer's funds, are also compensation in the eyes of the law and are treated as such by federal and state agencies for purposes of calculating income tax. Many workers in the hospitality industry earn more from tips than from wages.

Bonus is a term that refers to dollar amounts over and above an employee's regular wages or salary, given as a reward for some type of job performance. *Commissions*, on the other hand, are dollar amounts calculated as percentages of sales. Many travel agents and some banquet managers earn commissions on their sales.

INDIRECT COMPENSATION. Indirect compensation may include paid vacations, health benefits, life insurance, free meals, free living accommodations, use of recreational facilities operated by the employer, discounts on accommodations at other properties within a chain, and many other possibilities.

The paid vacation is among the most common forms of indirect compensation available to employees in the hospitality industry today. Paid vacations are typically linked to length of service with a given employer. In many instances, employees are awarded a basic vacation period with pay amounting to two weeks per year. Those whose length of service reaches some predetermined number of years—fifteen, for example—are given an additional week with pay. Another approach is to give each employee two days of paid vacation per year of service, up to a maximum of twenty days for ten years of service.

Health benefits, including medical, dental, and optical insurance, are among the most sought-after forms of indirect compensation. They are also among the most costly. Health benefits are commonly in the form of some or all of the costs of insurance being paid by the employer, who also assumes the entire cost of administering the plans. Administration requires hiring personnel in the human resources office to process forms, maintain records, and generally attend to the myriad details associated with these plans.

Life insurance, another popular form of indirect compensation, provides protection for the families of covered employees in case anything should happen to the employee. This saves employees the considerable costs that can be associated with life insurance coverage.

In those establishments that offer hospitality product lines in which food is the central element, it is common to provide meals to employees during their working hours. Thus, hotel or restaurant employees assigned to work from 7 A.M. to 3 P.M. may be permitted to have breakfast and lunch on premises. In those large properties where this is permitted, special facilities may be set up to be used by employees. In some cases, one or more members of the kitchen staff may be assigned exclusively to the preparation of employees' meals. Including meals in the hospitality compensation package is generally very popular with employees, who gain from this very tangible benefit.

In some hotel properties, part of an employee's compensation package may include living accommodations. This is particularly true in resort hotels but is not uncommon in some large transient hotels. In the former, living accommodations may be available to all employees; in the latter, accommodations would probably be limited to managerial staff members who are expected to be on call twenty-four hours a day.

Many resort properties include in their employees' compensation packages the rights to use various recreational facilities during the hours they are off duty. Thus, employees at ski resorts may have access to the slopes; whereas those at beach resorts may be able to use special beaches and such equipment as water skis and sailboats during their off hours.

Many hotel and motel chain organizations offer their employees special discounted rates on accommodations. Those who choose to travel during their vacation periods find this an extremely useful and valuable form of indirect compensation.

Deferred Compensation

Deferred compensation is compensation received by an employee after the conclusion of his or her period of employment. Two of the most important forms of deferred compensation are pension benefits and that collective group of benefits generally known by the term *Social Security.*

Human resources professionals are normally expected to play leading roles in formulating and administering appropriate compensation programs for hospitality employees. It is important, therefore, for managers in this area to have a comprehensive knowledge of the various forms of compensation found in the industry.

LABOR UNIONS

In some places, especially large cities, groups of workers in various hospitality operations have joined labor unions. The principal reasons for joining unions are dissatisfaction with wages, benefits, or working conditions and a belief by employees that their needs and desires are more likely to be satisfied through a united effort than by the individual efforts of workers. By definition, a *labor union* is an organization of employees united to bargain collectively with their employers on such issues as wages, benefits, and working conditions. Because unions offer this promise of collective effort on behalf of all members, many employees of hospitality operations have joined.

Once employees join a union, representatives of the union then serve as their bargaining agents in all matters relating to wages, benefits, and working conditions. A contract is negotiated between management and the labor union, and the contract is signed by both parties. This legal and binding document governs the relationship between the two for the period of the contract.

A union contract may cover all workers except those considered members of the management staff, or the coverage may be limited to specific departments or even simply to those employees who have chosen to join the union. These various possibilities exist because of differences in the laws from one state to another, as well as differences in common practice and belief from one area to another.

Union contracts normally provide some orderly system for the resolution of the disputes, both major and minor, that commonly arise between management and labor. Some of these disputes result in grievances. A *grievance* is a complaint filed when an employee or a union believes that the union contract is being violated by management. The orderly system for their resolution is known as a *grievance procedure.*

Although the details of grievance procedures vary, they generally include rules about specific steps that the parties must follow. These usually provide for efforts to resolve the grievance to begin at the lowest possible level. This may involve discussion among an individual employee, her union representative, the employee's immediate supervisor, and a representative of management—often a member of the human resources staff. If efforts to resolve the grievance at this first step are unsuccessful, another attempt is made at a higher level. This commonly brings into the process higher-level representatives of both union and management. The grievance will be moved from one level to another until it is finally resolved. At the highest level, an impartial third party, known as an *arbitrator*, may be brought in to listen to both sides and to render a judgment binding on both parties.

In those properties and locations where there are union contracts in effect, it is commonly the human resources staff that represents management in day-to-day interactions between the property and its union employees. Thus, it is very important that each member of a human resources staff be thoroughly familiar with all provisions of the contract and with any unwritten work rules. It is also desirable, where possible, that the human resources staff organize informational seminars for management, to be certain that they all understand the union contract and work rules. When there is a union contract, it is important for both workers and managers to understand their rights and obligations under the contract.

EMPLOYEE SAFETY

Another important concern in hospitality operations is employee safety. Accidents are costly to both employees and employers—costly in terms of lost wages, medical bills, and higher insurance premiums, among the many possibilities. Therefore, when feasible, responsible employers prefer to develop educational campaigns and training programs aimed at improving safety in the workplace and reducing the number of accidents. Efforts to do this normally come under the direction of human resources managers.

One agency of the federal government, the Occupational Safety and Health Administration (OSHA), sets safety and health standards for workers in the United States. The basic standard is that an employee's workplace should be free from recognized hazards—those that are likely to cause physical harm to the employee. Most states have also adopted legislation aimed at protecting workers from physical hazards.

The potential for physical harm in the hospitality industry is as great as that in many other industries. Such areas as kitchens, bars, stairwells, boiler rooms, elevator shafts, laundry rooms, and many others present great potential for physical harm. Management must take three important steps to enhance employee safety in the workplace.

1. Know the applicable federal, state, and local safety regulations, and take all necessary and appropriate actions to comply.
2. Develop written policies, procedures, methods, guidelines, and work rules aimed at maintaining a safe work environment for all employees.

3. Conduct appropriate safety training for all categories of employees, giving special emphasis to those who work with potentially dangerous materials and equipment.

EMPLOYEE ASSISTANCE PROGRAMS

An *employee assistance program (EAP)* is a coordinated effort developed by management to help employees deal with personal problems. The kinds of personal problems EAPs address include the following:

1. Substance abuse, including the abuse of alcohol and illegal drugs
2. Psychological problems, including depression, stress, and burnout
3. Family issues, including marital problems, spousal abuse, child care, and parent–child disputes
4. Financial issues, including debt counseling, retirement planning, and obtaining tuition assistance for job-related courses
5. Legal problems, including difficulties with landlords and leases
6. Health issues, including counseling related to AIDS, cancer, and chronic medical problems
7. Educational issues, including learning English and learning more about careers in the hospitality industry

Because unresolved personal problems are likely to influence job performance negatively, it is clearly in the interest of employers to provide assistance to employees who require it. Many employed in the hospitality industry have had limited education and may have considerable difficulty understanding and dealing with problems such as those listed without help.

In hospitality organizations with EAPs, it is likely to be the personnel of the human resources staff who are charged with responsibility for the efforts to help employees resolve their problems.

EMPLOYEE MORALE

In preliminary discussion at the beginning of this chapter, we introduced the term *employee turnover rates* and explained the method by which employee turnover rates are calculated. We also pointed out that many hospitality operations have very high rates of employee turnover and that 100 percent per year was not uncommon in the industry. This is a topic of great concern to owners and managers, and certainly to human resources personnel.

In those establishments with high employee turnover rates, trained and knowledgeable employees are continually leaving. They must be replaced quickly for business to continue in a reasonable manner. Replacing lost employees is costly in two ways: Recruiting and training costs are high, and the process requires time. Much of the burden falls on human resources personnel.

In addition, most managers would prefer to retain present employees rather than to recruit new ones. Although present employees may not be perfect, at least they have some knowledge of their jobs—more than new employees have before training. Therefore, it is preferable to retain employees and to devote some time and attention to their skills and their morale.

A number of ways exist to maintain or improve employee morale. Developing equitable and appealing compensation programs and instituting valued employee assistance programs are two of the more common. Some of the other possibilities include

1. permiting valued employees to work flexible schedules—so-called flex time—if possible;
2. developing a program of varied social and recreational events for employees and their families;
3. giving frequent positive feedback to those employees who are particularly good at their jobs;
4. identifying an "employee of the month" and providing special privileges or awards to employees earning this designation; and
5. providing employees with opportunities to make suggestions about improving the service product line or their own performance on the job.

Much of the work of the human resources staff is devoted to preventive maintenance programs designed to retain, retrain, upgrade, and improve the skills and knowledge of present employees—a more satisfying and less costly approach than constantly recruiting new employees to replace those who have become dissatisfied and quit their jobs.

SUMMARY

In this chapter, the term *human resources management* is defined. The elements of human resources planning are listed and discussed, and the information required for job analysis is identified. Three parts of a job description are described. The terms *job specification* and *recruiting* are defined, and ten possible sources for recruiting hospitality employees are discussed. A seven-step standard procedure for selecting the best candidate for employment is described. Three principal elements included in a basic orientation for new employees are dicussed. Five approaches for training groups of employees are identified and discussed in detail. Three primary objectives of performance appraisal are also discussed. The term *compensation* is defined, and distinctions are drawn between deferred compensation and the two forms of current compensation. The term *labor union* is defined, and grievance procedures are discussed. Three important steps taken by management to enhance employee safety in the workplace are described. The term *employee assistance program (EAP)* is defined, and seven issues often addressed by EAPs are listed. Finally, five ways to improve employee morale are identified.

QUESTIONS

1. Define the term *human resources management.*
2. List the elements of human resources planning.
3. Identify the information required for job analysis, and describe two common methods used for gathering the information.
4. List and discuss the three parts of a job description.
5. Define the term *job specification.*
6. Define the term *recruiting* as used in human resources management.
7. Identify ten possible sources from which human resources personnel can recruit applicants for employment.
8. List and discuss the seven basic steps that constitute a standard procedure for selecting the best candidate for employment.
9. Define the term *bona fide occupational qualification,* and provide one example of a BFOQ that may be used in the hospitality industry.
10. List four types of written tests commonly used to aid in assessing applicants' qualifications.
11. Distinguish between *direct* and *open-ended* questions.
12. Identify three principal elements that should be included in a basic orientation for new employees.
13. Distinguish between the following:
    a. Individual training vs. group training
    b. On-the-job training vs. off-the-job training
14. Describe each of the five approaches to training employees in groups, as listed below:
    a. Lecture/demonstration
    b. Role playing
    c. Seminar
    d. Case study
    e. Panel
15. List three primary objectives of performance appraisal.
16. Define the term *compensation.*

17. Distinguish between deferred compensation and current compensation, and identify the two forms of current compensation.
18. Define the term *labor union*.
19. Describe a grievance procedure and identify its purpose.
20. Identify three important steps taken by management to enhance employee safety in the workplace.
21. Define the term *employee assistance program* and list seven issues EAPs often address.
22. Identify five ways to improve employee morale.

Hospitality Accounting

18

LEARNING OBJECTIVES

After reading and studying this chapter, you should be able to:

1. *Define* accounting.
2. *Describe the six branches of accounting.*
3. *Identify the two major financial statements derived from accounting records, and list the principal parts of each.*
4. *Define the following terms:* asset, current assets, fixed assets, liquidity, accumulated depreciation, liability, current liability, long-term liability, owners' equity, income statement, revenue, expense, profit, loss, operating expenses, *and* fixed charges.
5. *Identify the following ratios: a. Food cost-to-sales; b. Beverage cost-to-sales; c. Labor cost-to-sales; d. Percentage of occupancy; e. Seat turnover; f. Inventory turnover; g. Current ratio; h. Quick ratio; i. Return on sales; j. Return on equity.*
6. *Define the following averages: a. Average rate per occupied room; b. Average sale per customer*
7. *Define the term* budget, *and identify each of the following types of budgets: a. Fixed operating budget; b. Flexible operating budget; c. Capital budget.*
8. *Discuss* cash management *and describe the development of a cash budget.*
9. *Discuss the importance of cost control to the management of hospitality operations.*

INTRODUCTION

Previous chapters have introduced various essentials of the hospitality industry — history, scope, operations, planning, management, marketing, and human relations, among others. One recurring theme in these chapters was the need to establish goals and objectives for hospitality operations.

A common goal shared by commercial hospitality operations is a financial goal: profit. Noncommercial operations also have financial goals: not profit, but keeping costs under control to break even, or keeping losses to predetermined amounts.

To determine if financial goals are being achieved, it is necessary to keep records. In many small, owner-operated establishments, the records may consist of nothing more than a checkbook showing deposits and expenditures. In most others, more complete and complex records are kept, and written summaries of those records are prepared. From these summaries, management can determine whether or not the financial goals of the operation are being achieved.

The objective of this chapter is to introduce the student to the nature of financial records and reports that assist in managing the finances of hospitality operations. The term used to describe this topic is *accounting*.

Accounting has frequently been referred to as "the language of business." Accounting is the language of business because the reports that come from accounting records are the best expressions of the financial condition of any hospitality operation. Accountants must keep complete records of all business transactions if the reports they provide are to reflect accurately the financial condition of that business.

DEFINITION OF ACCOUNTING

Accounting has been broadly defined as ". . . the process of identifying, measuring, and communicating economic information to permit informed judgments and decisions by users of the information."[1] In practical terms, it is the process of analyzing, recording, classifying, reporting, and interpreting data that reflect the financial condition of an organization. *Accounting principles* are the rules — generally accepted by the accounting profession — for analyzing, recording, classifying, reporting, and interpreting these financial data.

Anyone with sufficient knowledge of accounting principles should be able to look at information provided by an accountant for a hospitality organization, understand it, and make judgments about the financial condition of the organization.

---

[1] *A Statement of Basic Accounting Theory* (Evanston, IL: American Accounting Association, 1966), p. 1.

BRANCHES OF ACCOUNTING

There are six generally accepted branches of accounting. They are:

1. Financial accounting
2. Cost accounting
3. Management accounting
4. Auditing
5. Tax accounting
6. Accounting systems design

Financial Accounting

Financial accounting is concerned with analyzing, recording, classifying, and summarizing the day-to-day transactions that occur in an organization.

Analyzing means preparing data to be recorded. Recording means entering data into the formal records of the organization. Classifying is arranging the data into useful categories, so that data will be reported in a way that can be understood. Reporting is summarizing the information into statements for managers, owners, and others.

Some people think of financial accounting as "bookkeeping," and indeed bookkeeping is one part of financial accounting. Bookkeeping is record keeping. It is clerical in nature and a fundamental element in accounting.

Management Accounting

Management accounting is that branch of accounting that focuses on financial information used by managers within the organization for the purpose of decision making. One example is a management accounting report comparing actual expenditures with budgeted expenditures. Another example is a report that informs management of the organization's ability to pay its current bills.

Cost Accounting

Cost accounting is a branch of accounting that deals exclusively with the costs of operating a business and the control of those costs. *Cost control* is the process of regulating costs and guarding against excessive costs. Cost control procedures provide management with cost information in ways that enable management to make judgments about those costs. For example, one major cost in food service operations is the cost of food. Cost control procedures provide management with information about the level of food costs relative to food sales. Food cost totals can be compared with expected or planned costs and with past costs to determine whether or not the cost of food is excessive.

Auditing

Auditing is the branch of accounting that verifies that record-keeping is accurate and that financial statements truly reflect the financial condition of the organization. Audits may be internal or external. Internal audits are performed by employees for a specific purpose. External audits are usually performed by certified public accountants (CPAs) and are required in all public corporations.

Tax Accounting

Tax accounting is that specialized branch of accounting dealing with the preparation of tax forms for city, state, and federal governments. Tax accountants provide management assistance in tax planning—taking steps to minimize taxes—and in such other matters as payroll taxes, property taxes, sales taxes, and excise taxes.

Accounting Systems Design

Accounting systems design is that branch of accounting that deals primarily with computer information systems. Accounting systems design assesses the needs of an organization and develops an integrated accounting package to meet those needs. Because each hospitality operation is sufficiently different to require a computer information system tailored to its particular needs, systems designers have found fertile territory in the hospitality industry.

The following sections present some common financial, managerial, and cost accounting concepts and a number of related terms. These are intended to acquaint the student with a few of the many applications of accounting in hospitality management.

THE ACCOUNTING CYCLE

Accounting cycle is a term that refers to a sequence of procedures used to record and summarize transactions for an accounting period; to organize the summary data into financial reports, called *statements*; and to prepare for the next sequential accounting period. The normal accounting period is one year. Accounting data, however, are typically summarized monthly and used to prepare monthly statements.

The two most important financial statements prepared by accountants are the balance sheet and the income statement.

THE BALANCE SHEET

A *balance sheet* is a financial statement that lists the assets, liabilities, and the value of ownership claims to the assets of a business on a specific date. Figure 18.1 shows the balance sheet for the Value Lodge, described in Chapter 9.

FIGURE 18.1 *Value Lodge balance sheet*
December 31, 19XX

Assets				Liabilities and owners' equity			
Current Assets				**Current Liabilities**			
Cash		$3,560		Accounts payable	$2,300		
Accounts receivable		2,575		Wages payable	350		
Cleaning supplies		620		Sales taxes payable	375		
Office supplies		75		*Total Current Liabilities*			$3,025
Total Current Assets			$6,830				
				Long-Term Liabilities			
Fixed Assets				Mortage payable			$993,000
Land	$1,500,000			*Total Liabilities*			996,025
Building		$65,000					
Less accumulated				**Owner's Equity**			
depreciation	100,000	1,400,000		Roger and Jane Goodson			
Furniture and				Capital at January 1, 19XX		$353,300	
equipment	50,000			Net income for 19XX		76,400	
Less accumulated				*Total Capital*			$429,700
depreciation	14,285	35,715		*Total Liabilities and Capital*			$1,515,045
Automobile	12,500						
Less accumulated							
depreciation	5,000	7,500					
Total Fixed Assets			$1,508,215				
Total Assets			$1,515,045				

Assets

On the left hand side of the balance sheet are the assets of the Value Lodge. An *asset* is anything of value. Any asset belonging to an organization belongs on the organization's balance sheet. Examples of assets are cash, cleaning supplies, buildings, and automobiles.

TYPES OF ASSETS. Assets are classified as current assets or fixed assets.

Current Assets. *Current assets* are those that are not expected to last beyond one year. They are normally used up in the course of doing business. Current assets are listed on the balance sheet in order of liquidity. The term *liquidity* refers to the capacity to be converted into cash. Obviously, cash is the most liquid of all assets, so it is listed first. In Figure 18.1, accounts receivable (money owed the Value Lodge) and cleaning supplies are listed second and third, and represent other current assets.

Fixed Assets. *Fixed assets* are those that will last beyond one year. In Figure 18.1, these are land, building, furniture and equipment, and an automobile. Note that the values of some of the fixed assets have been reduced by amounts shown on the balance sheet as accumulated depreciation. *Accumulated depreciation* is a bookkeeping figure that indicates a theoretical lessening in value of those assets from the time they were purchased. It should be noted that accumulated depreciation is only a bookkeeping figure and that the real value of fixed assets—their market value—may be either higher or lower than shown on the balance sheet. For example, the building shown on the balance sheet as having a value of $1,500,000 less $100,000 in accumulated depreciation may really be worth more or less than shown if the motel were to be sold. Assets are listed at cost, because it is impossible to know their true market value until they are actually sold.

Liabilities

Liabilities are financial obligations to others. They are generally incurred during normal business operations. Liabilities are classified as current liabilities and long-term liabilities.

Current Liabilities. *Current liabilities* are those financial obligations that are due to be paid within the next accounting period. On the illustrated balance sheet, there are several current liabilities: accounts payable, wages payable, and sales tax payable. *Accounts payable* refers to amounts owed to suppliers for goods and services. *Wages payable* refers to wages earned by employees but not yet paid to them. *Sales tax payable* refers to sales taxes collected from customers but not yet remitted to the government agency that collects the tax.

Long-Term Liabilities. *Long-term liabilities* are financial obligations due beyond the current year. The Value Lodge has a large mortgage on the property, and the amount remaining on it is shown as a long-term liability.

Owner's Equity

Owner's equity is the term used to describe the owner's claims to the value of the assets listed on the balance sheet. The Goodson's *capital* (their claim to the assets) at the beginning of the year was $353,300. The motel made a profit of $76,400 last year, and that amount is added to the Goodson's original balance to arrive at the total capital figure of $429,700.

Figure 18.2 shows the balance sheet of the Steak Shack discussed in Chapter 6.

The balance sheet of the Steak Shack is very similar to that of the Value Lodge, but there are several significant differences. One is that the Steak Shack has large inventories of food and liquor—supplies not used in the Value Lodge. Another is the absence of any major long-term liability on the Steak Shack balance sheet. Unlike the Value Lodge, the Steak Shack leases its facilities and thus has no mortgage.

THE INCOME STATEMENT

The second important financial statement is the income statement. An *income statement* shows the revenues and expenses of an organization for a given time period. That period is normally one year, but income statements can be prepared for any period of time. *Revenue* is the amount of income an organization receives as a result of doing business. *Expenses* are the costs of doing business. The difference between total revenues and total expenses is defined as net income before taxes. If revenue exceeds expenses for the period covered by the income statement, the result is termed *profit*. If expenses exceed revenue for the period, the result is termed *loss*.

The income statement for the Value Lodge is shown in Figure 18.3. The Value Lodge has two sources of revenue. The major source is identified as room sales—income received from renting accommodations to guests. The secondary source is identified as miscellaneous income—that received from selling postcards, maps, and food in the vending machines.

The statement reveals two categories of expenses: operating expenses and fixed expenses, identified on this income statement as fixed charges. *Operating expenses* are those that are within the power of operating management to control. They are direct expenses, which tend to increase and decrease as business volume increases and decreases. These expenses include wages, linen, cleaning supplies, and office supplies. *Fixed charges*, in contrast, are those that are beyond the power of operating management to control in the near term. Fixed charges are not related

FIGURE 18.2 *The Steak Shack balance sheet*
December 31, 19XX

Assets			Liabilities and owners' equity		
Current Assets			**Current Liabilities**		
Cash		$9,322	Accounts payable	$4,250	
Accounts receivable		3,893	Wages payable	2,312	
Food		16,891	Sales taxes payable	1,567	
Liquor		9,633	Rent payable	2,000	
Supplies		4,540	*Total Current Liabilities*		$10,129
Office supplies		561			
Total Current Assets		$44,840	**Long-Term Liabilities**		
			Note payable		2,355
Fixed Assets			*Total Liabilities*		$12,484
Furniture and equipment	$243,600				
Less accumulated depreciation	23,678	$219,922	**Owner's Equity**		
Automobile	18,700		Capital at January 1, 19XX	$111,100	
Less accumulated depreciation	6,400	12,300	Net income for 19XX	153,478	
Total Fixed Assets		$232,222	*Total Capital*		$264,578
Total Assets		$277,062	*Total Liabilities and Capital*		$277,062

494

FIGURE 18.3 *Value Lodge statement of income for the period ending December 31, 19XX*

Revenue			
Room sales		$474,838	
Miscellaneous income		2,333	
Total Revenue		$477,171	
			Percent of Revenue
Operating Expenses			
Wages	$41,630		8.72%
Cleaning supplies	6,750		1.41
Office supplies	2,300		0.48
Automobile expenses	4,450		0.93
Laundry and dry cleaning	38,325		8.03
Uniforms	675		0.14
Commissions	3,334		0.70
Utilities	26,722		5.60
Telephone	11,115		2.33
Credit card fees	625		0.13
Repairs and maintenance	15,250		3.20
Reservation network fees	4,245		0.89
Franchise fees	22,450		4.70
Total Operating Expenses		$177,871	37.28%
Income Before Fixed Charges		$299,300	62.72%
Fixed Charges			
Property taxes	$34,600		7.25
Insurance	26,500		5.55
Interest expense	99,300		20.81
Depreciation	62,500		13.10
Total Fixed Charges		$222,900	46.71%
Net Income Before Income Taxes			
		$76,400	16.01%

---

to business volume. In the Value Lodge the fixed charges are property taxes, insurance, interest expense, and depreciation.

The income statement of the Value Lodge is comparatively simple and provides useful information about financial operations to the owners. The total amount in each category can be compared with anticipated or budgeted amounts. For example, if the amount shown for wages is higher than anticipated or budgeted, the owners can investigate, determine the cause, and take precautions to hold wages to a lower figure during the next period.

Many income statements show both dollar amounts and percentages. These percentages are based on total revenue, and indicate the percentage of total revenue represented by each dollar amount. For example, wages at the Value

FIGURE 18.4   *Steak Shack statement of income*
for the period ending December 31, 19XX

Sales			Percent
Food sales	$853,066		78.93%
Beverage sales	223,355		20.67
Miscellaneous income	4,356		0.40
Total Revenue		$1,080,777	100.00%
Cost of Sales			
Food cost	$349,757		32.36%
Beverage cost	51,372		4.75
Total Cost of Sales		$401,129	37.11%
Gross Operating Profit		$679,648	62.89%
Operating Expenses			
Wages	$312,240		28.89%
Cleaning supplies	22,300		2.06
Office supplies	2,400		0.22
Automobile expenses	5,345		0.49
Laundry and dry cleaning	4,600		0.43
Uniforms	520		0.05
China and glassware	12,400		1.15
Utilities	48,341		4.47
Telephone	2,350		0.22
Credit card fees	3,600		0.33
Repairs and maintenance	8,976		0.83
Total Operating Expenses		$423,072	39.15%
Income Before Fixed Charges		$256,576	23.74%
Fixed Charges			
Rent	$72,000		15.09%
Insurance	16,225		3.40
Interest expense	1,258		0.26
Depreciation	13,615		2.85
Total Fixed Charges		$103,098	9.54
Net Income Before Income Taxes		$153,478	14.20%

Lodge were $41,630 during a period when total revenue was $477,171. Thus wages were 8.72% of revenues, calculated as follows:

$$\frac{\$41,630}{\$477,171} = 8.72\%$$

Expressed as percentages of revenue, these figures can be compared with those for previous periods, or with industry averages. By making such comparisons, owners and managers can make judgments about performance during the period covered by the statement.

The income statement of the Steak Shack is shown in Figure 18.4.

Note the differences between the income statements of the Value Lodge and the Steak Shack. The income statement of the Steak Shack shows *sales* instead of *revenue*. This is simply a difference in terminology and is not significant. The Steak Shack, however, has a section labeled *cost of sales*, in which the food and beverage costs are subtracted from total sales to determine *gross operating profit*. This is customary in hospitality operations whenever there are expenses that can be attributed directly to a specific revenue source. The remainder of the income statement of the Steak Shack is similar to that of the Value Lodge. Because the Steak Shack leases the facility, a large payment is shown for rent; and relatively little depreciation is shown.

The data available to managers from income statements, balance sheets, and other sources can provide much useful information. Some of it is very basic and readily available to anyone taking the time to examine the statements. Room sales data for the Value Lodge, for example, are summarized on the income statement and someone merely glancing at the statement can obtain the total: $474,838. Information about food sales and beverage sales in the Steak Shack is just as easy to obtain.

The value of accounting information is not limited to the specific figures listed on these two statements. Additional useful information can be obtained by anyone willing to spend a few moments performing some comparatively simple calculations, several of which are described in the following sections. There are literally dozens of ratios, averages, and other figures that can be used to analyze business performance. The following are just a few, selected to suggest the broad range of possible calculations.

RATIOS

Ratios compare one number to another for purposes of making judgments. Students are normally familiar with the term, if not the concept. For example, if there are ten questions on a test, a student who answers eight correctly can be said to have performed well. Her ratio of correct answers to total questions is eight to ten, written numerically as:

$$\frac{8}{10} \quad \text{or } .8 \quad \text{or } 80\%$$

Thus we determine that the student's grade—an evaluation of performance—is 80 percent.

Ratios are used very commonly in hospitality operations to evaluate financial performance in one way or another. The following are a few of the ratios that can readily be calculated. Note that all answers are rounded.

COST-TO-SALES RATIOS: COST PERCENTS

Food and Beverage Cost-to-Sales Ratios.   The ratios of cost of food and cost of beverages sold to food sales and beverage sales respectively are very important in food and beverage operations. The ratio of food cost to food sales is also known as the *food cost percent;* the ratio of beverage cost to beverage sales is known as the *beverage cost percent.* These two ratios, or cost percents, indicate how well these important costs are being kept under control. Cost-to-sales ratios are calculated as follows:

$$\text{cost-to-sales ratio} = \frac{\text{cost}}{\text{sales}}$$

For the Steak Shack, the cost-to-sales ratios for food and beverages are calculated as follows:

$$\text{food cost-to-sales ratio} = \frac{\text{food cost}}{\text{food sales}}$$

$$= \frac{\$349,757}{853,066}$$

$$= .4099 \text{ or } 41.0\%$$

$$\text{beverage cost-to-sales ratio} = \frac{\text{beverage cost}}{\text{beverage sales}}$$

$$= \frac{51,372}{223,355}$$

$$= .23 \text{ or } 23\%$$

The food cost percentage is .4099 or 41 percent. This figure can be compared with planned cost percentage and with industry averages for other restaurants of that characteristic type.

The beverage cost percentage is .23 or 23 percent. As in the case of the food cost percent, managers would compare it with the planned cost percentage and industry averages. In this instance, both the food cost percentage and the beverage cost percentage compare favorably with industry averages.

Labor Cost-to-Sales Ratio.   Earlier in the chapter, in a discussion of Figure 18.3, we pointed out that income statements often include both dollar figures and percentages and that these percentages are based on total revenue. In the case of the Value Lodge, we calculated that wages represented 8.72 percent of total revenue, determined as follows:

$$\frac{\text{wages } \$41,630}{\text{sales } \$477,171} = .0872 = 8.72\%$$

This is a cost-to-sales ratio for labor, commonly known as *labor cost percent*. For the Steak Shack, it would be calculated as follows:

$$\frac{\text{labor cost } \$312,240}{\text{total revenue } \$1,080,777} = .2889 = 28.89\%$$

The labor cost-to-sales ratio or cost percentage is 28.89 percent. As with the food cost percent, managers would compare it with the planned cost percent and industry averages. In these cases, the labor cost percents compare favorably with industry averages for these types of establishments.

Some additional ratios that can be calculated very simply using readily available figures include the following:

OPERATING RATIOS. *Operating ratios* measure overall performance in a particular area. Three commonly used ratios are percentage of occupancy, seat turnover, and inventory turnover.

Percentage of Occupancy. *Percentage of occupancy* is used in lodging operations to express the ratio of occupied rooms to total rooms available for sale. It is calculated as follows:

$$\frac{\text{occupied rooms}}{\text{total rooms available for sale}} = \text{percentage of occupancy}$$

To illustrate, we will use the Value Lodge, which has 50 rooms. On a given night, 40 of those rooms are occupied, so the percentage of occupancy for that night is 80%, calculated as follow:

$$\frac{40 \text{ occupied rooms}}{50 \text{ rooms available for sale}} = .8 = 80\%$$

Lodging operations normally determine the percentage of occupancy each night. They then make comparisons with their percentages of occupancy the same night the previous week and the same night the previous year. By this means management is able to make a general assessment about the state of business for that one night, compared with other nights. In some major cities, night clerks in the major hotels normally exchange these percentages so that managers of the properties can compare their percentages of occupancy to those of their competitors.

Seat Turnover. *Seat turnover* relates the number of diners served in a given time period to the number of seats available for diners in the food service operation. Viewed another way, it indicates the average number of customers served per seat in the time period. Often called "turns" in the industry, it is cal-culated as follows:

$$\frac{\text{number of diners served}}{\text{number of seats available for diners}} = \text{seat turnover}$$

In the Steak Shack, with 100 tables seating 250 persons, the number of customers served on a given Friday night was 575. Seat turnover for that night is calculated as follows:

$$\frac{575 \text{ diners served}}{250 \text{ seats available for diners}} = 2.3 \text{ turns}$$

Food service managers often maintain records of the number of turns so that comparisons can be made between days and dates.

Inventory Turnover.   *Inventory turnover ratio* measures the rate at which inventories are used up and replaced during an accounting period. Although it is commonly used in food service operations, it does not readily apply to lodging operations without food service. The ratio is calculated as follows:

$$\text{inventory turnover ratio} = \frac{\text{cost of goods sold}}{\text{average inventory}}$$

For the Steak Shack, there are two inventory turnover ratios to calculate: one for food; the other for beverage. Food inventory turnover rate is calculated as follows:

$$\text{inventory turnover rate} = \frac{\text{cost of food sold}}{\text{average inventory}}$$

The inventory figures from the balance sheet of the Steak Shack are shown as $16,891 for food and $9,633 for beverages. We will assume that these represent the average inventories for food and beverage. Costs are shown on the income statement as $349,757 for food and $51,372 for beverage. Given this information, the inventory turnover rates would be calculated as follows:

$$\text{food inventory turnover rate} = \frac{\$349,757}{\$16,891}$$

$$\text{food inventory turnover rate} = 20.71$$

$$\text{beverage inventory turnover rate} = \frac{\$51,372}{\$9,633}$$

$$\text{beverage inventory turnover rate} = 5.33$$

The food inventory rate is 20.71 times per year or just under two times per month. This ratio would be considered about right for many restaurants. Because food is perishable, it should be used up and replaced about every other week.

The beverage inventory turnover rate is 5.33 per year or about every other month. Except for beer, alcoholic beverages are not considered perishable. Therefore, it is not uncommon for food service establishments to have large liquor inventories. This is particularly true for those that stock fine wines.

If inventories are used up and replaced very slowly, the organization may have too large an inventory and might not be utilizing its assets wisely. On the other hand, if inventories are used up too quickly, it is possible that the organization might run out of some inventory items and not be able to fill customers' orders for particular items.

LIQUIDITY RATIOS. *Liquidity ratios* are used by owners, managers, and creditors to measure an organization's ability to pay its bills. Two liquidity ratios can be computed readily from balance sheet figures: the current ratio and the quick ratio.

Current Ratio. The *current ratio* is used to measure the ability of the organization to pay its current bills out of current assets. It is calculated as follows:

$$\text{current ratio} = \frac{\text{current assets}}{\text{current liabilities}}$$

For the Value Lodge it is calculated as follows:

$$\text{current ratio} = \frac{\$6,830}{\$3,025} = \frac{2.26}{1}$$

For the Steak Shack it is calculated as follows:

$$\text{current ratio} = \frac{\$44,840}{\$10,129} = \frac{4.43}{1}$$

Most accountants recommend that a business maintain a current ratio of at least 2 to 1. If an organization has a ratio lower than 2 to 1, it may have trouble paying its bills in the event of a temporary downturn in business activity. Interestingly, accountants also state that current ratios should not be excessively high, such as 20 to 1, for example. If so, the business may not be using its funds to the best advantage.

Quick Ratio. The *quick ratio* is sometimes referred to as the *acid-test ratio.* It measures an organization's ability to pay its current obligations with its current cash assets or assets that can be immediately converted into cash. In hospitality, these tend to be limited to the so-called quick-assets cash and accounts receivable. The quick ratio provides an answer to an important hypothetical question: "If business were to cease for a period of time, would the organization be able to pay its current bills?"

The quick ratio is calculated as follows:

$$\text{quick ratio} = \frac{\text{quick assets}}{\text{current liabilities}}$$

For the Value Lodge, the quick ratio is:

$$\text{quick ratio} = \frac{\text{cash} + \text{accounts receivable}}{\text{current liabilities}}$$

$$= \frac{\$6,135}{\$3,025} = \frac{2.03}{1}$$

For the Steak Shack, the quick ratio is:

$$\text{quick ratio} = \frac{\text{cash} + \text{accounts receivable}}{\text{current liabilities}}$$

$$= \frac{\$13,215}{\$10,129} = \frac{1.3}{1}$$

Most accountants suggest that organizations maintain a quick ratio of no less than 1 to 1. Those with current ratios below the level recommended tend to rely very heavily on the sale of inventory to pay current expenses.

PROFITABILITY RATIOS. *Profitability ratios* measure the efficiency of organizations. They are very important to investors as well as to management, for they are an indication of the quality of management. Two important ratios are return on sales and return on equity.

Return on sales.   *Return on sales,* or *net profit margin,* shows the portion of each dollar of sales the organization earns as a profit. It varies considerably from one type of business to another. Return on sales is calculated as follows:

$$\text{return on sales} = \frac{\text{net income}}{\text{net sales}}$$

For the Value Lodge it is calculated as follows:

$$\text{return on sales} = \frac{\$76,400}{477,171}$$

$$= .16 \text{ or } 16\%$$

For the Steak Shack it is calculated as follows:

$$\text{return on sales} = \frac{\$153,478}{\$1,080,777}$$

$$= .142 \text{ or } 14.2\%$$

The ratios for the current year can be compared with those for prior years and with industry averages. Both ratios compare favorably with industry averages.

In both calculations, net income before taxes was used in the formula rather than net income after taxes, as is customary. Because both businesses are owner-operated, the profits would be subject to income taxes on the owners' personal tax returns.

Return on Equity.   The *return on equity ratio* provides owners with a means to measure the profitability of their investments. Anyone who considers investing in a business that has any degree of risk would want to measure the potential return on that investment, in order to compare it with industry averages and with investments of greater and lesser risk. The ratio is computed as follows:

$$\text{return on equity} = \frac{\text{net income}}{\text{owners' equity}}$$

For the Value Lodge, it is calculated as follows:

$$\text{return on equity} = \frac{\$76,400}{\$429,700}$$

$$= .1778 \text{ or } 17.78\%$$

For the Steak Shack, it is calculated as follows:

$$\text{return on equity} = \frac{\$153,478}{\$264,578}$$

$$= .58 \text{ or } 58\%$$

The owners of the Value Lodge are earning a 17.78 percent return on their investment, and the owners of the Steak Shack are earning a 58 percent return. As with the prior ratios, before-tax income was used in the formula. Both percentages appear to be excellent.

These are but a few of the dozens of ratios that can be calculated for hospitality operations. Other possibilities are solvency, debt-equity, fixed charge coverage, asset turnover, profit margin, and many others.

AVERAGES

In addition to ratios, owners and managers of food service and lodging operations commonly use various averages to evaluate business operations. An *arithmetic average*, the kind most commonly used, is determined by adding a series of figures to obtain a total, then dividing that total by the number of figures it includes. Suppose, for example, one wanted to determine the average grade earned by a student whose scores on four quizzes were 68, 82, 88, and 90. To determine the arithmetic average, one would add the scores on all quizzes and divide by the number of scores:

$$68 + 82 + 88 + 90 = 338 \text{ total of all scores}$$

$$\frac{328 \text{ total of all scores}}{4 \text{ scores}} = 82 \text{ average score}$$

Two of the most common arithmetic averages in hospitality are *average rate per occupied room*, used in lodging operations, and *average sale per seat*, used in food and beverage operations.

Average Rate per Occupied Room. An average room rate is calculated by adding all the rates charged for rooms occupied on a given night—the total of room sales for the night—then dividing that total by the number of occupied rooms. For example, if there were 40 rooms occupied in the Value Lodge on a given night and the total room sales for that night were $1,560, then the average rate per occupied room would be $39.00—calculated as follows:

$$\frac{\$1,560 \text{ total room sales}}{40 \text{ occupied rooms}} = \$39.00 \text{ average rate}$$

Lodging managers normally have in mind some desired average rate per occupied room. Many require that a daily average be computed, so that it can be compared to the desired daily average they have in mind. If it is above or below this desired average, they may attempt to determine the reasons for the difference. Some would attribute the difference to the performance of such employees as reservationists, room clerks, and sales representatives.

Average Sale per Customer. Average sale per customer is calculated by dividing total dollar sales for a given time period by the number of customers served in that period.

$$\frac{\text{total dollar sales}}{\text{number of customers}} = \text{average sale per customer}$$

In the Steak Shack, for example, total sales on a given day were $3,150.40. The number of customers served on the day was 220. Therefore the average sale per customer on that day was $14.32, calculated as follows:

$$\frac{\$3,150.40 \text{ total sales}}{220 \text{ customers}} = \$14.32 \text{ average sale per customer}$$

Average sales figures are always of interest to food and beverage managers and can be useful in various ways. They can be used to measure the effectiveness of menus or the ability of servers to increase dollar sales by selling appetizers, desserts, and other courses.

A variety of useful averages can easily be calculated, and many food service and lodging managers do so regularly. Some of the possibilities include average rate per guest, average sale per waiter, average sale per meal period, average number of guests per occupied room, average food sale, and average beverage sale, among others.

MANAGEMENT ACCOUNTING AND COST CONTROL

In the early part of this chapter, we described management accounting as that branch of accounting that focuses on the internal use of accounting information to assist managers in making better business judgments. We defined cost accounting as a branch of accounting that deals with the costs of operating a business and the control of those costs.

There are several specific responsibilities normally associated with management accounting and cost control that result in specific calculations and reports. Three are of special importance:

1. Budgeting
2. Cash management
3. Cost control

Although their application varies from one type of hospitality operation to another, some general observations should be made about them in an introductory text.

Budgeting

Financial accounting deals with past events. The ratios and other calculations previously discussed are all based on data from the past — previous days, or nights, or months, or accounting periods. In contrast, budgets deal with the future. A *budget* is a financial plan developed for a period in the future. Budgeting is a necessary element in business operations. Successful businesses need to look ahead and make specific plans to reach revenue targets while keeping expenses within certain predetermined bounds. Without planning, management is leaving the future health of a business to chance.

In Chapter 16, the importance of market planning was discussed in detail. Financial planning is no less important. Once financial plans have been developed, the plans become control devices: They provide guidelines to managers and others with authority to spend the organization's funds.

Several types of budgets exist. The two most important of these are the operating budget and the capital budget.

OPERATING BUDGET. An *operating budget* is a financial plan for generating a given amount of revenue at a given level of expenditure in the coming period. Operating budgets are normally prepared for periods of one year—the length of the normal accounting cycle—and then broken down into shorter time frames.

Operating budgets can be fixed or flexible. A *fixed operating budget* is one with precise forecasts of revenues and expenses. A *flexible operating budget* is really several fixed budgets, each one for a different level of business activity. For example, if the Steak Shack were to prepare a flexible budget for the coming accounting period, management might prepare forecasts for the expected level of sales and expenses as well as forecasts for sales and expenses at 5 percent, 10 percent, and 15 percent above and below the expected levels.

Once the operating budget is prepared, managers and others with the authority to purchase supplies and hire personnel have guidelines for doing so. The guideline is the budget. For example, once a flexible budget is prepared for the Steak Shack, the dining room manager will be given a budgeted amount for employees' salaries for the period—a figure limiting the amount that she can use for that purpose. From that budgeted figure, she will be able to determine the number of servers and other employees she can have on the payroll. Because management has developed a flexible budget, she will also have guidelines to follow if sales and the number of customers are higher or lower than were originally expected. Within the framework of the flexible budget, the dining room manager will have several levels of expense to work with.

In corporations and other large operations, many people are normally involved in budget preparation. The so-called bottom up approach to budgeting is common in these kinds of enterprises. When this procedure is used, department heads make budget requests based on the level of business volume anticipated by top management. All these budget requests go to a management committee, which either approves or changes each department's budget. The management committee then prepares an operating budget for the entire enterprise, adding necessary expenditures not included in departmental budgets.

CAPITAL BUDGET. A *capital budget* is a financial plan for the expenditure of funds other than those in the operating budget. These are funds used for such purposes as building or renovating facilities or for purchasing major equipment. These are expenditures on fixed assets that will last beyond one year. Examples of capital expenditures are the purchase of new equipment for a kitchen, or new furniture for guest rooms, and refurbishing of recreational facilities. Capital budgets include the anticipated costs of such capital projects and the anticipated sources of funds they require. Capital expenditures are separate from the operating budget.

The typical procedure for developing a capital budget is similar to that used for developing an operating budget. Requests for capital expenditures are made by department heads and sent to a management team that determines which of the capital projects will be undertaken in a given year. The number of capital projects suggested for a given year and their cost are normally beyond the capacity of an organization for any one year, and projects must be ranked in order of importance. Thus, the capital budget process imposes reasonable limits on the number and the extent of projects to be undertaken by an organization and aids in the organization's overall planning process.

Cash Management

Most businesses do not have equal flows of cash coming into and going out of the business. For example, it is not unusual for lodging operations to have peak seasons with high occupancy when they are charging the highest rates and slow seasons with low occupancy when rates are the lowest. During the peak periods they are likely to have great inflows of cash—far in excess of that needed to meet current financial obligations. During slow periods, the operation may be experiencing net outflows of cash—spending more each week than the enterprise is taking in.

If a business is to be prepared to deal successfully with these dramatic changes in the inflows and outflows of cash, it is obvious that planning must take place. There must be effective use of excess funds during peak times, so that reserves can be established to make up the cash deficiencies experienced during slow periods. If reserves cannot be set aside, other arrangements must be made. Moreover, if planned capital expenditures are expected to require additional cash expenditures, plans must also be prepared to deal with these needs.

SHORT-TERM CASH PLANNING. To plan for normal and seasonal changes in the inflows and outflows of cash, many establishments prepare a cash budget. A *cash budget* is a financial statement that predicts the sources and uses of funds for

TABLE 18.1 *Cash budget for the Value Lodge January 19XX*

Opening cash balance	$3,560
Receipts	
Cash revenues	$25,150
Accounts Receivable	$ 1,700
Total	$30,410
Disbursements	
Wages	$ 6,950
Supplies	$ 1,700
Utilities	$ 2,300
Telephone	$ 970
Mortgage	$ 8,790
Laundry	$ 3,160
Franchise Fees	$ 1,645
Reservation Fees	$ 353
Auto Expense	$ 470
Total	$26,338
Closing cash balance	$ 4,072

the period covered. Cash budgets are normally prepared for one year in advance but can cover any period of time. Table 18.1 is an excerpt from the annual cash budget for the Value Lodge. It illustrates anticipated inflows and outflows of cash for the month of January.

The closing cash balance for the month becomes the opening cash balance for the next month, February. It is affected by projected inflows and outflows of cash for February. The net of the opening cash balance for February, plus cash inflows, less cash outflows equals the closing cash balance for February. This, in turn, becomes the opening cash balance for March; and the procedure is repeated.

If the cash projections for January were to show insufficient cash available to cover expenditures for the month, the owners would make arrangements to bring cash into the business. This may be accomplished in several ways. One way is to deposit cash in some form of interest-bearing account during those periods when excess cash is coming into the business. Another is to arrange for a line of credit with a bank. A line of credit is a commitment from a bank to loan a business money when needed on a short-term basis. Lines of credit typically must be arranged well in advance of the time when the funds are needed.

Still another source of funds is trade credit. Most suppliers are willing to extend credit for purchases up to 30 days to businesses with satisfactory credit ratings. Some will extend credit for longer periods. Just as with banks, arrangements for credit should be made well in advance of need.

Cost Control

Cost control activities are very important to management of hospitality operations. As described earlier in this chapter, *cost control* is the process of regulating costs and guarding against excessive costs. The extent and types of cost information provided to management vary from establishment to establishment.

Managers need to know the costs of the hospitality service products they sell to customers and guests. For example, a hotel manager needs to know the total cost of preparing a vacated hotel room for the next guest. There are many elements to that total cost, including the wages of the housekeeper who will clean the room and the costs of the bed linen, bath linen, soap, and various other supplies that go into it. Restaurant managers need to know the costs of the ingredients in the menu items they prepare so that suitable prices can be established and printed in menus. Some need to know the labor cost of preparing standard quantities of particular menu items. Other cost information requested by managers includes heating costs for guest rooms or swimming pools, energy costs for air conditioning guest rooms, and fuel costs for kitchen equipment.

Determining the above costs, as well as many others, are part of the cost accounting activities that take place daily in hospitality operations. It is important that these costs be known before sales prices are established for hospitality service products. The costs associated with cleaning and maintaining a hotel room clearly should be known before one sets room rates. And the costs of food and beverage items on menus should be established before setting menu prices. One example will suffice.

One of the items on the luncheon menu at the Steak Shack is a charcoal-broiled hamburger served on a sliced sesame-seed bun. The standard portion size for a hamburger is six ounces. Hamburgers are made from ground chuck, which is purchased at $2.40 per pound. Hamburger buns are purchased fresh daily at $1.50 per dozen.

The cost of the six-ounce hamburger is $.90, determined by dividing 16 ounces into the $2.40 cost per lb. to find the $.15 cost per ounce, then multiplying by six ounces in each portion.

$$\frac{\$2.40 \text{ cost per pound}}{16 \text{ ounces in each pound}} = \$.15 \text{ cost per ounce}$$

$$\$.15 \text{ cost per ounce} \times 6 \text{ ounces per portion} = \$.90 \text{ cost per portion}$$

The cost of the bun is $.125, determined by dividing the cost of the dozen, $1.50, by the number of buns in the dozen, 12.

$$\frac{\$1.50 \text{ cost per dozen}}{12 \text{ buns per dozen}} = \$.125 \text{ per bun}$$

Thus the basic food cost per portion for the hamburger and bun is:

hamburger	$ .90
bun	.125
	$1.025

To this, one would add the costs of any other items accompanying the hamburger—ketchup, mustard, pickles, and so on—to determine the total cost of the item. If the other items are assumed to cost $.225, the total cost of the item would be $1.25.

It should be obvious that any food service operator should know the basic cost of every item on a menu before setting menu sales prices. If the hamburger above is listed on the menu at $1.50, the cost of the food alone will use up all but $.25 of the sales price. However, if the item can be priced at $2.50, the sale price will be twice the food cost.

In the first case, food cost percent would be 83.3 percent, calculated as

$$\frac{\text{food cost } \$1.25}{\text{menu sales price } \$1.50} = .833 = 83.3\%$$

In the second, food cost percent would be 50.0 percent, calculated as

$$\frac{\text{food cost } \$1.25}{\text{menu sales price } \$2.50} = .5 = 50.0\%$$

An important management activity is pricing the service product line such that the desired profit will result. For restaurants, the pricing of food and beverages is a critical issue. Some of the factors involved in the pricing decision for restaurant products were discussed in Chapters 7 and 17. The key to pricing restaurant products is that prices must be high enough to provide a sufficient gross profit to cover the other costs of operating the establishment and also to provide profit.

In the case of the Steak Shack, calculations earlier in this chapter indicated that overall food cost percent in the Steak Shack is 40.0 percent. If the food cost of the hamburger item described above is to be 40.0 percent of the menu sales price, an appropriate sales price could be calculated as follows:

$$\frac{\text{food cost } \$1.25}{40\% \text{ food cost } \%} = \$3.125 \text{ sales price}$$

Therefore, if the owner wanted food cost for the hamburger item to be 40.0 percent of its menu sales price, he would probably set the menu sales price at approximately $3.15.

From the foregoing, it should be apparent that accounting and financial record keeping play an important role in hospitality operations. Financial information and the various ratios and calculations flowing from it assist owners, managers, vendors, creditors, and various government agencies in assessing the financial condition of an enterprise for a number of different purposes. Those planning careers in hospitality management should expand their knowledge of accounting to include more information about the topics discussed in this chapter and about the detailed process and complex topics that no introductory chapter could cover.

SUMMARY

In this chapter, accounting is defined and the six major branches of accounting are identified and described. The balance sheet and income statement are identified as the two principal financial statements derived from accounting records. The contents of the balance sheet and the income statement are described in detail, as are a number of important terms, including *current assets, fixed assets, depreciation, current liabilities, long-term liabilities, owner's equity, revenue, expenses, operating expenses, fixed charges, net income before taxes, profit,* and *loss*. Various ratios are described and the formulas used to calculate a number of important ratios are provided, including food cost-to-sales ratio, beverage cost-to-sales ratio, labor cost-to-sales ratio, current ratio, quick ratio, percentage of occupancy, seat turnover, inventory turnover, return on sales, and return on equity. Two arithmetic averages—average rate per occupied room and average sale per customer—are defined and the methods for calculating these are illustrated. Budgeting, cash management, and cost control are described in detail and identified as three specific areas of responsibility associated with management accounting and cost control. Specific activities and reports associated with the three areas include operating budgets, fixed budgets, flexible budgets, capital budgets, cash budgets, and calculations related to the cost of cleaning a guest room and the cost of a portion of food. Finally, one basic method for determining an appropriate menu sales price for an item is illustrated.

QUESTIONS

1. Define *accounting*.
2. Describe the six branches of accounting.
3. Identify the two major financial statements derived from accounting records and list the principal parts of each.
4. Define the following terms:
   a. Asset
   b. Current assets

    c. Fixed assets

    d. Liquidity

    e. Accumulated depreciation

    f. Liability

    g. Current liability

    h. Long-term liability

    i. Owner's equity

    j. Income statement

    k. Revenue

    l. Expense

    m. Profit

    n. Loss

    o. Operating expenses

    p. Fixed charges

5. What is the formula for calculating the food cost-to-sales ratio?

6. What is the formula for calculating the beverage cost-to-sales ratio?

7. What is the formula for calculating the labor cost-to-sales ratio?

8. Given the following information, determine percentage of occupancy for the Kensington Hotel for the night of October 8th:

    number of occupied rooms: 252

    total number of rooms available for sale: 350

9. Given the following information, determine seat turnover for the Steak Shack for March 15th:

    number of diners: 900

    number of seats available for diners: 250

10. Identify each of the following terms:

    a. Inventory turnover

    b. Current ratio

    c. Quick ratio

    d. Return on sales

    e. Return on equity

11. Define the following averages:

    a. Average rate per occupied room

    b. Average sale per customer

12. Define the term *budget* and identify each of the following types of budgets:
    a. Fixed operating budget
    b. Flexible operating budget
    c. Capital budget
13. Discuss *cash management* and describe the preparation of a cash budget.
14. Discuss the importance of cost control to the management of a hospitality operation.

Tomorrow's Hospitality Industry

19

LEARNING OBJECTIVES

After reading and studying this chapter, you should be able to:

1. *Identify six social and economic changes that suggest a bright future for the hospitality industry.*
2. *Describe the growth in demand for the service products of the food service and lodging industries.*
3. *Identify and discuss specific issues that tomorrow's hospitality managers are likely to face in each of the following areas:*
   a. Marketing; b. Legal; c. Human resources; d. Operations;
   e. Consumer affairs

INTRODUCTION

In the preceding chapters, we have introduced a number of significant topics, including the history of the hospitality industry, the dimensions of its principal segments, and the application of major business principles to food service, lodging, and travel/tourism. Understanding these topics is of considerable importance to those planning careers in the industry. It is useful as a predecessor to later coursework or as a foundation for the experiential learning that can be of such great value to anyone pursuing a professional career in hospitality.

THE BRIGHT FUTURE OF HOSPITALITY

In recent years, a number of important social and economic changes have occurred that suggest a bright future for our industry. These have been addressed briefly in several previous chapters, but it is useful to review them here.

Social and Economic Changes

EARLY RETIREMENT. Today, many American workers are retiring at earlier ages than was the case in previous years. Our social security system provides benefits to those as young as 62 years of age, and many employee retirement programs are tied to years of service rather than to age. In some retirement programs, particularly government programs, it is possible to work twenty-five or thirty years and receive substantial retirement benefits at age 55 or younger. Greater numbers of people retiring early mean increased sales for hospitality operations, as these people use their time to see and experience the world.

LONGER LIFE SPAN. The average American can now expect to live well into his 70s, and many will live longer. This is in contrast to earlier generations, when the average life span was considerably less. The increasing population of older, retired citizens provides a larger base of potential customers for hospitality operations.

SHORTER WORK WEEK. Sixty years ago, the six-day work week was standard for most working people. Today, the five-day work week is standard, and the four-day work week is not uncommon—leaving several days for other activities. The resulting increase in leisure time, combined with faster and easier transportation, makes it possible for many to take weekend vacations, drive to friends and

In addition to a shorter work week, an increase in holidays, greater disposable income, greater mobility, early retirement, and longer life spans are among the social and economic changes contributing to the hospitality industry's healthy future, providing a larger base of potential customers for travel, food service, and lodging operations. (Photo copyright © 1990 Dan Bryant; courtesy Motel 6.)

relatives, attend weddings and receptions, and generally travel to a degree they could not have attempted a few years ago. Hospitality operations benefit from this increase in travel.

MORE HOLIDAYS. Greater numbers of holidays are now scheduled, and they are often observed on Mondays and Fridays. These create three- and four-day weekends that provide people with more opportunities for patronizing hospitality operations. One comparatively recent addition to the list of holidays is Martin Luther King's birthday. In most states it is celebrated on a Monday in mid-January. This has created a long weekend that has had a major impact. In the Northeast, for example, it has turned a relatively quiet weekend into a record weekend for the ski areas.

GREATER DISPOSABLE INCOME. The average family has more money to spend than ever before. Higher wages and two-earner households account for much of this. A large portion of the additional disposable income is being spent on consumer goods and services, and hospitality operations appear to be receiving an important share of it.

GREATER MOBILITY. Improved roads and better transportation make it easier to travel each year. The interstate highway system has reduced the time required for automobile travel between any two points. In addition, most Americans live close enough to an airport to select air travel more readily than would have been the case years ago. These increases in travel have had a strong positive impact on hospitality sales.

Growing Demand

Today, the food service industry ranks as one of the largest in the nation. A recent publication of the National Restaurant Association (NRA), the industry's principal trade association, states that "eating and drinking places are first among all retailers in the number of establishments and the number of employees." Today, there are over 710,000 eating and drinking establishments, employing over 9 million people. The number of managerial and administrative positions in the industry is approaching 500,000. One out of every four retail outlets in the nation is an eating or drinking establishment.

On a typical day, food service establishments provide approximately 30 percent of American adults with lunch and nearly 25 percent with dinner. Of those patronizing these establishments, over 50 percent are men. On this typical day, over 55 percent of adult men eat out, compared with under 50 percent of adult women. Well over 70 percent of the adult population eats at a restaurant once a month.

The growth of food and beverage sales has been continuous. In 1970, NRA figures placed food service sales at 42.8 billion dollars. By 1975, sales volume had grown to 70.3 billion. By 1980, it had grown to approximately 120 billion, and the 1980 figure had nearly doubled by 1990. Although these figures are not adjusted for inflation, they point out the extraordinary growth in that ten-year period. Today, food and beverage sales account for over $250 billion. This is nearly 5 percent of the GNP, the gross national product, of the United States—generally defined as the value of all goods and services sold. By any measure, this is indeed a major industry.

The demand for food service has grown at a very rapid pace in recent years. In today's world, even children are patronizing food service establishments at very early ages—having their Kid's Meals at Wendy's, then continuing to patronize Wendy's and restaurants in general in their adult years. Today, many adults eat out several times each week—more than ever before in our history. Various studies have shown that the average American eats more than one out of three meals away from home. The National Restaurant Association (NRA) reports that 43 percent of the money Americans spend on food is spent in food service establishments.

In addition, the frequency of eating out is increasing. Americans are consuming ever greater numbers of meals away from home each year, and nationwide food sales continue to increase dramatically. It has been predicted by experts that Americans will soon be eating half of all meals away from home.

The commercial lodging industry is also growing. The American Hotel & Motel Association reports that the commercial lodging industry in the United States now includes approximately 45,000 properties, ranging in size from small inns with fewer than 10 rooms to giant hotels with over 3,000 rooms. In total, the commercial lodging industry in the United States generates more than $57 billion in sales each year, representing about 1 percent of the gross national product. The industry employs approximately 1.6 million people, full time and part time. It is a major industry, and with the increases in leisure time and disposable income, it is continuing to increase in size and in economic importance.

The future of the hospitality industry is bright, in spite of the temporary setbacks that any industry must endure. In one region or another, changes will always occur that have negative implications for various segments of the industry. However, these are unlikely to last. In most areas, hospitality and tourism will continue to be important to the economic vitality of the region.

ISSUES IN HOSPITALITY

Although the future of the industry is bright, it is not without problems. Those pursuing careers in hospitality will find it necessary to acquire and maintain knowledge of a number of issues that the industry must address in the years ahead.

Students in degree programs commonly confront some of these in senior research seminars. Some have been issues for many years, but no final solutions for them have yet been found. Others are emerging issues, occasioned by social, economic, and technological change. A number of these issues are addressed below—not exhaustively, but to the extent that indicates the significance of each and the areas in which the impact is likely to be felt most.

The issues addressed in this chapter can be distributed under the following headings:

1. Marketing
2. Legal
3. Human resources
4. Operations
5. Consumer affairs

These issues are certainly not the only matters of concern to hospitality managers. They can perhaps best be described, however, as some of the major issues about which men and women planning managerial careers in this field should have some knowledge. Many are discussed in daily newspapers, in general periodicals, in trade publications, and at industry conferences. Sometimes they are the subjects of programs on broadcast television or on cable networks. They are often central topics for discussion at meetings of hospitality-related organizations. Numerous owners and managers are genuinely concerned about them. Many have to do with the social responsibility of those who own and operate food service and lodging enterprises—social responsibility toward customers, employees, the community, and the environment. Readers of this book are likely to discover that they, too, will become increasingly aware of these and other similarly important issues as their managerial careers progress.

Those considering these issues and the categories under which they are discussed in this chapter may disagree with our including a given issue under a particular category. Some, for example, might consider it more suitable to cover questions relating to diet/nutrition/health with operations issues, rather than with consumer issues. The difference would have more to do with the degree of emphasis given one or another of the elements.

The authors would certainly not disagree with anyone seeking to categorize any of these issues differently. We are less concerned about the particular category than we are about the significance of the issues. We are particularly interested in fostering the notion that responsible hospitality managers should know about, and be engaged in constructive consideration of, the issues that face the industry. In our view, all of the issues discussed here will be of considerable significance to hospitality managers in the years ahead.

Marketing Issues

Changing Demographics.   The population of America is aging. The median is now 33 years and is projected to go higher in the coming years. This is an issue of dramatic importance to the industry. An older population has preferences that differ significantly from those of a younger population, and hospitality providers will find it necessary to adjust their service products to the changing preferences of the market.

Another changing demographic characteristic is the increase in the number of single-parent households. Single-parent households traditionally have had lower levels of discretionary income and thus have not been as able to support hospitality businesses. To reach this market, hospitality providers will have to continue developing new service products that appeal to this demographic segment at affordable prices.

A third demographic change is the continuing growth in the number of people traveling for personal, rather than for business purposes. As indicated in Chapter 11, approximately 74 percent of domestic travelers are traveling primarily for a nonbusiness purpose. This group has accounted for growing percentages of the travel market in the past forty-five years, and the growth is sure to continue.

The fourth demographic change is the growth in the number of international travelers, in general, and in the number of international travelers to the United States, in particular. International travelers account for an ever-growing share of hospitality and travel revenues in the United States. The number of international visitors projected for 1992 is 44,000,000.

Changing Vacation Patterns.   Americans and the citizens of other industrialized nations are changing their vacation patterns. The traditional once-a-year vacation of two weeks or more is declining in popularity. For growing numbers of people, vacations are becoming shorter and more frequent. Today, more people are likely to plan minivacations, adding two of their annual vacation days to a three-day holiday weekend. By doing so, they manage to get away for a minivacation of five days while using only two actual vacation days. In one recent year, only 8 percent of the trips taken over 100 miles from home were for ten or more nights' duration.

Market Segmentation.   In the years since 1980, a key term in hospitality marketing has been *market segmentation*. Until the late 1970s, lodging establishments attempted to appeal to broad, general markets; their aim was to appeal to as broad a group of potential guests as possible. In more recent years, the success of the limited service properties has led to the development of other properties designed to appeal to carefully selected market segments at various points on the guest spectrum. Some of the types of lodging properties to emerge include all-suite properties, residence properties, subbudget properties, and a variety of budget properties differentiated by their varying services and amenities.

Examples of market segmentation have also been evident in food service, particularly in the past ten years. A number of the restaurants that traditionally have offered extensive something-for-everyone menus have begun to see reductions in business, as customers have chosen to patronize restaurants offering specialized service products.

As new market segments are identified, properties designed to appeal to those segments are likely to be developed.

Frequent Guest Programs.   With the proliferation of properties and the growing competition among them, some lodging operators have begun to develop programs to gain repeat business. Modeled on the frequent-flyer programs used so successfully by many airline companies, these plans typically give credits to regular guests. They can be redeemed in the form of reduced rates, upgrades, free accommodations, free meals, or any of a variety of amenities. As competition becomes even keener, the number of these kinds of programs is likely to grow. Many believe that these programs will gain in the lodging business the same degree of favor they have achieved among airline customers.

Maturation in Segments of the Fast-Food Industry.   Segments of the fast-food market are no longer expanding to the extent that was formerly possible. The demand for hamburgers is not growing as fast as it once did, and operators are finding it necessary to develop new products to maintain desired sales levels. Today, for example, establishments that once offered few products other than hamburgers are now test marketing or offering pizza, salads, or various poultry or other meat products. As public tastes continue to change, food service operators will need to keep pace—to develop new specialty products to retain an adequate share of the market.

Consolidation in the Commercial Lodging Industry.   Some experts are now suggesting that the number of large, nationwide lodging companies will decrease in the years to come. They are forecasting that a small number of firms will dominate the lodging industry by acquiring smaller chains of regional or national properties. This will enable successful firms to obtain the funds required to expand their operations internationally.

The trend toward consolidation will have significant impact on all commercial lodging operations. Both independent operations and smaller chains will have increasing difficulty competing with heavily advertised national and international brands.

One of the marketing issues impacting the hospitality industry is the maturation of various fast-food industry segments. Where bare-bones menus once facilitated the industry's rapid growth, fast-food establishments—as well as traditional restaurants and prepared food enterprises—are now developing and test marketing other product lines (top), including "health-conscious" or "light" items such as salads or grilled chicken or fish (bottom). (Top: courtesy Kentucky Fried Chicken; bottom: photo courtesy of Pierce Foods.)

Legal Issues

Liquor Liability.   In recent years, public concern has been growing over the alarming number of alcohol-related automobile accidents. Today, alcohol and drug use is a factor in over half of all automobile accidents This has led to increasing public pressure on state legislatures to act. Although the particulars vary from one state to another, it is generally true that legislators have responded

In response to the growing awareness of the negative effects of alcohol abuse, new state regulations increase liability for establishments that serve alcoholic beverages to intoxicated individuals. In reaction, some restaurant and bar owners either no longer serve alcohol, or promote nonalcoholic beverages (shown above). (Courtesy Ocean Spray Cranberries, Inc.)

by lowering the levels of blood alcohol at which an individual is considered intoxicated and by increasing penalties on offenders. In addition, many states have imposed new regulations on the serving of alcoholic beverages. In at least one state, new regulations have made the discounting of drink prices—the so-called happy hour—illegal. In many states, establishments and their owners can be held financially accountable if they serve alcoholic beverages to an intoxicated individual who causes damage or injury after leaving the establishment. In some places, this has caused such huge increases in the cost of liability insurance that some bar and tavern owners have chosen to go out of business. It has caused some restaurant owners to stop serving alcoholic beverages.

Some restaurant and bar owners have changed market strategy: They are now featuring and promoting nonalcoholic drinks. Others have encouraged groups of their patrons to select a designated driver and have provided various incentives for them to do so.

As societal attitudes toward alcoholic beverages continue to change, it will be necessary for food service and lodging operators to adjust.

Impact of the Americans with Disabilities Act of 1990. This landmark legislation prohibits discrimination against anyone with a disability. A *disabled person* is defined as one who has a physical or mental impairment that substantially limits one or more major life activities. Relevant to the hospitality industry, the Americans with Disabilities Act applies to both employees and guests in lodging establishments of more than five rooms and in all restaurants, bars, and similar establishments serving food or drink.

In practice, the act prohibits discrimination in hiring on the basis of disabilities. As applied to guests, it dictates that builders of new facilities must design and construct them to accommodate the disabled; whereas owners of existing facilities must make reasonable efforts to accommodate the disabled. In general, it holds that the disabled are entitled to full and equal enjoyment of goods, services, facilities, privileges, advantages, and accommodations.

Although the language of the act is subject to varying interpretations, these will, no doubt, eventually be resolved in the courts. In the meantime, hospitality owners and managers are likely to be addressing questions arising from the passage of this act for many years to come.

Ethics in Hospitality.   *Ethics* is an academic discipline that deals with the study of the codes of moral conduct practiced by individuals or groups. *Business ethics* is a term that refers to the application of a particular moral code to relationships, activities, and decisions made by those in business or industry. It is the code that enables the individual in business to distinguish right from wrong — to differentiate between ethical and unethical behavior.

Ethics in the hospitality industry has been an issue for thousands of years — since the tavern-keepers of earliest recorded history first diluted the drinks of unsuspecting customers. Although this and similar practices are illegal today, it is possible to question the business ethics of some hospitality operators. For example, a manager of a new restaurant may hire twenty servers, intending to keep only the twelve most able beyond the second week of operation. A room clerk may accept bribes to register guests without reservations, even when the property is overbooked. An owner may fail to report all sales on her income tax returns; and, similarly, a server may cheat on her income taxes by failing to report all tips. An owner may misrepresent his property, using idealized artists' renderings rather than photographs in his advertising. An employee in a purchasing department may accept gifts from vendors in return for purchasing inferior products. Another owner may cheat on his taxes by charging personal expenses to the business. The examples go on and on. Business ethics is likely to remain forever on any list of hospitality issues.

Human Resources Issues

Sexual Harassment.   The Federal Equal Employment Opportunity Commission defines *sexual harassment* as "unwelcomed sexual advances, requests for sexual favors, and other verbal or physical conduct of a sexual nature that takes place under any of the following conditions:

1. submission is made a condition of the person's employment;
2. submission to or rejection of such conduct is used as a basis for employment decisions affecting the person; or
3. it unreasonably interferes with the person's work performance or creates an intimidating, hostile, or offensive work environment."

Most cases of sexual harassment involve complaints by females about male co-workers or superiors. In the last ten years, as greater numbers of women have become willing to speak out, the number of these cases has grown.

Because employers are liable for the actions of their employees at work, it is particularly important for employers to take several important steps:

1. Institute a strict policy banning all forms of sexual harassment in the workplace.
2. Develop appropriate training programs for managers and employees so that all will understand and become sensitive to the nature of sexual harassment.
3. Establish procedures for handling all complaints promptly, fairly, and in a sensitive manner.

Employee Turnover.   As was pointed out in Chapter 17, employee turnover continues to be one of the major issues facing hospitality managers. With turnover rates averaging approximately 100 percent per year across the industry, managers are continually faced with the problem of losing experienced employees and hiring those with less experience as replacements. Faced with inexperienced replacements, many managers believe they have only two choices: to incur the high training costs associated with transforming new employees into valuable workers; or to suffer the equally high costs associated with operating with untrained workers. Too few realize that they have a third option: to take suitable steps directed toward retaining employees and reducing turnover.

Many hospitality managers understand the prerequisites to reduced turnover— which include adequate wages and benefits, reasonable working conditions, reasonable work schedules, and reasonable treatment of employees by enlightened managers. Comparatively fewer are willing to put these into practice.

A number of employers and managers still attempt to treat workers as if they were cogs in some gigantic wheel—metal parts, rather than people. They hire at the lowest possible wages, provide no training, then berate and belittle workers for failing to do work correctly. They assign workers to schedules without any regard to personal preferences, change their schedules without notice, and demand that they report for work on their days off if the need should arise. Then they complain about the ungrateful workers who quit their jobs at the first opportunity to accept seemingly equal jobs with other employers.

Employee Assistance Plans.   Employee assistance plans (EAPs) are included in this discussion of hospitality industry issues, because they are one of the several efforts by enlightened owners and managers to pay responsible attention to the real, human problems faced by their employees. The problems of those employed in hospitality are essentially the same as the problems of those in the general population. These include substance abuse; psychological problems; family issues; financial issues; legal problems; health issues; and educational issues.

The hospitality industry traditionally has been among the larger employers of those with limited education, including many of the foreign-born with limited knowledge of English. Because of this, the hospitality manager has an oppportunity to be of unique assistance to workers who might otherwise not have access to help with their problems.

The hospitality manager who establishes EAPs to benefit employees will be developing a more loyal work force—one that is willing to strive toward the operational goals of the enterprise. At the same time, the manager with the foresight to help employees is likely to see employee turnover reduced.

Employee Empowerment.   In several chapters of this book, we have made the point that service products cannot be mass-produced in advance—that they are produced only when ordered by a customer. To an important extent, each service product is tailored to suit the guest or customer who has ordered it.

In some hospitality operations, managers have developed extensive rules and procedures that all guest service employees are directed to follow. These can extend to the most minute details—rules forbidding free refills on coffee; strict limits on the number of hand towels per guest; directives prohibiting substitutions on special dinner menus; inflexible rules about checkout time. These—and the many others one sees daily in hospitality—lead to critical moments of truth that may affect a guest's overall impression of a particular food service or lodging enterprise. The negative moment of truth resulting from a refusal to give a guest an extra half cup of coffee may be enough to offset all the positive moments of truth that precede and follow it. For some guests, it may be enough to make them decide never to return.

Many hospitality owners and managers have come to realize, however, the futility of attempting to set strict rules governing every detail of guest service. Instead, they are now revising their approach, setting policies that are guest-oriented and training their employees to provide as many positive moments of truth as possible. They are giving their employees some latitude to tailor service products to the specific needs and preferences of guests. In effect, they are empowering their employees to make enlightened, educated decisions that will improve service quality for guests without having a negative impact on operations.

Operations Issues

Automation.   *To automate* means to use electronic and mechanical equipment and machinery to complete some or all of the tasks associated with a given enterprise. Three principal reasons are commonly cited for automating an enterprise:

1. To increase the speed of work
2. To reduce the cost of work
3. To standardize results

Historically, hospitality managers have always been ready to automate. A few of the historical examples of automation in the industry include peeling potatoes, washing dishes, washing tablecloths and napkins, preserving frozen foods, vacuuming carpets, recording reservations, and maintaining guest accounts.

Today, we are at the point where some food service and lodging establishments have automated to the extent that guests and customers no longer have direct contact with any human staff. There are lodging operations where one inserts a credit card in an electronic device, enabling one to check in without speaking to the room clerk at the desk. Checkout can be accomplished via a touch-sensitive screen on the television set in one's room. Food and beverages can be obtained from vending machines.

It is interesting that food service and lodging operations at the high end of the price spectrum have tended to maintain the appearance of service, even when automated devices have been installed. For example, some hotels with automatic elevators have continued to employ personnel to run the elevators. Guests are still treated to a high level of service but with more modern and efficient equipment than the older manual elevators.

Some are beginning to question whether the industry is pushing automation too far—whether those that automate too extensively are offering any degree of hospitality. Have they automated themselves out of the hospitality industry, so to speak? It is a question that owners and managers of hospitality enterprises, as well as their guests and customers, will continue to ask in the years ahead. And it is sure to be of growing importance, as well: The technological capacity to automate grows daily, and the industry will have to determine the extent to which it should use the technology.

Smoking/No-Smoking Areas.   As more and more customers and guests of food service and lodging enterprises demand smoke-free areas for dining and smoke-free sleeping accommodations, the industry will continue to make all reasonable efforts to meet these demands. This will be particularly true in those states and localities in which legislation mandates that appropriate facilities be made available.

To date, this trend has had the greatest impact on the food and beverage sector of the industry. Restaurants and related enterprises have found it desirable, if not necessary, to apportion sections of their dining facilities to accommodate the wishes of nonsmokers. Some have also found it necessary to install or improve ventilation equipment.

Many lodging operations have set aside accommodations for nonsmokers—rooms that are free of the lingering effects of tobacco smoke. In some properties, smoking is prohibited in public areas—lobbies, corridors, elevators, and other areas—often as a matter of law.

The prohibition of smoking in hospitality operations is an issue that will be of growing significance to owners and managers in the years ahead.

Sanitation and Public Health.   No subject is of greater importance in food service than sanitation. Everyone agrees that all responsible steps must be taken to prevent illnesses that can be traced to the manner in which food is handled, or to the food itself.

Insuring proper food handling has always been an issue in the industry. Managers must constantly check to see that food is purchased from responsible vendors. It also must be kept at suitable temperatures to prevent bacterial growth or under proper conditions to prevent infestation by insects and rodents. Equipment surfaces must be cleaned effectively to ensure that food is not contaminated during preparation. Washing is an ongoing necessity in food service—the washing of employees' hands, the washing of some fresh foods to remove chemical residues, and the thorough washing of all china, glassware, flatware, pots, and pans that are used in the preparation and service of foods and beverages.

State and local governments apply strict sanitary standards to food and beverage operations. Some conduct regular inspections and place sanctions on those found violating the applicable code. The sanctions range from imposing fines, to publishing lists of violators in newspapers, to closing flagrant violators.

In an effort to ensure their compliance with local sanitary codes, many food and beverage operators hire consultants to conduct regular inspections and to assist in the immediate correction of any violations. As consumers become increasingly aware of the potential for harm from improperly handled food, preventing possible violations of local codes will be an issue of growing importance to food and beverage operators.

Recycling/Solid Waste.   In recent years, there has been a gradual closing of the landfills traditionally used for disposing of solid wastes and growing awareness of the harmful effects of either burning solid waste or dumping it in the sea. This has led to major waste-disposal problems in some areas.

Although not often emphasized, sanitation is one of the most important operations issues in the hospitality industry. Ensuring proper food handling, supervising vendors, and the washing of foods, utensils, and equipment are all essential in meeting legal sanitary standards. (Courtesy Cryovac.)

In some major metropolitan areas, the cost of removing solid wastes is becoming higher than government and citizens are willing and able to pay. In many of these areas, separating recyclable plastic, glass, and metal items from other solid waste is now required by law. Eliminating these recyclables from other solid wastes greatly reduces the quantities requiring disposal.

This trend toward recycling is likely to grow. Many in the hospitality industry who have not previously been affected by this issue will find that their situations have changed. They, too, will eventually find it necessary to adopt a recycling program.

Consumer Affairs Issues

Fire and Safety. Fire and safety have always been issues of concern in hospitality. In earlier centuries, taverns, inns, and hotels, usually constructed of wood, were regularly demolished by fire. Many burned to the ground, and large numbers of people were killed or maimed.

During the twentieth century, various changes have made hotels, motels, and other hospitality operations much safer. Improvements in design and construction have made a great difference. So have improvements in the fire control systems installed in buildings—electronic smoke detectors, automatic systems to summon fire departments, better sprinkler systems, and so on. Because of these changes, people have never been safer.

A number of dangers associated with fire remain to be addressed, however. In the event of fire, the guests in some properties today may face danger from the toxic smoke resulting from the burning of furniture, fixtures, and fibers produced from manmade materials. In a fire, many of the artificial fibers used in wall coverings, carpets, draperies, and upholstery produce toxic fumes that can be more dangerous than fire.

Another problem relates to construction. In recent years, to reduce heating and cooling costs, new buildings were particularly well insulated. In some, the windows were not designed to be opened. Temperature and air were controlled by very complex central systems. In the event of fire in such buildings, some danger exists that smoke may be quickly dispersed throughout the building. As a consequence, a shift to individual room ventilation can be seen in properties being built today.

Truth in Menu.   For most food service operators, preparing truthful and accurate menus is an ethical practice that must never be violated. A small minority, however, have produced menus that were not always entirely accurate indicators of the foods served in their establishments. Some have merely abused such terms as *fresh* and *cooked to order.* Others have been more flagrant, serving U.S. Choice beef when their menus state *U.S. Prime.* Still others have served portions with fewer ounces than the number listed in the menu. Some have not used the actual ingredients suggested by their menus and have substituted one product for another: turkey for chicken, margarine for butter, generic products for name brands, and domestic products for imported.

In some areas, enough abuses have occurred to produce a groundswell of public opinion in favor of requiring food service operators to be entirely truthful. Where such consumer protection legislation exists, those who violate the regulations risk fines and loss of licenses. It is important that those in the industry conduct their operations ethically—in such a manner that consumers can have complete faith in the truth of their menus, the wholesomeness of their foods, and, generally, the honesty of their business practices.

Diet/Nutrition/Health.   With the public becoming increasingly concerned about healthy diets, containing less fat and fewer calories, many food service operators are adjusting or amending their menus to these changing public tastes. Some are devoting sections of their menus to foods for the diet conscious; others are designating certain of their menu items as appropriate for those interested in foods low in sodium and cholesterol. Growing numbers of restaurants are seeking to attract health-conscious diners. Some have eliminated "unhealthy" foods from their menus.

The trend to healthier dining is certain to continue, and successful food service operators will want to give greater attention to the nutritional content of foods in the years ahead.

SUMMARY

In this chapter, several social and economic changes likely to affect the future of the hospitality industry are described—including earlier retirements, longer life spans, shorter work weeks, more vacation time, greater disposable income, and increased mobility. Growing demand for the hospitality service products of both the food service and lodging industries is discussed. Many of the issues that will be addressed by tomorrow's hospitality managers are identified and categorized in five areas: marketing, legal, human resources, operations, and consumer affairs. Marketing issues include changing demographics, changing vacation patterns, market segmentation, frequent-guest programs, maturation in segments of the fast-food industry, and consolidation in the commercial lodging industry. Legal issues include liquor liability, impact of the Americans with Disabilities Act of 1990, and ethics in hospitality. Human resource issues include sexual harassment, employee turnover, employee assistance programs, and employee empowerment. Operations issues include automation, smoking/no-smoking areas, sanitation and public health, and recycling/solid wastes. Finally, consumer affairs issues include fire and safety, truth in menu, and diet/nutrition/health.

Selected Bibliography

Albrecht, Karl (1988). *At America's Service*. Homewood, IL: Dow Jones-Irwin.

Bardi, James (1990). *Hotel Front Office Management*. New York: Van Nostrand Reinhold.

Batterberry, Michael and Ariane (1973). *On the Town in New York*. New York: Charles Scribner's Sons.

Bell, Donald A. (1989). *Wine and Beverage Standards*. New York: Van Nostrand Reinhold.

Borer, Mary Cathcart (1972). *The British Hotel Through the Ages*. London, England: Lutterworth Press.

Borsenik, Frank (1987). *The Management of Maintenance and Engineering in the Hospitality Industry*, 2nd ed. New York: John Wiley & Sons.

Carlzon, Jan (1987). *Moments of Truth*. New York: Harper & Row.

Coltman, Michael C. (1990). *Beverage Management*. New York: Van Nostrand Reinhold.

———— (1991). *Financial Control for Your Hotel*. New York: Van Nostrand Reinhold.

———— (1991). *Financial Control for Your Foodservice Operation*. New York: Van Nostrand Reinhold.

———— (1990). *Hospitality Industry Purchasing*. New York: Van Nostrand Reinhold.

———— (1991). *Hospitality Management Accounting*, 4th ed. New York: Van Nostrand Reinhold.

———— (1989). *Introduction to Travel and Tourism: An International Approach*. New York: Van Nostrand Reinhold.

———— (1989). *Tourism Marketing*. New York: Van Nostrand Reinhold.

Dahmer, Sondra, and Kurt Kahl (1988). *The Waiter and Waitress Training Manual*, 3rd ed. New York: Van Nostrand Reinhold.

Dittmer, Paul R., and Gerald G. Griffin (1989). *Principles of Food, Beverage, and Labor Cost Controls*, 4th ed. New York: Van Nostrand Reinhold.

Dorsey, Leslie, and Janice Devine (1964). *Fare Thee Well*. New York: Crown Publishers, Inc.

Drummond, Karen Eich (1990). *Human Resource Management for the Hospitality Industry*. New York: Van Nostrand Reinhold.

Drummond, Karen Eich (1991). *Retaining Foodservice Employees*. New York: Van Nostrand Reinhold.

Earle, Alice Morse (1900). *Stage Coach and Tavern Days*. New York: Benjamin Blom, Inc.

Evers, Alf, et al. (1979). *Resorts of the Catskills*. New York: St. Martin's Press, Inc.

Fay, Clifford T., Jr., Richard C. Rhoads, and Robert L. Rosenblatt (1976). *Managerial Accounting for the Hospitality Service Industries*, 2nd ed. Dubuque, IA: William C. Brown Company, Publishers.

Firebaugh, W. C. (1923). *The Inns of the Middle Ages.* Chicago: F. W. Morris Co.
——— (1928). *The Inns of Greece and Rome.* New York: Benjamin Blom, Inc.
Flippo, Edwin B., and Gary M. Munsinger (1975). *Management*, 3rd ed. Boston: Allyn & Bacon, Inc.
Franck, Irene M., and David M. Brownstone (1989). *Restaurateurs and Innkeepers.* New York: Facts on File.
Gee, Chuck Y., James C. Makens, and Dexter J. L. Choy (1988). *The Travel Industry*, 2nd ed. New York: Van Nostrand Reinhold.
Gee, Chuck Y., et al. (1990). *Professional Travel Agency Management.* Englewood Cliffs, NJ: Regents/Prentice Hall.
George, Dorothy M. (1965). *London Life in the Eighteenth Century.* London, England: Penguin Books.
Gold, Hal (1990). *The Cruise Book: From Brochure to Bon Voyage.* Albany, NY: Delmar Publishers, Inc.
Haas, Irvin (1985). *America's Historic Inns and Taverns.* New York: Hippocrene Books, Inc.
Hilton, Conrad (1957). *Be My Guest.* Englewood Cliffs, NJ: Prentice Hall, Inc.
Hooker, Richard J. (1981). *Food and Drink in America.* Indianapolis: Bobbs-Merrill Company, Inc.
Inskeep, Edward, and Antonio Enriquez Savignac (1991). *Tourism Planning: An Integrated and Sustainable Development Approach.* New York: Van Nostrand Reinhold.
Iverson, Kathleen M. (1989). *Introduction to Hospitality Management.* New York: Van Nostrand Reinhold.
Kasavana, Michael L. (1983). *Effective Front Office Operations.* New York: Van Nostrand Reinhold.
——— (1983). *Hotel Information Systems: A Contemporary Approach to Front Office Procedures.* New York: Van Nostrand Reinhold.
Katsigris, Costas, and Mary Porter (1982). *The Bar and Beverage Book.* New York: John Wiley & Sons.
Kazarian, Edward A. (1988). *Foodservice Facilities Planning*, 3rd ed. New York: Van Nostrand Reinhold.
Keiser, James (1989). *Principles and Practices of Management in the Hospitality Industry*, 2nd ed. New York: Van Nostrand Reinhold.
Khan, Mahmood (1990). *Concepts of Foodservice Operations and Management*, 2nd ed. New York: Van Nostrand Reinhold.
King, Carol (1988). *Professional Dining Room Management*, 2nd ed. New York: Van Nostrand Reinhold.
Kramer, Jack (1978). *The Last of the Grand Hotels.* New York: Van Nostrand Reinhold.
Kreck, Lothar A. (1984). *Menus: Analysis and Planning*, 2nd ed. New York: Van Nostrand Reinhold.
LaGreca, Genevieve (1988). *Training Foodservice Employees.* New York: Van Nostrand Reinhold.
Langdon, Philip (1986). *Orange Roofs, Golden Arches.* New York: Alfred A. Knopf, Inc.
Lathrop, Elise (1926). *Early American Inns and Taverns.* New York: Tudor Publishing Company.
Lattin, Gerald W. (1985). *The Lodging and Food Service Industry.* East Lansing, MI: Educational Institute of the American Hotel and Motel Association.
Lefever, Michael M. (1988). *Restaurant Reality.* New York: Van Nostrand Reinhold.
Lewis, Robert C., and Richard E. Chambers (1988). *Marketing Leadership in Hospitality.* New York: Van Nostrand Reinhold.

Lundberg, Donald (1989). *The Tourist Business.* New York: Van Nostrand Reinhold.

Martin, Robert, and Donald Lundberg (1991). *Human Relations for the Hospitality Industry.* New York: Van Nostrand Reinhold.

McGinty, Brian (1978). *The Palace Inns.* Harrisburg, PA: Stackpole Books.

McIntosh, Robert (1984). *Employee Management Standards.* New York: Van Nostrand Reinhold.

McIntosh, Robert, and Charles Goeldner (1990). *Tourism: Principles, Practices, Philosophies,* 6th ed. New York: John Wiley & Sons.

Medlik, S. (1961). *The British Hotel and Catering Industry.* London, England: Sir Isaac Pitman & Sons, Ltd.

Metelka, Charles J. (1989). *The Dictionary of Hospitality, Travel, and Tourism,* 3rd ed. Albany, NY: Delmar Publishers, Inc.

Mill, Robert Christie (1989). *Managing for Productivity in the Hospitality Industry.* New York: Van Nostrand Reinhold.

———— (1990). *Tourism: The International Business.* Englewood Cliffs, NJ: Regents/Prentice Hall.

Miller, Floyd (1968). *Statler.* New York: The Statler Foundation.

Miller, Jack E. (1987). *Menu Pricing and Strategy,* 2nd ed. New York: Van Nostrand Reinhold.

Miller, Jack E., and Mary Walk (1991). *Personnel Training Manual.* New York: Van Nostrand Reinhold.

Moncarz, Elisa S., and Nestor de J. Portocarrero (1986). *Financial Accounting for Hospitality Management.* New York: Van Nostrand Reinhold.

Morrison, Alastair M. (1989). *Hospitality and Travel Marketing.* Albany, NY: Delmar Publishers, Inc.

Nykiel, Ronald A. (1988). *Marketing in the Hospitality Industry,* 2nd ed. New York: Van Nostrand Reinhold.

Palan, Earl R., and Judith A. Stadler (1986). *Preparing for the Foodservice Industry: An Introductory Approach.* New York: Van Nostrand Reinhold.

Palmer, John D. (1989). *Principles of Hospitality Engineering.* New York: Van Nostrand Reinhold.

Pillsbury, Richard (1990). *From Boarding House to Bistro.* Boston: Unwin Hyman, Inc.

Reid, Robert (1988). *Hospitality Marketing Management,* 2nd ed. New York: Van Nostrand Reinhold.

Reilly, Robert T. (1991). *Handbook of Professional Tour Management,* 2nd ed. Albany: Delmar Publishers, Inc.

———— (1988). *Travel and Tourism Marketing Techniques,* 2nd ed. Albany, NY: Delmar Publishers, Inc.

Rice, Kym S. (1983). *Early American Taverns.* Chicago: Regnery Gateway.

Richardson, Albert E. (1972). *Old Time Inns of England.* New York: Benjamin Blom, Inc.

Rowling, Marjorie (1987). *Everyday Life in Medieval Times.* New York: Dorset Press.

Rowling, Marjorie (1989). *Everyday Life of Medieval Travellers.* New York: Dorset Press.

Rushmore, Stephen (1990). *Hotel Investments: A Guide for Lenders and Owners.* Boston: Warren, Gorham & Lamont, Inc.

Rutherford, Denney G. (1989). *Hotel Management and Operations.* New York: Van Nostrand Reinhold.

———— (1990). *Introduction to the Conventions, Expositions, and Meetings Industry.* New York: Van Nostrand Reinhold.

Schmidgall, Raymond S. (1986). *Hospitality Industry Managerial Accounting*. East Lansing, MI: The Educational Institute of the American Hotel and Motel Association.

Schmidt, Arno (1987). *Food and Beverage Management in Hotels*. New York: Van Nostrand Reinhold.

Schneider, Madelin, and Georgina Tucker (1989). *The Professional Housekeeper*, 3rd ed. New York: Van Nostrand Reinhold.

Scriven, Carl R. (1988). *Food Equipment Facts*. New York: Van Nostrand Reinhold.

Scriven, Carl R., and James W. Stevens (1989). *Manual of Equipment and Design for the Foodservice Industry*. New York: Van Nostrand Reinhold.

Seaberg, Albin (1990). *Menu Design*, 4th ed. New York: Van Nostrand Reinhold.

Shames, Germaine W. (1989). *World Class Service*. Yarmouth, ME: Intercultural Press, Inc.

Spears, Marian C., and Allene G. Vaden (1985). *Foodservice Organizations*. New York: Macmillan Publishing Company.

Stevens, Laurence (1990). *Guide to Starting and Operating a Successful Travel Agency*, 3rd ed. Albany, NY: Delmar Publishers, Inc.

———— (1988). *Your Career in Travel, Tourism, and Hospitality*, 6th ed. Albany, NY: Delmar Publishers, Inc.

Strianese, Anthony J. (1990). *Dining Room and Banquet Management*. Albany, NY: Delmar Publishers, Inc.

Stutts, Alan, and Frank Borsenik (1990). *Maintenance Handbook for Hotels, Motels, and Resorts*. New York: Van Nostrand Reinhold.

Tanke, Mary L. (1991). *Human Resource Management for the Hospitality Industry*. Albany, NY: Delmar Publishers, Inc.

Tannahill, Reay (1973). *Food in History*. New York: Stein & Day.

Tarras, John (1991). *Practical Guide to Hospitality Finance*. New York: Van Nostrand Reinhold.

Tull, Donald S., and Lynn R. Kahle (1990). *Marketing Management*. New York: Macmillan Publishing Company.

Vallen, Jerome J., and James Abbey (1977). *Readings in Hotel and Restaurant Management*. New York: Van Nostrand Reinhold.

Vallen, Jerome J., and Gary K. Vallen (1991). *Check-In Check-Out*, 4th ed. Dubuque, IA: William C. Brown, Publishers.

White, Arthur (1970). *Palaces of the People*. New York: Taplinger Publishing Co.

Williamson, Jefferson (1975). *The American Hotel*. New York: Arno Press.

Yoder, Paton (1969). *Taverns and Travelers, Inns of the Early Midwest*. Bloomington, IN: Indiana University Press.

Index